Juvenile Delinquency and Justice in the United States

Juvenile Delinquency and Justice in the United States

SECOND EDITION

Lee Michael Johnson

Professor of Criminal Justice,
Department of Behavioral Sciences
Purdue University Northwest

Kimberly A. DeTardo-Bora

Professor of Criminal Justice and Criminology,
Department of Criminal Justice, Criminology, & Forensic Sciences
Marshall University

Frances P. Reddington

Professor Emeritus of Criminal Justice and Criminology
University of Central Missouri

CAROLINA ACADEMIC PRESS
Durham, North Carolina

Library of Congress Cataloging-in-Publication Data

Names: Johnson, Lee Michael author | DeTardo-Bora, Kimberly A. author | Reddington, Frances P. author
Title: Juvenile delinquency and justice in the United States / by Lee Michael Johnson, Kimberly A. DeTardo-Bora, Frances P. Reddington.
Description: Second edition. | Durham, North Carolina : Carolina Academic Press, 2025. | Includes bibliographical references and index.
Identifiers: LCCN 2025042447 | ISBN 9781531031633 paperback | ISBN 9781531031640 ebook
Subjects: LCSH: Juvenile justice, Administration of—United States | Juvenile delinquents—Legal status, laws, etc.—United States | Juvenile delinquency—United States
Classification: LCC KF9779 .J64 2025
LC record available at https://lccn.loc.gov/2025042447

Carolina Academic Press
700 Kent Street
Durham, North Carolina 27701
Telephone (919) 489-7486
www.cap-press.com
Printed in the United States of America

To Tiffany and Audrey.
—Lee Michael Johnson

To my students, who continue to teach me.
—Kimberly A. DeTardo-Bora

To my family, friends, and colleagues.
—Frances P. Reddington

Contents

Table of Cases

Table of Legislative Acts

Preface

In writing this textbook, we want to give equal and proper attention to what may be considered two different, yet overlapping and interrelated, subjects: juvenile *delinquency* and juvenile *justice*. Like its "parent concept," *crime*, delinquency refers to behavior prohibited by law, in this case, behavior by juveniles (typically, persons under the age of 18). Continuing, like its "parent system," the *justice system*, juvenile justice refers to society's governmental response to this behavior (delinquency)—in this case, the parts of the system which deal with juveniles either primarily (juvenile court and juvenile corrections) or differently (police). "Criminal justice" often refers to justice procedures experienced by adults, not juveniles; reasons for doing so are given in Chapter 1. Basically, delinquency (like crime) is "the problem" and juvenile justice (like criminal justice) is part of "the solution." In this way, delinquency and juvenile justice are different but linked subjects.

However, there is no neat line between the two subjects. For example, how the justice system responds to crime/delinquency depends on its nature, extent, and causes (e.g., if we know what causes it, we may thus know how to prevent it) as well as if a behavior is politically defined as illegal in the first place. If we are not careful, we will be unsuccessful at reducing it or even make the problem worse. The justice system likely has a causal impact on crime, to some extent. Thus, if one were to study "juvenile justice," one would necessarily also study some delinquency, and if one were to study "juvenile delinquency," one would necessarily also study some juvenile justice.

Accordingly, we wrote a textbook with twelve chapters that recognizes both the distinction and overlap between the subjects of juvenile delinquency and juvenile justice. These subjects divide the book into two parts. Part I contains six chapters where overall we describe the problem: what delinquency is exactly, how much of it occurs (and its relative seriousness), why it happens, and why it does not happen (informal social control). Since there are many possible causes of delinquency, and these causes operate in complex ways, we wrote three chapters on them. In them, we focus on theories and factors which receive significant research support. Here, much attention is given to life course and developmental theories, given their prominent place in contemporary criminology and that child development has long been a focus in understanding delinquency.

Then, in Part II, six more chapters describe what the juvenile justice system is doing (formal social control) and possibly should do to solve the problem of delinquency. The book goes beyond formal justice system structure and processes (policing, courts, and corrections) to address the major role that human/social service workers and non-profit agencies play in juvenile justice processes. This is important as most system-involved juveniles are not serious chronic offenders deeply entangled in the system; most are sanctioned in the community and may deal more with social service agents at a local level. Echoing the sentiments of early reformers, the goal is to do what is in the best interests of the child and ultimately what that means is treating the youthful offender instead of increasing punishment. Thus, much attention is given to diverting youth away from the formal system and linking juveniles to appropriate treatment and rehabilitation services. Further, we address broader issues of social justice and human rights. Unique to this book is a chapter devoted solely to juvenile justice reform (Chapter 11).

Chapter 1, "Introduction: What Is Delinquency?" asks the reader to think carefully and critically about the varying nature of juvenile delinquency. The chapter has two parts. The first part covers definitions of types of offenses. However, since specific legal definition of offenses varies across the country, the definitions covered in this chapter, many provided by official governmental agencies, are for research and understanding purposes. The second part places views on the nature of delinquency in a broader philosophical and social context. Definitions of illegal acts should not be taken for granted. Crime problems are "socially constructed." How "bad" certain acts are, or even whether they are considered bad at all, depends on the nature and extent of damage caused by them but also cultural norms, power, and conflicting interests in society. The chapter ends by entertaining the possibility that delinquency, to some extent, is "normal" adolescent behavior.

Chapter 2, "Extent of Delinquency: How Bad Is It?" asks the reader to think carefully and critically about the amount of delinquency that occurs and how many juveniles engage in it, especially the more serious forms. Without understating the problem of delinquency, the chapter provides information suggesting that delinquency has not increased and relatively few juveniles engage in the more serious forms of offending (e.g., violence). Incidence and prevalence rates from major sources of data are presented. This chapter addresses "newer" forms of offending such as cybercrime and neglected problems that are now receiving much attention such as bullying and harassment, and it examines gender, race, and class differences in arrests and offending. The chapter ends with a possible explanation for why many people falsely believe that delinquency rates are greatly increasing.

Chapter 3, "'Causes' of Delinquency: Characteristics of Individuals and Their Environments," begins a series of three chapters on theories and proposed causes of delinquent behavior. (Theoretical perspectives on why certain behaviors are illegal in the first place are addressed in Chapter 1.) Here, emphasis is placed on variables that research has shown to be related to delinquency. After describing how social scientists use scientific methodology to identify causation, this chapter covers attributes that exist within individuals' psychological and biological make-up and conditions of the communities and society in which individuals live that may play a role in causing delinquent behavior.

Chapter 4, "'Causes' of Delinquency: Social Processes," covers theories that do not just propose factors in individuals' lives that may cause them to act illegally but also how experiences over time, including from birth/childhood, can lead to problem behavior by juveniles (and eventually adults). In addition to covering three major process perspectives in criminology—social learning, social control, and labeling or societal reaction theories—this chapter provides an introduction to a prominent general perspective: life course and developmental criminology. Additionally, the chapter provides a critical, perhaps unique, perspective on the role of gangs in social processes leading to delinquency as well as a brief discussion of the possibility that social media facilitates violent behavior.

Chapter 5, "'Causes' of Delinquency: Life Course Processes," covers explanations of how risk factors in children's lives from birth and beyond operate to produce delinquency. Included are pathways to different types of offending as well as desistance. Featured are Moffitt's Developmental Typology, Sampson and Laub's Life Course Theory of Crime, Thornberry and Krohn's Interactional Theory of Delinquency, Farrington's ICAP Theory, and Hagan's Developmental Theory of Street Crime. The chapter also describes how life course processes leading to delinquency are affected by historical context and social change as well as how they differ according to individuals' race or ethnicity and sex or gender. A brief discussion of the life courses of juvenile sex offenders is also included.

Part I ends with Chapter 6, "Informal Social Control." Before moving into discussions of formal social control (e.g., the juvenile justice system) in Part II, this chapter describes the role that other social institutions have in preventing or causing juvenile offending. After describing what a social institution is and how social control is one of their functions, we cover three main institutions. First, *the family* is discussed, with an emphasis on socialization, punishment, and supervision of children. Second, *education* is discussed, with an emphasis on how problems at school can facilitate delinquent behavior and issues of school violence. Third, *religion* is discussed, with an emphasis on how religious beliefs, values, and practices discourage or interfere with juvenile offending. The chapter then ends with a brief discussion of how *peers* may be considered a social control institution.

Chapter 7, "A Brief History of Juvenile Justice in the United States," provides an overview of the history of the juvenile justice system in the United States, which, you will note, is very much entwined with the U.S. history of juvenile institutionalization. It is very important to understand the history and philosophies of how the United States has reacted to youthful offenders, as well as how society viewed the cause of juvenile offending historically, to appreciate the juvenile justice system's creation as a completely separate entity from the traditional criminal justice system. This chapter notes the cycles that have existed throughout the decades of American juvenile justice. We have tried, failed, and tried again to deal appropriately with our country's troubled children, sometimes returning to a practice or philosophy that had been abandoned in the past. This has been caused, in part, by a re-questioning of what causes juvenile delinquency and what are the best ways to reduce juvenile crime.

Chapter 8, "Policing Juveniles," includes a general overview of how members of law enforcement interact with juveniles and status offenders as well as neglected and abused youth in the community. We also describe the typical processes involved in policing youth, such as search and seizure, *Miranda* warnings, and taking youth into custody. The chapter also delves deeper into aspects of juvenile policing that are more troubling, such as using extra-legal factors in decision making when it comes to arrest, racial and gender bias, and discrimination. A central feature of this discussion hinges on police discretion and concepts introduced to the reader, such as diversion and net widening. Special attention is given to the developmental and neurological differences between youth and adults and how interrogating youth can lead to severe consequences (e.g., false confessions), especially when coercive tactics are used. The last part of the chapter describes some of the ways in which members of law enforcement facilitate youth programming, such as gang violence prevention programs and school-based programs.

Chapter 9, "Juvenile Court," begins by framing juvenile court jurisdiction in terms of age and behavior, signaling the distinction that the court processes both youths who commit delinquent crimes (similar to adults) and youth who commit status offenses (crimes with which adults cannot be charged), in addition to youth who experience abuse and neglect. The chapter also unfolds with descriptions about the intake process and intake officer, screening and assessment procedures, as well as detention and preventative detention measures. There are many key courtroom personnel at work in the court, including the juvenile court judge, defense counsel or guardian ad litem, the juvenile probation officer, and potentially treatment staff. More formally and depending on how far the youth's case stretches into the system, the court is also described from the point of filing a petition to the various hearings (e.g., preliminary, adjudication, disposition). We also describe how some states allow juveniles to be transferred to adult court via juvenile court petition pathways or criminal court petition pathways. The chapter concludes with a description of a few specialty courts, namely teen courts, drug courts, and mental health courts.

Chapter 10, "Juvenile Corrections," begins with a review of the current philosophies that guide juvenile corrections, with an emphasis on philosophies such as rehabilitation and reintegration. In this chapter, we outline the notion that juvenile corrections can be distinguished as being part of a state or local system. We explain to the reader that there are many correctional services carried out at the local level and among non-profit agencies. In addition, we present community-based alternatives, which are the more common way in which a juvenile's needs are met. Such alternatives reduce stigma and aim to maintain the youth's ties to the community. Moreover, the chapter features descriptions of day report treatment centers, foster care, and group homes. Other forms of less stigmatizing punishment are featured, including home confinement and electronic monitoring, probation, restitution, and community service. For juveniles who require more supervision, residential treatment centers and detention centers are discussed. Programming options are showcased in this chapter as well. Last, the chapter highlights the harms of placing youth into solitary confinement.

In Chapter 11, "Juvenile Justice Reform: A Human Rights Perspective," we begin by describing the United Nations' *Convention on the Rights of the Child* as a way to place juvenile justice reform in a social justice and human rights context. The chapter provides a more extensive discussion on social justice and human rights issues related to three key areas of the system: policing, the legal system and the courts, and corrections. First, we present a deeper discussion about policing juveniles, disproportionate minority contact, and the importance of narrowing the net so that more youth are not unnecessarily caught up in or trapped in the system. The second area of reform to address, the legal system and the courts, unveils the problems that ensue with adult court jurisdiction, the harms of criminalizing youth for minor misbehavior, and the problems with casting juveniles into the adult court system, which only worsens or deepens youth criminality. In terms of the correctional system, this third social justice area provides the reader with insights about labeling and exclusion and highlights institutional and professional misconduct. The chapter ends with a discussion about advocacy and showcases some of the most well-known, progressive, and active advocacy groups in the country, including the Annie E. Casey Foundation, the Coalition for Juvenile Justice, and the Children's Defense Fund, just to name a few.

Finally, Chapter 12, "Current Issues in Juvenile Justice," presents an overview of some of the most prominent current issues facing the juvenile justice system. Within this chapter are discussions about the age of criminal responsibility, conditions of confinement in juvenile correctional facilities, the use of solitary confinement on juveniles, juvenile life without parole, and sexting. Within each area, discussions include background information and an overview of current trends. All of the issues extend beyond national concern. The age of criminal responsibility is a very pertinent current international topic of discussion. Conditions of confinement, in part, have to answer the question of what we should provide for children we place in locked, secure correctional facilities. The use of solitary confinement on juveniles is being addressed on a state-by-state basis after being banned at the federal level. The last of these issues has been recently addressed at the Supreme Court level. While examining Juvenile Life Without Parole (JLWOP) there are recent Supreme Court cases that are defining its practice. Intertwined in all of these issues are three underlining themes: (1) the current sentiment of moving away from punishment in the juvenile justice system, (2) recent discoveries about the adolescent brain and developmental model building, and (3) creating an effective, efficient juvenile justice system based on an understanding of and response to adolescent development.

Acknowledgments

Chapters 4 and 5 were originally written with support from a 2018 Summer Stipend awarded by the College of Humanities and Social Sciences' Research Center for the Humanities and Social Sciences at William Paterson University of New Jersey.

Juvenile Delinquency and Justice in the United States

Chapter 1

Introduction: What Is Delinquency?

Chapter Learning Objectives

Students will be able to:

- Classify delinquent acts
- Recognize general crime types
- Recall specific crime definitions
- Classify status offenses
- Summarize the characteristics of cyber delinquency
- Judge the seriousness of offenses
- Clarify the culturally relative nature of delinquency
- Clarify the socially constructed nature of delinquency
- Determine offenses that fit a consensus model of law and crime
- Determine offenses that fit a conflict model of law and crime
- Deconstruct one's biases in beliefs about delinquency
- Reflect on one's progress in understanding delinquency

Introduction

Juvenile delinquency is a problem. Like any problem, we must know exactly what it is before we can solve it. Without giving it much thought, we may assume we know what delinquency is: it's bad, illegal behavior (crime) committed by kids (people under age 18). This is largely true but overly simplistic and incomplete. No one likes to over-complicate matters, but delinquency is a complex issue. Thus, a sufficient understanding of it is necessarily complex. When we approach a problem with just a vague or incomplete understanding of it, it is unlikely that we will be able to solve it. We may even make it worse. Like its parent concept "crime," delinquency is a changing, multi-dimensional umbrella term that refers to several quite different behaviors. Further, we (academics, students, government authorities, juvenile justice professionals, and the general public) do not completely agree on the set of behaviors that constitute delinquent acts.

Defining the nature of delinquency is very difficult, and we are very imperfect in both the definitions we create and how we go about creating them. An important first step toward understanding delinquency is to question not only our basic definition of it, but our overall perspective on it as well. Because of our ideologies—our moral, cultural, philosophical, and professional beliefs, for example—we may not be very willing to question our views on the nature of delinquency. Still, again, it is important to develop a critical view of the problem of delinquency to be able to solve it. Thus, the objective of this chapter is to help the reader develop a comprehensive and philosophical answer to the question: "What is delinquency?"

Basic definitions of delinquency are a good starting point for exploring the nature of delinquency. The federal governmental authority on delinquency and juvenile justice in the U.S. is the Department of Justice's Office of Juvenile Justice and Delinquency Prevention (OJJDP). The OJJDP defines a **delinquent act** generally as follows.

> An act committed by a juvenile which, if committed by an adult, would be a criminal act. The juvenile court has jurisdiction over delinquent acts. Delinquent acts include crimes against persons, crimes against property, drug offenses, and crimes against public order. (OJJDP, n.d.)

There is an important condition in this definition that needs to be recognized. For an act to be considered delinquent, it must be illegal for adults. Thus, if an act is not illegal for adults, it cannot be considered delinquent when committed by a juvenile. Technically then, "status offenses" (discussed later), those which apply to juveniles only, are not delinquent acts. Thus, delinquency is defined heavily by the persons committing the behavior, not just the behavior itself. A 16-year-old who shoplifts commits a delinquent act while a 21-year-old who does the same commits a crime. This is not a trivial or arbitrary distinction, however. As will be discussed in following chapters, even when juveniles and adults commit the same behavior, the causes, motives, and social significance of the behavior can be much different when committed by juveniles versus adults. Of immediate concern, however, is that the basic distinction between criminal and delinquent acts means that definitions of types of delinquent acts are, for the most part, the same as those for criminal acts. In other words, they are the same for juveniles and adults, hence the following discussion of "crime" types.

There is a maximum age, usually 17, at which an offender's behavior is considered delinquency. Is there a minimum age? The OJJDP (n.d.) defines a juvenile as "a youth at or below the upper age of original juvenile court jurisdiction." It says nothing about a lower age of jurisdiction. So, can a five-year-old, for example, be a delinquent? We probably do not customarily think of very young children as "juveniles." The term might seem more synonymous with "adolescent," which refers to about ages 12–17. Most states legally define a person under the age of 12 as a "child," one who generally lacks the capability to understand the potential consequences of certain behaviors.

A child therefore cannot form "criminal intent"—a component necessary for determining that one has committed a crime (McNamara & Bucher, 2012). Contrary to what some may think, the juvenile justice system assumes that juvenile offenders are generally aware that their actions are wrong and thus they can be held legally responsible for them, just not in the same way as adults. Since young children are not legally responsible for their behavior, it is difficult to label their law-violating behavior as delinquent. There does not appear to be an official minimum age by which to define delinquency, but it may be safe to say that acts committed by very young children are not ordinarily considered delinquency. Child and family services are more likely to handle cases involving young children.

Nature of Delinquency: Crime Types

When we think of "delinquency," certain criminal acts may come to mind, often serious ones like physical assault and theft of expensive items. Then again, we might instead think of more common acts such as shoplifting, vandalism, and fighting. At any rate, delinquency encompasses a wide variety of types and sub-types of behaviors. Some types tend to be more or less serious than others, although the harm associated with acts also varies quite a bit within most categories as well. Further, while good typologies have mutually exclusive categories, the truth is that some acts could conceivably be seen as multiple types. Robbery, for example, is both a violent and property crime. Still, for clarity's sake, we tend to place acts in only one category and point out when their characteristics cross over into other categories. Knowing the multiple categories and several specific acts of delinquency is a good start to understanding the multidimensional nature of delinquency. As stated previously, different people share different definitions of delinquency. Thus, this chapter addresses official, academic, and other professional definitions of crime types.

Specific *legal* crime definitions differ in criminal codes across the 50 U.S. states, the federal government, and local jurisdictions in each state. It is beyond the scope of this book to cover them. The purpose here is to provide useful *conceptual* definitions of crime and delinquency. The U.S. Federal Bureau of Investigations (FBI) has established what may be the most comprehensive set of crime definitions in its Uniform Crime Report (UCR) Program's National Incident-Based Reporting System (NIBRS). The UCR/NIBRS definitions are not the official definitions used for charging persons with offenses. Instead, they categorize and organize crimes committed throughout the U.S. It is important to remember then that some specific criminal codes may not reflect elements of these general definitions.

The NIBRS definitions are based on common-law definitions found in *Black's Law Dictionary* and the National Crime Information Center's (NCIC) 2000 Uniform Offense Classifications. Since most states' statutes are also based on common-law definitions, most offenses should generally fit into NIBRS classifications (FBI, 2021). However, the UCR/NIBRS definitions are *official* in that they are used by the federal government for conducting national-level crime research. (The next chapter will discuss this research in length.) The OJJDP too offers definitions, though they are based heavily on UCR definitions. Finally, another federal governmental authority on crime is the Bureau of Justice Statistics (BJS), which conducts the annual National Crime Victimization Survey (NCVS) (also discussed in the next chapter). The following sections cover UCR/NIBRS, OJJDP, and BJS/NCVS definitions, as well as some others.

Violent Offenses

Violent crimes, also known as "crimes against the person," usually involve some sort of an attack upon a person's body. It is important to know that it is not necessary for an attack to result in physical contact or injury to be considered violent; violent crimes also include attempted attacks. **Violent crime** is defined in the UCR as offenses involving force or *threat* of force and recognizes four categories: murder and non-negligent manslaughter, rape, robbery, and aggravated assault (FBI, 2019). The BJS defines "attempted/threatened violence" as "the unsuccessful attempt of rape, sexual assault, personal robbery or assault" including "attempted attacks or sexual assaults by means of verbal threats" (BJS, n.d.b). Accordingly, the following discusses the categories of (non-sexual) assault, robbery, homicide, and hate crime. Bullying and stalking are also discussed here because they are largely defined by violence. Since there are several forms of sexual offenses, they will be discussed separately.

Assault. Beginning with assault, a distinction can be made between less and more serious offenses. The NCVS points out that assaults range from "minor threats to nearly fatal incidents" (BJS, n.d.b). The common distinction is between "aggravated" and "simple" assaults. "Sexual assault" is defined separately (covered next). "Assault" as a stand-alone term usually refers to attacks of a non-sexual nature. The NIBRS defines **aggravated assault** as:

> An unlawful attack by one person upon another wherein the offender uses a dangerous weapon or displays it in a threatening manner or the victim suffers obvious severe or aggravated bodily injury, or where there was a risk for serious injury/intent to seriously injure. (FBI, 2021, p. 17)

The definition goes on to specify injury as "apparent broken bones, loss of teeth, possible internal injury, severe laceration, or loss of consciousness."

The category of assault also includes *battery* (or *assault and battery*), a statutory term (used in specific laws) that refers to completed, not just attempted, assaults, which usually result in injury (OJJDP, n.d.). The NCVS clarifies that an aggravated assault may occur without a weapon if serious injury results (e.g., severely beating a victim using one's fists) or without injury if a weapon was somehow used. Serious injuries include "knife or gunshot wounds, broken bones, loss of teeth, loss of consciousness" and other injuries requiring large amounts of hospitalization (e.g., for serious internal injuries) (BJS, n.d.b). Basically, then, charges of aggravated assault are usually reserved for attacks that are potentially lethal or require medical attention.

Moving on to less serious assaults, the NIBRS defines **simple assault** as:

> An unlawful physical attack by one person upon another where neither the offender displays a weapon, nor the victim suffers obvious severe or aggravated bodily injury involving apparent broken bones, loss of teeth, possible internal injury, severe laceration, or loss of consciousness. (FBI, 2021, p. 18)

The NCVS definition of simple assault adds more detail: "Attack without a weapon resulting either in no injury, minor injury (for example, bruises, black eyes, cuts, scratches or swelling) or in undetermined injury requiring less than 2 days of hospitalization. Also includes attempted assault without a weapon" (BJS, n.d.b). "With minor injury" is defined as "an attack without a weapon resulting in such injuries as bruises, black eyes, cuts or in undetermined injury requiring less than two days of hospitalization" and "without injury" is defined as "an attempted assault without a weapon not resulting in injury" (BJS, n.d.b).

The categories of aggravated and simple assault do not sufficiently cover threats of violence. Thus, the NIBRS offers a third category, **intimidation**, which it defines as unlawfully placing "another person in reasonable fear of bodily harm through the use of threatening words and/or other conduct without displaying a weapon or subjecting the victim to an actual physical attack" (FBI, 2021, p. 18).

Robbery. Robbery may also be considered a property crime, since it involves the taking of possessions (e.g., money, jewelry, cell phones) from victims. However, since it involves force or the threat of force against persons, it is classified as a violent crime. As will be addressed later, theft offenses such as larceny, burglary, and auto theft do not involve force and are often committed without the victim's immediate knowledge.

The NIBRS defines **robbery** as taking or attempting to take "anything of value from the control, custody, or care of another person by force or threat of force and/or by putting the victim in fear of immediate harm" (FBI, 2021, p. 38). "Armed robbery" may often come to mind (e.g., using a gun to "hold up" an employee or pedestrian), but robbery often takes place without a gun or other weapon. The NCVS further explains that robbery may be attempted or completed, occur with or without injury, and committed with or without a weapon. For example, an unsuccessful attempt to take property by force or threat without the use of a weapon that does not result in injury would still be considered a type of (attempted) robbery (BJS, n.d.b). An example of robbery without use of a weapon is *mugging*, which involves physically taking something from a victim's person but without resulting in major injury (Bergman, 2014).

Homicide. Homicide is generally the killing of one human being by another, though incidents may involve multiple victims and/or offenders. Acts of homicide may be committed intentionally, unintentionally, or intentionally but in the defense of oneself or others. Not an unlawful act, "justifiable homicide" is the killing of someone committing a serious crime by police or private citizens for the sake of protection (FBI, 2021). The NIBRS defines **murder and non-negligent manslaughter** as "the willful (nonnegligent) killing of one human being by another" and **negligent manslaughter** as "the killing of another person through negligence" (FBI, 2021, pp. 29–30). Negligent manslaughter is more commonly known as simply "manslaughter." Manslaughter refers to acts that are not purely accidental in nature; the deaths are caused by recklessness or gross negligence. Manslaughter includes "vehicular manslaughter" (OJJDP, n.d.), which excludes deaths occurring from actual traffic accidents.

We may be more familiar with the terms *murder* and *manslaughter*, the unlawful homicides. These are defined in criminal statutes, with each divided into two categories (Fox et al., 2012). *First degree murder* refers to murders that are premeditated, non-premeditated if especially heinous (brutal, cruel, or extreme), or occur during the commission of another dangerous felony (e.g., arson or robbery). Premeditation here refers to planning or considering the act in advance, although not necessarily well in advance. This category is also known as "murder one," and "capital murder" when the offense is punishable by the death penalty (Bergman, 2014). *Second degree murder* then refers to murders (not committed during a dangerous felony) that are non-premediated or involve unintentional deaths caused by recklessness or "depraved indifference" to human life. This category is also known as "murder two" (Bergman, 2014).

Ranking in seriousness behind first- and second-degree murder, manslaughter is a felony homicide for which the killer is less morally culpable (Bergman, 2014). Fox and colleagues (2012, p. 8) define *voluntary manslaughter* as "the intentional killing of another person under extenuating circumstances, such as provocation or emotional duress (the so-called heat of passion) without time or opportunity for cooling off." This includes excessive or unreasonable use of force to kill someone in self-defense. *Involuntary manslaughter* then refers to killing another person through reckless or negligent acts which do not constitute felonies. This includes failing to fulfill one's duty (e.g., part of one's job) to prevent others from dying, such as controlling dangerous situations like handling hazardous materials, medication, or guns (Fox et al., 2012).

Attempted homicide or *attempted murder* may be classified as a type of aggravated assault. The NIBRS definition of aggravated assault includes the use of a dangerous weapon or some other means to cause serious bodily injury (FBI, 2021). Also, the OJJDP (n.d.) points out that the aggravated assault category includes "assault with intent to kill, assault with intent to commit murder or manslaughter, atrocious assault, attempted murder, felonious assault, and assault with a deadly weapon."

Hate Crime. According to the UCR, **hate crimes** are crimes "motivated, in whole or in part, by the offender's bias(es) against a race, religion, disability, sexual orientation, ethnicity, gender, gender identity ... even if the offenders are mistaken in their perception the victim was a member of a certain group." Further, victims include "individuals (adults and juveniles), businesses, institutions, and society" (FBI, n.d.). At least one of three things must occur for the NCVS to classify an offense as a hate crime: the police confirmed that it was bias-motivated, "the offender(s) used hate language," or "the offender(s) left behind hate symbols" (BJS, n.d.a). While hate crimes can involve several specific criminal acts, including crimes involving property, they are more commonly associated with violent acts. For example, marking a building with a racial slur is an act of vandalism, but it may be seen as a violent expression, perhaps intended to intimidate, especially if violence is stated in the graffiti.

Bullying. Like hate crime, bullying does not refer to a specific illegal act, and as a category may include several specific types of offenses. Usually, violence in some form is associated with bullying, even when property is involved (e.g., forcefully taking or damaging the victim's property), although the violence need not be physical. Whereas "hate crime" organizes offenses by motivation, "bullying" organizes them by victimization patterns and victim-offender relationship. Generally speaking, bullying is abuse committed by other juveniles instead of adults. While it may occur in a variety of environments (e.g., neighborhood, work, non-school related sports), bullying is more widely examined as a school violence issue.

Bullying is difficult to define, and definitions vary among scholars, policymakers, and practitioners. However, Swedish psychologist Dan Olweus provides a definition that has perhaps had the most influence upon anti-bullying policy and programs in the U.S. and other countries. Olweus' definition has three criteria (Cornell & Limber, 2015). *First*, **bullying** is intentional physical, verbal, or social aggression. Physical acts may also be considered assault, especially if severe. Verbal and social aggression is more difficult to identify and includes name-calling, spreading rumors, "shunning," teasing, or horseplay. *Second*, bullying involves some kind of a power imbalance between aggressor and victim. This is also difficult to identify as power can be established several ways, including differences in physical size, peer status (e.g., level of popularity and involvement in activities such as sports), minority status (e.g., sexual orientation), level of self-confidence, physical and cognitive abilities, and situational factors. *Third*, bullying is repeated aggressive behavior. In fact, it may also be considered a type of harassment, not limited to sexual harassment. A single act that does not meet the first two criteria would not constitute bullying. However, there is probably not a "minimum number" of acts required to establish a "pattern" of behavior. In fact, a single incident may still be classified as bullying if it can be established, by the presence of factors associated with bullying, that it is likely to be repeated in some form. Otherwise, authorities would have to wait until it happens again to recognize it as a problem (Cornell & Limber, 2015).

Stalking. Stalking too is defined more by a pattern of behaviors which may include other offenses (e.g., trespassing, damage to property, intimidation, and assault). Stalking is not a recognized offense type in FBI, BJS, or OJJDP classifications but it is recognized in criminology and state and local law. **Stalking** is also difficult to define but it generally refers to repeated intrusions such as unwanted monitoring, continuous communication, unwanted physical presence, and intimidating acts which annoy, frighten, or otherwise distress people targeted by such behaviors (Marcum et al., 2014). Like bullying, stalking considerably overlaps with harassment. Physical violence may not always occur with stalking, but the threat is always present and stalking is at least suggestively violent as it is intrusive upon one's physical, social, or psychological personal space. Stalking may also be a sexual offense if the offender's motives and/or behavior are sexual or potentially sexual in nature. The National Intimate Partner and Sexual Violence Survey measured "stalking tactics" as the following behaviors: watching/following from a distance or spying with a listening device, camera, or GPS; unwanted approaching or showing up at places such as home, work, or school; leaving strange or threatening items to be found, sneaking into a home or car and doing something to show that one has been there to scare the victim; leaving unwanted messages such as texts and voice messages; making unwanted phone calls including hang-up calls; sending unwanted emails, instant messages, or messages through social media websites; and leaving unwanted cards, letters, flowers, or presents (Black et al., 2011).

Finally, violent offenses are not limited to actions toward humans. The NIBRS defines **Animal Cruelty** as:

> Intentionally, knowingly, or recklessly taking an action that mistreats or kills any animal without just cause, such torturing, tormenting, mutilation, poisoning, or abandonment. Included are instances of duty to provide care, e.g., shelter, food, water, care if sick or injured; transporting or confining an animal to fight with another; inflicting excessive or repeated unnecessary pain or suffering, e.g., uses object to beat or injure an animal. (FBI, 2021, p. 16)

It should be noted that this definition applies to "any animal," not just pets.

Box 1.1: Simple Assault and Vehicular Assault in New Jersey

Title 2C:12-1a of the New Jersey Code of Criminal Justice states that a person is guilty of *simple assault* if one:

1) Attempts to cause or purposely, knowingly or recklessly causes bodily injury to another; or

2) Negligently causes bodily injury to another with a deadly weapon; or
3) Attempts by physical menace to put another in fear of imminent serious bodily injury.

Notice the lack of the term "serious" when referring to cause of bodily injury. The code elaborates: "Simple assault is a disorderly persons offense unless committed in a fight or scuffle entered into by mutual consent, in which case it is a petty disorderly persons offense."

Section 2C:12-1c defines *assault by auto or vessel*:

> A person is guilty of assault by auto or vessel when the person drives a vehicle or vessel recklessly and causes either serious bodily injury or bodily injury to another.... Assault by auto or vessel is a crime of the fourth degree if serious bodily injury results and is a disorderly persons offense if bodily injury results. Proof that the defendant was operating a hand-held wireless telephone while driving a motor vehicle ... may give rise to an inference that the defendant was driving recklessly.

Thus, a person can be accused or convicted of assault even if one does not intend to hurt anyone, but acts carelessly or irresponsibly, such as driving an automobile while distracted.

Source: Title 2C: The New Jersey Code of Criminal Justice. (n.d.). https://lis.njleg.state.nj.us/nxt/gateway.dll/statutes/1/2765/2859?f=templates$fn=document-frameset.htm

Box 1.2: Aggravated Assault in New Jersey

Title 2C:12-1b of the New Jersey Code of Criminal Justice states that a person is guilty of *aggravated assault* (which involves "serious" bodily injury) if one:

1) Attempts to cause serious bodily injury to another, or causes such injury purposely or knowingly or under circumstances manifesting extreme indifference to the value of human life recklessly causes such injury; or
2) Attempts to cause or purposely or knowingly causes bodily injury to another with a deadly weapon; or
3) Recklessly causes bodily injury to another with a deadly weapon; or
4) Knowingly under circumstances manifesting extreme indifference to the value of human life points a firearm ... at or in the direction of another, whether or not the actor believes it to be loaded; or
5) Commits a simple assault as defined in paragraph (1), (2) or (3) of subsection a. of this section upon: [The item goes on to specify several circumstances including civil servants, educators, and health care workers performing their duties]; or

6) Causes bodily injury to another person while fleeing or attempting to elude a law enforcement officer ... or while operating a motor vehicle in violation ...; or

7) Attempts to cause significant bodily injury to another or causes significant bodily injury purposely or knowingly or, under circumstances manifesting extreme indifference to the value of human life recklessly causes such significant bodily injury; or

8) Causes bodily injury by knowingly or purposely starting a fire or causing an explosion ... which results in bodily injury to any emergency services personnel involved in fire suppression activities, rendering emergency medical services resulting from the fire or explosion or rescue operations, or rendering any necessary assistance at the scene of the fire or explosion, including any bodily injury sustained while responding to the scene of a reported fire or explosion ...; or

9) Knowingly, under circumstances manifesting extreme indifference to the value of human life, points or displays a firearm ... at or in the direction of a law enforcement officer; or

10) Knowingly points, displays or uses an imitation firearm ... at or in the direction of a law enforcement officer with the purpose to intimidate, threaten or attempt to put the officer in fear of bodily injury or for any unlawful purpose; or

11) Uses or activates a laser sighting system or device, or a system or device which, in the manner used, would cause a reasonable person to believe that it is a laser sighting system or device, against a law enforcement officer acting in the performance of his duties while in uniform or exhibiting evidence of his authority ...; or

12) Attempts to cause significant bodily injury or causes significant bodily injury purposely or knowingly or, under circumstances manifesting extreme indifference to the value of human life, recklessly causes significant bodily injury to a person who, with respect to the actor, meets the definition of a victim of domestic violence ...; or

13) Knowingly or, under circumstances manifesting extreme indifference to the value of human life, recklessly obstructs the breathing or blood circulation of a person who, with respect to the actor, meets the definition of a victim of domestic violence ... by applying pressure on the throat or neck or blocking the nose or mouth of such person, thereby causing or attempting to cause bodily injury.

The code elaborates:

> Aggravated assault under paragraphs (1) and (6) of subsection b. of this section is a crime of the second degree; under paragraphs (2), (7), (9) and (10) of subsection b. of this section is a crime of the third degree; under

paragraphs (3) and (4) of subsection b. of this section is a crime of the fourth degree; and under paragraph (5) of subsection b. of this section is a crime of the third degree if the victim suffers bodily injury, otherwise it is a crime of the fourth degree. Aggravated assault under paragraph (8) of subsection b. of this section is a crime of the third degree if the victim suffers bodily injury; if the victim suffers significant bodily injury or serious bodily injury it is a crime of the second degree. Aggravated assault under paragraph (11) of subsection b. of this section is a crime of the third degree. Aggravated assault under paragraph (12) or (13) of subsection b. of this section is a crime of the third degree.

Source: Title 2C: The New Jersey Code of Criminal Justice. (n.d.). https://lis.njleg.state.nj.us/nxt/gateway.dll/statutes/1/2765/2859?f=templates$fn=document-frameset.htm

Sexual Offenses

As stated earlier, rape and sexual assault are violent "crimes against the person." These are the most severe sexual offenses and are but a few examples. Because there are several specific types of sexual offenses, some of which may not be directly or overtly violent in nature, they are covered separately here. The NIBRS defines "sex offenses" as "any sexual act directed against another person, without the consent of the victim, including instances where the victim is incapable of giving consent" (FBI, 2021, p. 39). *Juvenile sex offenses* are limited to actions by youth who may be held criminally responsible. Sexually aggressive or otherwise inappropriate behaviors by children under age 12 are often not classified as sexual offenses, but rather as *sexual behavior problems*. These are potentially non-problematic as sexual behavior is a normal part of development. However, persistent, coercive, or very harmful acts are problematic and potential precursors to adolescent or even adult sex offending (McNamara & Bucher, 2012).

Rape. The UCR defines **rape** as "penetration, no matter how slight, of the vagina or anus with any body part or object, or oral penetration by a sex organ of another person, without the consent of the victim" (FBI, 2019). The NIBRS defined *rape*, separately from statutory rape, as:

> The carnal knowledge of a person, without the consent of the victim, including instances where the victim is unable to give consent because of his/her age or because of his/her temporary or permanent mental or physical incapacity. (FBI, 2021, p. 39)

The NIBRS also specifies *sodomy*—nonconsensual oral or anal intercourse, *sexual assault with an object*—unlawful use of an object or instrument to penetrate genital or anal openings (FBI, 2021). Further, the UCR also recognizes *attempted rape*—"assaults or attempts to commit rape" (FBI, 2019), thereby recognizing acts which are not completed. At least two elements of the NIBRS's definition of rape are worth pointing out, as they counter commonly held rape myths. One is the condition in which a victim is incapable of consenting to sex. This establishes that one does not have the burden of openly stating that they do not want to have sex, and that a struggle or overt force does not have to take place. This is important considering that some victims are unable to communicate or resist, as when given a drug. The other is the reference to a victim as "his/her," which recognizes that men can be victims of rape.

The NIBRS also defines sex offenses that do not include force. *Incest* is "nonforcible sexual intercourse between persons who are related to each other within the degrees wherein marriage is prohibited by law," and **statutory rape** is "nonforcible sexual intercourse with a person who is under the statutory age of consent" (FBI, 2021, p. 40). Under these conditions, sexual activity is unlawful even if all parties willingly engage in it. In the case of statutory rape, a minor is considered unable to consent to sex by virtue of young age. Statutory rape laws are intended to prohibit adults from having sex with minors. However, it is possible for minors to be charged and convicted of statutory rape against other minors—so-called "Romeo and Juliet" cases. However, perhaps partly because of "close in age exemptions" added to many state laws, these cases are rare (Bierie & Budd, 2016).

Sexual Assault. The term "sexual assault" typically refers to sexual attacks that do not involve sexual penetration. The NIBRS does not offer a distinct definition of sexual assault separate from rape but does include the sub-category of *fondling*—the nonconsensual touching of private body parts for the purpose of sexual gratification (FBI, 2021). The NCVS, however, provides a description of **sexual assault**:

> A wide range of victimizations, separate from rape or attempted rape. These crimes include attacks or attempted attacks generally involving unwanted sexual contact between victim and offender. Sexual assaults may or may not involve force and include such things as grabbing or fondling. Sexual assault also includes verbal threats. (BJS, n.d.b)

The NCVS makes two important clarifications about rape and sexual assault. First, it points out that *rape* includes forced sexual intercourse through "psychological coercion," not just physical force, and that "attempted rape includes verbal threats of rape" (BJS, n.d.b). Further, the NCVS directly states that offenses include those against both male and female victims as well as those which takes place in both heterosexual and homosexual contexts.

Pressured Sex. Social scientists and victim advocates may define sexual victimization more broadly than do state or federal laws. Due either to insufficiently written laws or the state's limited capacity to control behavior, legal definitions may exclude sexual behaviors that bring harm to others. Social scientists and advocates focus on studying and reducing acts of *sexual victimization*, often regardless of whether they formally violate the law. Thus, their definitions of sexual offenses may include more behaviors than legal definitions. It is important to recognize these other types of behaviors because they can be very harmful and because they have implications for the development of juvenile sexual offending. Some research examines *pressured sex*, which includes subtler forms of harassment and coercion. Laws may not apply well to these kinds of situations because it would be difficult to prosecute the offender. However, pressured sex may leave the victim feeling just as harmed as if one were coerced into sex with threats of violence. The National Intimate Partner and Sexual Violence Survey measured **pressured sex** (vaginal, oral, or anal) as sex that resulted from behavior such as telling lies, making false promises about the future, threatening to end relationships, threatening to spread rumors about the victim, wearing the victim down with repeated requests for sex or expressions of unhappiness, and using authority (e.g., as a boss or teacher) over the victim (Black et al., 2011). The last example also constitutes sexual harassment, which is of course formally prohibited by civil law as well as organizational or institutional policies.

Additionally, some offenses of a sexual nature do not necessarily involve direct physical contact or highly aggressive behavior, though they may be correlated with more serious sex offending (youth who commit the minor offenses are at risk of committing the major offenses). These include sexual harassment, voyeurism, and exhibitionism.

Sexual Harassment. Sexual harassment is not included in FBI, BJS, or OJJDP categories, perhaps because it is controlled more by organizational policies than criminal law. Sexual harassment was traditionally viewed as a workplace issue but now it is also seen as a problem in schools, including high schools. **Sexual harassment** may be defined in several ways, but in the context of school environments it usually refers to unwelcome sexual conduct—including cyber activity such as texting, email, and use of social media—that damages the educational environment and interferes with others' abilities to learn (Clear et al., 2014). Of course, sexual harassment can take place outside of school. Sexual harassment is usually non-physical. Physical sexual harassment could be considered sexual assault, especially if touching of private body parts occurs. In fact, sexual harassment may be viewed on one end of a sexual assault continuum, with rape at the other end. Some research utilizes the Sexual Experiences Questionnaire, which measures sexual harassment with items asking about telling sexual stories or making sexual jokes, making sexual gestures or rude remarks, using sexual body language, and repeatedly asking someone out on a date or to "hookup" (Clear et al., 2014). Making *obscene phone calls* is also considered a sexual offense (McNamara & Bucher, 2012), which may also be seen as a type of harassment, especially if it occurs within organizational contexts.

Voyeurism. There are multiple types of **voyeurism** (McNamara & Bucher, 2012) but one more well-known offense is termed "***peeping Tom***," which is the act of secretly looking into a room or building for the purpose of voyeurism. This offense often involves trespassing and is not always a trivial matter, as the offender may be planning a more serious offense or engaging in stalking.

Exhibitionism. Another type of sex offense is **exhibitionism** (McNamara & Bucher, 2012), which is also excluded in FBI, BJS, or OJJDP categories. This offense occurs when one exposes one's private body parts (usually genitals) to another person or persons in an unwanted way, often to unsuspecting strangers, for sexual arousal (Swindell et al., 2011).

Box 1.3: Sexual Assault in Illinois

Article 11.5, subdivision 1.20 of the State of Illinois Criminal Code states that a person commits *criminal sexual assault* if one "commits an act of sexual penetration and

1) uses force or threat of force;
2) knows that the victim is unable to understand the nature of the act or is unable to give knowing consent;
3) is a family member of the victim, and the victim is under 18 years of age; or
4) is 17 years of age or over and holds a position of trust, authority, or supervision in relation to the victim, and the victim is at least 13 years of age but under 18 years of age."

Subdivision 1.30(a) states that a person commits *aggravated criminal sexual assault*, a more serious felony, if one "commits criminal sexual assault and any of the following aggravating circumstances exist during the commission of the offense or, for purposes of paragraph (7), occur as part of the same course of conduct as the commission of the offense:

1) the person displays, threatens to use, or uses a dangerous weapon, other than a firearm, or any other object fashioned or used in a manner that leads the victim, under the circumstances, reasonably to believe that the object is a dangerous weapon;
2) the person causes bodily harm to the victim, except as provided in paragraph (10);
3) the person acts in a manner that threatens or endangers the life of the victim or any other person;
4) the person commits the criminal sexual assault during the course of committing or attempting to commit any other felony;
5) the victim is 60 years of age or older;
6) the victim is a person with a physical disability;
7) the person delivers (by injection, inhalation, ingestion, transfer of possession, or any other means) any controlled substance to the victim without the victim's consent or by threat or deception for other than medical purposes;
8) the person is armed with a firearm;
9) the person personally discharges a firearm during the commission of the offense; or
10) the person personally discharges a firearm during the commission of the offense, and that discharge proximately causes great bodily harm, permanent disability, permanent disfigurement, or death to another person."

Subdivision 1.30b-c adds two other conditions: if the perpetrator "is under 17 years of age and: (i) commits an act of sexual penetration with a victim who is under 9 years of age; or (ii) commits an act of sexual penetration with a victim who is at least 9 years of age but under 13 years of age and the person uses force or threat of force to commit the act" or "commits an act of sexual penetration with a victim who is a person with a severe or profound intellectual disability." (Article 11 also defines sexual offenses that do not involve sexual penetration, including "criminal sexual abuse.")

Source: Criminal Offenses (720 ILCS 5/): Criminal Code of 2012. (2012). http://www.ilga.gov/legislation/ilcs/ilcs3.asp?ActID=1876&ChapterID=53

Property Offenses

Whereas violent crimes are offenses against the person, property crimes are offenses against things belonging to persons. Property offenses include not only the taking of property ("stealing") but also damaging and misusing others' property. The UCR defines **property crime** as theft-type offenses involving the taking of money or property without force or threat of force and destruction of property, and recognizes four categories: burglary, larceny-theft, motor vehicle theft, and arson (FBI, 2019). Also covered here are other types of property offenses.

Larceny-Theft. The NIBRS defines "**larceny/theft** offenses" as "the unlawful taking, carrying, leading, or riding away of property from the possession or constructive possession of another person" (FBI, 2021, p. 32) and identifies several acts: pocket-picking, purse-snatching, shoplifting, theft from a building, theft from a coin-operated machine or device, theft of motor vehicle parts or accessories, and theft from (not "of") a motor vehicle. This includes attempted larceny (OJJDP, n.d.). The NCVS stipulates that larceny occurs "by stealth, without force or deceit" and "excludes receiving and/or reselling stolen property (fencing), and thefts through fraud or deceit," and it defines "theft" separately as "completed or attempted theft of property or cash without personal contact" (BJS, n.d.b). Theft crimes involve the taking of several different types of items widely ranging in value. Thus, states distinguish between "grand" and "petty" larceny or theft. Petty larceny is a misdemeanor act in which property with a value lower than a statutory amount, often $500, is stolen, whereas grand larceny is a felony act in which property with a value greater than the statutory amount is stolen (Bergman, 2014).

Purse-snatching may seem like a crime against the person because the victim could possibly get hurt in the act, especially if the purse is snatched from the victim's body. The NCVS does not classify it as a violent crime (BJS, n.d.b), perhaps because the act usually does not involve injury. However, the NCVS uses the term "nonforcible purse snatching" when mentioning it as an example of larceny, and defines purse snatching, along with pocket picking, as "theft or attempted theft of property or cash directly from the victim by stealth, without force or threat of force" (BJS, n.d.b). According to the NIBRS, an incident should be classified as strong-arm robbery if "the offender used more force than was actually necessary to snatch the purse from the grasp of the victim, or if the victim resists the theft in any way" (FBI, 2021, p. 33). Thus, purse snatching cases involving force, and especially injury, would seem to constitute violent offenses. These acts could be considered "mugging," which as a type of robbery is a more violent crime (Bergman, 2014).

Motor Vehicle Theft. The stealing of a motor vehicle is typically seen as a category separate from "larceny-theft." The NIBRS defines motor vehicles to include automobiles (cars), buses, recreational vehicles, trucks, and other vehicles such as motorcycles and snowmobiles and does not classify an incident as motor vehicle theft if the stolen vehicle is the "proceeds of another crime" (FBI, 2021, p. 36). The OJJDP (n.d.) defines **motor vehicle theft** as the "unlawful taking, or attempted taking, of a self-propelled road vehicle owned by another, with the intent to deprive the owner of it permanently or temporarily." One particular type of auto theft, *carjacking*, is a violent crime—a type of robbery that involves the use or threat of physical force to take a vehicle from a driver (Topalli et al., 2015). More frequent among juveniles is the typically nonviolent offense of **joyriding**, stealing a vehicle for the fun of driving it rather than for material gain (Kellet & Gross, 2006). This offense can, of course, be serious if an accident occurs or there is damage to the vehicle, or the owner never regains possession of the vehicle.

Burglary/Breaking and Entering. The NIBRS defines **burglary/breaking and entering** as "the unlawful entry into a building or other structure with the intent to commit a felony or a theft" (FBI, 2021, p. 18). The OJJDP (n.d.) defines burglary with a little more detail: "Unlawful entry or attempted entry of any fixed structure, vehicle, or vessel used for regular residence, industry, or business, with or without force, with intent to commit a felony or larceny." The NCVS definition of burglary "includes only crimes where the offender committed or attempted a theft," distinguishing it from trespassing into a place (not just on land) which "includes crimes where the offender did not commit or attempt a theft" (BJS, n.d.b). These definitions recognize that forced entry, such as breaking a window or picking a lock, does not need to occur for an act to be considered burglary. What is important is the intruder does not have a legal right to be in a structure. One particular type of burglary, *home invasion*, is a violent crime—a type of robbery that occurs when residents are home and the intruder or intruders confront them and use force or threat of force to take property (Kopel & Blackman, 2009).

Vandalism. The NIBRS defines "destruction/damage/**vandalism** of property," that is not arson, as the willful or malicious destruction, damage, defacing, or otherwise injuring of "any public or private property without the consent of the owner or the person having custody or control of it" (FBI, 2021, p. 22). The OJJDP (n.d.) includes attempted vandalism. Acts of vandalism are numerous, including breaking windows or other parts of buildings and automobiles, damaging playground equipment, and graffiti, to name just a few. Of course, some acts of graffiti vandalism express gang identity and territory, and some are committed by street artists (who may or may not be gang members) (McNamara & Bucher, 2012). However, it should be noted that much street art is not vandalism, as it is created with appropriate permission—murals for example.

Arson. The NIBRS defines **arson** as an unlawful and intentional "damage or attempt to damage any real or personal property of another person or entity by fire or incendiary device" (FBI, 2021, p. 16). Arson is thus a non-accidental act, committed for a variety of reasons including fun, revenge, curiosity, or attention (McNamara & Bucher, 2012). The OJJDP (n.d.) adds that burning may be done by "fire or explosion." It is also important to note that arson may also be considered a violent crime if it is committed with the intention of harming a person.

Weapon Law Violations. The NIBRS defines **weapon law violations** as "the violation of laws or ordinances prohibiting the manufacture, sale, purchase, transportation, possession, concealment, or use of firearms, cutting instruments, explosives, incendiary devices, or other deadly weapons" (FBI, 2021, p. 41). The OJJDP (n.d.) adds that "weapons offenses" also include weapon accessories, the alteration of weapons, and attempted offenses. Weapon law offenses are difficult to categorize. They are grouped under property offenses here because they involve the illegal handling of a type of property—weapons (which may or may not be stolen). They could be grouped under violent offenses because of the association between weapons and violence, and the preceding definition mentions the use of weapons, which may be violent in nature even if not used in an attack. Then again, many weapon law violations are not violent in nature, and the violent uses of weapons meet the definitions of separate offenses. Also, for juveniles, many weapon violations could be considered status offenses since weapons, especially firearms, are more strictly controlled for minors. Regardless, it is important to be aware of this type of offense, as illegal weapon possession among juveniles is a recognized problem in the U.S.

Stolen Property. Separately from acts of theft themselves, **stolen property** offenses are defined in the NIBRS as "buying, receiving, possessing, selling, concealing, or transporting any property with the knowledge that it has been unlawfully taken, as by burglary, embezzlement, fraud, larceny, robbery, etc." (FBI, 2021, p. 41). The category includes attempted offenses (OJJDP, n.d.).

Counterfeiting and Forgery. The NIBRS defines counterfeiting/forgery as:

> The altering, copying, or imitating of something, without authority or right, with the intent to deceive or defraud by passing the copy or thing altered or imitated as that which is original or genuine, or the selling, buying, or possession of an altered, copied, or imitated thing with the intent to deceive or defraud. (FBI, 2021, p. 21)

The OJJDP (n.d.) definition includes attempted forgery and counterfeiting.

Fraud. The NIBRS defines "fraud offenses," excluding counterfeiting/forgery, as "the intentional perversion of the truth for the purpose of inducing another person or other entity in reliance upon it to part with something of value or to surrender a legal right" (FBI, 2021, p. 24). More specifically, these offenses include *false pretenses/swindle/confidence game*—the use of deception to obtain things of value, *credit card/automated teller machine fraud*, *impersonation*—pretending to be someone else in order to obtain something of value, *welfare fraud*—using deception to obtain welfare benefits, *wire fraud*—the fraudulent use of electric or electronic communications facilities, *identity theft*—obtaining and/or using someone else's personal data, *hacking/computer invasion*—accessing the computer, software or hardware, or networks of another person or institution without permission, and *money laundering*—transforming profits of crime into legitimate assets (FBI, 2021). The NCVS elaborates on fraud against a business:

> Fraud may be committed by someone inside or outside the business. Includes instances in which a computer was used to defraud the business of money, property, financial documents, insurance policies, deeds, use of rental cars, or various services by forgery, misrepresented identity, credit card or wire fraud. Excludes incidents of embezzlement. (BJS, n.d.b)

Using bad checks may also be considered a type of fraud (OJJDP, n.d.).

Theft of Personal or Financial Data. The NCVS includes a separate category on the act of acquiring information that one does not have legal access to, which is likely to be used to commit fraud. The NCVS defines theft of personal or financial data as:

> The illegal obtaining of information that potentially allows someone to use or create accounts under another name (individual, business, or some other entity). Personal information includes names, dates of birth, Social Security numbers, or other personal information. Financial information includes credit, debit, or ATM card account or PIN numbers. Excludes theft of intellectual property such as copyrights, patents, trade secrets, and trademarks. Excludes theft of any other type of information. (BJS, n.d.b)

Illegally acquiring personal and financial data may be done for the purpose of identity theft. The NCVS defines ***identity theft*** as one of three types of offenses: "unauthorized use or attempted use of an existing account," "unauthorized use or attempted use of personal information to open a new account," or "misuse of personal information for a fraudulent purpose" (BJS, n.d.b). Personal or financial data and identity thefts involving the use of computer technology and the internet would constitute "cybercrimes," which will be discussed later.

Some offenses are rarely committed by juveniles. The NIBRS defines **embezzlement** as "the unlawful misappropriation by an offender to his/her own use or purpose of money, property, or some other thing of value entrusted to his/her care, custody, or control" (FBI, 2021, p. 23). The offender is usually an employee and acts include "instances in which a computer was used to wrongfully transfer, counterfeit, forge or gain access to money, property, financial documents, insurance policies, deeds, use of rental cars, or various services by the person to whom they were entrusted" (BJS, n.d.b). The NIBRS defines ***extortion/blackmail*** as unlawfully obtaining "money, property, or any other thing of value, either tangible or intangible, through the use or threat of force, misuse of authority, threat of criminal prosecution, threat of destruction of reputation or social standing, or through other coercive means" (FBI, 2021, p. 24). Since force may be involved, some cases may also be violent offenses. The NIBRS defines ***bribery*** as "the offering, giving, receiving, or soliciting of anything of value (i.e., a bribe, gratuity, or kickback) to sway the judgment or action of a person in a position of trust or influence" (FBI, 2021, p. 18).

Box 1.4: Larceny in New York

New York State law states: "A person steals property and commits larceny when, with intent to deprive another of property or to appropriate the same to himself or to a third person, he wrongfully takes, obtains or withholds such property from an owner thereof. Larceny includes a wrongful taking, obtaining or withholding of another's property" (Article 155.05). Regarding *petit (petty) larceny*, a Class A misdemeanor, Article 155.25 simply states: "A person is guilty of petit larceny when he steals property." *Grand larceny* is divided into four degrees of severity.

155.30. A person is guilty of grand larceny in the fourth degree (Class E felony) when:

1) "The value of the property exceeds one thousand dollars; or
2) The property consists of a public record, writing or instrument kept, filed or deposited according to law with or in the keeping of any public office or public servant; or
3) The property consists of secret scientific material; or
4) The property consists of a credit card or debit card; or
5) The property, regardless of its nature and value, is taken from the person of another; or
6) The property, regardless of its nature and value, is obtained by extortion; or
7) The property consists of one or more firearms, rifles or shotguns . . . ; or
8) The value of the property exceeds one hundred dollars and the property consists of a motor vehicle . . . other than a motorcycle . . . ; or
9) The property consists of a scroll, religious vestment, a vessel, an item comprising a display of religious symbols which forms a representative expression of faith, or other miscellaneous item of property which: (a) has a value of at least one hundred dollars; and (b) is kept for or used in connection with religious worship in any building, structure or upon the curtilage of such building or structure used as a place of religious worship by a religious corporation. . . .
10) The property consists of an access device which the person intends to use unlawfully to obtain telephone service.
11) The property consists of anhydrous ammonia or liquified ammonia gas and the actor intends to use, or knows another person intends to use,

such anhydrous ammonia or liquified ammonia gas to manufacture methamphetamine."

155.35. A person is guilty of grand larceny in the third degree (Class D felony) when:

1) "The value of the property exceeds three thousand dollars, or
2) The property is an automated teller machine or the contents of an automated teller machine."

155.40. A person is guilty of grand larceny in the second degree (Class C felony) when:

1) "The value of the property exceeds fifty thousand dollars; or
2) The property, regardless of its nature and value, is obtained by extortion committed by instilling in the victim a fear that the actor or another person will (a) cause physical injury to some person in the future, or (b) cause damage to property, or (c) use or abuse his position as a public servant by engaging in conduct within or related to his official duties, or by failing or refusing to perform an official duty, in such manner as to affect some person adversely."

155.42. A person is guilty of grand larceny in the first degree (Class B felony) "when the value of the property exceeds one million dollars."

Additionally, all four degrees include the option, or

The property consists of retail goods or merchandise stolen pursuant to a common scheme or plan or a single, ongoing intent to deprive another or others of the property or to appropriate the property to the actor or another person and the value of the property exceeds [dollar amount for each level] ...

Source: Laws of New York, Penal: Part 3—Specific Offenses. (n.d.). https://www.nysenate.gov/legislation/laws/PEN/P3TJA155

Drug Offenses

Drug offenses include the production, possession, use, distribution, and selling of controlled substances, including the illegitimate handling and use of prescription drugs. Many drug offenses do not have clear victims, other than perhaps the persons who use drugs to the detriment of their health. Thus, they may also be categorized as public order offenses, discussed next. However, other drug offenses and drug-related offenses could or do have victims or cause some other tangible problem, such as driving while under the influence, selling drugs to children, and operating dangerous drug labs. Thus, "drug offenses" is offered here as a separate category.

The NIBRS defines **drug/narcotic offenses**, excluding driving under the influence, as "the violation of laws prohibiting the production, distribution, and/or use of certain controlled substances and the equipment or devices utilized in their preparation and/or use" (FBI, 2021, p. 23). Specifically, ***drug/narcotic violations*** is defined as "the unlawful cultivation, manufacture, distribution, sale, purchase, use, possession, transportation, or importation of any controlled substance" and ***drug equipment violations*** is defined as "the unlawful manufacture, sale, purchase, possession, or transportation of equipment or devices utilized in preparing and/or using drugs or narcotics" (FBI, 2021, pp. 23). The second definition points out that drug equipment itself, a "meth lab" for instance, is illegal regardless of the presence of drugs. The BJS defines ***drug possession*** as an act that "includes possession of an illegal drug, but excludes possession with intent to sell" (BJS, n.d.b).

Driving Under the Influence. The NIBRS defines **driving under the influence** as "Driving or operating a motor vehicle or common carrier while mentally or physically impaired as the result of consuming an alcoholic beverage or using a drug or narcotic" (FBI, 2021, p. 43). Driving a vehicle while under the influence of a substance is difficult to classify. Since some cases involve an accident in which persons are physically injured or killed, it has some qualities of a violent crime. On the other hand, most cases likely do not involve the intentional use or threat of violence. People typically do not drink and drive, for example, with the intention of harming someone, although an impaired driver may be accused of "vehicular manslaughter" if one is involved in an accident in which another person is killed. Driving under the influence is grouped under drug offenses here because the act involves the illegal use of alcohol or drugs.

Box 1.5: Drug Offenses in Missouri

Regarding *drug possession*, Chapter 579.015 of the State of Missouri Statutes states:

1. A person commits the offense of possession of a controlled substance if he or she knowingly possesses a controlled substance....
2. The offense of possession of any controlled substance except thirty-five grams or less of marijuana or any synthetic cannabinoid is a class D felony.
3. The offense of possession of more than ten grams but thirty-five grams or less of marijuana or any synthetic cannabinoid is a class A misdemeanor.
4. The offense of possession of not more than ten grams of marijuana or any synthetic cannabinoid is a class D misdemeanor. If the defendant has previously been found guilty of any offense of the laws related to controlled substances of this state, or of the United States, or any state, territory, or district, the offense is a class A misdemeanor.

Regarding *delivery* of a controlled substance, Chapter 579.020 states:

1. A person commits the offense of delivery of a controlled substance if ... he or she: (1) Knowingly distributes or delivers a controlled substance;

(2) Attempts to distribute or deliver a controlled substance; (3) Knowingly possesses a controlled substance with the intent to distribute or deliver any amount of a controlled substance; or (4) Knowingly permits a minor to purchase or transport illegally obtained controlled substances.

2. Except when the controlled substance is thirty-five grams or less of marijuana or synthetic cannabinoid or as otherwise provided under subsection 5 of this section, the offense of delivery of a controlled substance is a class C felony.
3. Except as otherwise provided under subsection 4 of this section, the offense of delivery of thirty-five grams or less of marijuana or synthetic cannabinoid is a class E felony.
4. The offense of delivery of thirty-five grams or less of marijuana or synthetic cannabinoid to a person less than seventeen years of age who is at least two years younger than the defendant is a class C felony.
5. The offense of delivery of a controlled substance is a class B felony if: (1) The delivery or distribution is any amount of a controlled substance except thirty-five grams or less of marijuana or synthetic cannabinoid, to a person less than seventeen years of age who is at least two years younger than the defendant; or (2) The person knowingly permits a minor to purchase or transport illegally obtained controlled substances.

Regarding *possession of drug paraphernalia*, Chapter 579.074 states:

1. A person commits the offense of unlawful possession of drug paraphernalia if he or she knowingly uses, or possesses with intent to use, drug paraphernalia to plant, propagate, cultivate, grow, harvest, manufacture, compound, convert, produce, process, prepare, test, analyze, pack, repack, store, contain, conceal, inject, ingest, inhale, or otherwise introduce into the human body, a controlled substance or an imitation controlled substance in violation of this chapter or chapter 195.
2. The offense of unlawful possession of drug paraphernalia is a class D misdemeanor, unless the person has previously been found guilty of any offense of the laws of this state related to controlled substances or of the laws of another jurisdiction related to controlled substances, in which case the violation of this section is a class A misdemeanor. . . .
3. The offense of unlawful possession of drug paraphernalia is a class E felony if the person uses, or possesses with intent to use, the paraphernalia in combination with each other to manufacture, compound, produce, prepare, test, or analyze amphetamine or methamphetamine or any of their analogues.

Source: Revisor of Statutes, State of Missouri. (n.d.). *Title XXXVIII crimes and punishment: Chapter 579 controlled substance offenses.* http://revisor.mo.gov/main/OneChapter.aspx?chapter=579

Public Order Offenses

Although the term is frequently used in criminology, **public order offense** is difficult to define. However, it seems fairly clear this it refers to acts that do not involve an identifiable victim, other than sometimes the person committing the offense, and are prohibited because they are perceived to threaten society's moral well-being more than cause tangible harm (Dabney, 2004). Some acts such as prostitution, gambling, and drunkenness are considered "vice crimes" because they involve indulgence in a pleasurable activity in a way that goes against mainstream cultural norms. Perhaps another organizing element of public order offenses is that they do not fit elsewhere. Because tangible harm or victims are often difficult to identify, public disorder offenses can be difficult to categorize, although property is often somehow involved. At any rate, this section briefly defines types of offenses often identified as public disorder.

Disorderly Conduct. The NIBRS defines this offense as "any behavior that tends to disturb the public peace or decorum, scandalize the community, or shock the public sense of morality" (FBI, 2021, p. 43). The OJJDP (n.d.) defines it as "unlawful interruption of the peace, quiet, or order of a community, including offenses called disturbing the peace, vagrancy, loitering, unlawful assembly, and riot."

Curfew/Loitering/Vagrancy Violations. The NIBRS defines these offenses as:

> The violation of a court order, regulation, ordinance, or law requiring the withdrawal of persons from the streets or other specified areas; prohibiting persons from remaining in an area or place in an idle or aimless manner; or prohibiting persons from going from place to place without visible means of support. (FBI, 2021, p. 842)

Liquor Law Violations. The NIBRS defines these, separately from driving under the influence and drunkenness, as "the violation of laws or ordinances prohibiting the manufacture, sale, purchase, transportation, possession, or use of alcoholic beverages" (FBI, 2021, p. 43). This definition is more relevant to adults and could include the sale of alcohol to minors. Underage alcohol use is addressed under status offenses.

Trespassing. The NIBRS defines "trespass of real property" as unlawfully entering "land, a dwelling, or other real property" (FBI, 2021, p. 44). The OJJDP (n.d.) categorizes trespassing as a crime against property but distinguishes it from more serious offenses: "unlawful entry or attempted entry of the property of another with the intent to commit a misdemeanor other than larceny or without intent to commit a crime."

Prostitution. The NIBRS defines **prostitution** as engaging in "commercial sex acts for anything of value" (not just money) (FBI, 2021, p. 38). Prostitution offenders are also often victims as many are forced, coerced, deceived, or persuaded into engaging in acts of prostitution or otherwise exploited. This may be particularly true of juveniles who tend to be more impressionable than adults and are considered unable to consent to sex. In fact, prostitution offenses as a broader category also include purchasing and assisting or promoting sex services (FBI, 2021). Especially when juveniles are involved,

these two types, which may involve violence and sex offending, cannot be considered simple "disorder" and are thus discussed separately, later.

Gambling. The NIBRS defines gambling offenses as unlawfully betting or wagering money or something of value; operating, promoting, or assisting gambling activities; possessing or transmitting wagering information; gambling equipment violations; and sports tampering (FBI, 2021).

Family Offenses, Nonviolent. The NIBRS defines these as "unlawful, nonviolent acts by a family member (or legal guardian) that threaten the physical, mental, or economic well-being or morals of another family member and that are not classifiable as other offenses, such as assault, incest, and statutory rape" (FBI, 2016, p. 8).

Status Offenses

Status offenses are non-criminal offenses; they are not illegal for adults. As stated earlier, they are not technically delinquent acts, although they are illegal when committed by juveniles. This is likely because these offenses are, unlike criminal/delinquent acts, defined by the social position of the persons doing them more than the acts themselves (although status offenses are indeed harmful). However, for practical and informal purposes, it may be permissible to speak of status offenses in the same vein as delinquency. What may be more important is that both delinquent acts and status offenses are both matters of "juvenile offending," and that patterns of offending may include persistent, serious status offending or both delinquent and status offending. For example, a juvenile may commit both property or violent crimes and status offenses, and the same problems in their life may underlie both. The OJJDP (n.d.) defines a **status offense** as "acts or types of conduct that are offenses only when committed or engaged in by a juvenile and that can be adjudicated only by a juvenile court " and includes the following.

Curfew. A curfew violation is the violation of an ordinance that prohibits juveniles from being in public places during certain hours. These hours are usually nighttime hours (McNamara, 2008). Curfew as well as loitering were defined earlier along with vagrancy violations in a general category that also applies to adults. However, as juvenile status offenses, curfew and loitering refer to violations of local ordinances that only apply to persons under age 18 (OJJDP, n.d.). These ordinances vary greatly across locations, and some may apply to youth under age 16 or 17 rather than 18, but most include exceptions for youth who are accompanied by adults or traveling to or from an acceptable activity (such as school-related functions or work) (McNamara, 2008).

Ungovernability. The OJJDP (n.d.) defines ungovernability" as "being beyond the control of parents, guardians, or custodians or being disobedient of parental authority." This offense is also known as *incorrigibility*, which refers to habitually disobeying parents or legal guardians—not listening to them and following their rules (McNamara, 2008). The key term here is *habitually.* Most children disobey their parents to some degree. Some may do so minimally, some may do so moderately, and others may do so extremely. Although exactly what constitutes incorrigibility is subjective and varies across authorities, the term is reserved for more severe disobedience.

Running Away. Running away is defined as "leaving the custody and home of parents or guardians, or custodians without permission and failing to return within a reasonable length of time, in violation of a statute regulating the conduct of youth" (OJJDP, n.d.). Further, the NIBRS defines a runaway as "a person under 18 years of age who has left home without permission of his/her parent(s) or legal guardian" (FBI, 2016, p. 8).

Truancy. Truancy is the "violation of a compulsory school attendance law" (OJJDP, n.d.), or more simply being absent from school without permission (Falcone, 2010). Informally, it is known as "skipping" or "cutting" school or class.

Status Liquor Law Violations. The OJJDP (n.d.) defines these as "Violation of laws regulating the possession, purchase, or consumption of liquor by minors" and points out that "Some States treat consumption of alcohol and public drunkenness of juveniles as status offenses rather than delinquency." Thus, status liquor law violations involve more than just underage drinking.

Underage Smoking. Neither the FBI nor the BJS defines underage smoking, but it is illegal for juveniles to smoke or use other tobacco products. Tobacco products include cigarettes, cigars, pipe tobacco, and smokeless products such as "chew" and "snuff" (McNamara & Bucher, 2012).

Other Offenses

Obstruction of justice offenses are very difficult to group with other offenses because they do not directly confront property, violence, or drug issues, and some offenses could have serious harmful consequences while others may resemble a less serious public order type offense. However, they are important offenses to recognize. The OJJDP (n.d.) defines **obstruction of justice** as "Intentionally obstructing court or law enforcement efforts in the administration of justice, acting in a way calculated to lessen the authority or dignity of the court, failing to obey the lawful order of a court, escape from confinement, and violating probation or parole." Examples include contempt, perjury, bribing witnesses, failing to report a crime, and nonviolent resisting of arrest.

Some offenses are rarely committed by juveniles but often involve them as victims. Many of these involve violent and/or sexual offending. One is ***human trafficking***—using force, fraud, or coercion, or inducement or enticement if the victim is a minor, to make a person perform a commercial sex act, labor, or other services (FBI, 2021). It is important to know that human trafficking involves more than just sex trafficking. The NIBRS defines "commercial sex act" trafficking as "inducing a person by force, fraud, or coercion to participate in commercial sex acts, or in which the person induced to perform such act(s) has not attained 18 years of age" and "involuntary servitude" trafficking as obtaining "person(s) through recruitment, harboring, transportation, or provision, and subjecting such persons to force, fraud, or coercion into involuntary servitude, peonage, debt bondage, or slavery" excluding commercial sex acts (FBI, 2021, p. 31).

Other offenses overlap with or are similar to sex trafficking. ***Purchasing prostitution*** is defined as the buying or trading of "anything of value for sex acts," and ***assisting or promoting prostitution*** is defined as: "To solicit customers or transport persons for prostitution purposes; to own, manage, or operate a dwelling or other establishment for the purpose of providing a place where prostitution is performed; or to otherwise assist or promote prostitution" (FBI, 2021, p. 38). The NIBRS definition of sex trafficking above may be interpreted to mean that force, fraud, or coercion are not needed to induce minors. Thus, the pimping of juveniles may always be seen as sex trafficking.

Another related offense is ***pornography/obscene material***, defined as "the violation of laws or ordinances prohibiting the manufacture, publishing (publication), distributing (distribution), sale, purchase, or possession of sexually explicit material deemed legally obscene" (FBI, 2021, p. 37). Finally, another offense involving juveniles as victims more than offenders is ***kidnapping/abduction***, defined as "the unlawful seizure, transportation, and/or detention of a person against his/her will or of a minor without the consent of his/her custodial parent(s) or legal guardian" (FBI, 2021, p. 32).

Finally, there are also several offenses that we could label "***petty offenses***," defined specifically in local ordinances, that are difficult to place in the preceding categories and too numerous to cover. Falcone (2010, p. 179) defines a **petty offense** as "an infraction or lower level misdemeanor ... for which the sanction does not extend beyond six months confinement or a fine if not more than $500 or both." These may include

offenses such as jaywalking, littering, noise ordinance violations, and minor traffic violations. While typically not very severe, these offenses are still tangibly harmful (which is why it is difficult to categorize them simply as public order offenses) and could be dangerous. Jaywalking, for example, could cause a traffic accident.

Cyber Delinquency

Many of the types of offenses described above can be committed with the use of cell phones, computers, and the internet. Also, the development of this technology has been accompanied by the development of newer forms of crime. Subsequently, a new offense category has been created: **cybercrime**. With great access to computers and the internet, it is no surprise that juveniles also participate in cybercrime, or in their case, "cyber delinquency." The NCVS defined three general types of cybercrimes: cyber attacks, cyber theft, and other computer security incidents (BJS, n.d.c).

Cyber Attacks. **Cyber attacks** are "crimes in which the computer system is the target," consisting "of computer viruses . . . , denial of service attacks, and electronic vandalism or sabotage." A *computer virus* is "a hidden fragment of computer code which propagates by inserting itself into or modifying other programs," including "viruses, worms, and Trojan horses" but excluding "spyware, adware, and other malware." *Denial of service* is "the disruption, degradation, or exhaustion of an Internet connection or e-mail service that results in an interruption of the normal flow of information . . . usually caused by ping attacks, port scanning probes, or excessive amounts of incoming data." *Electronic vandalism or sabotage* is "the deliberate or malicious damage, defacement, destruction or other alteration of electronic files, data, web pages, or programs" (BJS, n.d.c).

Cyber Thefts. **Cyber thefts** are "crimes in which a computer is used to steal money or other things of value," including "embezzlement, fraud, theft of intellectual property, and theft of personal or financial data" (BJS, n.d.c). Embezzlement, fraud, and theft of personal or financial data were defined earlier and may also be committed without cyber technology. ***Theft of intellectual property*** is defined here because juveniles would rarely be able to commit this offense without electronic access. The NCVS defines theft of intellectual property as:

> The illegal obtaining of copyrighted or patented material, trade secrets, or trademarks (including designs, plans, blueprints, codes, computer programs, software, formulas, recipes, graphics) usually by electronic copying. Excludes theft of personal or financial data such as credit card or social security numbers, names and dates of birth, financial account information, or any other type of information. (BJS, n.d.b)

Piracy and *illegal file sharing* are examples of intellectual property thefts which have been facilitated by cyber technology (Kigerl, 2013). Piracy occurs when someone obtains copyrighted materials such as music, videos, and books without the copyright holder's permission with the intent of distributing it, for profit or simply for sharing. Although they are also used for legitimate distribution, P2P file sharing networks make it easier to illegally distribute these materials, which harms sales and distribution by authorized parties.

Other Computer Security Incidents. This category refers to illegal activities not covered under the other two: "spyware, adware, hacking, phishing, spoofing, pinging, port scanning, and theft of other information, regardless of whether the breach was successful" (BJS, n.d.b). *Hacking* is one of the more prevalent offenses among juveniles. Hacking may be motivated by fascination with learning about computer systems and programming and the challenge of gaining access (McNamara & Bucher, 2012), not necessarily financial gain or destructiveness. Particular forms of hacking include "cracking"—breaking into secure databases—or "spoofing"—gaining access by posing as a legitimate user. Hackers may get users' information through "social engineering"—pretending to be a user having trouble with a system (e.g., claiming to have lost a password)—or "dumpster diving"—searching through a company's trash to find login, personal, and other confidential information (McNamara & Bucher, 2012).

Cyberbullying. Bullying, defined earlier, existed long before cell phones, personal computers, and the internet and still takes place without their use. However, the use of modern digital communication to commit these offenses has recently become a major issue. The conceptual definition of cyberbullying is fundamentally the same as bullying in general; it is the mode of communication or contact that is different. Of course, digital communication replaces physical contact such as hitting victims, although this does not necessarily make cyber forms less dangerous. In fact, digital communication may actually facilitate bullying, enabling aggressors to impose their presence upon others more easily and from a distance. Thus cyberbullying, as well as cyberstalking (discussed next) may alternatively be seen as "cyber harassment." Digital communica-

Figure 1.1: Delinquency Typology

Violent		
Aggravated Assault Bullying Robbery Attempted Murder	Murder Simple Assault Stalking Hate Crime	Animal Abuse Manslaughter Intimidation
Sexual		
Forcible Rape Attempted Rape Statutory Rape (non-forcible)	Incest Rape (non-forcible) Sexual Assault Pressured Sex	Sexual Harassment Voyeurism Exhibitionism
Property		
Larceny-Theft Theft of Personal or Financial Data Stolen Property Arson Blackmail	Vandalism Motor Vehicle Theft Bad Checks Fraud Counterfeiting	Forgery Weapon Law Burglary/B&E Extortion Embezzlement
Drug		
Cultivation & Manufacture Sale & Distribution Transportation & Importation	Drug Equipment Purchase Possession & Use	Driving under Influence Drug Related Offenses
Public Order		
Disorderly Conduct Liquor Law Violations Prostitution Trespassing	Vagrancy Curfew Nonviolent Family Offenses	Gambling Drunkenness Loitering
Status Offenses		
Curfew Running Away	Truancy Incorrigibility	Liquor Law Violation Underage Smoking
Other Offenses/Juvenile Victimizations		
Human Trafficking Assisting/Promoting Prostitution	Purchasing Prostitution Kidnapping/Abduction Pornography/Obscene Material	Obstruction of Justice Petty Offenses
Cyber Offenses		
Virus Attacks Denial of Service Electronic Vandalism/ Sabotage	Theft of Intellectual Property (e.g. Piracy & File Sharing) Other Computer Security Incidents (e.g. Hacking)	Cyber-bullying Cyber-stalking Cyber Thefts

tion has especially facilitated verbal and social bullying. Through web postings, text messages, and tweets, for example, aggressors are able to repeatedly commit serious acts of public humiliation of others (Cornell & Limber, 2015).

Cyberstalking. Stalking is also a pre-existing offense facilitated by cyber technology, much in the same way as cyberbullying. For example, offenders can use the internet anonymously, easily, and efficiently to use personal information to threaten or intimidate victims, repeatedly send hostile emails or instant messages, and impersonate victims after stealing their email or social network login information (Marcum et al., 2014).

Delinquency and Control in Social Context

Understanding official definitions of delinquency is good but only a start. The nature of delinquency is a complex issue. The general limitation of official definitions is that they only cover behaviors which have been declared by legislative bodies to be illegal. This presents two problems. One is that it is possible that the legal "umbrella" or "net" covers behavior that is not seriously harmful. Law may in some ways be too inclusive. We cannot assume that someone is always doing something awful when violating a law. If someone is loitering, for example, are they really doing any harm, with the loitering itself? (Maybe, maybe not.) On the other hand, the other problem is that the law may not prohibit some behaviors which can be quite harmful. Law may also in some ways be too exclusive. Let's think for a minute: Are there some acts that should be illegal but are not? Some non-illegal acts may be more harmful than some illegal acts (Bohm & Vogel, 2015). For example, which is worse, loitering or making exaggerated claims in sales advertising? Maybe what we really need to be worried about, then, is harmful or potentially harmful behavior on the part of juveniles, more than simply what is or is not illegal.

Thus far, we have barely explored the nature of delinquency in terms of *seriousness*. Offenses range in the type and amount of harm they cause, which speaks to their nature—"what they are like." They may range from petty to serious offenses. The law does of course recognize crime seriousness. Bergman (2014) describes a three-level hierarchy of criminal offenses based on crime seriousness and punishment severity. Least serious are *infractions* or *violations*: petty offenses punishable only by small fines. Most common are traffic offenses such as speeding and running a red light. More serious are **misdemeanors**: offenses punishable by up to a year in jail and/or fines, probation, community service, or restitution. States may subdivide misdemeanors into more specific categories based on their seriousness such as degrees, classes (e.g., A–C), or specifying "gross misdemeanors." Also, cities may designate misdemeanors in local ordinances. Most serious are **felonies**: offenses resulting in serious harm to person or property punishable by imprisonment for one year or longer or by death. Felonies too may be subdivided into classes or degrees of seriousness. Of course, some incidents are borderline; they could be seen as misdemeanors or felonies, and their ultimate classification may occur during judicial processes. These offenses may be termed *wobblers* (Bergman, 2014).

Like definitions, official levels of crime seriousness are limited, and it is important to assess seriousness in other ways, such as the amount of delinquency that occurs. As covered in the next chapter, most juvenile offenses are status offenses and misdemeanors (much of which is petty). An answer to the question "What is delinquency?" must include a description of delinquency as a social problem, not just descriptions of delinquent acts. Further, we have not explored the development of our notions of delinquency in broader contexts. McNamara and Bucher (2012, p. 9) point out that "delinquency is a complex problem that requires a thorough understanding of the physical, social, economic, legal, and political context in which it occurs." The meaning of delinquency also depends on the circumstances surrounding it, such as historical period, geographic location, dominant culture, current public and political concerns, and specific situation. Thus, we turn now to these issues.

Cultural Norms

We often associate the terms crime and delinquency with "deviance." This is appropriate, as illegal behavior is a type of deviant behavior. The two are not synonymous however, as deviance includes more than just illegal behavior. Also, not all deviant behavior is "bad"; some may just be unusual and others innovative, challenging the way we think. **Deviance** can be defined generally as behavior that violates norms (Scott, 2014). Social **norms** are behavioral expectations, akin to a system of rules of conduct, shared by people in a given society (Scott, 2014). Norms tell us what the "dos and don'ts" of life are—which behaviors are appropriate or inappropriate, good or bad, in certain situations or always. The juvenile and criminal justice systems do not deal with most deviant acts. Individuals and other social institutions (e.g., friends, parents, school, church, and work) respond to most deviance. In fact, "norms" may customarily refer to expectations of average daily conduct more than laws and official organizational rules (e.g., at school and work) (Scott, 2014). They range in seriousness from issues of manners and politeness (e.g., shaking someone's hand, avoiding eye contact with strangers in an elevator, and taking off hats while the national anthem is playing) to sexual behavior (e.g., monogamy and avoiding sex before marriage). Laws, however, may be thought of as codified norms—those which presumably prohibit more serious behaviors. The study of delinquency is not concerned with deviance in general, then, just certain forms—violations of law and other behaviors associated with law breaking also thought to be harmful.

We know that norms involve rules that we are supposed to follow. They tell us which behaviors are right or wrong. But where do norms come from? Who says that these are the rules? Their origins can be difficult to trace, but one quick answer is that they develop in our cultures. Norms are expectations of what is considered culturally desirable and appropriate (Scott, 2014). As types of norms, laws too are largely reflections of culture. This would explain why laws differ across countries. What is illegal in one country may not be in another because the two have different cultures. For example,

while the legal age for drinking alcoholic beverages is 21 in the United States and some other countries, 18 is the most common legal age worldwide (among countries that permit alcohol consumption) and in some countries or under certain circumstances (e.g., alcohol content) it can get as low as 16 (International Alliance for Responsible Drinking, 2022).

Consider the following scenario then. A 16-year-old is having one glass of wine at dinner with their family. In the U.S., this teenager, and whomever supplied the wine, would be committing an illegal act. In some European countries, the teenager would not be committing an illegal act. What is the difference? Maybe it is culture. Although many people in the U.S. disapprove of them, underage drinking laws are largely consistent with the popular belief that young people should not drink "until they are old enough." Drinking can be dangerous and thus we would like people to abstain from it until they are mature enough to make wise decisions about alcohol. In the U.S., underage drinking is associated with poor academic achievement, health problems, risky sexual behavior, psychological problems, and auto accidents (McNamara & Bucher, 2012). In contrast, in some European societies, sharing wine with younger family members may be considered appropriate, even desirable. Allowing them to drink wine in their company may be a way of socializing them into properly consuming alcohol, thereby reducing the problematic consequences of drinking. Which culture is right? Can we really say? If the above scenario was changed to a 16-year-old getting drunk at a party, higher minimum drinking age laws may seem more justifiable. The main point here is that rather than being a matter of absolute and universal truth, much of law is an expression of culture, the dominant culture anyway, which greatly differs among societies. Thus, when we break the law, we may be defying our culture (which could itself be damaging) more than we are "doing evil."

The Social Construction of Deviance

Crime is also historically relative: what is deemed illegal and considered a crime changes. Over time new laws get passed while some acts become "de-criminalized" (no longer illegal or formally punished). One good illustration is the prohibition of alcohol in the United States during the early twentieth century. Prior to Prohibition, drinking alcohol would not itself be a crime. During prohibition, the same act would be considered a crime. Then, after prohibition ended, the same act is again not a crime. The basic act did not change; rather its designation as a crime changed. Also, juvenile status offenses are a relatively new creation. Using alcohol and tobacco products would not have been considered "offending" by 16-year-olds during the nineteenth century, perhaps because they were considered adults. The historical relativeness of law and crime does not mean that our definitions are illegitimate. As society changes so too should our rules. For example, with a more complex society and longer life spans, it makes sense that we now see 16-year-olds as "too young" to engage in some behaviors. Historical relativity does mean, however, that we should not consider the bases or rationale for all laws to be absolute, fixed realities. How do law and crime change over time then? Do we simply recognize the changing needs of society and adapt to them?

Regardless of its changing nature, crime is a continual part of reality. To understand the nature of crime, it is necessary to understand the nature of reality—social reality anyway, the reality that humans create. Unlike material parts of reality (e.g., earth, sun, rocks, water, trees), law and crime only exist because human beings create them. Realities of human society and behavior are **socially constructed**, meaning that social life is created through human social interaction (Scott, 2014). We do not perceive and behave in our world objectively; we create ideas about it. We think about, conceptualize, define, represent, and react to phenomena, through language and terminology, for example (Goode, 2016). This applies to crime and other forms of deviance. We may assume that our laws are "natural" parts of reality, but they are not. Remembering the simplest definition of crime, a violation of law, clearly a law must be made against a behavior before it can officially be considered crime (by the government). Like other forms of deviance, the existence of crime involves a broader social process of law making, law breaking, and response to law breaking. Thus, deviance, including crime, is not merely a characteristic of behaviors themselves nor the individuals doing them (Becker, 1963). In other words, deviance is not a "thing" but a process of social interaction. Crime is not just something that people commit; it is something that happens in society.

Humans are very imperfect and subjective beings. The realities we create (e.g., cultures, societies, institutions, communities, organizations) are thus far from perfect and "objective" (the absolute correct way to function or exist). We should not view law making and enforcement any differently. To understand the nature of crime and delinquency, we must understand the social processes behind law making and enforcement.

Crime is a political concept. Decisions to prohibit a certain kind of behavior with a law, to punish people who do it, and on how to punish are based on values, beliefs, and assumptions that are not universally shared (not in the exact same way anyway). This is not to say our laws and responses to breaking them are all unfair, but we would be misunderstanding the problem of crime and delinquency if we assumed that they are naturally correct and only serve the collective good. When someone breaks the law, our first reaction is probably to ask: Why did s/he do that? This is understandable, especially when one commits a violent crime. However, an equally important question to ask, which may not readily come to mind, is: Why is that illegal? Trying to answer the second question helps us develop a more complete view of the nature of crime/delinquency. To understand crime is to understand *social control*—efforts to ensure conformity to norms (Goode, 2016), or in this case, laws.

Some perspectives on the nature of crime challenge our traditional ways of viewing life. One such perspective, postmodernism, asks us to consider that there is no objective truth, that all truth is relative (not that there is no truth or that no truth has value, as some may think) (Arrigo, 2010). What we see as true depends on the paradigms—a system or structure of assumptions, beliefs, and values—we use to assess reality. Further, we can only see reality through paradigms. Again, humans are not instruments that simply detect the world "as it is." There are of course several different paradigms varying across people, situations, and historical periods. Basically, reality is open to interpretation. It may seem strange to ask ourselves the question "Why is it illegal?" because our biases lead us to assume that our rules are simply just right. How we think and act depend heavily upon the interests we draw from our political, religious, economic, cultural, and other social contexts, including our notions of right and wrong, justice, fairness, and accountability (Arrigo, 2010). We may not be conscious of the possibility that these social influences upon our thinking make us believe that our rules are right. However, what we think and how we feel about certain laws and behaviors are shaped by our social backgrounds and circumstances. Take marijuana use, for example. Those opposed to it and in favor of it being illegal may view it from paradigms having to do with health enthusiasm, religious discipline, or bad experiences involving marijuana. Those not in favor or at least not opposed to it, and against it being illegal, may on the other hand view it with scientific skepticism, a focus on individual freedom, or through favorable experiences with marijuana.

Further, postmodernism proposes that reality is shaped through language in its various forms (e.g., written and spoken words) (Arrigo, 2010). Through the use of language, we construct and exchange conceptualizations of the world—versions of reality. In fact, we cannot think or express ourselves without language. Language is thus a very powerful force in the social construction of reality. However, the structure of language is unavoidably limited; it does not allow us to comprehend reality in complete or neutral ways (Arrigo, 2010). Regarding deviance, language used to represent behavior in discourse suggests how good or bad it is. Euphemisms and exaggerations often have this effect. For example, imagine an incident in which a five-year-old child angrily pushes another to the ground. At one extreme one might dismiss it as "horsing around." At the other extreme one might call it "an assault." It is important to think about how much language impacts how we view crime, or anything else about reality. As an interesting exercise, one might (1) think of a type of delinquency currently receiving much media attention, (2) think of the popular terms used to identify and describe it, and (3) consider how these terms have impacted one's impression of how bad it is, as a singular act and as a social problem. For example, does "drug abuse" make marijuana use seem awful, and does "recreational drug use" make it seem harmless?

Mala in se versus Mala prohibita

In criminal justice studies we often use two Latin terms to divide offenses into two categories. "***Mala in se***" refers to offenses that are wrong by nature—bad in and of themselves—likely those which cause tangible harm to others. These include violent crimes such as murder and rape as well as serious property crimes such as burglary and arson (Ireland & Rush, 2011). It is likely that norms prohibiting these behaviors are cultural universals—these offenses are likely seen as bad in all societies. It is not difficult to identify the objective harm in these acts and thus explain why they should be illegal. "***Mala prohibita***" refers to offenses that are wrong simply because the law says they are wrong, not because they are inherently wrong (Ireland & Rush, 2011). They may offend others but without directly causing tangible harm. These include many public order and status offenses seen as "victimless crimes." We probably agree that intrinsically harmful acts like murder, rape, and theft should be illegal, but we might wonder why *mala prohibita* acts are illegal. Should law be restricted only to *mala in se* offenses? Who gets to say which non-tangibly offensive behaviors are prohibited by law, and why are they prohibited? After all, there are several highly offensive acts that are not illegal. What is the difference between these and those which are illegal?

As stated earlier, laws can be based largely on culture. This is also true regarding *mala prohibita* offenses. It was also pointed out that culture and laws vary across societies. But what happens when a society has multiple cultures, as is the case with the United States? We probably cannot create separate laws for people in each culture. Thus, which culture gets to create laws? It is likely to be the dominant culture. It is possible, then, that some laws are not embraced by many members of a society—those who do not identify with the dominant culture and those who disagree with the laws for other reasons. *Mala prohibita* based laws may be imposed upon diverse members of a society by the dominant culture. However, the powerful interests behind these laws are not always cultural. Law is not based *completely* upon cultural norms. Some may be based on other social interests such as economic or organizational goals.

Consensus versus Conflict Models of Law

Understanding law as socially constructed reality gives us a good general idea of *how* laws, and subsequently crime, come to exist. But what about *why* they exist? Why do we create the laws and punishments we have? This is an important question considering especially that some of our laws prohibit behavior that doesn't seem to be intrinsically bad. Two contrasting models of lawmaking, consensus and conflict, provide viable answers to this question.

One answer to the question "why do we make the laws we have" is that the behaviors they prohibit really are bad, so we have to make them. The cultural relativeness of law and criminalization is likely limited. Again, serious violent and property offenses are likely prohibited in all societies; laws against them reflect culturally universal norms. It should stand to reason then that these laws are universally accepted *within* a society. According to the **consensus model of legislation**, laws are passed and enforced because the diverse people of a society are in agreement as to the laws' value and necessity (Ireland & Rush, 2011). In other words, we all believe in and want them. Without them, we would be free to harm each other and thus not have a civil, organized society. Regardless of the groups and subcultures we belong to, we all likely agree, generally anyway, that acts such as murder, rape, and theft are "crimes."

However, power guides the social construction of reality, and power is not shared equally among the people of a society. The people who hold the most power (i.e., various segments of the population, organizations, groups, individuals) have more of an impact upon the development of institutions such as law and criminal justice. Humans are very self-interested beings; thus, it is likely that the powerful will attempt to impact social reality in ways which benefit them in some way. For example, Marxist criminologists argue that law is a tool used by the wealthy to protect their interests against the lower classes (Bernard et al., 2016). For example, selling drugs on the street is defined as illegal, but the widespread manufacture and distribution of expensive drugs, many with harmful side effects, by pharmaceutical companies ("big pharm") is not. Also, "street crimes" such as robbery and burglary are heavily punished while large-scale corporate crime may go virtually unpunished.

According to the **conflict model of legislation**, then, laws are passed and enforced to represent the interests of the more powerful groups in society, not everyone's (Ireland & Rush, 2011). Passing laws and catching and punishing people who violate them are powerful ways to promote a group's values, beliefs, and desires. Besides potentially improving public safety and security, law making and enforcing is often a moral enterprise (Becker, 1963). The "war on drugs," for example, gives moral satisfaction to citizens and interest groups who hope to improve the health of society by reducing or eliminating drug use. However, it also creates several economic opportunities, including in private criminal justice industries (Hobson, 2014).

Again, the role of language is important here. As stated earlier, a postmodernist perspective suggests that language shapes how we perceive and react to crime (Arrigo, 2010). Thus, individuals, groups, and organizations which gain control over language and communication, especially crime rhetoric, may have a major impact upon public perceptions of crime and, subsequently, support for certain laws, policies, and practices. Terminology plays a major role in propaganda intended to get public support behind efforts to criminalize or de-criminalize a behavior. We are probably more likely to see that which seems awful as something that should be illegal. If it does not seem awful, then we are probably less likely to think that it should be illegal.

At the surface, a conflict model of lawmaking may not apply well to laws against serious violent and property offenses. Not only does there seem to be consensus that these acts should be prohibited, we need not be too pessimistic about selfishness in human motivation. Decency and compassion play a role, hopefully a major one, in the social construction of law and crime. While norms against seriously harmful behavior are fairly universal, how we define and respond to them are not. Let's consider the case of rape. Forcing sex upon another person is universally wrong. But what are the boundaries of behavior considered to be rape? Definitions of what exactly constitutes rape varies across cultures. Just how bad of a behavior rape is considered to be, and how severely it is punished, also varies. There is social construction surrounding intrinsically harmful crimes as well, and even *mala in se* offenses are subject to the conflict model. Throughout U.S. history rape was greatly tolerated through narrow definitions, unreasonable burdens of proof, victim-blaming (including by criminal justice authorities), and frequently light punishments until recent feminist and victims' movements lead to greater criminalization of rape, although problems in controlling it continue to exist (Freedman, 2013). Thus, our worst offenses are subject to both consensus and conflict processes.

Victimless Crimes?

Some offenses lack clear victims, hence the term "**victimless crimes**." We may wonder why they are illegal. Many people are offended by the behaviors, but tangible harm such as physical injury and loss of property are not readily apparent in them. Are we simply *choosing* to be offended by them then? If we simply choose to be offended by behaviors, can we be considered victims? "Victimless crimes" often include public order and status offenses. Gambling is one example but much of it is legal, for adults anyway. For juveniles, then, it may be difficult to see who their victims are when they bet, possibly lose, their own money in organized gaming. Two of the most hotly debated offenses are prostitution and drug use. Critics of laws prohibiting these behaviors may argue that they exist because cultural special interests have been successful in getting the government to impose a rather subjective moral code upon others, in other words "criminalizing" behavior that is considered "sinful." Does the government have the right to tell people that they cannot sell their own bodies for sex, or put drugs into their own bodies? Perhaps it can, if it can be shown that these activities really have tangible victims.

First, prostitution and drug use can involve serious harm to the persons engaging in them, especially to their health. Thus it can be said that they are victimizing themselves. A person selling sexual services may, for example, contract a sexually transmitted disease, be exploited by a pimp, or be assaulted or robbed by a "john." Then again, can't one reduce the risk of STDs by using protection (e.g., condoms), and can't non-prostitution sex just as easily transmit STDs? (Should we ban "risky sex" altogether?) Also, being victimized by pimps and johns are separate crimes, not the act of selling sex itself. Perhaps then sex workers should be protected, not treated as criminals. There are also two sides to the drug use issue. One may become addicted to drugs and thus face deteriorating health and great financial expense, overdose or have some other immediate reaction, or injure oneself while impaired. Then again, is it also possible that people can use substances, at least some, responsibly? Aren't there several legal human activities that are potentially dangerous and require much precaution, such as driving a car, using power tools, and playing contact sports? Also, the dangers of illegal drug use also exist in legal drug use—alcohol and prescription drugs. Must the law completely ban other substances, or is it in society's best interest to control them as with alcohol and prescription drugs? Perhaps the main question here is: How far should the law go in protecting people from themselves? If self-harm justifies law, then can't we also make eating junk food and not exercising illegal?

One might assert that crimes are actions that hurt other people. It is certainly possible that one may harm others while engaging in prostitution or using drugs. For example, prostitution may facilitate the spread of STDs, thereby adding to a public health problem. Any of the parties involved may for example transmit to their other sexual partners. Again, however, perhaps this could be offset by regulation and protective sex. Prostitution may also involve infidelity and thus harm relationships, although one may just as easily "cheat" on one's partner without buying or selling sex. Drug use, too, can be associated with harm to others. Perhaps the most compelling argument is that being impaired by drugs makes one a danger to others. While "high," one may be less able to function and make good decisions, which could lead to accidents involving others. Some drugs may even increase the capacity to become violent. Also compelling is that drug addiction emotionally, and often financially, harms people close to the addicted person. It is tough to manage a relationship with a loved one who is addicted. However, can't all of these be true regarding persons involved in heavy legal alcohol use and gambling? Is criminalizing substance abuse a good approach, or should it be treated primarily as a health problem? Further, are *all* drugs this dangerous, including marijuana, for instance? Should only the drugs that can be shown to induce antisocial behavior ("dangerous drugs") be illegal?

At any rate, it is not the purpose of this chapter to take a side on the "victimless crime" debate, regarding adults anyway. The purpose in bringing this issue up is to understand how it pertains to juveniles. With juveniles, it is easier to argue against the notion of victimless crimes. To begin, making and enforcing laws to protect people from themselves is not as problematic regarding juveniles. As a society, we are responsible for controlling and protecting children. In fact, as will be discussed in Chapter 7, the juvenile justice system was developed to ultimately help and protect delinquent and victimized youth. Thus, prohibiting juveniles from engaging in substance use (including tobacco), prostitution, and gambling because "they are bad for them" is consistent with the mission of juvenile justice. Engaging in these behaviors disrupts development and may set them on a path toward severe health, financial, and legal problems in adulthood. Also, an adult who pays for sexual services from a juvenile is committing sexual abuse (McNamara & Bucher, 2012). Here, the juvenile is a victim of sexual abuse, sometimes statutory rape, even if the juvenile offered or seemed willing to provide sex services.

It is unlikely that juveniles engaging in sex work are making well-informed voluntary decisions (McNamara & Bucher, 2012). For example, contrary to what may be popular belief, female prostitutes, including juveniles, are rarely "entrepreneurs" with power who maintain a great deal of control over their lives (and their clients) and make good money. They are likely being exploited by others, such as pimps and johns, and have turned to prostitution because of a variety of social and psychological problems. For example, many runaway and homeless youth turn to prostitution to survive on the streets. Substance dependency and abuse victimization in the home are also contributing factors. Further, juvenile sex workers are exposed to many dangers including mental and physical health problems as well as violent victimization at the hands of clients, pimps, and other potential offenders (McNamara & Bucher, 2012).

Of course, actual incidents of juvenile offending will often not have a victim, including oneself. An older teenager having a little wine at a family function or playing cards for small amounts of money, for example, may be harmless (among low-risk youth anyway). However, laws are made against categories of behavior which may unavoidably include some low-danger scenarios. We cannot label juvenile offenses such as prostitution, drug or alcohol use, and gambling as "victimless" simply because some specific acts are victimless. Nonetheless, the potential for some offenses to lack clear victims is important in understanding their nature. They seem to be quite distinguishable from other offenses that always or almost always have distinct victims, namely violent and property crimes.

Ending Thoughts

A broad, philosophical perspective on the nature of delinquency and justice is important in understanding the impacts that different delinquent acts, and our responses to them, have on individuals, the community, and society. However, this is only part of what we need to know. At this point, we may have developed a good understanding of delinquent offenses, but what about the nature of *offenders* and *offending*? To properly, and justly, respond to delinquency, it is not enough to create a catalog of offenses and their appropriate responses. It is also necessary to understand the different patterns of behavior and social circumstances of individual offenders. Whether a juvenile has committed a minor vs. serious offense on one occasion may not be as important as what one does over time and what their environment is like. For example, committing several status offenses could be an indicator of a serious problem that justifies a serious intervention, even if each status offense is quite minor. When reading the following chapters, it is important that the reader also develop a good understanding of juvenile offenders, offending patterns, and responding to juvenile offenders.

Summary Points

- "Delinquency" is a complex term that refers to a wide range of illegal behaviors committed by juveniles—usually persons under the age of 18. The study of delinquency includes age "status offenses"—acts which are illegal for juveniles but not adults.
- Since specific *legal* offense definitions differ across the country, the study of delinquency often relies on official definitions provided by government agencies (e.g., FBI, OJJDP, and BJS) and "academic" definitions developed in theory and research.
- General categories of juvenile offenses include violent (nonsexual), sexual, property, drug, public disorder, status offenses, other offenses (including minor ones and those which are more often victimizations *against* juveniles), and cyber offenses (see Figure 1.1).
- "Delinquency" is culturally relative. Which acts are considered to be delinquent and how they are defined differ across cultures and countries.
- Delinquency is socially constructed and historically relative. Instead of being a "natural" part of reality, its existence is created through social interaction—through political processes of law making, breaking, and enforcement.
- There seems to be some public consensus that violent and property offenses are indeed harmful and should be prohibited by law. However, laws defining "victimless crimes," as well as how crimes involving victims are handled, may be the result of social conflict and a group's ability to gain power.

Key Terms

Aggravated Assault: an unlawful attack wherein the offender uses or presents a weapon or the victim suffers serious bodily injury.

Animal Cruelty: killing or physically abusing or neglecting any animal without just cause.

Arson: willful or malicious burning or attempted burning of a house or other building, motor vehicle, aircraft, or personal property of another.

Bullying: repeated intentional abuse—physical, verbal, or social aggression—committed by an aggressor who has some type of power over the victim.

Burglary/Breaking & Entering: unlawful entry into a structure with the intent to commit a felony or theft.

Computer Security Incidents: attempted or completed crimes involving spyware, adware, hacking, phishing, spoofing, pinging, port scanning, or theft of other information.

Conflict Model of Legislation: an argument proposing that laws are passed and enforced to represent the interests of the more powerful groups in society.

Consensus Model of Legislation: an argument proposing that laws are passed and enforced because the people of a society widely agree upon the laws' value and necessity.

Cyber Attacks: offenses targeting computer systems including infecting with viruses, denying service, and electronic vandalism or sabotage.

Cybercrime: offenses committed with the use of computers and the internet, including cyber attacks, cyber theft, other computer security incidents, "cyberbullying" and "cyberstalking."

Cyber Theft: the use of a computer to commit embezzlement or fraud or to steal other things of value such as intellectual property (e.g., piracy and file sharing) and personal or financial data.

Delinquent Act: an act committed by a juvenile, usually a person under the age of 18, that would be considered a criminal act if committed by an adult.

Deviance: generally, behavior that violates norms.

Driving Under the Influence: operating a motor vehicle while mentally or physically impaired due to alcohol or drug use.

Drug/Narcotic Offenses: illegal production, distribution, or use of certain controlled substances and equipment or devices utilized in preparing or using controlled substances.

Exhibitionism: exposing private body parts (usually genitals) to others in an unwanted way, often to unsuspecting strangers, for sexual arousal.

Felony: a category representing a range of offenses resulting in serious harm to person or property that are punishable by imprisonment for one year or longer or by death.

Hate Crimes: crimes motivated (whole or in part) by offenders' biases against victims based on race or ethnicity, gender, religion, disability, or sexual orientation.

Intimidation: unlawfully threatening a person with words and/or other conduct, excluding displaying a weapon or physically attacking the person.

Joyriding: stealing a vehicle for the fun of driving it rather than for material gain.

Larceny-Theft: unlawful taking of property from the possession of another person (e.g., pocket-picking, purse-snatching, shoplifting, and theft from a building, automobile, or vending machine).

Mala in se: expression used to refer to offenses that are wrong by nature—bad in and of themselves—likely those which cause tangible harm to others (e.g., violent and property crime).

Mala prohibita: expression used to refer to offenses that are wrong simply because the law says they are wrong, not because they are inherently wrong (e.g., public order and status offenses).

Misdemeanor: a category representing a range of less serious offenses punishable by up to one year in jail and/or fines, probation, community service, or restitution.

Motor Vehicle Theft: unlawful taking or attempted taking of a vehicle (e.g., car, truck, van, bus, RV, motorcycle) with the intent to deprive the owner of it.

Murder/Non-Negligent Manslaughter: the willful, unjustifiable killing of another person.

Negligent Manslaughter: ("manslaughter") the killing of another person through negligence (carelessness or recklessness).

Norms: culturally relative behavioral expectations or everyday rules of conduct shared by people in a society.

Obstruction of Justice: offenses committed with intent to interfere with the administration of justice (e.g., policing), such as perjury, failure to report crime, and non-violent resist of arrest.

Petty Offenses: lower-level misdemeanor offenses punishable by no more than six months confinement, $500 fine, or both, such as jaywalking, littering, noise, and minor traffic violations.

Pressured Sex: sex resulting from an aggressor's harassing or manipulative behavior, such as telling lies, making false promises, threatening to break up, threatening to spread rumors, excessive appeals for sex or expressions of unhappiness, and exploiting authority over the victim.

Property Crime: offenses involving the taking of money or property without force or threat of force (e.g., burglary, larceny-theft, motor vehicle theft) and destruction of property (e.g., arson).

Prostitution: engaging in commercial sex acts in exchange for money or other things of value.

Public Order Offenses: acts prohibited by law because they are thought to threaten society's moral well-being (e.g., "vices") more than cause tangible harm to others, such as disorderly conduct, loitering, trespassing, gambling, prostitution, and non-violent family offenses.

Rape: nonconsensual vaginal or anal penetration of another person with any body part or object, or oral penetration of another person with a sex organ.

Robbery: the actual or attempted taking of anything of value from a person by force, threat of force, or threat of other immediate harm.

Sexual Assault: Aside from rape or attempted rape, attempted or completed attacks involving unwanted sexual contact between victim and offender, including grabbing or fondling private parts and making verbal threats.

Sexual Harassment: unwelcome sexual conduct that damages the environment (e.g., school) and interferes with the victim's ability to function, such as telling sexual stories or jokes, making sexual gestures or insults, sexual body language, and repeated requests for dates or "hookups."

Simple Assault: an unlawful physical attack without a weapon that does not result in serious bodily injury to the victim.

Socially Constructed: a term that refers to how human collective action, rather than "natural forces," create social realities (e.g., morals, law, crime, punishment, and social institutions).

Stalking: repeated intrusions such as unwanted monitoring, continuous communication, unwanted physical presence, and intimidating acts which annoy, frighten, or distress victims.

Status Offenses: noncriminal offenses prohibited for underage persons only, including curfew violations, incorrigibility (being ungovernable), running away, truancy, drinking, and smoking.

Statutory Rape: nonforcible sexual intercourse with a person under the statutory age of consent.

Stolen Property: an offense in which one knowingly receives, buys, possesses, conceals, or transports stolen property.

Vandalism: willful or malicious destruction, damage, defacing, or injuring of property without the consent of the owner or the person responsible for it.

"Victimless Crimes": Illegal acts that appear to lack a victim (other than perhaps those committing them), such as many public order, status, and drug offenses.

Violent Crime: offenses involving force or threat of force against a person (e.g., murder, manslaughter, rape, robbery, and assault).

Voyeurism: monitoring another person in stealth for sexual arousal (e.g., "peeping Tom" acts).

Weapon Law Violations: offenses involving the manufacture, sale, purchase, transportation, possession, concealment, alteration, or use of firearms, cutting instruments, explosives, incendiary devices, other deadly weapons, or weapon accessories.

References

Arrigo, B. A. (2010). The peripheral core of law and criminology: On postmodern social theory and conceptual integration. In B. A. Arrigo & D. Milovanovic (Eds.), *Postmodernist and post-structuralist theories of crime* (pp. 27–52). Ashgate.

Becker, H. S. (1963). *Outsiders: Studies in the sociology of deviance.* The Free Press.

Bergman, P. (2014). *Criminal law: A desk reference* (2nd ed.). Nolo.

Bernard, T. J., Snipes, J. B., & Gerould, A. L. (2016). *Vold's theoretical criminology.* Oxford University Press.

Bierie, D. M., & Budd, K. M. (2016). Romeo, Juliet, and statutory rape. *Sexual Abuse: A Journal of Research and Treatment*, 1–26. https://doi.org/10.1177/1079063216658451

Black, M. C., Basile, K. C., Breiding, M. J., Smith, S. G., Walters, M. L., Merrick, M. T., Chen, J., & Stevens, M. R. (2011). *The National Intimate Partner and Sexual Violence Survey (NISVS): 2010 summary report.* National Center for Injury Prevention and Control, Centers for Disease Control and Prevention.

Bohm, R. M., & Vogel, B. L. (2015). An introduction to theory. In *A Primer on Crime and Delinquency Theory* (4th ed., pp. 3–18). Carolina Academic Press.

Bureau of Justice Statistics (BJS). (n.d.a). Bias-motivated/hate crime. https://bjs.ojp.gov/topics/crime/hate-crime

Bureau of Justice Statistics (BJS). (n.d.b). Glossary. https://bjs.ojp.gov/glossary

Bureau of Justice Statistics (BJS). (n.d.c). *Terms & definitions: Cybercrime.* http://www.bjs.gov/index.cfm?ty=tdtp&tid=41

Clear, E. R., Coker, A. L., Cook-Craig, P., Bush, H. M., Garcia, L. S., Williams, C. M., Lewis, A. M., & Fisher, B. S. (2014). Sexual harassment victimization and perpetration among high school students. *Violence Against Women, 20*(10), 1203–1219.

Cornell, D., & Limber, S. P. (2015). Law and policy on the concept of bullying at school. *American Psychologist, 70*(4), 333–343.

Dabney, D. A. (2004). Public order crime. In D. A. Dabney (Ed.), *Crime types: A text/reader* (pp. 239–254). Wadsworth.

Falcone, D. N. (2010). *Dictionary of American criminal justice, criminology, & criminal law* (2nd ed.). Pearson Education, Inc.

Federal Bureau of Investigation (FBI). (n.d.). *Hate crime statistics.* https://www.fbi.gov/how-we-can-help-you/more-fbi-services-and-information/ucr/hate-crime

Federal Bureau of Investigation (FBI). (2019). *2019 crime in the United States.* https://ucr.fbi.gov/crime-in-the-u.s/2019/crime-in-the-u.s.-2019

Federal Bureau of Investigation (FBI). (2021). *2021.1 National Incident-Based Reporting System user manual.* https://bjs.ojp.gov/sites/g/files/xyckuh236/files/sarble/data_common/nibrs-user-manual-2021-1041521.pdf

Fox, J. A., Levin, J., & Quinet, K. (2012). The lure and the law of homicide. In J. A. Fox, J. Levin, & K. Quinet (Eds.), *The will to kill: Making sense of senseless murder* (pp. 1–17). Pearson Education, Inc.

Freedman, E. (2013). *Redefining rape: Sexual violence in the era of suffrage and segregation.* Harvard University Press.

Goode, E. (2016). Constructing deviance. In E. Goode (Ed.), *Deviant behavior* (11th ed., pp. 57–83). Routledge.

Hobson, C. (2014). Privatising the war on drugs. *Third World Quarterly, 35*(8), 1441–1456.

International Alliance for Responsible Drinking. (2022). *Minimum legal age limits.* https://iard.org/science-resources/detail/Minimum-Legal-Age-Limits

Ireland, C. E., & Rush, G. E. (2011). *The dictionary of criminal justice* (7th ed.). McGraw-Hill.

Kellet, S., & Gross, H. (2006). Addicted to joyriding? An exploration of young offenders' accounts of their car crime. *Psychology Crime & Law, 12*(1), 39–59.

Kigerl, A. C. (2013). Infringing nations: Predicting software piracy rates, BitTorrent tracker hosting, and P2P file sharing client downloads between countries. *International Journal of Cyber Criminology, 7*(1), 62–80.

Kopel, D. B., & Blackman, P. H. (2009). To Heller and back. *Journal of Contemporary Criminal Justice, 25*(1), 106–112.

Marcum, C. D., Higgins, G. E., & Ricketts, M. L. (2014). Juveniles and cyber stalking in the United States: An analysis of theoretical predictors of patterns of online perpetration. *International Journal of Cyber Criminology, 8*(1), 47–56.

McNamara, R. H. (2008). *The lost population: Status offenders in America*. Carolina Academic Press.

McNamara, R. H., & Bucher, C. C. (2012). *Problem children: Special populations in delinquency*. Carolina Academic Press.

Office of Juvenile Justice and Delinquency Prevention (OJJDP). (n.d.). *Glossary of terms*. https://ojjdp.ojp.gov/sites/g/files/xyckuh176/files/pubs/jcs96/glos.html

Scott, J. (2014). *Oxford dictionary of sociology* (4th ed.). Oxford University Press.

Swindell, S., Stroebel, S. S., O'Keefe, S. L., Beard, K. W., Robinett, S. R., & Kommor, M. J. (2011). Correlates of exhibition-like experiences in childhood and adolescence: A model for development of exhibitionism in heterosexual males. *Sexual Addiction & Compulsivity, 18*(3), 135–156.

Topalli, V., Jacques, S., & Wright, R. (2015). "It takes skills to take a car": Perceptual and procedural expertise in carjacking. *Aggression and Violent Behavior, 20*, 19–25.

Chapter 2

Extent of Delinquency: How Bad Is It?

Chapter Learning Objectives

Students will be able to:

- Recognize incidence and prevalence rates
- Determine the relevance of sources of delinquency data
- Clarify the "age-crime curve"
- Differentiate rates for each type of delinquency
- Summarize gender, race, and class differences in delinquency rates
- Judge the overall seriousness of the delinquency problem in the United States
- Deconstruct one's biases concerning beliefs about the seriousness of delinquency
- Reflect on one's progress in understanding the extent and relative severity of delinquency

Introduction

So just how bad is the social problem of juvenile delinquency in the United States? There is a great deal of media coverage, research, and books and articles on it, so it must be serious to some extent. Has it been increasing in recent years or decades, and if so, how much? Is it skyrocketing? Are juveniles committing more violent delinquency? Are kids out of control these days? The accuracy of answers to these kinds of questions depends upon a calm, careful examination of a great deal of information. If we are not careful, our judgements will be clouded by emotions and misinformation. It is important to remember that answers to these questions lie in what is going on every day around the country, not just what happens in our personal lives, our neighborhoods, or the media. After the following discussion of research on the occurrence of delinquency, the reader can decide how bad the problem is.

The simplest way to think of the extent of delinquency is how much it happens—how many incidents of delinquent acts occur and/or how many juveniles commit them—in a given time frame such as a month, year, or decade. However, it would be incomplete to determine "how bad" the delinquency problem is based only on this measure of extent. Another kind is the extent of harm or damage caused by delinquency—by each delinquent act and by the sum of all delinquent acts that occur. Again, juvenile offenses range in the type and amount of physical, psychological, and financial harm they cause, from petty infractions or violations to misdemeanors to felonies involving serious harm to person or property (Bergman, 2014).

Thus, we have another layer of crime seriousness to account for: how much serious delinquency occurs relative to less serious forms. Truly, a great deal of delinquency occurs in the U.S. However, if most of this delinquency is minor—either causes little harm or no apparent tangible harm—then our delinquency problem may not be as bad as it seems. On the other hand, an offense may occur infrequently, but the act may cause severe damage that affects many people (e.g., mass violent attacks). Thus, we might give more weight to rarely occurring acts when determining their contribution to the overall severity of our society's problem with delinquency. It is possible then that a small number of offenses create a significant part of the problem.

Incidence, Prevalence, and Rates

It is also very important to understand the math and logic behind the way that researchers measure and report the extent of crime, namely incidence vs. prevalence and use of rates.

Incidence refers to the number of times something occurs in a place or population within a certain time frame, for example, the number of crimes committed in the U.S. last year. **Prevalence** refers to the number of people or other units (e.g., families) who produce or are affected by incidents, for example, the number of people victimized by crime in the U.S. last year. The incidence and prevalence of something are often not the same thing. For example, the number of crimes that occurred is not the same as the number of people who committed crimes because (1) some people commit more than one crime and (2) some crimes are committed by more than one person. This must be kept in mind when interpreting incidence and prevalence statistics.

Incidence is often reported as a rate instead of the total number of incidents, because the total itself may not give a good idea of how frequently something occurs. A **rate** is a measure of the quantity of something per a fixed unit of something else—a denominator. Some of the U.S. "crime rates" are calculated as the number of crimes that occur per 100,000 people in the population. This is calculated by dividing the number of offenses in the population by the number of people in the population and multiplying the result by 100,000. For example, if 1,350,000 acts of violent crime were detected in a year and the population at the time was 350,000,000 people, the rate would then be 385.7, meaning that for every 100,000 people in the country, there were 385.7 violent offenses detected. Note that this is not saying that about 386 "out of" every 100,000 people (or, about 0.39% of the population) committed a violent crime, as 385.7 refers to incidents, not people. (The rate is "per," not "out of.") The unit of 100,000 people gives a frame of reference for gauging how common crime is among people.

Also, very importantly, rates allow us to control for the effect of population change. The larger a population, the more behaviors that people do will occur in that population. For example, in a class of 25 students, maybe five get As, but in a class of 100, many more than five should get As. (If 20 students in the larger class get As, then the rate is the same for both classes: 5 As per 25 students.) With crime, it is possible that the number of offenses increases over time because the population increases. (Or, the number might stay the same or even decrease despite population increases.) To illustrate, imagine a city of 50,000 people that had 75 violent crimes in a year and another city with 100,000 people that had 125 in that same year. The larger city had more violent crimes but is twice the size of the smaller city. However, its number of violent crimes is not twice that of the smaller city (125 instead of 150). Thus, the larger city will have a lower violent crime rate, and perhaps a smaller violent crime problem, compared to the smaller city. The rate allows for comparisons between areas and time periods by controlling for changes in population. The rate statistic is per X number (e.g., 100,000) of people in a population regardless of how many people there are in a population at a certain time.

Prevalence of crime can be reported as a percentage or fraction of people who have committed an offense. For example, a study might find that 10% of, or one out of ten, juveniles in a sample reported committing an offense. This would give us an idea of how bad delinquency is in terms of how many juveniles are involved in it. However, sometimes, arrest rates are used as an indicator of involvement in crime. Caution must be taken with interpreting these as well. Although arrests are of persons, they are incidents that are measured just like known offenses—such as per 100,000 people in the population. For example, an arrest rate of 2,500 per 100,000 in a year would mean that for every 100,000 people there are in the population, 2,500 arrests were made that year, not that 2,500 individuals out of 100,000 (or 2.5%) were arrested. Arrest rates are calculated from the number of arrests made in a year, not the number of persons who have been arrested in a year. Some people are arrested more than once within a year. Still, differences in arrest rates suggest that more people are involved, or people are more extensively involved, in crime in one place or at one time.

Sources of Data

"The UCR"

Official data and statistics on crime in the U.S. are provided through the **Uniform Crime Reporting (UCR) Program,** which has been administered by the Federal Bureau of Investigation (FBI) since 1930. Now a leading source of indicators of crime, the UCR collects data on reported crimes and cleared cases (person arrested, charged, or turned over to the court) from more than 18,000 law enforcement agencies (city, county, state, federal, tribal, and college/university) nationwide. Data and statistics are available for the nation, regions, states, counties, cities, towns, tribal law enforcement, and colleges/universities. An interactive tool for viewing crime statistics, the Crime Data Explorer, is available free online (go to www.fbi.gov), although there is some time lag in release due to the time needed to complete data collection and analyses and process reports. The program also creates other special or supplementary reports on subjects such as hate crime and homicide (FBI, n.d.a).

The UCR program contains major steps in its methodology to ensure the accuracy, objectivity, utility, integrity, and overall quality of its data and statistics. Since crime definitions vary across states and localities, the FBI ensures uniform reporting by providing law enforcement agencies with materials and support explaining how to provide data according to uniform definitions, and training and consultation if needed. The main system used in the UCR to collect data from agencies is the National Incident-Based Reporting System (NIBRS). The NIBRS collects data for a total of 62 types of offenses (10 have arrest data only) on both single offense incidents and separate (multiple) offenses within incidents. Information on these offenses include that on known offenders and arrestees, victims, victim-offender relationships, time and place of offenses, property involved in crimes, and whether drugs, gang activity, and computers were involved in the crime (FBI, n.d.a).

Regarding arrests, statistics show the number of arrests, not persons arrested, per 100,000 people in the population. A person may be arrested multiple times in a year. Also, they do not show number of offenses resulting in arrest, as some single offenses are committed by multiple offenders. This is a special problem for estimating juvenile offending, as juveniles are more likely than adults to offend in groups. It is difficult to collect offender demographic data on *offenses* because often the offender is not known. The reporter often knows *that* a crime has been committed but not *who* committed it. Thus, the UCR cannot determine the number of offenses committed by juveniles (or race or gender categories). It can, however, reveal how many arrestees are juveniles and offer a juvenile arrest rate. Of course, arrests further underestimate offending since many crimes reported to the police do not result in arrest. Juvenile arrest rates may still be useful in giving some kind of indication of juvenile involvement in crime, especially serious crime.

Estimates of *juvenile arrests* based on UCR data are developed by the National Center for Juvenile Justice (NCJJ), the research division of the National Council of Juvenile and Family Court Judges (NCJJ, n.d.). The NCJJ is a private, non-profit organization that, among other projects, provides statistical analyses for the U.S. Department of Justice's **Office of Juvenile Justice and Delinquency Prevention (OJJDP)**—an important resource for students, scholars, and practitioners of juvenile justice. NCJJ's juvenile arrest estimates are available online through the OJJDP Statistical Briefing Book (www.ojjdp.gov).

It is important to note the UCR program's main limitations. To begin, it does not measure "crime" per se, because it does not include all acts of crime that take place.

It only covers those that are detected by the police, either through citizen reports or by direct discovery. Many crimes, of course, are not reported to or detected by police. In fact, the UCR may only detect crime's "tip of the iceberg." Many acts of crime are difficult to detect due to circumstances such as privacy or unnoticed damage (e.g., individuals often do not get caught possessing or using illegal drugs), or victims are hesitant to report because of fear (e.g., of their personal lives being exposed, offender retaliation, or stress associated with judicial processes) or a belief that reporting will do no good (e.g., a stolen item is not likely to be recovered). Thus, we cannot use official reports to assess how much crime takes place, with the exception perhaps of very serious offenses like homicide that are much less likely to go unnoticed by authorities.

Another limitation is that the NIBRS does not yet cover the entire U.S. population and all targeted law enforcement agencies. While all 50 states and the District of Columbia are participating, as of May 2024, 82% of the U.S. population was covered and 125 of 154 agencies serving cities and counties with 250,000 or more people were reporting to NIBRS. This is because the NIBRS is new. In 2021, it replaced the UCR's old Summary Reporting System (SRS), which had several major limitations. The NIBRS is a major improvement upon the SRS, but it is still in a late stage of development (BJS, n.d.a). Also, as with any major research project, some data may be inaccurate or missing due to errors and other problems with reporting, although the program undertakes several major efforts to keep these to a minimum. It should be noted that UCR statistics for years prior to 2021 are from SRS data, including the juvenile arrest rates presented in this chapter.

With such serious limitations, one may wonder why we should even use UCR data and statistics to indicate the extent of crime. While the UCR does not tell us "how much crime is out there," it does give us good information on crime trends. For example, it shows differences in the types of crimes detected by police; who is more likely to be arrested in terms of age, race, and gender; and changes in rates over time. For instance, we can see if rates of arrest and reported crimes change over time, which gives us a general idea of whether crime is getting better, worse, or staying the same. Of course, changes in rates may be due to changes in law enforcement policies and practices, but it is possible to account for them in analyses. Another advantage is that offenses are recognized by expert governmental authorities, so we have some assurance that they really did occur. UCR data and statistics are considered "official." If we do not use carefully produced, extensive information like the UCR, we may base our perceptions of the extent of crime on much less reliable or generalizable sources like personal experiences (anecdotal evidence), emotions, rumors and myths, false claims by biased organizations, and sensationalized media coverage. Nonetheless, the UCR is an insufficient source of information on the extent of crime, which is why we also use other sources.

Victimization and Self-Reported Offending

Another way to study the crime problem is to assess how many people are victimized by crime. Another major federal program, administered by the Bureau of Justice Statistics (BJS), is the **National Crime Victimization Survey (NCVS)**, which asks members of a large representative sample of U.S. households about their experiences with victimization (BJS, n.d.b). Since the survey asks about offenses that victims report and do not report to police, the NCVS detects more incidents of crime than the UCR. However, annually, both sources show many of the same *trends* regarding relative frequency of offenses, change or stability in crime rates, and differences in the population. Thus, the two corroborate each other to some extent. Another advantage is that this program collects more background data on victims and offenses than the UCR. However, depending on the circumstances, victims often do not know who their perpetrators are and cannot give information on them such as their age. Also, the NCVS does not detect cases in which there is no clear victim, such as drug use. Thus, the NCVS is limited in its ability to give estimates of juvenile offending rates. However, victimization data can give an idea of the extent of a problem; for example, it provides NCVS School Crime Supplement (SCS) data (Irwin et al., 2024).

Although it may sound strange, the best way to detect delinquency might be to ask juveniles if they offend. Of course, juveniles will often be reluctant to admit to committing offenses, especially serious ones, even under anonymous or confidential circumstances. On the other hand, others may exaggerate their offending to convey a rebellious self-image or out of mischief. However, studies have shown that juveniles are willing to report much offending and do so rather accurately. With rigorously planned research procedures, such as those which ensure confidentiality and privacy, self-report studies can collect much valuable information on offending (Benson, 2013). An advantage to **self-reported delinquency surveys** is that they can detect crimes overlooked by the UCR and NCVS—those which do not involve a clear victim or otherwise go unnoticed, such as drug use. Several self-reported delinquency surveys have been conducted over the years, but most are relatively small-scale studies that cannot be used for wide estimates of offending. They may use small or non-national samples (e.g., local or statewide), or they may not collect data on several types of offending.

However, some self-report surveys, which will be mentioned throughout the remainder of this chapter, are major studies that provide our best estimates of certain offenses. For example, since 1991, the Center for Disease Control and Prevention (CDC) has conducted the **Youth Risk Behavior Survey (YRBS)** biennially to collect data on a variety of behaviors that affect health, including those which are unlawful. The YRBS surveys a nationally representative sample of students in grades 9–12 (generally, high school students) at public and private schools in all 50 U.S. states and DC. In 2023, a little over 20,000 students participated in the survey (CDC, n.d.).

Also, estimates of the prevalence of juvenile substance use may be obtained from two major ongoing annual surveys. **Monitoring the Future (MTF)** is the leading study of self-reported substance use among young people in the U.S. MTF has been conducted by the University of Michigan's Institute for Social Research since 1975 with funding from the National Institute on Drug Abuse. In 2023, MTF surveyed 6,240 eighth-grade, 8,494 tenth-grade, and 7,584 twelfth-grade students at 235 schools nationwide, for a total sample of about 22,318 adolescents (Miech et al., 2024). The **National Survey on Drug Use and Health (NSDUH)** examines self-reported substance use by older adults as well as youth aged twelve or older, excluding the non-sheltered homeless and those in institutional settings. Conducted by the federal government's Substance Abuse and Mental Health Services Administration (SAMHSA), the NSDUH has sampled all 50 states and DC since 1999. In 2023, 67,679 valid interviews were completed, including those with 14,279 adolescents aged 12–17 (SAMHSA, n.d.). Unlike MTF, the NSDUH samples juveniles from the general population rather than select grades in school. Thus, the two may produce very different estimates of drug use.

Strengths and Weaknesses of Data Sources

Each of these three types of data sources—UCR, NCVS, and self-reports—have major limitations. Individually, each provides poor estimates of offending, by underestimating it (although not to the same degree). However, each also has strengths that the others do not have. For example, individuals are not likely to report serious offenses in surveys but tend to be willing to report minor offending, while law enforcement tends to detect more serious offenses than minor offenses (e.g., "victimless crimes" or

Figure 2.1: Strengths and Weaknesses of Data Sources

Strengths	*Weaknesses*
UCR	
Long-running, well-established, rigorous research program Identifies geographic, social, and temporal trends in crime Geographically covers most of the U.S. Crime incidents are expert-identified Fairly accurately measures some serious offenses, namely homicide Statistics, reports, and some data are freely available on the internet	Most illegal acts are not detected by police Police do not always formally arrest juvenile offenders Very limited and often unavailable data on offenders and victims Police detection is affected by biased, changing policies/practices Data from agencies are sometimes inaccurate or missing
NCVS	
Well established, rigorous research program Surveys a large representative sample of U.S. households Anonymous or confidential questioning increases reporting Detects more incidents of crime than the UCR Identifies geographic, social, and temporal trends in victimization Collects data on offenses and victims unavailable in the UCR Statistics, reports, and some data are freely available on the internet	Information on victimization is not always accurate Respondents often cannot provide offender information Covers a limited range of crimes Respondents still may not be willing to divulge victimization Under-samples homeless and transitory persons Excludes institutionalized persons (e.g., in treatment facilities) Excludes victims under age 12
Major Self-Report Surveys	
Well established, rigorous research programs Surveys large, sometimes national, samples of juveniles Anonymous or confidential questioning increases reporting Detects more incidents of crime than the UCR Collects data on offenses and offenders not in the UCR & NCVS Many reports are freely available on the internet	Respondents are less willing to admit to serious offending Some respondents may exaggerate their offending Self-reported offending is not always accurate Serious offenders are under-sampled (e.g., those incarcerated) Measures often do not identify number of offenses committed Samples may not be highly representative of juveniles in the U.S.

juvenile offenses handled informally). Thus, self-report studies may offer a good gauge of less serious offending while the UCR may offer a good gauge of serious offending. Taken as a whole, our major sources of crime data still underestimate offending, but they can give us a pretty good picture of how bad our crime problems are as well as how crime changes or differs. Figure 2.1 summarizes some of the main strengths and weaknesses of each of the three types of data sources.

Figure 2.2: 2014 Arrests by Age

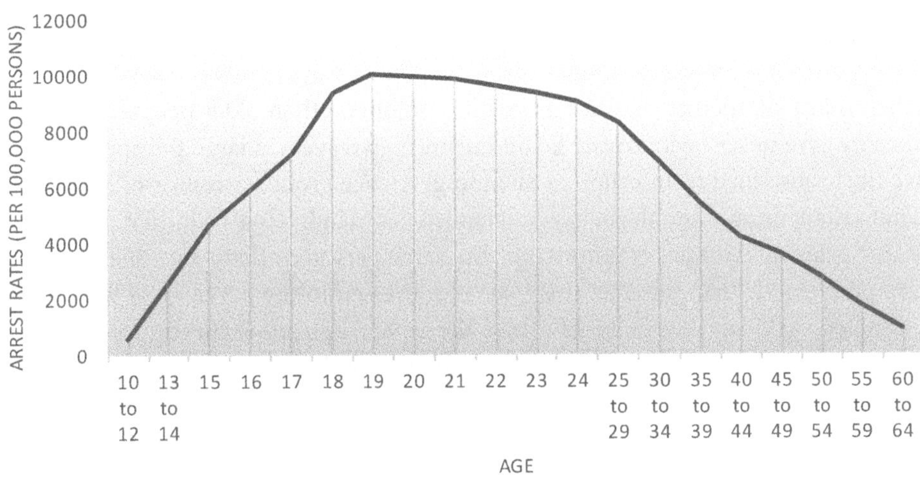

Source: Snyder, H. N., Cooper, A. D., & Mulako-Wangota, J. (2018, May 25). U.S. Arrest Estimates: Arrest Rates by Age for All Offenses. Bureau of Justice Statistics. Generated using the Arrest Data Analysis Tool at www.bjs.gov.

The Age-Crime Curve

Perhaps the first thing that should be noted about juvenile crime rates is that they are continuously high in comparison to other age groups. The **age-crime curve** is a graphed pattern that shows that offense or arrest rates rapidly increase in early adolescence, peak in late adolescence/early adulthood, gradually decline during the 20s, and then sharply decline with age. (Young adults, from 18 to about 25, also have relatively high rates.) Thus, some of the highest rates are going to be found among juveniles. After late adolescence, the older a person is, the less likely one is to offend (Benson, 2013).

Figure 2.2 shows an age-crime curve based on UCR estimated arrest rates for 2014. As to be expected, children aged 10 to 12 are not frequently arrested. When juveniles reach ages 15–17, they are much more likely to be arrested. The peak for arrests appears to be somewhere between 18 and 21, when arrestees are technically adults. However, it is important to remember that these are arrest, not offending, rates. Thus, they do not determine, for example, that 17-year-olds offend less than 18-year-olds. Regardless, juveniles are a noticeable category of arrestees (Snyder et al., 2018.

In comparing arrest rates, it should be noted that juveniles and adults may not have the same chances of being arrested for committing offenses. Juveniles are more likely than adults to offend publicly and thus have higher chances of getting caught (Benson, 2013). Perhaps due to immaturity, juveniles may be less capable of, or mindful about, concealing their offenses than adults. On the other hand, police officers are more likely to handle juvenile offenses informally (not make a formal arrest) compared to adult offenses. Here, juvenile offenders are less likely to get arrested. It seems that these two tendencies would cancel each other out, *to some extent*, in determining juvenile vs. adult arrest rates.

One must interpret the age-crime curve carefully. While it suggests that much crime is committed by adolescents, it does not show that they are highly involved in crime. Rather, it just shows that they are more likely to offend than older people. Most adolescents have never been arrested, and during a given year, a large portion of them have likely abstained from criminal offending. An age group's arrest or offense rates do not say anything about the behavioral tendencies of individuals within it, for example that some offenses are committed by the same person or that some offenders are more problematic than others. (This issue is addressed in the coverage of life course criminology in Chapters 4 and 5.) Further, the general age-crime curve does not show how many offenses are serious. To understand just how bad delinquency is, then, it is important to explore rates and patterns of specific types of offending.

Estimates of Arrests and Offending

Again, the juvenile arrest rate based on UCR data is the number of arrests of juveniles (ages 10–17) for every 100,000 juveniles in the U.S. population. After ranging from 6,074 to 7,339 in the 1980s then peaking at 8,476 in 1996, the *overall* juvenile arrest rate (all types of offenses) fairly steadily declined to 2,044.2 in 2019 (NCJJ, 2022). (The rate plummeted in 2020, the first year of the Covid-19 Pandemic.) These rates suggest that juvenile offending became the lowest it has been in at least three or four decades. Further, most of these arrests were not for violent offenses. Figure 2.3 shows annual overall juvenile arrest rates from 2000 through 2020.

Violent Offenses

To begin, the UCR calculates a **Violent Crimes** arrest rate that combines homicide, rape, robbery, and aggravated assault. The juvenile arrest rates for violent crimes ranged from 279 to 387 in the 1980s, peaked at 497.4 in 1994, steadily declined to 264 in 2004, rose to 290.3 in 2006, and then fairly steadily declined to 182.4 in 2012. Because of changes in the definition of rape, rates for rape and thus overall violent crime based on data from the old reporting system were not estimated past 2012. According to arrests, among violent offenses, juveniles most commonly commit aggravated assault and rarely commit homicide (NCJJ, 2022). In 2022, juveniles accounted for 9.7% of violent crime arrests including rape (FBI, n.d.b).

Figure 2.3: Juvenile Arrest Rates, 2000–2020

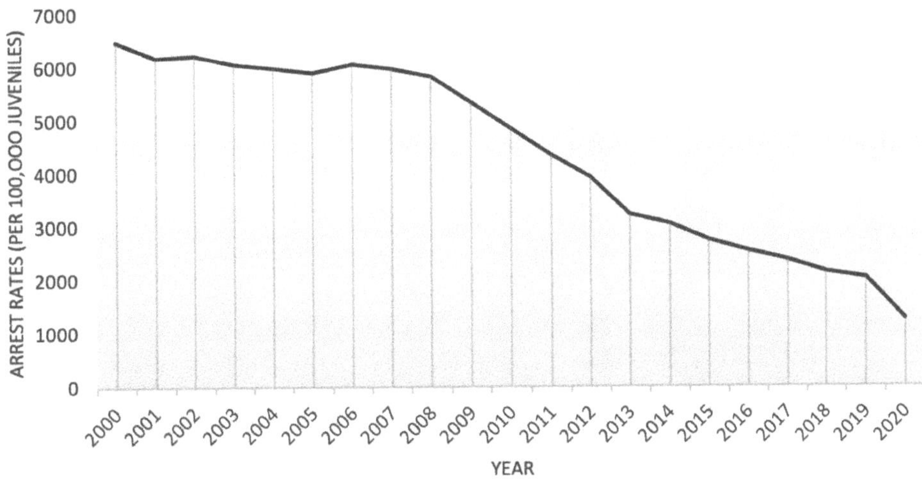

Source: National Center for Juvenile Justice. (2022, July 8). Juvenile arrest rates by offense, sex, and race. http://www.ojjdp.gov/ojstatbb/crime/excel/JAR_2020.xls

As stated earlier, victimization research detects more offenses than arrest research.

Assault. Returning to arrests, the juvenile arrest rate for *aggravated assault* ranged between 128 and 217 in the 1980s, peaked at 282 in 1994, steadily declined to 174.5 in 2004, rose to 177 in 2005, and then steadily declined to 80 in 2019. The juvenile arrest rate for *simple assault* ranged between 270 and 502 in the 1980s, peaked at 761.7 in 1997, fluctuated somewhat until 2005, and then declined to 369.7 in 2019 (NCJJ, 2022). In 2022, juveniles accounted for 7.5% of aggravated assault arrests and 12.1% of simple assault arrests (FBI, n.d.b). Juveniles are arrested for aggravated assault far more frequently than they are for the other serious violent crimes: robbery, rape, and homicide. (As will be shown, arrests for these other three offenses declined in recent decades as well.) Figure 2.4 shows annual aggravated assault arrest rates for juveniles from 2000 through 2020.

Robbery & Homicide. The juvenile arrest rate for *robbery* ranged between 111 and 147 in the 1980s, peaked at 183.5 in 1994, steadily declined to 72.7 in 2002, rose to 103.7 by 2008, and then decreased to 47.5 in 2019 (NCJJ, 2022). In 2022, juveniles accounted for 20% of robbery arrests (FBI, n.d.b). The juvenile arrest rate for *murder and nonnegligent manslaughter* ranged between 4.6 and 9.8 in the 1980s, peaked at 12.8 in 1993, steadily declined to 3.6 in 2000, remained fairly steady into 2009, decreased to 2.2 in 2012, and then rose to 2.8 in 2019 (NCJJ, 2022). In 2022, juveniles accounted for 10.8% of murder and non-negligent manslaughter arrests and 7.2% of negligent manslaughter arrests (FBI, n.d.b).

Hate Crime. As of the writing of this text, national estimates of the incidence or prevalence of bias offenses committed by juveniles appear to be unavailable. UCR data for 2021 show that of 8,237 *known* hate crime offenders on whom age was reported,

Figure 2.4: Juvenile Aggravated Assault Arrest Rates, 2000–2020

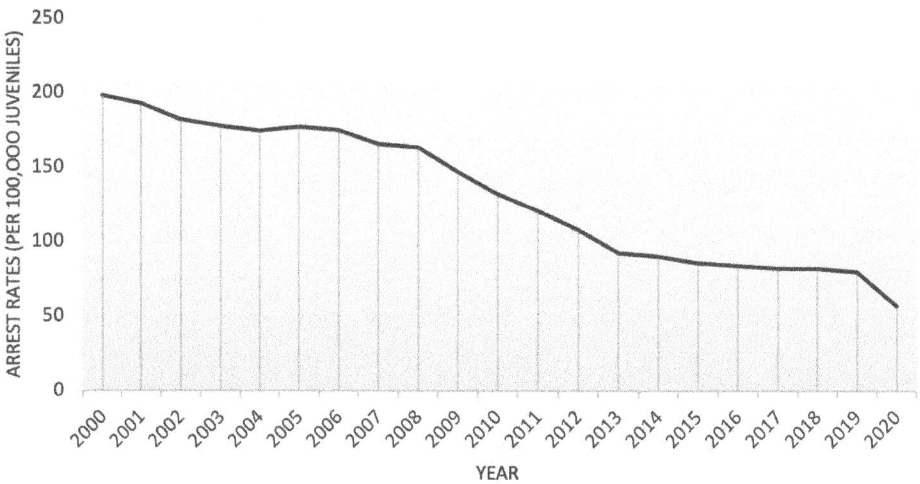

Source: National Center for Juvenile Justice. (2022, July 8). Juvenile arrest rates by offense, sex, and race. http://www.ojjdp.gov/ojstatbb/crime/excel/JAR_2020.xls

15.7% were younger than 18 (FBI, 2023). While this percentage does not provide a good estimate of the extent of juveniles' involvement in hate crime, it does suggest that it is a noticeable problem.

However, national estimates of hate victimizations committed at school are available. NCVS School Crime Supplement (SCS) data show that for the 2021–2022 school year, 7% of students aged 12–18 reported being called a derogatory word about their race, ethnicity, religion, disability, gender, or sexual orientation at school (in a school building, on school property, on a school bus, or going to and from school)—a decrease from 9% in 2010–2011. Also, 23% of them reported seeing hate-related graffiti (words or symbols written in classrooms, bathrooms, or hallways or on the outside of buildings) at school during the 2021–2022 year, which was a decrease from 28% in 2010–2011 (Irwin et al., 2024). Further, School Survey on Crime and Safety (SSOCS) data show that 3.5% of U.S. public schools reported that one or more hate crimes occurred at school during the 2021–2022 year, with a rate of 0.2 incidents per 1,000 students (Burr et al., 2024). Hate crime victimization in schools will be discussed further in Chapter 6.

Bullying. While bullying occurs in different environments, including online, much of it occurs at school. The U.S. Department of Education conducts a national School Survey on Crime and Safety (SSOCS), which asks public school principals to report disciplinary problems that occur at their schools during the school year. For the 2021–2022 school year, 14.3% of public-school principals reported that student bullying occurred at least once a week (at 28% of middle, 15% of high/secondary, and 10% of elementary schools) (Burr et al., 2024). This is up from the 2015–2016 school year, which had a rate of 11.9%, but still well below the rate of 29% in 1999–2000 (Musu-Gillette et al., 2018). Also, in 2022, juveniles accounted for 11.5% of arrests for intimidation (FBI, n.d.b), although how many of these occurred in the context of bullying is unknown. Bullying victimization in schools will be discussed further in Chapter 6.

Cyberbullying. According to SSOCS data, 15.6% of public-school principals reported that during the 2021–2022 school year, cyberbullying-repeated harm inflicted using computers, cell phones, or other electronic devices—among their students occurred at or away from school at least once a week (at 37% of middle, 25% of high/secondary, and 6% of elementary schools) (Burr et al., 2024). This is up from a rate of 12% during the 2015–2016 year (Musu-Gillette et al., 2018). Also, 2023 YRBS results show that 16.3% of high school students (20.7% of females, 12% of males) reported being electronically bullied (through texting or social media) during the past 12 months, up slightly from 15.9% (20.5% of females, 11.2% of males) in 2021 (CDC, n.d.), and results of a 2023 national survey of 13- to 17-year-olds collected by the Cyberbullying Research Center show that about 55% reported lifetime cyberbullying victimization and about 27% reported that it occurred in the past 30 days (Patchin & Hinduja, 2024).

Stalking. National estimates of juvenile stalking perpetration in the U.S. are currently unavailable. A few past studies examined its prevalence but only in non-nationally representative samples. Smith-Darden and colleagues (2016) found that among 1,182 sixth- and ninth-grade students from 13 schools who participated in a 2013 survey funded by the Centers for Disease Control and Prevention (CDC), 30% reported engaging in some form of stalking—identified from a list of 14 behaviors. However, only 3% reported high-frequency ("comprehensive") stalking. In a sample of 18,103 students (9th through 12th grade) from 26 high schools in one midwestern state, Fisher et al. (2014) found that 5.3% reported engaging in stalking. In this study, stalking was defined conservatively as engaging in *one* (not any) of three types of behavior *at least three times* in the past 12 months: followed, spied on, or monitored someone electronically; showed up or waited for someone who does not want you to; or sent unwanted messages. Using a more inclusive definition would have likely resulted in higher prevalence. Roberts and colleagues' (2016) international review of research suggests that adolescent stalking exists at levels at least as high as those of adults, although specific behavioral patterns between the two likely differ.

Juvenile Domestic Violence. Some juvenile violence occurs in domestic contexts. Juvenile domestic violence includes child-on-parent violence, dating violence, and sibling abuse. In addition to physical assault, these types of violence include verbal abuse, implicit or explicit threat or intimidation, and other types of psychological or emotional abuse.

Child-on-parent violence is relatively infrequent. These acts are more likely to be committed by youth between the ages of 12 and 16. Since many of these youth are themselves victims of abuse by their parents, some child-on-parent violence may be committed to prevent future victimization or even to retaliate (McNamara & Bucher, 2012). NCVS data show that from 2003 to 2012, the average number of domestic assault victimizations committed by a victim's child was 97,490 per year, making up 1.5% of all nonfatal violent crime victimizations and 6.9% of all nonfatal domestic violence victimizations. "Serious violent crime" made up 33.7% of these victimizations, and the rest were simple assaults. The rate was 0.4 victimizations by one's child per 1,000 persons 12 or older (0.1 for serious violent crime and 0.3 for simple assault) (Truman & Morgan, 2014).

Teen dating violence is more common. In past studies, percentages of youth in national samples reporting dating violence, also known as adolescent relationship abuse (ARA), ranged from less than 10% to 40%, depending on sampling differences and how many acts are included in the measures of violence (Taylor & Mumford, 2016). In 2013–2014, a National Survey of Teen Relationships and Intimate Violence (STRiV) was conducted with funding from the National Institute of Justice. Focusing on 12–18-year-old respondents from sampled households (1,804 youth), Taylor and Mumford (2016) found that of the 37% who reported dating currently or in the past year (667 youth), 62.7% reported that they engaged in ARA at some point in the relationship. Thus, the rate for the entire sample would be about 23%. Among those who dated, 62% reported psychological abuse, 12% reported physical abuse, and 12% reported sexual abuse. Also, most perpetrators also reported victimization; only 4.7% reported perpetration only. (Dating violence victimization of high school students will be discussed in Chapter 6.)

The extent of *sibling abuse* is very difficult to measure not only because of under-reporting and under-detection but because it is often difficult to distinguish between what is abuse or bullying and what is socially tolerable play. A great deal of teasing, "horsing" or "messing" around, and arguing is to some extent culturally accepted. A line is crossed when aggressive physical or non-physical acts become harsh, especially when repeated. (Abuse may also be more easily recognized when one sibling has power over another, by being older, stronger, or more mentally able, for example.) Many victims may not realize that what they experienced was inappropriate. However, some research suggests that sibling abuse is the most common form of intra-family violence, and children are more likely to be victimized by a sibling than a parent (McNamara & Bucher, 2012).

Tucker and colleagues (2013) examined data on 1,705 children, aged one month to 17 years who had only one sibling under 18 living in the same household, from the National Survey of Children's Exposure to Violence (NSCEV), a 2008 survey funded by the OJJDP. They found that 37.6% experienced at least one of three forms of victimizations by a co-residing sibling. Only 7.4% experienced more than one type. Just over 32% of all children were physically assaulted, with 3.9% experiencing assault involving a weapon or injury. Among 2–17-year-olds, 4.8% had property stolen, 6.3% had property vandalized, and 2.7% experienced psychological (verbal) cruelty. The rates peaked between ages two and nine and then declined. For example, among 14–17-year-olds, 27.6 % experienced some type of sibling victimization, 5.1% experienced more than one type, 23.1% were physically assaulted, none had property stolen, 3.6% had property vandalized, and 1.2% experienced psychological cruelty. However, 14–17-year-olds had the highest rate of assault involving a weapon or injury at 6.9%.

Sexual Offenses

Most juvenile sex offenders do not commit extremely violent acts; touching, fondling, and non-contact offenses like indecent exposure are more common (McNamara & Bucher, 2012). It is difficult to obtain estimates of juvenile sex offending in the U.S. National self-report studies rarely collect data on these more serious offenses and national sexual victimization studies rarely identify age of perpetrator. Victimization studies tend to show that sexual violence among juveniles is prevalent enough to be considered a serious problem. For example, 2023 YRBS results show that 5.9% of high school students (9.3% of females, 2.9% of males) reported that they experienced sexual dating violence (e.g., unwanted kissing, unwanted touching, and physically forced intercourse), which was down from 2021 (9.7% overall: 15.3% of females, 4% of males) (CDC, n.d.).

Rape. The juvenile arrest rate (per 100,000) for forcible rape rose from 14.9 in 1980 to 21.7 in 1989, remained fairly steady until about 1994, and then decreased fairly steadily to 7.6 in 2012 (NCJJ, 2022). In 2022, juveniles accounted for 15.8% of arrests for rape (new definition), 8% of arrests for *sexual assault with an object*, and 23.1% of arrests for *sodomy* (nonconsensual, including due to age or ability) (FBI, n.d.b).

Sexual Assault & Pressured Sex. In 2022, juveniles accounted for 19.9% of arrests for *fondling* and 17.3% of arrests for *sex offenses, nonforcible* (FBI, n.d.b). Also, sexual violence prevalence has been reported in some dating violence self-report studies. For example, as mentioned earlier, Taylor and Mumford (2016) found in their study that 12% of adolescents who recently dated reported committing sexual abuse against their partners. Of course, these studies leave out sexual assaults that do not occur in the context of dating. It is also difficult to find estimates of *pressured sex* or *sexual harassment* committed by juveniles. Williams et al. (2014) found in their statewide study that 3.6% of high school students (5% of males and 2.5% of females) reported threatening to end a friendship or romantic relationship, arguing, or begging to get another high school student to engage in sexual activity, at least once in the last 12 months.

"Sexting." Lamphere (2014, p. 57) reviewed several prevalence studies of sexting and concluded that "sexting is neither exceedingly common nor rare among youth populations." National studies of juveniles reported in popular media tended to show higher rates (as high as 19%) while studies that used stronger research methods tended to report much lower rates (as low as 4%). Rates are especially low when restricted to producing *sexually explicit images* (e.g., exposed sexual body parts). Further, younger teenagers appear to have lower rates than older teenagers (about 16–18), so teen sexting may be more common among legal or near-legal adults (Lamphere, 2014).

Madigan and colleagues (2018) conducted an international review and meta-analysis of juvenile sexting studies. (A little over half of the studies were done in the U.S.) They found that among youth aged 12 to 17, the mean prevalence rate was 14.8% for sending "sexts," 27.4% for receiving them, and 12% for forwarding them without consent, and that these rates were higher for older juveniles. Further, they found that more recent studies tended to show higher prevalence. This may suggest that juvenile

Figure 2.5: Juvenile Property Crime Arrest Rates, 2000–2020

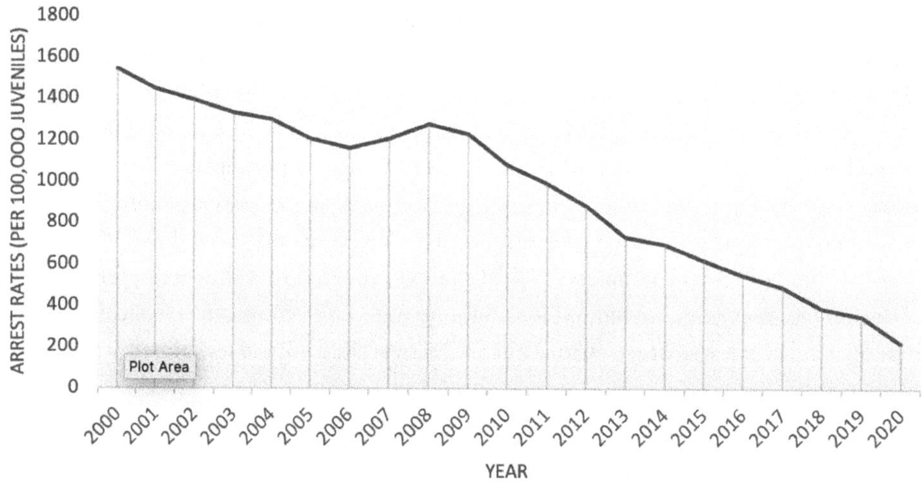

Source: National Center for Juvenile Justice. (2022, July 8). Juvenile arrest rates by offense, sex, and race. http://www.ojjdp.gov/ojstatbb/crime/excel/JAR_2020.xls

sexting is becoming more common, perhaps because of the increase in smartphone ownership among juveniles; the study also found that youth were more likely to sext with mobile devices than computers.

Property Offenses

To begin, the UCR calculates a **Property Crime Index** arrest rate that combines burglary, larceny-theft, motor vehicle theft, and arson. Clearly, juveniles are arrested for property crime much more than for violent crime. Since 1980, the property crime arrest rate for juveniles peaked at 2,543.1 in 1988, remained fairly steady through 1991, declined fairly steadily to under 1,000 in 2011, and then declined steadily until reaching only 351.9 in 2019. In comparison, the juvenile violent crime arrest rates from 1980 to 2012 ranged from about 175 to 478. Among the four property crimes, juveniles are arrested most frequently for larceny-theft and most infrequently for arson (NCJJ, 2022). Although it damages property, vandalism is not included in the property crime index, perhaps because unlike other property offenses, it typically is not done for financial gain. In 2022, juveniles accounted for 9.3% of property crime arrests (FBI, n.d.b). Figure 2.5 shows how annual overall property crime arrest rates for juveniles declined from 2000 to 2020. As shown next, arrests for each of the four property crime categories follow the same general trend.

Theft. Since 1980, the juvenile arrest rate for *larceny-theft* rose somewhat steadily to a peak of 1,668.4 in 1991, fluctuated somewhat through 1997, steadily declined to 799.5 in 2006, rose to 942.7 in 2008, and then steadily declined to 244.4 in 2019 (NCJJ, 2022). In 2022, juveniles accounted for 8.2% of larceny/theft arrests (FBI, n.d.b). The juvenile arrest rate for *burglary* in 1980 was 728.4. From then it fairly steadily declined

Figure 2.6: Juvenile Vandalism Arrest Rates, 2000–2020

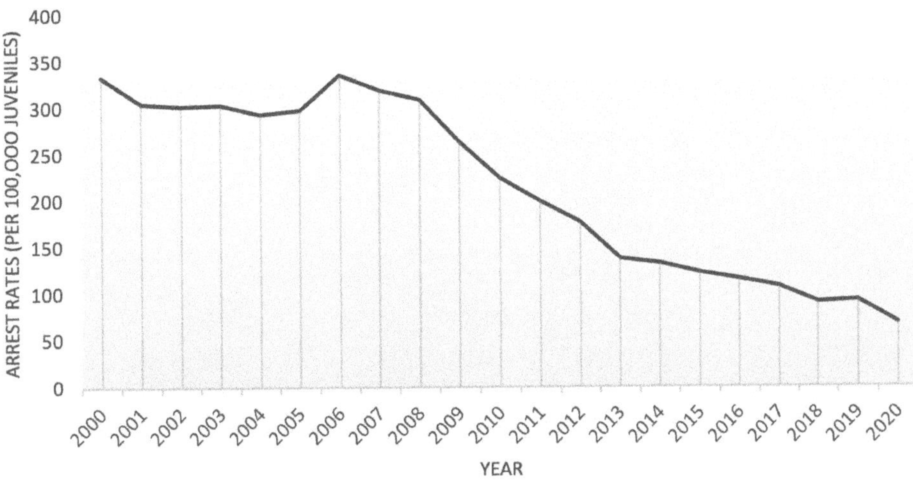

Source: National Center for Juvenile Justice. (2022, July 8). Juvenile arrest rates by offense, sex, and race. http://www.ojjdp.gov/ojstatbb/crime/excel/JAR_2020.xls

to 535.7 in 1989, to 298 in 1999, to 220 in 2009, and then to 62.1 in 2019 (NCJJ, 2022). In 2022, juveniles accounted for 10.4% of burglary/breaking and entering arrests (FBI, n.d.b). Since 1980, the juvenile arrest rate for *motor vehicle theft* peaked at 343.5 in 1989, decreased every year until reaching its lowest point of 35 in 2013, then steadily increased to 47.2 in 2016, but then decreased to 40.4 in 2019 (NCJJ, 2022). In 2022, juveniles accounted for 16.8% of motor vehicle theft arrests (FBI, n.d.b).

Arson & Other Property Offenses. The juvenile arrest rate for *arson* ranged between 21 and 24.9 in the 1980s, peaked at 33.9 in 1994, and then eventually declined to 5.1 in 2019 (NCJJ, 2022). In 2022, juveniles accounted for 16.2% of arson arrests (FBI, n.d.b). It should be noted that while the UCR categorizes arson under property crime separately from vandalism, financial gain may not be a major motive behind juvenile arson, although it may be for adult arson. Regarding other types of property offenses, in 2022, juveniles accounted for 10.1% of *stolen property* (buying, receiving, or possessing) arrests, 1.8% of *counterfeiting/forgery* arrests, 3.9% of *fraud* offenses arrests, and 4.9% of *embezzlement* arrests (FBI, n.d.b).

Vandalism. The juvenile arrest rate for vandalism ranged between 339 and 416 in the 1980s, peaked at 487.7 in 1994, and then fairly steadily declined to 93.2 in 2016 (except for coming down after a noticeable increase to 335.4 in 2006) (NCJJ, 2022). In 2022, juveniles accounted for 15.7% of all destruction/damage/vandalism arrests (FBI, n.d.b). As shown in Figure 2.6, juvenile arrest rates for vandalism follow the same general downward trend from 2000 to 2020 as other crimes against property.

Weapon Law Violations. The juvenile arrest rate for weapons offenses (e.g., carrying, possessing) ranged from 85 to 142 in the 1980s, peaked at 209.2 in 1994, steadily decreased to 102.8 in 2002, steadily increased to 135.5 in 2006, and then fairly steadily

Figure 2.7: Property Crimes, Violent Crimes & Simple Assaults, 2019

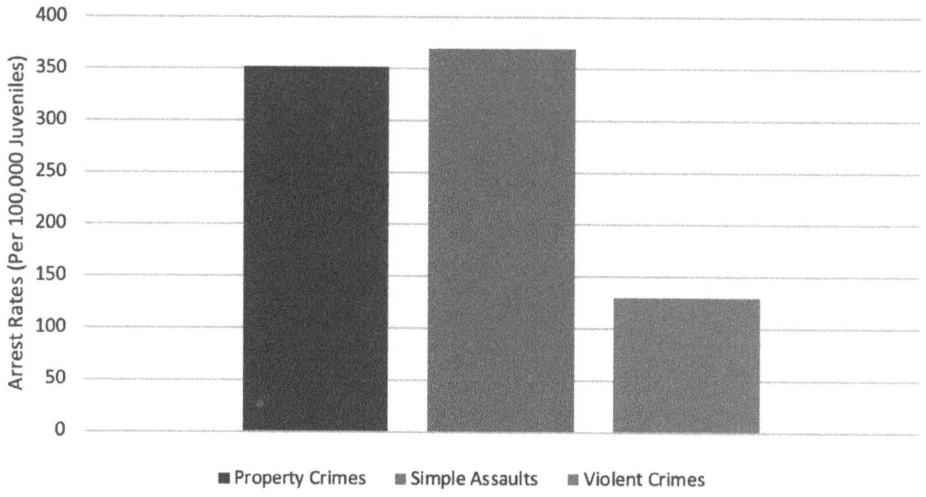

Source: National Center for Juvenile Justice. (2022, July 8). Juvenile arrest rates by offense, sex, and race. http://www.ojjdp.gov/ojstatbb/crime/excel/JAR_2020.xls

Figure 2.8: Property & Violent Offenses, 2019

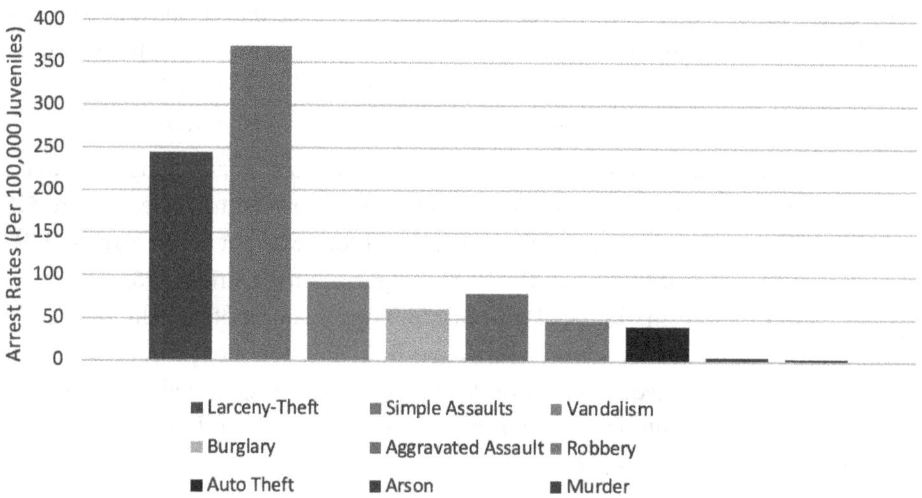

Source: National Center for Juvenile Justice. (2022, July 8). Juvenile arrest rates by offense, sex, and race. http://www.ojjdp.gov/ojstatbb/crime/excel/JAR_2020.xls

decreased to 47.5 in 2019 (NCJJ, 2022). Also, both 2021 and 2023 YRBS results show that 3.5% of high school students reported *carrying a gun* other than for the purpose of hunting or organized sports at least one day during the past 12 months (CDC, n.d.). (Carrying weapons at school will be discussed in Chapter 6.)

Figure 2.9: Illicit Drug Use Lifetime Prevalence, 2000–2023*

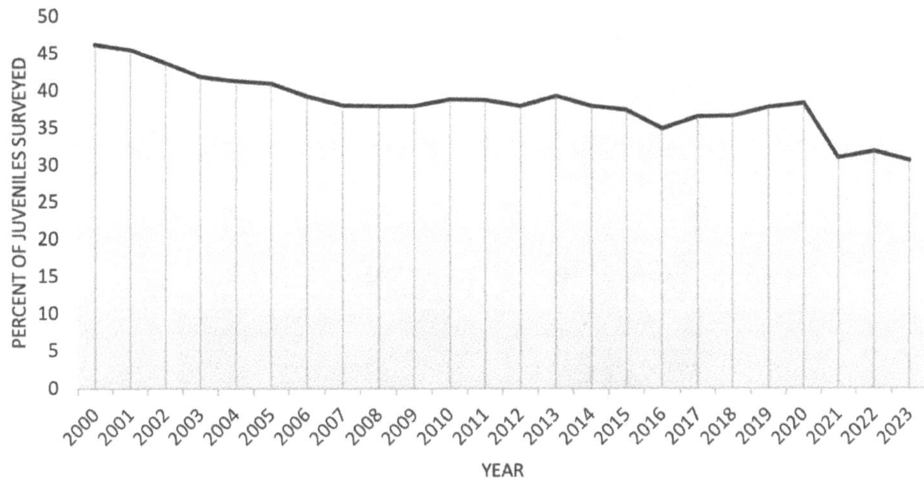

*Includes inhalants.

Source: Miech et al. (2024). *Monitoring the Future national survey results on drug use: 1975–2023: Overview and detailed results for secondary school students.* Institute for Social Research, University of Michigan.

Figures 2.7 and 2.8 help put the relative frequency of arrests for property and violent delinquency in perspective. Notice in Figure 2.7 that the UCR-defined group of property crime and simple assault arrests (those which do not meet the severity criteria for aggravated assault) occur much more frequently than the group of violent crime arrests. (Note: The 2019 violent crimes exclude rape, as incidents meeting the new definition of rape were not yet factored into the rates. However, juvenile arrests for rape are relatively infrequent; the juvenile arrest rate for rape in 2012 was only 7.6 per 100,000 juveniles.) Also notice in Figure 2.8 that, specifically, arrests occur most frequently for simple assaults and larceny-theft while those for serious violent offenses are much less frequent. However, the rate for simple assaults is higher than that of larceny-theft, suggesting that aggressive behavior by juveniles is relatively frequent.

Drug Offenses

Drug and Alcohol Abuse Arrests. The juvenile arrest rate for *drug abuse violations* (sale, manufacturing, and possession) ranged between 268 and 415 in the 1980s, peaked at 684.5 in 1997, and then somewhat steadily declined to 240.4 in 2019 (NCJJ, 2022). (We could speculate that the sharp increase into the 1990s could partly be due to increased arrests, as part of the "war on drugs," rather than increased offending.) The juvenile arrest rate for *drunkenness* was 144.8 in 1980 and since then non-steadily decreased to 57.5 in 1993, steadily increased to 78.7 in 1998, and then fairly steadily decreased to only 10.2 in 2019. Also, since 1980, the juvenile arrest rate for *driving under the influence* (of alcohol or drugs) peaked at 110.5 in 1982, steadily declined

Figure 2.10: Types of Illicit Drug Use Lifetime Prevalence, 2023

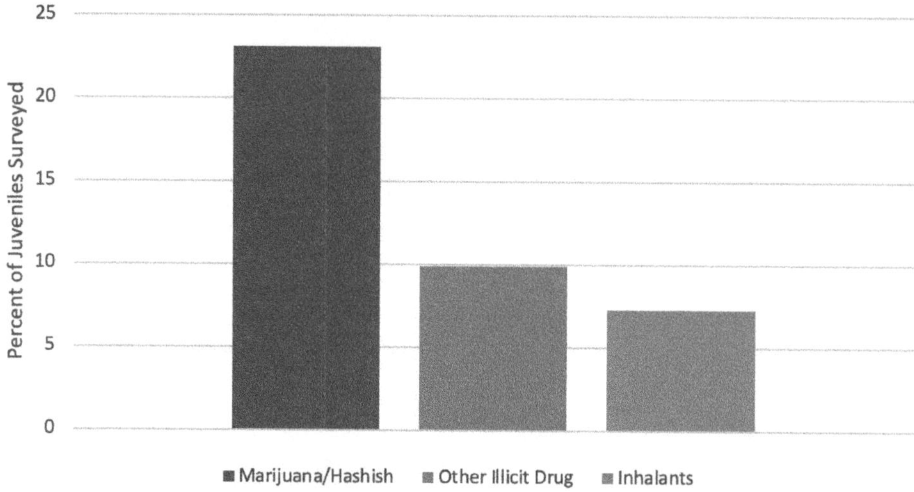

Source: Miech et al. (2024). *Monitoring the Future national survey results on drug use: 1975–2023: Overview and detailed results for secondary school students.* Institute for Social Research, University of Michigan.

from the late 1980s to 46.3 in 1994, increased to 69.3 in 1999, and then fairly steadily declined to only 16.7 in 2019 (NCJJ, 2022). In 2022, juveniles accounted for 1.4% of DUI arrests (FBI, n.d.b).

Self-Reported Drug Use. Monitoring the Future (MTF) data show that since 1991, the percentage of students in grades 8, 10, and 12 (combined) who reported *ever* using *any illicit drug including inhalants* peaked at 48.2% in 1997, steadily decreased to 37.9% in 2008, and fluctuated somewhat until decreasing to 30.6% in 2023. However, much of this was marijuana use. Self-reported *marijuana/hashish* use peaked at 37.8% in 1997, steadily decreased to 27.9% in 2008, increased to 32% in 2013, and then decreased to 23.1% in 2023. The rate for vaping marijuana was 8.5% in 2017, rose to 20.1% in 2020, and then decreased with some fluctuation to 16.6% in 2023. For *any illicit drug other than marijuana* (mostly "harder" drugs such as LCD, ecstasy, cocaine, heroin, and methamphetamine), the percentage peaked at 24.2% in 1996, steadily decreased to 16.5% in 2009, remained roughly stable through 2014, and then decreased to its lowest point of 9.9% in 2023. Heroin has the lowest prevalence, peaking at 2.2% in 1998–1999 and then somewhat steadily decreasing to its lowest point of 0.4% in 2020 and 2021, which was followed by 0.5% in 2022 and 2023 (Miech et al., 2024).

Since 1991, the percentage of these students who reported using any illicit drug including inhalants recently—*in the past thirty days*—peaked at 22.4% in 1996, steadily decreased to 16.1% in 2008, and fluctuated somewhat to 17.4% in 2020 before lowering to 13.4% in 2023. Again, much of this was marijuana or hashish use, which peaked at 17.9% in 1997, fairly steadily decreased to 12.4% in 2007, increased to 15.6% in 2013, and then decreased to 10.9% in 2023. The rate for vaping marijuana was 3.6% in 2017,

Figure 2.11: Illicit Drug Use Lifetime Prevalence MTF v. NSDUH

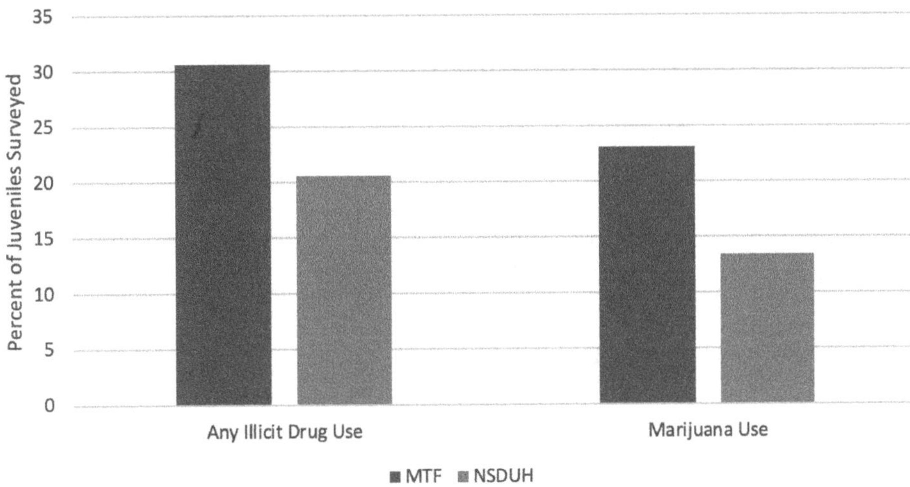

Sources: Miech et al. (2024). *Monitoring the Future national survey results on drug use: 1975–2023: Overview and detailed results for secondary school students.* Institute for Social Research, University of Michigan; Center for Behavioral Health Statistics and Quality. (2025). *Results from the 2023 National Survey on Drug Use and Health: Detailed tables.* https://www.samhsa.gov/data/report/2023-nsduh-detailed-tables

rose to 10.1 in 2019, and then fluctuated some to 8.6% in 2023. For any illicit drug other than marijuana, the percentage peaked at 8.4% in 1995–1997, then gradually decreased to its lowest point of 2.6% in 2021, followed by 2.8% in 2022 and 2023. For heroin, it was 0.2% in 1991, peaked at 0.6% in the late 1990s and then decreased to 0.2% or 0.1% in the years 2015 through 2023 (Miech et al., 2024).

National Survey on Drug Use and Health (NSDUH) data suggest lower prevalence (see Figure 2.11). First, it should be noted that the NSDUH greatly expanded its list of illicit drug categories in 2015. Ecstasy, inhalants, methamphetamine, and misused prescription drugs were added to marijuana, cocaine (including crack), heroin, LSD, and PCP. Thus, the NSDUH cannot offer longer-term trends for these newer categories and general illicit drug use. This said, in 2017, the percentages of juveniles reporting using any of the identified illicit drugs were 23.9% during one's lifetime, 16.3% in the past year, and 7.9% in the past month. The lifetime rate was 20.9% in 2022 and 20.6% in 2023, the past year rate was 14.3% in 2022 and 14.7% in 2023, and the past month rate was 7.3% in 2022 and 7.2% in 2023, showing a decrease (Center for Behavioral Health Statistics and Quality, 2025).

Specifically, NSDUH rates for marijuana were 15.3% lifetime, 12.4% past year, and 6.5% past month in 2017; 13.5% lifetime, 11.5% past year, and 6.4% past month in 2022; and 13.4% lifetime, 11.2% past year, and 6% past month in 2023. Rates for inhalants were 8.6% lifetime, 2.3% past year, and 0.6% past month in 2017; 7.5% lifetime, 2.2% past year, and 0.7% past month in 2022; and 7.4% lifetime, 2.2% past year, and

0.5% past month for 2023. Rates for hallucinogens were 2.8% lifetime, 2.1% past year, and 0.6% past month in 2017; 2.1% lifetime, 1.4% past year, and 0.4% past month in 2022; and 2% lifetime, 1.5% past year, and 0.4% past month in 2023. Rates for cocaine were 0.7% lifetime, 0.5% past year, and 0.1% past month in 2017 and then 0.3% or less for the time periods in 2022 and 2023 (those for crack cocaine specifically were 0.1% or less for any time period in any year). Rates for methamphetamine were 0.3% lifetime, 0.2% past year, and 0.1% past month in 2017 and then 0.3% or less for the time periods in 2022 and 2023. Rates for heroin were 0.1% or less for any time period in any year. Rates for misused prescription drugs were 4.9% past year and 1.5% past month in 2017; 2.5% past year and 0.6% past month in 2022; and 3% past year and 0.8% past month in 2023. Finally, rates for opioids (heroin or misused pain relievers including fentanyl) were 3.1% past year and 0.9% past month in 2017; 1.6% past year and 0.5% past month in 2022; and 2.3% past year and 0.6% past month in 2023 (Center for Behavioral Health Statistics and Quality, 2025). Like MTF data, NSDUH data suggest that juvenile drug use has generally declined over time.

Public Order & Status Offenses

Disorderly Conduct. The juvenile arrest rate for disorderly conduct ranged between 322 and 450 in the 1980s, peaked at 689.6 in 1996, were lower but fluctuated somewhat until 2008, and then steadily declined to only 161.2 in 2019 (NCJJ, 2022). In 2022, juveniles accounted for 20% of disorderly conduct arrests, as well as 10.2% of *trespass of real property* arrests and 2.1% of *family offenses, nonviolent* arrests (perhaps related offenses) (FBI, n.d.b).

Liquor Law Violations. Liquor laws may also be broken by adults, such as selling to minors or during prohibited hours. After reaching a peak of 621 in 1988, the juvenile arrest rate for liquor law violations decreased to 395.4 in 1993, rose to 515.5 in 1996, were lower but fluctuated somewhat until 2008, and then steadily declined to only 78.7 in 2019 (NCJJ, 2022). In 2022, juveniles accounted for 26% of liquor law violation arrests (FBI, n.d.b).

Curfew and Loitering. The juvenile arrest rates for curfew and loitering law violations ranged between 229 and 322 in the 1980s, peaked at 593.9 in 1996, and then somewhat steadily declined to only 43.9 in 2016 (NCJJ, 2022). In 2022, juveniles accounted for 45.7% of curfew/loitering/vagrancy violation arrests (FBI, n.d.b). It should be noted that using arrest records to estimate status offense rates is difficult as status offenders may not be formally arrested, and their cases may be handled by social services rather than the juvenile court (McNamara, 2008).

Truancy. School truancy is considered a major problem in the U.S. According to the U.S. Department of Education, the national rate of chronic absenteeism, defined as students missing at least 10% of school during the year, was about 28% for 2022–2023 (USDE, n.d.). Absenteeism can also be measured daily and monthly. National Center for Education Statistics data showed that the average daily non-attendance rate for public schools during November 2023 was 10% (NCES, n.d.).

Figure 2.12: "Been Drunk" Lifetime Prevalence, 2000–2023

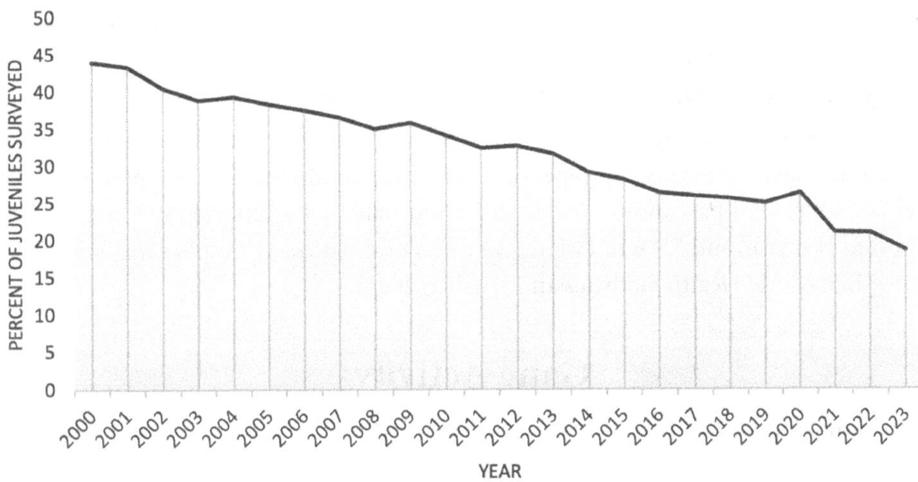

Source: Miech et al. (2024). *Monitoring the Future national survey results on drug use: 1975–2017: Overview and detailed results for secondary school students.* Institute for Social Research, University of Michigan.

Alcohol Use. MTF data show that in 1991, the percentage of adolescents surveyed who reported *ever* using alcohol was 80.1%. Since then, it fairly steadily decreased over time to 41.2% in 2018 before fluctuating a little and reaching its lowest point of 35.7 in 2023. After remaining close to 45% throughout the 1990s, the percentage of those reported having ever *been drunk* fairly steadily decreased to 18.7% in 2023. In 1991, the percentage who reported recently using alcohol—*in the past 30 days*—was 39.8%. Since then, it somewhat steadily decreased over time to 14.3% in 2023. After peaking at 21.2% in 1997, the percentage of those who reported recently being drunk eventually decreased to its lowest point of 6.2% in 2023 (Miech et al., 2024). NSDUH data show that 9.9% of juveniles reported using alcohol in the past month in 2017, which decreased to 6.8% in 2022 and 6.9% in 2023. In 2017, 5.3% reported "binge" use and only 0.7% reported "heavy" use, which decreased to 3.2% and 3.9% binge use in 2022 and 2023 and 0.2% and 0.5% heavy use in 2022 and 2023, respectively (Center for Behavioral Health Statistics and Quality, 2025).

Tobacco Use. MTF data show that since peaking at 57.8% in 1996, the percentage of adolescents who *ever* used *cigarettes* steadily decreased until reaching its lowest point of 9.9% in 2023. Since peaking at 26.3% in 1994, the percentage for using *smokeless tobacco* steadily decreased to 12.3% in 2008, eventually decreased to 8.7% in 2017, and then decreased to its lowest point of 5.9% in 2023 after a short spike to 12% in 2020. The rate for *vaping nicotine* was 18.9% in 2017, increased to 35% in 2020, then decreased to 24.8% in 2023. After peaking at 28.3% in 1996–1997, the percentage who reported recently using cigarettes—*in the past 30 days*—fairly steadily decreased to its lowest point of 2.1% in 2023. Since peaking at 9.7% in 1994, the percentage for recently using smokeless tobacco decreased to 4.9% in 2008, increased to 6.5% in 2010, but then eventually decreased to 2.1% in 2023 after a spike to 4.9% in 2020. The rate for vaping nicotine was 7.5% in 2017, rose to 18.1% in 2019, and then decreased to 11.8% in 2023. The percentages of those who reported smoking types of cigars or a hookah ranged from 3.3 to 5.6% in 2016 but then rather steadily declined to 0.8 to 1.3% in 2023 (Miech et al., 2024). NSDUH data show that 20.6% of juveniles reported lifetime tobacco use (cigarettes, cigars, smokeless, or pipe) or nicotine vaping, 14.9% reported past year use, and 7.3% reported past month use in 2022 and that 20.4% reported lifetime, 14.2% reported past year, and 7.4% reported past month tobacco use or vaping in 2023 (Center for Behavioral Health Statistics and Quality, 2025).

Gang Activity

Beginning in 1996, the **National Gang Center (NGC)**—a project funded by the U.S. Department of Justice—conducted an annual survey on a nationally representative sample of law enforcement agencies, the National Youth Gang Survey (NYGS), to measure the presence, characteristics, and behaviors of local gangs throughout the country. However, 2012 was the last year of the survey. For the survey, the NGC defined a youth gang as "a group of youths or young adults" that the law enforcement agency recognizes as a gang, excluding "motorcycle gangs, hate or ideology groups, prison gangs, and exclusively adult gangs" as these cannot be considered *youth* gangs per se (NGC, n.d.).

Analyses of NYGS data showed that the prevalence rate of gang activity markedly declined from the mid-1990s to the early 2000s, increased significantly between 2001 and 2005, and then remained fairly stable through 2012. From 2005 to 2012, about one-third of the law enforcement agencies reported experiencing gang problems. The highest rate (39.9% of agencies) was reported in the first year of the survey—1996, the lowest was reported in 2001 (23.9%), and the rate in 2012 was 29.6%. Thus, the 2012 rate, although higher than the 2001 rate, is still much lower than that of 1996. In fact, there was a slight decline from recent years (2009: 34.5%; 2010: 34.1%; 2011: 31.6%). However, this decline may be attributed solely to a decline in smaller cities (those with populations between 2,500 and 49,999), as it was the only area category to show a noticeable decline (from 34.8% in 2007 to 25.4% in 2012). The data show that gangs are more prevalent in larger cities, especially those with populations of 100,000 or more. For example, in 2012, 86% of agencies in larger cities reported gang problems compared to 50% in suburban counties, 25% in smaller cities, and 16% in rural counties.

However, estimates of the number of gangs that existed, based on law enforcement agency identification of specific gangs, suggested that gangs increased during the 2000s. In 1996 the number was 30,800 gangs, which steadily fell to the lowest point in 2003 (20,100), but then steadily increased to 30,700 in 2012—about the same number as in 1996. As may be expected, most gangs are in cities: 41.6% of gangs were in larger cities, 27.1% were in smaller cities, 25.8% were in suburban counties, and 5.5% were in rural counties. Also, the estimated number of gang *members* followed a vaguely

Figure 2.13: Student Reported Gang Presence at School, 2001–2021

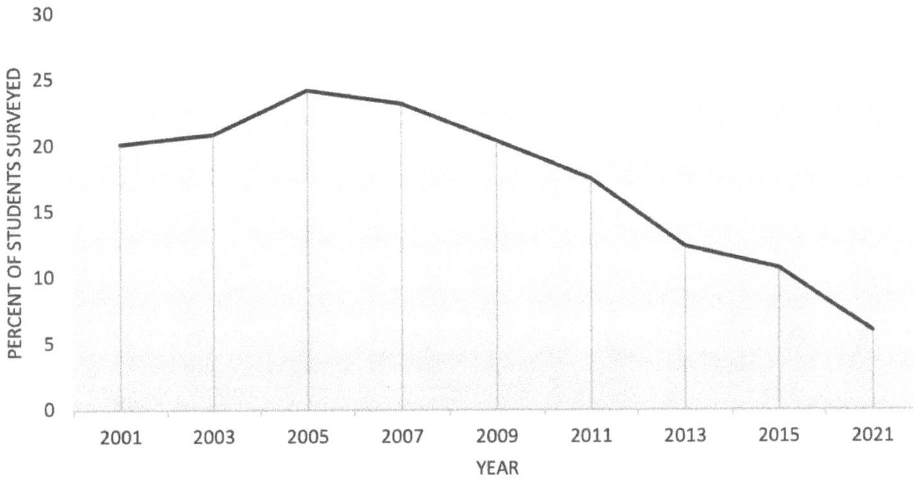

Sources: Musu-Gillette et al. (2018). *Indicators of School Crime and Safety: 2017* (NCES 2018-036/NCJ 251413). National Center for Education Statistics, U.S. Department of Education, and Bureau of Justice Statistics, U.S. Department of Justice; Irwin, V., Wang, K., Cui, J., & Thompson, A. (2024). *Report on indicators of school crime and safety: 2023* (NCES 2024–145/NCJ 309126). National Center for Education Statistics, U.S. Department of Education, and Bureau of Justice Statistics, Office of Justice Programs, U.S. Department of Justice. https://nces.ed.gov/use-work/resource-library/report/compendium/report-indicators-school-crime-and-safety-2023

similar trend. Except for an increase from 1998 to 1999 (780,000 to 840,500), the number decreased from 1996 (846,500) to the lowest point in 2003 (710,500) and then non-steadily increased to the highest point in 2012 (850,000). Over half of gang members were in larger cities—57.3%, compared to 24.4% in suburban counties, 15.6% in smaller cities, and 2.7% in rural counties.

It should be noted that according to the NYGS, most gang members are adults (aged 18 and over). In 1996, the split between juveniles and adults was even (50% each), but the portion of juveniles non-steadily decreased to 35% in 2011. Thus, much criminal gang behavior does not constitute delinquency (although we cannot assume that older gang members are just as active as younger ones). However, in 2011, adult gang members were only a slight majority (52%) in smaller cities, and there were more juveniles (58.9%) in rural counties (NGC, n.d.).

More recent information on gang activity, at schools for example, suggests that gang activity has decreased in the United States. According to SSOCS data, 10% of public-school principals reported that gang activity occurred at their schools during 2015–2016 (Musu-Gillette et al., 2018), but by 2021–2022, only 0.8% reported gang activities (Burr et al., 2024). Also, the NCVS-SCS asks students aged 12–18 to report if gangs are present at their schools during the school year. The percentage who reported gang presence increased from 20.1% in 2001 to 24.2% in 2005 but then consistently declined to 10.7% in 2015 (Musu-Gillette et al., 2018) and then 6% in 2021 (Irwin et al., 2024).

Figure 2.14: Gender Differences in Arrest Rates

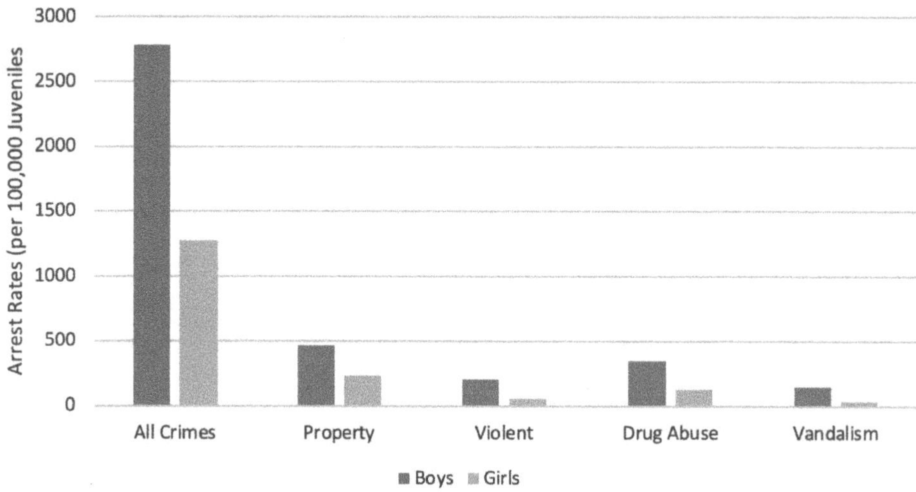

Source: National Center for Juvenile Justice. (2022, July 8). Juvenile arrest rates by offense, sex, and race. http://www.ojjdp.gov/ojstatbb/crime/excel/JAR_2020.xls

Gender, Race, and Class Differences in Arrests and Offending

Gender

Girls are far less likely than boys to commit crimes, especially those of a violent and sexual nature. This difference is continuously reflected in UCR juvenile arrest rates. In 2019, females were arrested for violent offenses at a rate of 55.4 compared to 202.2 for males. In 2019, females were arrested for property offenses at a rate of 236.0 compared to 463.1 for males. Girls are also much less likely to be arrested for other offenses: simple assault, vandalism, weapon law violations, drug abuse, driving under the influence, liquor law violations, drunkenness, disorderly conduct, and curfew and loitering (NCJJ, 2022). Further, YRBS data showed that in every survey year from 1993–2015, high school females were less likely to report carrying a weapon (such as a gun, knife, or club), at school or anywhere else, at least one day during the past 30 days. In 2015, 8% of females reported carrying a weapon compared to 24% of males (Musu-Gillette et al., 2018). YRBS results from 2023 show that 1.8% of females reported *carrying a gun*, specifically, (other than for the purpose of hunting or organized sports) at least one day during the past 12 months compared to 4.9% of males, which were about the same rates as in 2021 (CDC, n.d.).

Boys generally engage in more interpersonal violence than girls. For example, studies described earlier found that girls are less likely to engage in stalking behaviors. Smith-Darden et al. (2016) found that 37.5% of boys and 23.1% of girls reported

Figure 2.15: Gender Differences in Lifetime Prevalence of Substance Use

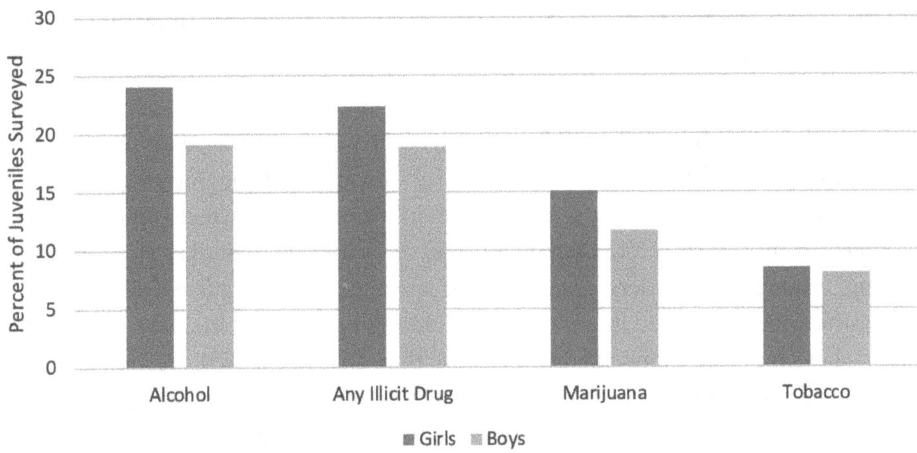

Source: Center for Behavioral Health Statistics and Quality. (2025). *Results from the 2023 National Survey on Drug Use and Health: Detailed tables.* https://www.samhsa.gov/data/report/2023-nsduh-detailed-tables

stalking, and that 6.4% of boys and 0% of girls reported high-frequency stalking. Also, Fisher et al. (2014) found that 6.5% of boys and 4.2% of girls reported stalking. However, this trend in interpersonal violence does not hold up in all contexts and studies. In the STRiV study, Taylor and Mumford (2016) found that girls were not less likely to engage in dating violence than boys, nor were they more likely to be victims. Girls reported engaging in physical abuse at a significantly higher rate than boys (14.7% vs. 9.3%). Boys engaged in sexual abuse at a higher rate (13.4% vs. 10.6% for girls) but the difference was not statistically significant. More specifically, while boys and girls had about the same rates of moderate psychological abuse (about 61%), girls had higher rates of serious psychological abuse (8.6% vs. 3.2%), moderate threats and physical violence (12.7% vs. 5%), and serious threats and physical violence (10.5% vs. 7.6%). However, the study did not examine these gender differences more precisely, such as if one group was more likely to threaten instead of physically assault or tended to inflict more serious injury.

There has been a shrinking of the gender gap in arrests in recent decades, meaning that females now make up a noticeably larger (but still relatively small) portion of arrests. This could be due to increased offending by females, increased tendency of officers to arrest females (a reduction in "chivalry"), or both. An analysis of 2010 National Incident-Based Reporting System (NIBRS) data found that while two-thirds of documented juvenile assaults were committed by boys, after controlling for offense severity, offender characteristics, and victim characteristics, girls were slightly but significantly *more likely than boys* to be arrested for their assaults. Further, female assaults were more likely than male assaults to be committed against parents, against 18- to 44-year-olds, and in the home. Thus, girls' assaults were more likely to be domestic, which are subject to mandatory arrest. Boys may be more likely to commit assaults that are subject to flexible discretion. The increased likelihood of girls to be arrested, then, could at least be partly due to changes in justice policies and procedures for certain offenses (Vaughan et al., 2015).

According to MTF data, boys generally have higher rates of self-reported drug use than girls, especially frequent use. However, over the years, the difference in marijuana use has disappeared. In 2023, girls' marijuana use (including through vaping) was even slightly higher than that of boys. Differences in alcohol use have also narrowed. In 2023, slightly more girls (25%) than boys (23%) reported any alcohol use in the past 30 days, but among 12th graders, *binge drinking* specifically (having five or more drinks in one sitting) was reported more by boys (12%) than girls (9%). In 2023, among 12th graders, boys reported more cigarette smoking than girls (3.5% vs. 1.6%, respectively), although vaping nicotine was higher for girls. Boys continue to have higher rates of smokeless tobacco use, although their rate in 2023 was low (3.2% of 12th graders, 0.8% for girls). Rates of nicotine pouch use were roughly equal (Miech et al., 2024).

However, NSDUH data show that girls were more likely to self-report drug use. For any illicit drug use, lifetime prevalence for girls was 23.4% in 2022 and 22.4% in 2023, but for boys was 18.5% in 2022 and 18.9% in 2023. Past year prevalence for girls was 15.5% in 2022 and 16.5% in 2023 but for boys was 13% in 2022 and 13.1% in 2023. Past month prevalence for girls was 8.4% in 2022 and 8% 2023 but for boys was 6.3% in 2022 and 6.4% in 2023. Further, when broken down by specific category girls had higher or equal self-report rates including for "hard drugs" such as cocaine, opioids, and meth. However, these rates are based on a measure of "any use" of drugs, not the frequency or amount of use during the time period. Thus, they do not determine how frequent or heavy girls' drug use is compared to that of boys. Also, that girls' rates are higher than boys' does not mean that girls' rates can be described as high; both boys' and girls' self-reported drug use is lower in comparison to past years.

Girls were also more likely to report alcohol use: lifetime prevalence for girls was 24.5% in 2022 and 24.1% in 2023 but for boys was 20.2% in 2022 and 19.1% in 2023, past year prevalence for girls was 18.9% in 2022 and 19.2% in 2023 but for boys was 14.7% in 2022 and 2023, and past month prevalence for girls was 8.3% in 2022 and 7.9% in 2023 but for boys was 5.4% in 2022 and 6% in 2023. Further, girls were more likely than boys to report past month binge use (4% in 2022 and 4.5% in 2023 vs. 2.6% in 2022 and 3.3% in 2023, respectively) while past month heavy use was reported about the same. Finally, girls were also more likely to report tobacco use or nicotine vaping: lifetime prevalence for girls was 22.8% in 2022 and 2023 but for boys was 18.4% in 2022 and 18.2% in 2023, past year prevalence for girls was 17.4% in 2022 and 16.6% in 2023 but for boys was 12.5% in 2022 and 12% in 2023, and past month prevalence for girls was 8.8% in 2022 and 9% in 2023 but for boys was 5.9% in 2022 and 2023. However, the rates for tobacco product use excluding vaping (what may be thought of as traditional tobacco product use) tended to be about equal, which means that girls are more likely to report nicotine vaping. Lifetime prevalence for girls was 8.4% in 2022 and 8.5% in

2023 and for boys was 8.9% in 2022 and 8.1% in 2023, past year prevalence for girls was 4.7% in 2022 and 4.6% in 2023 and for boys was 4.8% in 2022 and 4.9% in 2023, and past month prevalence for girls was 2% in 2022 and 2.1% in 2023 and for boys was 1.9% in 2022 and 1.6% in 2023. Girls were slightly more likely to report cigarette use but consistently less likely to report use of smokeless tobacco (Center for Behavioral Health Statistics and Quality, 2025).

Race/Ethnicity

UCR arrest data show that Black juveniles have the highest overall arrest rates followed by Native Americans, whites, and then Asians. The UCR does not define Hispanic as a separate race; youth of "Hispanic ethnicity" may be included under any racial category (NCJJ, 2022). The UCR's crude definitions of race and ethnicity must be heavily considered when interpreting differences. Theoretically, we might expect Black Americans to have higher rates of offending since they experience social disadvantages associated with crime (e.g., economic strain and racial discrimination) at high rates. However, we must keep in mind that differences in arrest rates may be due biases in the justice system rather than differences in actual offending. Thus, it is important to also consider other indicators of delinquency. Also, data do not always show that youth of color are at higher risk of offending.

In 2019, the juvenile arrest rate for violent offenses was 384.9 for Black youth, 117.4 for American Indian youth, 83.8 for white youth, and 31.2 for Asian youth. The juvenile arrest rate for property offenses was 903.1 for Black, 335.1 for American Indian, 254.9 for white, and 93.7 for Asian youth. The rate for drug abuse was 317.6 for Black, 274.5 for American Indian, 238 for white, and 61.7 for Asian youth. However, Black juveniles have some of the lowest arrest rates for other substance-related offenses. The 2019 juvenile arrest rate for driving under the influence was 26.1 for American Indian, 19.9 for white, 6.2 for Black, and 4.7 for Asian youth. The rate for liquor law violations was 241.9 for American Indian, 90.1 for white, 32.2 for Black, and 18.8 for Asian youth. The rate for drunkenness was 48.4 for American Indian, 10.6 for white, 7.5 for Black, and 1.9 for Asian youth (NCJJ, 2022).

American Indian juveniles had the highest arrest rates for the three alcohol-related offenses. Earlier research suggested that American Indians and Alaska Natives (AI/AN) are at higher risk of alcohol abuse. Thus, one may suppose that their arrests rates reflect alcohol abuse rates. However, past studies were done on local or regional samples that cannot be generalized to AI/AN nationwide. (Some may also be outdated.) More recent analyses of national survey data show that AI/AN alcohol abuse rates are about the same as those of white juveniles, white juveniles show higher light to moderate alcohol consumption, and AI/AN are more likely to abstain (Cunningham et al., 2016). Thus, any heighted risk of alcohol use problems experienced by AI/AN may be contextual (e.g., in certain geographic areas or extremely disadvantaged communities), and the difference in national arrest rates may be due to policing practices. However, some research also suggests that AI/AN youth start drinking at relatively younger ages (Enoch & Albaugh, 2017).

According to MTF data, for several past years, white adolescents had substantially higher rates of general self-reported drug use than African American adolescents, but these findings have largely reversed. Results from 2022 and 2023 show that Black/African American students' lifetime, annual, 30-day, and daily prevalence levels of most drug use were higher than those for whites and Hispanics. Much of this difference lies in marijuana use. Among 12th graders, annual marijuana use prevalence was 33% for Black, 26% for white, and 25% for Hispanic students, with little difference between them in 8th and 10th grades. Also among 12th graders, 30-day illicit drug use other than marijuana prevalence was 3.7% for Black, 2.8% for Hispanic, and 2.5% for white students. However, Black students often had rates lower than whites and Hispanics for certain drugs such as hallucinogens, inhalants, and prescription drugs. Among 12th graders, white students had the highest 12-month Vicodin, Ritalin, GHB, and steroid use prevalence, and Hispanic students had the lowest levels for all major drugs. In 2023, among 12th graders, Black students reported more alcohol use than Hispanics and whites. For example, 12-month prevalence for getting drunk was 34% for Black, 20% for white, and 16% for white students and 30-day prevalence for binge drinking was 16%, for Black, 8% for Hispanic, and 5% for whites. Also in 2023 among 12th graders, Black students reported the most nicotine use. For example, the 30-day prevalence for cigarette smoking was 5% for Black, 1.9% for Hispanic, and 1% for white students and the 30-day prevalence for nicotine vaping was 25% for Black, 13% for Hispanic, and 10% for white students (Miech et al., 2024).

However, 2023 NSDUH findings do not suggest that Black/African American youth are highest in risk of illicit drug use in general. Prevalence was highest for multi-racial youth, and lowest for Asian youth. Lifetime self-reported prevalence for any illicit drug use among juveniles was 26.8% for multi-racial youth, 22.4% for Black or African Americans, 21.9% for American Indian or Alaska Natives, 20.8% for Hispanic or Latinos, 20.3% for whites, and 12.8% for Asians. The past year prevalence was 20.1% for multi-racial youth, 16.4% for Black or African Americans, 16% for American Indian or Alaska Natives, 14.9% for Hispanic or Latinos, 14.7% for whites, and 6.5% for Asians. The past month prevalence was 12% for multi-racial youth, 8.2% for Hispanic or Latinos, 7.5% for Black or African Americans, 6.9% for whites, 4.5% for American Indian or Alaska Natives, and 2% for Asians. However, trends sometimes changed with specific categories. For example, Black or African American youth reported the lowest prevalence for cocaine use and Hispanic or Latino youth reported the highest for misuse of prescription pain relievers (Center for Behavioral Health Statistics and Quality, 2025). A comparison of Figures 2.16 and 2.17 suggests that racial differences in drug *use* may not be as pronounced as drug *arrests*, although some of the inconsistency may be explained by the UCR's exclusion of a multiracial category.

Regarding tobacco product use and nicotine vaping in general, in 2023, multi-racial youth consistently had the highest prevalence, and Asian youth consistently had the

Figure 2.16: Drug Abuse Arrest Rates by Race, 2019

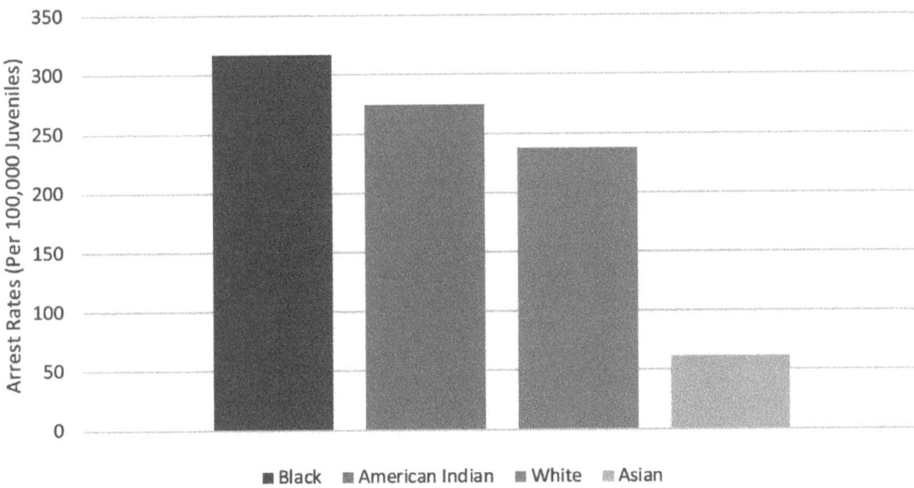

Note: Hispanic or Latino/a youth may be included in any category and are not reported separately.

Source: National Center for Juvenile Justice. (2022, July 8). Juvenile arrest rates by offense, sex, and race. http://www.ojjdp.gov/ojstatbb/crime/excel/JAR_2020.xls

Figure 2.17: Illicit Drug Use Past Year Prevalence by Race, 2023

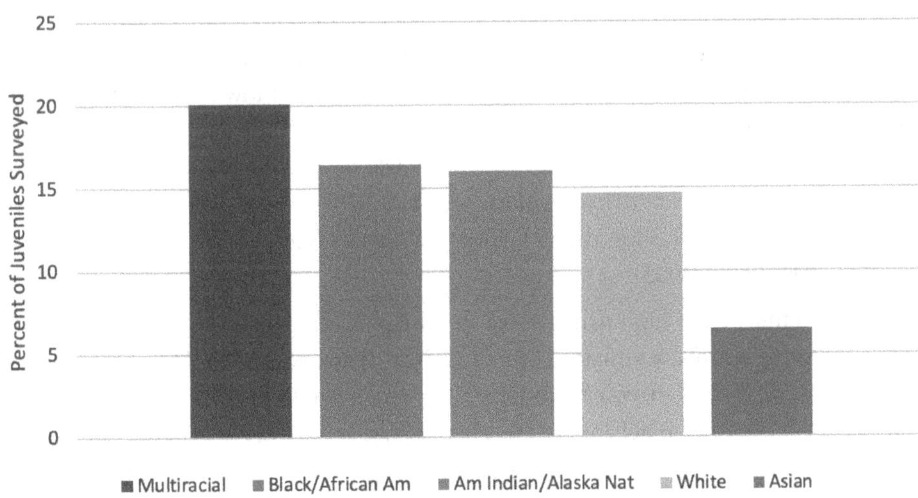

Note: Hispanic or Latino/a youth may be included in any category.

Source: Center for Behavioral Health Statistics and Quality. (2025). *Results from the 2023 National Survey on Drug Use and Health: Detailed tables.* https://www.samhsa.gov/data/report/2023-nsduh-detailed-tables

lowest, while white, Black or African American, American Indian or Alaska Native, and Hispanic or Latino youth had similar rates that varied according to time frame.

Figure 2.18: Alcohol Use Lifetime Prevalence by Race, 2023

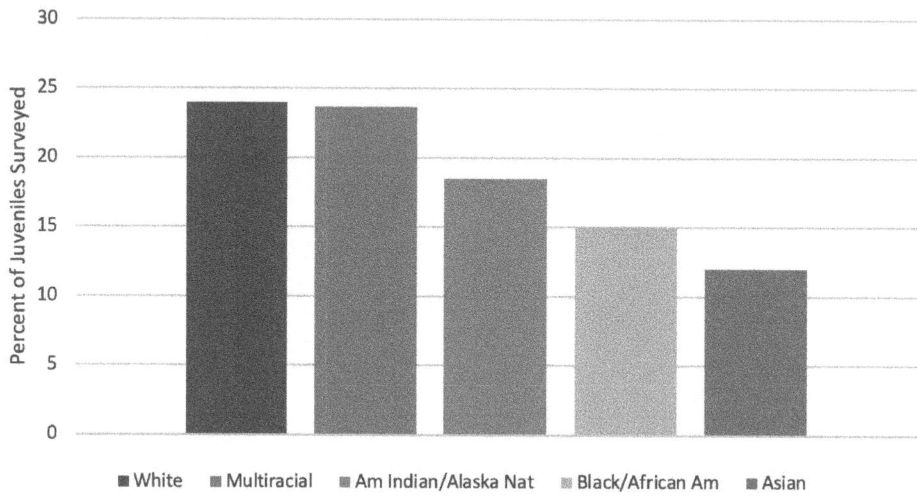

Note: Hispanic or Latino/a youth may be included in any category.

Source: Center for Behavioral Health Statistics and Quality. (2025). *Results from the 2023 National Survey on Drug Use and Health: Detailed tables.* https://www.samhsa.gov/data/report/2023-nsduh-detailed-tables

This trend largely held for cigarette use specifically, except that Black/African American youth consistently had the second lowest rates. White and multi-racial youth had the highest rates of general alcohol use followed by Hispanic and Latinos, and Black or African American and Asian youth consistently reported low rates. Getting more specific, past month binge alcohol use prevalence was 4.6% for whites, 4.2% for Hispanic or Latinos, 3.9% for multi-racial youth, 2.6% for American Indian or Alaskan Natives, 2.4% for Black or African Americans, and 0.7% for Asians. Past month heavy alcohol use prevalence was less than 2% for all categories (Center for Behavioral Health Statistics and Quality, 2025).

Black juveniles have high arrest rates for weapon offenses. In 2019, the juvenile arrest rate for weapon law violations was 122.3 for Black youth, 34.7 for white youth, 30.6 for American Indian youth, and 13.3 for Asian youth (NCJJ, 2022). However, YRBS data suggest that Black, as well as Hispanic, juveniles are less likely than white juveniles to carry weapons. In 2015, the percentages of high school students reporting carrying a weapon were, from highest to lowest: 26.3% of Pacific Islander youth, 22.4 % of American Indian/Alaskan Native youth, 20.8% of youth of two or more races, 18.1% of white youth, 13.7% of Hispanic youth, 12.4% of Black youth, and 7.1% of Asian youth (Musu-Gillette et al., 2018). In 2023, the percentages reporting carrying a gun, specifically, were: 8.7% of Native Hawaiian or Other Pacific Islanders, 4.1% of Hispanics or Latinos, 3.3% of whites, 3.2% of Black/African Americans, 3% of multiracial youth, 2.1% of American Indians or Alaska Natives, and 1.9% of Asians (CDC, n.d.).

Most studies show that socially disadvantaged racial and ethnic minorities make up a majority of gang members in the U.S. For example, in the National Youth Gang Survey (NYGS), from 1996 to 2011, law enforcement agencies most often reported gang members as Hispanic/Latino followed by Black or African American. The portions ranged from 45.2% to 50.2% for Hispanic/Latino, 30.9% to 37.8% for Black/African American, 7.9% to 13.4% for white, and 5.7% to 8.4% for "all other." This general distribution holds up across different areas except rural counties, where in 2011 agencies reported that 56.8% of members were Black/African American and only 24.8% were Hispanic/Latino. Also, in 2011, white gang members were more prevalent in smaller cities (14.6%) and rural counties (14.9%) compared to larger cities (9.7%) and suburban counties (9.1%) (NGC, n.d.). Racial and ethnic minorities are likely over-represented in gangs because they disproportionately experience the social and economic risk factors, such as adverse neighborhood conditions, associated with gang membership. However, there is a noticeable number of non-Hispanic white youth involved in gangs, and their pathways (experiences with risk factors over time) to gang membership may be similar to those of minority gang members (Mendez & Kerig, 2023).

Social Class

Theoretically, we might expect lower socio-economic status (SES) youth to commit more delinquency than middle- and upper-class youth because they are more exposed to criminogenic factors associated with economic problems and educational disadvantage. However, as will become apparent after reading the following chapters, there are many non-SES factors that produce delinquency, and higher status youth have deviant opportunities that lower status youth tend not to have. Thus, lower and higher status youth may engage in about the same rate of delinquency but experience different causes for doing so. Also, if low SES does put youth at higher risk of offending, it may only be for certain offenses or offending patterns, and the difference in offending rates between low and higher status youth may not be that great. Further, there may be class biases in how juvenile justice, school, and other agencies operate. Lower SES youth may not commit more crime; they may simply get caught more for it.

Contemporary research tends to suggest no class differences in rates of *minor* delinquency (which makes up most delinquency) but that lower SES youth are slightly more likely to engage in serious delinquency, perhaps because the set of factors associated with serious (e.g., violent) delinquency are more unique to disadvantaged environments (e.g., heavy direct exposure to violence) (Akers et al., 2017). For example, a study of boys in Pittsburgh suggests that the age-crime curve for violent crime takes on a different shape for youth growing up in socio-economically disadvantaged neighborhoods. Fabio and colleagues (2011) found higher and longer curves in more disadvantaged neighborhoods, suggesting that more boys from disadvantaged neighborhoods engage in violence and that they take longer to desist in comparison to boys in advantaged or even average SES neighborhoods.

Figure 2.19: Illicit Drug Use Past Year Prevalence by Family Income, 2023

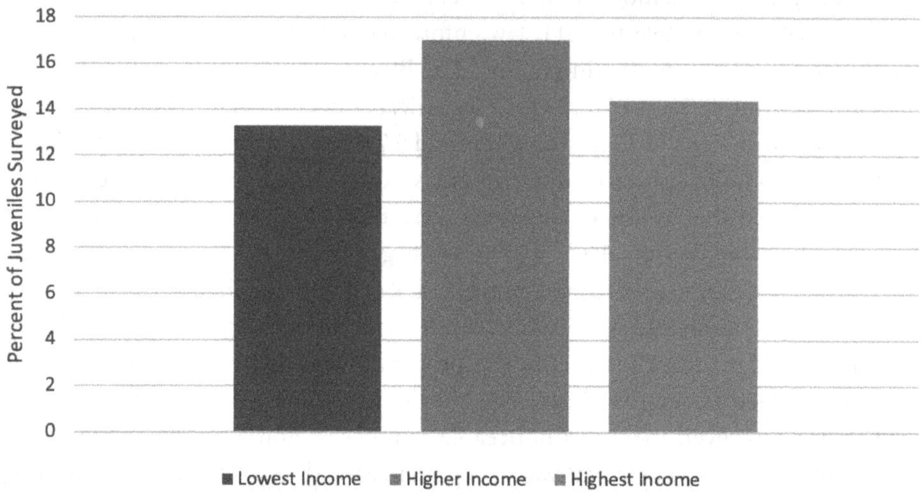

Source: Center for Behavioral Health Statistics and Quality. (2025). *Results from the 2023 National Survey on Drug Use and Health: Detailed tables.* https://www.samhsa.gov/data/report/2023-nsduh-detailed-tables

Unfortunately, our major sources of data do not measure and analyze social class as much as gender and race, perhaps because class is more difficult to measure categorically. Thus, it is difficult to find national estimates of differences in offending across class categories. The exception here is with substance use. According to MTF data, illicit drug use, including marijuana use, does not differ greatly by adolescents' socioeconomic status (SES), defined as the average level of education of their parents, and the general trend of decreased drug use has also been experienced by lower SES youth. Also, lower SES is not strongly associated with abusing alcohol (Johnston et al., 2018). In fact, a more recent analysis of MTF data revealed that 50.6% of 12th graders with at least one college-educated parent reported past-year alcohol use compared to 43.2% of those without a college-educated parent. Further, tobacco and nicotine use did not vary greatly according to parent college education (Miech et al., 2024).

NSDUH 2023 data show about the same trends in comparing three groups of juveniles: family incomes under 100% of the U.S. Census Bureau's poverty threshold (lowest income), family incomes at 100–199% of it (higher income), and family incomes at 200% or more of it (highest income). Past year prevalence for all illicit drug use was 13.3% for lowest income youth, 17% for higher, and 14.4% for highest. The past month prevalence was 7% for lowest income youth, 7.7% of higher, and 7.1% of highest. Regarding marijuana use specifically, past year prevalence was 9.8% for lowest income youth, 13.3% of higher, and 10.9% of highest and past month prevalence was 5.6% for lowest income youth, 6.5% of higher, and 6% of highest. Reported cocaine use was very low for all three categories (0.3% or less) (Center for Behavioral Health Statistics and Quality, 2025).

Figure 2.20: Alcohol Use Past Year Prevalence by Family Income, 2023

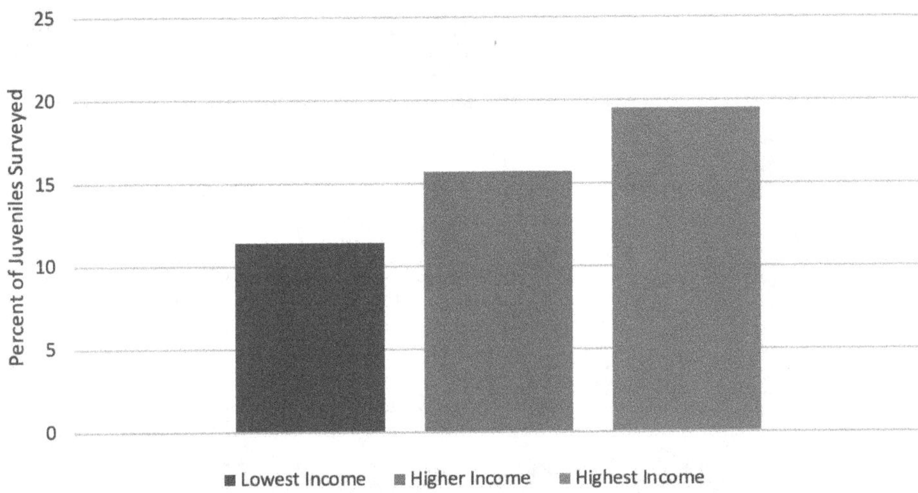

Source: Center for Behavioral Health Statistics and Quality. (2025). *Results from the 2023 National Survey on Drug Use and Health: Detailed tables.* https://www.samhsa.gov/data/report/2023-nsduh-detailed-tables

With alcohol use, the higher the family income category, the higher the prevalence. (Lowest income youth had the lowest rates.) The 2023 past year/past month rates were 11.4%/4.6% (lowest), 15.7%/6% (higher), and 19.5%/8.2% (highest). The trend was the same for past month binge use (2.8%, 3.3%, and 4.5%, respectively), and heavy use was very low for each level (0.5%, 0.4%, and 0.6%, respectively). Regarding tobacco and vaping, the highest income youth were less likely to report tobacco product use and nicotine vaping while lowest and higher income youth had about the same rates. Cigarette use, specifically, was very low for all three levels and did not vary much (all past year rates were about 3.5% and all past month rates were on or close to 1.3%) (Center for Behavioral Health Statistics and Quality, 2025).

Why Does It Seem Like Delinquency Is Increasing?

It is popularly believed that juvenile crime is increasing or somehow getting worse. Fear and concern over problems such as gangs and youth violence may lead the public, as well as law and policy makers, to think that "kids these days are out of control" and the juvenile justice system is incapable of handling them (McNamara & Bucher, 2012). The offending rates covered in this chapter show that such extreme views are unwarranted. In reality, serious violent offenders and offenses are relatively rare, and delinquency rates do not fluctuate that much and have even gone down recently. Simply put, most kids are good kids. Why then does it seem like delinquency is getting worse?

The media may be partly to blame, but we must not be too simplistic here. "Media" is a vague, general term referring to many different types of outlets—different types of television shows, news programs, films, newspapers, magazines, websites, and so on. We often speak of "the media" as if it were one thing—a single concrete entity. The quality of information greatly varies across outlets and individual reports. Much media attention sensationalizes or falsely portrays crime (Miller & Davis, 2008), but accurate information can also be found in the media. Also, the relationship between media and the public is reciprocal. Media coverage influences our perceptions, but our perceptions likely also influence media coverage. Media agencies require public consumption to be sustained and thus may tailor programming according to what they believe to be their audiences' expectations.

Regardless, a great deal of media attention is given to crime with coverage tending to focus on more alarming forms and cases, which may fuel public perceptions of crime, including delinquency, as a growing problem. However, much of the problem may lie in how audiences process media information. Media reports and images often do not directly state that crime is more serious than what it really is, but the emphasis or focus on incidents that shock and frighten us makes it seem like the problem is more severe than it actually is (McNamara & Bucher, 2012). We may confuse the alarming nature of some incidents with the frequency of their occurrence. Media agents are responsible for biased coverage here, but the public is responsible for consuming media information non-critically. If we are not careful, we may falsely believe that since we are continuously seeing a type of event in the media, or a great deal of media coverage of one catastrophic event, the type of event must be increasing or occurring at some alarming rate.

Similarly, we may confuse the severity of certain offenders with their frequency. Most delinquency is relatively minor and committed by youth temporarily involved in offending. However, a small group can be identified as *chronic juvenile offenders.* Longitudinal research shows that a small portion of juvenile offenders commit most of the serious offenses that occur (Benson, 2013). Chronic juvenile offenders, many of whom are involved with gangs, are at high risk of becoming a "career criminal": an individual who offends well into adulthood (McNamara & Bucher, 2012). These offenders pose a major problem for public safety and juvenile justice and draw a great deal of media attention. "Get tough" policies and practices have been developed with them in mind. Thus, citizens who believe that the problem of delinquency is getting worse or "out of control" may be focusing on harm done by chronic violent offenders, despite their statistical rarity.

Another possible reason has more to do with a reasonable perception of delinquency: there is indeed much of it. To point out that delinquency rates are somewhat stable as opposed to going up, or slightly going down, is not to say that *the rates are low.* Considering again the age-crime curve, it is apparent that juveniles commit a great deal of the crime that occurs in society. High delinquency rates appear to be a stable part of our society. Further, certain acts of mass violence committed by youth, such as mass school shootings, although statistically rare, may have increased in recent decades (May et al., 2014). Media representations aside, these are some of the most horrific acts imaginable. As such, they make major impressions upon us, which may include the notion that juveniles are becoming more violent, more criminal.

To some extent, the myth of skyrocketing delinquency may be an exaggeration of the appropriate recognition of delinquency as a continuing major problem. As we mature and morally develop, become more educated, and experience profound life transitions such as becoming parents, we may become more aware of and concerned over the consequences of social problems such as crime. Who knows, for some people, maybe the belief that crime is increasing is really an increase in how much one cares about it.

Summary Points

- The extent and severity of delinquency in society may be understood in terms of *incidence*—the number of times acts occur during a certain time, *prevalence*—the number of juveniles who commit acts, and *rates*—a measure that puts incidence or prevalence in context (e.g., a ratio or percent). These may be of all delinquency, certain categories (e.g., violent or property crime), or specific types (e.g., larceny-theft).
- It is impossible to know the true extent of delinquency or crime in the population since most minor and many major acts are undetected, but with careful research we can calculate useful estimates.
- Our major sources of data on delinquency and crime are official/governmental—namely the FBI's Uniform Crime Reporting (UCR) system, victim-provided—namely the National Crime Victimization Survey (NCVS), and self-reported (multiple studies).

These studies are better for identifying trends (e.g., if delinquency is going up or down or staying the same) than the true amount of offenses that take place.

- The *age-crime curve* shows that older adolescents and very young adults are the most likely to commit crime. However, this does not mean that most youth significantly engage in crime. Data also show that most delinquency is minor and non-violent, and most juveniles who engage in it do so temporarily (desisting by or in early adulthood).
- Arrest, victim-report, and self-report data suggest that like adult crime, delinquency has either decreased or remained relatively stable in recent years. This trend is true for violent, property, drug, and public order offenses. However, better estimates on "newer" forms of crime, such as the various cybercrimes, are needed.
- Boys are much more likely to commit delinquency than girls, especially violence. This gender gap has decreased in recent decades, meaning that girls show relatively higher rates of arrest or offending than in the past. However, some of this may be due to changes in justice system policies and practices (e.g., police are more likely to arrest girls for certain offenses than in the past), not just increased offending by girls.
- Recent research suggests that with most delinquency, racial and ethnic minority and lower SES youth are *not* more likely than whites and higher SES youth to offend, although minorities are more likely to be arrested. However, there seem to be racial differences for certain types of crimes, with whites sometimes being more likely to offend. Also, socially disadvantaged youth seem to be more likely to commit less frequent, more serious offenses.

Key Terms

Age-Crime Curve: a graphed pattern that shows that offense or arrest rates rapidly increase in early adolescence, peak in late adolescence/early adulthood, gradually decline during the 20s, and then sharply decline with age.

Incidence: the number of times something occurs in a place or population within a certain time frame (e.g., the number crimes committed in a country for one year).

Monitoring the Future (MTF): an annual survey of self-reported substance use among young people in the U.S. conducted by the University of Michigan's Institute for Social Research with funding from the National Institute on Drug Abuse.

National Crime Victimization Survey (NCVS): an annual survey administered by the Bureau of Justice Statistics (BJS) which asks members of a large representative sample of U.S. households about their experiences with victimization.

National Gang Center (NGC): a project funded by the U.S. Department of Justice that serves as a major source of information on gang activity and intervention in the U.S.

National Survey on Drug Use and Health (NSDUH): an annual survey of self-reported substance use by older adults as well as youth aged twelve or older in the U.S. conducted by the federal government's Substance Abuse and Mental Health Services Administration (SAMHSA).

Office of Juvenile Justice and Delinquency Prevention (OJJDP): an agency within the U.S. Department of Justice that serves as the federal authority on delinquency and juvenile justice, providing important information on research and interventions to professionals and the public.

Prevalence: the number of people or other units (e.g., families) who produce or are affected by incidents (e.g., the number of people victimized by crime in the U.S. last year).

Property Crime Index: the Uniform Crime Reporting Program's (UCR) combined measure of burglary, larceny-theft, motor vehicle theft, and arson.

Rate: a measure of the quantity of something per a fixed unit of something else—a denominator (e.g., number of arrests per 100,000 citizens) or a percentage of a sample or population (e.g., the percent of juveniles in a study who reported committing offenses).

Self-Reported Delinquency Surveys: various studies that anonymously and/or confidentially ask juveniles to report their own offending for research purposes.

Uniform Crime Reporting (UCR) Program: the leading source of official crime data provided by the Federal Bureau of Investigation (FBI), who collects data annually on reported crimes, arrests, and cleared (closed) cases from more than 18,000 law enforcement agencies (city, county, state, federal, tribal, and college/university) nationwide.

Violent Crime Index: the Uniform Crime Reporting Program's (UCR) combined measure of murder and nonnegligent manslaughter, forcible rape, robbery, and aggravated assault.

Youth Risk Behavior Survey (YRBS): a biennial survey conducted by the Centers for Disease Control and Prevention (CDC) to collect data on a variety of self-reported behaviors that affect health, including those which are unlawful, from a nationally representative sample of students in grades 9–12 at public and private schools in the U.S.

References

Akers, R. L., Sellers, C. S., & Jennings, W. G. (2017). *Criminological theories: Introduction, evaluation, and application* (7th ed.). Oxford University Press.

Benson, M. L. (2013). *Crime and the life course: An introduction*. Routledge.

Bergman, P. (2014). *Criminal law: A desk reference* (2nd ed.). Nolo.

Bureau of Justice Statistics (BJS). (n.d.a). *National Incident-Based Reporting System (NIBRS)*. https://bjs.ojp.gov/national-incident-based-reporting-system-nibrs

Bureau of Justice Statistics (BJS). (n.d.b). *National Crime Victimization Survey (NCVS)*. https://bjs.ojp.gov/data-collection/ncvs

Burr, R., Kemp, J., & Wang, K. (2024). *Crime, violence, discipline, and safety in U.S. public schools: Findings from the School Survey on Crime and Safety: 2021–22* (NCES 2024-043). National Center for Education Statistics. U.S. Department of Education. https://nces.ed.gov/pubsearch/pubsinfo.asp?pubid=2024043

Center for Behavioral Health Statistics and Quality. (2025). *Results from the 2023 National Survey on Drug Use and Health: Detailed tables.* https://www.samhsa.gov/data/report/2023-nsduh-detailed-tables

Centers for Disease Control and Prevention (CDC). (n.d.). *1991–2023 High School Youth Risk Behavior Survey data.* http://yrbs-explorer.services.cdc.gov/

Cunningham, J. K., Solomon, T. A., & Muramoto, M. L. (2016). Alcohol use among Native Americans compared to whites: Examining the veracity of the "Native American elevated alcohol consumption" belief. *Drug and Alcohol Dependence, 160*, 65–75.

Enoch, M. A., & Albaugh, B. J. (2017). Review: Genetic and environmental risk factors for alcohol use disorders in American Indians and Alaskan Natives. *The American Journal on Addictions, 26*, 461–468.

Fabio, A., Tu, L. C., Loeber, R., & Cohen, J. (2011). Neighborhood socioeconomic disadvantage and the shape of the age-crime curve. *American Journal of Public Health, 101*(S1), S325–S332.

Federal Bureau of Investigation (FBI). (n.d.a). *How we can help you.* https://www.fbi.gov/how-we-can-help-you/more-fbi-services-and-information/ucr

Federal Bureau of Investigation (FBI). (n.d.b). *FBI Crime Data Explorer.* https://cde.ucr.cjis.gov/LATEST/webapp/#/pages/home

Federal Bureau of Investigation (FBI). (2023). *Supplemental hate crime statistics, 2021.* https://cde.ucr.cjis.gov/LATEST/webapp/#/pages/explorer/crime/hate-crime

Fisher, B. S., Coker, A. L., Garcia, L. S., Williams, C. M., Clear, E. R., & Cook-Craig, P. G. (2014). Statewide estimates of stalking among high school students in Kentucky: Demographic profile and sex differences. *Violence Against Women, 20*(10), 1258–1279.

Irwin, V., Wang, K., Cui, J., & Thompson, A. (2024). *Report on indicators of school crime and safety: 2023* (NCES 2024-145/NCJ 309126). National Center for Education Statistics, U.S. Department of Education, and Bureau of Justice Statistics, Office of Justice Programs, U.S. Department of Justice. https://nces.ed.gov/pubsearch/pubsinfo.asp?pubid=2024145

Johnston, L. D., Miech, R. A., O'Malley, P. M., Bachman, J. G., Schulenberg, J. E., & Patrick, M. E. (2018). *Monitoring the Future national survey results on drug use: 1975–2017: Overview, key findings on adolescent drug use.* Institute for Social Research, The University of Michigan.

Lamphere, R. (2014). Prevalence and research methodology. In T. C. Hiestand & W. J. Weins (Eds.), *Sexting and youth: A multidisciplinary examination of research, theory, and law* (pp. 33–60). Carolina Academic Press.

Madigan, S., Ly, A., Rash, C. L., Van Ouytsel, J., & Temple, J. R. (2018). Prevalence of multiple forms of sexting behavior among youth. *JAMA Pediatrics, 172*(4), 327–335.

May, D. C., Henry, E., & Kimberling, S. (2014). Forty years of school homicides: Are our kids really more at risk in the 21st century? In D. C. May (Ed.), *School safety in the United States: A reasoned look at the rhetoric* (pp. 13–28). Carolina Academic Press.

McNamara, R. H. (2008). *The lost population: Status offenders in America.* Carolina Academic Press.

McNamara, R. H., & Bucher, C. C. (2012). *Problem children: Special populations in delinquency.* Carolina Academic Press.

Mendez, L., & Kerig, P. K. (2023). Gang membership among adolescents from distinct racial and ethnic backgrounds: The roles of neighborhood conditions and victimization. *Journal of Interpersonal Violence, 38*(11–12), 7556–7577.

Miech, R. A., Johnston, L. D., Patrick, M. E., & O'Malley, P. M. (2024). *Monitoring the Future national survey results on drug use: 1975–2023: Overview and detailed results for secondary school students.* Institute for Social Research, University of Michigan. https://monitoringthefuture.org/national-survey-results-on-drug-use-1975-2023-overview-and-detailed-results-for-secondary-school-students/

Miller, J., & Davis, R. C. (2008). Unpacking public attitudes to the police: Contrasting perceptions of misconduct with traditional measures of satisfaction. *International Journal of Police Science & Management, 10*(1), 9–22.

Musu-Gillette, L., Zhang, A., Wang, K., Zhang, J., Kemp, J., Diliberti, M., & Oudkerk, B. A. (2018). *Indicators of school crime and safety: 2017* (NCES 2018-036/NCJ 251413). National Center for Education Statistics, U.S. Department of Education, and Bureau of Justice Statistics, U.S. Department of Justice.

National Center for Education Statistics (NCES). (n.d.). *Public school leaders report 90 percent average daily student attendance rate in November 2023.* https://nces.ed.gov/whatsnew/press_releases/1_18_2024.asp

National Center for Juvenile Justice (NCJJ). (n.d.). *National Center for Juvenile Justice.* http://www.ncjj.org

National Center for Juvenile Justice (NCJJ). (2022). *Juvenile arrest rates by offense, sex, and race.* https://www.ojjdp.gov/ojstatbb/crime/excel/JAR_2020.xls

National Gang Center (NGC). (n.d.). *National Youth Gang Survey analysis.* https://www.nationalgangcenter.ojp.gov/survey-analysis

Patchin, J. W., & Hinduja, S. (2024). 2023 *Cyberbullying data.* Cyberbullying Research Center. https://cyberbullying.org/2023-cyberbullying-data

Roberts, K., Tolou-Shams, M., & Madera, K. (2016). Adolescent versus adult stalking: A brief review. *Journal of Forensic Psychology Practice, 16*(4), 236–252.

Smith-Darden, J. P., Reidy, D. E., & Kernsmith, P. D. (2016). Adolescent stalking and risk of violence. *Journal of Adolescence, 52*, 191–200.

Snyder, H. N., Cooper, A. D., & Mulako-Wangota, J. (2018). U.S. *arrest estimates: Arrest rates by age for all offenses.* Bureau of Justice Statistics. Generated using the Arrest Data Analysis Tool at www.bjs.gov.

Substance Abuse and Mental Health Services Administration (SAMHSA). (n.d.). *NSDUH: National Survey on Drug Use and Health.* https://www.samhsa.gov/data/data-we-collect/nsduh-national-survey-drug-use-and-health

Truman, J. L., & Morgan, R. E. (2014). *Nonfatal domestic violence, 2003–2012* (BJS Publication No. NCJ 244697). U.S. Department of Justice.

Tucker, C. J., Finkelhor, D., Shattuck, A. M., & Turner, H. (2013). Prevalence and correlates of sibling victimization types. *Child Abuse & Neglect, 37*, 213–223.

U.S. Department of Education (USDE). (n.d.). *Chronic absenteeism.* https://www.ed.gov/teaching-and-administration/supporting-students/chronic-absenteeism

Vaughan, T. J., Pollock, J., & Vandiver, D. M. (2015). Sex differences in arrest for juvenile assaults. *Violence and Gender, 2*(1), 24–34.

Williams, C. M., Cook-Craig, P. G., Bush, H. M., Clear, E. R., Lewis, A. M., Garcia, L. S., Coker, A. L., & Fisher, B. S. (2014). Victimization and perpetration of unwanted sexual activities among high school students: Frequency and correlates. *Violence Against Women, 20*, 1239–1257.

Chapter 3

"Causes" of Delinquency: Characteristics of Individuals and Their Environments

Chapter Learning Objectives

Students will be able to:

- Clarify the process of behavior causation
- Differentiate causal from other variable relationships
- Recall major factors of delinquency
- Classify categories of delinquency factors
- Determine the relevance of factors to types of offenses
- Summarize the main points of crime theories
- Judge the plausibility of theoretical explanations of delinquency
- Deconstruct one's biases concerning delinquency causation
- Reflect on one's progress in understanding delinquency factors

Social Science and Crime Causation

There are many beliefs about what causes crime, ranging from the absurd to the highly plausible. These beliefs are often influenced by very subjective forces such as culture, politics, self-interests, and personal characteristics. We often have some kind of "stake" in believing them, even if they may not be true. Social science seeks, although imperfectly, to find more objective reasons to believe that something causes crime—at least some evidence that it might. As opposed to other sources of belief, social science tells us that we are supposed to be critical of our own opinions as to what causes behavior. We are supposed to try to prove ourselves wrong, not just right, which is likely not the case when our crime-causation beliefs have, for example, economic motives behind them (e.g., the medical industry benefits more if drug abuse is seen as a disease

whereas corrections benefits more if it is just seen as a poor moral choice). Social science offers a systematic way to be very careful about deciding what causes crime, which is very important because if we are going to reduce it, we need to know what likely causes it. Unsupported beliefs may not only lead to ineffective interventions but actually make social conditions worse and unfairly benefit some people in society at the expense of others.

However, due to its limitations social science has not yet uncovered proven causes of crime. In fact, it is almost universally inaccurate to speak of social scientific research as "proof." To explore cause and effect, social science research heavily relies on indirect measures of human qualities and behavior, such as survey questions, organizational records, and non- or quasi-experimental observations rather than the direct experimental measures used in the natural sciences (e.g., biology, chemistry, physics). Social science has the general problem of humans studying humans. Humans are not likely objective in studying themselves, and in terms of being subjects, we are much more unpredictable compared to microorganisms, rocks, cells, other animals, and so on. Further, it would be inhumane to carry out natural science-type experiments on human beings. For example, many theories implicate child-rearing practices in crime causation, but we would not carry out a study in which we would purposely maltreat children to see if it might cause them to commit delinquency.

Social science research is better at finding *correlates* of crime. These are variables or **factors** that are shown, through statistical analysis or direct observation, to be somehow related to crime. A **correlation** is an empirically verified relationship between two variables. Some of these variables may indeed be causes but we cannot yet verify them as such. A correlate can also be something that just goes hand-in-hand with crime, or it can also be a consequence of crime (the causal order may be reversed). Further, a correlate may be both cause and consequence. For example, as will be discussed later, this may be true of deviant peer association. A juvenile who is already inclined to commit delinquency may seek out a peer group that engages in delinquency. The group may then further encourage the juvenile to commit delinquency.

Since we are unsure of exactly how correlates relate to crime, we often call them **risk factors**: conditions (personal or social) and events currently in a person's life that are (statistically) associated with a higher chance that something bad, like criminal behavior, will happen in the future (Carlsson & Sarnecki, 2016). Many correlates may be warning signs of crime. Conversely, **protective factors** are associated with a lower likelihood that something bad will happen. Protective factors against delinquency include nurturing parenting, family economic stability, having prosocial friends, and strong academic abilities. (These may be thought of as *potential causes* of prosocial behavior.) What every social science student and practitioner needs to always remember here is that *correlation does not equal causation.*

To prove causation, science has to do more than just show that a variable is correlated with an outcome. Social science has great difficulty meeting these other requirements. To begin with, obviously the proposed cause must have occurred before the effect, which we must show empirically. A problem is that many social science studies use **cross-sectional** designs that collect all data during one point in time (e.g., past 30 days or past year) and thus do not show which events or conditions occurred or existed first. Then again, some studies use **longitudinal** designs that measure the proposed cause at an earlier time and the effect at a later time. However, the fact that something happened first does not mean that it caused the outcome. (Clapping one's hands at 11:59:59 a.m. does not make a clock strike noon.) Thus, we need evidence of the process in which the prior event or condition made the outcome happen.

Several other events or conditions will have also occurred before our outcome, and we need to know that they didn't cause or help cause it. Many correlations, even time-ordered ones, could be **spurious**, meaning that the two variables are related because another variable causes them, not that one causes the other (e.g., ice cream sales and crime rates coincide largely because of changes in the weather.) We need to somehow exclude or control for these other confounding or competing variables. Experimental environment manipulations and statistical measures are helpful in doing this, but again, the nature of human subject research makes it virtually impossible to exclude or control for the numerous other potential causes in society, even if we restrict ourselves to plausible ones (e.g., we do not have to control for consuming ice cream when examining crime factors). Even in tightly controlled classic experiments, which are rarely done in criminology, we cannot completely rule out all relevant factors that may contribute to an outcome (e.g., unknown events in the lives of subjects before they begin an experiment).

Because of these empirical research limitations, we need theory to help us identify possible causes. This chapter discusses theoretical arguments as to which variables and processes create crime. Generally speaking, a **social scientific theory** is a proposed explanation of why human behavior, such as crime, occurs. A theory can be broken down into specific tenets or propositions (e.g., hypotheses or questions) that can guide research. The designation of "theory" establishes that it is not a statement of fact or "law" of human behavior (or else we would call them such). Theories are arguments that need verification, possibilities to be explored. Further, a theory cannot likely explain all types of crime, although some can explain a wide variety of them (general theories). Remember that "crime" is a very general concept or umbrella term that refers to many different types of behaviors. Different types of behavior require different explanations.

Believing that a correlate variable stands a good chance of being a cause, then, depends largely on its theoretical plausibility—how much sense it makes. Take the popular example of a spurious correlation: when ice cream sales increase, crime rates increase. It is rather inconceivable that consuming ice cream can make people commit crime. However, it is conceivable that something like the trauma of child abuse, an important variable in socialization theories, could induce antisocial behavior in its victims.

It is also important to avoid logical fallacies in causal reasoning. Causation is not as simple as we would like it to be. It is very complex, which makes crime and other social phenomena very difficult to study, understand, and respond to. First, human behavior rarely has a single cause. In fact, it likely has several. The set of causes, or, factors, of a behavior may be like a food recipe of ingredients. For example, being poor by itself may not make a person commit crime any more than flour itself can make up a cake. Further, "recipes" of crime causation may differ. Even similar behaviors, domestic assaults for example, can be explained by different sets of factors, just like different kinds of cake can have different ingredients. (Of course, there can certainly be common factors/ingredients across cases.) Thus, a variable like poor problem-solving skills may be a major cause of committing domestic assault for one offender but not another. It is important that we are careful about how we generalize factors of behavior. Factors do not have to be universal; a variable does not have to explain all cases of a behavior to be considered a possible cause. If a variable explains a majority of cases, it could be considered a major factor. A factor then can also be rare—it may only explain a few cases. These factors may still be important, but we must avoid broadly generalizing them to several other cases.

If social science cannot prove what causes crime, then why bother with it? Because it is better than assuming or completely guessing at causes, or letting special interests (political, economic, and so on) dictate what we believe about crime. If there is research support for a proposed cause of crime that also makes good theoretical sense, we have a good idea of what we can try as a response to crime. If the response seems to work well, then we have further evidence supporting the proposition. Accordingly, this chapter and the next two are attempts to cover the theories and factors which have received the most support from research and theoretical critique—our best attempts to date to identify what might cause delinquency.

Box 3.1: Logic Errors Due to Irrelevance

In addition to misidentifying information about cause and effect, such as flawed observations (sometimes things aren't as they seem), we also make mistakes in how we think about (cognitively process, interpret) information. One type is that we sometimes use irrelevant information in making decisions, such as the following examples.

Appeal to Authority. People who hold positions of authority are important sources of information and we must often rely on them. However, the fact that they are authorities does not guarantee that they are always right. (They are human and may sometimes make mistakes or have biases that skew their claims.) Error: "A prominent juvenile court judge states that the primary cause of delinquency is bad parents; thus, bad parenting must be the primary cause of delinquency." Maybe bad parenting is the primary cause, but that this judge said so, itself, doesn't make it true.

Appeal to Consequences. We may accept a causal argument because we are afraid of what will happen if we do, or do not, decide that something is a cause. Error: "If we do not incarcerate juveniles for serious offending, they will offend more; therefore, incarceration must be an effective way to reduce re-offending." Proof of the actual causal process, not speculation about the consequences of accepting something as a cause, establishes something as a cause.

Appeal to Force. We may accept a causal argument because we are explicitly or implicitly threatened with punishment if we don't. Error: "Being forceful is the best way to make youth in programs behave well; if you don't use force like the other staff, then youth will harm you, and other staff will not 'have your back.'" Such a threat does not make the claim true.

Appeal to Emotion. We may accept a causal argument because it will appear insensitive to some individuals or groups if we don't. Error: "Mike's parents never spend any time with him; no wonder he gets into fights." Lack of parental involvement may have something to do with Mike's behavior, but our compassion for him itself doesn't prove it.

Appeal to Popularity. We may accept a causal argument because many other people do, and it thus seems unquestionably true. Error: "Most parents in the neighborhood I grew up in used some form of physical punishment with their children; thus, physical punishment builds good character in children." The fact that many people believe in something doesn't make it true. For example, at one time many people thought that the sun orbits the earth rather than vice versa.

Argument from Fallacy. We may not believe that something is a cause because we listened to a bad argument for it—we confuse the nature of the argument with the causal process itself. Error: "Punishment can be associated with decreased delinquency because deterrence is the easiest theory to understand." How easy it is to understand a theory does not speak to its accuracy, so this is not a reason to accept or reject deterrence theory.

Red Herring. We may not accept a causal argument because we are distracted from its main propositions and diverted toward another topic. Error: "Incarceration has a negative impact on juveniles?... Tell that to their victims." Without a doubt, crime victims deserve our support. However, this has nothing to do with how incarceration impacts juveniles.

Strawman. We may reject a causal argument because we were exposed to, or created, a false version of it. It is easier to refute, or "burn down" (straw burns easily), a bad argument. Error: "Incarceration harms juveniles? So, we should just let violent offenders run the streets then [sarcasm]." The latter statement is a false representation of the first, but giving violent offenders unrestricted freedom is such an absurd position that it is easier to refute than the real one.

Source: Logically Fallacious. (2025, August 13). https://www.logicallyfallacious.com/logicalfallacies/search

Box 3.2: Logic Errors Due to Presumptions

In addition to logic errors involving the use of irrelevant information, we are sometimes too presumptuous in making cause-and-effect decisions, such as the following examples.

Affirming the Consequent. When we know that "variable A" tends to lead to "variable B," we may falsely assume that the reverse is also true: if "B" is present, then "A" must have occurred (ignoring the possibility that something else could have caused B). Error: "When people smoke marijuana, they become very hungry. My son is eating a ton of food; thus, he must be high." Here, the son *may have* smoked pot or may have not eaten all day or just finished working out.

Argument from Ignorance. We may accept a causal argument simply because someone cannot, at the time anyway, prove it wrong. Error: "I believe that violent video games cause delinquency. Research hasn't proven that it doesn't; thus, violent video games cause delinquency." The false assumption here is "if you can't prove me wrong, then I am right."

Begging the Question/Circular Reasoning. This fallacy might often be due to stubbornness more than honest mistakes in thinking. We may assert that a causal argument is true, "because it is true." Instead of giving a separate reason for believing something is true, we re-state the basic proposition and treat it as proof. Error: "Social disorganization theory affirms that bad neighborhoods cause delinquency; social disorganization theory is a very good theory; thus, bad neighborhoods are a cause of delinquency." Notice the first and third statements are the same. The claim might be true, but not because of what is said here.

Hasty Generalization. We may think that if a causal argument seems to be true in one or a few cases that we are familiar with, then it is true in all or most cases. Error: "A friend of mine had very strict parents, and she rebelled by partying and breaking laws; thus, strict parenting causes delinquency." We must be careful about generalizing from our personal experiences; they may be exceptions more than rules.

Sweeping Generalizations: "Accident Fallacy." We may also think that if a causal argument is frequently true, then it must be true in all cases. Variables often act as causes only under certain circumstances. Error: "Re-offending is high among under-educated violent offenders released after several years in prison. Sam didn't finish high school and just spent 10 years in prison for armed robbery. Sam is going to re-offend." Not all people in Sam's situation re-offend—it depends on several factors.

"Post Hoc." This fallacy involves the perception that because one thing occurred after another, the first thing caused the second. We probably understand that this is not true when we consider obvious examples, such as going to sleep at night does not make the sun rise. Mistakes are more likely when there is a plausible relationship between events one and two. Error: "A few days ago Jim made friends with Bob, a known neighborhood troublemaker; today, Jim got caught shoplifting; thus, Bob influenced Jim to shoplift." According to learning theory, Bob might have influenced Jim, but we cannot infer this just because Jim met Bob a few days before shoplifting.

Slippery Slope. Sometimes we falsely assume that an inevitable causal sequence of multiple events will occur. Causal "domino effects" do indeed occur; much crime is likely the result of them. The fallacy is believing that "one thing *must* lead to another," when it doesn't. Error: "If you smoke marijuana, you will want to try hard drugs, then you will become addicted, then you will turn to crime to support your habit, then you will get caught and sent to prison." This is not an impossible sequence: each phase in the statement does have some research support. The error is in thinking that *all of these will occur*. Most people who try marijuana do not end up in prison.

Source: Logically Fallacious. (2025, August 13). https://www.logicallyfallacious.com/logicalfallacies/search

Individual-Based Theories

Human behavior is studied at multiple levels of social life. For example, we can take a view of individual behavior, the behavior of groups and organizations as collective entities, the state of a community, or what an entire society (or even the world) is like. Further, we may study behavior at multiple levels, for example how groups impact individual behavior and how individuals impact the group. All of these levels are indispensable to explaining human behavior. It is important to understand that what appears to cause behavior will differ according to the perspective we take when studying it, and that we must avoid confusing our viewpoints with what we are viewing. If we examine only at the individual level, then individual attributes will appear to cause individuals' behavior. If we examine only environmental conditions, then the environment will appear to cause behavior. Which is right? In some ways, they both are. We just have to modify our understanding to accommodate the idea that behavior results from the interaction between individuals and their environments. Before proceeding to environmental theories, this section focuses on individual-level explanations of crime.

Rational Choice

People usually commit crime because it in some way benefits them. Stealing, for example, allows one to acquire desirable property that one did not have before. The general argument of **rational choice theory** (RCT) is that in their minds, humans perform a cost-benefit analysis of engaging in risky human action such as crime. If a person weighs the benefits of committing a criminal act against its risks—dangers in the act itself, chances of getting caught, and severity of punishment—and there appears to be a net gain, one is more likely to engage in crime. Individuals can of course be mistaken about just how risky, costly, or beneficial criminal acts are. RCT makes much sense when considering crimes that are done for monetary or other property gain ("instrumental crimes"), but benefits also include others such as expression, control, and excitement. Thus, there may also be rational motives behind non-economic crimes such as vandalism and fighting. Further, detection and punishment may come formally from justice authorities or informally from others such as parents/family members, school authorities, and friends. Thus, RCT suggests that individual beliefs about crime and justice are causes of crime. RCT research has associated offending or re-offending with variables such as perceived risk of arrest, certainty and severity of punishment (perceived or experienced), amount of illegal income, amount of legal income, and anticipated rewards of offending (Loughran et al., 2016).

Among RCT's limitations is that it does not seem to work well in explaining crimes that are committed "irrationally," namely those done more impulsively (without a cost-benefit analysis), which is the case with many violent crimes. Also, rational crime beliefs may only exist on the surface of crime causation; they may not be root causes. Maybe what we really need to know is why some people "rationally" consider and choose crime while others do not. Social conditions and other individual-level variables impact how people think about the prospect of committing crime. For example, even when crime appears to be rewarding, a person may choose not to do it because of moral objections or because it violates social norms (Mehlkop & Graeff, 2010).

Psychological

Psychological theories of delinquency implicate mental and emotional states or characteristics as factors and often place emphasis upon early childhood experiences (Hoffmann, 2011). Moore (2011) groups these theories into five major areas: learning, intelligence, personality, psychopathy, and cognitive and social development.

Learning theories of crime apply more general knowledge of how children, and adults, learn from the environment. We observe events and conditions in our environments through our senses, form symbolic representations of them (concepts), experience internal stimuli (e.g., emotions, pain, pleasure, confusion), and behaviorally react. Through this repeated process we acquire knowledge and other personal attributes, as well as behavioral tendencies. While growing up we learn from the people we are exposed to—who model behaviors for us, instruct us, and in some ways persuade us to act in certain ways—and then our behavior is conditioned over time through others' responses to it. This is not a simple process; we are not *simply* products of our environments. Albert Bandura and other social/cognitive learning theorists proposed that behavior results from the interplay among three types of factors: environmental conditions, cognitive and other personal attributes (what "kind of person" one is), and prior behavior. Behavior, then, results from what happens in a person's environment, how that person perceives it, and how the person experiences the consequences of prior behavior (Moore, 2011).

Criminal behavior is learned in the same way (the same causal process) as non-criminal behavior. What makes one learn criminal behavior has to do with what specifically occurs in this process. After all, children are exposed to different environmental events and conditions while growing up. Children may initially learn deviant (and non-deviant) behavior through imitation. However, this process applies more to younger children, and the long-term effects of imitation depend on broader developmental contexts—what else is going in the child's life. Criminologist Edwin Sutherland proposed that **differential association**, with offenders vs. non-offenders, may increase or decrease one's tendency to become criminal. If a child spends more time around family members, friends, and others who engage in or support criminal behavior than they do around people who do not, the child is more likely to learn criminal behavior. If a child spends more time around "non-criminal people," then the child is less likely to learn criminal behavior and more likely to learn prosocial behavior (Moore, 2011).

Significant others may express, directly or indirectly, **definitions favorable to crime**: attitudes, beliefs, and perspectives which present offending as somehow good or justified (and perhaps that conforming to the law is bad). They may also express *definitions* un*favorable to crime*: attitudes, beliefs, and perspectives which present offending as wrong (and conforming to the law as right). Children who are exposed to more definitions favorable than unfavorable to crime, largely achieved by stronger associations with offenders, are at higher risk of learning criminality. Further, differential association is impacted by the length and intensity of exposure to, and type and quality of relationship with, others (Akers et al., 2017). Thus, the theory does not simply argue that if one is exposed to criminal elements, one will become a criminal. (We are all probably exposed to criminal elements to some extent). A child may spend a great deal of time around offenders, but if the context is general (e.g., lives in the same neighborhood) and the relationship with the offenders is not close or favorable, the child may be more influenced by prosocial others with whom one has a better relationship (e.g., teachers).

However, learning theory does not just present deviant behavior as an end result. Associations, imitation, and definitions produce initial deviance in children, then this deviance initiates further causal sequences. The fact that a young child is exposed to "criminal elements" does not necessarily mean that becoming "a criminal" is one's fate. If the child experiences "the right consequences," the deviant behavior may not continue. Deviance has feedback and reciprocal effects which, over time, determine whether or not crime becomes a persistent part of a person's behavior during late adolescence and early adulthood. For example, experiences with sanctions and rewards may change or reaffirm a child's prior association with others, tendency to imitate, and definitions of deviance, which then affect future behavior (Akers et al., 2017). Thus, it is very important to understand what happens after a child engages in a deviant act.

Drawing from B.F. Skinner's work on *operant conditioning*, Robert Burgess and Ronald Akers added that **differential reinforcement** interacts with differential association. Generally speaking, operant conditioning is the process by which behaviors are rewarded and thus likely to continue, or not rewarded and thus not likely to continue (extinguished). When a behavior continues because it is rewarded, it is *reinforced*. This reinforcement can be *positive*—a desirable stimulus is added (e.g., taking a child out to dinner for earning good grades)—or negative—an undesirable stimulus is removed (e.g., a child gets out of doing chores for earning good grades). (Note: reinforcement is nearly the opposite of "punishment"—adding undesirable stimuli or removing desirable stimuli with the intent of *discouraging* the behavior, such as spanking or grounding. Thus reinforcement, including negative, cannot be confused with punishment.) If a type of behavior is frequently and strongly rewarded over time, the learned behavioral reactions are internalized, and the person sees them as likely to re-occur. Regarding differential association, then, if a child sees that significant others are being rewarded for criminal behavior such as gaining attention or money—*vicarious reinforcement*—one is more likely to offend. Conversely, if a child sees that significant others are not being rewarded for criminal behavior, or are being rewarded for prosocial behavior, one is less likely to offend (Moore, 2011). Further, one's own offending can be directly reinforced by directly receiving rewards, which do not always come from other people. *Nonsocial reinforcement* occurs when the act itself is rewarding, for example the excitement (thrill or rush) that occurs upon committing a deviant act (Akers et al., 2017).

Intelligence theories get support from the well-documented correlation between IQ (Intelligence Quotient) test scores and delinquency: delinquents tend to have lower IQ scores than non-delinquents. One's level of intelligence could plausibly have an impact upon one's tendency to commit crime. Participation in mainstream society, such as employment, requires literacy, analytic, and communication knowledge and skills.

Persons lacking in these abilities may have trouble functioning in "normal" activities and thus seek deviant activities such as crime. Many crimes likely do not require strong intellectual abilities. However, others, such as many white-collar and cybercrimes, do require high intelligence, which stands as one of the major limitations on intelligence theories. Indeed, many offenders are quite intelligent. Also, there is no universal definition of or way to measure "intelligence," and there are likely several types of intelligence (one test cannot measure all of them). Historically, IQ tests have been socially and culturally biased. The tests may reflect the backgrounds (e.g., white middle class) of the people creating them more than general knowledge. In recent decades, however, many changes have been made to "IQ" tests to address problems like culture and class bias.

Current studies still allow for the possibility of a causal link between IQ and crime but tend to assert that the relationship is indirect or mediated by the presence of other factors. For example, the underlying factor may be socio-economic disadvantages (e.g., low-income families and disorganized neighborhoods), which lead to low IQ which then lead to delinquency. Also, regardless of socio-economic background, school performance will impact IQ, which then impacts delinquency. Thus, even if a child comes from poverty, if they do well in school, they will probably have a higher IQ and thus a lower tendency to offend. Another possibility is that children born with brain development problems that impact intelligence do poorly in school, academically and socially, which increases their chances of delinquency (Moore, 2011). The core risk factor in all of this may be poor school performance rather than just test performance.

Learning disability, a related issue, is also a factor indirectly related to delinquency. **Learning disabilities** (LD) involve physical or mental conditions (e.g., neurological) that impair the development or acquisition of knowledge and skills, such as being less able to sort and store information due to language or sensory processing problems. LD youth tend to score in the average range on intelligence tests, so LD should not be confused with poor intelligence. LD youth may have difficulty completing tasks and working with others in school or other environments, which are often not designed to meet their unique needs. Having trouble distinguishing between socially acceptable and unacceptable behavior, they may develop poor relationships with peers and adult authorities (e.g., teachers and police) (Hoffmann, 2011). Situations are especially problematic for youth with undetected LDs, as their initial behavioral or performance problems may be falsely attributed to malicious intent, and they do not receive specialized educational services.

Personality trait theories implicate pathological (constituting some kind of "illness") qualities in the sets of psychological and behavioral characteristics that sets individuals apart from others (e.g., temperament, mannerisms, and thought patterns). Our personality traits can be inborn, products of socialization, or the results of interaction between inborn and environmental factors. Loosely, "personality" refers to who we are, psychologically speaking, as persons. Theories in the Freudian tradition (psychodynamics and psychoanalysis) and Erikson's work on identity development assert that deviant behavior results from how individuals deal with inner conflicts or crises.

Delinquency may often be a matter of "acting out"—ways of coping with inner turmoil or symbolically meeting unconscious needs, often upon experiencing changes in one's life (Moore, 2011).

Other personality theories may attempt to identify specific personality characteristics as crime factors, such as suspiciousness, uncooperativeness, destructiveness, defensiveness, and hostility (Moore, 2011). Some research using personality tests such as the MMPI (Minnesota Multiphasic Personality Inventory) found that delinquent youth, especially boys, are more likely to exhibit characteristics such as: immaturity, dishonesty, rebelliousness, conflicted thoughts, lack of conscientiousness, externalizing blame, disagreeableness, impulsiveness, insensitivity, aggression, lack of empathy, selfishness, unreliableness, sensation-seeking, and highly emotional (Hoffmann, 2011).

Personality theories have theoretical merit in explaining crime, but their propositions are difficult to empirically test, largely because internal psychological states cannot be directly observed. Thus, much personality research uses observable behavior to test propositions, which presents the problem of circular reasoning (Moore, 2011). For example, one might wonder if impulsivity—acting suddenly, without thinking of consequences—is a causal trait that explains the behavior or a description of the behavior that needs to be explained (or both). Further, "good vs. bad" personality traits is a very subjective matter, and some of the before mentioned traits may also predict prosocial behavior (Hoffmann, 2011). For example, rebelliousness can lead to beneficial changes, and aggressiveness is desirable when done for public good (e.g., police protection). Research has yet to convincingly identify types of personalities that are more criminogenic than others. However, research may have identified early personality risk factors and a more general "antisocial personality," discussed in the next two chapters.

Psychopathy theories differ from personality theories in that they implicate a broader criminogenic state of being in which multiple distinct traits comprise a "disorder," and in that they are typically used to explain more serious violent and chronic crime. (Offenders thought to severely personality-disordered may be more commonly referred to as "psychopaths.") Psychopathic disorders are identified more explicitly with psychiatric diagnoses. One example is antisocial personality disorder (APD), a pervasive pattern of disregarding the welfare and violating the rights of other people (Moore, 2011). Other diagnoses highly relevant to criminal behavior include borderline personality disorder (BPD) and, regarding adolescents, conduct disorder (CD) and oppositional defiant disorder (ODD) (Hoffmann, 2011).

Among limitations is that psychopathy explains very little crime and delinquency. A very small percentage of offenders are diagnosed with a psychopathic disorder, and extremely violent or otherwise serious acts make up a small portion of criminal offenses. Adolescents are especially unlikely to be diagnosed as they may not establish the required behavioral pattern until they become 18 or older, although they can show early signs. Also, psychopathy theories may offer after-the-fact labels more than predicting propositions. Only after one engages in serious offending can we know that one is "psychopathic." It is not unreasonable to believe that having such a disorder causes one to commit crime, and several other acts of harm, but in terms of causation it seems more important to know what causes the disorder. Does or can it result from highly traumatic socialization experiences (e.g., severe child maltreatment), biological conditions, or a combination of both? Research has yet to sufficiently sort this matter out.

Cognitive and social development theories draw from the work of theorists like Jean Piaget and Lawrence Kohlberg to find problems in the way individuals come to mentally process information in the world and choose behaviors accordingly. Important here is how children learn and acquire reasoning abilities and morals, which is done in developmental stages. A juvenile offender might be one who is delayed in advancing through stages (e.g., older adolescents who cognitively function as younger ones). Ideally, children are socialized to accept conventional beliefs, make good decisions, be productive, and exhibit concern for the welfare of others. Family, school, and peers of course have major impacts upon how children grow cognitively, morally, and socially. Both anti- and pro-social behaviors are cumulative—they result from experiences with environments in earlier stages which impact those in later stages. For example, if pre-school children lack prosocial influences in the home they are less prepared to function in school, and if they do not function well in school they may not acquire enough of the cognitive and social abilities, and prosocial peer relationships, schooling offers (Hoffmann, 2011; Moore, 2011). Over time, a child who experiences inadequate socialization experiences in the home (e.g., abuse), chronic problems at school, and deviant peer relationships is likely to acquire pro-crime perceptions (e.g., pessimism, "we live in a dog-eat-dog world"), moral beliefs (e.g., "greed is good"), and problem-solving strategies (e.g., using violence).

Cognitive problems affecting delinquency may include negative memory bias (emphasizing negative over positive memories), strong tendency to attribute blame or causation to external forces (including perhaps one's own illegal behavior), tendency to attribute others' actions to hostile or deceitful intent, and unusual or distorted scripts or schemas—mental representations or models of things in life. Youth who have trouble responding to social cues (information from one's environment) seem to be at higher risk of delinquency. Some research shows that aggressive youth tend to (1) be less attentive to important social cues (e.g., others' facial expressions, which indicate emotions), (2) misinterpret social cues (e.g., see hostile or deceitful intent behind others' actions when there is none), (3) generate fewer goals or desired outcomes upon interpreting cues, and consider more aggressive goals when they do, (4) access behavioral schemas from violent or otherwise negative memories (e.g., if fighting has been beneficial in the past), and (5) choose aggressive behaviors from alternatives. Further, these problems are associated with the problematic personality traits discussed earlier, as well as physiological factors (discussed in the next section on biosocial theories) (Hoffmann, 2011).

Psychological theories such as learning and cognitive and social development also discuss external forces such as parental socialization and group influences. Instead of just identifying individual attributes that promote antisocial behavior, they begin to explain *why* individuals have or do not have these attributes. Thus, theories may also be *social psychological* in that they describe the interplay between the person's psychological make-up and the person's social environment (our environment impacts us, but we also impact our environment). These theories, which describe social processes, are covered more in depth in the next two chapters.

Biosocial

A large body of contemporary research has found that biological factors can influence the development of antisocial behavior (Glenn & McCauley, 2019). However, modern biology-based theories do not assert that inborn traits directly cause antisocial behavior (e.g., that certain people are "born criminals"). Rather, **biosocial theories** tend to assert that biological factors interact with the environment to produce behavior. Instead of "nature vs. nurture," they tend to take the position of "nature *and* nurture."

Biological and environmental factors have a "reciprocal relationship": they impact each other. Environmental factors can alter biological states; for example, prolonged exposure to stress can impact the human stress response system. Also, biological factors impact how individuals respond to their environments, including how well juvenile offenders respond to interventions. Because of biological predispositions, individuals can be more or less sensitive to the same environment, whether the environment is a good or bad one. (A highly sensitive person has a higher chance of becoming antisocial if placed in a bad environment but also a higher chance of becoming pro-social if placed in a good environment.) Further, like environmental factors, biological factors vary widely in how they operate. Individuals engaging in antisocial behavior differ in how factors affect them, including that they are affected by different sets of biological abnormalities and environmental stressors (Glenn & McCauley, 2019). Biosocial theories typically do not explain specific offenses, separately. None speak of, for example, a shoplifting gene or a vandalism gene. Rather, they make more sense as general theories of crime (Beaver & Walsh, 2011). Biological factors may increase the likelihood that a person will have more general antisocial, impulsive, aggressive, or violent behavioral tendencies, which then make them more likely (but not certain) to break society's rules and harm others.

Genetics seems to be the most controversial subject in biosocial criminology. The main question here is: How much of our behavioral tendencies, including antisocial ones, are inherited? Many studies have examined kinship pairs, especially twins. These tend to show that (1) individuals who are genetically alike or similar behave quite similarly even if they do not heavily share environments and (2) those who are genetically different behave differently even if they share environments. More recently, molecular genetic studies have been done. These use DNA samples directly to identify "genetic polymorphisms" (specific DNA markers that vary in the population) that are correlated with antisocial behavior. Biosocial theory also posits that genetic factors can indirectly influence crime by determining environment. For example, a juvenile's attraction to antisocial peer groups may be driven by genetic predisposition, not just other environmental factors. Still, single genes are not likely to have a major effect on antisocial behavior unless they are paired with environmental risk factors (Beaver & Walsh, 2011).

In addition to genetic influences, Rudo-Hutt and associates (2011) identify several biological correlates of antisocial behavior in their extensive review of research. To begin with, *early health risks* are problems that occur prior to, during, or soon after a child's birth. (Some may have environmental origins, such as maternal drug use.) These include *prenatal nicotine and alcohol exposure* and *birth complications*, as well as *minor physical anomalies* (e.g., adherent ear lobe, single palmar crease, and furrowed tongue) which, if extensive, are indicators of central nervous system and brain development problems.

Another type is *hormones*: "molecules that are released into the bloodstream and travel to act at a different location of the body" (Rudo-Hutt et al., 2011, p. 23). *Reduced cortisol levels* make one less reactive to stress and thus perhaps less fearful of consequences for antisocial behavior, and *increased testosterone levels* may make one more aggressive. *Neurotransmitters* "are molecules that are used to signal between neurons in the central nervous system" and at least one, *reduced serotonin activity*, has been linked to aggressive behavior (Rudo-Hutt et al., 2011, p. 25). Regarding the brain, *structural abnormalities* have been found in the regions involved in making decisions (e.g., prefrontal cortex) and regulating emotions (e.g., amygdala and hippocampus), and *functioning impairments* have been found in regions such as the prefrontal and temporal cortex. *Psychophysiological* factors include *low heart rate*—a possible indicator of problems in the interaction between the sympathetic nervous system which drives the "flight-or-fight" response—and the parasympathetic nervous system—that acts to return the body to rest (may increase aggression). They also include *low skin conductance arousal* and *poor skin conductance conditioning*—possible indicators of emotional deficits and amygdala dysfunction (Glenn & McCauley, 2019; Rudo-Hutt et al., 2011).

Finally, *neuropsychological* factors include *low intellectual ability*, especially *verbal test skills* (e.g., defining words and solving math problems), and impaired *executive functioning*—the cognitive ability to understand goals as indicated by attributes such as mental flexibility, strategy formation, selective attention, and habitual response suppression (may largely be controlled by the prefrontal cortex) (Rudo-Hutt et al., 2011). Of course, while an individual's general intellectual potential may be genetically determined, it is unknown how much intelligence tests reflect "natural" abilities vs. those obtained through environmental exposure. Thus, we cannot classify intelligence as a strictly biological factor.

Many of the above problems have a genetic basis. For example, *polymorphic genes*—genes that come in different varieties among people—have been associated with problems with two neurotransmitters, dopamine and serotonin. Dopamine is released when we find experiences rewarding; they send messages to the brain indicating that the experience is pleasurable. However, dopamine can also be released in response to negative experiences and can be stimulated by aggression. (The danger here is that aggression can be rewarding.) Serotonin helps regulate mood and impulses. Imbalanced levels of it in the brain may lead to depression and antisocial behavior. *Alleles*—the specific varieties of polymorphic genes—related to dopamine and serotonin functioning have been associated with hyperactivity, conduct disorder, substance abuse, violence, and crime. Again, these kinds of associations are based on interactions with the environment. Possessing high-risk alleles may promote antisocial behavior in some environments but not others. For example, "low activity alleles" of a gene called MAOA are less efficient at metabolizing neurotransmitters, which can lead to imbalances in levels of serotonin and dopamine. Some research suggests that carrying these alleles will lead to antisocial behavior among abused children but not non-abused children (Benson, 2013).

A biological factor that is highly correlated with antisocial behavior may be considered a *biomarker*—an indicator of the presence of such behavior. Very few of these have been identified with certainty, but one possibility is low resting heart rate (one's heart rate when one is at rest—neither engaging in, nor just having engaged in, physical exertion). Several studies controlling for several other factors have found that low resting heart rate strongly predicts antisocial behavior, although its exact impact upon antisocial behavior is yet unknown. Theoretically, low resting heart rate may produce or work in association with other conditions such as increased desire for stimulation, fearlessness, low norepinephrine levels, and low right brain hemisphere functioning (Raine & Portnoy, 2012).

The above problems can significantly impair an infant's or child's temperament, emotional state, and cognitive functioning, creating a challenge for those responsible for raising the child. However, they are more closely related to antisocial behavior when combined with psycho-social risk factors (Rudo-Hutt et al., 2011). Still, when combined with protective factors, antisocial behavior is less likely. Consider a child born with a neurological problem. If the child is raised in a caring home and community with adequate discipline and educational and economic resources, the chances are very good that the child will not become a serious offender. On the other hand, if this same child were to be raised in an abusive and neglectful home and community, the child has a much higher risk of becoming a serious offender.

Social Structural Theories

Much crime involves clearly harmful behavior, that which seems to be indisputably wrong. It is certainly understandable if we think there is something wrong with a person who commits crime. Therefore, our impulse may be to attribute offenders' behavior to their pathological attributes, and we may sometimes be right. However, we must be aware of the limitations of individual analyses of behavior. When we find factors at the individual level, we are not showing that crime *originates* within individuals. Rather, the finding is the result of our examination—of using an individual-level perspective, and importantly, not using another level perspective. Used improperly, individual perspectives can be short-sighted, resulting in attribution errors. Individual factors are easier to "see" than those lying outside the individual, which may result in an attribution bias that inhibits us from seeing other factors. Even when we do correctly identify individual attributes, we need to know where the attributes came from. For example, if we see a child get into a fight and act very violently, the "data" are right in front of us: harmful blows to the other person, hostile words, angry facial expression, and so on. Thus, we may assume that "violent" is part of the child's personality and thus the cause of the behavior. What we do not see in front of us are things like the child's upbringing, neighborhood characteristics, and cultural experiences.

Another reason we may put so much emphasis on individual factors of crime is that doing otherwise might violate our sense of morality. Acknowledging that offenders' behavior results from environmental conditions might imply excuses for their behavior (it's "society's fault"). This implication is not the objective of social science. Science seeks factors, not excuses. For example, a theorist might argue that experiencing extreme child abuse may result in one growing up to be a violent offender, but this is not the same as saying that the offender is thus not responsible for their behavior. One could make the philosophical argument that these kinds of situations reduce individuals' responsibility for their behavior, if so desired, but this argument does not automatically flow from the theory itself (rather, one is using theory to make another argument). It is important, then, to avoid false assumptions about theoretical arguments and consider them objectively. To avoid making attribution errors, and to understand crime causation more completely, we must consider the various contexts of individual behavior. To work toward this end, this section covers social conditions, on a variety of levels, associated with crime.

Social structural theories are sociological in nature. They find factors of crime in social structures—ways in which society and its parts are organized into patterns of relationships and interactions. Social structures can be seen at macro (on a large scale), micro (on a small scale), and meso (in between) levels of social analysis. Our social institutions are good examples of macro structures, including the economy, the family, education, religion, the media, and the criminal justice system. These involve general tendencies for the people of a society to behave in similar ways, often according to rules. Systems of inequality such as race, class, gender, sexual orientation, age, and disability are also macro-structures. Micro structures on the other hand are found in everyday life, for example how we tend to interact in specific groups such as a particular family or in a particular neighborhood according to our perceived roles. Meso structures exist beyond small groups and local environments to include patterns such as social networks—systems of close and distant relationships with others (e.g., "connections") that helps shape our lives. Regardless of level, social structural theories tend to focus on poverty and inequality in community and cultural contexts.

Social Disorganization

Social disorganization theory finds roots of crime in the structure of neighborhoods, namely "structural disadvantages." These disadvantages include *poverty* (high unemployment and low average incomes), *high portions of single-parent homes* (fewer adults in the neighborhood), *high residential mobility* (people frequently moving in and out of the neighborhood), and *racial and ethnic background heterogeneity* (which may impede communication and collaboration among residents). These conditions tend to generate social processes that lead to neighborhood disorganization (e.g., dilapidation, noise, litter, unmonitored children) and crime (Kingston et al., 2009). Conversely, structurally advantaged (or at least non-disadvantaged) neighborhoods are characterized by economic sufficiency, lower portions of single-parent homes, and relative residential stability. These neighborhoods can be expected to experience significantly less crime.

In their early formulation of the theory, Shaw and McKay argued that structural disadvantages impair local social control processes; the people of the neighborhood are less capable of conforming to and enforcing societal norms. For example, single parents who work low-paying jobs and cannot find suitable childcare find it more difficult to monitor their children and keep them out of trouble. Later work attributes social disorganization and crime to social processes generated by three conditions. One is **weak social networks**. Individuals are associated, or "connected," with others both directly (e.g., friends) and indirectly (e.g., friends of friends) in somewhat limited systems of associations. These networks contain a pool of resources available for sharing among its members. A weak network offers a "weak pool" of resources, so to speak. For example, weak networks offer little social support (e.g., emotional support and financial assistance), social control (e.g., help with monitoring and disciplining children), and other resources (e.g., community programs) (Kingston et al., 2009).

Thus, secondly, disadvantaged neighborhoods tend to possess *low collective efficacy.* With a lack of collective resources, the community as a whole, notably the adults, are less able and willing to effectively create the kind of social order needed for conformity. **Collective efficacy** may be defined as "mutual trust and solidarity among neighbors combined with the willingness of local residents to intervene on behalf of the common good" (Kingston et al., 2009, p. 56). Residents are less likely to intervene in community matters when communal norms are unclear or problematic, and they mistrust or fear one another. For example, they may not do anything to stop neighbors' children from misbehaving because they believe that it is none of their business and/or are afraid of reactions by the children's parents.

Third, social disadvantages foster **delinquency opportunity structures** at the expense of conventional opportunity structures. Disadvantaged youth lack access to resources such as good schools and educational supports, libraries, computers, recreational centers, art programs, health services, and employment programs. However, they may be readily exposed to street crime and delinquent peers, as delinquent peer groups are more likely to emerge in neighborhoods lacking adult monitoring and sanctions for inappropriate behavior. In a neighborhood without enough material resources, social support, and informal social control needed to develop productive law-abiding residents, youth are more likely to develop weak bonds or ties to conventional society (with family, school, employers, and so on), and gravitate toward delinquent peer groups and activities. Further, youth comprehend the lack of opportunities surrounding them and may hold little hope about their chances of achieving conventional success (e.g., going to college and getting a good job). Thus, they may react by making decisions that in fact harm their future, such as quitting school, using drugs, and engaging in delinquency (Kingston et al., 2009).

Social disorganization theory does not argue that high crime is inevitable in "poor neighborhoods." Structurally disadvantaged neighborhoods vary significantly in their crime rates, including that some have relatively low rates. This may occur because disadvantaged neighborhoods vary in how they experience the structural characteristics and social processes that foster crime or conformity, as well as level of disadvantage. Neighborhoods may be more or less structurally disadvantaged. For example, a neighborhood may have high poverty, but it may also have a low portion of single-parent homes, which indirectly reduces delinquency through the ability to monitor children and inhibit delinquent peer association (which may block the formation of delinquency opportunity structures) (Kingston et al., 2009).

Strain

Strain theories argue that juveniles are more likely to engage in delinquency when they are harmed, especially when they are blocked from achieving goals. The people of a society commonly expect to be treated well by others and given opportunities to be successful. For example, we believe that we have certain rights. When we are treated in ways that appear unjust, we become upset (e.g., angry, frustrated, or anxious) and thus experience strain or stress. Unjust treatment comes in many forms, ranging, for example, from a verbal insult to systematic discrimination. The types of goals that are important to youth include those having to do with money, status, and respect; having fun; and autonomy from adults (Agnew & Brezina, 2018). Strain theory overlaps with social disorganization theory in that the deprivations experienced in disorganized neighborhoods are often mentioned as sources of strain, such as lack of economic, educational, and recreational opportunities as well as lack of safety and protection.

Merton's classic anomie strain theory argues that individuals are more likely to engage in deviant behavior when they find that they lack conventional means by which to obtain their goals, primarily those of acquiring money and material goods. ("Anomie" refers to a breakdown in society's ability to regulate the behavior of its members.) We are all supposed to achieve material success through things like hard work and education, but we do not have the same access to opportunities to do so (e.g., get a job or go to college). Further, a highly materialistic society that emphasizes goals over how to reach them creates the temptation to resort to controversial means. When lacking in opportunity, some might find different ways to reach their goals, or "innovate." This innovation is not always destructive but does include criminal behavior. Offenders are raised in the same society and come to want the same things as everyone else. They differ from "non-offenders" in the opportunities they have, and thus the methods they use, to get these things (Akers et al., 2017). Merton's argument seems to apply well to crime with an economic basis. For example, a young person living in poverty with poor education and job prospects for the future may be tempted to engage in theft or drug sales to make an income.

Later, theorists such as Albert Cohen added that youth deprived of the status available to middle-class youth formed delinquent subcultures (discussed in the next section) as a collective response to strain. Deprived youth find it hard to believe that they can attain statuses such as good student, good athlete, or popular at school. By forming a separate culture with values opposing those of the mainstream, deprived youth now have opportunities to acquire heightened status, for example gaining a reputation as a good fighter or a thief. Cloward and Ohlin added further that deprived youth also do not have equal access to *illegitimate* opportunities, and the type of deviance they engage in largely depends upon the type of delinquent subculture and opportunity structure available to them. For example, youth without local opportunities to engage in economic crime (e.g., someone to set them up with drug dealing or teach them how to steal) may instead respond to strain with group activities based on expressive violence

(e.g., fighting) or on escaping through substance use. These earlier kinds of additions to strain theory expanded it to explain non-utilitarian crime (Akers et al., 2017).

Messner and Rosenfeld's (2013) **institutional-anomie theory** more recently expanded on Merton's theory by thinking beyond the class system and addressing the interaction of social institutions. Institutions such as the family, education, government, and the economy have different, although overlapping, functions. Also, these institutions limit each other. For example, laws in the U.S. require parents to ensure that their children receive schooling. (The family does not completely control child-rearing.) Problems occur when there is an imbalance of social institutional functioning—if one dominates over the others. In the U.S., the free-market economy appears to dominate. Messner and Rosenfeld argue that the "American dream" has four main value orientations that facilitate crime: *achievement*—one's value is based on what one achieves or possess; *individualism*—one must achieve by oneself, in competition with others; *universalism*—one must pursue the same success goal as all others; and *money "fetishism"*—the accumulation of wealth itself is good. These values tend not to be expressed with clear limits (e.g., in advertising) such as "money is great, but it isn't everything." This mainstream cultural emphasis on monetary success and competition, then, helps motivate crime.

Further, these emphases weaken noneconomic institutions that are largely responsible for controlling crime. Informal social control, especially of juveniles, is a major function of the family and education, and formal control is a major function of government. Social control is not a major function of the economy, at least not the kind that inhibits crime. However, the economy is dominant in three interrelated ways.

First, other institutions are *devalued.* For example, education is largely thought of as a means to occupational ends while learning and knowledge for their own sake are not highly valued. Second, other institutional settings must be altered to *accommodate* the requirements of the economy (much more than vice versa)—the long hours that many parents work at the expense of time with their children, for example. Third, economic norms *penetrate* other institutional systems—the popular belief that government "should be run like a business" (although the purpose of government is different) for example. Thus, since the economy has primacy over social control institutions, diminishing their effectiveness, crime rates are higher than they should be (Messner & Rosenfeld, 2013).

Strain can be generated by undesirable events or conditions regardless of whether there is a specific goal at stake. Agnew's **general strain theory** argues that juveniles may engage in delinquency to cope with the negative emotions that result from *loss of positive stimuli* (something good is taken away, such as a break-up with a romantic partner) or *presentation of negative stimuli* (something bad is done, such as being assaulted or insulted). Types of negative treatment often associated with delinquency include parental rejection; parental discipline and supervision that is excessively strict, harsh, or erratic; abuse and neglect; negative school experiences; abusive peer relations; criminal victimization; homelessness; and prejudice and discrimination based on ascribed characteristics (e.g., race and gender) (Agnew & Brezina, 2018).

However, delinquency is only one way youth might choose to alleviate negative feelings. They may instead use one of at least three other types of strategies. *Cognitive coping* involves reinterpreting one's strain to minimize its impact. One might tell oneself that the situation is not that bad or important, or even that one deserved it. For example, if a teenager does not have a desired amount of money, one might choose to believe that "money isn't everything," one has enough money anyway, or that not having enough is one's own fault. Nondelinquent *behavioral coping* involves taking lawful actions to try to reduce strain. For example, one might get a job, or work more, to get more money. Delinquency then is illegal behavioral coping. Nondelinquent *emotional coping* involves lawful actions that alleviate the negative feelings which result from strain. For example, one might exercise, meditate, or listen to music. Delinquency can also be emotional coping, as when one takes drugs to feel better (Agnew & Brezina, 2018).

Thus, strain does not automatically lead to delinquency. After all, everyone experiences strain in some way, but most people do not react to it with crime. It is important then to know why some youth respond to strain with delinquency while others do not. Agnew and Brezina (2018) describe five circumstances under which youth are more likely to use delinquent coping. First, strain involving an *area of life considered important by the individual* creates more negative feelings, which may make it difficult to handle appropriately. For example, an insult directed at one's "manhood" might provoke a violent reaction by one with much masculine pride. One less concerned with masculinity on the other hand may ignore or deflect the insult. Second, those with *poor coping skills* are more likely to react to strain inappropriately. Juvenile offenders often lack the cognitive and emotional abilities (e.g., intelligence, problem-solving, social skills, and self-efficacy) needed to use the nondelinquent strategies covered earlier. Third, those with *few conventional social supports* lack external resources that can be used to properly alleviate strain, such as having family and friends who can give advice, material support, and emotional support. Fourth, consistent with rational choice theory, delinquent coping is more likely when the *perceived benefits of delinquency are high and the perceived likelihood of getting caught and seriously punished are low.* Fifth, youth experiencing a *variety of other criminogenic factors* (e.g., past reinforced delinquency, low self-control, deviant peer association, and weak moral beliefs) are more likely to respond to strain with delinquency.

Delinquent Subculture

The basic argument of **delinquent subculture theories** is that some youth are distanced from mainstream middle-class culture and instead participate in a subculture that espouses beliefs, attitudes, and behaviors—often illegal—that are different from or even oppose those of the dominant culture. Certain groups of juveniles (e.g., poor racial minorities or poor Southern whites) may engage in delinquency because of the systems of norms and values that they learn, just as culture influences any individual's behavior. For example, early subculture theorist Walter Miller argued that lower class youth have "focal concerns" different from those of middle-class youth in that they place more emphasis on ability to handle trouble, toughness, street smarts, excitement, fatalism, and autonomy from authority figures (e.g., parents, teachers, and police). Delinquent subculture is tied to social disorganization and strain in that it emerges from social and economic disadvantage. The delinquent subculture may seem to be part of the structurally disadvantaged, socially disorganized neighborhood. As stated earlier, youth in neighborhoods lacking adult social control and education, recreation, and economic opportunities are less likely to develop ties to conventional society, and thus, are more likely to turn to delinquent peer groups such as gangs. Lacking means by which to live up to middle-class standards of achievement, and be accepted by middle-class peers, lower class and minority youth create their own standards and sense of belonging (Bohm & Vogel, 2015).

Delinquent subculture theory seems plausible except that it does not sufficiently explain why many youth in disadvantaged communities, who would be exposed to the subculture, do not commit delinquency. Also, research failed to show that disadvantaged youth reject middle-class culture and prefer their own way of life, or even that values and beliefs held by disadvantaged youth correlate strongly with delinquency. (For example, one could value toughness and street smarts without committing crime.) A more specific subculture theory, Wolfgang and Ferracuti's **subculture of violence,** sought to explain violent offending on the part of poor African Americans and other minority groups. The theorists attributed inner city violent crime, namely homicide, to a pervasive belief among residents, especially youth, that violence is an appropriate or necessary (and therefore not morally wrong) response to being attacked, insulted, or otherwise provoked by others. Further, they modified the subcultural approach by pointing out that it is not problematic that disadvantaged youth embrace many mainstream cultural values, as a subculture is never completely different from its wider society, and one cannot expect those who advocate violence to act violently in all situations. Also, the theory distinguished violent from nonviolent (or, not very violent) offenders, which is important considering that most juvenile offenders are not violent. Perhaps the two groups present different types of delinquent subculture. However, research has also failed to show that poor minorities or whites embrace a pro-violence belief system (Bohm & Vogel, 2015).

One can question that a distinct delinquent subculture, separate from and largely in opposition to dominant middle-class culture, exists. Pro-delinquency values and beliefs can be found among juvenile offenders, but do these values and beliefs really represent a subculture? The problem lies in attributing delinquency to a distinct normative subcultural system rather than other social forces present in disadvantaged communities. Perhaps delinquency is better associated with parenting methods, limited opportunities/strain, treatment by others, or low self-control, for example. One cannot be certain that juveniles commit delinquency because "it's their culture." Still, the subcultural perspective may help us understand the context of delinquency causation—how disadvantaged youth experience delinquency factors.

A newer subculture of violence perspective, Anderson's (1999) **code of the street,** has received some research support. Anderson's propositions are drawn from an ethnographic study of inner-city African American youth in Philadelphia in the 1990s. Anderson describes a neighborhood street culture that pressures young African Americans to respond violently to perceived instances of disrespect. Disrespectful actions can range from prolonged eye contact to verbal insults to serous physical assault. From this culture evolved a street code of conduct, one that emphasizes respect, toughness, bravery, and retribution, and advocates violence as a means by which to achieve them. This code outlines how one should act to demand respect, defend honor, avoid becoming victimized, and thus achieve high status among peers. It also justifies the use of violence by individuals already inclined toward aggression.

Much of the code revolves around presenting oneself as tough (someone not to be messed with). Since reputation is very important, one must maintain the respect of all who adhere to the code, not just an individual who may or has committed an act of disrespect. For example, if one is verbally insulted, one must retaliate with a form of violence (could be a threat or physical act), not only to hold the insulter (perpetrator) accountable, but to demonstrate to others that one abides by the code and is not a coward or weak. Per Anderson (1999, p. 10), "repeated displays of 'nerve' and 'heart' build or reinforce a credible reputation for vengeance that works to deter aggression and disrespect, which are sources of great anxiety on the inner-city street." Individuals' adoption of the code, especially when strong, leads to increased violence in the neighborhood. Violence escalates as more youth engage in posturing and threatening actions, and come into conflict with one another, and more come to rely on violence for self-defense.

Anderson connects the subculture to problems such as structural disadvantage and discrimination. For example, a lack of job opportunities in the inner-city results in fewer gainfully employed men who may serve as role models to young African American males. The inner city is alienated from broader social institutions, as manifested in economic disadvantages, ineffective criminal justice protection, low informal control (e.g., familial and educational), and resulting high crime. The street culture is an adaptation to these circumstances. Inner-city youth tend to be pessimistic about the ability of authorities such as police and teachers to solve interpersonal problems. Thus, ordinary societal rules of civil law are weakened. The code of the street is not just a collection of beliefs then; it is a powerful system of norms that replaces the rule of law. Thus, it serves a social control function; it calls on individuals to settle their own disputes in peer settings. Anderson (1999, pp. 9–10) writes:

> At the heart of this code is a set of prescriptions and proscriptions, or informal rules, of behavior organized around a desperate search for respect that governs public social relations, especially violence, among so many residents, particularly young men and women. Possession of respect—and the credible threat of vengeance—is highly valued for shielding the ordinary person from the interpersonal violence of the street.

Thus, Anderson (1999) presents a multilevel view of the subculture: the "neighborhood street culture," which is a property of the structurally disadvantaged environment, and the individual's adoption of street code norms and values (embracing values, beliefs, and behaviors consistent with street culture norms). Becoming aware of the street culture through interaction with others (e.g., family and peers), and experiencing the dangers and disadvantages in the neighborhood, inner-city youth are pushed and pulled toward adopting street values as their own. The more one embraces the code, the more violence one is likely to commit. The internalized street culture, then, heavily influences how residents interact with one another.

However, individuals vary in the manner and extent to which they are alienated from mainstream culture and adopt the street code. Anderson identified two conflicting value orientations in the neighborhoods he studied. Families and individuals with a *decent* orientation still embraced mainstream cultural values—a civil code, whereas those with a *street* orientation embraced the oppositional culture—a street code. ("Decent" and "street" are labels that residents place on themselves and others in the neighborhood.) While few residents fully embrace the street culture, it applies to everyone. Parents in "decent families" are still tied to mainstream values and teach them to their children. However, understanding that their children need to respond to threats in the neighborhood, they also raise them to understand that they cannot ignore the street code. Even decent youth, who do not highly value violence, are pressured to use violence or aggression in some form to protect themselves and manage relationships and interactions. They too must maintain street credibility and a reputation of toughness. When circumstances seem to require it, decent youth may "switch codes"—from civil to street (Anderson, 1999).

Box 3.3: An Example of a Decent Family

Elijah Anderson (1999, pp. 43–45) discusses "Diane," a 46-year-old single mom who is "of average height, heavyset, and light-complexioned." She has been a single parent for 15 years. She separated from her husband in 1979. She has four sons, three of whom are grown. The oldest is 35 and the youngest is 15. One adult son works as a night watchman and another works as a security guard. Diane "works as an aide in a day care center" and part-time as a janitor. She has lived in her neighborhood since 1981.

Diane is very concerned about the drug problem in her area. She recognizes this as being part of living in a bad area but has "never seen it this bad." Several mothers are on crack, and many grandmothers take care of kids. Drug dealers and users are "all on the corner," and some use crack while sitting in front of apartments. They roam up and down the streets at night and litter used crack vials ("caps") near residents' front doors. Diane closely watches them every day ("stay on 'em") to guard against trouble and knows who many of the drug dealers are. She points out that parents must remove their children from playing outside ("sweep 'em up") when drug activities are going on. She finds it a constant struggle to raise kids in this environment.

Faced with these circumstances, Diane does everything she can to keep her 15-year-old boy straight, which she finds difficult. However, he is interested in auto mechanics, installing radios for example, and she feels that she can be successful if she keeps him interested in these kinds of things. Still, she said "it's not a day that goes by that I'm not in fear." Her son has friends who make good money and receive other benefits by selling drugs. She pays him a little money to "mop floors" and worries that selling drugs will appear more appealing than this. Thus, she teaches against materialism, that he should not worry about anything as long as he has a roof over his head. She warns him of severe punishment if he becomes involved in drug dealing. Dianne informed him that she knows some of his friends are drug dealers. She does not forbid him to talk to them but warns about her catching him "hangin' on the corner." She makes it clear to her son that she is not going to let him throw his life away.

Diane also has to contend with the excessive freedom other boys have. She requires her son to come into the house at certain times, and when he goes somewhere demands to "know where he's at and who he's with." This includes going over to a girlfriend's house. She does not allow it unless her parents are responsible and is particularly concerned about preventing teenage pregnancy. Her son's friends complain about his restrictions and may continue to sit outside on her stoop after he goes in or try to get him to go away with them. So far, her son resists their influences because he wants "no problem with my mama." Diane is currently able to keep track of her son by herself but feels she can go to her older sons for help if needed in the future.

She also finds that the threat of violence has become worse. For example, at one time with gangs "you fought 'em, and it was over" but now, if you fight others "they may come back and kill you." According to Diane: "You got to be street-smart to get along." However, she said that her son does not like to fight. Diane finds it unrealistic that parents can pick their kids' friends. Thus, she teaches her son that while it is unavoidable that he will be around bad kids, he cannot do the things that they do. She tells him: "You got to use your own mind."

In contrast, youth with an extreme street orientation more fully embrace violence and are more likely to use it. The street code is perpetuated more by "street families." Compared to decent families, which tend to have more socioeconomic resources (e.g., education, employment, and stability), street families are more removed from mainstream supports. They rely more on the street code for survival and become deeply entrenched in the street culture. Their view of relations with others is characterized by cynicism and distrust, assuming that others are going to try to "get over" on them and possibly believing that they must strike first. Parents in street families often have their own behavioral problems such as substance abuse, unstable relationships, and justice system involvement. Street parents may directly teach their children street values, but transmission also comes from abuse and neglect. Street parents are more likely to use harsh punishment and provide inadequate supervision. At earlier ages, their children spend more time on the street, learning the street code. Decent parents provide more supervision. Thus, their children do not get such early exposure to the street code. Street youth employ the street code universally and are less able than decent youth to code switch. Street youth thus tend to employ the code to interpret, often falsely, behavior outside of street contexts such as school or public settings shared by middle-class youth who do not understand the code (Anderson, 1999).

Based on Anderson's work, we may expect that youth residing in violent, disadvantaged areas are more likely to embrace subcultural norms of violence and are thus more likely to engage in violence. This proposition has been supported by some research (Stewart & Simons, 2010). Ironically, adopting the street code does not seem to reduce one's chances of violent victimization. In fact, Stewart and colleagues (2006) found that it increased it. Still, the perceived rather than actual value of violence may determine its use.

Anderson solves the problem that subculture theory has in explaining non-delinquency among disadvantaged youth. All youth in the neighborhood must recognize the code, but those with strong influences from prosocial adults, namely parents, do not readily translate street code beliefs and values into illegal behavior. Still, it is questionable that the street code as violent subculture explains violent rather than general offending. Youth who use violence to maintain control and respect often commit nonviolent offenses. Of course, it is unreasonable to expect that violent offenders would commit violent acts *only*. However, if violent norms really drive their delinquency, then violence should *dominate* their offending patterns. Research has yet to show that this is the case—that a pro-violence system of values and beliefs exists separately from a general delinquent orientation (McGloin et al., 2011). Thus, it seems that factors other than subcultural norms might separate the violent from the nonviolent offender.

However, it remains plausible that the code of the street increases acts of violence by amplifying the violence of youth who have general delinquent tendencies and by inducing victims to use retaliatory violence instead of legal responses. Also, the code seems to facilitate misunderstandings that could lead to preemptive and retaliatory violence. One may incorrectly perceive imminent or actual disrespect from another, then respond with violence. The code of the street perspective may be adopted to study populations other than inner-city African American youth. However, the modern subculture of violence theory is quite limited, perhaps only explaining the violent offending of disenfranchised minorities. While violence occurs disproportionately in poor urban areas, most delinquency in the U.S. is committed outside of this context.

Box 3.4: An Example of a Street Family

Elijah Anderson (1999, pp. 46–47) discusses "Joe Dickens," a "heavyset" 32-year-old Black man. Joe lives with his three children: two girls aged five and seven and a three-year-old boy. The children's mother, Joe's wife, is absent from the home. Joe separated from her allegedly because she became addicted to crack and turned to street prostitution to support her habit. He then took over the household and since then has kept the children fed, clothed, and housed. At first glance, Joe appears to be a "decent parent." Other information suggests that he is not.

Joe rents a house that "sticks out on the block." In addition to structural damage and bars on the front windows (which may be the landlord's fault), "the small front yard is filled with trash and weeds" and "the garbage cans at the side of the house are continually flowing." Joe's neighbors report that he yells and curses at the kids, "when he pays attention to them at all." Joe lets his kids run up and down the street unsupervised at all hours, "riding their Big Wheels and making a racket." They are joined by other kids who play on the sidewalks and streets without supervision.

Joe spends more time with "buddies" who frequently hang out at his place, on the porch when the weather is warm. They play loud music, drink beer, and play cards. Joe often spends the earlier part of the day preparing to entertain guests. His house looks like "the scene of an ongoing party." He does not seem to care about his neighbors. Noise from his house constantly bothers them. They become more frustrated after they call the police, who rarely respond to their complaints. "Decent neighbors" are afraid to confront Joe. They think that he must believe "in the principle that might makes right" and if they bother him, he and/or his friends will retaliate. Also, neighbors suspect or believe that he is a crack dealer. Anderson confirms that "people come and go at all hours of the day and night" (often leaving cars running, dashing into the house, quickly emerging, and then driving off).

Joe's children are exposed to much of his activities. They are sometimes made to stand outside on the porch, perhaps while Joe is conducting "business" inside the house. Anderson concludes that Joe's children are learning, by example, "the values of toughness and self-absorption: to be loud, boisterous, proudly crude, and uncouth—in short, street."

Conflict & Marxist

The conflict perspective was covered in Chapter 1, but not as an explanation of why individuals choose criminal behavior. Rather, it was an explanation of how law and justice authorities, and other powerful groups, determine what is illegal, who gets punished, and how people are punished in a society. The possibility was raised that some laws and legal responses are unjust, for example, prohibiting and punishing people for behaving in ways that are simply different than that of a dominant group or culture, not innately bad. It is also possible that group conflict creates innately harmful behavior such as violence and property crime, namely by motivating some group members to commit these kinds of acts. Groups with different norms, values, and goals compete for power, control, and resources. When stakes are high, groups can be hostile and aggressive toward each other. They may define each other with negative stereotypes, and members of one group may come to dislike members of another, even viewing them as enemies. While much aggressive behavior between groups is legal, intergroup hostility and struggles for limited resources make it more likely that some individuals will resort to illegal behavior in their relations with other groups—hate crimes, for example.

However, while intergroup conflict itself can motivate crime, contemporary conflict perspectives on crime causation center more on inequality—on conflict between groups or larger segments of the population that do not share power and status equally in a society. Dominant groups or segments are interested in retaining power and advantage over subordinate ones, and subordinate groups or segments are of course interested in gaining freedom and autonomy from the dominant ones. Vold's group conflict theory argues that "minority power groups"—those lacking the power to shape laws, policies, economic practices, and so on—are pressured to resort to crime to promote their interests (Bernard et al., 2016). Roughly speaking, **conflict perspective theories of crime** typically argue that pronounced inequality breeds crime. Thus, they overlap with the other structural theories. Inequality is a main feature of social disorganization, deviant subcultures, and many sources of strain (e.g., unequal opportunity and discrimination). The conflict perspective looks deeper in the roots of crime and can explain how socially disorganized neighborhoods, delinquent subcultures, and sources of strain emerge.

With an emphasis on economic inequality, conflict perspective criminology has roots in the work of Karl Marx, namely in arguing that capitalism-based economic systems are flawed in ways that produce crime. Strain theory points out that countries like the U.S. place heavy emphasis on acquiring and spending money, and individuals lacking ability to do so, namely those in the lower classes, may turn to crime to acquire money and material goods or cope with the frustration of being unable to acquire them. Some Marx-inspired theorists (e.g., Willem Bonger and Richard Quinney) find capitalism responsible for these circumstances. They argue that private industry and profit motives foster unchecked greed and self-centeredness. These tendencies affect the lower, middle, and upper classes, but the illegal behavior of the lower classes receives more scrutiny and differs in type. While various forms of white-collar or elite crime occur among the middle and upper classes, members of the lower classes tend to commit **crimes of accommodation** such as burglary and robbery, prostitution, and substance abuse to deal with class disadvantages (Akers et al., 2017).

According to Marxist criminologists, members of the lower classes may commit **crimes of resistance**. Experiencing disadvantages such as lower access to opportunities and interpersonal discrimination, members of subordinate groups may become angry and resentful toward the dominant group (and maybe dissatisfied with life in general). In response, they may engage in behaviors that demonstrate their dissatisfaction, which will include both prosocial and antisocial behaviors. For example, as often covered in the media, residents in disadvantaged minority neighborhoods concerned about unjust treatment by justice authorities have engaged in protests. Most of them are peaceful, but some individuals have expressed themselves with assault and property damage. Some of these acts may be, in part or full, acts of defiance or releases of frustration. Protesters may also break laws nonviolently—engage in civil disobedience—to make their points. Additionally, dominant group members are motivated to commit crimes to maintain advantages and control, such as corporate crime, police brutality, and political corruption (Akers et al., 2017). However, juveniles are unlikely to commit these crimes.

One might believe then that capitalism leads to a significant amount of crime, by simultaneously creating the exaggerated value of wealth and the lower class that covets but cannot attain it. However, "blaming capitalism" might be over-simplistic. It may be economic inequality itself that leads to crime, for example by adversely affecting family, school, and community functioning. After all, pronounced inequality and high crime are also found in other economic systems, socialist-based, for example (Akers et al., 2017). Still, capitalism plausibly has much to do with the development of the inequalities that can be directly linked to crime, as well as the over-emphasis on monetary goals described by strain theorists. Thus, the free-market economy may still be an important context for understanding factors of crime.

Feminist

Like other critical perspectives, the feminist perspective is applied toward understanding criminal justice systems and criminology itself. Feminism has also advanced knowledge on factors of crime, as discussed in depth by Chesney-Lind and Shelden (2014). Criminology is a historically male-dominated, and thus male-biased, discipline that largely ignored issues like female crime. It is true that females commit much less crime compared to males, but this does not make female criminality an insignificant issue. Female crime rates are not so small as to warrant dismissal, and it is now well recognized that girls are involved in gangs and significantly system-involved due to status offending. In the past, theories developed with male offending in mind were often assumed to apply to female offending, perhaps with slight modifications. However, traditional theories often do not make sense as explanations of female offending. Strain theory, for example, would seem to predict high rates of female offending, as gender discrimination results in fewer opportunities. This is not to say that established theories are irrelevant to female offending. However, the factors and processes behind female offending must be examined in their own respect, not just in comparison to male offending.

Also, the very "excuse" offered for the neglected study of female crime—that females commit much less crime—begged for an explanation. In addition to examining female crime-causation specifically, feminism has advanced knowledge of the role of gender in crime, and why males commit so much more of it. Considering that gender is more strongly related to crime than race and class (the male/female crime ratio is much more imbalanced compared to white/nonwhite and poor/nonpoor), it should be considered at least equally important to understanding crime causation. Perhaps the difference in tendency to commit crime is explained by gender socialization, by raising boys to be "masculine" and girls to be "feminine." After all, the aggressive, selfish nature of many crimes more closely matches stereotypical masculine characteristics (e.g., competitive and self-centered) than stereotypical feminine characteristics (e.g., cooperative and empathetic). In fact, some theorists have assumed that the females who commit violent or aggressive crimes are simply more like males, and thus male-centered explanations apply equally as well to them. However, while it seems that gender socialization and criminal behavior are somehow related, the impacts of masculinity and femininity are complex. For example, research has not clearly shown that "more masculine" males or females commit more crime (Chesney-Lind & Shelden, 2014). Thus, **feminist perspectives on crime** causation seeks better explanations for female offending and gender differences in offending.

Rather than supposed fundamental differences between boys and girls, the causes of girls' delinquency (many of which do indeed apply *similarly* to boys' causes) may lie in their experiences growing up. It is also important to look at differences among females, not just between males and females. Socialization occurs in multiple stages, rather than just during early childhood (e.g., infancy through five years). Thus, it is important to take a developmental view of gender differences. Perhaps girls acquire some crime-inhibiting characteristics early, but boys and girls do not simply learn different things—their pathways across stages differ. During adolescence, girls' experiences with gender may be more external. Gender-appropriate behavior, including non-criminality, may be more directly determined by how others (e.g., parents, teachers, and friends) interact with girls in institutional settings (e.g., family, school, and peer groups) than by internal traits acquired biologically or through early socialization. Boys however are freer to practice gender. Thus, boys and girls have different experiences with factors that encourage risk taking. For example, girls may associate with fewer delinquent peers, be subject to stricter control in the home and at school, and have lower access to legitimate and delinquent opportunities. Additionally, gender must be recognized as a pervasive system of inequality (one that impacts all aspects of life) not just one of differences (Chesney-Lind & Shelden, 2014).

To begin, the low female crime rate can be attributed to gender inequality. One argument is that girls commit delinquency because they are subject to more social control than boys. For example, Hagan and colleagues' power-control theory argues that parents tend to restrict the lives of their daughters more than their sons, which gives boys more access to delinquent opportunities. Boys are typically given more freedom and encouragement to engage in activities outside the home and tinker with adult roles, which means that they are more entrusted to regulate their own behavior. Compared to their brothers, girls are more watched, contained, and encouraged to limit themselves. This higher control of girls is more pronounced in "patriarchal" families—those in which fathers have more economic power than mothers (Bernard et al., 2016). A gendered theory of social control seems to make sense. However, it suggests that girls who are allowed as much freedom and responsibility as boys will commit more delinquency—perhaps almost as much as boys. However, research has not clearly shown this to be the case (Chesney-Lind & Shelden, 2014). (Here, one must avoid confusing freedom given by egalitarian parents with "freedom" gained through abandonment or neglect, as these factors are of course associated with increased delinquency in girls.)

The higher supervision of girls may be due in part to legitimate fears that parents and other authorities (e.g., school) have about girls' increased risk of sexual victimization, but it may have more to do with administering the sexual double standard: it is "natural" to express male sexuality, but female sexuality must be repressed. Thus, compared to boys, girls experience more external control over their sexual behaviors, or more importantly, situations that increase opportunities for sexual behavior (e.g., going to parties or on unchaperoned dates). However, this extra control can "backfire." Girls are also often viewed as more responsible than boys, which places girls in contradictory situations. Faced with what they find to be unjust treatment, girls may be motivated to engage in risky behaviors to pursue their interests. For example, they may lie about their activities or sneak out of the home, possibly to (ironically) enter unsafe environments such as parties involving substance use and presence of potential male offenders (Chesney-Lind & Shelden, 2014).

Another argument is that, simply speaking, the world of criminality is also quite sexist. Here, it is important to examine the power that females have should they decide to commit crime. With more power, and masculine expectations regarding the aggressive use of power, it may be no surprise that men commit not only more crime, but more serious (e.g., violent) crime. Marxist feminists argue that a "glass ceiling" also exists in illegitimate economic enterprises. Street crime is male dominated, and as such, gives females fewer opportunities to commit higher-impact street crimes. Instead, they are restricted to less serious, more self-destructive acts (Chesney-Lind & Shelden, 2014). For example, they have little access to drug sales but do get involved in drug possession or transport (e.g., holding or delivery) and use.

Gender inequality also explains some of the crime that females do commit. Modern American society is still largely patriarchal—male dominated (e.g., fathers and male siblings tend to have more power in the family). Under patriarchy, subordination of females, male aggression, and male control of females results in frequent physical or sexual victimization of females. Victimization is a factor of delinquency for boys and girls but works differently between them. Girls are more likely to be victims of sexual violence and experience longer durations of ongoing sexual abuse. Girls may react to this victimization with delinquency and status offending, such as running away or violating curfew to escape or evade abuse. Compared to boys, abuse may be a stronger factor in girls' decisions to run away. Girls may also use drugs or inappropriate behaviors ("act out") to cope with trauma generated by abuse (depression, anxiety, hostility, PTSD, and so on). Abuse also affects school performance and may lead to truancy. Girls who run away are then exposed to criminogenic environments such as living on the street or with others who engage in crime. They may commit offenses such as panhandling, theft, and prostitution—out of survival rather than due to antisocial tendencies. For example, girls' involvement in prostitution is driven more by males' interest in having sex with girls. Rather than seeking to defy the law and get males to pay them for sex, runaway girls choose prostitution because it is a street survival method made available to them (Chesney-Lind & Shelden, 2014).

Gender inequality also explains violent female crime—namely that directed toward other females or other oppressed groups. Male dominance and privilege make it difficult for girls to direct anger and frustration toward males, especially without severe consequences. Thus, they may take their anger and frustration out on, or seek to control, other girls. Rather than rejecting or escaping from traditional feminine roles to break into male domains, these girls often subscribe to patriarchal ideology and demonstrate loyalty to males. They may target victims because they perceive them as failing to live up to feminine standards (e.g., unattractive, allegedly sexually promiscuous, or even "too pretty") and thus deserving attack. This is not to say that these girls ensure that their own behavior is always consistent with feminine stereotypes; some (e.g., female gang members) may find advantages in behaving in ways similar to male peers and then view themselves as exceptions to the dominant view of women that they accept (Chesney-Lind & Shelden, 2014).

Then again, some female offenders may not see violence as a violation of feminine standards. Anderson's code of the street framework has also been applied to explain girls' violence. Like their male counterparts, girls who live in heavily disadvantaged neighborhoods are expected to abide by the code (although boys' and girls' experiences are not exactly alike). Distanced from white middle-class society and facing class, race, and ethnic (and for girls, gender) inequalities, girls and boys alter conventional ways to achieve strong feminine and masculine identities to fit their context. On the streets, girls are not acting "non-feminine" when they, similar to boys, use violence as a resource for control, self-protection, sense of accomplishment, and excitement (Chesney-Lind & Shelden, 2014).

Summary Points

- Accurately identifying factors of delinquency is made difficult by (1) the complex nature of social reality, (2) our biases and perceptual limitations, and (3) imperfect research.
- However, with ample research, plausible theories, successful policies and practices, and careful and honest consideration, we can identify the more likely causes of delinquency.
- Possible causes of crime are specific variables often called "factors." These variables may increase the likelihood of offending—"risk factors"—or decrease the likelihood of offending—"protective factors."
- Factors of crime are those which are shown to be "correlated" with offending; they vary in a systematic way with crime or delinquency variables. However, a correlation itself does not prove causation. Two variables may be "spuriously" related, meaning that one does not actually cause the other, and instead they are both caused by a third variable.
- Individual-level theories find factors in rational thought, psychological states, and how human biological conditions interact with environmental conditions.
- Social structural theories find factors in neighborhood or community characteristics, strain and stress that people experience, subcultural systems, and social inequality.

Key Terms

Biosocial Theories: theories arguing that biological factors—e.g., genes, early health risks, hormones, brain structures, and neurological conditions—interact with the environment ("nature *and* nurture") to produce general types of behavior, including crime.

Code of the Street: a particular system of street culture beliefs, found primarily in African American inner cities, that emphasizes respect, toughness, bravery, self-protection, and retribution, and advocates violence as a means by which to achieve them.

Cognitive & Social Development Theories: theories that find problems in ways that children learn and acquire reasoning abilities and morals and choose behaviors accordingly, over time.

Collective Efficacy: mutual trust and solidarity among local residents combined with their willingness to intervene for the common good.

Conflict Perspective Theories of Crime: theories argue that crime by lower class and other minority individuals is often committed to resist or cope with inequality.

Correlation: an empirically verified relationship between two variables, not synonymous with *causation*—a process in which a variable in fact creates a change in another.

Crimes of Accommodation: crimes committed by lower classes persons to deal with class disadvantage, such as burglary, robbery, prostitution, and substance abuse.

Crimes of Resistance: crimes committed by socially disadvantaged persons to express dissatisfaction with struggles such as lack of opportunities and interpersonal discrimination.

Cross-Sectional: a type of research study in which all data are collected at one point in time and thus does not directly show which events or conditions occurred or existed first.

Definitions Favorable to Crime: attitudes, beliefs, and perspectives which present offending as somehow good or justified (and perhaps that conforming to the law is bad).

Delinquency Opportunity Structure: an alternative structure of opportunities made available through exposure to crime and delinquent peers that emerges when conventional opportunities are not available in a community.

Delinquent Subculture Theories: theories that argue that some youth are distanced from middle-class culture and instead participate in a subculture that espouses beliefs, attitudes, and behaviors—often illegal—that differ from or even oppose those of the dominant culture.

Differential Association: a learning theory concept that represents the ratio at which a child spends time with others who advocate crime vs. those who do not.

Differential Reinforcement: the extent to which children recognize, directly or vicariously, that certain behaviors, including crime, are rewarded or not rewarded.

Factor: a variable that is shown, through statistical analysis or direct observation, to be somehow related to another variable, such as criminal behavior (a.k.a. "correlate").

Feminist Perspectives on Crime: inquiries into crime causation that seeks better explanations for female offending and gender differences in offending, with a focus on gender inequality.

General Strain Theory: a theory that argues that juveniles engage in delinquency to cope with negative emotions that result from loss of something positive (e.g., a break-up with a romantic partner) or presentation of something negative (e.g., being assaulted or insulted).

Institutional-Anomie Theory: a strain theory that argues that a society will experience more crime when its economy dominates over social control institutions (e.g., family and education)—when these other institutions are devalued, altered to accommodate economic requirements, and penetrated by economic norms.

Learning Disabilities: physical or mental conditions (e.g., neurological) that impair the development or acquisition of knowledge and skills, such as being less able to sort and store information due to language or sensory processing problems.

Longitudinal: type of research study in which data are collected at multiple points in time, often measuring a proposed cause at an earlier time and its proposed effect at a later time.

Personality Trait Theories: theories that implicate pathological qualities in the sets of psychological and behavioral characteristics that set individuals apart.

Protective Factors: variables in a person's life that are (statistically) associated with a *lower* chance that something bad, like criminal behavior, will happen.

Psychopathy Theories: theories of more serious violent and chronic crime that implicate broader criminogenic states of being in which multiple distinct traits comprise "disorders."

Rational Choice Theory: a theory that proposes that humans choose actions, including crime, after performing a mental cost-benefit analysis that favors the actions.

Risk Factors: variables in a person's life that are (statistically) associated with a *higher* chance that something bad, like criminal behavior, will happen.

Social Disorganization Theory: a theory that finds root causes of crime in disadvantages embedded in the structure of neighborhoods, namely poverty, high portions of single-parent homes, high residential mobility, and racial/ethnic background heterogeneity.

Social Scientific Theory: a proposed explanation of why human behavior, such as crime, occurs.

Social Structural Theories: theories that find causes of behavior in the ways in which society and its parts are organized into patterns of relationships and interactions (e.g., social institutions).

Spurious: a type of correlation in which two variables are related because another variable causes them, not because one causes the other.

Strain Theories: theories that argue that juveniles engage in delinquency as an adaptation or reaction to stress or strain they experience from being mistreated or restricted by others.

Subculture of Violence: a subculture found among lower class youth, especially racial minorities, that focuses on violence and presents it as an appropriate or necessary (therefore morally acceptable) response to being attacked, insulted, or otherwise provoked by others.

Weak Social Network: a system of relationships in which the persons who comprise it are unable to pool together and share ample resources such as emotional and financial support and supervision over children.

References

Agnew, R., & Brezina, T. (2018). Strain theory. In *Juvenile delinquency: Causes and control* (6th ed., pp. 115–130). Oxford University Press.

Akers, R. L., Sellers, C. S., & Jennings, W. G. (2017). *Criminological theories: Introduction, evaluation, and application* (7th ed.). Oxford University Press.

Anderson, E. (1999). *Code of the street: Decency, violence, and the moral life of the inner city*. W.W. Norton & Company.

Beaver, K. M., & Walsh, A. (2011). Biosocial criminology. In K. Beaver & A. Walsh (Eds.), *The Ashgate research companion to biosocial theories of crime* (pp. 3–15). Ashgate.

Benson, M. L. (2013). *Crime and the life course: An introduction*. Routledge.

Bernard, T. J., Snipes, J. B., & Gerould, A. L. (2016). *Vold's theoretical criminology*. Oxford University Press.

Bohm, R. M., & Vogel, B. L. (2015). Microsociological theories. In *A primer on crime and delinquency theory* (pp. 121–144). Carolina Academic Press.

Carlsson, C., & Sarnecki, J. (2016). *An introduction to life-course criminology*. Sage Publications.

Chesney-Lind, M., & Shelden, R. G. (2014). *Girls, delinquency, and juvenile justice* (4th ed.). Wiley-Blackwell.

Glenn, A. L., & McCauley, K. E. (2019). How biosocial research can improve interventions for antisocial behavior. *Journal of Contemporary Criminal Justice*, *35*(1), 103–119. https://doi.org/10.1177/1043986218810608

Hoffmann, J. P. (2011). Psychological theories of delinquency. In J. P. Hoffmann (Ed.), *Delinquency theories: Appraisals and applications* (pp. 58–81). Routledge.

Kingston, B., Huizinga, D., & Elliot, D. S. (2009). A test of social disorganization theory in high-risk urban neighborhoods. *Youth & Society*, *41*(1), 53–79.

Loughran, T. A., Paternoster, R., Chalfin, A., & Wilson, T. (2016). Can rational choice be considered a general theory of crime? Evidence from individual-level panel data. *Criminology*, *54*(1), 86–112.

McGloin, J. M., Schreck, C. J., Stewart, E. A., & Ousey, G. C. (2011). Predicting the violent offender: The discriminant validity of the subculture of violence. *Criminology*, *49*(3), 767–794.

Messner, S. F., & Rosenfeld, R. (2013). *Crime and the American dream* (5th ed.). Wadsworth.

Moore, M. (2011). Psychological theories of crime and delinquency. *Journal of Human Behavior in the Social Environment, 21*, 226–239.

Raine, A., & Portnoy, J. (2012). Biology of crime: Past, present, and future perspectives. In R. Loeber & B. C. Welsh (Eds.), *The future of criminology* (pp. 30–39). Oxford University Press.

Rudo-Hutt, A., Gao, Y., Glenn, A., Peskin, M., Yang, Y., & Raine, A. (2011). Biosocial interactions and correlates of crime. In K. M. Beaver & A. Walsh (Eds.), *The Ashgate research companion to biosocial theories of crime* (pp. 17–44). Ashgate.

Stewart, E. A., Schreck, C. J., & Simons, R. L. (2006). I ain't gonna let no one disrespect me: Does the code of the street reduce or increase violent victimization among African American adolescents? *Journal of Research in Crime and Delinquency, 43*, 427–58.

Stewart, E. A., & Simons, R. L. (2010). Race, code of the street, and violent delinquency: A multilevel investigation of neighborhood street culture and individual norms of violence. *Criminology, 48*(2), 569–605.

Chapter 4

"Causes" of Delinquency: Social Processes

Chapter Learning Objectives

Students will be able to:

- Recall major factors of delinquency
- Classify categories of delinquency factors
- Determine the relevance of factors to types of offenses
- Summarize the main points of crime theories
- Judge the plausibility of theoretical explanations of delinquency
- Clarify possible relationships between gangs and delinquency
- Judge violent video games as a potential factor of delinquency
- Recognize the main concepts of the life course perspective
- Summarize the main features of the life course perspective
- Recognize the main concepts of life course/developmental criminology
- Summarize the main features of life course/developmental criminology
- Deconstruct one's biases concerning delinquency causation
- Reflect on one's progress in understanding delinquency factors

Social Process Theories

The social structural theories covered in the prior chapter identify risk factors in the conditions under which people live. However, most of the people who live under what could be called criminogenic conditions do not engage in serious crime. Social process theories consider what actually happens in individuals' lives that may lead them to criminal behavior, and in so doing, helps explain why many structurally disadvantaged people do not offend. **Social process theories** focus on interpersonal relationships within key socialization environments such as families, peer groups, schools, and

religious organizations, and how interaction with others, especially authority figures, shapes our personalities and behavior. Social process theories tend to incorporate individual-, group-, and community-level perspectives, thus drawing from psychology, social psychology, and sociology.

Social Learning

The psychological and social psychological perspectives on learning covered earlier can be integrated with sociological perspectives. Mechanisms of learning may be fundamentally the same for most children, but the social contexts within which they live, including the immediate environment (e.g., home, school, and neighborhood), shape the *content* learned. For example, a child living in an abusive home in a high-crime, impoverished neighborhood learns in about the same manner as a child living in a nurturing home in a middle-class, low-crime neighborhood, but "what they learn" is different. Conceivably, the first child is at higher risk of learning criminality.

Sociologist Ronald Akers expanded upon his earlier work with Robert Burgess in developing an integrated **social learning theory**. Akers identified four dimensions of social structure that impact learning processes (differential association, imitation, differential reinforcement, and definitions of deviance). *Differential social organization* refers to community or society characteristics associated with crime rates, such as age composition, population density, and employment rates. *Differential location in the social structure* refers to sociodemographic characteristics of individuals and groups that indicate their positions in social hierarchies, such as social class, sex and gender, sexual orientation, race and ethnicity, marital status, and age. *Theoretically defined structural variables* refers to conditions believed in popular theories to foster crime, such as social disorganization, anomie, and group conflict as well as class, race, and gender oppression. *Differential social location in groups* refers to individuals' membership, hierarchical position, and roles in important groups such as families and friends or peers as well as recreational, civic, and work groups (Akers et al., 2017). Each of these dimensions, as experienced by individuals, may be more or less criminogenic, and an individual may experience anywhere from one to four criminogenic dimensions, which will affect one's criminogenic risk. It should also be noted that an individual may experience both criminogenic and non-criminogenic dimensions. For example, a child may live in a socially disorganized neighborhood but with an economically viable and prosocially supportive family. Here, the family may offset the criminogenic risk created by the neighborhood.

Social learning theory also accounts for how both adults and juvenile peers impact learning criminality, as well as how parenting impacts juvenile peer associations. **Deviant peer association** is a major predictor of delinquency. Children also learn from their peers, as friends and other associates provide instruction, encouragement, rewards, punishment, and opportunities for criminal or noncriminal activities. Older peers can serve as "mentors" in this regard. During later adolescence, youths' behavioral choices may even be more directly influenced by peers than parents. However, parents largely determine their children's choice of peers. For example, parents who engage in poor parenting practices (e.g., lack of monitoring and abuse) and/or engage in deviant behavior themselves are more likely to steer their children toward deviant peer association, whereas parents who do otherwise tend to steer their children toward prosocial peer association. Children who have learned aggressive, antisocial behavior from parents are more likely to be rejected by well-behaved children at school and thus develop friendships with other children like themselves (Akers et al., 2017).

Box 4.1: Xavier and Jamie

Juveniles are not necessarily drawn to deviant peers by an interest in offending. Otherwise "good kids" may associate with deviant peers for other reasons such as safety and social support. In one study, young men in violent, low-income neighborhoods were interviewed about their adolescent peer networks. Two of them were Xavier and Jamie (Patton & Roth, 2016, pp. 126–128).

Xavier is a Latino man who grew up in a low-income apartment complex that he described as unsafe. He recalled often hearing gunshots. However, he said that he was used to the danger and wasn't afraid. However, he was aware he was in danger, especially after his apartment was broken into, and his father was mugged—when he was twelve. Soon after, he met some older adolescents while playing soccer. He noticed that nobody wanted "to mess with these guys," and eventually realized that they were in a gang. To gain this kind of respect, for himself and his family, he spent more time with them. This led to Xavier getting into fights with members of other gangs, but he noted that this family was no longer being victimized. He attributed this to his reputation of being associated with the gang members. Thus, protection seemed to be an important motivation behind Xavier's gang affiliation.

Xavier reported that his father "was never around." It seems then that his father was unavailable for guidance and support. Some older members of the gang gave him advice on how to stay safe in the neighborhood and avoid conflicts that lead to trouble. They even sometimes drove him to school and waited until he was inside, which was very helpful considering that he did not have a car, there was no bus stop nearby, and his high school was too far away for walking. Xavier was a good student. He made it to school on time and never received detention. However, he found himself in violent confrontations with rival gang members, at school and in the neighborhood. On one occasion, they threatened him in his apartment complex, and he nonfatally shot them with a gun he obtained from a friend. Subsequently, he was sentenced to four years in prison.

Jamie was also a good student at school who formed relationships with deviant peers for protection from neighborhood violence. About a group of gang members, Jamie said that he hangs with them but does not call himself one of them. He hangs with them "cause of a little safety"—because of the neighborhood he's in. He said that he "could walk away from it" but noted that he likes to come outside in the neighborhood, and implied that it would be unsafe to do so if he walked away: "You gotta be with, like, the right person, like, the right clique."

Jaimie has a friend who smokes marijuana. Despite this, Jaimie sees him as a role model, largely because the friend has a daughter and he takes care of her. He also dates Jamie's sister and comes to all of Jaimie's football games. Jaimie said that when he is feeling down or stressed out, he is "always there to come talk to me" and is the only person he can go to and express his feelings. He listens because he knows "the same way I'm coming from." Thus, in addition to protection, Jaimie finds mentorship and emotional support in deviant peer association.

Source: Patton, D. U., & Roth, B. J. (2016). Good kids with ties to "deviant" peers: Network strategies used by African American and Latino young men in violent neighborhoods. *Children and Youth Services Review, 66*, 123–130.

Control

Most theories assume that crime is not a "natural" behavior, and that something must go wrong in one's life to make one offend. **Control theories**, however, assume that all humans have the potential to offend, and that something must happen in our lives to stop us from doing it. Making this assumption, it is important to figure out why some people *do not* commit crime, not just why others do. In other words, we should know what is stopping people from committing crime, or controlling them. When these factors that control people are weak in an individual's life, one is more likely to offend. Thus, it is important to identify these mechanisms of control. Before proceeding, an important point needs to be raised about these mechanisms. A breakdown in social control means that one is released from the pressure to conform but it does not make one offend. Rather, future behavior becomes uncertain. Inhibited control leads one to *drift* toward offending, unless something happens to stop it (Matza, 1964).

Several terms have been used to identify basic types of social control, but Agnew (2003) sums them up with three types: direct, stake in conformity, and internal. To begin, *direct control* involves the ability of others to monitor and sanction an individual's behavior—to deter deviance. For juveniles, parents are the strongest force here given that they have raised them. However, others such as other family members, neighbors, school authorities, and police may also exert control. There are at least four components of direct control. One is setting clear rules that prohibit and limit temptations and opportunities for crime. Another is monitoring one's behavior to detect any rule violations, either directly (watching, observing) or indirectly (e.g., questioning a juvenile or others about the juvenile). A third is recognizing that violations have occurred. The fourth is sanctioning violations and behavior conducive to crime (e.g., associating with offenders) in a consistent, meaningful, and just (not overly harsh) way (Agnew, 2003).

Stake in conformity refers to what a person has to gain by conformity and lose by engaging in deviance, which has two components. One is a person's emotional attachment to conventional others such as parents and teachers. If a juvenile has good relationships with conventional others (i.e., likes, respects them), then deviance jeopardizes one's relationships with them and the benefits they offer. For example, a juvenile who commits a delinquent act may lose the esteem of significant others as well as any opportunities they can provide (e.g., a coach who decides if one may remain on a team). The other component is a person's investment in conventional activities such as schoolwork, building social networks, seeking employment, and pursuing wealth. A juvenile who is counting on good grades, a fine reputation, and a good job to succeed in life has a great deal to lose by engaging in behavior like delinquency (Agnew, 2003).

Internal control refers to a person's ability to restrain oneself when presented with the impulse or temptation to commit deviant acts. Control theory is similar to learning theory in that it explains that the attributes that inhibit or facilitate offending are acquired during socialization. In fact, one's ability to refrain from offending largely depends on what one has learned, such as moral beliefs, although biological factors may also contribute. One's "conscience" and the fear of feeling guilt plays a major part in controlling one's own behavior. Thus, an individual may refrain from committing a criminal act because one condemns it. Offenders do not necessarily have overt "immoral beliefs" (e.g., that stealing is a good thing); they may have "amoral" views of crime which reduces their inhibition about committing it. As will be discussed soon, internal control also involves a more general "self-control" tendency that is a function of multiple personality traits (e.g., impulsiveness and irritability) (Agnew, 2003).

At first it may seem that the higher the level of a type of social control, the better. Often it will be true that these controls will have independent or additive effects. For example, understanding that a behavior is wrong may make a child apprehensive about committing it, which may be enough for conformity, but also being subject to direct control may better ensure conformity. However, the three types of social control also interact in complex ways, especially with regard to childhood socialization experiences. First, they have causal impacts upon one another. For example, across time, children's experiences with direct control and demonstrated stake in conformity should produce in them a belief that illegal and other inappropriate behaviors are bad. However, another possibility is that a high level of one type of control reduces the level of another. For example, if authorities recognize that certain youth have a high stake in conformity, they may subject the youth to less direct control, which may produce more opportunities for them to offend. Also, in more immediate situations, controls can combine to produce effects. For example, just how bad a child thinks an act is might depend on their level of stake in conformity: an act that would not seem to be too costly if detected may not seem to be that bad (thus direct control may be needed to ensure conformity) (Agnew, 2003).

Thus, the appropriate type, level, or combination of controls likely depend on particular circumstances. For instance, if a child believes that a behavior is wrong and has a high stake in conformity, a moderate approach may be needed to ensure conformity, while excessive direct control may make the child resentful and ready to act in defiance. The causes of behavior then lie in the interaction of internal and external controls. After all, to even begin to follow rules, individuals must be aware of them; there must be transmission between the external forces of control and the individuals who receive and internally process messages from them. Thus, social control depends on the social ties or bonds that individuals have with others (e.g., family, school, peers, work, the community).

Hirschi (2004) describes four dimensions of **social bonds** (ties or attachments to others) that facilitate social control. If these four bonds are strong, internal and external social control is likely to be high. If they are poor, social control is lower, and deviance is more likely. *Attachment* refers to the emotional bond (e.g., love and respect) between individuals and conventional others such as parents, other family members, friends, and even institutions such as school. *Commitment* refers to one's investment toward success in achieving conventional goals, which speaks largely to "stake in conformity" as described above. *Involvement*, put simply, refers to the extent to which one is too busy engaging in conventional activities (e.g., sports, outdoor activities, work, spending time with parents, watching TV) to find opportunities to commit crime. The fourth, *belief*, refers to one's acceptance of the moral validity of conventional rules. A large body of research suggests that *attachment to parents* is most important, upon which the other bonds depend (Gottfredsen & Hirschi, 2003).

Regarding the *belief* dimension, some research suggests that the moral beliefs of offenders are similar to those of non-offenders. This makes us wonder why offenders seem to be acting against their own beliefs. One possibility is that they alter conventional beliefs and thus do not espouse them in the same manner or degree as non-offenders (Hirschi, 2004). Considering the role that conscience plays in social control, it seems that feelings of guilt can be an effective internal force of control. Feeling guilty after doing something wrong should decrease the likelihood that we will do it again. Also, we may foresee that we would feel guilty about doing something wrong and therefore not do it in the first place. Feelings of guilt however may not prevent future offending if they are neutralized by justifications, excuses, defenses, or "spins" on the meaning of one's behavior. Conceivably, then, a person is more likely to offend if one can deceive oneself about the wrongness of an act.

Sykes and Matza (1957) argued that juvenile offenders learn cognitive **neutralization techniques** to alter conventional beliefs and values and identified five types. To begin, one may *deny responsibility* for one's behavior, claiming that it was committed by accident or driven by forces beyond one's control. For example, one may get physically rough with another as a form of teasing and unintentionally cause serious injury, then claim that it wasn't one's fault because "I didn't mean to do it"—ignoring the fact that one caused the dangerous situation. Next, one may *deny injury*, claiming that no actual or significant harm was done. For example, one might claim that one's assault victim was not actually physically hurt. One may also *deny the victim*, claiming that a person harmed by one's actions does not deserve sympathy, due perhaps to the victim's character or behavior. For example, one might claim that one's assault victim "had it coming" because of something the victim allegedly did or said. Similarly, one may *condemn the condemners*, claiming that sanctioning authorities themselves engage in wrongful behavior. Offenders may be on the lookout for hypocrisy: "Who are you to judge me?" While offenders may at times be correct, to some extent, about the flaws of their condemners, this technique diverts attention from the nature of one's own choices and behavior. For example, one might cite high-profile cases of corruption in arguing against the legitimacy of the justice system. Finally, one may *appeal to higher authorities*, claiming that an act was done out of loyalty to significant others. "Peer pressure" is often at work here. For example, one who joined a group of friends in committing vandalism might claim that not doing so would have risked one's friendships.

Social bonds support the interplay between internal and external controls (Agnew, 2003). Hypothetically, a juvenile could have fairly strong internal controls (e.g., moral beliefs) and is subjected to much direct control (e.g., parental monitoring) but still commit deviant behavior if one's relationship with the community is not strong. This may occur if something happens, such as a traumatic experience (e.g., violent victimization or death of a loved one), that severs the bond between the juvenile and others. However, it is likely that strong internal controls, external controls, and social bonds tend to go hand-in-hand, as each facilitates the others. For example, a child raised by nurturing parents who administer proper discipline will probably acquire strong

internal controls and develop close bonds with the parents, and these bonds facilitate both the child's further development and the parents' ability to control the child.

Bonds between children and parents may be most important because internal controls are developed largely through interaction with parents. Accordingly, Gottfredsen and Hirschi (2003) developed a theory implicating level of self-control in crime causation. For many offenders, crime may be a restraint more than a motivation problem. Most people are presented with motives to commit crime, such as material gain or venting anger. Most also likely have several opportunities to commit *some kind* of crime. Yet most people stop themselves from acting upon these motives and opportunities. What gives us the ability to stop ourselves, to ward off the impulse to steal something of value or hit someone who angers us, for example? An obvious answer may be that we simply understand that this is wrong and, in the long run, have more to lose than gain by the act. There is a good chance that we will be in trouble with the law and/or other authorities (e.g., one may lose one's job or get expelled from school) if we steal, hit someone, and so on. But what gives us the ability to comprehend this right away? Why do people commit crimes that often, perhaps usually, offer little to gain but much to lose? This ability to hold oneself in check is called self-control.

A person lacking in self-control—the ability to restrain one's behavior in a prosocial manner—then seems to be more likely to offend. People with **low self-control** tend to be impulsive, thrill-seeking, insensitive, short-sighted, nonverbal, and combative. Since they are less likely to immediately comprehend, or even be concerned with, the consequences of their actions, they are more likely to engage in risky behavior. It is important to note here that several offenses are committed spontaneously; they are not premeditated. People with low self-control are more likely to offend because crime often offers easy immediate gratification without requiring much skill and planning (Gottfredsen & Hirschi, 2003; Hirschi, 2004).

Self-control is largely a product of early childhood socialization. Parenting has the strongest impact upon self-control development, although other influences such as school and other family members also contribute. Children raised by parents or guardians who meet their physical and emotional needs and maintain structure and discipline are likely to acquire sufficient levels of self-control. Abuse, neglect, and permissiveness on the other hand facilitate the development of low self-control ("LSC"). One appeal of this theory is that it is a general theory: it explains a wide variety of illegal and other antisocial acts. For example, it explains substance abuse, domestic violence, fraud and status offending, just to name a few. LSC is a general trait that makes one less inhibited from offending, not necessarily determined to do it. Like other risks, LSC only increases the chances of offending. The type of act one commits may depend on circumstances such as opportunities to commit a specific offense. For example, a juvenile seeking excitement may not be able to steal a car, because one cannot drive or a car is not accessible, but can steal a bicycle (Gottfredson & Hirchi, 2003; Hirschi, 2004). (Depending upon the presence of other factors, a person with LSC may not offend at all.) LSC offers a plausible explanation as to why juvenile offenders tend to commit a variety of antisocial acts.

"Self-control" is often distinguished from internal "social control." Whereas an internal control like moral beliefs is a part of an individual's perceptions of the rules and principles of community and society (hence, "social"), self-control is closer to a psychological attribute. In theory, a person could have LSC but still believe that crime is wrong. Regardless, LSC is plausibly an immediate cause of crime. However, LSC is allegedly something that is brought on by parents or other primary caretakers. While it is important to understand the nature of LSC and how it operates, to dig deeper into crime causation, we must be able to identify the parenting behaviors which *create low self-control.* Particularly helpful here is life course and developmental criminology, covered later in the chapter.

A newer control theory that has received some empirical support is Tittle's (2004) **control-balance theory**, which views control not just as the extent to which society exerts pressure upon individuals to avoid offending, but as a ratio between it and individuals' desires to exert their own control. This theory holds the assumption that humans naturally desire autonomy, to have control over their lives. Deviant behavior can be seen as an individual's attempt to gain autonomy and control, to do or get what one wants. Social control then involves others' efforts to suppress this behavior. Individuals who experience *control imbalance* are more likely to become motivated to engage in deviance. There are two types. A *control deficit* occurs when the control a person can exert is less than that to which they are subjected. A *control surplus* occurs when the control a person can exert is more than that to which they are subjected. Individuals who experience *control balance*—a state in which the control they can exert is equal to that which they are subjected—are more likely to conform.

However, to become motivated toward deviance, one must first be provoked by certain events or circumstances into recognizing that one is experiencing control imbalance and deviance is a possible solution to the problem. Tittle (2004) writes:

> Those with deficits are provoked by realizing that they do not have enough control to manage life circumstances or to avoid humiliation while those with surpluses are provoked by recognition that the control they have become accustomed to exercising or expect to exercise is not sufficiently acknowledged. (p. 411)
>
> The greater the provocation, relative to the control imbalance, the stronger the motivation, and the stronger the motivation, the greater the chances the person or entity will turn to some form of deviant behavior. (p. 414)

For example, a 16-year-old who is not allowed to go out at any time during the evening without parental supervision, and has several friends who can, may recognize a control *deficit* and become motivated to sneak out at night. Also, another 16-year-old who is given unlimited freedom by parents to go out at night, but is not allowed to go out at night when visiting another relative, may recognize a control *surplus* and too become motivated to sneak out.

Further, an imbalanced control ratio that produces motivation interacts with at least three other factors to determine the type of deviance committed or if it is committed at all. These are: opportunity to engage in deviance, anticipated cost of "counter control" reactions by others, and level of self-control. In general, a variety of acts are possibly committed by individuals experiencing either control deficits or control surpluses. Having a deficit vs. a surplus itself does not dictate a specific type of deviance (Tittle, 2004). While not its main point, control balance theory brings up the possibility that offending can occur because a person is subjected to too much or too little external control (relative to the amount of personal control one needs).

Labeling/Societal Reaction

Chapter 1 brought up the possibility that the state creates some crime simply by making laws against certain behaviors. Some illegal acts are not inherently harmful or antisocial. They are illegal because powerful interest groups were successful in making them illegal. Some argue this is the case with marijuana laws, for example. History offers blunter examples such as racial segregation laws. Thus, some crime may exist only because the state *labels* it as crime. If this argument applies, the cause of the individual's behavior in violating the law is irrelevant, to the issue of crime-causation anyway. However, also included under **labeling theory** are causal explanations of antisocial behavior. The basic idea here is that we can make juveniles offend by defining them and treating them as offenders; punishment may have an ironic effect. However, the different processes by which this occurs are complex.

Labeling theory may alternatively be called *societal reaction theory* because it focuses on how others (individuals, groups, organizations, communities, and so on) perceive and react to offending and offenders, more so or at least as much as offenders' behavior. The perspective does not ignore the offender's behavior, however. Labeling arguments often address relationships between offenders and their "audiences"—those who evaluate and respond to their offending, locating factors of crime in social interaction between the two. Thus, with roots in symbolic interactionism, labeling theory takes *an interactionist perspective on crime.* It might be better to consider labeling a broader perspective rather than a specific theory. In fact, there may be multiple labeling theories (one being the macro-sociological version covered in the first chapter). Arguments that focus on societal reaction may emphasize audience behavior—what the "labeler" does to directly increase the offender's tendency to commit crime. However, interactionist arguments may be more indirect; for example, the labeler facilitates a deviant sense of self in the offender, or the labeled, and it is this "spoiled identity" that leads one to offend (Schur, 1971). This is not to say that labelers (e.g., the courts, law and policy makers, employers, and administrators) necessarily *drive* the person to offend, but it does illustrate that the labelers' definition of the labeled had more of an impact than the labeled person's self-definition.

In the tradition of George Herbert Mead, an interactionist labeling perspective examines how individuals develop a sense of self: the sets of self-concepts and identities that one defines oneself with—loosely speaking, how we see ourselves (Schur, 1971). Our self-concepts and identities are acquired over time through interactions with significant others. Our experiences with our families, communities, and society while growing up tell us who were are. These self-concepts and identities also tell us how to behave. For example, "math student" suggests one should solve math problems, "athlete" suggests one should play sports, and "gang member" suggests one should engage in illegal activities. In the self-concept version of labeling theory, societal reaction has an indirect effect upon delinquency: others instill in a child a deviant sense of self, then the child engages in delinquency as identity-consistent behavior.

Here it is important to note that labeling—placing a social definition upon someone—is not simply name-calling. For example, telling a child that they are "a delinquent" in one instance is not likely to immediately make the child see oneself as delinquent. Rather, labeling is a developmental argument (Lopes et al., 2012). While one experience might have a profound influence upon one's sense of self (e.g., being arrested and going to court), or initiate a sequence of events that have effects upon one's sense of self, a "deviant self-identity" usually develops over a period of time in which the child receives feedback from others affirming and reaffirming the notion that one is deviant. For example, a young child may often hear from parents and other family members that they are "a bad kid." Due to conflict in the home, the child might act out at school and thus be considered "unruly" by teachers and rejected by prosocial peers. Associating with deviant peers, the child then gets into trouble with the law, thereby acquiring the label of delinquent. After this sequence of profound experiences, the child may indeed come to "identify with" being a delinquent in adolescence.

Thus, it is important to understand the pathway from defining a child as deviant to that child's deviant behavior. It is essentially a self-fulfilling prophecy. When a child that we have defined and treated as deviant misbehaves, we will probably believe that we were right—"see, the child *is* deviant." What we may fail to realize is that the child's misbehavior is not due to their nature, but to the way we treated the child. Of course, we are often right in disapproving of a child's behavior that first catches our attention. While one can be incorrectly labeled (e.g., falsely accused), a child usually misbehaves in some way to draw a negative reaction. Lemert (1994) termed this initial misbehavior *primary deviance*. Primary deviance is that which is caused by several possible factors but not by being labeled. However, if the social reaction to this primary deviance has the impact upon self-concept described above, the child may engage in further, perhaps more serious, misbehavior. Lemert (1994) termed this subsequent misbehavior **secondary deviance**. Secondary deviance is caused, at least partially, by labeling.

To illustrate, let's say that a child, seeking excitement or responding to a dare, spontaneously shoplifts an item from a store and gets caught. This is the child's first illegal act—a case of primary deviance. This one act should not be reason to believe that the child is by nature "a bad kid." However, after being shamed by the community, the child comes to view oneself as an offender and resent authorities. Subsequently, perhaps as an act of defiance, the child joins with a group of other youth to commit serious acts of vandalism in the neighborhood. This vandalism would be a case of secondary deviance.

In proceeding from primary to secondary deviance, the child experiences **stigmatization**, the process by which an individual's identity is degraded because of shaming by authorities. The authority sanctioning the child's behavior imposes what sociologist Harold Garfinkel termed a **status degradation ceremony**, an often ritualistic event or series of events which shames rule violators, restricts their freedom, and lowers their social standing. The juvenile justice process of arrest, detention, going to court, adjudication, and disposition is one such ceremony; a child going through it is exposed to several implicit or explicit messages that one is a bad person. The potential flaw in how we respond to child misbehavior is that we may over-react to it, exaggerating its harm, the extent to which it measures the child's character, and the punishment needed for the behavior. Early labeling pioneer Frank Tannenbaum termed this the *dramatization of evil*. It is this dramatization that stigmatizes the child, alters one's sense of self, and ultimately worsens the child's behavior (Schur, 1971).

As Becker (1973) explained, such an experience changes a person's public identity, as the community learns of one's deviant behavior and sanctioning and assigns "deviant"—e.g., offender, delinquent, or criminal—as the person's master status trait. When we perceive that a person has such a trait, we assume that the person will behave accordingly to that trait, that a "delinquent child" for example will commit illegal acts and other antisocial behaviors. Thus, we tend to treat that child differently than others. Here, the status of delinquent is used to differentiate and likely segregate the child from others—nondelinquents, thereby making one an *outsider*—someone who is different from, and inferior to, "normal" youth in the community. The trouble with basing a child's status on their delinquent behavior is twofold: it is usually incorrect, as most youth offenders spend most of their time engaging in legal activities, and even if seemingly correct, assigning the deviant status may only worsen the child's behavior. If we must assign it, "delinquent" should be a temporary status. Without a ceremony or gesture to terminate such a status, it may become persistent or even permanent. If a punished child is never given the opportunity to redeem oneself and return to the good graces of the community, the child is more likely to keep offending.

One contradiction to the theory is that labeling often seems to work. Punishment inspires some youth to improve behavior, to shed the label and restore a prosocial identity. Braithwaite (1989) helps explain this contradiction by distinguishing between two types of shaming. **Reintegrative shaming** occurs when authorities do only what is necessary to hold someone accountable for misbehavior, condemn the behavior but not the person who did it, and offer a ceremony or gesture marking one's return to good social standing (e.g., expunging one's record or a program graduation). In short, the consequences administered do not segregate the offender from the mainstream community and steer one toward deviant peer association. System-involved youth who desist may have experienced this kind of shaming. In contrast, **disintegrative shaming** is consistent with the idea of the degradation ceremony: consequences are intended more as retribution, the person is shamed, and there is no terminal ceremony to reintegrate one into the group or community. System-involved youth who re-offend may have experienced this kind of shaming.

However, it can also be argued that it is as, or even more, important to consider how the labeler defines the labeled, not how the labeled define themselves. In contrast to the self-concept approach, societal reaction may have a more direct impact upon one's behavior. Typically, labelers have power over the labeled and will thus have a major impact in shaping their present and future circumstances. What the labeler "does to" the labeled person depends largely on how the labeler defines that person. In fact, it is possible for a labeling effect to occur even if the labeled person does not define oneself negatively. For example, employers, educational programs, and social groups may refuse to give opportunities to an ex-prisoner with a felony record. Even if this ex-prisoner became rehabilitated and does not identify with being a criminal, they may be "steered toward" offending, for example, by using substances to cope with distress or committing property or drug crimes to make money. This is not to say that an individual with a criminal history has no impact upon the current outcome. Indeed, earlier offending and system involvement damages relationships and future opportunities.

To explain how earlier offending and other problems lead to later offending, the next two sections introduce two broader social process theoretical perspectives that incorporate the processes identified so far in this chapter and the factors identified in the prior chapter: the life course perspective and developmental criminology. The next chapter will then elaborate by presenting more specific life course/developmental arguments on crime causation.

The Life Course Perspective

The **life course perspective** is a multidisciplinary approach to understanding human behavior. It draws from social and behavioral sciences such as psychology and sociology, as well as natural science such as biology. The perspective allows for a multi-level (or perhaps multi-dimensional), and arguably more complete, view of human development. Throughout the life span, humans proceed through interactive biological, psychological, and environmental changes, which are seen to occur in stages. However, the perspective does not simply recognize stages. What a person is like—one's personality and behavioral tendencies—does not simply naturally unfold over time. Rather, one is the product of complex interactions among biological states and processes, psychological states and processes, and external social conditions and processes. It is not just the individual that develops over time; one's surrounding environment also develops. Each person has a biography, but our biographies are shaped by the time, place, and structure of the society in which we live (Carlsson & Sarnecki, 2016). In short, the life course perspective provides a conceptual framework for understanding how individuals' lives "play out."

The life course perspective is thus a broad social scientific perspective, one utilized in multiple disciplines to study a wide variety of behaviors. ("Life course criminology" refers to the application of the perspective to studying crime.) Applying the general life course perspective implies adherence to a set of interconnected principles or guidelines (Carlsson & Sarnecki, 2016). *First*, human development depends on the historical nature of time and place—where and when a person lives. Social conditions vary from place to place—across different communities, regions, or countries for example—but they also vary according to the historical period in which one lives in a place. For example, in the U.S., a child growing up in a working-class neighborhood in the industrial Midwest during the 1950s and 1960s would have a very different developmental experience there in the 1980s and 1990s, due to large job losses and decreased neighborhood quality during the latter period. The child would likely "take a different path in life" because of the economic conditions. Perhaps in the 1960s, the child would have immediately gone to work in a factory after completing high school but would have decided to go to college in the 1990s to get a suitable job. This difference in historical periods may also differentially impact a child in a middle-class Midwest suburb, but not in the same way as the working-class child.

Second, the **timing** of events in human lives is very important. Events throughout life help shape our personalities, behavior, circumstances, and futures. The nature and magnitude of events (positive or negative, of minor or major importance) is of course a major determinant of their impact upon development. However, the impact of events also depends on *when* they occur. An event that took place at one point in life would not have had the same effect if it had occurred at another point in life. In other words, the impact of life events is age-graded. A person changes throughout life. Events that happen to an individual over time are, in a way, happening to a different person, in different circumstances. The effects of event timing depend upon biological and psychological stages but also on the organization of the society in which one lives. When events "should happen" is often prescribed by laws, public policies, and cultural norms. For example, in the U.S., a 17-year-old is considered "too young" to drink alcoholic beverages. When the timing of an event is normal, it may be called *on time*—having a child after one has graduated high school and obtained gainful employment for example. Having a child while still an adolescent however would be *off time*. As will be discussed later, off-time events are often problematic, potentially altering lives in an undesirable way.

Of further importance is the *ordering* of events. For example, if a young person gets into serious legal trouble *prior* to finishing high school, one may have trouble acquiring the education needed to lead a productive life, but if one gets into trouble *after* finishing high school, one may be better equipped to move on from the experience and stay out of future trouble. This is not to say that it is always better to have negative experiences while older. An older adult who gets into serious trouble with the law may thus lose a good job and have trouble finding another one.

Third, human lives are linked. What we do as individuals impacts those around us, and of course, what others do impacts us—our thoughts, feelings, and behavior. Not all actions are highly significant, but some have major impacts upon a person's future. Again, it is important to account for the individual's social context in development. What kinds of families, friends, and other groups we grow up with have major impacts upon how we proceed in life, and we in turn impact others in these groups. Take, for example, delinquent vs. non-delinquent peer groups. Members of delinquent groups encourage each other to commit crime. Members of non-delinquent, or, prosocial, groups encourage each other to engage in conventional activities. Which type of peer group a child becomes established with will have a major impact on what the rest of the child's life will be like.

Fourth, the above three do not dismiss individual human agency. We often behave in habitual and routine ways, without putting much thought into our actions, but we also engage in very *purposive* behavior. We think about our experiences and assess current situations, then choose actions (within social constraints, available options) that can have a major impact on our lives (e.g., choosing a college and choosing a major). As one may assume, the individual has a great deal of control over determining one's own path in life. Human agency is also dynamic. Over time a person may significantly change in terms of one's motivations, perceptions, and behavior, switching to a different career or ending a long period of criminal offending, for example. Human agency helps account for the fact that people proceed through life stages in different ways, and can be quite unpredictable (Carlsson & Sarnecki, 2016). Many do not follow "culturally scripted" pathways (often with beneficial results). For example, some people wait awhile after high school to go to college, and some are able to retire early.

It is important to know exactly what is meant by the term **life course**. Rather than simply the duration of a person's life from birth to death, it is "a sequence of age-graded stages and social roles that are socially constructed and recognized as being different

from one another" (Benson, 2013, p. 3). Here, **age-graded** means that these stages and roles are fairly predictable according to age, based on what commonly occurs in a society. In short, the experiences that one "should" have at some point depend largely on age. For example, going to school is age-graded. In the U.S., children typically begin kindergarten between four to six years of age. It is "age-inappropriate" to begin kindergarten upon turning four or, for most children, after turning six. Individuals are expected to take on different age-graded social roles as they age across the life span. For example, children are expected to enter high school during adolescence.

Further, the life course consists of social pathways or developmental lines across time, called **trajectories**. These pathways involve individuals' participation in social institutions. One's life typically includes educational, employment, and family trajectories, for example. For education, we typically move through elementary, junior high, and high school, and for many college, before marking the end of our education with our highest degree. However, for some, criminal behavior is a trajectory. Trajectories may be viewed within three domains of human functioning: biological (e.g., biological maturation), psychological (e.g., advancing through cognitive development stages), and social (e.g., education). These types of trajectories can impact each other. For example, reaching puberty causes changes in an adolescent's thoughts and emotions as well as the way one behaves at home and at school (Benson, 2013).

Embedded within trajectories are **transitions**, major life events that mark the passage from one social role into another, such as college graduation—an event that often signifies the change from "student" to "worker." Similarly, high school graduation could mark the transition from high school student to college student or directly to worker. First marriage is also a popular transition. For an offender, joining a gang or first arrest may be a transition. A focus on the life course then is a consideration of both changes and continuations (expected or unexpected) in individuals' thoughts, feelings, and behavior as they *age* through various *transitions* and move along *trajectories* (Carlsson & Sarnecki, 2016).

Life Course/Developmental Criminology

The theories addressed thus far tend to focus on differences *between* offenders and non-offenders: offenders experience the factors or lack of factors which cause crime; non-offenders do not. Life course and developmental criminology also examines differences *within* individuals (Carlsson & Sarnecki, 2016), for example how non-offenders become offenders, offenders become more (or less) serious offenders, or offenders become non-offenders. In doing this, however, life course criminology still retains the goal of explaining why some people offend and others do not. It does so by examining how criminal behavior develops over time in some people, but not or not as much in others.

Thus, **life course criminology** is largely a matter of perspective—on how an individual's life changes, or stays about the same in some ways, over the life span—but one that has major implications regarding crime causation. In fact, as a wider perspective rather than single theory, life course criminology explains how many of the factors and specific processes identified in traditional theories work. Instead of simply identifying whether a person is exposed to "crime causes" and commits offenses, we should learn how one "becomes an offender"—more broadly, how one develops as a person. Applying the life course perspective to crime recognizes that criminal trajectories interact with other types of trajectories (e.g., education and employment). Crime trajectories represent only one part of someone's life course. (Even serious chronic offenders spend most of their daily lives engaging in noncriminal behavior). Thus, it is important to view them within the total context of a person's life and development (Benson, 2013).

Human development occurs in **life stages**: socially constructed, culturally relative, and approximately defined periods within the life course. Later stages are dependent upon experiences that occur in earlier stages. One does not simply leave one stage and enter another; one transitions across stages (Carlsson & Sarnecki, 2016). In terms of crime causation, the forces at work may begin long before offending begins, perhaps very early in children lives. Biological processes are important to the study of child development, but so too are socialization processes involving parents and the family, as well as schools, peers, and the community. The life course perspective may generally be seen as a merging of sociology and history with developmental psychology. The theories covered in this chapter build upon earlier, well-known stage theories in psychology. A particularly relevant example is Lawrence Kohlberg's theory of moral reasoning, which describes how youth develop (or "grow") cognitively and socially.

Based on his research, Kohlberg argued that there are three progressive levels of general moral reasoning. Within each level are two stages—thus six stages total. The first reasoning level is *preconventional*. In stage one, "naïve moral realism," young children are motivated to avoid punishment and obey authority figures. In stage two, "pragmatic morality," children tend to think in a utilitarian but egocentric manner, seeking to maximize benefits and minimize punishments to oneself. The second level is *conventional.* In stage three, "socially shared perspective," older children tend to be motivated by approval or disapproval from others with whom they are in relationships. In stage four, "social system morality," individuals (e.g., adolescents) are concerned with upholding society's rules and laws, which they see as the basis for a moral society. The third level, which is ideally reached by early adulthood, is *postconventional.* In stage five, "human rights and social welfare," individuals understand that laws are based on a social contract between them and the community, although circumstances sometimes dictate that laws be broken. In stage six, "universal ethical principles," adults guide themselves by principles of fairness and justice regardless of circumstances. Kohlberg pointed out that most individuals do not advance through all stages, especially the sixth (Hoffmann, 2011). Youth who are delayed in progressing from earlier stages may be more prone to behavior problems.

Kohlberg's original model was met with several criticisms. For example, scholars such as Carol Gilligan pointed out that Kohlberg's theory needed to be modified to accurately describe the development of females, who may base reasoning more on empathy and concern for others—which are not inferior methods of judgement—more than abstract justice principles. More generally, it is unclear that the reasoning described in a stage is truly superior to that of its preceding stage, and it appears that some individuals may skip or even move backwards from stages, depending on life circumstances. Also, the theory may not predict behavior well, as one's actions may not correspond with one's apparent moral reasoning capabilities (e.g., an action may reflect a lower stage). More recent research supports modifications to Kohlberg's theory. For example, some research shows that delinquent youth exhibit a lower stage of moral reasoning than their nondelinquent peers, although this relationship is reciprocal (delinquency also impacts moral reasoning). Also, while Kohlberg saw childhood peers as the main early influence upon how individuals evaluate moral situations, some research suggests that the main early influence is parenting (Hoffmann, 2011).

According to Le Blanc (2012, p. 124), **developmental criminology** "describes within-individual changes, along the life course, for all forms of deviant behavior and explains their development (onset, continuity, and extinction). It shares many constructs and empirical results with the criminal career paradigm" and "adopts concepts from developmental psychology" Developmental criminologists explain crime as the result of multiple types of influences that exist across the life course, such as biological, psychological, social, and cultural forces (Le Blanc, 2012). For some scholars, *life course criminology* and *developmental criminology* are about the same. For others, it is not. This purpose here is not to differentiate between the two, but it should be noted that some scholars see "developmental" as a perspective that focuses more narrowly on the unfolding of stages that seem to be natural for all humans, perhaps more in the tradition of earlier developmental psychology theories. "Life course" may refer to a broader perspective that sees life as more fluid, dynamic, and unpredictable, and places human development within a larger social and historical context (Carlsson & Sarnecki, 2016). For simplicity's sake, this chapter assumes "developmental" within the use the term "life course," as life course criminology necessarily accounts for progression across developmental stages.

The importance of studying intra-individual offending over time is underscored by two general phenomena. First, the consistency of the age-crime curve pattern (covered in Chapter 2) across generations suggests not only that younger people offend more but also that most stop or decrease offending by their late twenties. Second, research during the later twentieth century uncovered a pattern not readily apparent in the age-crime curve: most of the serious offending recorded in the curve is committed by a small portion of offenders. Criminologists then became concerned not simply with offenders and non-offenders, but at least two distinct categories of offenders—the minority "serious chronic" offenders and the majority short-term offenders—and with understanding not just what causes criminal acts but also what causes long- vs. short-term offending. In other words, we wanted to know why many juvenile offenders soon quit while some keep offending well into adulthood. Because of the interest in individual change over time, life course scholars rely on longitudinal (data collection at multiple times) more than cross-sectional (data collection at one time) research (Carlsson & Sarnecki, 2016).

The span of an individual's offending may be termed a **criminal career**. "Career" is more commonly associated with employment occupations, but the term can be used broadly (perhaps more loosely) to include other sequences of involvement in a type of activity (e.g., a "college career"). Technically, a person who commits only one crime in life has a criminal career (Carlsson & Sarnecki, 2016). However, multiple offense careers are of more concern. To be clear, in this context, criminal career does not *specifically* refer to crime as a profession (e.g., the activities of expert thieves and assassins dramatized in movies and television), although "professional criminals" may certainly be studied within a life course perspective.

Offenders vary on six key dimensions of the criminal career (Carlsson & Sarnecki, 2016). To begin, *onset* of offending refers to one's first commission of a criminal act. One could also speak of onset of antisocial behavior in young children, as it is often a precursor to delinquency. Important is one's "age of onset," as committing the first offense at younger ages (which does not occur in most careers) is associated with more severe long-term offending. While onset is marked by a single act, it is not defined by it. Onset is not synonymous with "first offense." Rather, onset is a process concept that represents the initiation phase of a criminal career. Next, *frequency* of offending refers to one's rate of offending—the number of offenses committed in a certain time-period (e.g., 30 days, six months, or one year). Perhaps self-explanatory is the *seriousness* of one's offending, for example if it includes only petty crimes or also violent crimes. It is important to note that seriousness and frequency also vary within individuals; the nature and extent of offending changes over one's career.

Continuing, *duration* refers to the overall length of the criminal career, from onset to the point at which one stops offending. We are, of course, highly concerned with long durations of offending. *Persistence* refers to continuity or repetition of offending, usually in long (but varying) durations. There is no universal standard of length of time, and frequency of offending within that time, that establishes what counts as persistent offending, but it likely requires more than two offenses across life stages (e.g., multiple offenses in adolescence followed by at least one in adulthood). Further, persistent offending need not be done in regular intervals. Some repeat offenders engage in intermittent or sporadic offending, which may contain long periods of non-offending. One may intermittently offend because (1) for varying reasons, one chooses to take time off from offending or (2) one intends to desist but eventually offends again.

Finally, *desistance* refers to the point at which one stops offending (quits). Desistence is the norm even for chronic offenders. Very few offend into their elderly years. However, the existence of intermittent offending means that desistence, too, is a complicated concept, as one may "desist" more than once. Defining desistance too strictly is problematic, as death is the only point at which we know for sure that someone will no longer offend. We cannot even be sure a persistent non-offender will not someday offend. Many individuals make multiple attempts to desist offending before stopping for good. Thus, like onset, desistance may be more of a process than distinct event (Carlsson & Sarnecki, 2016). Desistence may take place gradually, for example through a decrease in the frequency or variety (specialization) of offenses or refraining from committing more serious offenses (Le Blanc, 2012). Desistence may refer to reaching a stage in which one is not more likely to offend than people who were not persistent offenders. Of further interest to life course criminologists, then, is how individuals maintain desistence (Carlsson & Sarnecki, 2016).

Since individuals often do not get caught committing certain acts, one may distinguish between "actual" and "observed" incidents regarding these concepts. For example, one may have offended prior to one's first detected criminal act (e.g., by parents, teachers, or police), which would mean that the observed onset is not the same as the actual onset (Carlsson & Sarnecki, 2016). To sum up, the most problematic offenders are those who start offending very young (onset), regularly commit very harmful acts (frequency, seriousness), and take a long time (duration, persistence) to stop offending (desistance).

Three types of theories explain criminal careers. One is **static** (or, propensity) **theory**. Perhaps a persistent offender is someone who acquired a trait or set of traits early in life that causes one to offend throughout life. The person keeps offending because one continues to have this trait or set of traits (i.e., the condition is static). They experience circumstances and events that many other theories would view as causes of crime, such as having delinquent peers, being labeled, or unemployment. However, this is due to **self-selection**—a process by which individuals seek out environments and experiences that are consistent with their personality characteristics. The basic view here is that an offender persists because one experienced major problems very early in life which set one on a fairly stable developmental offending trajectory (Benson, 2013). Further, changes in offending, such as increasing or decreasing in frequency or seriousness, over time are due to the normal changes that most people experience as they age (e.g., going through puberty or growing old). An example of a static approach is Gottfredson and Hirschi's low self-control theory covered earlier, which argues that a person acquires low self-control as a young child, from insufficient parenting, and continues to possess it throughout one's life course. The underlying cause of this person's offending during childhood is the same as during adulthood—low self-control. In short, static theories find explanations for criminal careers in how individuals are about the same throughout life (Carlsson & Sarnecki, 2016).

Another type is **dynamic theories**, which do not assume that behavior is set or argue that early-acquired traits by themselves determine one's future. Perhaps the persistent offender is someone who experienced an event or condition during one stage which made transition to subsequent stages and thus prosocial functioning difficult. In short, dynamic theories find explanations for criminal careers in how individuals change throughout life (Carlsson & Sarnecki, 2016). Offending may be initiated and sustained through a kind of domino effect. Imagine, for example, a five-year-old kindergartener who begins to suffer abuse at home. The child's distress will make it difficult to focus at school and get along with peers, and the child may use misbehavior to try to cope with stress (i.e., "act out"). In consequence, the child may frequently draw disciplinary actions from teachers (e.g., time-outs, admonishments), which interferes with the child's learning. If the child does not acquire adequate academic and social skills, they are less likely to succeed in later schooling and more likely to engage in delinquency. Life course/developmental theories of crime tend to make or include dynamic arguments.

A third approach is an integration of static and dynamic theory (Carlsson & Sarnecki, 2016). Developmental propensity and dynamic life course perspectives are not necessarily incompatible. Individuals may have certain propensities to offend, but how this propensity is expressed could depend on the environment (Benson, 2013). Perhaps chronic offending results from a continuation of an intra-individual problem *and* environmental changes, and the two affect each other. A problem such as low self-control leads to behavior that adversely affects one's social environment, which then worsens one's behavior. This interplay of internal and external influences then makes it more likely that a person will have problems in later stages. Imagine, for example, a five-year-old child with low self-control who goes off to school. The child misbehaves at school, frequently drawing disciplinary actions from teachers, which interferes with the child's learning. If the child does not acquire adequate academic and social skills, they are less likely to succeed in later schooling and more likely to engage in delinquency. However, what happens if "something good" happens in one's social environment—can it somehow "cancel out" the impact of an individual trait? As will be discussed later, a person may have a problematic trait but refrain from offending because of a profound change in life circumstances, such as getting a job or getting married. However, lending merit to each approach does not necessarily mean integrating them. It is also possible that some offenders' careers are due to a static condition whereas others' are due to a series of connected problematic experiences.

Criminal career research often focuses on risk factors present during certain points in a person's life course, especially when dynamic perspectives are used. Risk factors tend to come in clusters—problems in one area of life (e.g., family) are accompanied by problems in others (e.g., school). They also tend to accumulate over time, increasing the risk of offending: the more risk factors to which a person is exposed, the higher the probability that one will offend. Risk factor analysis may be used to predict persistence, not just onset, of crime, as clusters of risks change over time, and the ones that explained a person's onset may not be the same ones that explain one's persistence in the future (although early risk factors do heavily influence the character of a criminal career). The main types of risk factors associated with criminal careers are those having to do with biological and psychological states, family, peers, school, and neighborhood and community (Carlsson & Sarnecki, 2016).

Obviously, all criminological theories and perspectives have flaws or limitations. However, most also have merit. Since no one theory sufficiently explains crime, it seems reasonable to combine and reconcile them—to take the "best parts" of them and form hybrid theories that offer more comprehensive, and accurate, explanations. This is the basic idea behind **integrated theory**. Akers' social learning theory, covered earlier, is a good example. Instead of simply merging theories, it is helpful to use a broader integrative framework. As a broad, multi-disciplinary perspective, the life course perspective presents a good opportunity for integrating theories. Many, if not all, traditional arguments on crime causation may be rearticulated within a life course view. Perhaps most apparent are the social process theories (learning, control, and labeling), as they essentially make developmental arguments. However, social structure is also quite important in life course theory. Structural conditions help explain why some individuals' pathways are more likely than others. For example, persistent offenders may tend to come from environments with structural conditions such as poverty, neighborhood disorganization, and disadvantaged families.

As will become evident, the prominent life course/developmental theories covered in the next chapter integrate multiple theories. However, before turning to them, this chapter ends with a discussion of different social processes which may be involved in gang activity.

The Gang: Cause, Correlate, or Outcome?

The role that gangs play in creating delinquency is complicated. To begin, "gang" is difficult to define. Scholars, practitioners, media agents, and general citizens alike have differing opinions as to what constitutes a gang. Notions of what qualifies may range from simply a group of juveniles who are misbehaving to a highly organized group deeply involved in criminal enterprise. However, it is problematic to base theory, research, and policy and practice upon the belief that just about any group of troublesome youth may be considered a gang. Thus, criminologists tend to use more exclusive definitions that delineate the criteria for what constitutes a gang. These definitions still vary, but most require that the group is at least slightly organized, the members identify with the group (not simply that others label them as a gang), and illegal activity is a major (although not necessarily sole) purpose of the group's existence. Prominent gang researcher Malcolm W. Klein and a group of other gang scholars worked together to create a general consensus definition of crime: "any durable, street-oriented youth group whose own identity includes involvement in illegal activity" (cited in Durán, 2013, p. 4).

However, there is debate over if, and to what extent, illegal behavior should be used to define gangs. First, that some members of a group engage in some illegal activity is not enough to identify the group as a gang, or else we could call just about any group of youth a gang. Organized groups with several members who regularly engage in illegal activities such as drug and gun sales, theft, violent attacks, and graffiti are more easily identifiable as gangs (*assuming* that crime defines gangs). Also, collective illegal behavior itself is not enough to identify a gang. It is common for juveniles to engage in delinquent acts with others, to *co-offend*, but most do not identify with or organize themselves into "a gang," nor do they engage in much serious delinquency. It is important to distinguish between gangs and "delinquent groups," as the two have different factors and social processes which characterize their existence, those of gangs perhaps being the more problematic (McNamara & Bucher, 2012).

According to the National Gang Center, the term *street gang* may be more practical, as "street" suggests that the group has a street presence, which is important because "street socialization is a key feature of adolescent gangs," and that the group's offenses—"street crimes"—tend to be of a more serious and violent nature (NGC, n.d.). The NGC criteria for classifying groups as gangs are:

- The group has three or more members, generally aged 12–24.
- Members share an identity, typically linked to a name, and often other symbols.
- Members view themselves as a gang, and they are recognized by others as a gang.
- The group has some permanence and a degree of organization.
- The group is involved in an elevated level of criminal activity.

Second, however, criminal definitions of gangs may not capture their true essence. These definitions are placed on gangs by outsiders and reflect their vested interests. Criminologists often define gangs as criminal to warrant "criminological" study of them, law enforcement does so to facilitate its control of gangs, and media does so to attract audience attention. Criminal definitions may lack an anthropological or ethnographic view of what gang members' lives are like and what the gang means to and does for them. It is important here to realize that even if gang members commit crime, they spend most of their time doing legal activities (e.g., recreational activities, simply hanging out with friends and family, going to school, and working). In other words, criminal definitions do not convey what a gang is in its own right. In response, contemporary gang scholars such as David C. Brotherton, Luis Barrios, and Robert J. Durán propose that we move toward gang definitions that recognize the role of marginalization (namely class, racial, and ethnic) and opportunities for positive identity development (e.g., "resistant identity"), individual and collective empowerment, speaking back to and challenging the dominant culture, escaping stress and strain in disadvantaged neighborhoods, and generating and practicing a group's own sacred rituals (Durán, 2013, p. 5).

Box 4.2: Why Do Girls Join Gangs?

In one study, interviews with Latin Queens in New York City (Brotherton & Salazar-Atias, 2003) revealed some reasons that girls in particular join gangs. These are listed below, each with a quote from an interviewee.

1) Acquire an empowered female, ethnic minority self-*identity*: "To me, being a Queen and Queenism is like being strong, being independent, on your own, having the right to speak your mind, being a woman" (p. 193).
2) Gain a replacement or supplement *family*: "I have a father through the Nation. He adopted me through the court system. That's when I first joined the nation and I was in trouble with the law and they helped me out big time" (p. 198).
3) Connect to a larger *community network*: "I have cousins … and people I grew up with, everybody in it, and then my family was in it so wherever I would go there was Kings—always Kings … so I started hanging out with them" (p. 201).
4) *Economic survival* (social support): "if they need an economic way with money we always there.… It comes out of our pockets. They ain't nothing to it. If somebody needs something, there you go. There's always a helping hand" (p. 200).
5) Seek *dignity and respect* within the *working or under-class experience:* "I seen how they carried themselves, I seen how they showed each other so much love. They like were so proud of themselves. I was like really I would really like to get to know more about them" (p. 203).

Source: Brotherton, D., & Salazar-Atias, C. (2003). Amor de reina! The pushes and pulls of group membership among the Latin Queens. In L. Kontos, D. Brotherton, & L. Barrios (Eds.), *Gangs and society: Alternative perspectives* (pp. 183–209). Columbia University Press.

Another controversy is the exact role that gangs play in delinquency causation. Gangs are groups of peers; thus, gang membership is a type of peer association. Peer influence is considered a major factor of youth behavior: delinquent peers increase one's tendency to offend while prosocial peers reduce it. Gangs of course would be an example of delinquent peer associations. However, many delinquent groups are not gangs; they are groups of youth who collectively or individually engage in delinquency without a gang structure. Since non-gang groups may also engage in a large amount of delinquency, could the key variable be delinquent peer association, not gangs specifically? Or is the gang a special kind of delinquent peer group, one that has a more powerful effect on delinquency compared to other groups? Further, since gang membership is a type of peer association, it is subject to the same questions we have about how peer association works. Do individuals choose groups that behave like them? Do groups choose individuals and make them behave like them? Can both be true?

When an offender is in a gang, it may be assumed that one's offending is due to being in the gang. When a gang member commits an offense, it may be seen as "gang-related," even if the offense was not committed with other gang members or distinctly for gang purposes (McNamara & Bucher, 2012). It also seems possible that gang members have individual-level motives for offending. Perhaps other factors, more than gang membership itself, explain offending that occurs in gang contexts. The relationship between gang membership and offending may be spurious, meaning that one does not cause the other although they coincide to some extent.

Children who develop "antisocial tendencies" are more likely to offend, but they may at the same time be more likely to join delinquent groups such as gangs. Like other youth, they are interested in joining groups that share their inclinations. Youth with antisocial behavior problems are not likely to have many opportunities to affiliate with prosocial youth, so gangs may be among the few choices they have for peer relationships. Thus, youth may "already be delinquent" before joining the gang. This is an example of **social selection**, a process in which persons pre-disposed to engage in activities performed by a type of group gravitate toward that group (Thornberry et al., 1993). Thus, gang membership itself may not cause crime. Rather, it is an *outcome* of individuals' pre-existing tendencies to commit crime. If true, we must concern ourselves more with individuals' tendencies to offend rather than gang affiliation.

In contrast, the perhaps traditional view of gang behavior is generally consistent with the peer influence aspect of learning theory: youth not highly inclined toward delinquency are "lured" into the gang, which then strongly encourages and enables them to engage in serious delinquency. This is an example of **social facilitation**: the group instills the tendencies to engage in its activities in persons who are not strongly pre-disposed to engage in them. Youth facilitated by gangs tend not to strongly identify with them, and they tend to stop offending upon leaving the gang (Thornberry et al., 1993). Perhaps "pretty good kids" can "fall in with the wrong crowd," such as a gang, and then become involved in serious delinquency. If true, the facilitation model suggests a promising delinquency prevention approach: keep children from joining gangs, and we keep them from committing delinquency.

There is a third possibility: selection and facilitation both occur. Youth inclined toward delinquency may be attracted to gangs or other delinquent groups, but after joining the group they become even more inclined to commit delinquency, perhaps increasing the seriousness and frequency of it. This is an example of **social enhancement**: the group takes persons inclined to engage in its activities and makes them do more (Thornberry et al., 1993). Thus, we do not have to rule out a selection effect to show that gang membership itself increases delinquency; we just have to account for selection. It is reasonable to expect that the gang have some kind of impact on how much delinquency its members commit, given that peer influence is a powerful force in general. If true, the enhancement model suggests that we must be concerned with two things: individuals' tendencies to offend and the effects of their gang affiliation.

One causal model does not explain all cases of gang affiliation. Whether selection, facilitation, or enhancement takes place may depend on circumstances such as the developmental stage at which a juvenile joins a gang and individual offender characteristics. For example, perhaps selection explains the gang affiliation of more serious offenders who engaged in antisocial behavior as young children and are more likely to continue offending into adulthood, and facilitation explains the gang affiliation of less serious, late-starting offenders who are more likely to be temporarily engaging in delinquency (Wong et al., 2013). Still, the question remains: If gang members were not in gangs, would they commit less delinquency?

Studies that measure delinquent behavior before and during gang membership may be used to examine the causal role of gangs. Evidence that youth did not engage in delinquency prior to gang membership but did so after joining a gang would suggest social facilitation. Evidence that youth engaged in some delinquency or other antisocial behavior prior to gang membership but engaged in more or worse behavior after joining a gang would suggest enhancement. However, it would be difficult to control for the many other factors present in youths' lives before and after joining gangs that could also explain the onset or escalation of delinquency. For example, delinquency that occurs after one has joined a gang may actually be due to aging. As youth develop, they may become more physically able to engage in violent behavior and more cognitively able to engage in more sophisticated crimes. Also, other social relationships may facilitate their delinquency, or a variety of events may occur which place strain upon youth (e.g., family problems such as illness/injury or unemployment). It is possible that youth would have started or increased their delinquency even had they not joined a gang.

Thus, another approach is to compare gang delinquent youth to non-gang delinquent youth. In this kind of research, the two groups would need to have very similar backgrounds except that the members of one group are not in gangs. If gang members are "more delinquent" than non-gang offenders, we can suppose that gangs do create more delinquency. If there are no significant differences between the two groups, on the other hand, it would appear that membership itself does not make gang members commit delinquency. In this case, gang membership would be an expression, not a cause, of delinquency, and it would appear that offenders merely *select* gang membership.

Research thus far has been fairly consistent in supporting the argument that gangs cause more delinquency than non-gang delinquent peer groups (Pyrooz et al., 2016). Thus, gangs do appear to be especially problematic. Gangs may even influence non-gang youth. Ang et al. (2012) found that non-gang youth with friends in gangs offended more than non-gang youth without friends in gangs (although non-gang youth with friends in gangs did not offend as much as gang youth). Gang membership is thus distinguishable from general delinquent peer association, and it may especially impact violent and other serious offending (Dong & Krohn, 2016; Gordon et al., 2014; Melde & Esbensen, 2013). Although gangs are usually not highly organized, they may be more delinquent because they tend to be more organized than other delinquent peer groups. Gangs may have somewhat more order, planning, and coordination that increase criminal incentives, capabilities, and opportunities. In short, the gang may boost the criminal productivity of its members (Bouchard & Spindler, 2010). Thus, perhaps it is a delinquent group's level of organization that elevates offending, not simply that one is a gang. We might then expect that more highly organized gangs offend more than less organized gangs, or even that a relatively organized non-gang delinquent group offends similarly to a gang.

So, why do kids join gangs? There may be a variety of reasons, and not all youth share the same ones. Youth may feel pressured to join a gang, by being coerced to join a neighborhood gang or as a strategy to protect oneself from other gangs, for example. They may also be attracted to what the gang has to offer, including a meaningful social identity, a sense of importance, close peer relationships, financial opportunities, and fun and excitement (McNamara & Bucher, 2012). However, a "reason" is not necessarily the same thing as a "cause." Ultimately, that gang members engage in delinquency may be more important than the fact that they are in gangs. Even if gangs do worsen group delinquency, they may have the same causes as delinquency. For example, gangs are much more likely to exist in highly disadvantaged communities. Thus, the key to eliminating gang activity may lie more in confronting the root causes of delinquency.

Box 4.3: Why Do People *Leave* Gangs?

In a study of former gang members in Los Angeles and Phoenix, O'Neal and colleagues (2016) found that women and men share reasons for leaving gangs. Awareness of these reasons is important for helping individuals disengage from criminal gang life. Participants in the study rated how influential certain matters were in their decisions to leave the gang, as well as how helpful certain sources of support were in transitioning out of the gang. (Note: lower ratings do not mean that the reasons or sources were unimportant.)

Most Influential Reasons

- Tired of the gang lifestyle, felt that it was time to grow up and move on
- Started a family
- Got a job or began working more
- Got into trouble with the law (e.g., arrested, incarcerated)
- Moved residences

Less Influential Reasons

- Exposure to violence (e.g., was assaulted or friends were assaulted)
- Being subject to police harassment or pressure
- Because of a girlfriend or boyfriend
- The gang fell apart or disbanded
- Family members left the gang

Most Helpful Sources of Support

- Family
- Job
- Significant Other
- Church

Less Helpful Sources of Support

- School
- Criminal Justice System
- Service Agency

Source: O'Neal, E. N., Decker, S. H., Moule, R. K. Jr., & Pyrooz, D. C. (2016). Girls, gangs, and getting out: Gender differences and similarities in leaving the gang. *Youth Violence and Juvenile Justice, 14*(1), 43–60.

Box 4.4: Does Social Media Promote Delinquency?

Teenagers in the U.S. spend a great deal of time on the internet. Most have access to a smartphone, and much of their online activity is on social media sites. Using social media has become a normal part of growing up in today's digital world (Stockdale & Coyne, 2020), and much research suggests that social media use can have positive effects like those associated with building relationships and connectedness (Coyne et al., 2019). However, social media has been widely criticized for providing platforms for spreading misinformation and disinformation, bullying, and other negative influences. These potential problems are particularly worrisome regarding teenagers, who are thought to be more impressionable.

Can social media use encourage and facilitate delinquent behavior? In a systematic review and meta-analysis of published studies, Purba (2021) found that frequent social media use was associated with increased risky behavior by adolescents, including substance use, gambling, and anti-social behavior, and that increased time and exposure to unhealthy behavior content was associated with increased harmful alcohol use by adolescents. Purba (2021) suggests that exposure to harmful social media content might increase adolescents' likelihood to engage in harmful behavior.

When they examined reasons for social networking site use, Stockdale and Coyne (2020) found that while an increase in using social networking sites to seek information from adolescence to emerging adulthood was not related to negative outcomes, levels of social media use to alleviate boredom during late adolescence were associated with problems such as anxiety and pathological social networking site use (which interferes with daily functioning, relationships, school, work, and so on) at emerging adulthood, and increases in using social networking sites to socially connect over time was related to problems such as anxiety, delinquency, and pathological social networking site use at emerging adulthood. Thus, using social media for certain reasons, such as to alleviate boredom and socially connect, may increase adolescents' risk of developing psychological and behavioral problems. However, Stockdale and Coyne (2020) also found that using social media to alleviate boredom and socially connect were related to empathy, so not all outcomes were negative.

Coyne et al. (2019) found in a sample of adolescents studied over a six-year period, into early adulthood, that about 83% were moderate users (reported steady social media use over time, about 30–60 minutes per day), 12% were "increasers" (had low social media use that gradually increased to a high level), and 6% were "peak users" (had low social media use that increased quickly but returned to baseline levels). Increasers and peak users tended to show lower self-regulation and reported higher levels of depression, aggression, delinquency, social media problems, and cyberbullying than the moderate users, although peak users may have improved self-regulation considering that their social media use returned to a moderate level. These results suggest that youth lacking the ability to regulate their thoughts, feelings, and behavior are more prone to over-use social media and be negatively impacted by it.

These recent studies suggest that in high amounts or under certain circumstances, social media use can have an adverse effect on adolescent development, mental health, and behavior. However, this kind of research is still relatively new, and more studies are needed to better understand the impact of social media on these types of outcomes.

Sources: Coyne, S. M., Padilla, W. L. M., Holmgren, H. G., & Stockdale, L. A. (2019). Instagrowth: A longitudinal growth mixture model of social media time use across adolescence. *Journal of Research on Adolescence, 29*(4), 897–907. https://doi-org.pnw.idm.oclc.org/10.1111/jora.12424; Purba, A. K., Henery, P. M., Thomson, R. M., Pearce, A., Henderson, M., & Katikireddi, S. V. (2021). Social media use and adolescent engagement in health risk behaviours: A systematic review and meta-analysis. *Lancet, 398*, S93. https://doi-org.pnw.idm.oclc.org/10.1016/S0140-6736(21)02636-2; Stockdale, L. A., & Coyne, S. M. (2020). Bored and online: Reasons for using social media, problematic social networking site use, and behavioral outcomes across the transition from adolescence to emerging adulthood. *Journal of Adolescence, 79*, 173–183. https://doi.org/10.1016/j.adolescence.2020.01.010

Figure 4.1: Correlates of Delinquency

Individual		
Rational Choice		
Risk of Detection Crime Rewards	Certainty of Punishment	Severity of Punishment
Psychological		
Criminal Behavior Modeling Lack of Empathy Delayed Social Development	Reinforced Delinquency Untreated Learning Disabilities Personality Disorders	Intelligence Cognitive Problems Psychopathy
Biosocial		
Brain Structure Abnormalities Neurophysiological Problems	Psychophysiological Problems Genetic Risks	Early Health Risks
Social Structure		
Social Disorganization		
Residential Mobility Strength of Social Networks	Neighborhood Heterogeneity Collective Efficacy	Portion Single Parent Families Delinquent Opportunities
Strain		
Income & Wealth Recreational Opportunities Negative School Experiences Family Conflict & Disruption Poor Peer Relations Prejudice & Discrimination	Economic Opportunities Monetary Goal Emphasis Harsh, Erratic Discipline Stressful Life Events Romantic Troubles Coping Strategies	Education Opportunities Homelessness Child Abuse & Neglect Substance Abuse Criminal Victimization Social Support
Subculture		
Gang Membership Rejection of Mainstream Culture	Neighborhood Street Culture Pro-Violence Beliefs	Adoption of Street Culture Neighborhood Crime Level
Social Inequality		
Group Conflict Sex/Gender Inequality	Economic Inequality	Racial/Ethnic Inequality
Social Process		
Social Learning		
Relationships with Adult Offenders Exposure to Violence	Peer Association School Performance	Definitions Favorable to Crime Violent Video Games?
Control		
External Control Neutralizing Beliefs Idle Time	Stake in Conformity Parental Bonds Control Imbalance	Self-Control Community Bonds
Labeling		
Definitions of Persons as Deviant Exclusion/Marginalization	Negative Status Labels Deviant Self-Identity	Disintegrative Shaming Poor Self-Concept

Summary Points

- Social process theories find factors in the ways that children learn in various social settings, are subject to control, and are defined and treated by others.
- Studying how children develop over the life course helps us understand that delinquency is not just the result of immediate factors, but also how earlier events and conditions shape the biological/psychological/social development of individuals.
- Offenders not only differ in the frequency and seriousness of their offenses, but also in when they start (onset), how long they offend (duration), their changes in offending (e.g., escalation and decline), and when and if they stop (desistance).
- Life course/developmental criminology draws from several disciplines (e.g., psychology, sociology, history, and biology) and integrates components from several different individual (e.g., biosocial and psychopathy), social structural (e.g., social disorganization and strain), and social process (e.g., control, labeling, and learning) theories.
- Gangs present a special kind of peer association that appears to have a more potent impact upon delinquency than non-gang delinquent peer groups.
- Some research suggests that excessive or other problematic use of social media can lead to mental health and behavioral problems.
- Chapters 3 and 4 cover several types of factors thought to impact delinquent behavior. Figure 4.1: Correlates of Delinquency summarizes of them.

Key Terms

Age-Graded: a concept that refers to how an individual's experiences (e.g., roles and events) are fairly predictable according to age, based on what commonly occurs in a society.

Control-Balance Theory: a theory that argues that a person is more likely to offend if one experiences a control imbalance—either a control deficit, which occurs when the control a person can exert is less than that to which they are subjected, or a control surplus, which occurs when the control a person can exert is more than that to which they are subjected.

Control Theories: theories that argue that individuals are more likely to offend if they lack inner inhibitions, self-control abilities, and/or external pressures toward conformity.

Correlation: an empirically verified relationship between two variables, not synonymous with *causation*—a process in which a variable in fact creates a change in another.

Criminal Career: The span of an individual's criminal offending, characterized by five key behavioral dimensions: onset, frequency, seriousness, duration, and desistance.

Developmental Criminology: an approach based heavily in developmental psychology that describes within-individual changes across the life course for antisocial behavior and explains their development (onset, continuity, and desistence), with a focus on criminal careers.

Deviant Peer Association: having close ties with youth who espouse and encourage antisocial beliefs, values, and behaviors, and who may provide opportunities for delinquency.

Disintegrative Shaming: administering retributive sanctions without a reintegration ceremony, which threatens prosocial identity and bonds with prosocial individuals and mainstream institutions and thus increases one's likelihood of re-offending.

Dynamic Theory: a type of theory that finds explanations for criminal careers in how individuals change throughout life, for example, how events or conditions during one stage makes transitions to subsequent stages difficult.

Integrated Theory: theoretical arguments that are constructed by combining and reconciling aspects of different existing theories, to offer better explanations of behavior.

Labeling Theory: a theory that argues that others' reactions to a person's actual or perceived deviance can itself help bring about future deviant behavior on the part of that person.

Life Course: "a sequence of age-graded stages and social roles that are socially constructed and recognized as being different from one another" (Benson, 2013, p. 3).

Life Course Criminology: a perspective that views criminal behavior as the result of human developmental processes and experiences occurring within social contexts—one that focuses on differences *within*, not just between, individuals in explaining crime.

Life Course Perspective: a multidisciplinary theoretical framework (drawing from fields such as psychology, sociology, and biology) that views human behavior as the result of interactive, multi-level processes and experiences (e.g., biological, psychological, and environmental changes) which occur in sequences or stages across the life span.

Life Stages: socially constructed, culturally relative, and approximately defined periods within the life course.

Low Self-Control: an individual's apparent lack of ability to restrain one's behavior in a prosocial manner, characterized by impulsiveness, thrill-seeking, insensitivity, short-sightedness, being nonverbal, and combativeness.

Neutralization Techniques: cognitive techniques allegedly used by juvenile offenders to reframe conventional beliefs and values and thus evade moral accountability for offending, including denying responsibility, harm, and victim worth as well as redirecting attention to the hypocrisy of accusers and appealing to higher loyalties.

Reintegrative Shaming: administering sanctions that hold offenders accountable and condemn their behavior without segregating them from the community and offer a ceremony or gesture marking one's return to good social standing (e.g., expunging a record or a program graduation).

Secondary Deviance: deviant behavior thought to be caused by negatively labeling a person who has committed "primary deviance"—earlier misbehavior not caused by labeling.

Self-Selection: a process by which individuals seek out environments and experiences that are consistent with their personality characteristics.

Social Bonds: individuals' ties or attachments to others that facilitate social control, such as attachment to parents and commitment to school.

Social Enhancement: a process in which a group takes persons inclined to engage in its activities and makes them do more (e.g., an offender committing more serious offenses after joining a gang).

Social Facilitation: a process in which a group instills tendencies to engage in its activities in persons who are not strongly pre-disposed to engage in them (e.g., non-offenders committing delinquency after joining a gang).

Social Learning Theory: a contemporary learning theory that integrates knowledge of interpersonal learning processes with the contextual factors that impact them: differential social organization, differential location in the social structure, theoretically defined structural variables, and differential social location in groups.

Social Process Theories: theories that focus on interpersonal relationships within key socialization environments such as families, peer groups, schools and religion, and how interaction with others, especially authority figures, shapes our personalities and behavior.

Social Selection: a process in which persons pre-disposed to engage in activities performed by a type of group gravitate toward that group (e.g., antisocial youth seeking out gang membership).

Stake in Conformity: a person's realization of the relationships and benefits one has to gain by engaging in conventional activities and lose by engaging in deviance.

Static Theory: (a.k.a. propensity theory) a type of theory that identifies a persistent trait or set of traits acquired early in life that causes individuals to offend throughout life.

Status Degradation Ceremony: an often ritualistic event or series of events which shames rule violators, restricts their freedom, and lowers their social standing (e.g., arrest and going to court).

Stigmatization: the process by which a person's identity is degraded because of shaming.

Timing: A life course concept that acknowledges that *when* and in what *order* certain events happen in the life span shapes the impact that these events have upon development.

Trajectories: pathways or developmental lines across the life span which contain transitions across social roles (e.g., education, employment, and criminal behavior).

Transitions: major life events that mark the passage from one social role into another (e.g., high school or college graduation and first marriage).

References

Agnew, R. (2003). The interactive effects of social control variables on delinquency. In C. L. Britt & M. R. Gottfredson (Eds.), *Control theories of crime and delinquency* (pp. 53–76). Transaction Publishers.

Akers, R. L., Sellers, C. S., & Jennings, W. G. (2017). *Criminological theories: Introduction, evaluation, and application* (7th ed.). Oxford University Press.

Ang, R. P., Huan, V. S., Chua, S. H., & Lim, S. H. (2012). Gang affiliation, aggression, and violent offending in a sample of youth offenders. *Psychology, Crime & Law, 18*(8), 703–711.

Becker, H. S. (1973). *Outsiders: Studies in the sociology of deviance, revised edition*. Free Press.

Benson, M. L. (2013). *Crime and the life course: An introduction*. Routledge.

Bouchard, M., & Spindler, A. (2010). Groups, gangs, and delinquency: Does organization matter? *Journal of Criminal Justice, 38*(5), 921–933.

Braithwaite, J. (1989). *Crime, shame, and reintegration*. Cambridge University Press.

Carlsson, C., & Sarnecki, J. (2016). *An introduction to life-course criminology*. SAGE.

Dong, B., & Krohn, M. D. (2016). Dual trajectories of gang affiliation and delinquent peer association during adolescence: An examination of long-term offending outcomes. *Journal of Youth and Adolescence, 45*, 746–762.

Durán, R. J. (2013). *Gang life in two cities: An insider's journey*. Columbia University Press.

Gordon, R. A., Rowe, H. L., Pardini, D., Loeber, R., White, H. R., & Farrington, D. P. (2014). Serious delinquency and gang participation: Combining and specializing in drug selling, theft, and violence. *Journal of Research on Adolescence, 24*(2), 235–251.

Gottfredson, M. R., & Hirchi, T. (2003). Self-control and opportunity. In C. L. Britt & M. R. Gottfredson (Eds.), *Control theories of crime and delinquency* (pp. 5–19). Transaction Publishers.

Hirschi, T. (2004). Self-control and crime. In R. F. Baumeister & K. D. Vohs (Eds.), *Handbook of self-regulation: Research, theory, and applications* (pp. 537–552). Guilford Press.

Hoffmann, J. P. (2011). Psychological theories of delinquency. In J. P. Hoffmann, *Delinquency theories: Appraisals and applications* (pp. 58–81). Routledge.

Le Blanc, M. (2012). Twenty-five years of developmental criminology: What we know, what we need to know. In R. Loeber & B. C. Welsh (Eds.), *Future of criminology* (pp. 124–133). Oxford University Press.

Lemert, E. M. (1994). Primary and secondary deviation. In S. H. Traub & C. B. Little (Eds.), *Theories of deviance* (4th ed., pp. 298–303). F. E. Peacock Publishers, Inc.

Lopes, G., Krohn, M. D., Lizotte, A. J., Schmidt, N. M., Vásquez, B. E., & Bernburg, J. G. (2012). Labeling and cumulative disadvantage: The impact of formal police intervention on life chances and crime during emerging adulthood. *Crime & Delinquency, 58*(3), 456–488.

Matza. D. (1964). *Delinquency and drift.* Wiley.

McNamara, R. H., & Bucher, C. C. (2012). *Problem children: Special populations in delinquency.* Carolina Academic Press.

Melde, C., & Esbensen, F. (2013). Gangs and violence: Disentangling the impact of gang membership on the level and nature of offending. *Journal of Quantitative Criminology, 29,* 143–166.

National Gang Center (NGC). (n.d). *Frequently asked questions about gangs.* https: //nationalgangcenter.ojp.gov/about/faq#0-0

Pyrooz, D. C., Turanovic, J. J., Decker, S. H., & Wu, J. (2016). Taking stock of the relationship between gang membership and offending: A meta-analysis. *Criminal Justice and Behavior, 43*(3), 365–397.

Schur, E. M. (1971). *Labeling deviant behavior: Its sociological implications.* Harper and Row.

Sykes, G. M., & Matza, D. (1957). Techniques of neutralization: A theory of delinquency. *American Sociological Review, 22,* 664–670.

Thornberry, T. P., Krohn, M. D., Lizotte, A. J., & Chard-Wierschem, D. (1993). The role of juvenile gangs in facilitating delinquent behavior. *Journal of Research in Crime and Delinquency, 30*(1), 55–87.

Tittle, C. R. (2004). Refining control balance theory. *Theoretical Criminology, 8*(4), 395–428.

Wong, I. J., Toh, D. P., Hung, P. L., & Ang, R. P. (2013). Delinquency in gangs—selection or socialization? *Aggression & Violent Behavior, 18*(6), 784–791.

Chapter 5

"Causes" of Delinquency: Life Course Processes

Chapter Learning Objectives

Students will be able to:

- Clarify how problems moving across developmental stages leads to delinquency
- Differentiate longitudinal and immediate processes of causation
- Summarize the arguments of major life course theories of crime
- Judge the plausibility of life course theories of crime
- Classify offenders according to individual patterns of behavior
- Recognize ways in which social inequality impacts life course development
- Deconstruct one's biases concerning proper child development
- Reflect on one's progress in understanding human development processes

---

The last chapter introduced the life course and developmental criminology perspectives. This chapter continues first by covering four prominent life course/developmental theories: Moffitt's Developmental Typology, Sampson and Laub's Life Course Theory of Crime, Thornberry and Krohn's Interactional Theory of Delinquency, and Farrington's ICAP Theory. Then the chapter proceeds by discussing how contexts of history and social change, race and ethnicity, and sex and gender impact life courses and criminality.

Life Course/Developmental Explanations of Criminal Careers

Moffitt's Developmental Typology

It is apparent that offenders have different types of criminal careers. Based on several longitudinal studies, Moffitt (2011) developed what is likely the most well-known developmental offender typology. Moffitt focuses on two categories of offenders: ado-

lescent limited and life-course persistent. Both represent a different model of crime causation. To begin, most offenders are **adolescent limited** (AL); they limit their offending to the peak years of adolescence. AL offending is characterized by *discontinuity*. AL offenders desist by early adulthood, and their offending is inconsistent across situations and environments. For example, they often behave well at home and do well at school and work but get into trouble in their spare time. Further, AL offenders tend not to have early childhood behavior problems. Of interest, then, is why they "suddenly" begin engaging in antisocial behavior during adolescence.

Here we must recognize the significance of the stage of adolescence, in its historical context. After going through puberty, adolescents become physiologically closer to adults. For example, increased physical size, dexterity, and cognitive abilities means that they are able to engage in many activities associated with adulthood (e.g., working and driving a vehicle), and biological maturity means that they can engage in sexual reproduction. Thus, we can expect adolescents to desire these kinds of activities and want more freedom and autonomy over their lives (to be grown up). However, in our contemporary complex society, adults have found it necessary to extend pre-adulthood—to limit many activities that adolescents are capable of, and were historically allowed to do, and heavily restrict their independence. Of course, adolescents still (perhaps innately) desire to engage in adult activities. All of this places modern adolescents in a *maturity gap*. It should be no surprise then that adolescents are discontent with these limitations and behave in ways that defy authority. But why delinquency?

Learning and strain theories may provide the answer. As will be discussed shortly, some offenders are more persistent across the life course—they chronically misbehave in early childhood, prior to engaging in delinquency. Prosocial young children, who are still largely interested in pleasing authorities and acquiring benefits from them, tend to disfavor other children who act disruptively (e.g., at school). However, upon reaching adolescence, and experiencing the previously discussed restrictions, prosocial youth may become attracted to offenders. Antisocial youth defy authority, have a major impact upon their environments (albeit disruptively), and get a great deal of attention. They may also gain economically from their offending (e.g., cars and money). Thus, chronic offenders may appear to possess the freedom and autonomy desired by other youth. They also seem to lash out at the authorities who other youth may now be at odds with (e.g., parents, teachers, police). On the other hand, teenagers who continue to be "good kids" or "good students" may seem too passive and naïve, accepting their inferior status and adult rules too readily. Thus, even prosocial youth may come to perceive offending as rewarding and then mimic the behavior of chronic offenders.

Thus, adolescent-limited offending may be in large part rebellion and a "roundabout" way of gaining control—living more like an adult. By adulthood, however, offending becomes unnecessary and unrewarding, as the desired level of independence is achieved and the adult costs of illegal behavior are higher (they inhibit autonomy and freedom). For example, adult criminal sanctions interfere with desired goals such as going to college, getting a good job, and enjoying economic success. (In contrast, an adolescent offender still has the right to schooling and to be cared for economically.) Further, since they lack a history of early behavior problems, they likely retain the personal attributes and social resources needed to function conventionally in society. Consequently, prosocial youth are no longer "charmed" by the behavior of chronic offenders, and they desist offending. ALs are taking a risk by offending, however. One could get caught in a "snare"—a consequence of offending that makes it difficult to participate in conventional activities and successfully transition into adulthood, such as incarceration, a criminal record, drug addiction, or disrupted education. These snares could delay desistance.

In contrast to AL offenders, **life course persistent** (LCP) offenders begin engaging in aggressive, antisocial behavior during early childhood (e.g., hitting and biting) then continue with minor delinquency prior to adolescence, serious delinquency during adolescence, severe violence by early adulthood, and offending well into adulthood. LCPs make up a small number of offenders but pose a serious challenge to treatment and crime reduction. Compared to ALs, they commit a wider variety of offenses, including violent and other serious forms. Their offending is also persistent across situations and environments, behaving in an antisocial manner at home, school, and work, for example. Whereas AL offender backgrounds are near normative (more closely resemble non-offenders), LCPs' can be described as pathological.

Moffitt gives a biosocial explanation as to why LCPs begin engaging in antisocial behavior so young and then persist. Some children are born with neurological problems (with the nervous system) that adversely affect their neuropsychological make-up (e.g., temperament and cognitive abilities). These neuropsychological problems then facilitate the development of characteristics such as hyperactivity, ill-temperament, low self-control, low IQ, and poor social skills. However, these problems can be corrected or managed through environmental influences, namely effective parenting and strong family resources (e.g., economic stability). However, children with neurological deficits tend to be born to disadvantaged parents, many with health and behavior problems of their own. A situation then arises in which parents who lack parenting abilities must nurture a child who is hard to care for—one with special needs and behavior that is difficult to manage. The result is often neglect and abuse, which worsens the child's neuropsychological problems. Such children are off to a bad start in terms of prosocial personality and behavioral development, and thus at high risk of very early onset of antisocial behavior.

These early childhood problems lead to long-term offending in both direct and indirect ways. One is a static traits explanation. As the child grows older, one continues to possess the characteristics that get them into trouble. This is termed *contemporary continuity*. For example, one's bad temper that led to severe tantrums as a toddler can be the same that causes disruptions at school and eventually conflict at work and violent offending. The other is a dynamic explanation. The original problems also set in motion a "snowball" process. Problematic traits produce negative experiences that then worsen these traits. Thus, as the child ages, one accumulates personal and social disadvantages that increase risk for offending. It becomes more difficult over time to desist, as one misses out on opportunities for prosocial alternatives (e.g., learning social skills and developing strong relationships) during each developmental stage. This is termed *cumulative continuity*. Thus, for example, disruptive temper tantrums at school can lead to low educational attainment, which then can lead to lowered employment capabilities. Lack of employment, then, creates a higher risk of criminal offending.

Moffitt cautiously offers a third category of juvenile offenders: **low-level chronic or childhood limited**. This is a very small group of offenders who behave antisocially as young children, engage in low to moderate delinquency in later adolescence, and then, unlike LCPs, significantly reduce their rate of offending. As adults, they engage in *intermittent* offending. Some may stop criminal offending in early adulthood, but these cases are likely rare. Research identifying those who *recover* from severe early childhood problems may simply be detecting the non-offending phase of intermittent offenders. (They would have to be monitored into later adulthood to see if they truly stopped offending.) Still, it is possible that some childhood chronic offenders stop criminal offending early, although their personality and behavior problems do not necessarily go away. Low-level chronic offenders may have psychological and social functioning problems that differ from those of LCPs—those that promote social isolation such as inability to make friends (even with delinquent peers), phobias, depression, and anxiety. Distancing oneself from others then reduces peer influences and opportunities to offend (Moffitt, 2011).

Before moving on to the next theory, we should note that biology helps explain adolescent-limited, not just life-course persistent, offending. Changes associated with puberty such as hormonal surges ("raging hormones") and rapid increases in size, endurance, and strength can contribute to rebelliousness and misbehavior. Also, changes in the brain during the early teenage years have recently been associated with antisocial behavior. The brain, of course, is a very complex organ, with many interactive structures and layers. There is now evidence that "the teenage brain" works differently than "the adult brain." Teenagers have yet to develop their full cognitive capacities, and different parts of their brains will keep developing into their early twenties (right about the time most stop offending). Further, just how one's brain develops depends on how one uses it and responds to the environment. For example, a juvenile who spends a great deal of time playing a musical instrument will develop the associated part of the brain differently than one who does not. Life experience is important to conformity here in that (1) the brain needs it to develop and (2) teenagers are lacking in it (Benson, 2013).

One potential problem is that the prefrontal cortex, which is responsible for making sound judgements, is one of the last parts of the brain to mature, but the limbic system, which generates deep emotions, matures earlier. This reduces teenagers' abilities to manage emotions, judge situations, and make good decisions. (Once their prefrontal cortexes mature, during early adulthood, they will be better able to do these things.) For example, some research shows that, compared to adults, teenagers are less able to read facial expressions. This means that teenagers are more likely to make mistakes in perceiving others' feelings, for example believing that someone is angry or hostile when one is not. Heightened emotions and under-developed capacities to read social cues and make rational decisions are a volatile mix that increases the likelihood of acting in ways that harm self and offend others, including delinquency. In general, conformity is easier for adults (Benson, 2013).

Sampson and Laub's Life-Course Theory of Crime

Sampson and Laub have developed a theory that integrates social control, and some other theories, with the life course perspective (Laub et al., 2011). Their main contention is that age-graded informal social control—primarily in the contexts of family, school, and work—explains onset, continuity, and changes in offending.

Important to Sampson and Laub's argument is the developmental nature of social control itself. Again, social control involves the interaction of intra-individual controls (e.g., moral conscience and self-control) and external controls administered by primary groups such as family and close friends and organizations such as schools, employers, and justice agencies. The external controls to which the individual is subject changes across life-stages—in type, potency, and combinations of type (in most stages, we are subject to multiple systems of control at once—school, family, and religion, for instance). The nature and extent, and impact, of social control is thus life-course dependent. For example, parents and other family members are primarily responsible for regulating the behavior of young children. However, when these children become teenagers, much (not all) of this responsibility shifts to school and peers. When they become adults, employment and the families they create (e.g., through marriage) are more influential. In measuring the impact of social control upon the individual's tendency to offend, we must consider not only the source of control but the relevance of the source to the individual's current life stage. For example, peer influence is a major predictor of delinquency, but it is not likely to have an impact upon small children, who are still more closely tied to their parents.

Sampson and Laub proposed three main themes. *First, the impact of structural variables (e.g., poverty and family disruption) must be understood in relation to social process variables, namely those involved in social control.* Structural conditions do not directly cause antisocial behavior during childhood and adolescence. Instead, they are contextual factors that are mediated by social controls, namely that provided through the family—consistent discipline, monitoring, and attachment to family—and school—school performance and attachment to school. Also important are peer attachments, as type of peers (delinquent vs. non-delinquent) inhibit or promote delinquency. For example, low socio-economic status youth with low self-control may come into more conflict with parents and perform poorly at school, which inhibits attachment to parents, school, and conventional peers (which guides one toward delinquent peers). Weak family and school bonds and delinquent peer association, then, directly cause delinquency.

Second, when social bonds are weak, antisocial behavior is more likely to continue across adolescence (e.g., misconduct, delinquency, and temper tantrums) and into adulthood (e.g., substance abuse and crime). This behavior occurs in a variety of life domains, again, such as home, school, and work. Antisocial behavior itself helps bring about this continuity, as such behavior during adolescence may lead to weak social bonds, often in the form of poor educational achievement, employability, and romantic relationships. These kinds of weak adult bonds then increase the likelihood of offending. Thus, the consequences of offending itself can cause future offending, not just factors that existed before the initial offending.

Sampson and Laub take a dynamic view of persistent offending. They do not believe that early formed personality traits and behavior patterns alone determine adult offending; rather, these impact the immediate situational aspects that do determine continuity or desistance. Important here is the concept of *cumulative continuity* (also employed by Moffitt), or as Sampson and Laub termed it, **cumulative disadvantage**: a developmental process by which earlier antisocial behavior is met with sanctions that harm the offender's social bonds, which in turn reduces one's future legitimate opportunities. For example, young adults whose early antisocial behavior got them into trouble at school and with juvenile justice authorities may not have developed the skills and social relationships needed to gain adequate employment and are thus more likely to turn to illegal means of subsistence. It is important to remember here that close bonds to mainstream society (e.g., family, school, and employment) provide benefits to individuals, and enable society's control over them.

Although social control differs by life stage, control in one stage shapes control experienced in subsequent stages. In other words, social control is **state-dependent**:

the nature of one's existence at one point depends upon its nature at prior points. For example, schools do not simply "take over" from parents as agents of control when their children begin school or advance into higher grades (e.g., from elementary to middle school or junior high). Rather, one's experiences with school influence depends largely on one's experiences with parental influence. Parents have a major impact upon what kinds of students their children become. Nurturing parents who model prosocial behavior are more likely to raise children with the social and academic skills needed to behave and perform well in school. Children who did not form prosocial bonds with their parents are less likely to bond well with teachers and other students. Going further, individuals who did not form strong school bonds, and did not perform well in school, are less able to find good jobs as adults (forming strong employment bonds).

Basically, social control and offending are reciprocally related (they impact each other) over the life course. For example, committing a delinquent act at one point in time may serve as an independent variable, causing a change in a social bond (weakening it), which is thus a dependent variable. This weakened social bond then becomes an independent variable, causing future offending—now a dependent variable. Still, this does not mean that poor social control experienced in an early stage "dooms" one to experience poor social control in each subsequent stage (to experience a fatalistic chain reaction throughout life). Rather, it is possible that significant experiences during stages or transitions significantly alter individuals' susceptibility to social control (Laub et al., 2011).

Sampson and Laub (2001) also incorporate labeling theory to explain how antisocial behavior results in diminished bonds and disadvantages. Authorities representing institutions of social control (e.g., parents, teachers, and bosses) regulate, or sanction, individuals' behavior, for example labeling persons who violate rules as deviant and punishing them for it. Serious sanctions may "knife-off" future opportunities for the sanctioned person. Take, for example, juveniles who are expelled from school for misbehavior. While away from school, the school now has little or no ability to control them, and they are missing out on opportunities to develop academic and social skills that will be needed later in life (e.g., to work). Excluded from conventional life as a student, a juvenile then becomes more likely to engage in delinquency, which will be met with punitive justice system sanctions. In short, antisocial behavior met with harsh sanctions "mortgage" the future of offenders.

In Sampson and Laub's (2001) cumulative disadvantage approach to labeling theory, *formal* social control becomes more relevant. The criminal justice system has much power in limiting the lives of late adolescent and adult offenders. Criminal justice labeling often results in major structural constraints upon offenders, including in other institutional settings. For example, "convicted offenders" or "ex-prisoners" often have trouble finding educational, employment, and housing opportunities. As discussed earlier, this denial of legitimate opportunities puts one at risk for committing future crime. Antisocial behavior, then, can have a "snowball effect." It initiates a chain reaction that makes future antisocial behavior more likely: sanction —> diminished bonds —> reduced opportunity —> more antisocial behavior —> sanction.... As this sequence is repeated over long periods of time, the offender becomes increasingly alienated from mainstream society, cut-off from legitimate opportunities, and more likely to continue offending. In other words, as one's social disadvantages accumulate, one's stake in conformity decreases. Further, recalling the indirect effects of social structure upon development, these cumulative disadvantages and labeling effects are more severe among impoverished youth and adults.

Third, despite earlier childhood tendencies, adult family and employment social controls explain changes in offending, including desistence. Sampson and Laub suggest that "adult social bonds have a direct negative effect on adult criminal behavior, controlling for childhood delinquency" (Laub et al., 2011, p. 317). Thus, even chronic youth offenders are not "doomed" to become chronic adult offenders. (Perhaps changes in social control help explain the offenders categorized by Moffitt as low-level chronic or childhood limited.) Sampson and Laub's perspective on criminal careers thus places emphasis on individual-environment interactions over time and the potential for change in human trajectories.

Again, while a large portion of crime is committed by adolescents, most adolescent offenders desist by early adulthood. The eventual liberation from parental control during later adolescence helps explain why so much offending takes place during adolescence—youth are freer to commit behaviors that were previously too difficult to perform, and associate with deviant peers. During late adolescence, the bonds that fostered control and conformity during childhood are weakened and forever changed (which may be necessary for the eventual transition to adulthood). In the transition to adulthood, however, most youth experience changes that increase their conventional social capital (beneficial social relations) and re-strengthen their bonds to society. For example, bonds with family take on a different form.

Just as they do with continuity, Sampson and Laub focus on the immediate situational aspects of a person's life to explain changes in offending into adulthood. Important here is the concept of **turning points**: major changes to individuals' life-course trajectories. These include experiences such as military service, employment, and marriage. Turning points are often generated by life course transitions, such as from adolescence to young adulthood, a time in which persons are expected to do things such as go to college or get a job. Turning points can serve to cut off the impact of the past upon the present. They potentially foster new relationships and social support, sources of supervision and control, conventional daily routines, and identity changes. Thus, "turning points may modify trajectories in ways that cannot be predicted from earlier events" (Laub et al., 2011, p. 314). This also means that a non-offender can become an offender, if a turning point serves to weaken social bonds. These may include negative experiences such as losses of loved ones, romantic partners, or employment.

Some of Sampson and Laub's research shows that chronic youth offenders may indeed desist from criminal offending in early adulthood. These individuals do not necessarily change dramatically (problems such as low self-control do not suddenly disappear), but their circumstances do. Provided one can attain them, good jobs, supportive romantic relationships, and other opportunities may steer chronic offenders toward conformity. Major adult-stage social control institutions such as marriage, employment, and the military may be effective at preventing offending even if child-stage controls were not. Thus, Sampson and Laub hypothesize that even among adults with long histories of offending, the stronger their ties to family, work, or other important institutions, the less crime they will commit. The question is: How is it that someone who has not been amenable to social control in the past now exhibits manageable behavior? Theoretically, one somehow finds new opportunities to form prosocial bonds and acquires a stake in conformity that may not have previously existed.

Youth with persistent personality and behavior problems are not necessarily void of any desire to obtain conventional goals, or any abilities to care for others and make practical decisions in one's own best interests (most are not "psychopaths"). A person with a past of chronic offending may realize that the benefits of good romantic relationships (e.g., emotional and material support, intimacy, a strong social network) and jobs (mainly income, but also benefits such as a boost to social networks and self-esteem) will become unavailable if one continues to offend and may thus become disinclined to do so. Some may continue to struggle with problems such as substance use, anger management, and non-illegal forms of socially unacceptable behavior, but criminal offending itself becomes less likely.

To the above three themes, Sampson and Laub added that situational context, represented by the extent to which individuals engage in structured *routine activities* (one's normal, regular behaviors, e.g., daily or weekly), and individuals' choices of actions—purposeful *human agency*—interact with social control and structural conditions (and with each other) to determine continuity or change in offending into adulthood. Thus, independent of background factors and past behavior, "Weak informal social controls, minimal structured routine activities, and human agency explain persistence" while "strong informal social control, highly structured routine activities, and human agency explain desistance" (Laub et al., 2011, p. 322).

The effect of social controls on offending is conditioned by how relatively structured or unstructured a person's routine activities are over the life course. Structured routine activities also modify the choices available to a person, typically limiting opportunities for deviance and facilitating opportunities for conventional activities (e.g., working—especially with prosocial co-workers, working at home, caring for children, and organized recreational and fitness activities). Too much idle time and unstructured socializing (i.e., hanging out) will fail to suppress deviance. Marriage, for example, has obligations (which often involve spending time with one's partner) that disrupt immediate causes of crime. This includes reducing idle time and leisure activities with peers (especially males), which might include risky behaviors like drinking and drug use. Of course, to reduce one's chances of offending, a romantic relationship must be, to a sufficient extent, mutually beneficial (a pretty good relationship). A partner who also behaves antisocially is not likely to administer effective social control, and an offender who is abusive or neglectful to one's partner is less likely to receive guidance and support from the relationship.

However, Sampson and Laub do not see the offender as a passive being in these processes. They recognize the role of human agency—individuals' abilities to impact their environments and circumstances. Individuals, of course, make choices, and these choices play a causal role in determining the circumstances that make one more, or less, likely to offend in the future. There is a reciprocal relationship, then, between individual choice and one's social structural context: "structures are in part determined by individual choices, and in turn structures constrain individual choices" (Laub et al., 2011, p. 323).

The most obvious choice would be whether to continue offending, and some offenders make conscious choices to continue (perhaps because of the perceived rewards of crime). One may also insist upon quitting, but desisters do not necessarily make an initial choice to quit. Other choices may lead them on a path to desistence. Choices indirectly related to future offending include those to become more involved in education, employment, and interpersonal relationships. In time, one might "find oneself in a situation" in which one no longer wants to offend, as doing so risks new investments made in these areas. Thus, desistence can be a process more than an event. However, human agency interacts with social control and support; a person with intent to desist is more likely to do so if one has strong social bonds. After all, individual choice is situated within structural constraints (we cannot do anything we want), and by other intra-individual forces such as motivation. Bonds with conventional others and institutions both compel individuals to avoid offending and enable them to choose alternative behaviors (Laub et al., 2011).

Thornberry & Krohn's Interactional Theory of Delinquency

Thornberry and Krohn (2005) also offer a theory that explains both continuity and change in offending. First, the theorists do not find that offenders can be placed into simple categories such as those who start early and persist into adulthood versus those who start late and desist by early adulthood. They point out that "early starters" can begin offending at different times, as can "late starters." It is more accurate to speak of onset in relative terms: *earlier* or *later*. They also point out that while the two are correlated, age of onset does not always predict length of persistence (or age of desistence). Thus, a juvenile could be an early starter but also an early desister, or a late starter but also a late desister. More specific patterns of offending between onset and desistence can also vary. For example, some persistent offenders may, as stated by other theorists, offend intermittingly ("on and off again"), and adolescent-limited offenders may offend frequently during their short careers.

Interactional theory has three fundamental principles. First, delinquency is a behavioral trajectory subject to *life-course influences*. Causes of delinquency vary according to life stages; the mix of causes present during one stage is not necessarily the same as in other stages. However, current causes may be linked to past causes, as success or failure in past development stages impact the success or failure in future stages. For example, prior antisocial behavior has major developmental consequences, impacting later states and behaviors.

Thus, secondly, there is *bidirectional causality* between delinquency and many of its causes (and between legal behavior and its causes). It is important to remember that delinquency is also an "independent variable"—it has a causal impact on other things. Both prosocial and antisocial behavior patterns result from interactions between a person and one's environment, not just the environment acting upon the person. Delinquent acts may result in or worsen later events or conditions which themselves cause more delinquency. For example, delinquent peer association may cause someone to commit delinquency, which then distances one further from prosocial peers and deepens association with delinquent peers. The social interactions resulting from antisocial behavior impact future opportunities and reduce important "life chances" (e.g., of educational and employment success). In short, delinquent careers are sequences of "mutually reinforcing causal loops." Also important is that these interactional processes are embedded in (produced by and related to) social structural factors such as class, race, and neighborhood.

The third principle is *proportionality of cause and effect*. Crime has multiple causes, but not all factors need to be activated to produce it. What matters is the magnitude of the **causal force** of a set of factors, which varies across individuals. Causal force is determined by the strength or potency of each factor, the number of factors in the environment, the accumulation of factors weighted by each one's strength or level, and the presence of offsetting assets (protective factors). Thus, delinquency is more likely when juveniles experience several strong delinquency-producing factors and few or no delinquency-reducing factors. Further, as the magnitude of the causal force increases, the likelihood and magnitude of the effect increases—here, the likelihood and severity of involvement in crime. Crime severity has many dimensions in addition to seriousness and frequency, including onset, persistence, and changes in offending.

The onset of antisocial behavior may occur in one of four broad developmental stages: preschool years, childhood, adolescence, and late adolescence/early adulthood. Instead of sharply defined stages, these are "areas or regions of the more gradual, continuous process of human development" (Thornberry & Krohn, 2005, p. 189). As other life course/developmental theorists argue, children who initiate serious antisocial behavior during the preschool years often experience problematic individual characteristics (some inborn), ineffective parenting, and low socio-economic status. These children are most likely to persist in offending. Ineffective parents lack in their abilities to monitor children's behavior, reward good behavior, punish bad behavior, provide guidance, and help children develop problem-solving skills. Thornberry and Krohn (2005, p. 190) wrote: "Parenting deficits include low affective ties and involvement with the child, explosive physical disciplinary styles, frequent irritable exchanges, poor teaching and problem-solving strategies, and inconsistent standard setting."

Keeping with the principle of bidirectional causality, the child's individual-level problems (e.g., negative emotionality, poor regulation of emotions, impulsiveness, and greater fearlessness) become reciprocally causal with the parent's ineffective style. Each worsens each other over time. A child with poor temperament is difficult to handle, but more so for a parent with poor parenting abilities. The parent may respond by becoming even more hostile toward the child. The situation of dealing with a difficult child thus makes one's ineffective parenting worse. Consequently, this ineffectiveness more potently damages the child's development, as the child meets the parent's hostility with hostility. Being cared for by a highly ineffective parent makes a child's problematic individual traits and behavior worse. If this "back and forth" causal exchange continues over time, the child's and the parent's problems become progressively worse. It may be no wonder then that the child, as an adolescent, has several major personal and social deficiencies, and thus engages in serious delinquency.

Again, as other life course/developmental theorists argue, the difficult child-ineffective parenting interaction just described tends to occur in problematic social structural contexts. It may be tempting to simply blame delinquency on parents and their children, but developing and administering effective parenting techniques—and, for children, growing up well—is difficult in environments characterized by poverty, social and physical disorganization, racial and other forms of discrimination, and other problems. Under these conditions, there is higher stress, which interferes with parenting, and fewer social and material resources that can be used to support parenting. Also, some research shows that children born into disadvantaged environments are more likely to have neuropsychological problems. In short, early onset is most likely to occur when the causal force behind antisocial behavior is extremely high—when social adversity, difficult temperament, and ineffective parenting intensely interact.

Compared to the preschool years, more youth initiate antisocial behavior in the childhood years (about ages 6–12), especially toward later childhood. This later onset may be due to the "uncoupling" of the three types of factors that produce preschool onset, which presents a weaker causal force for antisocial behavior. For example, a child may have been born with a positive temperament but has ineffective parents and lives in a disadvantaged neighborhood. Because of the child's temperament, their behavior may be manageable during the preschool years. However, as the child gets older, and has deeper contact with school and peers, the lack of guidance and instruction from parents may lead to misbehavior at school and rejection by prosocial peers and association with antisocial peers. The child will have difficulty forming strong social bonds. Social disadvantage may create blocked opportunities and anger or frustration (strain) that motivate offending. Also, as the child gets closer to adolescence, one becomes more exposed to delinquent opportunities such as a gang and drug involvement.

A child could also be born with poor temperament but into a strong household with effective parents. Effective parenting may manage the behavior of the child at home, but again, as the child ages, their poor temperamental qualities may lead to behavioral problems when interacting with school authorities and peers. Thornberry and Krohn believe that environmental qualities, especially impoverished and disorganized families and neighborhoods, not temperamental qualities, cause childhood onset of antisocial behavior. Exactly when onset occurs during the childhood years, earlier or later, depends on the strength and number of deficits (ineffective parenting, weak social bonds, and deviant opportunities). Stronger deficits will bring about earlier childhood onset. However, weaker deficits (e.g., if prosocial bonding increases and deviant opportunities decrease), will tend to delay onset until late childhood or even adolescence.

As stated earlier, most onset of offending begins in early to mid-adolescence. Adolescent starters typically have not experienced the extreme, interwoven causal forces described thus far. They were not likely born with poor temperament, nor were they likely to be raised in severely disorganized neighborhoods by highly ineffective parents. (Even if one grew up in a "bad neighborhood," one may not be very likely to initiate offending early if one also had a positive temperament and effective parents.) Still, children's characteristics and behavior, parenting styles, and environmental factors also interact to produce adolescent-onset offending. However, these causal forces are weaker, and their source is unique to the stage of adolescence. As argued by other theorists, adolescent offending may be a consequence of puberty and the tension between (1) the expectation that teenagers begin the transition to adulthood by becoming more autonomous and independent and (2) the need for further guidance and support from parents and other adults (e.g., teachers).

Child, parent, and environment factors also remain mutually causal during adolescence, including that adolescents' traits and behavior influence their parents' current style of parenting. (To some extent, children socialize their parents, not just vice versa.) For example, some parents who were effective at supervising young children may respond to their teenagers' demands for increased freedom by decreasing supervision (perhaps too much). With more freedom, and more capabilities from physical and cognitive maturation, teenagers spend more time around peers and in environments outside of the home and school (e.g., shopping centers, public areas, or parties). This increased mobility presents new opportunities, including to engage in substance use and other (usually minor) delinquent acts. These problems might be faced more by socially disadvantaged families, who lack resources to provide their teenagers with prosocial alternative activities, namely those that cost money (e.g., recreational and personal development programs).

For a small group, onset begins in late adolescence (or early adulthood). It may be surprising that someone would make it through most of adolescence without offending and then begin, when others are starting to age out or have aged out. However, the causal force needed to produce offending may not have been strong enough until later. Late starters may have had deficits during childhood and/or adolescence, such as low intelligence and academic competence, that make them less able than their peers to build social capital. However, during childhood and most of adolescence, these deficits were offset by other aspects of their lives such as supportive, socially advantaged families and schools. These youths adapt to their deficiencies and may become amenable to the high degree of structure (support and control) provided by well-resourced environments. (With readily available conventional alternatives to deviance, and less desire to break away from adult control, these youths are not drawn into adolescent onset as much as their peers.) However, in emerging adulthood, when they are expected to become independent, their lack of personal abilities and social capital makes it difficult for them to secure employment, live independently and form new relationships, which places them under a great deal of stress. Also, losing the protection of the family and school leaves them more vulnerable to deviant peer influences and temptations such as drugs and alcohol.

Continuity and change in offending are explained in generally the same way as onset, through variations in interwoven crime causal factors and offsetting assets. Again, continuity in offending across the life course is most likely for early starters. This could be due to one of two developmental processes. First, the causal factors of onset and early offending remain stable. Personal, familial, and structural deficits that are numerous and strong enough to produce early onset are also more likely to remain stable in a person's life, and thereby also produce later offending. Second, antisocial behavior, especially the more serious forms, itself has cumulative developmental consequences that make future antisocial behavior more likely. Antisocial behavior often elicits coercive responses from parents, and as the behavior persists, so too do the coercive responses. This loop sustains a coercive behavioral style on the part of a child, which extends into other settings such as at school and with peers. By later childhood, such a child has formed weak bonds with parents, school, and prosocial peers—circumstances that may produce delinquent behavior, but also further deficits such as poor academic ability and employability that may produce offending during adolescence and adulthood. However, the later the onset of behavior during childhood, the less stable the causal factors and less severe the developmental consequences will be, which should shorten the duration of continuous offending.

Conversely, sets of causal factors that were not strong enough to produce early onset are less likely to be stable, and thus produce persistent offending. Also, the negative developmental effects of early serious antisocial behavior are not present. This explains why most "on-time" (during early to mid-adolescence) starters stop offending by early adulthood. However, there is a significant level of persistence in some adolescent-onset offenders. Some may begin in early adolescence and continue throughout adolescence and even well into early adulthood (e.g., mid-twenties). These youth experience more than the ordinary, temporary conflicts of adolescence, such as clashes with parents. Thornberry and Krohn believe that adolescent-onset persisters experience more profound reciprocal consequences of their offending and have deeper deviant peer association compared to adolescent-limited offenders. Some teenagers do not escape substance use and other offenses with minor consequences, especially when detected by school or justice authorities. More severe consequences make it difficult to finish high school well, go on to college or into employment, and form quality relationships with significant others—areas of success vital to avoid being drawn into crime. Also, with weakened ties to school, work, and prosocial others, one may drift further into relations with peers who encourage crime. In short, the causal force behind offending becomes more powerful for some adolescent starters.

Considering late-onset persistent offending, it is important to note that Thornberry and Krohn find the relationship between onset age and offending persistence to be U-shaped. That is, older onsets are associated with less persistence, until a certain point at which the reverse is true. Childhood starters tend to have shorter antisocial careers than preschool starters, and early adolescent starters tend to have shorter careers than childhood starters. However, although late adolescent or early adult starters began very late, they tend to engage in persistent offending. Again, late starters tend to have stable personal deficits that are camouflaged by strong pre-adult stage environments (namely family and school). Since they possess strong, persistent individual-level criminogenic factors, and lose the offsetting assets available to them in pre-adulthood, perhaps permanently, they are at risk of experiencing continuous economic, relationship, and substance use problems that sustain offending.

Finally, Thornberry and Krohn (2005) explain offending de-escalation and desistence with three developmental processes. *First*, for most youth, the strength of causal force behind offending is lower with older ages of onset. Causal factors associated with late onset are less numerous, extreme, interwoven, and stable over time, and thus diminish more quickly and easily. For example, parents with marginal but not absent job skills find better work, families move to somewhat better neighborhoods with better schools, parental stressors such as family conflict ease, and weakened but not severed bonds between children and parents improve. As the moderately strong causal force diminishes, desistence becomes more likely. As the environment changes, so too does an individual's behavior (regardless of age or age of onset). Again, youth who initiate offending closer to the normal period of onset may experience more environmental and less severe causal factors, many of which exist temporarily during adolescence. Thus, desistence is, in a sense, easier for late childhood through middle adolescent starters.

Second, some youth have major deficits that produce offending, but they are not intensely coupled with other types of causal factors. For example, a child may live in a distressed family and neighborhood but is intelligent and does well in school. In a sense, some youths' lives need less repair. The causal force they experience is enough to produce offending but is moderate. Thus, fewer offsetting assets are needed to produce desistence. Once they acquire these assets, like a high school or college degree and a good job, desistence becomes more likely. *Third*, when youth acquire protective assets, they are less harmed by the negative consequences of offending, and thus less likely to experience the amplified loop toward deeper involvement in offending. In other words, they are more resilient when confronted with the negative effects of labeling. For example, upon being punished, a teenager with strong academic abilities will be more likely to continue pursuing educational accomplishments, and thus acquire the abilities needed to make a successful transition to adulthood and stop offending.

Farrington's ICAP Theory

By the end of the prior chapter, it was probably clear that criminological theory (social theory in general, really) is very complicated. Employing a life course perspective probably makes it even more complicated. However, this is because crime causation, especially as it occurs over time, is very complicated. By now it should be clear that many things, and many different combinations of things, cause crime. Also, what causes an individual's offending "today" may not cause it "tomorrow." Farrington's Integrated Cognitive Antisocial Potential (ICAP) theory provides a nice framework for understanding how potential causes of crime work over the life course. This theory integrates ideas from multiple theories including strain, rational choice, learning, control, and labeling (Farrington, 2007).

At various points in life, individuals are exposed to several risk and protective factors associated with antisocial behavior. Some of these factors may remain throughout one's life, but the entire set of factors changes. To determine someone's potential for offending, we must identify and evaluate the factors presently at work in the person's life. These factors may be biological, individual (e.g., psychological), familial, peer, neighborhood, socio-economic, or situational. Protective factors may either increase the likelihood of prosocial behavior (e.g., prosocial peers) or interact with risk factors to diminish their effects (e.g., good parenting may alleviate the impact of biological problems). Assessing only risk factors is incomplete, as youth who experience multiple risk factors may not be very likely to offend because they also experience multiple protective factors. (It would be redundant to include measures of protective factors that are simply the linear opposite of risk factors). However, in general, the likelihood of engaging in antisocial behavior increases with the number of risk factors in a person's life.

The key construct in Farrington's theory is **antisocial potential**: the varying potential that individuals have to engage in criminal and other antisocial behavior. The degree of one's antisocial potential (AP) determines whether one offends (rather than any specific variable). Youth with very high AP are likely to offend. Youth with very low AP are unlikely to offend. Further, Farrington distinguishes between short-term and long-term AP. Short-term AP is determined by motivational and situational factors. Long-term AP is determined by impulsiveness, strain, behavioral modeling (e.g., by parents, siblings, and peers), attachment and socialization processes (e.g., parental warmth, reinforcement, and punishment) and transitional life events (e.g., marriage or loss of a partner), as well as interactions between these types of factors. Few people are high in long-term AP; they are the more serious, persistent offenders. In the population, overall levels of AP vary according to age and peak during the teenage years, because the factors within individuals that influence long-term AP change. For example, parental influence decreases while peer influence increases in the transition from childhood to adolescence.

Drawing from strain theory, Farrington sees desire for material goods, status among close peers, excitement, and sexual satisfaction as main *motivating factors* that could lead to long-term AP. However, this will only occur if youth habitually choose antisocial methods (e.g., violence, defiance, and theft) of satisfying these motivations. According to Farrington (2007, p. 38): "Antisocial methods tend to be chosen by people who find it difficult to satisfy their needs legitimately, such as people with low income, unemployed people, and those who fail at school." These methods also depend upon one's ability to use them, such as skill and physical capabilities (e.g., being old or big enough to do them, like stealing a car). However, whether someone will offend depends on the interaction between one's immediate AP level and the social environment, namely criminal opportunities and the availability of victims, which are shaped by one's routine activities. "Short-term energizing factors" (e.g., boredom, anger, intoxication, frustration, and male peer encouragement) can be at work in this interaction: "Encountering a tempting opportunity or victim may cause a short-term increase in AP, just as a short-term increase in AP may motivate a person to seek out criminal opportunities and victims" (Farrington, 2007, p. 39).

Even with opportunities, the translation of AP into actual antisocial behavior depends on how individuals cognitively process (perceive) their circumstances and make subjective rational-choice decisions. This includes considerations of costs and benefits, likelihood of getting caught, and ideas or information from prior experience (memory). However, since AP interacts with rational choice, persons low in AP are unlikely to offend even though it may seem rational to do so, while persons high in short-term AP often offend even though it is irrational to do so (e.g., becoming violent when angry or drunk). Further, through learning and labeling processes, the consequences of antisocial behavior may impact long-term AP, and individuals' future thoughts, decisions, and behavior. For example, AP will increase if the consequences of an antisocial act are rewarding but decrease if they are punishing. However, AP may increase if the punishment involves stigmatization that restricts future legitimate opportunities.

ICAP theory accounts for the possibility that different people commit offenses, even similar ones, because of different primary causes and reasons. For example, some youth may act violently because they have high violence potential, some may do so because they are in violent situations, some may do so because of short-term influences, and some may act violently due to how they perceive potentially violent situations and make decisions. Farrington (2007) believes that offender typologies are useful, but that people should be classified according to their most influential risk factors and important reasons for committing antisocial acts. The processes of AP development and interaction with cognitive and external factors operate differently at different ages. Thus, it should be noted that high AP differs from Gottfredson and Hirschi's concept of low self-control (covered in the last chapter). Low self-control is a life-course stable personality trait, whereas AP is a dynamic condition composed of individual and environmental factors. However, level of self-control could be included in one's overall antisocial potential (Carlsson & Sarnecki, 2016).

Box 5.1: Juvenile Sex Offenders: Adult Sex Offenders in the Making?

As life course and developmental criminologists point out, there is little specialization in offenses by juvenile offenders, other than that most restrict themselves to less serious offenses. Individual youth tend to commit multiple types of offenses (e.g., one may engage in drug use, vandalism, and petty theft). Thus, it would be inaccurate to label most juvenile offenders according to specific crime type. One who has committed an act of arson, for example, is not necessarily "an arsonist," as the offense could be non-typical of the child's general behavior. Or, one may commit both arson and other offenses frequently. Thus, most offender typologies (e.g., Moffitt's) are based on multi-dimensional patterns of offending, although they may recognize distinctions between violent/serious and nonviolent/minor offending. However, some juvenile offenders, while they may commit a variety of offenses, have a persistent, focal problem that warrants special attention. Thus, while it must be understood that inventing categories based on behavior does not itself *explain* the behavior, some crime specialization typologies have been created that describe and therefore help us understand certain forms of juvenile offending. One category of major concern is "the juvenile sex offender."

Sex offenders are often seen as unique types of offenders who are unlikely to stop offending. It may be assumed then that juvenile sex offenders (JSO) are destined to become adult sex offenders. A juvenile who has committed a sexual offense is statistically more likely to commit another sexual offense *in comparison to* an adolescent who has not. However, we must be careful with logic here. This does not mean that one who has committed a sexual offense *is likely* to commit another. Put another way, committing an offense is simply a risk factor for later offending. Thus, a juvenile could be at higher risk of offending compared to others, but still not have a very high chance of re-offending. Chances of re-offending vary across individuals and are also determined by many other factors.

Evidence thus far strongly suggests that most juveniles who commit a sexual offense do not become adult sex offenders. Some research even suggests that most JSOs commit only one sexual offense. Put another way, many if not most adult sex offenders did not sexually offend as juveniles. Most JSOs more closely resemble adolescent-limited rather than chronic offenders. Even many of those in the small group of persistent sexual offenders desist at some point. It is important here to recognize that JSOs are not all alike. "JSO" is a broad category containing diverse subgroups of offenders. For example, JSOs vary in the frequency, seriousness, and duration of their offenses as well as who they tend to victimize (e.g., if they target children). However, those who do continue sex offending into adulthood are more likely to repeat sexual offending (recidivate) during adulthood. The belief that "sex offenders never stop" may be an overgeneralization of this very small category of offenders.

Further, while adult sex offenders may tend to specialize in sex offending, it appears that most juvenile sex offenders commit a variety of other offenses as well. Most sex offenders are probably general offenders who have included one or a few sexual offenses in their offending pattern. JSOs tend to resemble juvenile *non-sexual* offenders (JNSO) in terms of background and risk vs. protective factors. It is possible, then, that much juvenile sex offending is caused by the same factors and processes that cause nonsexual offending. The motivation for sexual offenses committed by general offenders may not even be sexual in nature; it may have more to do with general antisocial tendencies (e.g., interest in harming others).

However, causes do not likely operate the same way in producing sexual and nonsexual offending. For example, earlier age of criminal onset, sexual abuse victimization, and some psychological disorders may be more strongly associated with sexual offending while minority race, antisocial peer association, and household violence and substance abuse may be more strongly associated with nonsexual offending. Further, it is possible that the causes of one's sexual offending are different from the causes of one's nonsexual offending. Also, JSOs may not follow the same developmental trajectories as JNSOs. The two may differ in their *patterns* of risk and offending over time. Interestingly, some studies suggest that JSOs experience fewer risk factors and are less likely to non-sexually re-offend compared to JNSOs. Thus, while there are similarities, there are also notable differences between JSOs and JNSOs.

People may also assume that virtually all sex offenders are male. Girls sexually offend much less than boys but more than what many may think, especially when considering non-violent or non-aggressive offenses and sexually problematic behaviors. There may also be lower detection of female sex offending. Because females are widely considered to be sexually harmless, victims may be less likely to report them, and authorities may be less likely to identify their offending. Criminologists too seem to have overlooked female sex offending, as there has been very little published research on it. Further, most of the research available is on adult female offending. However, the small body of research on female JSOs is informative.

The backgrounds and development of female and male JSOs appear to be similar in many ways. Both often have histories of victimization such as child abuse and neglect, dysfunctional families, school problems, inadequate social skills, psychological disorders, mental health problems, self-harm behaviors, and non-sexual offending. However, a major difference is that female JSOs seem to have experienced more, and more serious, abuse and neglect, especially sexual abuse. Their sexual victimization seems to begin at younger ages and more frequently involve penetration and multiple perpetrators, compared to male JSOs. Other differences are that female JSOs tend to commit sex offenses at younger ages and are more likely to commit a sex offense with a co-offender.

Finally, some studies find that female JSOs are more likely to victimize younger children, but their findings have been contradicted by other studies. (Findings that girls have younger victims than boys may not account for contexts such as caretaking—that girls are more likely than boys to babysit or otherwise be around young children.)

Sources: Beaudry-Cyr, M., Jennings, W. G., Zgoba, K. M., & Tewksbury, R. (2017). Examining the continuity of juvenile sex offending into adulthood and subsequent patterns of sex and general recidivism. *International Journal of Offender Therapy and Comparative Criminology, 61*(3), 251–268; Cale, J., Smallbone, S., Rayment-McHugh, S., & Dowling, C. (2016). Offense trajectories, the unfolding of sexual and non-sexual criminal activity, and sex offense characteristics of adolescent sex offenders. *Sexual Abuse, 28*(8), 791–812; Faniff, A. M., Schubert, C. A., Mulvey, E. P., Iselin, A. R., & Piquero, A. R. (2017). Risk and outcomes: Are adolescents charged with sex offenses different from other adolescent offenders? *Journal of Youth and Adolescence, 46*, 1394–1423; Fox, B. (2017). What makes a difference? Evaluating the key distinctions and predictors of sexual and non-sexual offending among male and female juvenile offenders. *Journal of Criminal Psychology, 7*(2), 134–150; Leroux, E. J., Pullman, L. E., Motayne, G., & Seto, M. C. (2016). Victim age and the generalist versus specialist distinction in adolescent sexual offending. *Sexual Abuse, 28*(2), 79–95; Lussier, P. (2017). Juvenile sex offending through a developmental life course criminology perspective: An agenda for policy and research. *Sexual Abuse, 29*(1), 51–80; Oliver, B. E., & Holmes, L. (2015). Female juvenile sexual offenders: Understanding who they are and possible steps that may prevent some girls from offending. *Journal of Child Sexual Abuse*, 24(6), 698–715.

History and Social Change

It would be short-sighted to think of antisocial behavior development as something that simply occurs in family or community settings. We must also consider it in the context of history and social change. As stated earlier, one major life course perspective principle is that causal processes occurring throughout an individual's life are influenced by the historical time-period in which one lives—what society is like at the time. Over time, major changes occur in how social institutions operate, and how people live their lives. Think, for example, of the impact that social media (e.g., Facebook, Twitter, Instagram) has had on culture and public life. Life before social media was much different. Major changes also occur in the ways that businesses and the government operate. Things like public opinion and social policies can even resemble a "pendulum swing" between dominant beliefs about what is good for society. For example, we may go back and forth over time in emphasizing rehabilitation versus punishment in corrections (e.g., favoring rehabilitation in the 1960s, then favoring punishment in the 1980s and 1990s, then after 2000 questioning laws and policies that lead to mass incarceration). The impact of events, circumstances, and personal choices upon someone's life course may depend on major shifts in macro-social conditions and governmental and economic policies and practices (Benson, 2013).

Many major social changes come in the form of state (political, governmental) actions. The state can impact individuals' offending trajectories in how they criminalize or de-criminalize behaviors through changes or variations in laws, social policies, enforcement activities, and punishments. Take, for example, the "war on drugs" that began the 1980s, which included harsher sanctions such as longer jail or prison sentences. Imagine a young person caught possessing a moderate amount of marijuana prior to the war on drugs, and what kind of trouble that person would have been in. Now imagine if that same person, at the same age, was caught during the height of the war on drugs. The magnitude of labeling and cumulative disadvantage effects one would experience would likely be higher during the later period (Benson, 2013).

Social policies and programs may also have an indirect effect on individuals' criminal trajectories, for example those impacting public needs in the areas of housing, transportation, health care, and education. These policies and programs impact many aspects of a person's life such as where one lives, goes to school, and works as well as one's overall health. For many people, these policies and programs regulate how much strain they experience from not having their needs met. Social disadvantages are considered in criminology not only as immediate causes of offending but also as important influences upon how an individual develops over time. History shows that governmental support for public welfare varies over time. How individuals' lives are affected by this support or lack thereof varies accordingly. For example, if the government decides to cut funding for social programs and increase funding for prisons, it decreases the state's capacity to help initiate prosocial behavior trajectories among disadvantaged children. At the same time, this increases the state's capacity to separate offenders from legitimate opportunities, potentially helping to sustain criminal careers (Benson, 2013).

Individual life courses are also influenced by social changes not engineered by the government. One example is the "maturity gap" discussed earlier (the gap between biological and psychological adulthood and social and legal adulthood created by the historical process of re-defining young adults as adolescents). Another includes changes in the "American family." Three major developments since World War II may impact crime trajectories. First, nonfamily households—those whose members are not related by birth, adoption, or marriage (e.g., roommates)—increased dramatically. Second, divorce rates increased sharply and then stabilized. Coupled with this change is that single-parent homes increased. Third, more young adults now wait longer to get married or never marry. These changes are not necessarily bad or disastrous. Delaying marriage until one finds the right person and time, for example, is a good thing. However, these changes do not have a positive or neutral effect on everyone.

These family developments have likely affected social bonding and control processes. Individuals in their early adult years, a life stage that is still associated with higher rates of offending (compared to older adults), who are living alone or with non-relative others due to moving away from parents or guardians, delaying marriage, or divorce are not exposed to the support and control usually offered by parents, spouses, or other family members. Thus, they are freer (not destined) to engage in deviance. Typically, someone like a roommate will not discourage deviance as much as a family member, although there are exceptions of course. (Some roommates offer better support and control than some family members.) Further, divorce makes it more difficult (but not impossible of course) for parents to bond with and control children. For example, divorced parents may find it difficult to spend enough time having fun with and supervising their children. These problems alone are not enough to make a person offend; they have more impact upon those who are at-risk for other reasons—chronic offenders who could use family or spousal encouragement to desist, for example (Benson, 2013).

Box 5.2: The War on Drugs

"The War on Drugs" refers to major policy and law enforcement efforts to control and criminalize the manufacture, distribution, and use of illicit drugs (Lassiter, 2015). In the U.S., the origins of this "war" can be traced back to the earlier twentieth century, but it became more formal in the 1980s under President Ronald Reagan. Changes included mandatory minimum sentences which increased the length of sentences for drug offenses and the use of incarceration for minor offenses (e.g., possession of relatively small amounts of marijuana) that previously earned community sanctions. These policies contributed heavily to the sharp increase of the prison population beginning in the 1980s. Records of various political lobbying and publicity campaigns reveal that these changes were fueled in large part by exaggerated dangers of drug use, particularly marijuana, myths about how drugs are manufactured and distributed, and the racially biased demonization of drug dealers and users.

The war on drugs was largely launched by political conservatives, but liberal politicians and activists representing poor urban minority communities also played a role. Their rhetoric complained that authorities were complacent about problems in these communities, for example, in detecting and punishing drug dealers. Hypothetically, if the police and courts were more aggressive in removing dangerous drug offenders, then these communities would improve. Thus, some liberal reformers joined with conservatives in creating legislation and policies that cracked down on drugs and drug-related crime in poor urban communities. Some participants in the war, then, may have been trying to help poor minority communities. However, the war may have been more about protecting the interests of middle-class suburbia. Much pressure for stricter drug policies came from activism focused on the welfare of suburban youth, although it sought to de-criminalize suburban drug offending—unlike that of poor urban youth (Lassiter, 2015).

While it has its advocates, and not all analysts are sharply critical of it, the War on Drugs is not widely seen as successful in improving society, for example in significantly reducing drug use and crime, ensuring proper and equitable punishment, and improving the health of individuals and communities. One might find some benefits in it, for example that it increases our ability to incapacitate serious violent drug offenders. However, most of the offenders "caught in the net" of changes to drug policy and law enforcement are relatively minor, non-violent offenders—those who do not typically pose major threats to community safety, and whose drug problems may not be solved by incarceration or other severe punishments.

Race and Ethnicity

How individuals experience social change varies according to many conditions, such as social status and geographic location. The roots of developmental differences between whites and racial or ethnic minorities seem to be in the differences in circumstances under which humans develop. The social changes and historical developments in law and public policy discussed above also negatively impacted the lives of disadvantaged racial and ethnic minorities.

To begin, the increased incarceration due to harsher drug polices was experienced the most by young African American males living in urban areas. Much evidence shows that drug crimes committed by poor minorities are punished more severely than those committed by middle-class whites. Also, transportation, housing, and economic development throughout the twentieth century had a profound detrimental effect upon American inner cities. Minorities were displaced by "urban renewal" programs at a higher rate compared to whites (lower income minorities could no longer live in the areas), interstate highways were built through the heart of low-income communities, housing discrimination was tolerated, and public housing projects were not allowed in well-to-do areas. These actions destroyed the social organization of lower income communities and led to a concentration of poor African Americans and Hispanics into highly disadvantaged areas. Being born into and growing up in these areas heavily impact children's development, and because of race and class segregation, youth of color face certain developmental challenges at a higher rate (Benson, 2013).

Box 5.3: A "War" on Minorities?

Much of the anti-drug rhetoric of the second half of the twentieth century presented poor urban minority drug dealers and users, namely African Americans and Latino/as, as dangerous criminals deserving of strict punishments. Their white suburban middle-class counterparts, on the other hand, were framed as troubled, otherwise law-abiding, youth in need of treatment—victims perhaps of "others" (e.g., non-whites, immigrants) who supply and tempt them with drugs. Correspondingly, poor urban communities of color were framed as bad places where drug and crime threats originate—where law enforcement crackdowns are needed—and middle-class suburban white communities were framed as good places in need of public health campaigns.

Racial disparities in sanctions for drug offenses led some analysts to argue that the U.S. criminal justice system and war on drugs were designed to maintain racial segregation: poor minority drug offenders are incarcerated and thus separated from middle-class white drug offenders who receive community sanctions. The 100-to-1 crack to powder cocaine sentencing disparity established by the Anti-Drug Abuse Act of 1986 is often presented as a case of institutionalized racial discrimination. This ratio meant, for example, that possessing only 5 grams of crack would trigger the same penalty as 500 grams of powder cocaine. By the late 1980s, crack became associated with the poor, black, inner city (although more recent research tends to show that the market for crack is mainly white), while the more expensive powder cocaine is associated more with middle-class whites (perhaps because they can better afford it).

Whether a deliberate attempt to maintain racial inequality, a misguided attempt to solve problems associated with drug use, or a combination of both, there is strong evidence of a racial double standard in how the war on drugs is "waged." For example, some research shows that while whites likely make up a majority of illegal drug dealers and users in the U.S., the majority of drug offenders in state prisons are African American or Latino/a. Also, despite that urban and suburban teenagers likely sell and use illegal drugs at equal rates, inner-city minorities are more likely to be arrested and incarcerated for these offenses. In short, drug law, policy, and enforcement practices seem to steer poor minority drug offenders toward jail and prison and middle-class white offenders away from them (Lassiter, 2015).

Deindustrialization beginning in the late 1970s made these matters worse. Some manufacturing jobs declined because of advances in technology and equipment (automation), but many were lost because large manufacturing corporations (e.g., steel, auto, and appliance makers) relocated operations overseas in search of cheaper labor, lower taxes, and less regulation. This change hurt U.S. labor workers in general but caused more harm to minority workers. Manufacturing plants are environmentally undesirable and tend to be located nearer lower income residential areas, such as inner cities. (Middle-class suburbs tend to be developed away from environmental hazards and have the resources to keep them away.) Along with a decline in manufacturing, jobs became more available in suburban areas, especially white-collar positions requiring advanced education. Labor jobs required training, but higher education degrees were not needed for most of them. Thus, jobs accessible to less educated inner-city residents disappeared. These jobs supported families and sustained communities. Also, now finding the community undesirable, wealthier residents moved out. Criminals and people with substance abuse and mental health problems then moved in. With poorer residents, small businesses failed or left, leading to further divestment in the community. Consequently, many residents turned to vice crime and violence as ways to make a living (Benson, 2013).

Hagan's Developmental Theory of Street Crime

Hagan (1997) developed a theory of social capital to explain the relationship between economic changes during the late twentieth century and minority street crime in the U.S. Hagan incorporates ideas from strain and social disorganization theories but goes further to explain *how* communities can become strained and disorganized, or more so. The context here is the change from the economic "golden age" (about 1954 to 1974)—which included employment growth, increased governmental support of public welfare, and reductions in social and economic inequality—to the slowdown, which brought about a reversal of these trends. This downward economic turn included national policies and processes of reduced investment in industry and public welfare—what Hagan termed "capital disinvestment." This disinvestment more adversely affected lower and working-class minorities, largely through losses of manufacturing jobs.

It is important here to understand different types of "capital." Hagan employs definitions developed by sociologist James S. Coleman. We may be used to thinking of capital as financial capital (money) or *physical capital*: tangible resources such as tools, equipment, and land that can be used to make money. However, there are less tangible yet important forms of capital that can be used for a variety of gains in life. To begin with, *human capital* refers to individual-level attributes such as knowledge, skills, and credentials, which are largely acquired through education and training, that enable persons to be productive and achieve goals. However, other forms of capital are social, not individual, attributes.

Social capital refers to resources embedded in social relations, which are thus possessed by collective entities such as groups, social networks, communities, or even cultures. It is the property of social structures, not individuals. However, individuals who belong to these collectivities may draw from these resources, such as social support (financial, emotional, or informational), to serve their purposes. Social capital is often used to increase human capital, using community resources to find educational opportunities for children, for example. Higher social capital is found in communities with strong social bonds. (Collective efficacy—the ability and willingness of the people of a community to help each other out, such as supervise and care for children, covered under social disorganization theory in Chapter 3—serves as an example of social capital.) The more access that individuals, groups, communities, and so on have to human, social, financial, and physical capital, the more they can accomplish in life.

Groups and individuals adapt themselves to the capital available in the settings in which they live. These adaptations are expressed through the formation of *cultural capital*. When social capital is abundantly available, these adaptations may include a higher portion of residents acquiring college degrees and increased participation in art, music, and heritage activities (e.g., museums and theatres). Children in the communities thus have access to cultural capital that increases their chances of attainment. However, disadvantaged communities—those lacking in social capital—are inhibited in forming cultural capital. Thus, when a community experiences a loss in social capital, its ability to form and maintain cultural capital is reduced. With less social and cultural capital, families are less able to provide their children with opportunities. In low-capital communities, survival is more of a struggle, and residents must adapt to the circumstances, including the reformation of capital.

Recapitalization is a process by which available resources are reorganized to attain goals. In disadvantaged areas, recapitalization may produce poor substitutes, but they may be the best available options for generating capital. Cultural capital in advantaged communities connects residents to the larger mainstream society, to its systems of norms/values, and to the advantages it affords. In other words, strong social and cultural capital enables individuals to become productive and successful in broadly conventional and desirable (e.g., legal) ways. The low social capital in disadvantaged communities does not promote adaptation in normative ways. Thus, capital in these areas is sometimes subcultural or even countercultural, in that they cultivate attitudes and behavior which contrast with mainstream norms and values. One possible form is **criminal capital**—that which centers on instrumental crime opportunities.

Community losses in capital result from **capital disinvestment**: a process by which forms of capital used to sustain valued human activities are reduced or eliminated. Capital disinvestment is "destructive of conventional forms of social and cultural capital" (Hagan, 1997, p. 296). Hagan identified three overlapping processes of capital disinvestment in communities of color. *First*, along with discriminatory housing and transportation policies and practices, the loss of manufacturing jobs limited minorities' residential mobility, thus making residential segregation more pronounced. *Sec-*

ond, along with a backlash against affirmative action policies and anti-discrimination laws, job losses increased racial inequality, for example by increasing the earnings and education gaps between African Americans and whites (Blacks became poorer and less educated relative to whites). *Third*, the higher job losses in poorer communities of color weakened their attachment to the labor force, which increased the concentration of poverty into them. Hagan uses Wacquant and Wilson's expression that the "traditional ghetto" of the earlier twentieth century was transformed into a "hyperghetto." These forms of disinvestment then increased motives to commit crime (e.g., by producing economic and psychological strain upon individuals) and decreased social control and conventional opportunities in poorer urban minority communities. Further, they indirectly increased criminal opportunities.

With these disinvestments, African American and Hispanic urban communities experienced a major reduction in social capital. As a result, individual residents had fewer communal resources from which they could draw to live productive, satisfying lives. Basically, residents were pressured to look for new ways to survive, which involves a search for new capital to replace the old. Some of the lost conventional social capital was replaced with criminal capital. This recapitalization further developed **deviant service industries**: organized economic structures for the sale of illegal goods and services, including those associated with "vice" such as drugs, sex services, and gambling. Disadvantaged minority neighborhoods may serve as "deviance service centers" where illegal goods and services may be bought. In short, when members of a community are not able to participate in legal labor markets, they are more likely to participate in illegal markets.

Lack of conventional sources of social and cultural capital (in the case of disinvestment, losses of capital) and the presence of criminal capital impact how children in disadvantaged communities develop across the life course. One problem is that the lack of jobs inhibits youth from making successful transitions from adolescence to adulthood. Many grow up believing that options such as going to college and getting a good job are unavailable to them. Low-paying, part-time service industry jobs (e.g., in fast food restaurants) may be available, but (right or wrong) disadvantaged youth driven by mainstream ideals of material success do not perceive them as viable options. However, opportunities presented by deviant service industries may be more available and appear attractive, and some youth choose them. For example, they may join gangs that participate in drug sales and other crime for profit.

As explained earlier, criminal behavior has consequences, especially when detected by authorities, that further separate offenders from conventional opportunities. For instance, lack of employment may steer one into offending, and then offending decreases one's chances of getting a good job. Criminal behavior and its punishment stand in the way of developing human capital (e.g., job skills and a clear criminal record) as well as social ties which connect individuals to conventional social capital (e.g., friendships with prosocial, employed peers). Over time, as one's employability decreases, one becomes more reliant upon and involved in crime. This is known as

criminal embeddedness, which is a source of criminal capital that offers short-term benefits but serves as a liability for conventional prospects. For example, one can make money by participating in the illegal drug economy (e.g., selling or delivering), but one risks dangers such as getting caught and labeled by justice authorities or injury from violent victimization.

Criminal embeddedness also works the same at the community level. For example, wealthier individuals from outside of the community may come in to purchase illegal goods and services, which brings more money into the community. However, establishing itself as a deviance service center, the community further distances itself from conventional opportunities. For example, businesses and educational, cultural, and recreational centers may not want to locate in or near places know to be centers for vice. Further, awareness of criminal enterprise in an area may draw law enforcement responses such as crackdowns. These may result in the arrest and incarceration of many residents who use crime to support families, putting the community under greater economic strain. These points may make it seem that disadvantaged communities of color are simply making a poor choice with criminal recapitalization. However, it is important to remember the context of disinvestment, and thus the bind that these communities are in. Major job losses and other social changes have severely limited their alternatives.

Hagan's (1997) theory may be summed up as follows. Macro-social changes such as deindustrialization (which creates large manufacturing job losses), reductions in public welfare programs, weakened anti-discrimination efforts, and divisive transportation projects create capital disinvestments which particularly harm vulnerable communities—namely less wealthy urban minority communities. These disinvestments impair conventional social and cultural capital at the community level (e.g., the ability to support local educational and cultural facilities and programs), which then leads to subcultural adaptations including illegal recapitalization efforts—the generation of criminal capital. With many fewer legitimate conventional opportunities, namely employment, and an increase in illegal economic opportunities, crime rates in disadvantaged urban minority communities increase. Further, as groups and individuals become more reliant upon crime for subsistence (more criminally embedded), and without external support to recapitalize in conventional ways, the community becomes more segregated from mainstream society and the conventional opportunities it offers. Thus, capital disinvestment also explains the *persistence* of high community crime rates.

Sex and Gender

How youth experience risk factors across the life course also differs according to sex and gender. Factors and processes range in their severity and impact. While boys and girls share many risks, some studies find that abuse, neglect, and mental health problems are stronger predictors of female offending, and that sexual abuse is a more common risk factor for girls (Carlsson & Sarnecki, 2016). Further, while few persistent offenders are female, some research finds that female offenders experience risk factors more severely compared to male offenders, including drug abuse and childhood risk factors such as poverty, parent alcohol abuse, parent mental health problems, and father's criminality. This suggests that it "takes more" (risk) to produce serious offending in females. Also, female offending may "cost more" in terms of social exclusion. Female offenders may be more stigmatized because crime violates cultural expectations regarding feminine behavior. Thus, while offending reduces men's and women's social inclusion opportunities such as employment and marriage or cohabitation with conventional partners, the effect may be stronger for women (Estrada & Nilsson, 2012).

Box 5.4: Becca, Laura, and Cindy

In one study, female prisoners in a maximum-security prison were interviewed about their childhood experiences. Three of these women were Becca, Laura, and Cindy (Bowles et al., 2012, pp. 683–684).

Becca divulged that she was sexually abused by her father; he "did things to her that shouldn't have been done." However, she did not appear to hold that against him, even later as an adult, because she found that "he still showed that he loved her." Her mother on the other hand was verbally abusive. The week before her eleventh birthday, Becca's father died. She overheard a phone conversation in which her mother was accused of killing him for the insurance money. After her father died, she felt that she died, and her life began a downward spiral. At age twelve, she began using a variety of drugs. At a young age, Becca had already reached a point in her life when she no longer felt that there was a reason to live.

Laura divulged that she was sexually abused by her stepfather and physically abused by her mother. She recalled one event in which her mother kicked and punched her and held her to the floor. Laura then punched her mother and ran to her room. Her mother almost kicked in her door and then told her that she could not leave; her mother made her stay there. Laura reported that she became an alcoholic at age fifteen. She was aware that her parents kept a liquor cabinet for guests. She found that being drunk made it easier to deal with her stepfather's sexual abuse.

Cindy divulged that she was physically abused by her mother. For discipline, her mother used broomsticks and drop cords and would strike her "upside the head" and punch her. Cindy reported getting beaten like this four days per week, and that she sometimes did not know what she was being punished for.

Source: Bowles, M. A., DeHart, D., & Webb, J. R. (2012). Family influences on female offenders' substance abuse: The role of adverse childhood events among incarcerated women. *Journal of Family Violence, 27*, 681–686.

Gender differences can be found in antisocial behavior trajectories. For example, male offenders seem more likely than female offenders to begin early and persist, while females seem more likely to be low-level offenders. They may also have different tendencies to engage in subtypes of behavior, such as violent and nonviolent offending. In a large sample of youth, Zheng and Cleveland (2013) identified four classes of offenders: low (little or no offending), desister (stopped offending), decliner (reduced offending), and chronic (persisted at high levels). The researchers compared males and females in each class and found the following differences. Females were more likely than males to be *low*-level offenders. *Desister* males reported more antisocial behavior than desister females. Also, desister females reported more nonviolent than violent offending in adolescence, whereas desister males reported more violent than nonviolent offending. *Decliner* males reported about equal amounts of violent and nonviolent offending, whereas decliner females primarily reported nonviolent offending. Only males were *chronic* offenders. This does not mean that females do not engage in persistent offending. They just may not do it at very high levels. For example, some may decline but persist. The researchers pointed out that some female decliners somewhat resembled the chronic group.

In another study using a large sample of youth, Salvatore and Markowitz (2014) found gender differences in the influences of social bonds upon offending patterns. Educational attachment was associated with decreased offending more for males than females. This may be due to bonds in other areas that may be stronger for females. Friendship bonds during earlier adolescence predicted offending for boys only, perhaps because girls tend to be more strongly bonded to parents during this time. However, parental attachment appeared to be equally important for males and females. Job satisfaction reduced offending during emerging adulthood for women but not men. Perhaps men are less likely to experience stable employment during emerging adulthood because they tend to take longer to complete education and find employment. Religious participation reduced offending earlier for men but eventually became a stronger predictor for women. In early adulthood, women may become more involved in religious activities and form stronger religious bonds, which may be connected to their increasing roles as caregivers in the family. Low self-control increased offending more for males, perhaps because external controls compensate for low self-control more in females.

Salvatore and Markowitz (2014) also found differences in the influences of turning points and economic factors. Interestingly, having a child reduced offending during emerging adulthood more for men. It is uncertain if this is true during later stages (eventually, the reverse may become true). Contrary to expectations, cohabitation *increased* offending, and more so for women. Perhaps cohabitation is a more causal bond than marriage and thus does not provide the same types and level of control and support. (Or, with whom one cohabitates may be the key variable here.) Marriage reduced offending during emerging adulthood more for men, consistent with the notion that marriage "works" more for men. Although it would seem to be too early, marriage during adolescence also decreased offending but only for females. Also, higher level of education achieved was associated with higher offending for boys but lower offending for girls during adolescence. These findings may have occurred because females tend to socially mature earlier. Increasing hours at work during adolescence increased male offending only, suggesting that working more may increase delinquent associations and opportunities for males but not females. However, economic stability and higher income in adulthood reduced offending, more so for women, perhaps because they are key in offsetting women's higher risk of poverty.

Finally, men and women likely differ in what typically makes them desist. For example, some research associates marriage with desistance much more among men than women. Female offenders might have more difficulty finding good partners—those who foster an environment that discourages offending. Other research suggests that wanted adult pregnancies and parenthood are associated with women's desistence. Recalling Sampson and Laub's arguments, having and raising children offers opportunities to develop new bonds, identities, and routines that are incompatible with offending. Parenting may also promote desistence for men, but since crime is inconsistent with femininity in terms of gender stereotypes, the cultural pressure to be a "good mom" may be stronger than it is to be a "good dad." Thus, mothers may have an increased stake in refraining from offending (Carlsson & Sarnecki, 2016).

Final Remarks

Benson (2013, p. 193) states the main points of the life course perspective well: "The shape of your life course is determined by *when* you are born, *where* you are born, who your parents are, *how* they treat you, and *who* you meet as you age," or in other words "by history, geography, genes, family environment, and other people." Benson adds that one's life course is also shaped by *luck*. Much of what happens in life is beyond our control. As Sampson and Laub (Laub et al., 2011) also point out, many significant life events are unpredictable. Often, things like meeting a good friend or romantic partner or being presented with a good job opportunity occur by happenstance. (It seems that some opportunities find us). Thus, chance may be one reason that turning points, including those which bring about changes in criminal offending, are experienced by some people but not others.

Summary Points

- Most offenders are adolescent limited; they are typically well behaved as children, begin to offend during adolescence, tend to commit less serious offenses, and stop offending when they gain the autonomy and assume the responsibilities of adulthood. Serious crime is more attributable to the small category of *life course persistent* offenders: those who engage in antisocial behavior as small children, start committing illegal behavior by early adolescence, tend to commit more serious offenses, and persist well into adulthood.
- *Reciprocal* or *bidirectional* causation is a key concept in life course/developmental criminology, as the effects of actions can become causes of future actions, especially in terms of antisocial behavior and its consequences. For example, committing a delinquent act can weaken one's bond with significant others (e.g., parents and teachers) and result in costly punishments (e.g., expulsion from school or being fired from a job), then these weakened bonds and opportunity-reducing punishments increase the chances that one will reoffend.
- An individual's offending is determined by one's present level of *risk*: a complex state determined by a multitude of inter-related factors, including those that inhibit offending (protective factors), with each factor varying in its potency from person to person. There are many possibilities with risk, including that a child experiences several risk factors (e.g., those associated with poverty) but still does not offend because one also experiences strong protective factors (e.g., good parents and friends).
- How a person begins and develops in life is determined not only by biological factors and family and community life, but also the historical period in which one lives, the nature of society at the time, and major social changes that occur.
- Although individuals from different backgrounds proceed through the life course in generally similar ways, how they experience events, stages, transitions, risk and protective factors, and behavioral consequences is shaped race, ethnicity, sex, and gender.

Key Terms

Adolescent-Limited Offenders: the largest category of criminal offenders: those who limit their offending to the peak years of adolescence.

Antisocial Potential (AP): the varying potential of individuals to engage in antisocial behavior, due to interacting sets of risk and protective factors, which determine whether one offends.

Capital Disinvestment: a process by which conventional forms of social capital used to sustain valued human activities are reduced or eliminated, such as those initiated by deindustrialization.

Causal Force: the magnitude of a set of factors that varies across individuals—determined by the strength of each factor, the number of factors in the environment, the accumulation of factors weighted by each one's strength or level, and the presence of protective factors.

Criminal Capital: social capital that centers on instrumental crime opportunities.

Criminal Embeddedness: a process by which an individual becomes more reliant upon criminal capital and crime opportunities to make a living and consequently less able to access conventional social capital and opportunities.

Cumulative Disadvantage: a developmental process by which earlier antisocial behavior is met with sanctions that harm the offender's social bonds, which in turn reduces one's future legitimate opportunities.

Deindustrialization: a heavy exit of manufacturing industry from an area that results in major job losses and damage to community support.

Deviant Service Industries: organized economic structures for the sale of illegal goods and services, including those associated with "vice," such as drugs, sex services, and gambling.

Low-Level Chronic or Childhood-Limited Offenders: a very small category of offenders who behave antisocially as young children, engage in low to moderate delinquency in later adolescence, and then significantly reduce their rate of offending in adulthood.

Life Course Persistent Offenders: the small category of criminal offenders who commit antisocial behavior during early childhood then offend during adolescence and into adulthood.

Recapitalization: a process, provoked by a loss of capital, in which available resources are collectively reorganized to attain goals.

Social Capital: resources available to individuals which are embedded in social relations and thus possessed by collective entities such as groups, social networks, communities, and cultures.

State-Dependent: a concept recognizing that the nature of one's existence at one point in time depends upon its nature at prior points in time.

Turning Points: major changes to individuals' life-course trajectories, often generated by transitions such as adolescence to adulthood (e.g., military service, employment, and marriage).

References

Benson, M. L. (2013). *Crime and the life course: An introduction.* Routledge.

Carlsson, C., & Sarnecki, J. (2016). *An introduction to life-course criminology.* SAGE.

Estrada, F., & Nilsson, A. (2012). Does it cost more to be a female offender? A life-course study of childhood circumstances, crime, drug abuse, and living conditions. *Feminist Criminology, 7*(3), 196–219.

Farrington, D. P. (2007). Origins of violent behavior over the life span. In D. J. Flannery, A. T. Vazsonyi, & I. D. Waldman (Eds.), *The Cambridge handbook of violent behavior and aggression* (pp. 19–48). Cambridge University Press.

Hagan, J. (1997). Crime and capitalization: Toward a developmental theory of street crime in America. In T. P. Thornberry (Ed.), *Developmental theories of crime and delinquency* (pp. 287–308). Transaction.

Lassiter, M. D. (2015). Impossible criminals: The suburban imperatives of America's war on drugs. *The Journal of American History, 102*(1), 126–140.

Laub, J. H., Sampson, R. J., & Sweeten, G. A. (2011). Assessing Sampson and Laub's life-course theory of crime. In F. T. Cullen, J. Wright, & K. Blevins (Eds.), *Taking stock: The status of criminological theory* (pp. 313–333). Transaction.

Moffitt, T. E. (2011). A review of research on the taxonomy of life-course persistent versus adolescence-limited antisocial behavior. In F. T. Cullen, J. Wright, & K. Blevins (Eds.), *Taking stock: The status of criminological theory* (pp. 277–311). Transaction.

Salvatore, C., & Markowitz, M. W. (2014). Do life course transitions and social bonds influence male and female offending differently? Gender contrasts and criminality. *Deviant Behavior, 35*(8), 628–653.

Sampson, R. J., & Laub, J. H. (2001). A life-course theory of cumulative disadvantage and the stability of delinquency. In A. Piquero & P. Mazerolle (Eds.), *Life-course criminology: Contemporary and classic readings* (pp. 146–169). Wadsworth.

Thornberry, T. P., & Krohn, M. D. (2005). Applying interactional theory to the explanation of continuity and change in antisocial behavior. In D. F. Farrington (Ed.), *Integrated developmental & life-course theories of offending*. Advances in criminological theory (Vol. 14, pp. 183–209). Transaction.

Zheng, Y., & Cleveland, H. H. (2013). Identifying gender-specific developmental trajectories of nonviolent and violent delinquency from adolescence to adulthood. *Journal of Adolescence, 36*, 371–381.

Chapter 6

Informal Social Control

Chapter Learning Objectives

Students will be able to:

- Classify social control of individuals' behavior by social institutional context
- Summarize arguments on how family structure and parenting practices impact offending
- Summarize arguments on how religious organizations and practices impact offending
- Summarize arguments on how school structure and educational practices impact offending
- Deconstruct one's biases concerning proper child development
- Reflect on one's progress in understanding institutional social control

---

Social Institutions and Social Control

It is important to avoid assuming that preventing and reducing crime and delinquency is mostly the job of the criminal and juvenile justice system. Simply speaking, the responsibility falls upon society as a whole, with all of its social systems or institutions. In fact, the justice system may not be the most effective at regulating antisocial behavior. The justice system is unavoidably reactive; it usually responds to individuals after they have committed, or are suspected of committing, harmful acts. There are exceptions of course, such as when police conduct general safety patrols or collaborate with the community in prevention programs (e.g., D.A.R.E.). While the subject of this book is delinquency and formal social control—that of the juvenile justice system—it is important to acknowledge the other main institutions of social control, as the juvenile justice system is expected to function cooperatively with these other institutions, and in some cases, pick up where they have failed.

As described in Chapter 3's discussion of social control theory, **social control** refers to processes by which the behavior of the people of a society is regulated or sanctioned. Social control includes both mechanisms for ensuring conformity (adherence to norms and values) and responding to deviant behavior. These processes operate at multiple social levels, such as nationally or locally in communities and groups. This control is brought about by processes of socialization (instilling values, beliefs, attitudes, and habits in individuals), attachment (e.g., close bonds with parents and teachers), supervision and monitoring (e.g., watching children at home and school, and police patrol), and behavioral sanctions (e.g., rewards for normative behavior and punishments for deviant behavior). Social control takes place within social institutional contexts.

A **social institution** is a macro-social structure developed within a society to meet social needs. It is a complex network of interdependent positions (e.g., student, teacher, staff, and administrator in education) that perform social roles (e.g., teaching, learning, management) that reproduces itself over time. Social institutions shape the behavior of groups and individuals within it (Conley, 2017). They also contain systems of norms and values, which produce general tendencies for people of a society to behave in similar ways (patterns). For example, students are expected to study hard and perform well on tests and assignments, and teachers are expected to create challenging tests and assignments and grade them according to high standards. Examples of social institutions are the economy, the family, education, religion, medicine, the media, and the criminal justice system. This chapter addresses *institutions of social control*: those important to the regulation of individuals' behavior.

Social science distinguishes between two general types of social control. First, **informal social control** refers to control administered, often spontaneously, in everyday institutional life, such as at home, school, work, a place of religious worship, and a neighborhood. Examples of informal sanctioning include: a parent grounding a child for not doing homework or taking the child out to dinner for good grades; a teacher making a child stay in for recess for disrupting class or putting a happy face sticker on an assignment done well; and a neighbor yelling at a child for trespassing or paying the child well for taking care of the lawn. Informal control is particularly relevant to the functioning of institutions developed to meet a variety of social needs, a major one being the regulation of behavior. Regarding the control of delinquency, the family, education, and religion are major *informal social control institutions*. Work is also important to crime control but more so for adults. Knowing right from wrong and behaving accordingly are, of course, very important matters in these environments. Institutions such as the economy and media are usually not considered to be those of social control, as controlling deviant behavior is not one of their major functions. (This is not to say that they do *nothing* to regulate behavior.)

Formal social control refers to control administered procedurally by authorities in formal organizational settings such as the military, employment, school, and government. The formal authority most responsible for crime control is the government-based criminal justice system—a social institution designed purposely and primarily for the prevention and punishment of prohibited behavior. (Schools are also very involved in the formal control of misbehavior, but since their focus extends well beyond illegal behavior, criminology focuses more on education's capacity for informal social control.)

Criminal justice control is formal in that prohibited acts are coded as law, and most sanctions for committing them are guided or mandated by law and policy and determined through complex legal processes. For example, in response to committing an act of theft, a person may be arrested, tried or allowed to plead guilty, and then sentenced to probation. The criminal justice system is thus a *formal social control institution*, which contains more distinct subsystems (or even smaller institutions in themselves) such as juvenile justice. Since juveniles are not supposed to be treated as "criminals," "criminal justice" is often used to refer to the part of the system experienced by adults only—an adult justice system.

Importantly, we must remember that social control involves socialization and social bonding (proactive, preventative behavior control processes), not just punishments and rewards for behavior (reactive processes). Agents of informal social control are more involved in socialization and bonding. For example, educators may most effectively control delinquency by providing children with the knowledge and skills needed to go on to college and work. The formal justice system, on the other hand, focuses more on behavioral sanctions, especially punishment. Of course, agents of formal control tend to administer formal sanctions whereas agents of informal social control tend to administer informal sanctions. In this context, "formal" and "informal" refer to the nature of a specific response to behavior, not the general type of social control. However, justice authorities may also administer informal sanctions, especially to low-risk offenders for minor violations. For example, instead of formally processing a child who has committed trespassing, a police officer may have a long talk with the child and then turn him/her over to parents. In fact, as will be discussed later in the chapter, what sets the juvenile justice system apart from the adult criminal justice system is juvenile justice's mission to be more involved in socialization and bonding processes and the use of informal sanctions.

In this chapter, three major institutions of informal social control—the family, education, and religion—are discussed, including problems of control. Juvenile justice as a formal institution of social control is discussed in the next chapter.

The Family

There is no universal definition of *a family*, but it can be thought of generally (especially for the purposes of this chapter) as a group of individuals related through blood or adoption, or bonded through marriage or other close partnership, that contain children and function as an economic unit. **The family** is the social institution initially and primarily responsible for raising children. During the first years of life, children are primarily exposed to parents or guardians and other close family members (e.g., siblings) before eventually "phasing" into other environments. Thus, usually, by the time youth become deeply involved in school, peer, and community relations, much of their development has already been shaped by the family. Ideally, the family prepares children to live independently, productively, and harmoniously within society—to re-

spect and care for others and behave in socially acceptable and beneficial ways. Later, other institutional environments will hopefully reinforce children's tendencies to live in this way.

In short, the family is most (not solely) responsible for producing law-abiding citizens. Since families, especially parents or other guardians, likely have the most influence upon children's behavior, the family may be the most important institution of social control. Parents and guardians are usually personally interested in their children's legal behavior, but they are also morally and legally obligated to society to make genuine efforts to keep their children from breaking the law. As will be discussed later, the juvenile justice system is expected to activate only when informal institutions, primarily the family, need assistance in controlling the behavior and protecting the well-being of minors.

While multiple social institutions impact criminal behavior, the family receives the most attention from criminologists, as delinquency is thought to be rooted in the family. Early childhood trajectories are initiated within the family. In the first years of life, when children undergo rapid biological changes, family members, especially parents or guardians, are primarily responsible for socializing children. Primary caregivers thus have a major impact upon how children develop from infancy. Caregivers are responsible for providing children with basic necessities (e.g., food, shelter, and clothing), emotional support, discipline, and instruction in many areas of life (Benson, 2013).

Problems in family functioning can establish antisocial trajectories, especially when they are combined with biological disorders in children. Parents who maltreat (abuse or neglect) or have hostile relationships with their children, engage in crime themselves, and are hostile toward each other are more likely to have children who engage in delinquency. This is not to say that parents are solely responsible for creating chronic offenders. For example, parents are affected by inborn biological problems (e.g., temperament) with children as well as the type of neighborhood in which they must raise their children (e.g., structurally disadvantaged). Young children who are highly affected by familial risk factors may be set on a path toward serious antisocial behavior and criminal offending. They are not destined to stay on this path; indeed, many high-risk young children with behavior problems do not advance into serious offending. However, it can be difficult to transition out of this path (Benson, 2013).

Families are never perfect in how they support and control their children. Even a "good parent" occasionally acts in a manner consistent with some of the problems just described. It is likely that family problems must be rather severe (high-impact, persistent) to cause delinquency. To varying degrees, then, family problems interfere with the development of cognitive, emotional, and behavioral abilities as well as prosocial bonds and conventional opportunities. Arthur (2007) described eight interconnected types of family factors that contribute to the development of antisocial behavior. Family problems should be viewed as a "web of causation," as they "are all specific expressions of a common underlying propensity to problem behaviour that contributes to a syndrome of antisocial behaviour that runs wider than offending" (p. 32).

To begin with, *inadequate parenting* may be generally defined as a lack of child-rearing skills and effective family management practices. Exactly what constitutes good or bad parenting can be a matter of opinion. Social scientists must define inadequate parenting as objectively as possible, with support from research. It may be helpful to think of what children need from parents and understand inadequate parenting as failing to act in ways that sufficiently meet these needs. In general, competent parents are extensively and productively involved in their children's lives. Those who offer inadequate parenting, in contrast, fail to sufficiently express warmth, give support, articulate rules and standards for behavior, administer logical and consistent discipline, and show interest in the child's activities and development.

Poor parental supervision refers to a lack of monitoring of children's activities and awareness of their whereabouts. It is often part of a more general inadequate parenting style, especially regarding enforcement of rules of conduct. Parents who provide lax supervision allow their children to become more of a danger to themselves and others (they are not around to stop bad things from happening), for example when they allow children to roam the streets, especially at night. Also, it cuts down on time that parents can use to teach and mentor their children. In low degrees, poor parental supervision can be seen as part of a permissive parenting style. In high degrees, it can be seen as abandonment. It may also constitute a type of neglect.

Family disruption, for the most part, refers to a separation of a primary caretaker from the home, often through divorce but sometimes through serious illness or death. Disrupted families are also known as "broken homes." Like "good parent," what is widely considered a "good home" is subject to opinion. Thus, it is also important to objectively and empirically identify problematic family structures and processes.

Social science lays no claim to an ideal family constellation. For example, a dual-parent home is not automatically superior to a single-parent home, especially when there are problems like child maltreatment in the dual-parent, but not single-parent, home. It is the relatively sudden change in a family's structure or functioning that causes problems. Disruption brings about several possible types of stress upon children and other family members including emotional distress (e.g., anger, depression, or anxiety), loss of income, and reduced capacity to supervise children. The more immediate causes of delinquency are unresolved problems created by disruption, such as family conflict and adverse changes in parenting practices, which may also exist in non-disrupted homes. Most families can recuperate from disruption (after all, most children of divorced parents do not go on to commit serious offending), but those which cannot have trouble fostering children's prosocial development.

Unstable living conditions for the most part refers to youth homelessness, including living in shelters or other temporary housing. This type of factor is likely the result of one or more of the other family factors. For example, many homeless youths run away to escape abuse or have strayed away in response to neglect. Living on the streets is dangerous of course, and youth are exposed to several pressures and temptations to engage in crime. Also, homeless youth lack the family and community supports needed to achieve success in adulthood, for example in the areas of education, employment, and interpersonal relationships. Youth housing assistance programs can help, but it is difficult for them to offer the same support as "a stable family."

Having *teenage parents* increases children's risk of delinquency and other problems, primarily because teenagers lack the experience, cognitive-emotional maturity, education, and resources needed to provide adequate parenting quality and a stable living environment. Also, the risk factors that led to teen pregnancy, such as economic disadvantages, are often the same as those for delinquency and will likely be experienced by the child. This is not to say that a teen parent is a bad one. Indeed, many teen parents become good parents, and most children of teen parents do not become persistent offenders. Again, parenting is more difficult for teen parents.

Parent and sibling criminality refers generally to criminal behavior committed by a parent or a sibling, usually to the knowledge of the child, but is often measured by whether the relative has a criminal record. The exact relationship between child and parent/sibling criminal behavior has varying possibilities. Plausibly, the offending relative may transmit pro-crime beliefs and values to the child through social learning. However, research has not established that children typically receive overt encouragement from their relatives' criminality. It may be more that criminal relatives do not do enough to discourage delinquency. Criminal parents are less likely than non-criminal parents to provide adequate parenting, and thus it is inadequate parenting that leads to their children's offending. Other possibilities include that child and relative are both exposed to the same risk factors, and a relative's incarceration, especially of one who provides financial or other support, places criminogenic stress upon the child and family.

Finally, family structure and processes are inhibited by the *effects of economic disadvantage*. As discussed earlier, poverty or underemployment and living in disadvantaged neighborhoods make successful child rearing and family management more difficult. Economic hardship limits the personal and social resources from which parents may draw to properly raise their children. For example, financial stress may reduce parents' abilities to offer emotional support, stimulating activities, supervision, and expressions of conventional beliefs and values. Also, parents' low-income backgrounds may have inhibited them from acquiring the education and skills needed to provide adequate parenting.

Lastly, *child abuse and neglect* (a.k.a. maltreatment) may also be part of an inadequate parenting style. Children tend not to emotionally attach to abusive and neglectful parents in a healthy way (e.g., with mutual love, respect, admiration, caring). **Child abuse** is not limited to physically assaultive behavior such as hitting. It can be emotional (or "psychological"), which often takes a verbal form (e.g., name-calling, insults, or belittling). Also, abuse can be sexual, which can be physical (some form of sexual assault) or emotional (e.g., sexually inappropriate communication and exposure to pornography). **Child neglect** is the failure to provide for a child's basic needs, which too can be physical or emotional. Examples are inadequate food, shelter, and clothing as well as withholding affection and failing to ensure that a child receives schooling. These forms often overlap. For example, being hit and yelled at can cause physical injury and send the message that one is not loved or valued. Also, child maltreatment may be committed by other relatives, including siblings, who have power or influence over a child, and children are also traumatized by witnessing family violence such as spousal or partner abuse.

Child maltreatment includes acts of punishment that are severely harsh or cruel, such as physical strikes that cause injury, verbal threats to one's safety, and withholding food for long periods. Research has found that harsh punishment predicts delinquency and other problems (Arthur, 2007). This may not be surprising, as it basically repeats that maltreatment is associated with antisocial behavior development. However, what about the use of physical punishment—corporal punishment—that does not cause physical injury or seem to be very harsh? What kind of impact does it have upon children's development and behavior?

Box 6.1: "Mike"

Reflecting on his days as a childcare worker at a residential treatment center for troubled youth, Professor Everette B. Penn discusses "Mike" (a pseudonym): "a 12-year-old African American boy with a very small frame but a very large braggadocios presentation" (p. 209). Mike boasted that he was better than anyone at fighting, dating girls or women, sports and other physical activities, and dancing. Outwardly, then, he appeared to have high self-esteem. Mike was in residential treatment for committing a delinquent act—under peer pressure, he stole items from a store—but also because he was neglected by parents and thus was in need of assistance.

In the program, family members could visit youth over the weekend. Sadly, unlike other residents, Mike never received visits from parents or other family members. Thus, weekends were a tough time for him. (Most youth look forward to the weekend.) One might wonder if Mike's expressions of bravado were used to cope with or hide feelings of loneliness and insecurity. With exposure to deviant peers, and no family support system, Professor Penn worried that Mike was on a path toward gang involvement and crime. He does not know how Mike turned out—hopefully for the better. A caring and supportive family (biological, adopted, foster, or otherwise) would have certainly helped.

Source: Penn, E. B. (2012). Working with minority youth in residential treatment. In L. M. Johnson (Ed.), *Experiencing corrections: From practitioner to professor* (pp. 199–212). SAGE Publications.

Corporal Punishment

Straus et al. (2014, p. 3) define **corporal punishment** as: "the use of physical force with the intention of causing a child to experience pain, but not injury." In contrast, **harsh corporal punishment** may be physical punishment used either with the intention to injure or without regard to injury (done with excessive force or recklessly). Acts of harsh corporal punishment often meet official and academic definitions of physical abuse. Corporal punishment, harsh or not, includes acts intended to correct behavior. It can be seen as an example of *instrumental violence*: attacks used to achieve a purpose through the inflicting of pain, not simply to inflict pain (i.e., pain is a means, not an end). Corporal punishment excludes acts which are strictly forms of *expressive violence*: those that are committed for the purpose of causing harm, often to release anger or frustration at someone. However, an act of violence can be both instrumental and expressive. Corporal punishment sometimes has an expressive element, for example when a parent is extremely angered by a child's repeated misbehavior and experiences a release of negative emotions upon spanking the child for the misbehavior.

Perhaps one can make the argument that physical punishment that "goes too far"—harsh corporal punishment—causes developmental problems leading to outcomes such as delinquency, but that non-harsh physical punishment, for example what we commonly call "spanking," does not. Perhaps spanking administered judiciously and sparingly by skilled, supportive parents is effective child-rearing. However, in their book, *The Primordial Violence: Spanking Children, Psychological Development, Violence, and Crime*, Straus and colleagues (2014) argue that even regular spanking harms child development. They base their conclusions about the effects of spanking on several years of their own research as well as a review of other studies.

First, we must understand how the researchers define spanking. *Spanking* is a more familiar, non-academic term for non-harsh corporal punishment. It is limited to socially acceptable actions, such as slaps or paddling on the buttocks or hand. Strikes on other parts of the body such as the face, and the use of instruments such as belts, may not be considered spanking because they seem crueler and dangerous, especially when delivered with strong force. Terms such as beat, hit, or smack are sometimes used synonymously with spank, but they also refer acts of harsh corporal punishment whereas spanking does not.

Spanking, then, does not refer to incidents meeting legal definitions of *physical abuse*. Although spankings can range in severity, and the line between spanking and abuse is often unclear, abuse is usually defined as an attack resulting in injury (e.g., a bruise). However, although many people do not consider spanking to be aggressive or socially unacceptable enough to be considered violent, Straus et al. (2014) argue that *spanking is a form of violence*. After all, spanking is physical contact delivered to cause pain—to hurt someone, even if mildly. (Perhaps much spanking is mild violence.) The researchers make the point that if acts of spanking were committed against adults, there is a good chance that they would be considered assaults. Also, how does spanking appear from the perspective of the child who receives it? Not only might it hurt considerably, it can be frightening. Violence is known for inflicting pain and fear.

Many parents believe that the infliction of physical pain is sometimes necessary to respond to child misbehavior that is repeated, dangerous (e.g., running into a street), or highly immoral (e.g., hitting someone)—that associating pain with the behavior is the most effective way to "teach a lesson." However, the lesson learned may be that it is okay to hit others when they do things we do not like. Research shows that children who are spanked are more likely to hit others and less likely to comply with parents' requests to behave properly. This could simply mean that some children are aggressive and continue to receive spankings for misbehavior (which might suggest the spankings do not work). However, Straus et al. (2014) found a "boomerang effect" (another term for reciprocal causation): children who received spankings for misbehavior engaged in above average levels of antisocial behavior after a two-year period, and antisocial behavior increased the more children were spanked. Further, those who were not spanked engaged in lower-than-average levels of antisocial behavior. Thus, children may first hit others or fail to comply with parents' requests, then receive spankings for it, but the spankings then make it more likely that the children will elevate their antisocial behavior in the future.

Further, these results were obtained controlling for the impact of factors thought to stipulate the conditions under which spanking is beneficial. Spanking increased antisocial behavior even among children with parents who provide high levels of emotional support and cognitive stimulation. The relationship also occurred among girls and racial minorities, although it was stronger for boys and white children. The relationship also held up regardless of child's age group (at the time of spanking: 3–5, 6–9, or 10+ years of age), which contradicts the popular belief that spanking is appropriate if limited to preschool age children. Straus et al.'s (2014) review found that several longitudinal studies conducted later found similar results. Again, research such as this shows that children are at risk of offending, *not that they will offend.* Thus, many children who are spanked will not engage in antisocial behavior because of it. However, spanking puts them in more danger of doing it.

Many people believe that spanking is appropriate if not done "out of anger," in other words, if not done impulsively—immediately upon becoming alarmed by the child's behavior. Some advocates recommend controlled spanking—calming down first and then spanking methodically and dispassionately (which might seem "cold" to some people). One concern is that impulsive spanking teaches children to be impulsive, and impulsivity is of course a characteristic associated with delinquency. When a parent spanks immediately while upset, it may appear to the child that it happens because of the nature of the parent, not of one's behavior (which may create resentment that interferes with bonding). It may also seem chaotic and confusing to the child. Straus et al. (2014) found that impulsive spanking does have a stronger impact upon antisocial and impulsive behavior, but that non-impulsive spanking still has an impact.

Another popular belief is that the effects of spanking are culturally relative. There is likely some truth to this, as the impact of spanking may be more severe for children raised in certain cultural contexts. However, a controversial assertion is that spanking is beneficial in certain cultural contexts. One example is the belief that spanking works within African American families, especially those in inner cities. Some claim that spanking is more embedded in African American tradition, which further legitimizes its use in the minds of parents and their children, and that spanking is needed to offset the increased crime risk factors present in disadvantaged neighborhoods. However, Straus et al. (2014) found that studies consistently show that spanking is associated with increased adult violence in African American as well as Hispanic samples.

The saying "spare the rod, spoil the child" is a sort of hypothesis. It predicts that children who do not receive corporal punishment for misbehavior are more likely to develop antisocial behavioral tendencies. Advocates of spanking do not just claim that it is harmless; they claim that it sustains or promotes good behavior. Straus et al. (2014) found that the opposite hypothesis is supported: children who were *never spanked* committed less antisocial behavior than those who were spanked. Remembering the problem of causal order, this could have occurred simply because children did not misbehave and thus receive spankings during the study period. However, the researchers detected that many non-spanked children did misbehave and likely received alternative disciplinary actions (e.g., sent to room, time-outs, or reparation tasks).

It may be easier to theoretically connect spanking with physically aggressive behavior in children, as spanking seems to model such behavior. However, spanking is associated with a variety of antisocial and risky behaviors that may not seem to follow from it, such as property crime and risky sexual behavior. This may occur because corporal punishment has indirect effects upon delinquency; it is associated with the development of problems that put youth at increased risk of delinquency. Straus et al. (2014) also found that spanking (1) weakens child-to-parent bonds, (2) lowers mental reasoning abilities, possibly through stress and more reliance on physical rather than verbal interaction with the child, (3) reduces one's chances of earning a college degree, possibly as a consequence of problems such as impulsivity and poor mental abilities, and (4) increases the chances of experiencing depression. These relationships occurred even when controlling for possible conditional factors such as parental nurturing, age of child, and type and frequency of spanking. These factors often had significant independent impacts but did not eliminate the impact of spanking. For example, parental emotional support decreased antisocial behavior and other problems, but negative outcomes of spanking were found even among children with nurturing parents. This, however, does mean that parental emotional support probably *competes with* spanking in producing behavior.

Straus et al. (2014) found that spanking was also associated with offending in adulthood. One adult outcome is violence against romantic partners or spouses. It may be difficult to theoretically link spanking with these outcomes as well, since their seriousness does not resemble that of spanking. However, again, spanking causes problems through developmental processes that include causal chains of mediating variables. Many processes are possible, but Straus et al. (2014) found research support for four. Three are that spanking: (1) "teaches that it is morally correct to hit to correct misbehavior" (a social learning process), which carries over to adult relationships, (2) "limits development of nonviolent conflict-resolution skills that results in a high level of conflict with partners," and (3) "increases the probability of depression, which in turn increases the probability of aggression" (pp. 170–171). The fourth is that spanking contributes to the development of a general antisocial personality—a trait associated with violent offending, including sexual coercion and assault.

Social scientists are usually tentative about making practice and policy recommendations, often to meet the expectation of being an objective researcher and/or to recognize the limitations of research. However, based on their interpretations of available research, Straus et al. (2014) take the firm position that spanking should not be used at all. To some people, it may seem odd to consider that spanking, even less severe forms, harms children's development and behavior. Spanking is very common. It is practiced in most countries throughout the world. In the U.S., it seems that many adults are critical of spanking, and its use seems to be in decline, but many still practice it at least occasionally (Straus et al., 2014). The value of spanking may seem to be common sense, assuming humans naturally seek to increase pleasure and reduce pain. It seems plausible that if children experience pain after behaving a certain way, especially multiple times, they will associate pain with the behavior and stop doing it. However, as life-course and developmental social and behavioral science shows, how humans respond to punishing circumstances is very complex and life-stage dependent.

The research and interpretations by Straus et al. (2014) are subject to the usual limitations and cautions regarding social scientific research. They of course have not "proven" that spanking is bad for children. They do however strongly support their argument. As always, it is up to the individual to decide if the researchers made a strong case. It should also be noted that they do not claim that spanking is as bad as severe abuse. Before one dismisses (or uncritically accepts) their argument, one should ponder answers to important questions such as: Why do parents spank, really, and who does it "help," really? Do parents tend to spank in a dispassionate, methodical way, with conscious well-meaning intent? Or do parents tend to spank because they are angry or frustrated with their children, and are lashing out at them as a release? (Is "this is going to hurt me more than it's going to hurt you" true?) Some parents may tend toward the former and some toward the latter, but it is difficult to believe that a parent who spanks never does so while angry or frustrated. So, we may wonder: Is spanking a good parenting technique or a poor approach to coping, problem solving, anger management, or conflict management?

Obviously, most children who experience corporal punishment do not grow up to engage in serious antisocial behavior. (However, this is true of children experiencing any single risk factor.) Many of us can relate to the statement: "I was spanked, and I turned out okay." Some might even credit their good character to being spanked and may express gratitude to their parents for doing it. However, to really understand the impact of spanking upon child development and adult behavior, we must be willing to question some of our deepest held assumptions and beliefs (including those of us who strictly oppose spanking).

First, just because spanking did not seem to harm some people, does this mean that it did not harm others? We must avoid making a generalization mistake in logical reasoning here: what is true of oneself or some people is often not true of many others. *Second*, do people who were spanked turn out okay *because of* or *despite* spanking? Remember the criteria for causation: just because something happened before something else, it does not necessarily mean that it caused it; something else that exists may have caused it. Parents who administer spanking often do several other things with and for their children, such as maintain consistent discipline, reward good behavior, meet basic needs, and act in warm, loving ways. Is it possible that the combination of these "other things," not spanking, made one develop in a healthy way? In other words, is spanking a risk factor that can be offset by a strong set of protective factors? *Third*, did one who was spanked really turn out "okay"? Is it possible that although spanking did not result in antisocial behavior such as crime, it resulted in other problems such as emotional problems, low educational and economic achievement, and strained relationships?

Box 6.2: Pennsylvania's Definition of Child Abuse

Pennsylvania Statute (23 Pa.C.S. 6303 b.1) defines *child abuse* as "intentionally, knowingly or recklessly doing any of the following:

1) Causing bodily injury to a child through any recent act or failure to act.
2) Fabricating, feigning or intentionally exaggerating or inducing a medical symptom or disease which results in a potentially harmful medical evaluation or treatment to the child through any recent act.

3) Causing or substantially contributing to serious mental injury to a child through any act or failure to act or a series of such acts or failures to act.
4) Causing sexual abuse or exploitation of a child through any act or failure to act.
5) Creating a reasonable likelihood of bodily injury to a child through any recent act or failure to act.
6) Creating a likelihood of sexual abuse or exploitation of a child through any recent act or failure to act.
7) Causing serious physical neglect of a child.
8) Engaging in any of the following recent acts:
   i. Kicking, biting, throwing, burning, stabbing or cutting a child in a manner that endangers the child.
   ii. Unreasonably restraining or confining a child, based on consideration of the method, location or the duration of the restraint or confinement.
   iii. Forcefully shaking a child under one year of age.
   iv. Forcefully slapping or otherwise striking a child under one year of age.
   v. Interfering with the breathing of a child.
   vi. Causing a child to be present at a location while a violation ... (relating to operation of methamphetamine laboratory) is occurring, provided that the violation is being investigated by law enforcement.
   vii. Leaving a child unsupervised with an individual, other than the child's parent, who the actor knows or reasonably should have known: (A) Is required to register as a Tier II or Tier III sexual offender ..., where the victim of the sexual offense was under 18 years of age when the crime was committed. (B) Has been determined to be a sexually violent predator ... (C) Has been determined to be a sexually violent delinquent child ...
9) Causing the death of the child through any act or failure to act.
10) Engaging a child in a severe form of trafficking in persons or sex trafficking ..."

Source: Pennsylvania General Assembly. (n.d.). *Section 6303.0—Title 23—Domestic Relations.* https://www.legis.state.pa.us/cfdocs/legis/li/consCheck.cfm?txtType=HTM&ttl=23&div=00.&chpt=063.&sctn=003.&subsctn=000

Using the Family to Reduce Delinquency

Considering the parenting and other family problems described above, it may be easy to see families as the source of the problem of delinquency. However, might we see them more as the solution to the problem, or at least a major part of the solution? If we can identify risk factors and useful resources during early childhood, can we work with families to prevent offending or re-offending? Perhaps strengthening families' abilities to provide informal social control yields better results than waiting until later to rely on formal juvenile justice system control.

Some research on interventions shows that strengthening family management and conflict resolution skills, children's opportunities for active involvement in the family, and parental reinforcement of children's prosocial behavior and improvement (e.g., at school) may strengthen at-risk children's bonds with their families (attachment and commitment) and reduce their tendency to offend later during adolescence and even early adulthood (Hawkins et al., 2012). Also, interventions such as parent education, parenting skill training, access to preschool or daycare, and home visits by nurses for expecting and new parents may reduce delinquency by improving children's cognitive abilities and school performance, as well as family well-being (e.g., reduced child maltreatment). Family-level education, training, and therapy can also be effective in reducing re-offending among system-involved youth (Welsh, 2012). Family-based interventions will be discussed in more detail in later chapters.

Education

Children also spend much time at school. **Education** is a formal system of transmitting the skills, knowledge, and values determined to be needed in a population to make a society function well. (Given the subject, the discussion here is limited to elementary through high schools, although post-secondary schools such as colleges and universities also perform social control functions.) To meet learning objectives, schools must regulate children's behavior. Schools do more than just teach academic material. Directly or indirectly, schools teach many of the same values and beliefs taught by families—those having to do with respecting authority, honesty, hard work, concern for others, becoming well-educated, and so on. Students who embrace these values and beliefs should be less likely to engage in antisocial behavior.

While parents "had them first," school authorities, namely teachers, acquire responsibility over children beginning at very young ages—from 4–6 in kindergarten, and earlier for preschool. Thus, schools begin to influence children while they are still quite "impressionable." Even as students get older, schools continue to influence them through rule enforcement, teaching and learning, role modeling, and availability of desired opportunities. While schools tend to play a secondary role to families, they are still major agents of socialization; they help shape what children become. It should seem clear then that schools play a major role in preventing delinquency, and in efforts to rehabilitate juvenile offenders (those who do better in school are less likely to reoffend).

Schools and the juvenile justice system respond to antisocial behavior in similar ways. Sometimes, like parents, school authorities spontaneously respond to misbehavior at their own discretion, such as with verbal admonishment and issuing small sanctions like time-outs and reflective assignments. However, compared to parents, teachers and other officials are guided or mandated more by policies and procedures to respond to serious misbehavior in prescribed ways. For example, criteria must be met before a student may be expelled, and corporal punishment is either prohibited or highly restricted. School sanctions can be very costly and stigmatizing. Thus, care must be taken in using them. Responses such as expulsion may even feel as severe as some justice system sanctions. Like juvenile authorities, educators are tasked with somehow responding to antisocial behavior in ways that do not damage children's futures but properly hold them accountable and maintain the safety of others.

As with families, it is important to strengthen schools' abilities to provide social control and support. In fact, development of prosocial behavior is more likely when the efforts of educators, such as teachers, and family members, especially parents, are mutually supportive, as when parents reinforce children's academic and other achievements at school. Some research on interventions shows that strengthening teachers' use of better methods of instruction and classroom management, children's opportunities for active involvement in the classroom, and teacher *and peer* reinforcement of children's prosocial behavior during elementary grades may improve at-risk children's academic performance and school bonds, thereby reducing their tendency to offend later during adolescence and adulthood. Hawkins et al. (2012, p. 180) believe that "improving opportunities and rewards at school and thereby strengthening children's bond of commitment and attachment to school" will make children "more likely to seek success in life by completing high school, furthering their education and finding gainful employment, and ... less likely to risk this success by engaging in delinquent or other problem behaviors." Without such interventions, many schools will be ill equipped to respond to root causes of delinquency.

School Problems and Delinquency

We often believe that if families do not function properly and parents "do not do their job," their children may engage in delinquency. We may also believe that if schools do not function properly and authorities (e.g., teachers) "do not do their jobs," their students will engage in delinquency. However, the functioning of schools is closely dependent upon and intertwined with other social systems such as family, community, and government. Thus, it is difficult to argue that school problems are *major root causes* of delinquency. It might be said that poor schools fail to stop delinquency more than cause it. Schools are largely reflections of the wider communities in which they exist (e.g., the type of neighborhood), and of course receive children after they have been primarily socialized within their families. Thus, if a child does poorly in school, one may not be able to determine if this is because the school, family, community, or government failed the child. In some cases, all can be responsible. (Lack of government funding leaves schools in disadvantaged communities without enough resources to meet the needs of children who live in disorganized homes and neighborhoods.) To help children develop intellectually and socially, schools must overcome major external problems such as those associated with funding and other resources, communal support and cooperation, diverse student needs (e.g., disabilities and learning deficits), and social inequality.

Some research finds that school characteristics—various aspects of organization and social climate—may directly or indirectly impact delinquency among students. These include communication patterns, role relationships and perceptions, sets of behavioral norms, reward structures, student and faculty morale, discipline (clarity, fairness, and consistency in enforcement of rules), collective student attachment to school, levels of supportive relationships, extent to which common goals are embraced, percentage of certified teachers, and student-to-staff ratio (Kim, 2016; Limbos & Casteel, 2008; Lowe et al., 2008). However, these factors may not be as strong as neighborhood-level factors, and some school characteristics are influenced by neighborhood characteristics (Kim, 2016).

Further, the nature of mass schooling itself presents some challenges. Schools offer several important opportunities for students to grow and engage in conventional activities. However, since they bring several juveniles together into an environment in which they dominate in numbers, schools also have the potential to increase opportunities to engage in deviant behavior. For example, students may obtain drugs from other students. Youth Risk Behavior Survey (YRBS) data show that in 2015, 22% of high school students in the U.S. reported that an illegal drug was offered, sold, or given to them on school property in the past 12 months, although this was down from 32% in 1995.

Still, some research finds that schools can influence delinquency independently from neighborhood factors, including that schools counter the negative impacts of wider social disadvantages. One study found, in a sample of primarily African American and Hispanic students at public urban middle schools, that incidence of delinquency and drug use were lower among students at schools that delivered "value-added education"—better than expected student academic achievement and attendance—after controlling for individual, home, and community factors (Tobler et al., 2011). These results make sense considering that youth who perform well at school are less likely to offend. Efforts to improve attendance, curriculum development, and teaching practices are essential for improving learning outcomes, but at the same time seem to be promising strategies for reducing delinquency and other risky behaviors.

If not remedied, early poor academic performance and behavior problems at school may have developmental effects resulting in serious educational deficits, including failure to finish high school. An important mediating factor here is suspension, which disrupts students' abilities to engage in learning activities and proceed to graduation. Those who fail to finish high school are at high risk of engaging in serious offending and becoming imprisoned. The pathway from school problems to imprisonment facilitated by school policies and practices has become known as the **school-to-prison pipeline**, which is a problem experienced more by youth of color in economically disadvantaged homes and communities. The concern here is that punitive responses such as suspension help push at-risk youth out of school and toward justice system involvement (May & Stokes, 2014).

School authorities experience dilemmas in responding to student misbehavior: keeping disruptive youth in school may harm others but suspending them worsens their development and risk of offending. Teachers and administrators often deal with students who have problems attributable to family and community deficiencies. Thus, they may be dealing with problems that are "not their fault." However, problems also exist in how schools deal with student misbehavior. There is evidence that school suspension is used too much and in a racially discriminatory way. Youth are at times suspended for being unruly rather than dangerous, and African American and Hispanic youth are more likely to be suspended for misbehavior compared to white youth (May & Stokes, 2014).

Improper use of suspension may be due to over-reactions to and/or misunderstandings of student behavior. Regardless, inappropriate and unjust responses to student misbehavior potentially facilitate developmental pathways toward incarceration as well as the disproportionately high incarceration of racial minorities—Black and Hispanic youth are more likely to be "funneled through the pipeline." It is important then to develop more effective alternatives to suspension, incentives for proper behavior, culturally aware and sensitive training and strategies for behavior management, and equip schools with resources needed to meet the needs of students experiencing racial and economic inequality (May & Stokes, 2014).

School Violence

The threat of violent victimization at school is a serious problem that interferes with schools' abilities to educate children and foster their prosocial development, especially at schools located in economically disadvantaged areas. However, there are several myths and misconceptions surrounding this issue. These may include exaggerated rates of violence, false reports of incidents and studies, beliefs that youth are becoming more violent, and beliefs that schools have become largely unable to maintain law and order. In general, it may appear that schools are unsafe places. These misunderstandings are based partly in fear, which is perhaps fueled by media attention. Parents, and others, are of course very worried about the possibility of their children being harmed, especially when children are away from their protection. Students too may overestimate violence at school. However, upon careful examination, we should be able to see that schools are still relatively safe places. For example, children are much less likely to be victims of homicide at school than elsewhere in their communities. In the U.S., homicides of youth at school were about 1% of all youth homicides each year between 1992–1993 and 2020–2021 (National Center for Education Statistics, 2024).

This is not to say that students, parents, teachers, and others should not be concerned about school violence. Violence, especially less severe forms, can still be considered common in schools. School Survey on Crime and Safety (SSOCS) data collected from school principals show that for the 2021–2022 school year, 67.3% of public schools in the U.S. had at least one recorded violent incident and the national rate was 18 incidents per 1,000 students, and 19.7% of schools had at least one *serious violent* incident specifically and the national rate for this was 1.5 per 1,000 students (Burr et al., 2024). Reporting of overall violence did not change much over recent years, but there is a noticeable increase in serious violence specifically. For the 2015–2016 school year, 68.9% of public schools had at least one recorded violent incident and the national rate was 17.5 per 1,000 students, and 15.5% of schools had at least one recorded serious violent incident and the national rate for this was 0.8 per 1,000 students (Musu-Gillette et al., 2018).

SSOCS data also show the following recorded incidents for 2021–2022:

- Possession of a knife or sharp object: 32.6% of schools, 1.2 rate
- Physical attack or fight with a weapon: 4.3% of schools, 0.5 rate
- Physical attack or fight *without* a weapon: 61.2% of schools, 11.6 rate
- Threat of physical attack with a weapon: 9.9% of schools, 0.4 rate
- Threat of physical attack *without* a weapon: 35.2%, 4.9 rate
- Robbery (with or without a weapon): 4.2% of schools, 0.3 rate
- Hate crime: 3.5% of schools, 0.2 rate.

(Burr et al., 2024)

It is also important to consider students' reports of violence at school. Youth Risk Behavior Survey (YRBS) data on high school students in the U.S. show the following.

- In 2021, 3.1% reported carrying a weapon on school property at least once in the past 30 days, up from 2.8% in 2019 but down from 3.8% in 2017. In 2021, males (3.9%) were more likely to report than females (2.1%), LGBQ+ categories (ranging 3.1–5%) were more likely than heterosexuals (2.3%), and whites (2.4%) were more likely than Asians (1.9%) but less likely than American Indians or Alaskan Natives (3.3%), Blacks (4.6%), Hispanics (3.3%), Native Hawaiians or Pacific Islanders (5.1%), and multiracial students (4%). Reports did not include the motives for carrying a weapon, for example whether for defense or to attack.
- In 2021, 6.6% reported being threatened or injured with a weapon on school property at least once in the past 12 months, down from 7.4% in 2019 but up from 6% in 2017. In 2021, males (7%) were more likely to report than females (5.9%), LGBQ+ categories (ranging 8.1–8.7%) were more likely than heterosexuals (5.7%), and whites (6.2%) were more likely than Asians (3.2%) but less likely than American Indians/Alaskan Natives (8.3%), Blacks (7.9%), Hispanics (6.5%), Native Hawaiians or Pacific Islanders (7.4%), and multiracial students (8.5%).
- In 2021, 5.8% reported being in a physical fight on school property at least once in the past 12 months, down from 8% in 2019 and 8.5% in 2017. In 2021, males (8.1%) were more likely to report than females (3.2%) and whites (5.4%) and Hispanics (5.4%) were more likely than Native Hawaiians or Pacific Islanders (0.9%) and Asians (1.7%) but less likely than American Indians or Alaskan Natives (3.1%), Blacks (8.5%), and multiracial students (7.6%). There was little difference in fighting between heterosexuals and LGBQ+ students in general.
- In 2021, 8.6% reported that they didn't go to school because they felt unsafe at, or on their way to or from, school at least once in the past 30 days, roughly the same as 8.7% in 2019 but up from 6.7% in 2017. In 2021, females (10.5%) were more likely to report than males (6.6%), LGBQ+ categories (ranging 12.6–14.4%) were more likely than heterosexuals (6.6%), and whites (6.6%) were more likely than Asians (4.5%) but less likely than American Indians or Alaskan Natives (13.3%), Blacks (12.1%), Hispanics (11.3%), Native Hawaiians or Pacific Islanders (8.5%), and multiracial students (8.2%). (CDC, 2024)

It should be noted that 2021 YRBS data were collected during the pandemic, when many students were attending school remotely. Thus, we might expect a decrease in some at-school problems. However, percentages of reported problems were not always significantly lower compared to pre-pandemic years.

Also, National Crime Victimization Survey (NCVS) data show that in 2022, the nonfatal at-school violent victimization rate for students aged 12–18 was 16 victimizations per 1,000, down from 29 in 2012 (Irwin et al., 2024) and 18 in 2016 (Musu-Gillette et al., 2018). NCVS School Crime Supplement (SCS) data show that comparing 2010–2011 to 2021–2022, student-reported gang presence decreased from 18% to 6%, being called hate-related words decreased from 9% to 7%, and seeing hate-related graffiti decreased from 28% to 23%. However, in 2021–2022, 3.8% of students reported that they had been afraid of attack or harm at school (higher than the 2.2% reporting that they had been afraid of attack or harm elsewhere), which was not measurably different from 2010–2011, and 3.6% reported avoiding school activities or classes because they thought someone might attack or harm them, an increase from about 2% in 2010–2011 (Irwin et al., 2024).

Many of us can think of times when we or others were assaulted or threatened in some way at school. Of course, teachers and other workers at school also face threats of victimization. Thus, concern over school violence is warranted. Further, fear of victimization among students and school employees itself, whether rationally or irrationally based, is a problem. In addition to personal victimization, others' victimization, perceived potential victimization, and knowledge of dangers such as weapon possession by peers distract students and school officials from concentrating on educational activities. However, we must have accurate information on the nature, extent, and factors of school violence if we are to properly understand the effectiveness of education as a social control institution.

One particularly sensitive topic is school shootings. Contrary to popular belief, homicides at school (which primarily involve firearms) did not increase but instead decreased throughout the 1990s and then stabilized. Perhaps the most frightening type, mass or rampage shootings (in which one or a few assailants attack multiple victims in a short time period), was particularly rare during this time. Intense media coverage of school shootings may make it appear that they are more frequent than what really occurs. However, May et al. (2014) found evidence that while the number of school shooting *incidents* did not significantly increase throughout 1966–2013, the number of school shooting *victims* significantly increased beginning in the late 1990s, suggesting that multiple-victim school shootings increased. According to FBI data, from 2000–2022, 50 active shooter incidents occurred at elementary and secondary schools in the U.S. Annual numbers ranged from zero to six during this time. Four incidents occurred in 2022 that resulted in 52 casualties (29 wounded, 23 killed), the second highest number since 2000; in 2018 there were 81 casualties (52 wounded, 29 killed) (Irwin et al., 2024).

Mass school shootings warrant special attention from social scientists and policymakers, but an increase in them would be subject to a small numbers effect. If something is very rare, and it occurs a few more times than usual, the increase will appear very large when stated proportionally. For example, if an event occurred once last year but three times this year, it "tripled," although it happened only two more times. When counts become larger, increases of a few cases become less significant (e.g., from 97 to 99), and large percentage increases become more significant, for example if 100 doubles to 200 (an increase of 100 cases!). Basically, even if mass school shootings have noticeably increased, they are still rarely occurring events.

Although statistically rare, school shootings and other severe physical attacks (some attacks are committed with other weapons) are a matter of grave concern because they cause severe harm to many people (e.g., families and friends) throughout the community. It is understandable that parents, schools, the government, and others want to be prepared to handle such situations or better yet take steps to prevent them. However, we must not exaggerate or otherwise misunderstand school violence, as this fosters hasty decisions about what to do about the problem, negative views of schools and educators, and poor public-school relations—none of which helps solve the problem (and may even make it worse).

As discussed in Chapter 2, a relatively prevalent problem in schools is bullying. Although it too should not be exaggerated, mistakes about bullying include underestimating it, by misidentifying acts of bullying and failing to recognize its harm, for example. Bullying may be mistaken for "just joking around" or "horseplay." Bullying is not simply teasing or fighting with others. Rather, it involves repeated aggressive actions toward a victim by one or more others who have more power than the victim (e.g., through physical strength, older age, mental ability, or popularity). Bullying includes many types of behaviors including teasing, insults, threats, practical jokes, physical attacks, taking money or property, spreading rumors, or exclusion from groups. The effects of bullying upon victims can be as serious as other forms of abuse: physical injury, mental health problems, poor social development, poor academic performance, and increased risk of the victim becoming an offender. The effects upon offenders are also serious (May et al., 2014).

SSOCS data show that in 2021–2022, 14.3% of public schools reported that student bullying occurred at least once a week, and 15.6% reported that cyberbullying among their students occurred at least once a week (Burr et al., 2024). YRBS data show that in 2021, 15% of high school students reported being bullied on school property during the past 12 months, down from 19.5% in 2019 and 19% in 2017. In 2021, females (17%) were more likely to report being bullied than males (12.8%) and LGBQ+ categories (ranging from 21.1–26.4%) were more likely than heterosexuals (12%). Whites (17.9%), American Indians or Alaskan Natives (17.8%), and multiracial students (17.5%) were more likely to report bullying than Hispanics (12.4%), Asians (10.8%), Native Hawaiians or Pacific Islanders (8.9%), and Blacks (8.5%) (CDC, 2024). According to NCVS-SCS data, in the 2021–2022 school year, 19% of students aged 12–18 reported being bullied during school, down from 28% in 2010–2011. In 2021–2022, 21.8% of females and 16.7% of males reported being bullied, and the racial breakdown was as follows: multiracial: 30.1%, white: 21.6%, Black: 17%, Hispanic: 16.4%, and Asian: 9% (a rate could not be calculated for American Indians/Alaskan Natives and Pacific Islanders) (Irwin et al., 2024).

Without intervention, bullies' offending may become worse and develop into persistent criminal offending and other problems, and victims may develop persistent behavioral and mental health problems. To respond, schools worldwide have implemented anti-bullying programs. These programs have generally demonstrated effectiveness at reducing bullying perpetration and victimization, especially among younger children and those who are highly victimized, although some of these effects are small. However, more needs to be done to increase and better evaluate their effectiveness, and programs may need to be tailored to certain students' needs, such as according to age group and victimization levels (Hensums et al., 2023). Components of successful anti-bullying programs include those at the school level (e.g., having an anti-bullying policy), classroom level (e.g., rules and management practices), parent level (e.g., providing information), peer level (e.g., formal and informal peer involvement and encouraging bystander intervention), and individual level (e.g., working with victims and groups) as well as intervention-specific ones (e.g., providing curriculum materials, socio-emotional skill-building, and mental health support) (Gaffney et al., 2021).

Sexual violence and aggression at school is another relatively prevalent problem. While aggravated sexual assault and rape are rare in secondary schools, acts such as inappropriate touching, sexual comments and gestures, and coerced or pressured sexual contact are more common. Many sexually aggressive acts, especially non-physical ones, are considered sexual harassment. Adolescents' risk of this particular kind of victimization may be higher at school than elsewhere. Some studies suggest that most students experience some type of sexual harassment. Many victims experience repeat or even chronic (ongoing) sexual assault or harassment, which increases the harmful effects of victimization such as poor mental health, educational attainment, and self-esteem (Tillyer et al., 2016). Although more prevalent in high schools, sexual victimization is also a problem in middle or junior high schools. Also, while several cases of peer sexual offending involve male perpetration against females, same-sex, and female against male perpetration may also frequently occur (Levine, 2017).

There is some overlap in the phenomena of bullying and sexual violence, although the two terms should not be confused. Some acts of bullying are of a sexual nature—ongoing sexual harassment and sexual orientation-based teasing, for example (Tillyer et al., 2016). SSOCS data show that in 2021–2022, 1.6% of public schools reported that sexual harassment among students occurred at least once a week, and 2.1% reported that student harassment based on sexual orientation or gender identity occurred at least once a week (Burr et al., 2024).

Another related problem is dating violence, which includes both sexual and non-sexual forms. YRBS data show that in 2021, of high school students who dated or went out with someone, 9.7% reported that they experienced sexual dating violence in the past 12 months, up from 8.2% in 2019 and 6.9% in 2017. In 2021, females (15.3%) were more likely to report than males (4%) and LGBQ+ categories (ranging 12–20.8%) were more likely than heterosexuals (6.6%) to report dating violence. Multiracial students (11.7%), American Indians or Alaskan Natives (11%), whites (10.7%), and Hispanics (10%), were more likely to report than Asians (5.5%), Native Hawaiians or Pacific Islanders (5.5%), and Blacks (5.3%). Also in 2021, of students who dated or went out with someone, 8.5% reported that they experienced physical dating violence (e.g., being hit) in the past 12 months, up from 8.2% in 2019 and 8% in 2017. In 2021, females (10.2%) were more likely to report physical dating violence than males (6.7%) and LGBQ+ categories (ranging 14.1–16.1%) were more likely than heterosexuals (6.2%). American Indians or Alaskan Natives (14.6%) and Native Hawaiians or Pacific

Islanders (13.8%) were more likely to report physical dating violence than multiracial students (10.4%), whites (9.1%), Blacks (8.1%), Hispanics (7.4%), and Asians (5.3%) (CDC, 2024). Levine (2017) found in a sample of middle school students that dating increased the risk of sexual victimization and perpetration. Bullying, sexual harassment, and teen dating violence among students appear to be correlated. For example, those who commit bullying may be more likely to commit sexual harassment, and those who commit bullying or sexual harassment may be more likely to commit dating violence (Cutbush et al., 2016).

While schools possess elements that should reduce sexual misconduct, such as policies and faculty/staff supervision, the general context of school may facilitate it. In bringing many children together into an environment with a limited number of adults who can serve as protectors, schools potentially expose students to deviant peer influences, and potential victims to potential offenders, which increase opportunities for offending. Further, in this kind of environment, victims and offenders are not necessarily exclusive. Students who perpetrate sexual aggression are also at higher risk of being victimized by it (Tillyer et al., 2016). These circumstances present difficult social control challenges that schools must overcome. School-based violence and other delinquency interventions are discussed in more detail in later chapters.

Box 6.3: Olweus Bullying Prevention Program

One of the most widely known and utilized anti-bullying programs is the Olweus Bullying Prevention Program, which is supported by decades of research evidence initiated by its developer, the late Dr. Dan Olweus, a psychologist and researcher at the University of Bergen in Norway. The program is endorsed by Blueprints for Healthy Youth Development, a project that provides a registry of interventions shown to effectively reduce anti-social behavior and promote healthy human development. It is used in elementary, middle, and high schools worldwide and designed to more broadly reduce delinquent and criminal behavior, truancy, and violent victimization as well as to promote prosocial peer interactions. Secondary goals of the program include "increased awareness and knowledge about bullying, involvement of teachers and parents in bullying prevention, development of clear rules against bullying, and providing support and protection to victims" (Blueprints). The program has three levels, each with multiple components.

At the school level, "components consist of an assessment of the nature and prevalence of bullying in the school, the formation of a committee to coordinate the prevention program, and development of a system ensuring adult supervision of students outside of the classroom" (Blueprints). The strategy at this level includes an anonymous questionnaire about bullying at the school administered to students, as well as a conference day convened by school administration to discuss findings from the student survey, familiarize themselves with the program, form a Bullying Prevention Coordinating Committee (also consisting of other constituencies such as teachers, counselors, health care professionals, parents, and students), and plan for program implementation. Components "also involve[] increased adult supervision of school areas that are frequently the setting for bullying (i.e., the playground, cafeteria, and restrooms)" (Blueprints).

At the classroom level, "components include defining and enforcing rules against bullying, discussions and activities to reinforce anti-bullying values and norms and active parental involvement in the program" (Blueprints). The strategy here is to establish "clear and consistently enforced rules against bullying," have "regular class discussions and activities designed to reinforce rules and anti-bullying values and norms," cover "the harm caused by bullying and strategies for preventing it," and encourage "parental involvement through meetings and discussion of the problem and efforts to address it" (Blueprints).

At the individual level, components include interventions with students with histories of bullying perpetration and/or victimization and their parents intended to eliminate the bullying behavior and provide support to victims.

Training and technical assistance is available for schools interested in implementing the program. For more information about the Olweus Bullying Prevention Program, visit https://www.blueprintsprograms.org/programs/11999999/olweus-bullying-prevention-program/print/.

Source: Blueprints for Healthy Youth Development. (n.d.). *Olweus Bullying Prevention Program: A multi-level bullying prevention program designed to reduce and prevent school bullying in elementary, middle, and high schools.* https://www.blueprintsprograms.org/programs/11999999/olweus-bullying-prevention-program/print/

Religion

Religion can be defined as a cultural system of sacred beliefs, values, and rituals that provide adherents with identity and a sense of meaning and purpose in life. Examples include Christianity, Islam, Hinduism, Judaism, and Buddhism. Religions may be divided into more specific denominations such as Catholic and Baptist under Christianity, Sunni and Shia under Islam, and Orthodox, Conservative, or Reform under Judaism. Denominations are groups of congregations—more local organizations that share the same general doctrine and are governed by a common administration. For example, Catholic churches and organizations adhere to the system governed by the Roman Catholic Church (Conley, 2017).

Religious belief and practice separate the *sacred*—matters in life that are of a special holy or mystical nature—from the *profane* or secular—everyday matters that do not have direct religious significance (working, playing, shopping, housework, and so on). Religions may center on theism—the worship of one or more supernatural beings (deities or gods), ethicalism—adherence to a set of moral principles, or animism—the belief that spirits inhabit the natural world (Conley, 2017). Religion has, of course, existed for thousands of years. Most people in the world believe in some form of religion, and many nations have a dominant or official state religion. Religion is a social institution in that it meets a variety of collective social needs. The social functions of religion include providing social cohesion and support, answers to important questions in life, and moral regulation of behavior (Stark, 2015).

Religious doctrines contain sets of moral principles and rules of behavior that should and should not be done, and often prescribed punishments for violating them. There is, of course, major overlap between behaviors defined as crime and those forbidden by religion, such as murder and theft. Criminal justice in the U.S. and other countries even have roots in religious doctrine. According to Akers (2010, p. 1), we should expect to find that "religion generally provides institutional support for conformity to conventional norms."

Hirschi's social bond theory seems particularly relevant to religion: individuals who strongly *attach* themselves to religious organizations and members, *commit* to religious ideology, hold religious *beliefs*, and *involve* themselves in religious activities will have much less desire, time, and opportunity to engage in deviance (Adamczyk et al., 2017; Akers, 2010). Religion also offers direct control. Out of concern for the spiritual well-being of other members, and interest in upholding the ideals of the belief system, members and religious authorities may monitor others' behavior and administer punishments (e.g., verbal admonishment, shunning, or lost privileges). Thus, we may expect to find that religious affiliation reduces criminal behavior.

However, because religious doctrine and practice can be intolerant of other beliefs and practices, support inequality (e.g., gender, sexual orientation, or caste), claim supremacy over governmental law, and advocate violence in some circumstances, we could also suppose that religion increases crime. Perhaps religion does promote crime under certain circumstances, but of interest here is what *tends* to happen. Except for the connection between religious extremism and terrorism (Akers, 2010), research usually finds that religious involvement (e.g., church attendance, volunteering, prayer, and charitable giving) and belief are negatively correlated with crime and drug abuse (Adamczyk et al., 2017; Kelly et al., 2015).

Religious control may operate both coercively, such as through fear of negative earthly and supernatural consequences (e.g., shame, loss of group membership and social support, and an undesirable afterlife), or non-coercively such as through fostering social cohesion and positive emotions, identity, and sense of self. Further, religiosity may buffer against the effects of crime factors, for example by equipping individuals with personal and social resources for coping with strain and safety threats or finding opportunities in socially disorganized communities (Adamczyk et al., 2017; Kelly et al., 2015). It may also reduce offending by decreasing mental health problems like depression and suicidal ideation (Ji et al., 2011). In short, religion helps many people, including juveniles, deal with problems in life that affect behavior.

Instead of conceptualizing more abstract religious entities—institutions, organizations, and general belief systems—as "independent variables" directly impacting one's tendency to offend, it is better to understand how "religious contexts" impact crime. As argued by scholars such as Rodney Stark, religion may only reduce crime to the extent that it constitutes a "moral community." Individuals must accept their religious organizations and belief systems as legitimate bases for action and sustain them through interaction in social contexts such as friendship networks, local areas, states, and countries. Areas with high levels of religiosity should experience lower offending as a result, perhaps even among persons who do not strongly identify with the religion but are tied to the same community (Adamczyk et al., 2017).

The relationship between religion and crime, especially serious offending, could be spurious, however. Religiosity may not cause law abidingness; rather, the two may be caused by individual characteristics, such as level of *self*-control. Persons high in self-control may be more likely to be religious than those with low self-control (it takes a great deal of self-control to be devout), and of course those with high self-control are less likely to offend. However, religiosity may promote high self-control (e.g., through mediation and reflection), and thus indirectly reduce criminal behavior (Reisig et al., 2012). If true, these relationships do not deny the importance of religion as a crime control institution. Rather, they may reveal what is true of all control institutions: their effectiveness depends heavily upon individuals' susceptibility to control via personal characteristics, experiences within the institutional setting, and the strength to which individuals are tied to the institution (social bonds).

Like family and education, religion faces current problems which interfere with its ability to provide socialization and social control and support. Local religious organizations (e.g., churches, mosques, synagogues, and faith-based activist or advocacy groups) vary in social and material resources needed to offer control and support, and conditions such as economic strain and low social cohesion may be disruptive of religious, not just familial and educational, social control. The ability of religious organizations to counteract criminogenic influences is particularly important for disadvantaged communities of color.

For example, the "African-American church" may be an institution in itself—one that compensates for some of the disadvantages faced by low-income African Americans. Two studies found that attending religious services, especially very frequently, helped reduce Black youths' risk of serious offending due to neighborhood disorder (Johnson, Jang, et al., 2000; Johnson, Larson, et al., 2000). However, the studies did not differentiate if church attendance makes disadvantaged youth prosocial and thus less likely to offend, or if disadvantaged youth who are already prosocial (e.g., have higher self-control) choose both attending church and avoiding crime. Also, one of the studies found that religious salience, the perceived strength of the role that religion plays in one's life, was not related to offending. Religious involvement appears to play an important part in the resiliency of inner-city youth, but the exact nature of this relationship seems unclear.

Religious affiliation clearly has benefits for individuals deeply involved in religious practice. However, religion is also thought to have community-level impacts, such as lowering community crime rates. The presence of religious organizations should help develop community-wide social networks, social capital, and collective efficacy, thereby increasing the community's capacity for crime control and dealing with other social problems. In this way, religion has more than just direct impacts upon the behavioral tendencies of devout members. One may even expect to find that having several churches, for example, will lower neighborhood crime rates. However, the community-level impacts of religious organizations are varied and complex (Triplett et al., 2013), as demonstrated in two studies.

Box 6.4: Religion, Family, and Social Services

Social institutions do not exist or operate separately from each other. We are often in environments and situations in which family, school, religion, and other institutions are influencing us at the same time. For example, families often engage in religious activities together, parents may be involved in the PTA (Parent-Teacher Association), and some parents send their children to and become involved with religion-affiliated schools. Thus, social institutional forces may work together to provide social control and support for individuals. (Or they may fail to work together to provide control and support, such as when families and schools in communities are at odds with or distant from one another and thus do not function in harmony to steer children away from antisocial behavior.)

One study identified a way that religion, family, and social services may collaborate to provide support and guidance to at-risk youth. Children who are abused or neglected must sometimes be removed from the home and placed in foster care. These children are at heightened risk of developing persistent mental health and behavioral problems. Thus, it is essential that foster caregivers are highly motivated and able to meet these children's special needs. Foster parents with altruistic motives are thought to be more committed and better prepared to meet the challenges of fostering, since their motivation doesn't depend solely upon personally rewarding circumstances. ("Altruism" refers to putting the welfare and interests of others over one's own.) People have several reasons for foster parenting, one of them being religious beliefs.

An analysis of data from the National Survey of Current and Former Foster Parents showed that religiously motivated potential foster parents scored higher on altruism and were more likely to have altruistic reasons for foster parenting. For example, while they often identified non-altruistic reasons for fostering, 83.5% of religiously motivated persons identified "Wanted to help community/ society" as a reason compared to 52% of those not religiously motivated, and 79.5% of the religiously motivated identified "Give home to child who would've been in an institution" compared to 65.5% of the non-religiously motivated.

Importantly, considering that not all religiously motivated persons were highly altruistic, the study also found that it was those who were both religiously and altruistically motivated (not just religiously) who most frequently offered their homes to foster children. Of course, more than just altruism and good intentions are needed to provide effective foster care. Resources such as money and community support are also needed. Still, this study suggests that engaging in foster parenting is one way that agents of religious institutions can reduce problems among juveniles, including delinquency.

Source: Howell-Moroney, M. (2014). The empirical ties between religious motivation and altruism in foster parents: Implications for faith-based initiatives in foster care and adoption. *Religions, 5*, 720–737.

Religion is also a particularly important control institution in Latino/a communities, perhaps especially for newly forming immigrant communities in the U.S. Immigration reforms beginning in the 1980s directed or drew Latino/a immigrants away from traditional locations such as Texas and California into newer parts of the country such as the Southeast. Unlike established, traditional Latino/a communities, those in "new destination areas" may have not yet developed the social networks that offer protective social capital. Also, these newer communities tend to be more segregated from other racial and ethnic groups, and more disconnected from mainstream institutions. Thus, new destination areas may contain more social disorganization and disadvantages, which may increase residents' reliance upon informal institutions such as religion for social control and support. Shihadeh and Winters (2010) found that in new destination counties in the U.S., Latino/a homicide victimization rates tender to be lower in counties with a strong Catholic presence but *higher* in counties with a strong Protestant presence.

Shihadeh and Winters (2010) tentatively suggested that immigrants to new destination Catholic areas benefitted from (1) the Roman Catholic Church's centralized authority that dictates that members engage in coordinated action, (2) the established tradition of the Catholic Church in Latino/a life, and (3) the Church's focus on community outreach. Perhaps new destination Protestant areas were less accommodating to the recent influx of ethnically different, mostly Catholic, immigrants—who may have been viewed by current residents as competition for scarce jobs and threats to their cultural way of life. This may have distanced immigrants from the area's institutional social support and control mechanisms, which led to an increase in violent crime among Latino/as. (Note: most homicides were Latino-on-Latino; the study did not suggest that current residents became hostile and began violently assaulting Latino/as at a high rate.)

However, Shihadeh and Winters (2010) found that Latino/a homicides were not higher in heavily Protestant traditional destination counties, perhaps because Latino/as were already established in these areas, and many Protestant churches were in the habit of offering assistance to and recruiting Latino/a immigrants. (Recently, a noticeable portion of Latino/as have shifted from Catholic to Protestant affiliation.) Their study more broadly suggests that religion's capacity to control crime depends on what else is going on in a society, such as social policy changes, immigration patterns, and organizational differences between religious denominations.

In a study of one U.S. city, Triplett et al. (2013) found, oddly, that the higher the number of churches, the higher the neighborhood street and domestic violent crime rates tended to be—a result that was also found in a study on a city in another part of the country. It is not likely that churches facilitate or encourage a significant amount of crime. By offering services to the poor, churches could attract people experiencing a great deal of strain and frustration, who may be more likely to engage in violence, to the area. (Also, some denominations may advocate corporal punishment of children, traditional gender roles, and strong patriarchal family structure, which may translate into abuse when combined with other factors such as economic strain and poor coping and problem-solving skills.) However, the relationship is more likely spurious. High crime and number of churches could both be the result of other neighborhood characteristics. For example, for space, churches may be drawn into commercial (nonresidential) zones, which attract nonresidents and have more potential for criminal opportunities. The findings suggest that churches in some neighborhoods lack the capacity to control crime.

Peers as a Social Institution?

"Peers"—one's wider group of friends or other close, non-relative associates—may or may not be considered a social institution. However, as explained in prior chapters, peers constitute a social system that is very much involved in social control. While much attention is given to bad influences from adolescent peers, peer influence is not inherently bad. Peers can also encourage desirable behaviors such as volunteering (Choukas-Bradley et al., 2015). Peers can help instill prosocial values and beliefs, support involvement in conventional activities, and offer rewards for prosocial behavior and punishments for antisocial behavior. Or, they can help instill antisocial values and beliefs, support involvement in deviant activities, and offer rewards for antisocial behavior and punishments for prosocial behavior (e.g., teasing). Individual youth may self-identify with the characteristics of the groups to which they belong. One who is part of a group of "good kids" is more likely to see oneself as a good kid, while one who is part of a group of "bad kids" is more likely to see oneself as a bad kid. Peer groups play a major role in determining their members' individual attitudes. While people often do not behave in ways consistent with their attitudes, attitudes and behaviors are correlated. For example, youth with negative attitudes toward delinquency commit less of it (Carson, 2013).

However, peer groups are neither completely delinquent nor completely prosocial ("prosocial groups" would refer to those that are *primarily* prosocial.) In support of learning theory, Carson (2013) found that perceptions of peer behavior as prosocial was associated with more unfavorable attitudes toward delinquency while competing perceptions of peer behavior as antisocial was associated with more favorable attitudes toward delinquency, but that the impact of perceived prosocial peer behavior was more stable than that of perceived antisocial peer behavior. However, although having attitudes, behaviors, and peer association at one time increases the likelihood that one will have them later, an individual's peer group changes over time. This includes choosing different groups as well as changes of people, attitudes, and behavior within the same group. Uncomfortable with "imbalances" between qualities of themselves and their groups, individual youth may change their attitudes and behavior to match changes in the group, to maintain consistency with the perceived nature of the group.

Carson (2013) also found that as perceptions of antisocial peer behavior increased, so too did attitudes favorable toward delinquency. Attitudes became less favorable toward delinquency as perceptions of prosocial peer behavior increased, but this impact was not as strong as that of increased perceived antisocial peer behavior. Similarly, Farrell et al. (2017) found that peer pressure for fighting and friends' delinquent behavior were associated with adolescents' aggression, drug use, and delinquent behavior and friends' prosocial behavior was associated with adolescents' prosocial behavior. While these studies suggest that high-risk youth would benefit from an increase in prosocial peer association, they underscore the importance of *maintaining* highly prosocial peer relations. Prosocial peer behavior has a powerful impact upon a juvenile's prosocial beliefs, but these beliefs may be susceptible to the damaging effects of significant increases in peer antisocial behavior.

Like families, peer groups may serve as the source of both the problem and the solution to delinquency. If antisocial peers help cause delinquency through encouragement and learning processes, it can be equally claimed that prosocial peers help cause non-delinquency in the same manner. Thus, peers may be considered systems of informal social control, with conventional (prosocial, non-delinquent) peer groups providing adequate control and deviant (antisocial, delinquent) peer groups providing inadequate control. However, like other informal control systems, the ability of prosocial peer groups to regulate individuals' behavior depends on the extent to which individuals are involved with and tied to them. Thus, cultivating prosocial, or "positive, peer association should be included in efforts by families, schools, and religious organizations, as well as the juvenile justice system, to prevent and reduce antisocial behavior.

Summary Points

- To understand antisocial behavior and its prevention, it is important to understand processes of social control, which take place in different institutional environments. Most social control is "informal," that which is provided by social institutions other than criminal/juvenile justice—namely the family, education, and religion. The juvenile justice system provides "formal" social control.

- The family is a particularly important institutional context for human development, as trajectories are initiated within the family. Parents or guardians are primarily responsible for nurturing children during their first years of life, and the family continues to be the main agent of socialization during childhood and a major influence during adolescence.
- Families face several internal and external based problems that interfere with their ability to provide social control, including poor parenting practices, family unit disruption, unstable living conditions, teen parenting, parent and sibling criminality, economic disadvantage, and child abuse and neglect.
- Education is a social institution that provides social control through continued socialization, access to conventional activities, supervision and monitoring, punishments and rewards, and teaching knowledge and skills that make individuals productive members of society and less likely to offend. Current problems faced by schools include lack of material and social resources, disadvantaged surrounding communities, and school violence (physical and sexual assault, carrying weapons, bullying, sexual harassment, and dating violence).
- Religion is a social institution that provides social control through additional socialization, access to conventional activities, assistance with supervision and monitoring, punishments and rewards, social cohesion and support, positive identity, and sense of meaning and purpose in life. Like families and schools, the ability of religious organizations to provide social control is affected by social disadvantage, community disorganization, and social change.
- While it appears that many causes of delinquency arise or are worsened in certain institutional contexts like families and schools, it is important to remember that these contexts may also often present the best opportunities for reducing delinquency, for example through preventative or reparative interventions.

Key Terms

Child Abuse: harmful acts committed against children by older persons including those of a physical (e.g., hitting), emotional (e.g., insults or belittling), and sexual (e.g., inappropriate touch and speech and exposure to pornography) nature.

Child Neglect: is the failure of responsible persons to provide for a child's basic physical and psychological needs (e.g., inadequate food, withholding affection, and failure to educate).

Corporal Punishment: the infliction of physical pain, without intent to injure, upon a child with the purpose of correcting the child's behavior.

Education: a social institution—a formal system of transmitting the skills, knowledge, and values determined to be needed in a population to make a society function well.

The Family: the social institution that is initially and primarily responsible for raising children.

Formal Social Control: control administered procedurally by official governmental authorities within a social institution designed purposely and primarily for the prevention and punishment of prohibited behavior—the criminal justice system.

Harsh Corporal Punishment: physical punishment used upon a child either with the intention to injure or without regard to injury (done with excessive force or recklessly).

Informal Social Control: control administered in everyday institutional life, such as home, school, work, place of religious worship, and neighborhood. Informal social control takes place within the context of informal social control institutions (e.g., family, school, and religion).

Religion: as a social institution, is a cultural system of sacred beliefs, values, and rituals that provide adherents with identity and a sense of meaning and purpose in life.

School-to-Prison Pipeline: the research-identified pathway from school problems to imprisonment facilitated by school policies and practices, which is experienced more by economically disadvantaged youth of color.

Social Control: processes by which the behavior of the people of a society is regulated, which includes mechanisms for ensuring conformity (adherence to norms and values) and responding to deviant behavior.

Social Institution: a macro-social structure developed within a society to meet social needs—a complex network of interdependent positions that perform social roles that reproduces itself over time.

References

Adamczyk, A., Freilich, J. D., & Kim, C. (2017). Religion and crime: A systematic review and assessment of next steps. *Sociology of Religion, 78*(2), 192–232. https://doi.org/10.1093/socrel/srx012

Akers, R. L. (2010). Religion and crime. *The Criminologist, 35*(6), 1–6.

Arthur, R. (2007). *Family life and youth offending: Home is where the hurt is.* Routledge.

Benson, M. L. (2013). *Crime and the life course: An introduction.* Routledge.

Burr, R., Kemp, J., & Wang, K. (2024). *Crime, violence, discipline, and safety in U.S. public schools: Findings from the School Survey on Crime and Safety: 2021–22* (NCES 2024-043). National Center for Education Statistics. U.S. Department of Education. https://nces.ed.gov/pubsearch/pubsinfo.asp?pubid=2024043

Carson, D. C. (2013). Perceptions of prosocial and delinquent peer behavior and the effect on delinquent attitudes: A longitudinal study. *Journal of Criminal Justice, 41*, 151–161.

Centers for Disease Control and Prevention (CDC). (2024). Youth Risk Behavior Surveillance System (YRBSS). *YRBSS results*. https://www.cdc.gov/yrbs/results/index.html

Choukas-Bradley, S., Giletta, M., Cohen, G. L., & Prinstein, M. J. (2015). Peer influence, peer status, and prosocial behavior: An experimental investigation of peer socialization of adolescents' intentions to volunteer. *Journal of Youth and Adolescence, 44*(12), 2197–2210. https//doi.org/10.1007/s10964-015-0373-2

Conley, D. (2017). *You may ask yourself: An introduction to thinking like a sociologist* (5th ed.). W.W. Norton & Company.

Cutbush, S., Williams, J., & Miller, S. (2016). Teen dating violence, sexual harassment, and bullying among middle school students: Examining mediation and moderated mediation by gender. *Prevention Science, 17*, 1024–1033. https://doi.org/10.1007/s11121-016-0668-x

Farrell, A. D., Thompson, E. L., & Mehari, K. R. (2017). Dimensions of peer influences and their relationship to adolescents' aggression, other problem behaviors, and prosocial behavior. *Journal of Youth and Adolescence, 46*(6), 1351–1369. https//doi.org/10.1007/s10964-016-0601-4

Gaffney, H., Ttofi, M. M., & Farrington, D. P. (2021). What works in anti-bullying programs? Analysis of effective intervention components. *Journal of School Psychology, 85*, 37–56. https//doi.org/10.1016/j.jsp.2020.12.002

Hawkins, J. D., Catalano, R. F., Hill, K. G., & Kosterman, R. (2012). Taking effective crime prevention to scale: From school-based programs to community-wide prevention systems. In R. Loeber & B. C. Welsh (Eds.), *The future of criminology* (pp. 178–185). Oxford University Press.

Hensums, M., de Mooij, B., Kuijper, S. C., Cross, D., DeSmet, A., Garandeau, C. F., Irwin, V., Wang, K., Cui, J., & Thompson, A. (2024). *Report on indicators of school crime and safety: 2023* (NCES 2024-145/NCJ 309126). National Center for Education Statistics, U.S. Department of Education, and Bureau of Justice Statistics, Office of Justice Programs, U.S. Department of Justice. https://nces.ed.gov/pubsearch/pubsinfo.asp?pubid=2024145

Ji, C. C., Perry, T., & Clarke-Pine, D. (2011). Considering personal religiosity in adolescent delinquency: The role of depression, suicide ideation, and church guideline. *Journal of Psychology and Christianity, 30*(1), 3–15.

Johnson, B. R., Jang, S. J., De Li, S. & Larson, D. (2000). The "invisible institution" and black youth crime: The church as an agency of local social control. *Journal of Youth and Adolescence, 29*(4), 479–498.

Johnson, B. R., Larson, D., De Li, S., & Jang, S. J. (2000). Escaping from the crime of inner cities: Church attendance and religious salience among disadvantaged youth. *Justice Quarterly, 17*(2), 377–391.

Joronen, K., Leadbeater, B., Menesini, E., Palladino, B. E., Salmivalli, C., Solomontos-Kountouri, O., Veenstra, R., Fekkes, M., & Overbeek, G. (2023). What works for whom in school-based anti-bullying interventions? An individual participant data meta-analysis. *Prevention Science, 24*(8), 1435–1446. https//doi.org/10.1007/s11121-022-01387-z

Kelly, P. E., Polanin, J. R., Jang, S. J., & Johnson, B. R. (2015). Religion, delinquency, and drug use: A meta-analysis. *Criminal Justice Review, 40*(4), 505–523. https://doi.org/10.1177/0734016815605151

Kim, Y. S. (2016). Examination of the relative effects of neighborhoods and schools on juvenile delinquency: A multilevel cross-classified model approach. *Deviant Behavior, 37*(10), 1196–1214. https://doi.org/10.1080/01639625.2016.1170537

Levine, E. (2017). Sexual violence among middle school students: The effects of gender and dating experience. *Journal of Interpersonal Violence, 32*(14), 2059–2082. https://doi.org/10.1177/0886260515590786

Limbos, M. P., & Casteel, C. (2008). Schools and neighborhoods: Organizational and environmental factors associated with crime in secondary schools. *Journal of School Health, 78*(10), 539–544.

Lowe, N. C., May, D. C., & Elrod, P. (2008). Theoretical predictors of delinquency among public school students in a mid-southern state: The roles of context and gender. *Youth Violence and Juvenile Justice, 6*(4), 343–362.

May, D. C., Cornelius, C., Stokes, E., Rogers, C., & Walters, A. (2014). Evaluating the effectiveness of a bullying prevention program: Evidence from a quasi-experimental design. In D. C. May (Ed.), *School safety in the United States: A reasoned look at the rhetoric* (pp. 119–136). Carolina Academic Press.

May, D. C., Henry, E., & Kimberling, S. (2014). Forty years of school homicides: Are our kids really more at risk in the 21st century? In D. C. May (Ed.), *School safety in the United States: A reasoned look at the rhetoric* (pp. 13–28). Carolina Academic Press.

May, D. C., & Stokes, E. (2014). Reducing disproportionate minority contact in schools: Stemming the school-to-prison pipeline. In D. C. May (Ed.), *School safety in the United States: A reasoned look at the rhetoric* (pp. 137–153). Carolina Academic Press.

Musu-Gillette, L., Zhang, A., Wang, K., Zhang, J., Kemp, J., Diliberti, M., & Oudkerk, B. A. (2018). *Indicators of school crime and safety: 2017* (NCES 2018-036/NCJ 251413). National Center for Education Statistics, U.S. Department of Education, and Bureau of Justice Statistics, U.S. Department of Justice.

National Center for Education Statistics. (2024). *Violent deaths at school and away from school, and active shooter incidents. Condition of Education*. U.S. Department of Education, Institute of Education Sciences. https://nces.ed.gov/programs/coe/indicator/a01

Reisig, M. D., Wolfe, S. E., & Pratt, T. C. (2012). Low self-control and the religiosity-crime relationship. *Criminal Justice and Behavior, 39*(9), 1172–1191.

Shihadeh, E. S., & Winters, L. (2010). Church, place, and crime: Latinos and homicide in new destinations. *Sociological Inquiry, 80*(4), 628–649.

Stark, R. (2015). *Triumph of faith: Why the world is more religious than ever.* ISI Books.

Straus, M. A., Douglas, E. M., & Medeiros, R. A. (2014). *The primordial violence: Spanking children, psychological development, violence, and crime.* Routledge.

Tillyer, M. S., Gialopsos, B. M., & Wilcox, P. (2016). The short-term repeat sexual victimization of adolescents in school. *Crime & Delinquency, 62*(1), 81–106. https://doi.org/10.1177/0011128713501026

Tobler, A. L., Komro, K. A., Dabroski, A., Aveyard, P., & Markham, W. A. (2011). Preventing the link between SES and high-risk behaviors: "Value-added" education, drug use and delinquency in high-risk, urban schools. *Prevention Science, 12,* 211–221.

Triplett, R. A., White, G., & Gainey, R. (2013). Churches as neighborhood organizations and their relationship to street and domestic violent crime: The role of denomination, stability, and heterogeneity. *Deviant Behavior, 34*(10), 803–823.

Welsh, B. C. (2012). Preventing delinquency by putting families first. In R. Loeber & B. C. Welsh (Eds.), *The future of criminology* (pp. 153–158). Oxford University Press.

Chapter 7

A Brief History of Juvenile Justice in the United States

Parts of this chapter were previously published in Chapter 9: "'Getting Tough' and the Adultification of Juvenile Justice" in Flawed Criminal Justice Policies, *2nd Edition (2019). Permission was gained from the publisher, Carolina Academic Press, to republish those paragraphs in this work.*

Chapter Learning Objectives

Students will be able to:

- Clarify the historical underpinnings that lead to the creation of "juvenile justice"
- Determine how societal attitudes towards children shaped the focus of the juvenile justice system throughout its existence
- Summarize outside interventions by the Supreme Court and Congress that reshaped juvenile justice
- Recognize the language of the juvenile justice system with reference to its historical intention
- Reflect on one's progress in understanding the history of juvenile justice

---

Introduction

This chapter provides a brief overview of the history of the juvenile justice system in the United States, which you will note, is very much entwined with the U.S. history of juvenile institutionalization. It is very important to understand the history and philosophies of how the United States has reacted to youthful offenders to appreciate the juvenile justice system's creation as a completely separate entity from the traditional criminal justice system. As you read this chapter, note the cycles that have existed throughout the decades of American juvenile justice. We have tried, failed, and tried again to deal appropriately with our country's troubled children, sometimes returning to a practice or philosophy that had been abandoned in the past.

The Beginnings of Juvenile Justice (Before the 1800s)

In the young United States, children who broke the law were treated as children were in other countries under English Common Law. If they were younger than seven, they were presumed to not have legal responsibility for their actions, and thus they could not be prosecuted in court. This was known as the **infancy defense**. That same belief held for youth ages 7 through 13; however, the prosecution could attempt to prove that the child in question did have the moral responsibility to know the consequences of their actions and/or know right from wrong. If the prosecution was successful in that attempt, the child would be tried in criminal court. All children over age 13 were considered responsible for their actions and the **infancy defense** did not apply to them (Shepherd, 1999). These children were subjected to all criminal sanctions including capital punishment. However, juvenile crime was not a major issue in the colonies; it was not until much later that misbehaving youth became an issue of social concern in the United States.

Early 1800s

While the literature remains mixed on the forces driving the movement—social control of immigrants or humanitarian concerns—how to deal with misbehaving youth in American society became an issue of major importance during the early 1800s (see McNally, 1982; Platt, 1969). Many factors in American history, such as immigration, industrialization, and urbanization combined to create a changing culture. This change resulted in youth being arrested and housed with adults in prison in unprecedented numbers. It did not take long for the unintended, unanticipated negative consequences of housing youth with adults in prison to catch the attention of early social reformers. Initiatives known as "the child saving movements" to reform this unhealthy practice began to spring up in major metropolitan areas. New York City became the first area to make notable changes (McNally, 1982; Platt, 1969).

The New York City House of Refuge (1825)

Combined concerns that youth were in harm's way in the criminal justice system and that juries began to nullify cases with some regularity if the defendant was young, led to reform measures in New York City (Shepherd, 1999). In 1816, some New York City activists banded together and formed the Society for the Prevention of Pauperism. The society, led by the strong Quaker influence of most of its members, decided to conduct a nationwide study of American prisons in 1820 and 1821. A report of the findings was adopted by the society in 1824. As the results condemned most of the "modern" correctional practices of the time, the society began to consider the idea of creating separate housing opportunities for young offenders (New York State Archives, 1989).

This society morphed into The Society for the Reformation of Juvenile Delinquents. This group was the impetus in the creation and passage of an 1824 bill to create the New York City House of Refuge. This bill also included the first legal definition of the term *juvenile delinquent*. The New York House of Refuge opened in New York City on January 1, 1825. It was located in the rural area of Broadway and 23rd Street in Manhattan. The House of Refuge was modeled after adult prisons, but it was unique in that it housed only youth (New York State Archives, 1989).

The House of Refuge held young people who were "deemed still to be reformable" without "the contamination of incorrigible adults" (Fox, 1996, p. 30). Who were "reformable" youth? Any youth who was delinquent, idle, abandoned, or abused could be considered in need of reform. Children who had not committed crimes could be sent to the House of Refuge because there was also a preventative component associated with the House of Refuge. This philosophical belief would play a major role in the creation of the first juvenile court (Fox, 1996).

When the House of Refuge first opened, the population was six boys and three girls. By the end of the first decade, 1,678 children had passed through its doors (New York State Archives, 1989). The sentences for the children were indefinite. For most of the day, the children worked to help make money for the House of Refuge. Males tended to produce "brushes, cane chairs, brass nails and shoes" (New York State Archives, 1989). The young women sewed uniforms, did laundry and performed other domestic type tasks. After about eight hours of physical labor, the children studied reading and religion (New York State Archives, 1989). For children who misbehaved, the punishments were physical in nature and included beatings, hanging children from their thumbs, and use of the "ducking stool" for girls (Sheldon, 2005).

The concept of separate housing for troubled juveniles spread very quickly. By 1850, eight cities had acquired houses of refuge. Despite some practical and philosophical differences, the houses of refuge appeared to share three common threads: the segregation of children from adults, the rehabilitation of troubled youth, and the restriction of the youth admitted to those who seemed amenable to treatment. The other youth remained in prisons (Fox, 1996). The houses of refuge became so accepted as the "cure" for troubled children that soon there was almost no focus on the legal processes for committing a child to the houses of refuge. Law enforcers, and even parents, were allowed to send a child to a house of refuge.

Ex Parte Crouse (1839)

It stood to reason that eventually the houses of refuge would be questioned legally about their absolute authority over youth and the means by which youth were committed. In the 1830s, the mother of Mary Ann Crouse stated that Mary Ann was "by reason of vicious conduct" beyond her mother's control. After visiting a judge in Philadelphia who agreed with her, Mary Ann was sent to the Philadelphia House of Refuge. Her father, who was very upset with the actions of his wife, went to the judge and said that it was illegal to hold a child against her wishes if she had not been afforded the right to a trial by jury (*Ex parte Crouse*, 4 Whart. 9; 1839 Pa.). The case made its way to the Philadelphia Supreme Court. The court came back with a strong ruling that set the stage for the future institutionalization of troubled children.

The Pennsylvania Supreme Court decided that the Bill of Rights, including trial by jury, did not apply to children. Thus, Mary Ann's rights were not violated—because she had none. The Pennsylvania Supreme Court explained that when natural parents fail to do their job as parents, the court can intervene in the life of a child without parental consent as long as the court's action is in the best interest of the child. This, the Pennsylvania Supreme Court said, was implied in the **doctrine of parens patriae**. Furthermore, the Pennsylvania Supreme Court explained that if the institution acted with good intentions, its true function was the protection of the child. A House of Refuge which operated in the best interest of the child did not have to afford the child constitutional rights. Who needed rights against their protectors (*Ex parte Crouse*, 4 Whart. 9; 1839 Pa.)?

In the words of the Pennsylvania Supreme Court: "The infant has been snatched from a course which must have ended in confirmed depravity; and not only is the restraint of her person lawful, but it would be an act of extreme cruelty to release her from it" (cited in Pisciotta, 1983 p. 259). The Court continued:

> The object of the charity is reformation, by training the inmates to industry; by imbuing their minds with principles of morality and religion; by furnishing them with means to earn a living; and above all, by separating them from the corrupting influences of improper associates. To this end, may not the natural parents when unequal to the task of education, or unworthy of it, be super-

> seded by the **parens patriae**, or common guardian of the community? (cited in Pisciotta, 1983, p. 259)

The rulings in *Crouse* set precedent throughout the nation (Ventrell, 2005). However, the goals of the house of refuge were never fully realized. According to Barry Krisberg:

> While the houses of refuge had many prominent supporters, the new youth prisons also suffered the problems that would plague later juvenile correctional facilities. For example, there is ample evidence of the use of solitary confinement, whipping, and other forms of corporal punishment. The labor system within the houses of refuge was managed by outside contractors who sometimes abused the children.... Violence was commonplace in these prisons and one historian estimates that 40 percent of the children escaped from the institutions or from their post-release placements. (1988, p. 3)

Reformatories (1840s–1890s)

To make a long story short, during the mid to late 1800s, governments began to be involved with the housing of troubled children and the concept of the house of refuge began to turn into a more reformatory approach. According to Anthony Platt (1977) reformatories were actually designed to be more punitive than houses of refuge. Reformatories carried the following goals: separate troubled children from adult offenders, benefit the child by removing them from a poor environment to a good environment (home to institution) for as long as it was needed (indeterminate sentencing), and to remove the court from the process as much as possible (Shepherd, 1999; Platt, 1997).

The first reform school in the United States was the Lyman School for Boys located in Westborough, Massachusetts, and opened in 1847.

Box 7.1:

While reorganizing the Westborough Room in the Westborough Public Library, Local History Librarian Anthony Vaver discovered a film in a plastic bag labeled "Lyman School" and gave it to Westborough TV to digitize. The film turned out to be a silent black-and-white movie of boys from the Lyman School performing chores, playing games, and preparing for a Thanksgiving dinner. Westborough TV asked Rev. Frederick "Bob" Brown, to add narration to the film, which put the scenes depicted into context. When the Lyman School for Boys replaced the former Westborough Reform School in 1884, delinquent boys aged twelve to seventeen were sentenced to this facility on Route 9 to be rehabilitated, educated, and trained in useful jobs. At one point, the Lyman School housed as many as 590 boys (Henderson, 2018, para 1–2). You can watch the video at http://71.248.188.158/vod/6978-Lyman-School-narrated-by-Bob-Brown-High-v1.mp4.

By 1890, most northern states had reform schools fully in place. Many states which had these mostly government-run institutions had enough institutions to segregate children by gender and race. These facilities held all "troubled youth"—delinquents, status offenders, throwaways, and neglected children. Reformatories held the power to decide the length of stay for each youth and to transfer unreformed youth into the adult prison system (Krisberg, 1995). As with the houses of refuge, the reformatory model soon came to the attention of reformers, who questioned its effectiveness.

Placing or Farming-Out (1850s)

The house of refuge and reformatory movements spawned the philosophy that troubled children would be best served by removing them from their environment. When Charles Loring Brace was confronted by the number of young children thrown away onto the streets of New York City, his thoughts also turned to removing them from the streets. Taking the practice of institutionalizing children in a different direction, the concept of *placing* or *farming-out* was born. Through the Children's Aid Society, founded in 1853 by Charles Loring Brace and a group of social reformers, the relocation of thousands of youth began. The practice of *placing-out* forced many inner-city youth to relocate to farms in the Midwest. It was believed that once the children were situated in the Midwest, the fresh air, chores, and receiving families would turn the child around. The reality is that many of the children placed out were children of immigrants, were abused, and were never returned to their real homes and families (McCarty, 2007; PBS, 1995). It seems that Charles Loring Brace's dream "If enough families can be found to serve as reformatories institutions, is it not the most practical and economical method of reforming these children?" was not fully realized (cited in Mennel, 1972, p. 76).

The Movement toward a Separate Juvenile Court System (1899)

Many factors combined to steer reformers into yet another avenue to deal with troubled youth. Reform schools were experiencing occasional attacks by social reformers questioning their power to institutionalize children without granting them any legal recourse. In addition, there was an increasing incidence of jury nullification when the jury learned that, if convicted, the youth would be housed with adults (Shepherd, 1999).

Reform groups in Illinois worked long and hard to get the Juvenile Court Bill passed. The "Act to Regulate the Treatment and Control of Dependent, Neglected and Delinquent Children" held many significant underpinnings. These include: the court was founded on the belief of rehabilitation, not punishment (Krisberg, 2005); the cornerstone of the court's philosophy was parens patriae (Ferdinand, 1991); the court was more concerned with the actor and not the act (Del Carmen et al., 1998); and, the court's jurisdiction established treatment of all "troubled" youth, which included delinquent, dependent, and neglected children (Ventrell, 2005). In essence, the court was designed as a system of welfare and not a legal system.

What these philosophical beliefs translated into in practice was the following: the court served youth under age 16, employed the use of juvenile probation, set age limits for incarceration, was informal in nature (Shepherd, 1999), and offered youth no constitutional rights. The philosophy of the court—stepping in for unfit parents and providing treatment "in the best interests of the child" indicated no need for legal protections of the child. By the 1920s all but two states had juvenile courts (Krisberg, 2005).

Changes Coming to Juvenile Justice

The juvenile justice system remained essentially unchanged until the 1960s after the creation of the juvenile courts, but its effectiveness did not go unquestioned. And the question of its effectiveness still focused on what many considered to be the historical heart of juvenile justice—the institutions. By the 1960s, juvenile correctional institutions numbered around 200, spent about $300 million to operate, admitted 100,000 juveniles per year, and averaged a recidivism rate of 80% (Wooden, 2000).

The 1960s were a time of change and social unrest. There were movements to challenge traditions, ideologies, and people's rightful places in American society, especially in regard to certain groups. One of these groups was children and troubled children in particular. The concern with children was not just a national movement. In 1959, the United Nations (UN) created the United Nations Declaration of the Rights of the Child and declared 1959 as the Year of the Child. The principles of the Declaration were to protect the fundamental rights of children, including children who broke the law. The UN relied on the same basic fundamental belief that the American juvenile court touted—that rights ensured for youth be based on "the best interests of the child." The UN, in addressing the issue of troubled youth and society, followed suit. This, coupled with a growing distrust of governmental institutions, seemed to shine a spotlight on juvenile correctional facilities. In addition to reports of ineffectiveness, reports of abuse within the institutions began to surface as well.

Criticisms of the juvenile justice system leveled at this time ran the whole spectrum. The court and institutions were accused of holding unchecked discretion, affording juveniles no due process rights, and labeling youth (Mahoney, 1987; McNally, 1982). Perhaps the most serious and most repeated allegations were those of physical and sexual abuse, allegations that had existed since the houses of refuge.

> Since the founding of the New York House of Refuge in 1825, the history of juvenile corrections has been governed by a repetitive cycle of institutional abuses and scandals, public exposure of these severe problems, and spurts of reformist activity. After brief periods of positive change, the juvenile corrections system usually has drifted back to its tragic cycle of abusive practices. (Breed & Krisberg, 1986, p. 14)

However, the system was also accused of being too lenient and too ineffective with true criminal youth. The 1967 Task Force Report, *Juvenile Delinquency and Youth Crime*, authored by the President's Commission on Law Enforcement and Administration of Justice concluded that the juvenile court "has not succeeded significantly in rehabilitating delinquent youth, in reducing or even stemming the tide of juvenile criminality, or in bringing justice and compassion to the child offender" ("President's Commission," 1967, p. 80).

The commission cautioned that the juvenile justice system was ready to self-destruct. The increasing youth population and the increasing number of youth arrests were taxing the system. Furthermore, the commission stated, the numbers of incarcerated youth would increase by 70% unless there were some significant changes made (Schwartz, 1989).

Outside Interventions

Due Process

Prior to the 1960s, the judicial attitude towards the rights of prisoners, both juvenile and adult, was referred to as the "hands-off" doctrine. For over a century, courts had consistently refused to consider any complaint by a prisoner about the conditions of his confinement; they had taken the well-known "hands-off" position. A prisoner was, in the words of one court, the property of the state (Singer, 1980). The reasons for non-intrusion were many. For example, many judges assumed correctional administrators were best able to administer prisons (Fairchild, 1984). In addition, there existed a lack of judicial expertise in penology and some judges feared intervention would undermine prison authority and discipline (Palmer, 1985). Still other judges believed that courts lacked jurisdiction over inmate grievances (Hanson, 1984). Obviously, the judicial attitude towards adult inmates was mimicked in the juvenile justice system.

Despite this nonintervention, the amount of litigation filed by adult inmates increased dramatically while growing media exposure drew attention to the conditions inside of both adult and juvenile correctional institutions. The courts were forced to address the due process rights of those accused of crime, as well as those already convicted and incarcerated (Molanphy, 1984). "It was only when the complaints began to detail conditions so crass, so gross, as to shock the minds of all decent people that the courts became involved" (Singer, 1980, p. 3). By 1975, the old philosophy that prisoners had no rights was a legacy of the not-too-distant past.

As previously stated, prisoners were becoming more litigious. In 1964, the Supreme Court held in ***Cooper v. Pate*** (378 U.S. 546) that state inmates could bring suit against correctional administrators under Title 42, Section 1983, of the Civil Rights Act. Cases began to pour into courts.

In 1970, a controversial case changed the focus of judicial intervention, when a state's entire prison system was challenged as being in violation of the Eighth Amendment. Arkansas' entire prison system was declared unconstitutional in the 1970 district court case, *Holt v. Sarver* (309 F. Supp 362, E.D. Arkansas). However landmark the case was in judicial intervention, it was not to be unique. By 1983, a total of eight states—Texas, Florida, Mississippi, Tennessee, Alabama, Oklahoma, Michigan, and Rhode Island—had their entire adult prison systems declared unconstitutional. Judicial intervention did not stop with the adult criminal justice system. The Supreme Court and also lower courts did not keep their "hands off" of the juvenile justice system in their reform efforts. In 1966, the Supreme Court of the United States decided its first significant juvenile justice case. In 1967, the Supreme Court decided one of the most significant juvenile justice cases, *In re Gault*, which resulted in far-reaching changes of the juvenile justice system.

The Case That Opened the Door

In September of 1961, sixteen-year-old Morris Kent was taken into custody and charged with breaking into a house, robbery, and rape. Morris was currently on juvenile probation for several home invasions and an attempted purse snatching. Kent's attorney asked for a hearing on whether Kent should be transferred to the adult court and for access to Kent's records. There was no hearing in the case, yet the judge, stating that he had made a full investigation, waived the jurisdiction of the case to the criminal court. The judge gave no reasons for his decision to send the case to the criminal court. After the case was transferred to the adult system, a grand jury indicted Kent. Morris Kent went to trial and was found not guilty by reason of insanity on the rape charges and found guilty on numerous counts of breaking and entering and robbery. He was sentenced to a total of 30 to 90 years in prison (*Kent v. U.S.*, 383 U.S.541).

The question that the Supreme Court was to answer from the *Kent* case was whether juveniles being transferred to adult court have any due process rights during that waiver process. In 1966, the Supreme Court held that juveniles facing transfer to the criminal courts should have certain due process rights that were to be upheld in the transfer process. These rights were:

- A transfer hearing
- An attorney for the hearing
- Access to the records that the juvenile court holds about the juvenile
- A statement of reasons for an affirmative transfer decision (*Kent v. U.S.*, 383 U.S.541)

These rights are very significant as they signaled the first time that juveniles were afforded constitutional rights by the Supreme Court. However, the case dealt only with juveniles being considered for transfer to the adult system, thus not a large percentage of juveniles were impacted by the decision. However, perhaps of most significance was the forewarning that the Supreme Court gave juvenile courts. The Court was not done accepting juvenile justice cases as it certainly did not hold great faith in the practice of juvenile justice in the United States.

> While there can be no doubt of the original laudable purpose of the juvenile courts, studies and critiques of recent years raise serious questions as to whether actual performances measures well enough against purpose to make tolerable the immunity of the process from the reach of constitutional guarantees applicable to adults. There is much evidence that some juvenile courts ... lack the personnel, facilities and techniques to perform adequately as representatives of the State in a *parens patriae* capacity, at least with respect to children charged with law violation. There is evidence, in fact, that there may be grounds for concern that the juvenile receives the worst of both worlds: that he gets neither the protections accorded to adults nor the solicitous care and regenerative treatment postulated for children. (*Kent v. U.S.*, 383 U.S.541)

Notice that while this Court granted juveniles in the process of being transferred some basic fundamental rights, the Court commented on the continued failure of the facilities, and institutions, to rehabilitate troubled youth.

A Case of Major Significance

On June 8, 1964, mid-morning, a 15-year-old named Gerald Gault and his friend, Ronald Lewis, were taken into custody for reportedly making an obscene phone call to a female neighbor, Mrs. Cook. In the words of the Court, "it will suffice, for purposes of this opinion, to say that the remarks or questions put to her were of the irritatingly offensive, adolescent, sex variety" (*In re Gault*, 387 U.S. 1, 1967, 387, 1, 5). Supposedly, the lewd comments consisted of "are your cherries ripe today" and "do you have big bombers" (Snyder & Sickmund, 2006, p. 100). Gerald was already on probation for being with a boy who had taken a wallet out of a woman's purse.

No one informed the Gaults of Gerald's arrest. Later that evening, after investigating his whereabouts, his mother learned that he was being held in detention. She traveled to the detention center, only to be told that Gerald was to have a hearing the next day. The next day, Mrs. Gault, Gerald, Gerald's brother, and the superintendent of the detention center were all present in the judge's chamber. They were the only people present. Apparently, at the hearing, there was some confusion about whether Gerald had made the offensive statements at all or made only some of the statements. The judge sent Gerald back to detention while he pondered the case. Six days later, there was another hearing. This time Gerald, his co-defendant, and parents were present. There was, again, general discussion about the role that Gerald played in the alleged offense. The neighbor who had made the allegation was not present at this hearing either (*In re Gault*, 387 U.S. 1).

After the hearing, the judge committed Gerald to the State Industrial School. The court order stated, as was common practice, that Gerald was to remain there until the age of majority, which was 21 at that time. In essence, Gerald, 15 years old, had just received a possible six-year sentence for making a lewd phone call. If Gerald had been an adult, the maximum punishment for a lewd phone call would have been two months in the local jail or a maximum $50 fine (*In re Gault*, 387 U.S. 1).

After the hearing, the Gaults obtained an attorney who filed a writ of habeas corpus on the grounds that several of Gerald's basic constitutional rights had been violated. In reality, the writ was asking the Supreme Court to hold that juveniles in juvenile court, in fact, *did* have constitutional rights, and as such, this child had been denied his.

The Supreme Court held in the 1967 decision that juveniles who are in an adjudication hearing where an affirmative finding of guilt could result in institutionalization do have certain due process rights. These rights are:

- the right to receive notice of the charges
- the right to counsel
- the right to confront and cross-examine
- the right to remain silent—the right against self-incrimination (*In re Gault*, 387 U.S. 1)

The *Gault* case was, and perhaps still is, the single most important juvenile case ever heard by the Supreme Court, especially in a historical context. By giving juveniles due process rights, the Supreme Court was tinkering with a juvenile system that had specifically *not* given due process rights to juveniles for 68 years, because children needed no due process protection against a system designed to protect them. What the Supreme Court believed about the juvenile justice system is demonstrated in the majority opinion.

> We do not mean by this to denigrate the juvenile court process or to suggest that there are not aspects of the juvenile system relating to offenders which are valuable. But the features of the juvenile system which its proponents have asserted are of unique benefit will not be impaired by constitutional documentation. For example, the commendable principles relating to the processing and treatment of juveniles separately from adults are in no way involved or affected by the procedural issues under discussion.... It would be extraordinary if our Constitution did not require the procedural regularity and exercise of care implied in the phrase "due process." ***Under our Constitution, the condition of being a boy does not justify a kangaroo court.*** (*In re Gault*, 387 U.S. 1, emphasis added)

The Case about Burden of Proof

Twelve-year-old Samuel Winship was adjudicated delinquent for the theft of $112 out of a woman's purse that he had removed from a locker (*In re Winship*, 397 U.S. 358). As was New York juvenile law at the time, Winship was found guilty on a preponderance of the evidence. Winship was committed to the state system of juvenile corrections. He was sent to a facility for an initial 18 months and then could be subjected to extensions up until his 18th birthday, which could total six years. The judge who presided over the case acknowledged that there might not have been enough evidence for an adjudication if the burden of proof in juvenile court was "beyond a reasonable doubt," but the burden in juvenile court was the much lower standard of "preponderance of the evidence" (*In re Winship*, 397 U.S. 358).

The single question that the Supreme Court decided in 1970 was of "whether proof beyond a reasonable doubt is among the 'essential of due process and fair treatment' required during the adjudicatory stage when a juvenile is charged with an act which would constitute a crime if committed by an adult" (*In re Winship*, 397 U.S. 358). Were juveniles accused of committing a delinquent act entitled to the same burden of proof as adults accused of committing a crime? The Supreme Court decided, in a split 5–3 decision, that juveniles were entitled to proof beyond a reasonable doubt in a juvenile adjudication hearing. Furthermore, said the Supreme Court, "We conclude, as we concluded regarding the essential due process safeguards applied in *Gault*, that the observance of the standard of proof beyond a reasonable doubt 'will not compel the states to abandon or displace any of the substantive benefits of the juvenile process'" (*In re Winship*, 397 U.S. 358). In this case, the Supreme Court specifically mentions that an accused child deserves the highest burden of proof to determine guilt in juvenile court when that finding could result in institutionalization (*In re Winship*, 397 U.S. 358).

The Case That Changed Direction

In 1968, 16-year-old Joseph McKeiver was charged with robbery, larceny, and receiving stolen goods. A group of many youth, including Joseph, pursued three other children and robbed them of 25 cents. Joseph requested that he be given a jury trial. His request was denied; he was adjudicated delinquent by a juvenile court judge and placed on juvenile probation. The case that was decided in 1971 by the Supreme Court answered the question of whether juveniles were entitled to a trial by jury in a juvenile adjudicatory hearing. In a 6–3 decision, the Supreme Court held that juveniles were not constitutionally entitled to a trial by jury during an adjudication hearing. In the words of the court, the "requiring of a jury trial might remake the juvenile proceedings into a fully adversarial process, with the attendant delay, formality, and clamor of such process, and would effectively end the juvenile system's idealistic prospect of an intimate, informal, protective procedure" (*McKeiver v. Pennsylvania*, 403 U.S. 545). However, the Supreme Court added, states could grant the right to trial by jury in juvenile adjudication hearings through their state constitutions, were they so inclined.

Federal Intervention

The concerns about juvenile justice in the United States extended to Congress. By the 1960s a series of congressional hearings took place. Many employees and clients of the juvenile justice system testified to mistreatment and even abuse within the system and especially within the institutions. In 1968 Congress passed the Juvenile Delinquency and Control Act, which encouraged states to develop community-based delinquency prevention programs with a promise of federal funding for approved programs ("Juvenile Justice FYI," n.d.).

By the early 1970s, with a national momentum to address juvenile justice and close to six years of research by a Senate sub-committee designated to study juvenile justice, Congress passed a stronger piece of legislation that replaced the Juvenile Delinquency and Control Act. This was the Juvenile Justice and Delinquency Prevention Act of 1974 (known as the JJDPA). JJDPA held a broader mandate aimed at prevention, rehabilitation, and improving the juvenile justice system ("JJPDA Booklet," n.d.). There are four major requirements that the JJDPA is known for, though the last two were added in later years through amendments. In 1974 the primary focus of the act called for the deinstitutionalization of status offenders and the separation of adult and juvenile offenders in jails and institutions. In 1980, the act was amended to include the removal of juveniles from adult jails and lockups; in 1988 the act called for the study of disproportionate minority confinement (DMC); and in 2002, the act expanded that study to all areas of the juvenile justice system process, not just confinement (relabeled Disproportionate Minority Contact) (Snyder & Sickmund, 2006). Compliance with these mandates affected the level of federal funding for juvenile programming within individual states.

Box 7.2: Status Offenses, Status Offenders, and the JJDPA

"A status offense is a noncriminal act that is considered a law violation only because of a youth's status as a minor. Typical status offenses include truancy, running away from home, violating curfew, underage use of alcohol, and general ungovernability" (Development Services Group, 2015, para 1).

"The deinstitutionalization of status offenders (DSO) core requirement of the JJDPA established that youths charged with status offenses, and/or abused and neglected youths, shall not be placed in secure detention or locked confinement. The intent of this requirement was to encourage states to divert status-offending youths away from the juvenile justice system and place them in less restrictive, service-intensive, community-based programs. The DSO requirement reinforces the idea that status offenders should be dealt with differently than juvenile delinquents, and should not be placed in secure detention or correctional facilities" (Development Services Group, 2015, para 7).

Reforms Follow

The preceding cases afforded juveniles many due process rights that were not guaranteed in juvenile court before. These procedural differences changed the face of juvenile justice. In addition, federal intervention and the Juvenile Justice and Delinquency Prevention Act prompted changes in the process of juvenile justice. States removed status offenders from delinquency proceedings, removed juveniles from adult jails, and reexamined institutionalization practices for delinquents. In addition, many states faced judicial intervention as lawsuits challenging the conditions of confinement for juvenile offenders were filed on behalf of institutionalized juveniles. Some truly good programs were created during this time of change. However, the sentiment driving these progressive reforms soon began to waiver. It appears that during this time, the main goal of juvenile reform was to reserve juvenile institutions for those children who truly needed to be locked away from society and to find alternative placements, such as diversion programs, status offender programs, mental health programs, and drug treatment programs, for those who didn't need to be in secure custody. However, despite the strong push for deinstitutionalization, federal intervention, and the rhetoric of reform, the movement was not successful. Yes, many states took status offenders out of the juvenile delinquency statutes, many states invested in diversion programs, and some states even closed juvenile facilities. However, despite these movements, and a falling juvenile crime rate, the numbers of children in juvenile institutions still increased, and inappropriate placements still found their way into the institutions. In the late 1970s, something else began to affect the juvenile justice process in the United States. The general sentiment towards juvenile offenders and the appropriate action to take with them began to shift. People began to look at juvenile offenders less as children needing to be treated fairly and rehabilitated and more as offenders who needed to be punished.

The Coming of the Super-Predator

The more conservative political shift of the late 1970s and 1980s made a significant impact on the juvenile justice system. Monies for new and innovative juvenile programming dried up and forced the system to again rely primarily on institutionalization as a standard response to juvenile offending. The media fueled public sentiment that juvenile crime was getting out of control and that rehabilitation did not work. The public called for a tougher juvenile justice system, one that relied more on punishment and sending a tough message to would-be offenders.

When the juvenile crime rate began to rise in the late 1980s and early 1990s, including violent juvenile crime, the sentiment to "get tough" on juvenile offenders became increasingly stronger. Scholars warned of juvenile crime rates doubling, of the impending juvenile "super-predator" and of an unsalvageable generation of youth (Krisberg, 2005).

> Social scientists such as James A. Fox, John DiIulio, and others promulgated doomsday scenarios. In 1995, for example, Fox predicted a "bloodbath in

> about 10 years." In 1996, DiIulio predicted that there would be "270,000 more young predators on the streets" (DiIulio, 1996). Pronouncements like these were wrapped in racialized, demonizing language that further inflamed public alarm. "The black kids who inspire the fear seem not merely unrecognizable but alien," wrote DiIulio (1996), calling young people who came into contact with the justice system "radically impulsive, brutally remorseless" (Bennett et al., 1996). The most memorable and damaging description was "superpredator" (DiIulio, 1995). (as cited in McCarthy et al., 2016, p. 3)

The federal government and state legislatures responded accordingly. Congress amended the JJDPA to include transfer to adult court for some juvenile offenders, 40 states changed their laws, making it easier to transfer juveniles to adult court, and both "zero tolerance" and curfew laws for juveniles were widely enacted (Krisberg, 2005). Statues mandating the goals of juvenile justice expanded beyond "rehabilitative" language to include the language of deterrence, punishment, accountability, and public safety (Fass & Pi, 2002). The result of these actions for many states was a dramatic change in the handling of juvenile offenders. The system that had once focused on the needs of the child now focused on the acts of the child. Punishment eclipsed, and in some cases replaced, rehabilitation as the standard treatment for juvenile offenders. "Get Tough" measures were enacted long after the juvenile crime rate began to come down in the mid-1990s (McCarthy et al., 2016). The Violent Crime Control and Law Enforcement Act of 1994 encouraged states to update or build prisons incentivized by billions in federal funds. "Much of that money went to states which built, expanded, or renovated youth prisons and detention facilities, and contracted for additional detention and correctional beds" (McCarthy et al., 2016, p. 4). By the end of the 1990s, the number of youths incarcerated in American juvenile training schools reached its peak at 109,000 (McCarthy et al., 2016).

The predictions of the super predator were wrong and based on faulty analytical techniques (McCarthy et al., 2016). Near the end of the 1990s, it appeared as if, perhaps, the pendulum was beginning to swing back to a more rehabilitative approach to juvenile justice. In a FOCUS report by the National Council of Crime and Delinquency presented in 2007, while it was reported that 90% of people polled believe that juvenile crime was still a major concern, 91% of people polled also believe that rehabilitative services for young offenders can deter future crime as well as save tax dollars (Krisberg & Marchionna, 2007).

The End of Capital Punishment for Juveniles

Softening feelings toward juvenile offenders and their punishment did not go unnoticed in the law and policy making arena. The United States Supreme Court once again tackled juvenile and criminal justice practice when it heard the case ***Roper v. Simmons*** in the early 2000s. In 1993, at 17 years old, Christopher Simmons planned and carried out the particularly heinous murder of Shirley Cook. He was convicted and sentenced to death. His appeal was heard all the way to the U.S. Supreme Court. In a 5–4 decision that overturned previous U.S. Supreme Court cases, the Supreme Court "found that executing juveniles served neither the deterrence nor retribution (just desserts) functions of the death penalty" (Weiner, 2005, p. 84). Furthermore,

> Justice Kennedy reasoned that juveniles have diminished culpability for their crimes because, compared to adults (page 1195): They show "lack of maturity and an underdeveloped sense of responsibility," which results in "impetuous and ill-considered actions." They "are more vulnerable or susceptible to negative influences and outside pressures. The character of a juvenile is not as well formed" so that "personality traits of juveniles are transitory, less fixed" (Weiner, 2005, p. 84).
>
> The Court cited adolescent development research finding that children's brains—not just their bodies—are not fully developed, and as a result, they do not have adult levels of judgment or ability to assess risks and the consequences of their actions. The Court noted that children are more susceptible to peer pressure than adults and have little power to escape harmful environments. Because of where they are developmentally, children also have greater potential for rehabilitation. The Court concluded that children are categorically less culpable than adults. (The Campaign for Fair Sentencing, 2018)

The Supreme Court decision also held international implications. This decision put the United States closer to compliance with the United Nations' *Convention on the Rights of the Child.*

Juvenile Life without Parole

Perhaps one of the most significant issues today in juvenile justice is Juvenile Life Without Parole. Once the Supreme Court held that sentencing anyone under age 18 at the time of crime to the death penalty constitutes cruel and unusual punishment, Juvenile Life Without Parole (JLWOP) was used to replace the death penalty as the toughest sentence that could be given to juvenile offenders. The Supreme Court has taken cases involving JLWOP and has narrowed that it can only be handed out for first degree murder and that it cannot be a mandatory sentence (Rovner, 2018). JLWOP is covered in more detail in Chapter 11.

The Juvenile Justice System Today

Most juveniles that come into the juvenile justice system are referred by law enforcement, even though the juvenile justice system can, under strict guidelines, sometimes accept children through other referral sources such as schools or parents. Juveniles go through an intake or screening process to determine if they need to come to the attention of the juvenile court or if there are other appropriate actions that can be taken. If a juvenile goes to juvenile court, they will receive a disposition. This will be covered in detail in the following chapters.

Box 7.3: The Language of Juvenile Justice

The juvenile justice system, since 1899, has had its own language. As it developed to be different from the criminal court system, it adopted its own language. The language used in the juvenile justice system is much softer and much more treatment oriented.

Criminal Justice	Juvenile Justice
Criminal Court	Civil Court
Defendant	Juvenile
Crime	Delinquent Act
Arrest	Take into Custody
An information or indictment	A petition
Trial	Adjudicatory Hearing
To Convict	To Adjudicate Delinquent
Conviction	Adjudication
Guilty Plea	Admission
Sentencing Hearing	Dispositional Hearing
Pre-Sentence Investigation	Predisposition Investigation
Sentence	Disposition
To Incarcerate	To Commit
Parole	Aftercare

In practice, the juvenile justice system is making significant changes in treatment and programming of juveniles based on two relatively recent revelations about children. One is about the development of the adolescent brain. Recent research suggests that the adolescent brain remains immature or not fully developed for a longer span of time than was once believed. Second, research suggests that the youth who come into the juvenile justice system have been exposed to violence at alarming rates and are in trauma. The juvenile justice system needs to take and is taking this recent information and moving forward in creating a system that understands both the physiological aspects of its youth as well as acknowledges that most youth come into the system with trauma.

The Development Model

The system appears to be moving into a new model called the developmental model. That model is changing the way the juvenile justice system makes decisions about programming, policy, and sanctions based on an understanding of adolescent development and what is truly effective in promoting adolescent behavior change.

> Recent research on adolescent development has underscored important behavioral differences between adults and adolescents with direct bearing on the design and operation of the justice system, raising doubts about the core assumptions driving the criminalization of juvenile justice policy in the last decades of the 20th century. (National Research Council, 2013, p. 1)

The underlying crux of the adolescent brain research suggests three important factors that distinguish juveniles from adults. First, if an adolescent is in a position where emotions take over, they are less capable of controlling their emotions than are adults. Second, juveniles are much more influenced by external stimuli such as friends and immediate gratification. Third, juveniles are much less likely than adults to be able to make decisions based on what impact that decision may have in the future. These three factors obviously have a great impact on adolescent development and behavior (National Research Council, 2013).

> Evidence of significant changes in brain structure and function during adolescence strongly suggests that these cognitive tendencies characteristic of adolescents are associated with biological immaturity of the brain and with an imbalance among developing brain systems. (National Research Council, 2013, p. 2)

Trauma-Informed Care

Research suggests that some youth, especially youth coming into the juvenile justice system, are suffering from trauma. This information is important to the juvenile justice system as it will have a major impact on how those youth should be treated and what treatment will be most effective. Underlying trauma must be addressed in their treatment.

> Each year, millions of children are exposed to violence in their homes, schools, and communities. Left unaddressed, these experiences can lead to mental health and substance use disorders, school failure, increased risk taking, and delinquency (Ford et al., 2007; Ford et al., 2010; Saunders et al., 2005; Tuell, 2008). The majority of youth involved with the juvenile justice system have experienced traumatic events, with at least 75 percent having experienced

> traumatic victimization (Sprague, 2008). A recent study of youth in detention found that over 90 percent of youth had experienced at least one trauma, 84 percent experienced more than one trauma, and over 55 percent reported being exposed to trauma six or more times (Abram et al., 2013). (as cited in National Center for Mental Health, 2016, p. 1)

Benefits of a trauma-informed care based juvenile justice system appear to be significant. According to the National Center for Mental Health and Juvenile Justice, trauma-informed care contributes to public safety, overall understanding of youth trauma, and in the long term will produce financial savings (National Center for Mental Health, 2016).

Into the Future

The juvenile justice system is breaking new ground in its treatment of juveniles who violate the law. The juvenile justice system is studying the aforementioned information regarding the adolescent brain and trauma-informed care recommendations and moving forward in creating a system that understands both the physiological aspects of its youth as well as acknowledges that most youth come into the system with trauma. There have been tremendous changes.

However, there have been some troubling fluctuations in the crime rates. While crime rates still remain below rates of thirty years ago, variations in crime during the 2000s have some very concerned (Butts & Snyder, 2006). A 2018 publication by the Office of Juvenile Justice and Delinquency Prevention notes, "Juvenile arrest rates for violent crimes, such as robbery and aggravated assault, have declined in the last 5 years. Conversely, juvenile arrest rates for murder have increased since 2012" (Puzzanchera, 2018, p. 1). An additional spike in juvenile crime between 2020 and 2022 has some worried, although the 2023 data show decreasing crime rates. The media, public, and policymakers are taking particular interest.

Will this impact juvenile justice? Citing concern with the change in juvenile crime rates, lawmakers in "Louisiana and North Carolina have passed laws that roll back recent reforms and allow more of these teenagers to be prosecuted as adults" (Loudenback, 2024, para 2). The North Carolina bill expanded the crimes that call for automatic transfer of juveniles to criminal court. The bill was vetoed by the North Carolina governor, Roy Cooper, who stated "There are cases where sentences would be more effective and appropriate to the severity of the crime for teenagers if they were handled in juvenile court, making communities safer" (cited in Loudenback, para 17, 2024). The bill became law in 2024 after the governor's veto was overridden by the legislature. Is this an isolated incident or a glimpse into future changes?

Summary Points

- This chapter has reviewed the history of juvenile justice and juvenile institutionalization in the United States. This chapter especially focused on the philosophical beliefs that led to a separate juvenile justice system—more of a social welfare system than a legal system.
- This chapter also discussed the concerns of unchecked power and abuse that have plagued juvenile justice reforms from the houses of refuge in the early 1800s to today. Reforms to the system, including the intervention of the federal government and the United States Supreme Court, significantly changed the practice of juvenile justice in the United States.
- The public's perception in the United States regarding children who break the law affects the way society treats those children and the way that the legislature and state governments form laws to deal with juvenile delinquents. We are in an interesting time. After decades of juvenile crime rates falling we have seen recent increases that are of concern. What the future holds for juvenile justice remains uncertain.

Box 7.4: Informational Websites

For more information about the history of juvenile justice, visit one of the following websites.

Juvenile Detention in New York: Then and Now

http://www.correctionhistory.org/html/chronicl/djj/djj20yrs3.htm#1800

Lyman Boys School in Westborough, Massachusetts (1848–1971)

http://freepages.history.rootsweb.ancestry.com/~history/grafton/LymanSchool.html

For information about the current juvenile justice system, visit one of the following websites.

Office of Juvenile Justice and Delinquency Prevention

https://www.ojjdp.gov/

National Center for Juvenile Justice

http://www.ncjj.org/about/History.aspx

Key Terms

Doctrine of Parens Patriae: translates roughly into Father of the Child. Used in the history of juvenile justice in the U.S. to give the state the authority to take custody of troubled children.

Ex parte Crouse: 1839 Pennsylvania Supreme Court case which held that troubled children had no basic constitutional rights and that the authority of the state superseded the rights of parents whose children were troubled. The holdings of the case were widely followed.

Infancy Defense: in the young United States, children who broke the law were treated as children were in other countries under English Common Law. If they were younger than seven, they were presumed to not have legal responsibility for their actions, and thus they could not be prosecuted in court.

JJDPA 1974: the Juvenile Justice and Delinquency Prevention Act held a broader mandate aimed at prevention, rehabilitation, and improving the juvenile justice system ("JJPDA Booklet," n.d.). There are four major requirements that the JJDPA is known for, though the last two were added in later years through amendments.

New York City House of Refuge: The New York House of Refuge opened in New York City on January 1, 1825. It was located in the rural area of Broadway and 23rd Street in Manhattan. The House of Refuge was modeled after adult prisons, but it was unique in that it housed only youth (New York State Archives, 1989).

Status Offender: a juvenile who commits an offense that is only an offense because that person is a juvenile and not an adult. Examples include running away from home, truancy, and being beyond parental control.

Super-Predator: scholars warned of juvenile crime rates doubling, of the impending juvenile "super-predator" and of an unsalvageable generation of youth in the early 1990s. (Krisberg, 2005). Use of the term became widespread.

References

Breed, A. F., & Krisberg, B. (1986). Juvenile corrections: Is there a future? *Corrections Today*, *48*(8), 14–20.

Butts, J. A., & Snyder, H. N. (2006, November). *Too soon to tell: Deciphering recent trends in youth violence*. Issue Brief #110. Chapin Hall Center for Children at the University of Chicago.

The Campaign for the Fair Sentencing of Youth. (2018, January 28) *Roper v. Simmons* (2005). https://www.fairsentencingofyouth.org/court-case/roper-v-simmons-2005/

Cooper v. Pate, 378 U.S. 546 (1964).

Del Carmen, R. V., Parker, M. L., & Reddington, F. P. (1998). *Briefs of leading cases in juvenile justice*. Anderson Publishing Company.

Development Services Group, Inc. (2015, September). *Status Offenders*. Literature Review, a Product of the Model Programs Guide. Office of Juvenile Justice and Delinquency Prevention. U.S. Department of Justice. https://www.ojjdp.gov/mpg/litreviews/Status_Offenders.pdf

Ex parte Crouse, 4 Whart. 9; 1839 Pa. (1839).

Fairchild, E. S. (1984). The scope and study of prisoner litigation issues. *The Justice System Journal, 9*(3), 325–351.

Fass, S. M., & Pi, C. R. (2002). Getting tough on juvenile crime: An analysis of costs and benefits. *Journal of Research in Crime and Delinquency, 39*(4), 363–399.

Ferdinand, T. N. (1991). History overtakes the juvenile justice system. *Crime & Delinquency, 37*(2), 204–224.

Fox, S. J. (1996). The early history of the court. *The Future of Children, 6*(3), 29–39.

Hanson, R. (Ed.) (1984). Prisoner litigation: Problems, processes and solutions. *Justice System Journal, 9*, 252–350.

Henderson, K. (2018, March 27). *Historical film on Lyman School for Boys*. Westborough TV. https://westboroughtv.org/screening-of-discovered-film-on-lyman-school-for-boys/

Holt v. Sarver, 309 Fed. Supp 362, E.D. Ark. (1970).

In re Gault, 387 U.S. 1 (1967).

In re Winship, 397 U.S. 358 (1970).

Juvenile Justice Delinquency Prevention Act Booklet (JJDPA). (2002). It's the law. www.cj.msu.edu/_outreach/jj/booklet_2002.html

Juvenile Justice FYI. (n.d.). www.juvenilejusticefyi.com/history_of_juvenile_justice.html

Kent v. United States, 383 U.S. 541 (1966).

Krisberg, B. (1988). *The juvenile court: Reclaiming the vision*. National Council on Crime and Delinquency.

Krisberg, B. (1995). The legacy of juvenile corrections. *Corrections Today, 57*(5), 122.

Krisberg, B. (2005, August 14). *Reforming juvenile justice*. The American Prospect. https://prospect.org/special-report/reforming-juvenile-justice/

Krisberg B., & Marchionna, S. (2007, February). *Attitudes of US voters toward youth crime and the justice system*. FOCUS. Views from the National Council of Crime and Delinquency.

Loudenback, J. (2023). After juvenile justice reform, two states move to prosecuting more teens as adults. *The Imprint: Youth and Family News*. https://imprintnews.org/top-stories/after-juvenile-justice-reforms-two-states-return-to-prosecuting-more-teens-as-adults/251395

Mahoney, A. R. (1987). *Juvenile justice in context*. Northeastern University Press.

McCarthy, P., Schiraldi, V., & Shark, M. (2016, October). *The future of youth justice: A community-based alternative to the youth prison model*. National Institute of Justice.

McCarty, J. (2000). They rode the orphan trains. www.rootsweb.com/-mogrundy/orphans.html

McKeiver v. Pennsylvania, 403 U.S. 528 (1971).

McNally, R. B. (1982). Nearly a century later: The child savers-child advocates and the juvenile justice system. *Juvenile Court Digest*, *33*(3), 47–52.

Mennel, R. M. (1972, January). Origins of the juvenile court: Changing perspectives on the legal rights of juvenile delinquents. *Crime and Delinquency*, *18*, 68–78.

Molanphy, H. C. (1984). The U.S. courts and prison reform: *Ruiz v. Estelle*. *The Prison Journal*, *64*(2), 68–75.

National Center for Mental Health and Juvenile Justice. (2016). *Trauma among youth in the juvenile justice system*. https://www.ncmhjj.com/wp-content/uploads/2016/09/Trauma-Among-Youth-in-the-Juvenile-Justice-System-for-WEBSITE.pdf

National Research Center. (2013). *Reforming juvenile justice: A developmental approach*. Committee on Assessing Juvenile Justice Reform, R. J. Bonnie, R. L. Johnson, B. M. Chemers, & J. A. Schuck (Eds.). Committee on Law and Justice, Division of Behavioral and Social Sciences and Education. The National Academies Press.

New York State Archives. (1989). "A Brief History." In *The greatest reform school in the world: A guide to the records of the New York House of Refuge* (pp. 4–5). http://www.archives.nysed.gov/common/archives/files/res_topics_ed_reform.pdf

Palmer, J. W. (1985). *Constitutional rights of prisoners* (3rd ed.). Anderson Publishing Company.

Pisciotta, A. W. (1983). Race, sex, and rehabilitation: A study of differential treatment in the juvenile reformatory, 1825–1900. *Crime & Delinquency*, *29*(2), 254–269.

Platt, A. (1969). The rise of the child-saving movement: A study in social policy and correctional reform. *The Annals of the American Academy of Political and Social Science*, *381*(1), 21–38.

Platt, A. (1977). *The child savers*. University of Chicago Press.

President's Commission on Law Enforcement and the Administration of Justice. (1967). *Task force report: Corrections*. U.S. Government Printing Office.

Public Broadcasting Service (PBS). (1995, November 27). The orphan trains. *The American Experience*. www.pbs.org/wgbh/amex/orphan/

Puzzanchera, C. (2018). *Juvenile arrests, 2016*. Juvenile Justice Statistics: National Report Series Bulletin. Office of Juvenile Justice and Delinquency Prevention. U.S. Department of Justice.

Rovner, J. (2018). *Juvenile life without parole: An overview*. The Sentencing Project.

Schwartz, I. (1989). *(In)Justice for juveniles: Rethinking the best interests of the child*. Lexington Books.

Sheldon, R. G. (2005). *From houses of refuge to "youth corrections": Same story, different day*. Paper presented at the Midwestern Criminal Justice Association Meeting in Chicago, September 29–October 1, 2005.

Shepherd, R. E. (1999). The juvenile court at 100 years: A look back. *Juvenile Justice, 6*(2).

Singer, R. G. (1980). Prisoner's rights litigation: A look at the past decade and a look at the coming decade. *Federal Probation, 44*(4), 3–11.

Snyder, H. N., & Sickmund, M. (2006). *Juvenile offenders and victims: 2006 national report.* Office of Juvenile Justice and Delinquency Prevention. U.S. Department of Justice.

Ventrell, M. (2005). The practice of law for children. *Montana Law Review, 66*(1), 1–19.

Weiner, R. (2005). Judicial notebook: Outlawing the juvenile death penalty. *Monitor on Psychology, 36*(7). The American Psychological Association.

Wooden, K. (2006). *Weeping in the playtime of others: America's incarcerated children.* Ohio State University Press.

Chapter 8

Policing Juveniles

Chapter Learning Objectives

Students will be able to:

- Describe how the police respond to juvenile delinquents, status offenders, and abused and/or neglected youth
- Explain the role of discretion and legal and extralegal factors that influence police decision-making in juvenile encounters
- Interpret juvenile arrest data, including violent and property offenses
- Assess the differences in female juvenile offending versus male juvenile offending
- Interpret and explain racial and ethnic disparities in the juvenile justice system
- Explain a juvenile's *Miranda* rights and the concerns with juvenile police interrogation
- Determine which cases involving youth are appropriate for protective custody
- Identify program efforts that strengthen the relationship between juveniles and law enforcement

Introduction

In 2013, the International Association of Chiefs of Police (IACP) gathered for a summit on law enforcement leadership in juvenile justice. Conversations centered around the idea of juvenile reform and how reform can best be achieved by law enforcement fostering positive development and new initiatives. While there have been advancements in technology to enhance law enforcement practice, participants of the summit agreed that little has been done to advance police-juvenile interactions. Furthermore, there needs to be more alternatives other than arrest for juveniles, and greater support is needed for troubled youth and their families. Despite the adoption of paramilitaristic policing strategies after 9/11, rehabilitative strategies remain necessary and at the forefront when a police officer encounters a youth. At the same time, it is of equal importance to recognize and maintain officer and public safety. At the summit, Riverside Police Department Chief Thomas Weitzel remarked, "My officers receive so much firearms training, and yet they rarely fire a shot," he said, "and in some cases may never fire their weapon in the line of duty. Meanwhile they have multiple contacts each day with juveniles" (Bahney, 2014, p. 13).

Characterizing the various ways that police officers interact with juveniles is no easy task. There is obviously a myriad of factors that go into police-youth interactions. For one, youth are minors. So unlike police interactions with adults, officers are expected to make decisions that are in the best interest of the youth and the community. This may include cases where the officer needs to protect the youth from harm or when the officer needs to protect society from the potential harm that the youth may cause. Second, interactions are compounded by the fact that there is no one-size-fits-all procedure for police to follow; although the courts, state legislation, and academy training serve as a guide for law enforcement officers. Third, officers have considerable power and discretion to do what is necessary within the confines of the law. In brief, what can be said with certainty is that police officers often find themselves as the point of first contact with youth victims, delinquents, and status offenders, demonstrating the significant role that they play when it comes to encounters with juveniles.

Police Encounters with Juvenile Delinquents

Again, there is no simple way to describe the numerous encounters with juvenile delinquents. Rather, it must be reiterated that police officers serve as gatekeepers to the juvenile justice system given the amount of discretion they possess in situations that involve juveniles. It is also worth noting that decisions are not made completely in a vacuum; officers are trained to consider the least restrictive alternative, and avoiding arrest is pivotal unless a serious crime has been committed. What follows is a description of the common elements involved in police interactions with juveniles. Furthermore, each state has its own legal code, so there is no way to truly capture all of these nuances. Some of these procedures fall right in line with policing adults; however, since juveniles are involved, there are often differences and exceptions.

Detection

Most police work involves basic patrol, which means the officer is tasked with providing a presence that will aid in preventing crime, along with responding to calls and completing duties that may be requested by the officer's superior (Hess et al., 2015). Traditional law enforcement also involves the detection and investigation of a crime in order to apprehend the person or persons responsible for an alleged crime. Most often, the police detect crimes simply by virtue of their routine patrols and/or by responding to the complaints of a citizen, a victim, or a family member. For drug or liquor law violations, police may take part as undercover officers in order to apprehend the wrongdoers. Also, traditional law enforcement patrols center around known "hot spots" in a community where delinquent activity is known to occur.

In situations that involve violent crimes, 2018 and 2019 statistical data compiled from the National Incident-Based Reporting System (NIBRS) suggests that officers commonly respond to incidents of juvenile violence after school and in the evening on weekends (OJJDP, 2022). The violent crime rate among youth was the highest at 3 p.m., with a rate of 64.6 per 1,000 juvenile violent offenders, followed by a rate of 35.6 per 1,000 at 5 p.m. The chance of violent offending decreases as the evening goes on during a school night. On weekends, violent crimes among juveniles peak between the hours of 7 p.m. and 8 p.m. On weekends or non-school days around 7 p.m., the violent juvenile crime rate is around 26.6 per 1,000. As the evening wears on, there is not much difference in violent offending on school days or non-school days. For example, at 9 p.m. on a weekend, the violent juvenile crime rate is 23.5 per 1,000 versus a rate of 22.6 per 1,000 on school days. Statistical findings like these lend themselves to implementing more school-based prevention programs for youth, which is discussed later in this chapter.

Agency Policies and Training

Bostic and colleagues (2014) claim that little to no training is devoted to preparing police officers for arresting youth. As a result, some youths are arrested for "contempt of cop" or some other display of disrespect to a police officer. Due to a lack of training, officers may rush to judgment and may not consider the developmental factors that can explain a youth's misbehavior. This is not to say that police departments do not take juvenile matters seriously. For example, in partnership with the Police Foundation, officers in California have resources at their disposal, such as the *Toolkit for California Law Enforcement: Policing Today's Youth*, which describes the teen brain and consists of examples of how officers can better assist and interact with young people. This document calls for a tailored approach to responding to youth and informs officers that based on neuroscience, a youth's brain is not fully developed until age 20 or 22 (see Box 8.1).

Throughout the years, law enforcement agencies and organizations have made various attempts to improve how young people are handled at the point of first contact. The IACP (2015), through a partnership with the Office of Juvenile Justice and Delinquency Prevention (OJJDP), offers ten ways to promote positive police-youth relations. They are:

1. Approach youth with a calm demeanor, conveying that you are there to help them.
2. Establish rapport.
3. Be patient.
4. Model the respect you expect in return.
5. Use age-appropriate language.

6. Repeat or rephrase their statements. Affirm their emotions.
7. Take caution with nonverbal communication.
8. Model and praise calm confidence.
9. Empower them through choices.
10. Serve as a positive adult role model. (IACP, 2015, p. 4)

Considering recent high-profile cases involving unarmed, Black youth, the IACP and the Police Foundation have encouraged departments to implement specific policies when encountering youth. This knowledge can, in turn, assist officers in knowing how a teen thinks, and as a result, can help de-escalate a situation and avoid arrest of the juvenile, if warranted. In Grand Rapids, for example, Michigan police officers are provided with the following directives.

Officers shall take the following factors, if known, into consideration when interacting with youth, including but not limited to:

- Nature of the complaint or contact, including probability of possessing a weapon
- Age, intelligence, mental capacity, and physical condition
- Prior contacts/history with officers
- Likelihood to comply with parental control
- Cooperation and attitude of all parties and the likelihood of the offense being repeated
- Likelihood that the youth can be successfully referred to a supporting social service agency. (City of Grand Rapids, MI, 2018, p. 1–2)

The National Policing Institute, formerly known as the Police Foundation (2016), also put forth a number of general recommendations to assist police departments when interacting with youth, and these include:

- Teach officers to respond appropriately to youth with mental health and substance abuse history; through proper training, utilizing crisis intervention and de-escalation techniques to increase the safety of those involved.
- Develop roles for officers to engage youth and families in a positive manner and promote opportunities to engage in community-based activities.
- Promote alternatives to arrest, court referral, or detention by developing protocols in partnership with schools, counselors, treatment providers, and families for diversion options for law enforcement, when possible, to avoid directing youth to the juvenile justice system.
- Educate juveniles about the justice system and the consequences relating to their actions to aid in developing healthy relationships with police, who can serve as role models, guides, and resources; can promote law enforcement careers with youth and can increase safety in schools and neighborhoods. (Police Foundation, 2016, p. 3)

Box 8.1: Neuroscience and Policing the Teen Brain

It was once thought that the human brain was fully developed by age five or six (Blakemore & Choudhury, 2006). Neuroscientists have discovered using Magnetic Resonance Imaging (MRI) and by studying samples of youth brain development over time that the prefrontal cortex region of a youth's brain is still undergoing changes in gray matter. The *prefrontal cortex* is known to be the area of the brain responsible for what is called executive function. Here, the brain helps a person "think" before they act and weigh good behavior with bad behavior as well as weigh future consequences of current behaviors. So, for a youth where the frontal cortex (which supports concrete rule learning) is still underdeveloped, the youth's brain will rely more on the amygdala than an adult's brain. The *amygdala* is the region of the brain that is part of the limbic system and is developed earlier in life to assist with immediate reactions, namely the response of fear or aggression. What this means for an officer is that youth are more likely, given their underdeveloped prefrontal cortex, to act on impulse, get into accidents, get into fights, engage in more risky behaviors, and exhibit more resistance to authority.

Source: Blakemore, S. J., & Choudhury, S. (2006). Development of the adolescent brain: Implications for executive function and social cognition. *Journal of Child Psychology and Psychiatry*, *47*(3/4), 296–312. https://doi.org/10.1111/j.1469-7610.2006.01611.x

Search and Seizure

Because the U.S. Constitution affords us the right to privacy, the government or agents of law enforcement cannot encroach on these protections. These Fourth Amendment protections involving **search and seizure** are in theory no different for juveniles than adults. For police officers, a search may be conducted of a juvenile and their property, but the law reaffirms that the search must be reasonable, that is, the officer must have probable cause, and a warrant is required (Hess et al., 2015). Should there be objects or persons that are related to a crime, these items or persons can be seized. With this said, there are exceptions, commonly called warrantless searches. For example, if the juvenile is an immediate threat or danger to another person, the search is allowed. Another example would be if the juvenile was found to be intoxicated while driving. Clearly, in this case, the juvenile would most likely be taken into custody, and the right to search their vehicle would be warranted. There are also exceptions where the juvenile consents to the search, and therefore the need for a warrant is void.

Since education is compulsory for most minors until the age of sixteen in most states, juveniles spend a lot of time in school, where searches are also conducted. States have varying search laws when they are conducted on school property. Some states may afford more power to the police officer to conduct the search on school grounds as there is a need to protect students, employees, and the physical grounds. Such a case reached the U.S. Supreme Court in 1985—*New Jersey v. T.L.O.*—where the court ruled that the Fourth Amendment's protection of unreasonable searches and seizures was not just limited to searches that are carried out by police officers but public school officials as well (see Box 8.2). However, public school officials are afforded the opportunity to conduct a warrantless search notwithstanding the probable cause standard.

Box 8.2: *New Jersey v. T.L.O.* (1985)

The case of *New Jersey v. T.L.O.* involved a 14-year-old freshman girl in a New Jersey high school and her peer, who were smoking cigarettes in the school bathroom (Stoddard, 2011). A teacher discovered the girls and escorted them to the principal's office. The school's assistant vice-principal questioned the girls about smoking in the bathroom, to which T.L.O. denied smoking in the bathroom and denied smoking whatsoever. Subsequently, the vice-principal asked to see the young girl's purse and opened it to find a pack of cigarettes as well as rolling papers. In addition, he found marijuana, a pipe, and plastic bags. The search of the contents of her purse also revealed a large sum of money and a list of students who owed the girl money. The search yielded strong evidence that the girl was involved in dealing marijuana, which led to delinquency charges.

Arguments were brought forward by the defendant's counsel that the evidence found in her purse should be suppressed as the search itself was illegal (Stoddard, 2011). She later admitted to selling drugs, was adjudicated by the juvenile court, and was sentenced to one year of probation. So, was it legal for school officials to search her purse? Did the **exclusionary rule**, which states that evidence obtained from an unreasonable search is a violation of the Fourth Amendment (e.g., *Mapp v. Ohio*), apply to her case? If so, the contents of her purse would have been inadmissible. The case was initially heard in the Juvenile and Domestic Relations Court of Middlesex County in New Jersey, where it was ruled that the search was legal as the school official had reasonable suspicion that a crime had been committed. The New Jersey Appellate Court also responded to arguments in the case and ruled that there was no Fourth Amendment violation, yet the court requested that the case return to juvenile court to reassess whether T.L.O. had voluntarily waived her Fifth Amendment rights against self-incrimination. Eventually, the case reached the New Jersey State Supreme Court. Support was given to the lower court's ruling regarding the Fourth Amendment and its applicability to searches conducted by school officials. However, the state supreme court did not agree that the search was reasonable as simple possession of cigarettes was not in violation of the school rules. This meant that the vice-principal did not have any justification for searching T.L.O.'s purse.

Ultimately, the U.S. Supreme Court was left to consider whether the Fourth Amendment protections of unreasonable searches and seizures were applicable to searches conducted by school officials. The court ruled that youth are afforded such protections and are granted an expectation of privacy while on school grounds (Stoddard, 2011). Accordingly, school officials do not have the same authority as a student's parents, although, in the present case, the school officials acted quite reasonably. The bottom line is that public school officials, in this case, were believed to conduct a reasonable search and are generally permitted to do so if they have "reasonable grounds," especially if there is a suspicion that a school rule has been broken.

Source: Stoddard, B. (2011). *New Jersey v. T.L.O.*: School searches and the applicability of the exclusionary rule in juvenile delinquency and criminal proceedings. *Brigham Young University Education & Law Journal, 2*, 667–700. https://digitalcommons.law.byu.edu/elj/vol2011/iss2/19

Miranda Warnings

Similar to the adult system, *Miranda* rights also extend to juveniles. These rights were issued in the landmark case *Miranda v. Arizona* in 1966. Even though the Supreme Court of the United States did not include specific language, the typical wording of a *Miranda* warning includes:

> You have the right to remain silent. Anything you say can and will be used against you in a court of law. You have the right to an attorney. If you cannot afford an attorney, one will be provided for you. Do you understand the rights I have just read to you? With these rights in mind, do you wish to speak to me?

Upon more detailed inspection, the *Miranda* decision prescribed five key elements that must be present in a ***Miranda* warning**, as noted in the excerpt above. First, these warnings address one's right to silence, the consequences of surrendering this right, the privilege and right to receive counsel, the right to obtain indigent defense counsel, should it be necessary, and the fact that these rights can be extensive and ongoing as one proceeds forward into legal processes that may involve interrogation (Rogers et al., 2016). After the warning is read, police officers in most states are also expected to affirm that the individual understands these rights with a follow-up question, such as "Do you understand these rights?" (Hess et al., 2015). Nonetheless, many different versions of the *Miranda* warning exist for both adults and juveniles. Constitutional protections of *Miranda* were not extended to juveniles until the 1970s in the case *In re Gault*, which is explained in Chapter 7.

There are a few caveats to *Miranda* that warrant further discussion. Since youth are involved, the language used in the warning must be fully understood by the juvenile. To examine this issue further, Rogers and colleagues (2016) conducted an experiment to investigate a juvenile's comprehension and recall of *Miranda* warnings. Youth held in detention and at-risk youth, who were ordered into an educational alternative program, were given a crime vignette along with a *Miranda* warning that was issued both orally and in written fashion. Afterward, they were given a test to recall the content of the warning, in addition to a cognitive and psychological functioning assessment.

Results showed that the juveniles were unable to recall even half of the details in the *Miranda* warning. Interestingly, the researchers found that *Miranda* recall was more successful when youth were given the chance to read the warning as opposed to being presented with the warning in an oral fashion. It also led the researchers to call into question a larger issue, that is, whether juveniles are forfeiting their rights as they have little understanding of the rights that have been stated to them.

In an earlier study, Rogers et al. (2010) sought to analyze the content of 293 juvenile *Miranda* warnings that were obtained from county prosecutors and public defenders. They assessed the length of each warning in addition to the reading level of the warning using the Flesh-Kincaid reading ease standards. Close to 65% of the warnings were found to be too long. For instance, some warnings were over 175 words to 224 words in length, as opposed to 64 words shown in the earlier example, suggesting additional challenges would follow in *Miranda* comprehension and recall. Also, for nearly 92% of warnings, the comprehension level was higher than a sixth-grade reading level. A few were even written above the twelfth-grade reading level. Again, the research here lends itself to policy changes among police departments and careful consideration that must be given to the length and reading level of *Miranda* warnings that are issued to juveniles.

Over the years, other factors and situations have cast *Miranda* warnings into question. For instance, what about a youth who does not speak or understand English? Previous rulings have stated that if the youth does not understand English, a translation of these rights must be provided. There are other circumstances where it is just as important to understand when *Miranda* warnings are not dictated by law. For example, if the juvenile is casually speaking to an officer or if the youth is not in custody, *Miranda* rights are not applicable. Additional issues have been raised concerning juveniles waiving their *Miranda* rights, in which case, the juvenile must possess sound judgment and choose to waive their rights voluntarily. Moving forward, there is grave concern that juveniles may not fully understand and comprehend their rights, suggesting that a lot of legal and policy-based work still needs to be done.

Taken into Custody

In the adult system, it is common to use the term *arrest*. However, efforts have been made to reduce the stigma associated with this term and process when it involves a juvenile. Recall the labeling perspective from Chapter 4 and the ways in which a youth's self-identity may be impacted as they receive messages of being a "bad kid," especially as they travel through the formal processes of the court system. Thus, youth advocates and juvenile court personnel claim that while a juvenile is "arrested" in the traditional sense, the appropriate terminology is **taken into custody**, which refers to a process where a juvenile is physically apprehended by a police officer.

From a formal training perspective, officers must deal with situations that involve youth according to legal codes and protocol. Above all, the police officer's duty is to

make sure the juvenile is protected first. Police are expected to forgo punitive options in lieu of taking a rehabilitative role as much as the situation calls for. Second, the officer has the responsibility to investigate the situation and determine if the youth was victimized or if a delinquent act or a status offense occurred. Next, the objective is to seek a proper response. In order for a youth to be taken into custody, in many states, the responding officer only needs **reasonable suspicion**, which is a standard or presumption made by the officer that under the circumstances there is reason to believe that a person is committing a crime, and not **probable cause**, which involves a higher standard of proof where facts support that a crime has been, is being, or will be committed. The use of the reasonable suspicion standard by a police officer in situations involving status offenders is particularly upheld in the Uniform Juvenile Court Act that was formally adopted by the National Conference Commissioners on Uniform State Laws in 1968 (Arthur, 1969). Section 13 of the act states:

> (a) A child may be taken into custody:
>
> (1) pursuant to an order of the court under this Act;
>
> (2) pursuant to the laws of arrest;
>
> (3) by a law enforcement officer [or duly authorized officer of the court] if there are reasonable grounds to believe that the child is suffering from illness or injury or is in immediate danger from his surroundings, and that his removal is necessary; or
>
> (4) by a law enforcement officer [or duly authorized officer of the court,] if there are reasonable grounds to believe that the child has run away from his parents, guardian, or other custodian.

(b) The taking of a child into custody is not an arrest, except for the purpose of determining its validity under the Constitution of this State or of the United States.

Police Discretion

As mentioned earlier, even though there is protocol and state legal code to follow, there is often no formula or definitive approach for dealing with juveniles, and on many occasions, there is situational ambiguity, which opens the door for an officer to use discretion. **Discretion** refers to the decision-making power afforded to a police officer that may be based on personal opinion but is administered within a given legal framework. An advisory legal framework is not only part of the officer's training but also part of the administrative policy of most police departments. Officers are trained to use their discretion with juveniles in the sense that they apply the least restrictive alternative and that they seek other options beyond making an arrest.

To break this down further, Schulenberg and Warren (2009) outline how discretion is used among police officers at three critical stages involving minors. The first decision-making point occurs when the police officer takes into consideration whether an incident occurred or is substantiated. Next, the officer must decide if it is appropriate to address the situation formally by taking the youth into custody or handling the situation informally. Formal action entails taking the youth into custody and filing a petition, alleging the juvenile is a delinquent, while informal action includes, but is not limited to (1) releasing the youth with no verbal warning, (2) verbally warning the youth about the consequences of their behavior and releasing them to the custody of a parent or legal guardian, or (3) diverting the youth away from juvenile justice system by referring the youth to community-based or social service agencies (Potter & Kakar, 2002; Wilson & Hoge, 2012).

Legal Factors

In a system that is fair and just, it is presumed that an officer will rely on **legal factors**, which are objective and legally supported reasons for a juvenile's behavior, before arresting a juvenile (Walker et al., 2018). To illustrate this further, the Fairfax County Police Department in Virginia (2017) provides a set of decision-making guidelines to assist officers in determining whether juveniles should be managed informally or formally and which factors should be taken into consideration. Officers are instructed to consider the following factors: (1) the seriousness of the offense, (2) the prior record of the juvenile, (3) the juvenile's age, (4) cooperation and attitude of all parties (juvenile, parent, victim), (5) the possibility of the offense being repeated, (6) the degree of wrongful intent, violence, premeditation, and knowledge of violation, and (7) the likelihood that the juvenile or parent can be successfully referred to a social services agency.

There are several legal factors that an officer takes into consideration, and for the sake of brevity, researchers have identified the most common legal factors to be: the nature or seriousness of the offense, past history of the offender or previous involvement in the juvenile justice system, and evidence of suspicious behavior. When it comes to the first factor, the seriousness of the offense, if the juvenile's behavior is not serious and if there is no evidence of wrongdoing, the likelihood of arrest is extremely low (Myers, 2002). On the contrary, if there are conditions to support probable cause and the crime involves a minor property offense or a more severe public disorder crime, the likelihood of arrest increases. As expected, when the case involving a juvenile extends to a more serious property crime or a serious personal crime, the likelihood of taking the youth into custody yet again increases. Here, the circumstances are usually a bit more straightforward. If the youth is found breaking the law or if there is evidence to support that the law has been broken, it is reasonable for the officer to take the youth into custody. For example, if the youth is found in possession of a controlled substance with intent to sell, the logical step is for the officer to take the juvenile to the police department for questioning. The second factor is the juvenile's offense history. Police officers coming into contact repeatedly with the same juvenile will lead to the same outcome—taking the youth into custody. Evidence of suspicious behavior is the third factor. If youths are hanging out past curfew and in groups of two or more, it is more likely that the police officer will stop and question the youths. Among a group of police officers surveyed in Cleveland, Ohio, it is assumed that young people hanging around together are probably up to no good, and there is a strong likelihood that a delinquent act may occur (Allen, 2005). Such suspicious behavior places youth under the microscope, resulting in a higher likelihood that the youth will be questioned or taken into custody.

Extralegal Factors

Extralegal factors are subjective reasons about a juvenile or their behavior that a police officer may use in arrest decisions that are not found in the legal code (Walker et al., 2018). These factors are unrelated to the crime and may be linked to prejudice and bias. It is not unusual for factors like pressure from the public, media representations of youth, or prior encounters and experiences to be part of the toolkit an officer uses in making arrest decisions either. As shown in the research, three common extralegal factors that may play a role in a police officer's decision to arrest and that will be described next include attitude, race, and gender. Here, these factors are also framed as bias.

Attitudinal Bias

One of the most common and predictive factors used by a police officer when taking a youth into custody involves the youth's demeanor or attitude. More specifically, juveniles who demonstrate a lack of respect toward the officer or who are more hostile and assertive have a higher likelihood of being arrested than youth who are more cooperative and compliant with an officer. Allen's (2005) study supported this notion as 76% of the Cleveland police officers surveyed agreed that "adolescents who disrespect police officers should be taken into custody" (p. 126). As stated earlier in the chapter, a youth's demeanor and outward appearance may be indicative of their age and response to authority figures. This is where police officers have to consider the age of the individual and how even some behaviors may not be a matter of disrespect but of nervousness or fear of an authority figure.

Aside from the displays of attitudes that police officers perceive among youth, alternatively, the attitudes youth have toward police officers are important to consider. Several qualitative studies have shown that non-white youth are more likely to have negative attitudes about the police than white youth (Brick et al., 2009; Romain & Hassell, 2014; Sanden & Wentz, 2017). Nordberg and colleagues (2016) analyzed peer-reviewed qualitative studies in the United States that focused on the experiences and attitudes of minority youth during a police encounter. The results of this study yielded four major themes: dangerousness, control, prejudices, and ineffectiveness. First, Black and Latino/a youth expressed an inherent level of dangerousness when encountering the police, especially when police would misinterpret their behavior as threatening, and when the youth believed their behavior to be either innocent or benign. Second, youth of color found that police encounters involved a strong level of control. For instance, they reported how they were often monitored, followed, or questioned within a certain geographical space such as their school or neighborhood. Moreover, Black and Latino/a youth perceived police to exhibit power and control over their movements throughout the community. Third, Hispanic youth cited experiences where the police demonstrated little to no understanding of their rights as American citizens, and for Black and African American youth, police would use racial slurs and make derogatory comments. For females of color, police encounters were reportedly compounded by their race and also their gender. Lastly, police were described as ineffective, as they would often take their time to respond to calls in disenfranchised neighborhoods.

Race and Racial Bias

Race as an extralegal factor has received the most widespread attention. While race should not be a factor in the decision to take a youth into custody, official statistics indicate that a disproportionate number of minority youth come into contact with the juvenile justice system. This concept is known as disproportionate minority contact (DMC). To illustrate further, the U.S. Census Bureau (2023) estimates that from 2020 to 2023, African Americans as a whole made up 13.7% of the population in the United States, and non-Hispanic whites made up 58.4% of the United States population. When it comes to children and adolescents from birth to age seventeen in the general population in 2022, 14% were Black and non-Hispanic compared to 49% who were white and non-Hispanic (ChildStats, 2023). Thus, if Black or African American youth make up 14% of the entire youth population, then only 14% of Black or African American youth should be arrested, and that is clearly not the case. However, it is important to recognize that the issue is not the sheer number or volume of youth who are arrested. As a matter of fact, when examining total arrests, 2019 data show that more whites (62.5%) were arrested than Blacks or African Americans (33.9%) (FBI, 2020) (see Table 8.2). The key distinction to be made here is that Blacks and African Americans are over-represented in these arrests. Statistics like these have garnered much attention from our federal government and have led to more research, theorizing, and monitoring of disproportionality in each state system. The bottom line is that understanding the dynamics of police encounters with youth of color continues to be a priority for law enforcement agencies around the country.

Before drawing any conclusions, it is important to understand that while rates of disproportionate minority contact are very troubling, research regarding whether this is attributed to racial prejudice is mixed. It is possible that some police officers may possess unconscious bias and employ racial profiling tactics or engage in targeted patrols of certain "hot spots," which lends itself to more contact with non-white youth as they are under a more watchful eye. Like many others, Walker et al. (2018) support this notion that there may be no evidence of **systemic discrimination**, where discrimination is widespread at all stages of the justice system, but that there is a greater likelihood of contextualized discrimination. **Contextualized discrimination** occurs in various circumstances or situations where there is some interplay of actions and decisions being made based on a person's race. This is evident in situations involving the use of racial profiling techniques for making traffic stops or the implementation of harsher sentences for the use or possession of crack cocaine versus powder cocaine. In a meta-analysis of research examining race and arrests, Kochel and colleagues (2011) concluded that race does matter, and it is a contributing factor where people of color are more likely to be arrested than their white counterparts. In a study examining NIBRS data and juveniles, divergent results were found by Pope and Snyder (2003), who did not find any significant difference in police arrests of white and non-white juveniles. Others have found that race may not be the sole or only factor used by an officer, but it can make its way into the decision-making schema along with other extra-legal and legal factors (Brown et al., 2009). Nonetheless, arresting non-white youth using extra-legal factors has serious consequences, and to date, many states have taken it upon themselves to examine the rates at which youth of color are arrested in comparison to their white counterparts (see Box 8.3).

Box 8.3: Racial and Ethnic Disparities (R/ED)

The concept of disproportionate minority contact (DMC) gained national attention when in 1988 the Coalition for Juvenile Justice (formerly the National Coalition of State Juvenile Justice Advisory Groups) issued a report to Congress titled, *A Delicate Balance* (Coleman, 2011). The report was convincing enough that Congress mandated that all states that subscribed to Part B of the Title II Formula Grant Program were required to assess disproportionality in any adult detention or correctional facility. A few years later, in 1992, the issue of disproportionality became a core requirement of the reauthorization of the 1974 Juvenile Justice Delinquency Prevention (JJDP) Act. Again, states seeking any type of JJDP Act formula grant were required to assess if DMC existed in their state along with determining possible causes for DMC (Penn, 2006).

The most recent authorization of the JJDP Act in 2018 continued to call for a reduction in the number of non-white youths at key points in the juvenile justice system. This means that state or local jurisdictions that seek federal funding are expected to conduct their own assessment to identify and reduce racial and ethnic disparities. It is important to note that the term DMC has been retired by some practitioners and researchers and replaced with the term **racial and ethnic disparities**, using the acronym R/ED, instead. In practice, assessing **R/ED** refers to an examination of data regarding racial and ethnic youth as they are processed at different points of the justice system. The stages that are examined typically include arrest, diversions, pre-trial detention, confinement, and transfer to adult court. If overrepresentation of non-white youth at a certain stage is found, states that receive federal support and funding are expected to develop and implement strategies to reduce racial and ethnic unfairness.

Sources: Coleman, A. R. (2011). Disproportionate minority contact: A historical and contemporary perspective. In N. Parsons-Pollard (Ed.), *Disproportionate minority contact: Current issues and policies* (pp. 19–33). Carolina Academic Press; Puzzanchera, C., Hockenberry, S., & Sickmund, M. (2022). *Youth and the juvenile justice system: 2022 National report*. National Center for Juvenile Justice. https://ncjfcj.org/wp-content/uploads/2023/01/2022-national-report.pdf

Gender Bias

It is no surprise that one of the factors identified by Allen (2005) in a study of Cleveland police officers was related to the youth's gender. In this case, male youth were more likely to be taken into custody than female youth. More explicitly, male youth, especially when in groups and when exhibiting suspicious behaviors, would be perceived by police as if the group were probably up to no good.

Despite the fact that more male juveniles are arrested than females, there is still a degree of gender bias when officers are in contact with female youths. Such bias can either favor the female juvenile (leniency) or be unfavorable to the female juvenile (protection). The interplay of both leniency and protection that police officers express toward female juveniles lies at the root of gender-based perceptions and gender role expectations. The latter form of bias has manifested in examining what is known as the **chivalry hypothesis**. The hypothesis suggests that females are inherently or biologically weaker and, in turn, are granted more leniency either in arrest or sentencing decisions (Van Wormer & Bartollas, 2011). Females may receive more lenient treatment than their male counterparts as they are viewed as dependent, less dangerous, and passive. As a result, the police officer may be less likely to take a female juvenile into custody, or the officer may reduce the charges that are filed on the petition. In contrast, police officers may believe that females need protection and that they should not be "acting" the same way as male juveniles. For instance, female youth who run away from home are more likely to be taken into custody and charged with certain status offenses than male youth.

Diversion

It must be emphasized that officers also have the discretionary power to divert youth away from the formal trappings of the system. More formally, **diversion** involves the process of referring youth who have committed an offense or exhibit at-risk behaviors to social service and community-based treatment agencies, while still holding the youth accountable for their actions. Diversion is based on the theoretical foundation of labeling theory. Not only are stigmatizing effects supposed to be reduced, but the rates of recidivism are supposed to be reduced as well. Unfortunately, what exists in theory does not always manifest in practice. Concerns about the effectiveness of police diversion practices have been raised. Some argue that it aggravates the situation and has led to an increase in self-labeling and future delinquency (Lipsey et al., 1981). Even though removing low-risk and minor youthful offenders from the system has been standard practice since the 1970s, policymakers and academics have argued that diversion "widens the net" (Potter & Kakar, 2002). **Net widening** means that instead of reducing the number of youths that are formally processed through the juvenile justice system, such early prevention and intervention programs essentially capture more youth who are subject to just as much formal social control. As a result, net widening also depletes the necessary resources that are needed for more serious youthful offenders, and minor youthful offenders are left stigmatized. Additional points in the system to divert youth from the formal system are discussed in Chapter 9.

Booking

Police officers do not need probable cause to take a youth into custody. Once this occurs, in many states, the parents or guardians must be immediately notified. Depending on the severity of the situation, some elements of the process mirror that of the criminal justice system for adults. For example, some state laws may require fingerprinting or photographing the youth when they are apprehended and booked. In some states, like Florida, and in cases where a suspected felony offense occurred, the process may involve taking a DNA sample from the juvenile. The youth will undergo a screening process (typically by an intake officer), which entails assessing the youth's drug and alcohol history, conducting a mental and physical health evaluation, and reviewing the youth's prior arrest history. These factors often determine whether the youth should be detained or released to the custody of their guardians. Ultimately, a judge or magistrate will make these initial decisions in concert with information about the type of crime committed by the juvenile, the juvenile's offense history, and the juvenile's current situation.

Juvenile court reports showed that in 2022, law enforcement was the most common entity for referring delinquent youth to juvenile court; that is, they referred roughly 85% of delinquency cases, namely for cases involving property offenses and drug law violations (Hockenberry & Puzzanchera, 2024). Schools made up 4% of delinquency referrals. It is important to remember that while a large percentage of youths may be referred to the juvenile court, close to 44% of petitioned cases were handled informally that same year. The remaining percentage of youth who do not proceed to court received a referral to a social service/welfare agency, an assigned probationary or improvement period, or payment or fine.

Arrest Data

In 2019, law enforcement agencies from around the country arrested an estimated 696,620 youth who were under the age of 18 (Puzzanchera, 2021) (see Table 8.1). While this may seem like an extraordinary number of arrests, it is important to keep in mind that over the past few years, estimates show that there are around 73 million people under the age of 18, and around 50 million ages 5 to 17 (Puzzanchera et al., 2025). In terms of violent crimes, most youths were arrested for aggravated assault, followed by robbery and murder. Given the change to the FBI's definition of rape, these results were not reported. Among property crimes, an estimated 83,690 juveniles were arrested for larceny-theft, more than any other type of property crime. Estimates also revealed a decline for most offenses when comparing juvenile offenses from 2010 to 2019 or even when using shorter parameters and examining the time frame from 2015 to 2019. It is important to recognize that what is presented here reflects the estimated number of offenses and not rates as described in Chapter 2.

Table 8.1: Estimated Number of Juvenile Arrests, 2019

Most Serious Offense	2019 Estimated Number of Juvenile Arrests	Percent Change		
		2010–2019	2015–2019	2018–2019
Total	696,620	-58%	-24%	-4%
Violent Crime Index	44,010	-40	-8	-5
Murder and nonnegligent manslaughter	860	-15	10	-6
Rape[1]	NA	NA	NA	NA
Robbery	16,080	-41	-13	-7
Aggravated assault	27,070	-40	-6	-3
Property Crime Index	119,790	-67	-43	-9
Burglary	20,700	-68	-42	-7
Larceny-theft	83,690	-70	-46	-10
Motor vehicle theft	13,610	-14	-7	-8
Arson	1,800	-61	-33	-2
Nonindex				
Other assaults	126,130	-40	-4	1
Forgery and counterfeiting	850	-50	-17	-18
Fraud	3,690	-39	-18	-22
Embezzlement	540	22	-8	-7
Stolen property (i.e., buying, receiving, possessing)	8,940	-39	-14	-4
Vandalism	31,950	-59	-23	4
Weapons (i.e., carrying, possessing)	16,080	-49	-17	-6
Prostitution and commercialized vice	290	-73	-51	9
Sex offenses (except forcible rape and prostitution)	NA	NA	NA	NA
Drug abuse violations	81,320	-52	-18	-10
Gambling	190	-86	-60	7
Offenses against the family and children	3,060	-19	-11	-8
Driving under the influence	5,570	-54	-16	2
Liquor law violations	26,650	-72	-38	1
Drunkenness	3,470	-73	-37	6
Disorderly conduct	53,990	-65	-24	-7

Vagrancy	350	-84	-68	-49
All other offenses (except traffic)	144,160	-51	-14	3
Curfew and loitering	14,650	-80	-59	-27

Note: [1] Beginning in 2013, the FBI broadened the definition of rape, removing the phrase "forcible" from the offense name and description. Due to differences in agency reporting practices, national estimates for the offenses of "rape" and "sex offenses" are not available after 2012. The "violent crimes" category (which includes murder, robbery, and aggravated assault) replaces the Violent Crime Index (which included "forcible rape"), as the latter category is no longer compatible with prior years. In any given year prior to the change in the rape definition, these three offenses accounted for more than 95% of arrests for Violent Crime Index offenses.

Source: Puzzanchera, C. (2021, May). *National report series bulletin: Juvenile arrests, 2019* (NCJ 256032). U.S. Department of Justice, Office of Justice Programs, Office of Juvenile Justice and Delinquency Prevention. http://www.ncjj.org/Publication/Juvenile-Arrests-2019.aspx

Table 8.2: Percent of Juvenile Arrests by Race,[2] 2019

Most Serious Offense	2019 Estimated Number of Juvenile Arrests	White	Black	American Indian	Asian
TOTAL	696,620	63%	34%	2%	1%
Violent Crime	44,010	49	48	2	2
Murder and nonnegligent manslaughter	860	47	50	3	0
Rape[3]	N/A	N/A	N/A	N/A	N/A
Robbery	16,080	36	62	1	2
Aggravated assault	27,070	56	40	2	1
Property Crime	119,790	55	42	2	2
Burglary	20,700	57	40	2	2
Larceny-theft	83,690	55	41	2	2
Motor vehicle theft	13,610	47	50	2	1
Arson	1,800	69	27	2	1
Nonindex					
Other (simple) assault	126,130	59	38	2	1
Forgery and counterfeiting	850	62	36	1	2
Fraud	3,690	50	46	2	1
Embezzlement	540	47	50	0	3
Stolen property (i.e., buying, receiving, possessing)	8,940	35	62	1	2
Vandalism	31,950	70	27	2	1

Weapons (i.e., carrying, possessing)	16,080	56	41	1	2
Sex offense (except rape and prostitution)	N/A	N/A	N/A	N/A	N/A
Drug abuse violation	81,320	75	21	2	2
Gambling	190	58	38	0	3
Offenses against the family and children	3,060	67	23	10	0
Driving under the influence	5,570	89	6	3	2
Liquor laws	26,650	86	7	6	1
Drunkenness	3,470	77	12	10	1
Disorderly conduct	53,990	5	42	3	1
Vagrancy	350	75	25	2	1
All other offenses (except traffic)	144,160	67	29	2	1
Curfew and loitering law violations	14,650	66	30	3	2

Notes: [2] UCR data do not distinguish the ethnic group Hispanic; Hispanics may be of any race. In 2019, 88% of Hispanics ages 10–17 were classified racially as white. Detail may not add to totals because of rounding. [3] NA: Data for rape and sex offenses are not available because of the change in the definition for reporting rape.

Source: Puzzanchera, C., Hockenberry, S., & Sickmund, M. (2022, December). *Youth and the juvenile justice system: 2022 national report.* [table modified]. National Center for Juvenile Justice. https://ncjfcj.org/wp-content/uploads/2023/01/2022-national-report.pdf

Arrest Data and Minority Youth

Over the past decade, the arrest rate for all juveniles has steadily declined, but that does not mean that all arrests are equal. As described in Chapter 2, arrest rates for non-white youth are still disproportionately higher than for white youth. For example, in 2019, Black youth made up 34% of all juvenile arrests even though they only made up 17% of the general youth population, ages 10–17, in the United States (Puzzanchera et al., 2022). For white youth, who made up 75% of the general population of that same age group, 63% accounted for all juvenile arrests. Such disparities highlight that Black youth continue to be arrested at disproportionately higher rates than white youth, underscoring persistent racial inequalities in the justice system.

As shown in Table 8.2, and when examining the variable of race even further, white youth were arrested the most for crimes such as driving under the influence (89%), liquor law violations (86%), and drunkenness (77%) in 2019 (Puzzanchera et al., 2022). In comparison, Black youth were most likely to be arrested for the crime of receiving, buying, or possessing stolen property (62%). Looking more closely at violent crimes alone, white youth were arrested at higher rates for aggravated assault (56%), whereas Black youth were arrested more frequently for robbery (62%).

If we examine these figures through the lens of disproportionality, it is evident that white youth are over-represented when it comes to being arrested for crimes such as drug offenses, liquor law violations, and driving under the influence (see Table 8.2). Yet, white youth are clearly under-represented for several violent and property crimes, including murder, robbery, and motor vehicle theft. In contrast, Black youth, given that they only made up 17% of the population in 2019, were under-represented among arrests for only three crimes—driving under the influence, liquor law violations, and drunkenness (Puzzanchera et al., 2022). Among arrests of all other offenses, Black youth were over-represented. Although it is not shown, similar patterns of disproportionality exist for Hispanic youth.

Interrogation

There may be times when it is necessary to interrogate a juvenile about a crime or the potential commission of a crime. Such circumstances necessitate extreme sensitivity to the youth and their needs. In both the adult and juvenile systems, police officers are trained to use various interrogation methods and interviewing techniques. **Interrogation methods** are those techniques used when a police officer asks questions of a suspect to obtain information that may or may not involve the use of threats or intimidation. One of the most popular techniques is known as the **REID technique**. Using this method, law enforcement officers are formally trained to decipher whether the individual is telling the truth by way of conducting a Behavior Analysis Interview (BAI). That is, a set of behaviorally provoking questions is delivered with the intent of eliciting verbal and nonverbal responses that are subsequently analyzed to determine the truthfulness of the suspect's response. Ultimately, the BAI assists officers in identifying any inconsistencies with the suspect's statements as well as behavioral indications of truthfulness or deception, and whether the individual committed the act in question.

Even still, very little is known about police interrogations of juvenile suspects. However, some studies have recently begun to shed some light on how techniques are used and the consequences they may have on youth. When comparing interrogation and interviewing techniques for both adults and juveniles, Cleary and Warner (2016) found that simple information gathering is of primary concern to the officers. Contrary to the images of popular culture and those from primetime television, it was reported that in both juvenile and adult suspect cases, officers most commonly used pre-interrogation elements such as building rapport with the suspect, observing body language, offering items such as food or drink for comfort, and observing speech patterns.

While some may think that the techniques used for juvenile and adult suspects may differ, the researchers also found that some aggressive tactics are used with youth (Cleary & Warner, 2016). Among over half of the officers who had REID training, there was a higher likelihood that they used interrogation techniques prior to the interview, and there was a higher likelihood that they employed deception detection techniques during the interview. Fewer officers used statement analyses or youth-based interviewing practices. Yet, one of the most alarming findings was that coercive tactics were used more frequently among officers who are also video recorded during the interrogations. One would expect this would not be the case, but officers seemed to have little concern about any legal ramifications. Overall, results underscore the need for more law enforcement interrogation training in general, especially with juvenile suspects, and highlight the value of training as an avenue for reducing interrogation-induced miscarriages of justice. Adoption of the PEACE model may allow for more "just" interrogation processes when minors are involved.

As the antithesis to the REID technique, the **PEACE model** is based on a non-accusatory and non-confrontational practice that is widely used in the United Kingdom. PEACE stands for Preparation and Planning, Engage and Explain, Account, Closure, and Evaluate. An interview takes place with the interviewee only after developing a thorough written interview plan (College of Policing, 2018). The protocol is much more in line with journalistic approaches, and instead of seeking a confession, the primary goal is to gather information to either prove or disprove theories. At this preparation and planning stage, steps are taken to review the case, the characteristics of the interviewee, such as age, gender, cultural background, physical and mental health status, and so on, the location of the interview, the topics to be covered, and any material that may assist in the investigation, among others. During the next stage, police officers are trained to use active listening skills and to establish rapport with the interviewee. The conversation starts by clearly stating the purpose and objectives of the interview and asking the interviewee if the purpose is understood. The account stage involves the use of active listening skills when the interviewee reports what happened, along with making clarifying statements as prompted by the interviewer. The interviewer is to refrain from asking multiple and leading questions. Closing the interview is not abrupt but planned. At this stage, the interviewer summarizes what has been said and asks any additional questions or allows the interviewee to make any clarifications. Closure also involves informing the interviewee about what happens next. The final stage is evaluation, where the interviewer conducts a brief analysis of the interviewee's account and the facts of the case and makes decisions about any necessary further action.

To complicate matters further, police interrogation and use of the REID technique may lead to false confessions, which are more common for youth ages fourteen to sixteen than for adults (Gudjonsson et al., 2016). In addition, male youth are more vulnerable to false confessions along with youths who have been diagnosed with Attention Deficit Hyperactivity Disorder (ADHD) or other mental disabilities. As discussed earlier, advances in the medical profession and neuroscience have made it widely known that a youth's brain is not fully developed, and with that comes a higher degree of vulnerability to suggestions, ideas, and pressure. This has drawn the attention of advocacy groups to shield youth from excessive interrogation methods altogether. Advocates who work for the Center on Wrongful Convictions of Youth, for example, support this notion and have found that youth have a greater chance of giving a false confession as opposed to an adult (see Box 8.4). More specifically, youth are two to three times more likely to falsely confess during an interrogation when compared to their adult counterpart. The risk of false confessions among juveniles is so troubling that it has been recognized by the U.S. Supreme Court. What this suggests is that officers who use the REID technique need to exercise extreme caution and care when interrogating juvenile suspects; however, this may not be emphasized in police training enough.

Box 8.4: Brendan Dassey's False Confession

On November 3, 2005, 25-year-old Wisconsin native Teresa Halbach was reported missing by her parents, who lived next door to her (Garrett, 2018). A few days later, her burnt vehicle was found by a Calumet County Sheriff in Wisconsin along with what appeared to be her remains. Her personal belongings were on the scene, allowing officers to recover important, identifiable information. This case received national attention and was aired on Netflix's *Making a Murderer.*

Forensic evidence from Halbach's car was found to be the blood of Steven Avery. Subsequently, he was arrested and charged with kidnapping and murder (Garrett, 2018). Avery's alibi was a sixteen-year-old named Brendan Dassey, who was brought in for questioning. However, it was reported that Dassey's interrogations took place without his or his mother's consent. The interrogations involved the use of the REID technique for over a 48-hour period. There was no legal representation during these interrogations or a parent present. Eventually, Dassey confessed to Halbach's rape and murder as a co-conspirator. In sum, he confessed to first-degree homicide, sexual assault, and mutilation of a corpse. As a result, Dassey was sentenced to life in prison. A habeas petition was filed disputing that his confession was not voluntary. At the federal level, a few of the judges of the Seventh Circuit Court of Appeals supported the petition that there was evidence of physical coercion and intimidation leading to the false confession. However, the decision was reversed later by the entire circuit. Another element of the case that warranted further scrutiny was that Dassey received a clinical evaluation where it was concluded that he was a highly suggestible individual. Moreover, Dassey even recanted his confession and reported to the judge that he obtained the details from a book he had read by James Patterson, titled *Kiss the Girls.* To date, the ruling that Dassey made a voluntary confession still stands, and the U.S. Supreme Court has refused to hear his case.

Source: Garrett, B. (2018, June 9). Brendan Dassey's false confession shows we need to be more careful when interrogating juveniles. *USA Today.* https://www.usatoday.com/story/opinion/policing/2018/06/09/brendan-dasseys-false-confession-supreme-court-column/652915002/

Again, recognizing that a child's or adolescent's prefrontal cortex is not fully developed, the IACP (2012) put forth several guidelines for interrogating juveniles. Besides the diligent care with reading and reviewing *Miranda* rights with the juvenile, the next step involves a comprehensive understanding of child and adolescent behaviors. During an interrogation of a juvenile, the youth may not make eye contact, may slouch, or may be fidgety. These behaviors may be indicative of an adult trying to be deceptive or lying, but among young people, these behavioral cues may simply be a matter of how a youth responds to an authority figure or parental figure. These behaviors should not be interpreted as guilty behaviors, necessarily. Next, the IACP also recommends that a friendly adult be present during the interrogation. That person could be a parent or trained youth officer, who serves the role of child advocate. Furthermore, it is suggested that officers question youth during the day instead of late at night. Sleep deprivation, coupled with stress, has the potential to lead to a false confession. Lengthy questioning sessions should also be avoided. One hour is appropriate for a juvenile to be questioned, and then, there must be time for a substantial break. In total, the session should last no more than four hours. Last, officers are encouraged not to use deceptive techniques with juveniles. For example, presenting the youth with false evidence may lead the youth to assume that they have no other option but to confess, or the juvenile may start doubting their own memory, even if they are innocent.

Police Encounters with Abused and/or Neglected Youth

Not all youth encountered by the police are juvenile delinquents. As a matter of fact, it is more likely that the police will interact with a youth who has been abused or neglected. These cases warrant a different set of actions and a more sophisticated level of care and expertise from the responding officer. In cases of abuse or neglect, officers take the role of mandated reporters. For example, if the police officer suspects any type of abuse or neglect, they must report such cases to child and family services, where a child social services worker will be assigned to further investigate the case. Such cases involve cooperation between law enforcement and child protective services personnel.

For the responding officer, the initial step is to determine whether the child is in danger and needs protection or in some cases what is known as placing the youth in **protective custody**: an act where a police or child welfare professional has the authority to remove a child who is reasonably believed to be in imminent danger and to place them in a safe facility. This decision-making point for the officer must first and foremost follow the state code. However, to guide an officer's decision, the Office of Juvenile Justice and Delinquency Prevention (2014) states, "officers should consider all the information and ask themselves, 'If I leave and obtain a court order to remove this child, is the child likely to be injured before I return?' If the answer is 'yes,' the officer should remove the child" (p. 9).

Depending on state law, a police officer may be able to remove the child given their own judgment and culmination of observations of the present circumstances or if the child discloses that some type of physical or sexual abuse has taken place (OJJDP, 2014). The home environment may also be so unsuitable and dangerous that it warrants immediate removal of the child from the home. Researchers indicate that children are often placed into protective custody as a result of their parents having a known substance abuse disorder (Rivera & Sullivan, 2015). Most children who are placed into protective custody are placed in a foster home, while others may be placed in a temporary emergency shelter or with a kinship relative.

Then, there are additional steps that need to be taken by the officer when investigating the case. These steps would be covered in the officer's training; however, an example of these investigation proceedings is provided by the Office of Juvenile Justice and Delinquency Prevention (OJJDP).

Obtaining Information for the Preliminary Report

- Inquire about the history of the abusive situation. An accurate timeline of events is crucial to the successful investigation and prosecution of all types of child maltreatment.
- Obtain any elements of the crime necessary for the report.
- Inquire about the instrument of abuse or other items at the scene. Check the scene for potential instruments of abuse.
- Do not discount children's statements about who is abusing them, where and how the abuse is occurring, or what types of acts occurred.
- Save your opinions for the end of the report and provide supporting facts. Highlights the atmosphere of disclosure and the mood and demeanor of participants in the complaint. (OJJDP, 2014, p. 4)

A child abuse case involves a **multidisciplinary team approach**. This means that members of the medical profession, law enforcement, child services, victim advocacy, mental health services, and prosecutors come together in a coordinated and collaborative fashion to respond to the needs of the child or adolescent. Even though some may argue that a police officer's role is tangential to these cases, and they are simply a matter for child protective services alone, the importance of law enforcement handling a case properly cannot be overstated, as they are typically the first ones at the scene. Following the protocol is of utmost importance, especially given that the officer is responsible for obtaining information, documenting findings, preserving the crime scene, if there is one, and conducting appropriate follow-up investigations. If the officer does not do these things correctly, it could result in the dismissal of the case (OJJDP, 2014).

Police Encounters with Status Offenders

Recall from Chapter 1 that status offenders are youth who commit certain offenses that are not punishable if committed by an adult. Status offenses typically include problematic behaviors such as running away, truancy, ungovernability (also known as incorrigibility), violating curfew, and underage liquor law violations (Hockenberry & Puzzanchera, 2024). For many, these may seem like typical adolescent behaviors, but from a professional perspective, these behaviors signal that the juvenile may be at risk of future offending or more serious offending. Police and social service workers may even view these behaviors as indicative of deeper systemic issues related to family, school, or other personal problems. On the other hand, police officers may be lenient with teenage youth who are drinking or smoking underage or when the youth is out past curfew. In situations like underage drinking, the officer can utilize a greater degree of discretion. They can reprimand the youth and send them home or take the youth into custody and contact their parents or legal guardians. Depending on the factors of the situation, the officer could also refer the youth to counseling services or file a petition and refer the youth to court.

Approximately 62,200 petitioned status offense cases were managed by juvenile courts across the country in 2022 (Hockenberry & Puzzanchera, 2024). Among these cases, over half involved cases of truancy (64%), followed by cases of ungovernability or incorrigibility, which made up a much smaller percentage of cases (9%). Curfew violations made up the smallest number of petitioned cases (3%).

In terms of referrals of petitioned status offenses, the police do not make as many referrals as they do with cases involving delinquent acts. In 2022, law enforcement made up 14% of petitioned status offense referrals. The majority of status offense referrals are made by the schools (62%) (Hockenberry & Puzzanchera, 2024). Among the referrals that police officers made, most were for curfew violations or liquor law violations, whereas the schools made a larger number of referrals for truancy, as expected.

Over the years, researchers have noted some important gender and race-based differences when it comes to status offenses. When examining all status offenses in 2022, male juveniles (54%) were more likely to be petitioned for status offenses than female juveniles (46%) (Hockenberry & Puzzanchera, 2024). However, the gap between male and female status offenders has become much narrower over the past 15 years. Another interesting point to examine about gender is the status offense of running away. In 2022, these cases made up 27% of petitioned status offense referrals for law enforcement. Females accounted for a larger percentage of petitioned cases for running away (58%) in comparison to males, who made up a larger percentage of petitioned cases for violating curfew (65%). As mentioned in Chapter 3, female cases of running away need to be managed with sensitivity and not just a knee-jerk reaction to the situation. Running away could be the result of physical or sexual abuse and not that the female juvenile is running away for some other reason.

In terms of race, white youth (58%) were more likely to be petitioned for a status offense in comparison to Black (25%) and Hispanic youth (11%) (Hockenberry & Puzzanchera, 2024). Truancy, which is typically reported by the school, is the most common status offense among all racial groups, and it has increased among all racial groups since 2005. Curfew violations, however, have seen a larger decline since 2006, particularly for white and Hispanic youth.

While the police may deal with youth who have committed a status offense, it is important to keep in mind that characterizing youth as solely a delinquent or solely a status offender is not very realistic. In other words, status offenders are not really a unique category of juvenile offenders unto themselves, and using such a dichotomy is problematic (Feld, 2009). Status offenders may also commit delinquent offenses, such as shoplifting but may have never been caught. On the one hand, where it is probable that status offenders are at risk of future offending, it is equally probable that the majority of youth will eventually age out and adopt prosocial values.

Programming: Police and Juveniles

The most common image we have of a police officer is that of a first responder. There is no denying that this is a major expectation we have of the men and women in uniform who serve us. Aside from being a first responder, police officers are also tasked with keeping our communities safe. In this capacity, the police officer's duty is to prevent crime too. One way police officers are tasked with doing so is by being immersed and entrenched in the community. For young people, that community for most of the day is within the school system. Here, officers can have a positive influence on the lives of young people and serve as educators, role models, and peace-keepers. What follows are two leading examples of law enforcement community- and school-based efforts.

Gang Resistance Education and Training (G.R.E.A.T.)

Not all communities are riddled with gang violence in the United States, but there are a number of communities that are. The National Youth Gang Survey found that in 2012, there were approximately 30,700 gangs in the country with an estimated 850,000 gang members (Egley et al., 2014). What is alarming is that gang-related homicides increased by nearly 20% from 2011 to 2012. Such violence poses a significant number of challenges to the community and law enforcement. While urban areas may have their share of gang problems, smaller cities and rural communities are not immune from gang activity either.

Efforts to quell gang violence have been mediated by national programs like Gang Resistance Education and Training (G.R.E.A.T.). The program was created in 1991 by the Phoenix, Arizona, Police Department (PD), and financial assistance was provided by the Bureau of Alcohol, Tobacco, and Firearms (ATF) (Esbensen et al., 2013; Ramsey et al., 2003). The main goal of G.R.E.A.T. is to reduce gang involvement and activity through a series of life skills development programs, delivered by police officers. G.R.E.A.T. was expanded in 1992 in partnership with the Federal Law Enforcement Training Center (FLETC). The program was later administered in 2011 by the U.S. Department of Justice, Office of Justice Programs, where administrative control was granted to the Bureau of Justice Assistance (BJA).

According to the G.R.E.A.T. website, the program now touts six components, including one for elementary school children and another that caters to middle school children. Fourth or fifth graders in elementary school are provided with six different lessons that help them develop strong communication skills, strategies to manage their anger, and lessons about violence prevention, among other topics, such as respect for others. For middle schoolers, the curriculum is more in-depth and allows youth to examine the factors related to violence, drugs, gangs, and crime. The third component is a summer instructor curriculum development program, and the fourth component is centered on curriculum development strategies, where a review committee aids in researching and incorporating various behavioral, cognitive, and constructivist learning approaches. Encouraging family support and providing resources and programming to families is the fifth aspect of the program. The remaining component involves research. This last component demonstrates how research findings are incorporated into curriculum design. For instance, recent research shows that targeting certain risk factors and building and strengthening resiliency will shield youth from gang activity.

Overall, G.R.E.A.T. has been known to produce favorable results and is hailed as an evidence-based program. Esbensen et al. (2013) found that in a preliminary sense, the effect of the program is positive. Youths who completed the G.R.E.A.T. program were less likely to be associated with a gang and were less likely to be involved in other forms of delinquency when compared to the control group. They also noted that G.R.E.A.T. participants had developed more prosocial and positive attitudes about the police than the participants in the control group. In contrast, and in an urban middle school in Tennessee, other researchers found that when it came to positive attitudes about law enforcement, there was no difference among youth who participated in the program curriculum versus a control group who did not receive the curriculum (Ramsey et al., 2003).

School Resource Officer Programs

The first well-documented School Resource Officer (SRO) program can be traced back to a school in Flint, Michigan, in 1953 (Weiler & Cray, 2011). These programs became more widespread in the 1990s as news of school shootings hit the airwaves, leading to a national social-political discourse on violent youth offending. Funding for SRO programs during this time was backed by the Clinton administration through a federal initiative known as COPS in Schools (Community Oriented Policing Services). Over $750 million was earmarked in the late 1990s to go toward hiring school police

officers. This was also around the same time when criminologist, John DiIulio, declared that there was a wave of juvenile "super-predators" that would lead to an increase in serious violent juvenile offending. He preached about youth religious salvation and projected that these "morally impoverished youth" would permeate not just inner-city streets but the entire country.

> On the horizon, therefore, are tens of thousands of severely morally impoverished juvenile super-predators. They are perfectly capable of committing the most heinous acts of physical violence for the most trivial reasons (for example, a perception of slight disrespect or the accident of being in their path). They fear neither the stigma of arrest nor the pain of imprisonment. They live by the meanest code of the meanest streets, a code that reinforces rather than restrains their violent, hair-trigger mentality. In prison or out, the things that super-predators get by their criminal behavior—sex, drugs, money—are their own immediate rewards. Nothing else matters to them. So for as long as their youthful energies hold out, they will do what comes "naturally": murder, rape, rob, assault, burglarize, deal deadly drugs, and get high. (DiIulio, 1995, para. 29)

Another contributing factor to bolster SRO programs was the Columbine High School tragedy in 1999 in Littleton, Colorado, where twelve students and one teacher were brutally murdered by fellow students, Dylan Klebold and Eric Harris. Besides instilling a police officer presence in schools, these efforts have coincided with a **zero-tolerance approach**, where harsher disciplinary codes are imposed for the most minor offenses or misbehaving.

Most programs follow a triad model where the **School Resource Officer (SRO)** assumes the responsibilities of (1) a sworn officer with the power to arrest, (2) a law-related educator, and (3) a law-related counselor (Barnes, 2016; Weiler & Cray, 2011). The police officer is usually a member of local law enforcement, such as the sheriff's office or municipal police department, who is assigned to a certain school or school district. As mentioned earlier, the rationale for these programs falls in line with **community-oriented policing**, which entails a problem-solving approach where members of law enforcement serve to protect and secure a safe environment in concert with members of the community (Barnes, 2016). The school is seen as an extension of the community and also a place where early intervention can take place for juveniles. In brief, SROs can protect the lives and property in the school community, develop crime prevention activities, communicate prosocial values to youth, and serve as liaisons to assist youth with social services.

Research on SRO programs is lacking, and results are not very clear. On one hand, many would argue that SROs increase school security. It has been found that officers around the country confiscate drugs or weapons from students and their mere presence affords the students and staff a highly trained individual who is equipped to respond to a serious problem immediately. On the other hand, recent research has painted a slightly different picture and raised additional concerns about SROs. In a small qualitative study, Barnes (2016) found that SROs often felt frustrated with the lack of knowledge from school personnel about their actual role. Officers reported that they were asked to impose school rules and policies, monitor school restrooms, and deal with school infractions. Yet, their role is a police officer first and not a member of the faculty. Following the community-policing model, and on a positive note, officers reported that they were able to establish rapport and cultivate healthier relationships with youth, thereby upholding a positive image of law enforcement.

It seems like the appropriate reaction to school violence was to place police officers on patrol inside school walls. Yet, SRO programs are not without controversy. For one, the presence of SROs has led to an increase in criminalizing the behavior of youth, especially Black youth. Price (2009) argued that responding to common misbehaviors such as temper tantrums with a police response not only undermines the role of the SRO but also dismantles police-youth relations. The greater cause for concern though is that such intolerance of youth misbehavior has led to what scholars refer to as the school-to-prison pipeline, which was previously described in Chapter 6. Youth are thereby deprived of a solid, uninterrupted education, and in turn, find themselves in juvenile facilities with more low-risk youth of color. Documented cases also have been found where school-aged youth have been handcuffed for minor disruptive behaviors such as refusing to participate in gym class. Second, Shaver and Decker (2017) highlight several cases involving handcuffing youth with Attention Deficient Hyperactivity Disorder or other disabilities, when, in fact, these individuals possess certain protections from restraints under the Individuals with Disabilities Education Act (IDEA). Third, lawsuits have also been filed against schools in cases where SROs were using unnecessary and excessive force, which are unquestionably violations of a youth's Fourth and Fourteenth Amendment rights.

In 2010, the Southern Poverty Law Center filed a class-action lawsuit against school board officials in Birmingham, AL. Several students reported that while witnessing a physical altercation they were sprayed with pepper spray and in cases where students were physically restrained, officers and school officials would use pepper spray as an additional form of punishment (Shaver & Decker, 2017). In response to such accounts, Shaver and Decker call for extensive SRO training programs where the role of the SRO is clearly delineated by school policy and training that fosters appropriate interactions between SROs and youth with disabilities.

Summary Points

- Police encounters with juveniles are shaped by a number of factors and situations. Such ambiguity affords the police officers a great deal of discretion. Training, department policies, and state legal codes articulate some guidelines for police officers to follow when interacting with youth.
- Legal and extralegal factors may be used by police officers to make decisions about taking youth into custody. Legal factors include the seriousness of the offense, past history of the offender, and evidence of suspicious behavior, whereas extralegal factors are those such as the juvenile's attitude or demeanor, race, and gender, just to name a few.
- Police officers are essentially the gatekeepers for youth to enter the juvenile justice system and have the ability to divert youth away from the system. Diversion, while a common practice in the juvenile justice system, has been linked to increased stigmatization, increased recidivism, and net widening.
- Youth who are taken into custody may be booked, receive an intake evaluation, and may be interrogated depending on the nature of the crime committed. Classic interrogation methods do not work well with juvenile populations and increase the risk of false confessions. Police officers are encouraged to adopt non-confrontational methods instead of methods that provoke the youth or rely on deceptive tactics.
- Arrest rates for juveniles have been steadily declining. However, concerns about the disproportionate number of non-white youths who are taken into custody compared to white youth remain at the forefront.
- Juveniles have been afforded many of the same Fourth Amendment protections as adults regarding search and seizure and in receiving *Miranda* warnings. Searches must be handled and managed carefully by school officials as youth are granted some level of privacy even when at school.
- Not all youth are delinquent. Police officers also encounter youth who have been abused or neglected, requiring a proper response and care. Police officers also have to properly handle and manage cases involving status offenders, which includes run-

away and truant youth as well as youth who are incorrigible, violate curfew, or drink underage.

- Police officers are involved in a number of community and prevention-based programs. School Resource Officer Programs allow a trained member of the law enforcement community to supervise and attend to the safety and security of youth at school and provide opportunities to foster prosocial attitudes about the police. Programs such as G.R.E.A.T. are carried out by members of law enforcement to reduce the number of juveniles joining gangs.

Key Terms

Chivalry Hypothesis: the proposition that females are inherently or biologically weaker and in turn are granted more leniency either in arrest or sentencing decisions.

Community-Oriented Policing: a problem-solving approach where members of law enforcement serve to protect and secure a safe environment in concert with members of the community.

Contextualized Discrimination: occurs in various circumstances or situations where there is some interplay of actions and decisions being made based on a person's race.

Discretion: the decision-making power afforded to a police officer that may be based on personal opinion but is administered within a given legal framework.

Diversion: involves the process of referring youth who have committed an offense or exhibit at-risk behaviors to social service and community-based treatment agencies, while still holding the youth accountable for their actions.

Exclusionary Rule: evidence obtained from an unreasonable search is a violation of the Fourth Amendment and cannot be used in court.

Extralegal Factors: subjective reasons about a juvenile or their behavior that a police officer may use in arrest decisions that are not found in the legal code.

Interrogation Methods: techniques where a police officer asks questions of a suspect to obtain information that may or may not involve the use of threats or intimidation.

Legal Factors: objective and legally supported reasons about a juvenile's behavior before making an arrest of a juvenile.

***Miranda* Warning:** a warning issued by a member of law enforcement that addresses one's right to silence, the consequences of surrendering this right, the privilege and right to receive counsel, the right to obtain indigent defense counsel, and the fact that these rights can be extensive and ongoing as one proceeds up and throughout the processes that may involve interrogation.

Multidisciplinary Team Approach: members of the medical profession, law enforcement, child services, victim advocacy, mental health services, and prosecutors who come together in a coordinated and collaborative fashion to respond to the needs of the child or adolescent.

Net Widening: attempts made to reduce the number of youths who are formally processed through the juvenile justice system, such as by early prevention and intervention programs, essentially capture more youth who are subject to formal social control.

PEACE Model: interrogation techniques used by police officers that are based on a non-accusatory and non-confrontational practice that is widely used in the United Kingdom (Preparation and Planning, Engage and Explain, Account, Closure, and Evaluate).

Probable Cause: involves a higher standard of proof where facts support that a crime has been, is being, or will be committed.

Protective Custody: an act where a police or child welfare professional has the authority to remove a child who is reasonably believed to be in imminent danger and to place them in a safe facility.

Racial and Ethnic Disparities (R/ED): the examination of data about how youth from different racial and ethnic backgrounds are processed at different stages of the justice system such as arrest, pre-trial detention, disposition, and transfer to adult court and for states to develop plans to address any racial and ethnic disparities that are found.

Reasonable Suspicion: a standard or presumption made by the officer that under the circumstances there is reason to believe that a person is committing a crime.

REID Technique: interrogation techniques used by police officers that involves behaviorally provoking questions with the intent of eliciting verbal and nonverbal responses that are subsequently analyzed to determine the truthfulness of the suspect's response.

School Resource Officer (SRO): a member of law enforcement in the school system who assumes the responsibilities of a sworn officer with the power to arrest, as well as to serve as a law-related educator and counselor.

Search and Seizure: a search of a juvenile and their property by a police officer, but the law reaffirms that the search must be reasonable, that is, the officer must have probable cause, and a warrant is required.

Systemic Discrimination: widespread discrimination at all stages of the justice system.

Taken into Custody: a process where a juvenile is physically apprehended by a police officer.

Zero-Tolerance Approach: harsher disciplinary codes that are imposed for the most minor offenses or misbehaving.

References

Allen, T. (2005). Taking a juvenile into custody: Situational factors that influence police officers' decisions. *The Journal of Sociology & Social Welfare, 32*(2), 121–129. https://doi.org/10.15453/0191-5096.3074

Arthur, L. G. (1969). The uniform juvenile court act. *Juvenile & Family Court Journal, 19*(4), 153–156.

Bahney, A. (2014, July). *Law enforcement's leadership role in juvenile justice reform: Actionable recommendations for practice and policy*. International Association of Chiefs of Police. http://www.modelsforchange.net/publications/642

Barnes, L. M. (2016). Keeping the peace and controlling crime: What school resource officers want school personnel to know. *The Clearing House, 89*(6), 197–201. https://doi.org/10.1080/00098655.2016.1206428

Bostic, J. Q., Thurau, L., Potter, M., & Drury, S. S. (2014). Policing the teen brain. *Journal of the American Academy of Child & Adolescent Psychiatry, 53*(2), 127–129. https://doi.org/10.1016/j.jaac.2013.09.021

Brick, B. T., Taylor, T. J., & Esbensen, F. A. (2009). Juvenile attitudes toward the police: The importance of subcultural involvement and community ties. *Journal of Criminal Justice, 37*, 488–495. https://doi.org/10.1016/j.jcrimjus.2009.07.009

Brown, R. A., Novak, K. J., & Frank, J. (2009). Identifying variation in police officer behavior between juveniles and adults. *Journal of Criminal Justice, 37*, 200–208. https://doi.org/10.1016/j.jcrimjus.2009.02.004

ChildStats. (2023). *America's children: Key national indicators of well-being, 2023. Demographic background*. Forum on Child and Family Statistics. https://www.childstats.gov/pdf/ac2023/ac_23.pdf

City of Grand Rapids, Michigan. (2018). *Grand Rapids police department youth interaction policy*. https://www.grandrapidsmi.gov/Government/Departments/Police-Department/Policies-and-Procedures/Patrol-Operations-General/Grand-Rapids-Police-Department-Youth-Interaction-Policy

Cleary, H. M., & Warner, T. C. (2016). Police training in interviewing and interrogation methods: A comparison of techniques used with adult and juvenile suspects. *Law and Human Behavior, 40*(3), 270–284. https://doi.org/10.1037/lhb0000175

College of Policing. (2018). *Investigation: Investigative interviewing*. https://www.app.college.police.uk/app-content/investigations/investigative-interviewing/#peace-framework

DiIulio, J. (1995, November 27). The coming of the super-predators. *The Weekly Standard*. https://archive.org/details/the-weekly-standard-1995-11-27

Egley, A., Jr., Howell, J. C., & Harris, M. (2014). *Highlights of the 2012 national youth gang survey. Juvenile justice fact sheet* (NCJ 248025). Office of Juvenile Justice and Delinquency Prevention. https://files.eric.ed.gov/fulltext/ED553642.pdf

Esbensen, F. A., Osgood, W., Peterson, D., Taylor, T. J., Carson, D., Freng, A., & Matsuda, K. (2013). *Process and outcome evaluation of the G.R.E.A.T. program*. U.S. Department of Justice. https://www.ojp.gov/pdffiles1/nij/grants/244346.pdf

Fairfax County Police Department. (2017). Juvenile procedures: Purpose and policy. https://www.fairfaxcounty.gov/police/sites/police/files/assets/images/chief/generalorders/605_-_juvenile_procedures.pdf

Federal Bureau of Investigation. (2020). *Crime in the United States, 2019* (Table 43B, Arrests under 18). https://ucr.fbi.gov/crime-in-the-u.s/2019/crime-in-the-u.s.-2019/topic-pages/tables/table-43

Feld, B. C. (2009). Violent girls or relabeled status offenders? An alternative interpretation of the data. *Crime and Delinquency, 55*(2), 241–265. https://doi.org/10.1177/0011128708330629

Gudjonsson, G. H., Sigurdsson, J. F., Sigfusdottir, I. D., Asgeirsdottir, B. B., Gonzalez, R. A., & Young, S. (2016). A national epidemiological study investigating risk factors for police interrogation and false confession among juveniles and young persons. *Social Psychiatry Psychiatric Epidemiology, 51*, 359–367. https://doi.org/10.1007/s00127-015-1145-8

Hess, K. M., Orthmann, C. C., & Cho, H. L. (2015). *Introduction to law enforcement and criminal justice*. Cengage.

Hockenberry, S., & Puzzanchera, C. (2024). *Juvenile court statistics 2021*. National Center for Juvenile Justice. https://ojjdp.ojp.gov/library/publications/juvenile-court-statistics-2021

International Association of Chiefs of Police (IACP). (2012). *Reducing risks: An executive's guide to effective juvenile interview and interrogation*. https://www.theiacp.org/resources/document/reducing-risks

International Association of Chiefs of Police (IACP). (2015). *The effects of adolescent development on policing*. Office of Juvenile Justice Delinquency Prevention (OJJDP). https://www.theiacp.org/sites/default/files/2018-08/IACPBriefEffectsofAdolescentDevelopmentonPolicing.pdf

Kochel T. R., Wilson, D. B., & Mastrofski, S. D. (2011). Effects of suspect race on officers' arrest decisions. *Criminology, 49*(2), 473–511. https://doi.org/10.1111/j.1745-9125.2011.00230.x

Lipsey, M. W., Cordray, D. S., & Berger, D. E. (1981). Evaluation of a juvenile diversion program: Using multiple lines of evidence. *Evaluation Review, 5*(3), 283–306. https://doi.org/10.1177/0193841X8100500301

Miranda v. Arizona, 384 U.S. 436 (1966).

Myers, S. (2002). *Police encounters with juvenile suspects: Explaining the use of authority and provision of support* [Unpublished doctoral dissertation]. School of Criminal Justice, University at Albany.

New Jersey v. T.L.O., 469 U.S. 325 (1985).

Nordberg, A., Crawford, M. R., Praetorius, R. T., & Hatcher, S. S. (2016). Exploring minority youths' police encounters: A qualitative interpretive meta-synthesis. *Child Adolescent Social Work Journal, 33*, 137–149. https://doi.org/10.1007/s10560-015-0415-3

Office of Juvenile Justice and Delinquency Prevention (OJJDP). (2014). *Law enforcement response to child abuse: Portable guide to investigating child abuse.* U.S. Department of Justice, Office of Justice Programs. https://www.ojjdp.gov/pubs/243907.pdf

Office of Juvenile Justice and Delinquency Prevention (OJJDP). (2022, April). *Statistical briefing book [Juveniles offenders: Time of day]*. https://www.ojjdp.gov/ojstatbb/offenders/qa03301.asp?qaDate=2019

Penn, E. B. (2006). Black youth: Disproportionality and delinquency. In E. B. Penn, H. T. Green, & S. Gabbidon (Eds.), *Race and juvenile justice* (pp. 47–64). Carolina Academic Press.

Police Foundation. (2016). *A toolkit for California law enforcement: Policing today's youth.* Teen brain: Preparing your officers to engage with youth. https://www.policinginstitute.org/wp-content/uploads/2016/08/PF_IssueBriefs_TeenBrain_Final.pdf

Pope, C. E., & Snyder, H. N. (2003). *Race as a factor in juvenile arrests.* Office of Juvenile Justice Delinquency and Prevention. http://www.ncjj.org/Publication/Race-as-a-Factor-in-Juvenile-Arrests.aspx

Potter, H. R., & Kakar, S. (2002). The diversion decision-making process from the juvenile court practitioners' perspective: Results of a survey. *Journal of Contemporary Criminal Justice, 18*(1), 20–36. https://doi.org/10.1177/1043986202018001003

Price, P. (2009). When is a police officer an officer of the law? The status of police officers in schools. *The Journal of Criminal Law & Criminology, 99*, 541–570. https://scholarlycommons.law.northwestern.edu/jclc/vol99/iss2/6

Puzzanchera, C. (2021, May). *National report series bulletin: Juvenile arrests, 2019* (NCJ 256032). U.S. Department of Justice, Office of Justice Programs, Office of Juvenile Justice and Delinquency Prevention. http://www.ncjj.org/Publication/Juvenile-Arrests-2019.aspx

Puzzanchera, C., Hockenberry, S., & Sickmund, M. (2022, December). *Youth and the juvenile justice system: 2022 national report.* National Center for Juvenile Justice. https://ncjfcj.org/wp-content/uploads/2023/01/2022-national-report.pdf

Puzzanchera, C., Sladky, A., & Kang, W. (2025). *Easy access to juvenile populations: 1990–2023.* https://www.ojjdp.gov/ojstatbb/ezapop/

Ramsey, A., Rust, J., & Sobel, J. O. (2003). Evaluation of the Gang Resistance and Training (GREAT) program: A school-based prevention program. *Education, 124*(2), 297–309. https://link.gale.com/apps/doc/A112480004/AONE?u=anon~d3587921&sid=googleScholar&xid=750b312f

Rivera, M., & Sullivan, R. (2015). Rethinking child welfare to keep families safe together: Effective housing-based supports to reduce child trauma, maltreatment recidivism, and re-entry to foster care. *Child Welfare, 94*(4), 185–204. https://www.jstor.org/stable/48623250

Rogers, R., Blackwood, H. L., Fiduccia, C. E., Steadham, J. A., Drogin, E. Y., & Rogstad, J. E. (2010). Juvenile *Miranda* warnings: Perfunctory rituals or procedural safeguards? *Criminal Justice and Behavior, 39*(3), 229–249. https://doi.org/10.1177/0093854811431934

Rogers, R., Steadham, J. A., Carer, R. M., Henry, S. A., Drogin, E. Y., & Robinson, E. V. (2016). An examination of juveniles' *Miranda* abilities: Investigating differences in *Miranda* recall and reasoning. *Behavioral Sciences and the Law, 34*, 515–538. https://doi.org/10.1002/bsl.2243

Romain, D. M., & Hassell, K. D. (2014). An exploratory examination of the sources of socialization influencing juvenile perceptions of the police. *International Journal of Police Science & Management, 16*, 36–51. https://doi.org/10.1350/ijps.2014.16.1.326

Sanden, M., & Wentz, E. (2017). Kids and cops: Juveniles' perceptions of the police and police services. *Journal of Contemporary Criminal Justice, 33*(4), 411–430. https://doi.org/10.1177/1043986217724536

Schulenberg, J. L., & Warren, D. (2009). Police discretion with apprehended youth: Assessing the impact of juvenile specialization. *Police Practice and Research, 10*(1), 3–16. https://doi.org/10.1080/15614260802128609

Shaver, E. A., & Decker, J. R. (2017). Handcuffing a third grader? Interactions between school resource officers and students with disabilities. *Utah Law Review, 2017*(2), 229–282. http://dc.law.utah.edu/ulr/vol2017/iss2/1

United States Census Bureau. (2023). *Race and Hispanic origin.* QuickFacts. https://www.census.gov/quickfacts/fact/table/US/PST045222

Van Wormer, K. S., & Bartollas, C. (2011). *Women and the criminal justice system.* Prentice Hall.

Walker, S., Spohn, C., & DeLone, M. (2018). *The color of justice: Race, ethnicity, and crime in America* (6th ed.). Cengage.

Weiler, S. C., & Cray, M. (2011). Police at school: A brief history and current status of school resource officers. *The Clearing House, 84*, 160–163. https://www.jstor.org/stable/41304327

Wilson, H. A., & Hoge, R. D. (2012). The effect of youth diversion programs on recidivism: A meta-analytic review. *Criminal Justice & Behavior, 40*(5), 497–518. https://doi.org/10.1177/0093854812451089

Chapter 9

Juvenile Court

Chapter Learning Objectives

Students will be able to:

- Explain the key factors that determine juvenile court jurisdiction
- Identify the characteristics of the juvenile court that make it unique and specialized
- Characterize the trends of petitioned juvenile delinquency cases and status offense cases
- List the steps involved in which juvenile cases are processed by the courts
- Describe the roles of the key personnel who work in the juvenile court
- Explain the dispositional options that can be assigned to a juvenile by the court
- Compare and contrast the different types of specialty courts
- Summarize the different types of waivers to criminal court

Introduction

The juvenile court is a very remarkable and special court. In the past, juveniles were tried and convicted with little to no representation and intermingled with adults in holding cells. Recall from Chapter 7 that in the late nineteenth century, Progressives in Chicago, Illinois, called for massive reform and ushered in a separate court system that was designed exclusively for neglected, dependent, and delinquent children. The new court was predicated on the doctrine *parens patriae*, which essentially means that the state or government has the power to act as the ultimate parent or guardian of a child. After the Juvenile Court Act of 1899 was passed in Illinois, other states followed suit, and almost every state in the nation had a separate juvenile court by the mid-1920s. Even though this was a landmark event in our country's history, paving the way for just and humane juvenile treatment and reform, Whitebread and Heilman (1988) claim that the modern transformation of the juvenile court did not fundamentally begin until the late 1960s, during a time when juvenile rights were being expanded by the U.S. Supreme Court.

What follows is a description of how a juvenile is processed throughout the court system, including a description of key court personnel. This process can be somewhat messy, and it helps to remember that what is being characterized here are the steps a youth takes before, during, and after entering the court system. Similar to the ways in which processes were described in Chapter 8 regarding law enforcement and youth, here too are a myriad of decisions that are embedded in each stage of the juvenile court system. The process is presented in a simplistic way; however, it is important to recognize that it is not always this straightforward, and it is impossible to capture all of the nuances of each state's court system.

Jurisdiction

Jurisdiction over juvenile matters is defined by each state's legislature. To put it more simply, each state legislature frames jurisdiction based on the juvenile's age and behavior (Hess et al., 2013). Many states have clearly defined upper, lower, and even extended age limits by which cases will be heard in juvenile court. In terms of behavior, those who are status offenders, juvenile delinquents, and neglected or abused youth fall within the jurisdiction of the juvenile court. As described later in this chapter, not all cases may be handled in juvenile court, especially if the state has provisions for waiving cases involving serious juvenile offenders to adult court.

Age

Since there is no federal requirement as to what age defines a juvenile, the decision has been left to each state to determine the upper, lower, and extended age limits of juvenile court jurisdiction. In 2019, forty-six states and the District of Columbia held that the traditional upper age for court jurisdiction over cases involving juvenile delinquents was age seventeen (OJJDP, 2021b). At least five states have an upper limit of age sixteen, where the courts preside over juvenile delinquency cases. These states include Georgia, Michigan, Missouri, Texas, and Wisconsin. There are a handful of states that also specify lower age limits for managing juvenile delinquency cases. However, at least thirty-one states do not specify any lower age limit at all. California and Massachusetts have the lower age limit set at age twelve, and Nebraska, set the lower age limit at age eleven. Ten states specify that age ten is the lowest age limit for handling juvenile delinquency cases. Arizona sets the limit even lower at age eight, while New York, Connecticut, and Maryland set the age limit at seven. North Carolina's legal code specifies the lowest age limit in the country at six years of age.

For status offenders, there is more common ground with the upper age limits; that is, fifty states and the District of Columbia have set the upper age limit to seventeen years of age (OJJDP, 2021b). Alabama is the only state in the nation that has set the age of eighteen as the upper age limit for status offenders. When looking at the lower age limits for status offenders, forty-six states have no specified lower age limit. The exceptions are Mississippi and Connecticut, where the lower age limit of court jurisdiction for status offenders is age seven, and North Carolina and Massachusetts, where the age limit is set at age six. Arizona is the only state with a lower age limit of eight for status offenders.

Some may wonder if juveniles forfeit their case being heard in juvenile court once they reach the age of eighteen. It is worth mentioning that many states have also extended the upper age limit for juvenile court jurisdiction. These legal provisions are in place not only to do what is in the best interest of the youth and the public but may also be hinged on certain types of offenses (e.g., murder, robbery) or certain patterns of juvenile offending (e.g., habitual offending, violent offending). Thirty-four states impose an extended upper age limit of twenty (OJJDP, 2021a). This means that a juvenile court does not have jurisdiction over the youth once they turn twenty-one. South Carolina and Vermont extend juvenile court jurisdiction until the age of twenty-one, while Kansas and New York have extended juvenile court jurisdiction for those who are twenty-two years of age. Four states, Colorado, Montana, Oregon, and Wisconsin, have set the upper age limit to twenty-four.

Behavior

As stated in earlier chapters, the juvenile system handles cases involving status offenders—youth who commit certain crimes or behaviors for which an adult cannot be legally punished, and juvenile delinquents—youth who can be prosecuted for the same crimes as adults. It is important to make the distinction between the two when examining official statistics. Recall from Chapter 2, that one of the most easily accessible sources for official crime statistics is the Federal Bureau of Investigation's Uniform Crime Report (UCR) from which juvenile crime data is analyzed by agencies such as the Office of Juvenile Justice and Delinquency Prevention (OJJDP). Delinquent offenses are divided into categories, such as crimes against persons, property offenses, drug offenses, and public order offenses. The definitions for each of these categories follow the FBI's definitions as stated in the UCR. Crimes against persons include criminal homicide, rape, robbery, aggravated assault, simple assault, and other violent sexual acts, as well as other offenses against persons such as kidnapping, reckless endangerment, and harassment, just to name a few (Hockenberry & Puzzanchera, 2024). Crimes against property are those such as arson, burglary, larceny, motor vehicle theft, and vandalism. Offenses that involve the "unlawful sale, purchase, distribution, manufacture, cultivation, transport, possession, or use of a controlled substance or drug paraphernalia" are considered drug law violations (Hockenberry & Puzzanchera, 2024, p. 98). The last delinquent offense category—crimes against public order—include crimes that involve weapons (e.g., selling, distributing, manufacturing, transporting, or possession of a deadly weapon), nonviolent sex offenses (e.g., statutory rape, indecent exposure, lewdness, prostitution), liquor law violations (e.g., public intoxication), disorderly conduct (e.g., disturbing the peace, vagrancy, loitering), obstruction of justice (e.g., impeding the processes carried out by law enforcement or court officials in the administration of justice), or other offenses prohibited against the public (e.g., bribery, gambling, hitchhiking). Here, status offense data is broken down very easily into the categories of curfew violations, liquor law violations, running away, truancy, and ungovernability (e.g., disobedience, unruliness, or unmanageable to parents or guardians).

Juvenile Delinquency

In 2022, juvenile courts across the country processed 549,500 cases involving juvenile delinquents (Hockenberry & Puzzanchera, 2024) (see Figure 9.1). Overall, delinquency case rates have been steadily declining since 2005, most notably for property and public order offenses. Looking at each offense category, person offenses (40%) made up the majority of cases managed by the courts. Cases involving property offenses (27%) were next, followed by public order cases (22%) and drug cases (11%). Most youth processed by the court were fifteen or younger (57%) as opposed to youth ages sixteen and older. Capturing a snapshot of the types of delinquency cases referred to the courts for processing in 2022 and the juvenile's age category, cases involving crimes against persons were the most common among youth fifteen years of age or younger (43%), and for youth sixteen years of age or older, cases involving crimes against persons accounted for 36% of the cases. For youths who were sixteen or older, property cases (28%) were the second most common, which was similar to youths fifteen years old or younger (27%). Public order cases were also similar for both age groups, where 23% of cases were among those sixteen and older, and 21% of cases were among those fifteen and younger. For both age categories, drug offenses comprised the fewest number of referred cases at 9% among the younger age group and 13% among the older age group, respectively.

Examining gender, there are some additional insights worth noting. As males are more likely to be taken into custody, it is no surprise that the same finding is true when examining delinquency caseloads. Yet, it is important to recognize that delinquency caseloads have been declining for both males and females since 2005, with the decline most pronounced among male juveniles (Hockenberry & Puzzanchera, 2024). The actual number of delinquency cases for males in 2022 was the highest for person offenses (37%), followed by property offenses (30%), public order offenses (23%), and drug offenses (10%). For female juveniles, the pattern was quite different, especially when comparing person offenses (45%). Unlike male juveniles, the number of delinquency cases was lower for property offenses (22%) yet similar for both public order offenses (21%) and drug offenses (11%).

National data in 2022 regarding race shows that the most delinquency cases involved white youth (43%), followed by Black youth (37%), Hispanic youth (17%), American Indian youth (2%), and Asian youth (1%) (Hockenberry & Puzzanchera, 2024). In that same year, 52% of delinquency cases for white youth involved property offenses, followed by 43% which involved both person and public order offenses, and 39% which were drug offenses. Comparatively, whereas white youth had a larger number of cases involving property offenses (52%), Black youth had the largest number of delinquency cases involving person offenses (40%) and drug offenses (40%). Moreover, Black youth had a slightly lower number of delinquency cases for public order offenses (37%) compared to white youth and significantly fewer property offense cases (20%).

Status Offenses

In 2022 alone, juvenile courts across the country processed approximately 62,200 cases involving status offenders (Hockenberry & Puzzanchera, 2024). In general, the number of status offense cases formally processed by juvenile courts nationwide has been trending downward since 2005. More specifically, there was a 74% decrease in the number of status offense cases processed between 2005 and 2021. However, from 2021 to 2022, there was a 21% increase in status offense case processing. The data clearly show what may have led to a slight increase during this time frame. Among all of the status offenses (e.g., running away, truancy, curfew violation, ungovernability, or liquor law violation), the number of petitioned status offenses has steadily declined with the exception of truancy. To illustrate, from 2005 to 2007, petitioned truancy cases increased by 15%, then declined steadily until 2021, and then increased by 34% in 2022.

When examining age, data from 2022 showed that it was more common for a juvenile who was sixteen years of age to be petitioned for a status offense than a youth who was fifteen years of age or younger (Hockenberry & Puzzanchera, 2024). Even at age sixteen, overall cases of running away, truancy, and ungovernability were higher in comparison to seventeen-year-olds in 2022. However, when examining each status offense type separately, petitioned cases for liquor law violations were the highest among youth who were seventeen years of age. Other important demographic differences among status offenders are discussed later in the chapter.

Intake

Intake represents the potential gateway into the juvenile court system and perhaps is one of the most fundamental parts of the system that is often overlooked. Essentially, this is the starting place for youth to be referred to the court, and it is most common for a juvenile to be brought to intake by a police officer, as described in Chapter 8. According to Hockenberry and Puzzanchera (2024), at least 85% of the cases brought to juvenile court were the result of law enforcement referrals in 2022. However, in the remaining cases, a parent, truancy officer, social service worker, probation officer, or victim made the referral. Among status offenders, law enforcement made fewer referrals (14%), signaling that parents, truancy officers, social service workers, and so on make up a larger percentage of the referrals. Nonetheless, the **intake** stage is char-

Figure 9.1: Juvenile Case Processing, 2022

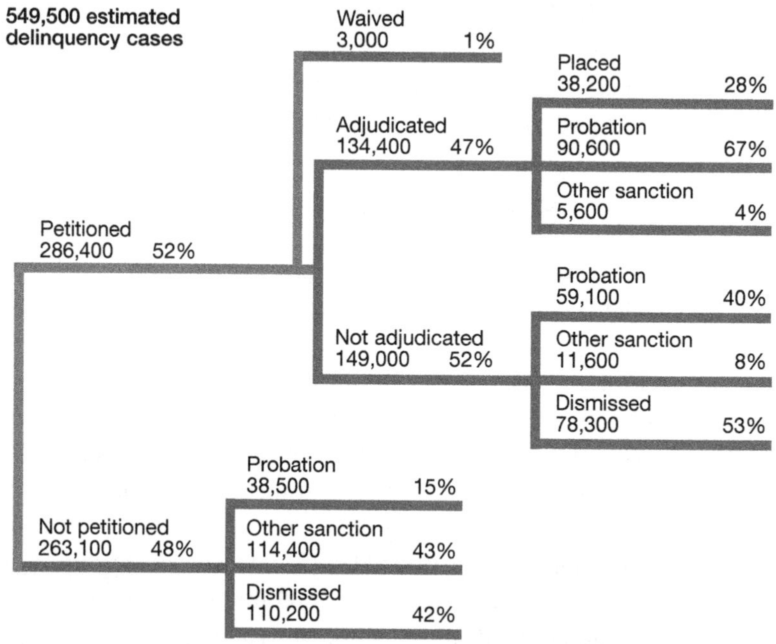

Note: Cases are categorized by their most severe or restrictive sanction. Detail may not add to totals because of rounding.

Source: Hockenberry, S., & Puzzanchera, C. (2024). *Juvenile court statistics 2022* (p. 52). National Center for Juvenile Justice. Office of Juvenile Justice and Delinquency Prevention. https://ojjdp.ojp.gov/publications/juvenile-court-statistics-2022.pdf

acterized best as a process by which an officer of the court assesses the juvenile's case and decides how to proceed.

The Intake Officer

Typically, the intake process is the responsibility of the juvenile probation department or the prosecutor's office (Hyland, 2018). The **intake officer**, who is often a juvenile probation officer, will first carry out an evaluation by gathering information about the youth, which is similar to the booking stage in the adult system. Unlike the adult system, however, not all states have provisions for granting a juvenile bail. **Bail** is the conditional and temporary release of an accused person with the condition that the individual is not a risk to the community and will promise to return to court. One of the most important roles an intake officer fulfills is conducting an evaluation of the youth to determine what type of action is required.

Screening. At intake, an evaluation is conducted in order to review the juvenile's offense history, mental health status, family situation, and educational background, among other factors that may be relevant to decision making. In addition, many states require the intake officer to conduct a more sophisticated clinical assessment to evaluate the youth. It is important not to confuse the term *screening* with the term *assessment* even though they are used interchangeably by most individuals (Vincent, 2012). **Screening** involves a process of gathering information to reach an immediate conclusion about a youth. **Assessment**, which is described in more detail later in this chapter, involves more extensive information gathering and detailed interviewing of a youth using a comprehensive psychometric instrument to determine a youth's risk level and to address a youth's needs.

Based on the results of screening and evaluation, the intake officer must arrive at some type of decision, which generally involves one of the following outcomes: dismissal, informal action, or formal action (Hyland, 2018). After reviewing the details of the complaint, the case may be dismissed on account of a lack of probable cause. Therefore, no petition is filed, and the youth is returned to the custody of a parent or guardian. Informal action implies that the petition is not filed, yet there may be enough evidence to warrant that the juvenile is at risk but is in need of a referral to social services, drug and alcohol counseling, and so on. In some cases, the youth may be placed on some type of improvement period with very "light" conditions that they must follow under the supervision of a probation officer. Informal action may also include an order for the juvenile to pay restitution to the victim or perform community service. If the crime is serious in nature, a decision is made to file a petition and let the case go forward to juvenile court. Another type of formal action would be to detain the youth and refer the case to adult criminal court, which is discussed later in this chapter. Even with such formal action, the juvenile may not necessarily be held in detention. Contrary to popular belief, most youths are released back to the custody of a parent or legal guardian.

To put this into perspective, 2022 data showed that nearly 110,200 delinquency cases among 549,500 delinquency cases were actually dismissed upon intake (Hockenberry & Puzzanchera, 2024). This translates roughly to about 20% of delinquency cases overall, and most cases are either dismissed as a result of the intake officer lacking legal grounds to file a petition. Approximately 152,900 non-petitioned cases were handled informally. As described earlier, this means that the juvenile agrees to another alternative sanction such as probation, community service, or restitution. Among the total overall cases of juvenile delinquency, 52% (286,400 cases) resulted in formal action and the filing of a petition (see Figure 9.1). Here, decisions need to be made about whether the youth should be detained. This decision does not come lightly as the intake officer weighs whether an out-of-home placement or an alternative to confinement will best serve the youth and their community. Such decision-making has been supported by the Juvenile Detention Alternatives Initiative (JDAI), which is credited to the Annie E. Casey Foundation. More about this effort can be found in Box 9.1.

Before moving to the next stage of processing in the juvenile court, it is important to note that the intake officer's role encompasses more than just serving as a gatekeeper. In many jurisdictions, the officer is involved in making referrals to link youth and families to community resources and in providing youth with any necessary crisis intervention. Their job also entails maintaining records and corresponding with youth, their parents or legal guardians, social workers, and attorneys. In some cases, the intake officer may even transport juveniles to court or detention hearings.

Even though it may seem like the job of the intake officer is rather straightforward, it has not escaped scrutiny. Lindner (2008) addressed both the positive and negative aspects of the intake process. On a positive note, the intake process is listed as one of the main reasons the juvenile court has been so successful. Youth are pre-screened, and only the most troublesome cases are brought forth to the court. Without this decision-making stage, the juvenile court would be overwhelmed with cases. Also on the positive side, intake helps to divert young people away from the system, often by way of handling cases informally. This coincides with the overarching philosophy of the court. Third, intake saves the court time and energy by focusing on only those cases that warrant serious attention. In contrast, there are some negative aspects too. The juvenile intake officer oftentimes has to make value judgments in borderline cases. This is likely the case when the intake officer does not use a formal assessment or set of guidelines but instead relies solely on gut instinct. The subjective nature of decision-making can be the result of using non-legal factors or a biased approach. To limit subjective decisions, intake officers in some jurisdictions may rely on and administer valid risk screening instruments to make these determinations to ensure that a fair decision is made. With this said, the intake officer still wields great discretionary power and plays a vital role in the system.

Box 9.1: Juvenile Detention Alternatives Initiative (JDAI)

The Annie E. Casey Foundation launched the Juvenile Detention Alternatives Initiative (JDAI) in 1992 to address the overuse of juvenile detention. This was considered a radical approach amidst the "get tough era," which included increasing juvenile arrest rates and the popular use of detention. Essentially, the initiative calls for creating state and local networks to reduce reliance on detention, seeking and utilizing community-based alternatives, improving public safety, and creating a more equitable juvenile justice system. JDAI also promotes a data-driven, problem-solving approach and emphasizes collaboration among many stakeholders (i.e., community organizations, law enforcement, and the judiciary), as can be seen from the current list of eight core strategies listed below.

- promoting collaboration between juvenile court officials, probation agencies, prosecutors, defense attorneys, schools, community organizations and advocates;
- using rigorous data collection and analysis to guide decision making;

- utilizing objective admissions criteria and screening instruments to replace subjective decision-making processes;
- implementing new or expanded community-based alternatives to locked facilities—such as day and evening reporting centers, home confinement and shelter care;
- instituting case processing reforms to expedite the flow of cases through the system;
- reducing the number of youth detained for probation rule violations or failing to appear in court, and the number held in detention awaiting transfer to a residential facility;
- improving racial and ethnic equity by examining data to identify policies and practices that may disadvantage youth of color at various stages of the process, and pursuing strategies to ensure a more level playing field for youth regardless of race or ethnicity; and
- monitoring and improving conditions of confinement in facilities. (JDAI, n.d.)

Elaborating on this list of core strategies, one of the core principles of JDAI is to ensure that detention is used only for youth who pose a significant risk to public safety or are likely to fail to appear in court. Thus, non-violent status offenders or youth who commit technical violations should not be held in lock up. Moreover, the initiative encourages the use of objective screening tools to assess the risk level of each youth and to make informed decisions about detention. This approach helps to prevent the unnecessary detention of low-risk youth, who can be better served through community-based alternatives.

JDAI also focuses on addressing racial and ethnic disparities in the juvenile justice system. Since youth of color are disproportionately represented in detention facilities, JDAI works to implement policies and practices that promote racial equity. This includes engaging with youth, families, and communities to ensure that their voices are heard and their needs are met.

Since its inception, JDAI has expanded to numerous jurisdictions across the United States. Some notable examples of state systems that have successfully implemented JDAI include the following:

1. **Indiana**: Indiana adopted JDAI in 2006 in Marion County, and now it exists in 32 counties in the state. The state has focused on reducing racial and ethnic disparities and improving outcomes for youth. Efforts included creating a steering committee, training staff, increasing data collection and analysis methods, and hiring detention strategists, just to name a few. Indiana's JDAI sites have reported reductions in detention admissions and lengths of stay, as well as increased use of community-based alternatives.

2. **Massachusetts**: Massachusetts has implemented JDAI in several counties, with a focus on reducing the use of detention for low-risk youth. The first counties to adopt these strategies were Worcester and Suffolk County in 2006. Efforts were made to create an expansive state-wide network that is coordinated by the Massachusetts Department of Youth Services. The state has seen positive results, including decreases in detention admissions and improvements in public safety. Massachusetts has also worked to address racial and ethnic disparities in its juvenile justice system.
3. **Missouri**: Missouri has adopted JDAI in multiple jurisdictions, with a focus on improving outcomes for youth and reducing reliance on detention. The initiative was implemented originally in three counties and was later expanded to 16 of the 17 jurisdictions by 2018. One of their notable efforts involved the creation of a state-wide data collection system to keep track of youth in the system. The state has reported reductions in arrests, detention admissions, and lengths of stay, as well as increased use of community-based alternatives.
4. **New Mexico**: One of the first pilot efforts began in Bernalillo County in 1999. Expansion grew to four counties, covering 56% of the youth population in the state. New Mexico's JDAI efforts focused on passing legislation to mandate detention screening for juveniles, coupled with a large-scale initiative to formalize and monitor case processing of juveniles throughout the legal system. Not only has the state seen a reduction in the use of detention for low-risk youth but they have also made policy changes to support youth with mental health treatment needs and alternatives to detention.

Sources: Guckenburg, S., Stern, A., Sutherland, H., Lopez, G., & Petrosino, A. (2019). *Juvenile detention alternatives initiative scale-up: Study of four states.* WestEd. https://assets.aecf.org/m/resourcedoc/wested-jdaiscaleup-2019.pdf; Juvenile Detention Alternatives Initiative (JDAI). (n.d.). *JDAI core strategies.* https://www.aecf.org/work/juvenile-justice/jdai/jdai-core-strategies

Detention

Should the intake officer decide that the youth needs to be detained, a detention hearing must be held within 24 to 72 hours (Hess et al., 2013). At the detention hearing, the juvenile court judge decides whether detaining the youth is justified or whether additional time in detention is warranted up until the adjudication hearing. Here, the judge may use detention in a similar vein as in the adult system, where the youth is held in detention because they are seen as a flight risk, a risk to society, or if the youth needs protection from their home environment or community. The use of pretrial or **preventative detention** or holding a youth temporarily for reasons other than posing a flight risk was once contested (see Box 9.2); however, it was deemed fair and permissible, especially if the juvenile court judge has reason to believe that the youth may engage in criminal behavior prior to their adjudication hearing. Even still, there are risks to consider when placing a youth in detention, such as the youth committing suicide or contemplating suicide (see Box 9.3). On a different note, keep in mind that later down the road, a juvenile may receive a detention hearing if they are sentenced to "serve time" in detention or if they are awaiting transfer to another court-ordered placement. Detention as a disposition is described in more detail in Chapter 10.

Box 9.2: *Schall v. Martin* (1984)

In the landmark case *Schall v. Martin* (1984), the Supreme Court ruled that it was constitutional for youth to be held in preventive detention (also known as pretrial detention). The crime took place on December 13, 1977, and involved a young man by the name of Gregory Martin, who was charged with first-degree robbery, second-degree assault, and criminal possession of a loaded weapon that had been used to hit another youth to steal his jacket and shoes (Weiss, 1984). Martin, who was fourteen at the time, was not forthcoming with the police and was kept in detention overnight. He lied to the police about where he resided and the fact that he lived with his grandmother. The next morning, the family court judge ordered that Martin be kept in detention on account of possessing a dangerous weapon, lying to the police, and being out past curfew the night the crime occurred. Five days later, a probable cause hearing was held, citing that Martin was guilty of both robbery and possession of a weapon. The disposition hearing was held on February 14, where Martin was sentenced to probation for two years.

Before the adjudication hearing, and at the point where Martin had been detained for a total of fifteen days, his legal counsel filed a habeas corpus petition, arguing that pretrial detention was akin to punishment and a violation of his Fourteenth Amendment rights as well as a violation of his Fifth Amendment due process rights (Weiss, 1984). In other words, the claim was that Martin was being punished as he was held in detention, yet he had not been found guilty of any wrongdoing. The U.S. District Court for the Southern District of New York agreed that pretrial detention was a violation of Martin's due process rights as it served as a punitive measure prior to the adjudication hearing, and the U.S. Appeals Second Circuit Court agreed that pretrial detention was not being used for the purpose of prevention in this case. Upon hearing these arguments, the U.S. Supreme Court reversed the decision of the lower court and held that pretrial detention not only protected society but prevented juveniles from future offending. The high court contended that pretrial detention was fair, as the state has to also consider the best interests and protection of society, which, in this case, outweighed the juvenile's liberty interests. The Supreme Court also addressed whether pretrial detention was considered a punishment, and therefore a violation of the juvenile's due process rights. Here, the court ruled that "preventative detention of juveniles was not punishment because the statute did not state that the detention was meant as punishment and the circumstances of the incarceration did not constitute punishment" (Weiss, 1984, p. 860).

Source: Weiss, L. A. (1984). Fourteenth Amendment—Due process and the preventive detention of juveniles. *Journal of Criminal Law & Criminology, 75*(3), 855–874. https://doi.org/10.2307/1143647

In 2022, national data revealed that 134,900 delinquency cases led to detention (Hockenberry & Puzzanchera, 2024). Compared to the number of cases in 2005 requiring detention (401,400), this was a considerable decline. Examining these cases from 2022 even further showed that 45% of delinquency cases involving crimes against persons resulted in detention, followed by 28% of cases involving property offenses, and 25% of cases involving public order crimes. Delinquency cases related to drug crimes (6%) were the least likely to result in detention. Moreover, delinquency cases involving white youth (32%) were less likely to result in detention when compared to Black youth (44%). Delinquency cases involving females (19%) were also less likely to result in detention than cases involving delinquent males (27%). The picture for status offenders is a little different. Here, 2,000 cases were processed in 2022, and among them, cases involving runaway youth (24%) were more likely to receive detention than cases involving youth who were truant (23%) or who were ungovernable (19%), for example. Cases involving curfew violations (5%) were the least likely to result in detention.

Box 9.3: Juvenile Detention and Suicide

While detention may be the best option given the circumstances of the crime and the needs of the youth, suicide is the single and foremost concern among detained youth. In juvenile detention facilities across the country, suicide is the leading cause of death (Hayes, 2009). Comparisons of youth in detention and youth who are not incarcerated show higher rates of suicide among those youth who are placed in detention. Research studies typically examine this issue in terms of actual suicides that have taken place or suicidal ideation, which means that the youth has contemplated suicide or has suicidal thoughts.

Only a handful of studies have examined suicidal thoughts and behaviors among detained youth in the United States. For example, Hayes (2009) conducted a national study to examine the suicides that had taken place among juvenile detention facilities, camps, secure facility/training schools, and reception centers from 1995 to 1999. Reportedly, 110 juvenile suicides took place during this time frame. Closer inspection of seventy-nine of these cases showed that most suicides occurred at a secure facility (41.8%), yet a significant number of suicides also occurred in detention centers (36.7%) and residential treatment centers (15.2%). The fewest suicides took place at reception/diagnostic centers (6.3%). A breakdown of suicides that occurred among state versus county or private agencies showed that nearly half (48.1%) of suicides took place in state-administered facilities, followed by 39.2% of suicides that took place in county facilities. The fewest number of suicides occurred in privately run agencies (12.7%).

Some select findings of Hayes's (2009, p. vii–viii) work as shown below, demonstrate the ongoing need to be attentive to the factors that place a youth at risk of suicide when the youth is held in detention.

- More than two-thirds (68.4 percent) of victims were Caucasian.
- A substantial majority (79.7 percent) of victims were male.
- More than two-thirds (69.6 percent) of victims were confined for nonviolent offenses.
- Approximately two-thirds (67.1 percent) of victims were held on commitment status at time of death, with 32.9 percent on detained status; the vast majority (79.3 percent) of victims held in detention centers were on detained status.
- A substantial majority (78.5 percent) of victims had a history of prior offenses; most of these (72.7 percent) were of a nonviolent nature.
- All detention center suicides occurred within the first four months of confinement, with more than 40 percent occurring within the first 72 hours.
- Nearly three-quarters (73.4 percent) of victims had a history of substance abuse, 19.0 percent had a history of medical problems, 44.3 percent had a history of emotional abuse, 34.2 percent had a history of physical abuse, and 27.8 percent had a history of sexual abuse.
- A majority (65.8 percent) of victims had a history of mental illness (with 65.3 percent of these victims suffering from depression at the time of death); 53.5 percent of victims were taking psychotropic medications.
- Almost all (98.7 percent) the suicides were by hanging; 71.8 percent of these victims used their bedding (e.g., sheet, blanket) as the instrument. A variety of anchoring devices were used in the hangings, including door hinge/knob (20.5 percent), air vent (19.2 percent), bedframe (19.2 percent), and window frame (14.1 percent).
- A large majority (85.0 percent) of victims who died by suicide while on room confinement status died during waking hours (6 a.m. to 9 p.m.), a higher percentage than those victims who died by suicide during waking hours but were not on room confinement status (70.9 percent).

Source: Hayes, L. M. (2009). *Juvenile suicide in confinement: A national survey.* National Center on Institutions and Alternatives. Office of Juvenile Justice and Delinquency Prevention. https://www.ojp.gov/pdffiles1/ojjdp/213691.pdf

Characteristics of the Juvenile Court

Aside from the historical context in which the juvenile court evolved, several characteristics distinguish the juvenile court from the adult court, and foremost, it is truly meant to be a "separate court." This allows the focus to be centered on what is in the best interest of the youth, plus, it can be argued that separate provisions afford a more safe and humane system for minors. Another characteristic is that the juvenile court is supposed to be non-adversarial (Hess et al., 2013). In theory, the court is not a place for drawn-out arguments and sparring among courtroom players. Instead, it is meant to house civil conversations where decisions can be made to provide the youth with the best treatment and safety alternative (Platt, 2009). Third, it is to be used most sparingly. As a juvenile is processed through the court system, there are various "exit doors" by which youth can be diverted away from the formal court system, such as treatment, programming, community-based alternatives, or court warnings and reprimands that still hold the youth accountable, in lieu of formalized punishment. Along these same lines, a fourth characteristic is to keep juvenile matters private and confidential. Minors are not on public display in an open courtroom and their case files are not subject to scrutiny by the public or news media. Last, not only is the process of labeling a young person as a juvenile delinquent avoided, but it is also a system predicated on the notion that youth deserve second, third, and sometimes fourth chances to correct their wayward behaviors. In other words, and as previously mentioned, the characteristics framing the court are treatment and rehabilitation. Youth are considered malleable, so treatment is afforded to juvenile delinquents and status offenders and is seen as one of the greatest options for teaching youth right from wrong during their formative years. There is one small caveat. Even though the juvenile court possesses these characteristics, there are situations where a juvenile's case can be waived to adult criminal court. Ironically, the court that was originally designed to protect and rehabilitate youth and to keep youth matters separate from adults was eventually deemed incapable of serving some of them.

Organizational Structure

What follows is a general description and overview of the juvenile court system and process. Again, the organizational structure from state to state may be similar, but state legal codes carry some differences. Nonetheless, like most descriptions of the justice system, the courts make up a very important part of the system. Several key personnel seek to rehabilitate the youth and at the same time maintain public safety.

Personnel

When peering into the juvenile court from the outside it may seem like there are only a handful of individuals who fill a role in the juvenile court. Because the system is centered on managing what is in the best interest of the child and operating under the guise of *parens patriae*, many courtroom players are involved. Although there are many, the main courtroom personnel described next include the juvenile court judge, prosecutor, defense counsel/guardian ad litem, and probation officer.

Juvenile Court Judge. The juvenile court judge has one of the most prominent roles in the juvenile justice system as they wield a significant amount of power and discretion. They may be elected to the position or appointed by the governor or legislature. The **juvenile court judge** is essentially an administrator of the court and is primarily responsible for overseeing how it is managed. This includes hiring staff, creating court policies, and monitoring the court budget. The role of the judge that garners the most attention is one of presiding over juvenile cases and issuing dispositions involving adjudicated delinquents and status offenders. It is unrealistic to think that the juvenile court judge is solely involved in determining the juvenile's accountability in a case. Before an adjudication hearing, the judge has the authority to place a youth in a secure facility while the case is being processed or return the juvenile to their parents or guardians. Should the case go to the adjudication stage, the judge presides over the adjudication hearing and weighs the facts of the case. Depending on the outcome, the judge also determines the appropriate disposition or sentence. Keep in mind that oftentimes the judge relies heavily on the recommendation of the juvenile probation officer and the findings outlined in the probation officer's predisposition report. The authority of the judge does not stop here. The judge can also issue mandates to the juvenile's parents or guardians, especially if the parent/guardian has been negligent in some way, and the judge has the power to remove a juvenile from their home if necessary.

Prosecutor. The **prosecutor** in juvenile court proceedings is commonly known for serving the interests of the state. In addition, while police officers were depicted as gatekeepers to the juvenile justice system in Chapter 8, and as intake officers were described as gatekeepers earlier in the chapter, prosecutors are yet another gatekeeper to the juvenile court, as they too wield a significant amount of power and discretion. For example, prior to any official court hearings, the prosecutor can decide to dismiss a case, especially if there is a lack of evidence. Second, the prosecutor may decide that the case is less serious, and the youth is diverted to other relevant programs or services. Last, the case may warrant formal action, and the prosecutor prepares the case for adjudication. This role typically comes to mind where the prosecutor sets in motion what charges should be filed against the juvenile. As adjudication processes are set to move forward, the prosecutor will likely consider reducing the charges in exchange for information. This is known as a **plea bargain**—an agreement made between the prosecutor and the defendant where the defendant enters a guilty plea in order to receive a lighter sentence. Depending on state law as discussed later in this chapter, the prosecutor may also have the ability to waive a juvenile case to criminal court.

Juvenile Defense Counsel/Guardian Ad Litem. Even though the juvenile court is not supposed to be adversarial in nature, juveniles must have legal defense representation. Recall from Chapter 7, the case *In re Gault* solidified a juvenile's due process right to representation by counsel. A juvenile's **defense counsel** is essentially an attorney, who may be appointed to the juvenile's case (such as a public defender), or the youth could hire a private attorney. Public defenders are state-employed lawyers who represent individuals who cannot afford an attorney on their own. There are many misconceptions about defense attorneys, namely that they are morally bankrupt individuals who protect those who are guilty of a crime. Such misconceptions are far from the truth in the justice system. Defense counsel serves a very noble role in ensuring that the constitutional rights of an individual are protected. In cases involving neglected and abused youth, the court may appoint a **guardian ad litem** to investigate and oversee the findings of the case.

The public defender system is not without its faults, however. Our courts process numerous cases each year, and, as a result, public defenders find themselves overburdened with very high caseloads. Sometimes this may not afford the juvenile the most specialized attention that their case requires. Despite these criticisms, The National Juvenile Defender Center (2012) as part of the Models for Change initiative, set forth the following standards for public defenders.

1. Juvenile defenders play a critical role in the fair administration of justice for children;
2. Juvenile defense is a specialized practice anchored in juvenile-specific training and practice skills;
3. Juvenile defense requires zealous advocacy;
4. Juvenile defense requires competence and proficiency in court rules and the law;
5. Juvenile defense requires legal representation that is individualized;
6. Juvenile defense requires representation that is developmentally appropriate;
7. Juvenile defense is based on the clients' expressed interests;
8. Juvenile defense requires that clients be meaningful participants in their defense;
9. Juvenile defense includes counseling clients through the legal and extralegal processes;
10. Juvenile defense includes ensuring that clients and their families are treated with dignity and respect and that there is decorum in the courtroom;
11. Systemic barriers and deficiencies impair juvenile defenders' abilities to provide high-quality representation; and
12. Systemic barriers and deficiencies lead to disproportionate representation of vulnerable, underserved populations at every contact with and stage of the juvenile delinquency court process. (National Juvenile Defender Center, 2012, p. 9)

Juvenile Probation Officer. The role of the **juvenile probation officer** is quite diversified, as they are known to wear many "hats" (Hess et al., 2013). Even though the role of the probation officer may vary slightly by state, the best way to think of their role is two-fold. First, and foremost, they are an officer of the court. Nearly every case that reaches the juvenile court will be handled by a juvenile probation officer. When a juvenile case is filed, the juvenile probation officer is expected to compile a predisposition report, with a recommendation for the judge on the appropriate disposition. The investigation can be time-consuming, and the report can be lengthy. Second, the juvenile probation officer acts as the supervisor for the adjudicated youth who has been placed on probation. In turn, surveillance of the juvenile may be a more prominent role that the officer takes, making home and school visits. However, probation officers perform rehabilitative duties, serving in the capacity of a counselor and linking youth to appropriate and available treatment services. This is not always done in isolation, but rather with a team of other practitioners, such as school counselors, treatment specialists, caseworkers, and even the youth's family members.

Clinical Evaluations and Assessment

When it comes to making decisions about a youth's risk level and treatment needs, standardized clinical assessments can be used to remove or limit subjectivity among practitioners. Another way to think about the utility of these assessments is that they take out the guesswork or diminish the use of hunches that so many practitioners have relied on in the past. Even though the use of these instruments is described as a function for probation officers, it is important to recognize that they are often used at various points in the juvenile justice system (e.g., diversion, adjudication, and disposition), and also by staff in detention, day treatment facilities, and secure juvenile institutions. Some examples of commercially available risk assessments include the Youth Level of Service/Case Management Inventory (YLS/CMI) and the Structured Assessment of Violence Risk in Youth (SAVRY) (Baird et al., 2013). The overarching premise of modern-day assessments is that predicting future juvenile offending is possible and treatment services can be matched to a juvenile's needs (Andrews & Bonta, 1994). Clinical assessments are not developed or implemented in a haphazard way. Instead, assessments are statistically validated and theoretically grounded in a set of three main principles: risk, need, and responsivity (Andrews et al., 1990).

The **risk principle** involves predicting the youth's likelihood of reoffending (Andrews & Bonta, 1994). Clearly, this principle is related to public safety concerns and the safety of the youth themselves. When risk scores are produced, they indicate whether a juvenile is high-risk, medium-risk, or low-risk. In addition, risk assessment instruments signal the appropriate type and level of matched services. For example, youth who score as high-risk offenders are expected to receive services that are more intensive in order to reduce the risk of reoffending. In turn, youth who score as low-risk offenders should receive minimal treatment services or no intervention. The level of risk also allows the probation officer, for example, to determine what type of disposition is appropriate, which may be probation or no supervision for low-risk offenders, but for high-risk juvenile offenders, detention, intensive treatment, or placement in a secure facility may be necessary.

The **need principle** consists of two categories: criminogenic factors and non-criminogenic factors (Andrews & Bonta, 1994). Criminogenic factors are also consid-

ered to be **dynamic factors**, which means that by nature they can change, and if these attributes can change, the probability of recidivism is reduced (Vincent et al., 2012). Examples of criminogenic factors are criminal attitudes, delinquent peers, antisocial values, and skills deficiencies, just to name a few. **Static factors** are those that cannot be changed, such as age, gender, and past delinquent offense history. To clinicians, identifying a juvenile's criminogenic needs in a precise way provides for targeted and individualized treatment, and once again, with targeted and successful treatment, the juveniles are less likely to reoffend. Non-criminogenic factors are also dynamic in nature but are not likely to impact future offending. Non-criminogenic factors include the youth's mental health, physical health, and intelligence, for example.

The third principle in clinical assessment is **responsivity**. What this means is that the results from the instrument indicate whether the youth is amenable to change and is responsive to treatment (Baird et al., 2013). Underlying this principle is also the notion that specific treatments should be tailored to fit the youth's risks and needs. For example, if the youth has anger management issues, the youth should receive the appropriate anger management treatment. Only youth who have substance abuse problems require substance abuse treatment, and so forth, unless this has been a factor that was clinically identified. To have the maximum benefit, these assessments must be conducted before alignment with treatment services (Van Voorhis et al., 1997).

Even though a properly executed risk assessment is a valuable tool in understanding a juvenile's problems and determining solutions, there are numerous barriers and limitations to consider. One of the leading problems is that risk assessments may further label and stigmatize youth (Seymour, 2013). This is especially true for youth of color, as risk assessment may magnify individual- and family-level factors while neglecting large-scale social factors such as poverty, discrimination, and segregation. Thus, it may underestimate what is really needed to keep youth from reoffending. Furthermore, the results may appear to justify residential or community placement, in which case socially disadvantaged youth are placed deeper within the justice system. Second, not all states or local jurisdictions may have the necessary funding to pay for the licenses to use commercial risk instruments. If this is the case, the agency may rely on more generic "web-based" assessment instruments that cannot make sound risk predictions (Hess et al., 2013). Third, a great deal of criticism has pointed to the fact that the instruments, even though standardized, have not been properly validated with the population they serve (Vincent et al., 2012). Such validation requires the skill of trained professionals or academicians to examine the instrument's ability to make sound risk predictions without the potential for bias on the specific population that it was meant to serve. A fourth and related issue is training. Implementation of a clinical risk assessment requires hours of training and practice before it is used. However, not all states or local jurisdictions have the resources to train juvenile justice staff adequately (Ho et al., 2018).

The Predisposition Report

A predisposition report is typically compiled by the assigned juvenile probation officer. A **predisposition report** (also known as a presentence report) is an official document that summarizes the juvenile's conduct and current situation with the purpose of providing the juvenile court judge with an appropriate disposition recommendation (see Box 9.4). Additionally, the report chronicles the factors related to the juvenile's home environment, parental status, family relationships, school attendance and activities, the presence of any physical or mental health issues, and previous status offense or juvenile delinquent history. As mentioned, and based on the report's findings, the juvenile probation officer provides a sentence recommendation to the juvenile court judge that falls in line with the state legal code. The juvenile probation officer may even include the results of the clinical assessment that was administered to the youth to determine their risk level, needs, and treatment options.

Box 9.4: Outline of a Predisposition Report

(1) Court Information

- Docket number and report date
- Petition number
- Offense
- Presiding judge
- State counsel
- Defense counsel
- Codefendant (if applicable)

- Custodial status

(2) Case Assignment

- Report prepared by (probation officer's name)
- Date completed

(3) Biographical Information

- Name of the defendant and any aliases
- Address
- Social Security number
- Race
- Citizenship
- Age
- Place of birth
- Sex
- Education
- Religion
- Family history
- Health and habits

(4) Offense Information

- Summary of crime
- Prior juvenile adjudications
- Victim Impact Statement
- Defendant's version
- Codefendant's version (if applicable)
- Statement of witnesses and complainants

(5) Evaluation

- Results of risk/needs assessment

(6) Sentencing options and recommendations

- Scheduled sentencing date

Figure 9.2: Outline of Delinquency Case Processing

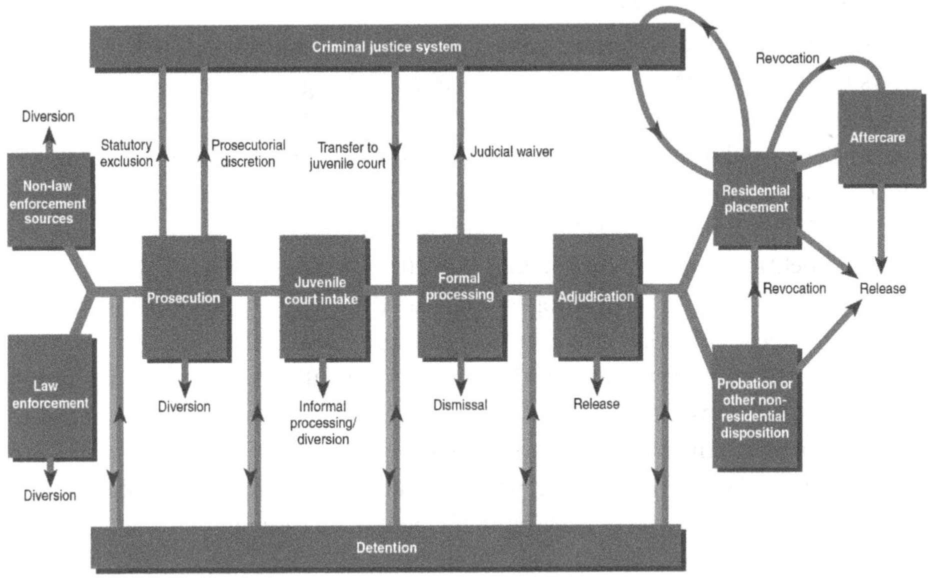

Source: Snyder, H. N., & Sickmund, M. (2006). *Juvenile offenders and victims: 2006 national report*. U.S. Department of Justice, Office of Justice Programs, Office of Juvenile Justice and Delinquency Prevention. https://ojjdp.ojp.gov/library/publications/juvenile-offenders-and-victims-2006-national-report

Juvenile Court Processes

Juvenile court processes involve a series of key decision-making points among key court personnel. The primary goals are to handle as many cases as possible informally, or dispose of the case entirely, and to provide youth with treatment services that will curb future delinquency or status offending. In this section, the process starts from the point of filing a petition. Keep in mind that just because a petition is filed does not necessarily mean that the juvenile will automatically go to court, as shown in Figure 9.2. Also, a significant number of cases do not result in a petition at all; these cases are diverted out of the system, or the case is dismissed (shown earlier in Figure 9.1). Should a juvenile continue through the entire process and should they be detained, they are entitled to a series of hearings.

Petition

Upon intake, one of the most important decisions that is made in a juvenile's case is whether a **petition** or formal charge should be filed with the court alleging that the juvenile is an adjudicated delinquent or adjudicated status offender (Hess et al., 2013). In some cases, the petition may also state whether the child is simply in need of supervision. Depending on the state or jurisdiction, this decision may be made by the prosecutor, police officer, or probation officer. In some states, parents or schools may be permitted to file a petition.

As stated earlier in this chapter, among the 549,500 delinquency cases that intake officers handled in 2022, over half (52%) resulted in filing a petition, with most petitions filed for cases involving crimes against persons (40%), followed by property offenses (29%), public order offenses (24%), and drug offenses (8%) (Hockenberry & Puzzanchera, 2024). In comparison to previous years, the number of delinquent cases resulting in a petition has been declining. The largest relative decreases in the number of petitioned cases between 2005 and 2022 were seen among cases involving drug offenses (79%), followed by property offenses (73%), public order offenses (71%), and person offenses (51%). When examining age groups in 2022, slightly more youth ages sixteen and older were petitioned (55%) versus youth ages fifteen and younger. Formal processing was also more likely for male youth (55% of all male cases resulted in a formal petition) than for female youth (where 44% of all female cases resulted in a formal petition). As described before, when examining youth of color combined, 59% were formally petitioned in comparison to the petitioned cases among white youth as a racial group (48%).

Recall from earlier in the chapter, and in comparison to petitioned cases involving delinquent acts, that there were an estimated 62,200 petitioned status offense cases in 2022, and of these, the majority were for truancy (64%) (Hockenberry & Puzzanchera, 2024). Overall, running away and ungovernability were both the second-highest petitioned status offense (9%), followed by liquor law violations (8%). Very few petitioned status offense cases were for curfew violations (3%). The largest decline among petitioned status offenses since 2005 was for cases involving liquor law violations.

As discussed in Chapter 8, males in comparison to females are most likely to be petitioned for a status offense, except for running away and truancy. What is overwhelmingly evident, however, is that since 2006 trends show that the gap between the two genders has narrowed significantly (Hockenberry & Puzzanchera, 2024). Even though the largest number of petitioned cases for males in 2022 was for truancy (63%), for females petitioned cases of truancy were not much different (64%). Among the remaining cases involving male status offenders, 8% of cases involved liquor law violations, followed by cases of ungovernability (9%), running away (7%), and curfew violations (3%). A slightly different picture emerged for female status offenders. Consistent with the research literature, the second most common petitioned status offenses for females were running away (12%), whereas ungovernability (9%), liquor law violations (7%), and curfew violations (2%) made up fewer cases. Again, the stark differences in petitioned status offenses between males and females are not as dramatic as they once were.

Additional insightful patterns of status offending can be found by examining the juvenile's race. The majority of petitioned status offense cases involved white youth (58%), compared to Black youth (25%), Hispanic youth (11%), American Indian youth (4%), and Asian youth (2%) (Hockenberry & Puzzanchera, 2024). Trend analyses show that the most significant decline in petitioned status offense cases has been for white youth and Black youth—both a 70% decrease from 2005 to 2022. Similarly, a decline in petitioned status offenses was noted for Hispanic youth (65%) as well. Regardless of race, the largest number of petitioned cases was for truancy. Aside from truancy, American Indian and Alaskan Native youth had the largest number of petitioned cases for liquor law violations (23%), followed by Black youth, who had the largest number of petitioned cases for running away (18%).

Preliminary Hearing

A preliminary hearing takes place prior to adjudication, and yet again, this stage represents another potential stop before processing the youth more formally. The hearing itself involves many decision-making points. For one, the judge reviews the intake officer's report in consultation with the juvenile probation officer to determine if the case warrants further judicial action. The hearing also entails informing the youth of the charges that they face as described in the petition. In some states, this hearing is devoted to determining whether there is probable cause. If the judge or magistrate believes this to be the case, then the juvenile and the juvenile's parents or guardians are informed of the juvenile's legal rights, and the judge must ensure that they fully understand these rights. Moreover, the hearing is to ensure that the juvenile is provided with legal counsel or retains their own counsel in order to proceed to the adjudication stage. The last decision that the judge must make is whether to release the youth back to their parents or guardians until the adjudication hearing or whether the youth needs to be further detained. In sum, formal action puts into motion the petition alleging that the youth is a delinquent or a status offender, and a request for an adjudication hearing is scheduled.

Adjudication

The **adjudication** stage in the juvenile court is when the juvenile is found guilty and thus adjudicated or charged as a delinquent. At this stage, and by law, they are also informed again of their rights, which include: (1) the right to counsel, (2) the right to an adjudication hearing, (3) the right to be free of self-incrimination, (4) the right to cross-examine witnesses, (5) the right to have witnesses testify on their behalf, and (6) the right to have charges proved beyond a reasonable doubt, should the juvenile be facing incarceration. Once the juvenile has been informed of their rights, they are asked to enter a plea. However, it is important to keep in mind that more than half of the petitioned cases go forward to an adjudication hearing, as shown in Figure 9.1.

Adjudication hearing. To put this into perspective, the adjudication hearing in the juvenile court is similar to a criminal trial in the adult system. At this stage, the court is fully involved in an effort to determine whether the juvenile committed the alleged offense. Unlike the criminal court, however, jury trials are not common in juvenile proceedings. As a matter of fact, juveniles are not afforded the constitutional right to a jury trial as ruled by the U.S. Supreme Court in the case *McKeiver v. Pennsylvania*. A juvenile court judge or juvenile referee considers the evidence and testimony that is provided by the prosecutor and defense counsel. There are two important facets of the juvenile court proceedings based on standards of proof. In cases involving status offenders, the judge will have to determine if there is a **preponderance of the evidence**. This is a lower standard of proof where the judge will consider the evidence and determine if it is likely that the juvenile committed said offense. Matters involving delinquent offenses require a higher standard of proof, that is, the level of proof is more certain, demonstrating **beyond a reasonable doubt** that the youth is guilty of committing the crime. In these cases where delinquency is evident, the juvenile court judge will order a predisposition report.

National data from 2022 showed that only 52% of the petitioned delinquency cases were adjudicated (Hockenberry & Puzzanchera, 2024). Among those adjudicated cases, delinquent offenses were mostly crimes against persons (39%) or property crimes (29%). Twenty-five percent of the adjudicated cases involved crimes involving the public order, and only 7% of the cases involved drug crimes. In terms of race, Hispanic, American Indian, and white youth were slightly more likely to have their cases adjudicated than Black or Asian males. Also, males (49%) overall experienced a higher likelihood of being adjudicated than females (40%). Looking at age, there was not much difference overall in terms of the chances that their case would be adjudicated. For status offenders in 2022, truants (47%) were more likely to be adjudicated than youth who committed any other status offense. Male status offenders also were more likely to be adjudicated in all status offense categories compared to females, except for ungovernability. White youth (30%) also were more likely to be adjudicated as status offenders than Black (27%) or Hispanic (18%) youth.

Disposition

Once a juvenile has been adjudicated, the next step is for a dispositional hearing to take place. The hearing itself may occur immediately after the adjudication hearing or a few weeks after adjudication. The dispositional hearing is similar to the sentencing stage in the adult system. By deduction here, the term **disposition** equates to a sentence, but since juveniles are concerned, the disposition also refers to treatment and custody options. Thus, at the hearing, it will be determined, above all, what is in the best interests of the youth, and depending on the crime, what is in the best interests of the community. Because the juvenile court is separate and in theory distinctly different than the adult court, the dispositional hearing is supposed to be informal, where each case is managed individually, and with the most suitable form of treatment for the juvenile in mind. In most jurisdictions, the probation officer also plays an important role in summarizing the findings of the predisposition report and a key part of that report is a recommendation to the judge. Once again, it is evident that this stage involves judicial discretion. The juvenile court judge is expected to rely on the facts of the case presented by counsel, the seriousness of the offense, and any prior history of offending to determine the most appropriate disposition. As discussed in Chapter 8, extra-legal factors may be taken into consideration even though, in a fair and just system, legal factors should bear greater weight in decision-making. Ultimately, the judge can decide to impose an improvement period, especially if there is cooperation from the juvenile to abide by certain conditions such as attending a treatment program. The judge could also recommend probation (as shown in Figure 9.2). Other options include mental health treatment or drug treatment, day report, a fine, community service, or intensive supervision probation. Last, and considered the most restrictive alternative, the judge can order the youth to an out-of-home placement or a residential facility. Residential placements range from foster homes and group shelter homes to something more punitive like a juvenile correctional center.

Examining national juvenile court data in 2022 revealed that 67% of adjudicated delinquents were assigned to juvenile probation, whereas 28% were ordered to a residential facility (Hockenberry & Puzzanchera, 2024) (see Figure 9.1). Interestingly, residential placement was most common for youths who had committed a public order offense, followed by those who had committed a crime against another person or a property crime. Adjudicated youths who had committed a drug crime were the least likely to be ordered to placement out of the home but assuredly received an order to drug treatment or other appropriate disposition. Moreover, out-of-home placement was the most common disposition for males, youth ages sixteen and older, and youth of color.

For status offenders, out-of-home placement as a court-ordered disposition has been declining. That is, in 2022, 1,800 status offenders were placed in a residential facility versus 11,100 status offenders in 2005 (Hockenberry & Puzzanchera, 2024), and youth were more likely to receive this disposition for ungovernability. Aside from residential placements, far more youth received probation for status offenses. In 2022, among petitioned cases, 11,400 adjudicated status offenders received probation, and among them, probation was commonly ordered for runaway or truant youth. Adjudicated males were assigned to probation slightly more than females, especially for status offenses like running away and truancy.

Transfer to Adult Court

In the late 1980s and early 1990s, national discourse arose about lawless and dangerous youth predators who would wreak havoc on society. Naturally, such rhetoric began to instill fear in the public. The public outcry was met with an answer by lawmakers to increase the penalties against these so-called "super-predators" (Dilulio, 1995) by transferring them to criminal court. This was primarily due to the fact that the juvenile court did not have the power to impose maximum penalties, but the adult court could. Plus, the juvenile court was deemed ill-equipped to rehabilitate violent youth. After several states changed their age limits and created transfer laws, juvenile waivers peaked in 2006, where 6,800 cases were judicially waived to adult court (Hockenberry

& Puzzanchera, 2024). The number of cases fell to a little over 3,000 cases in 2015. In 2021, there were fewer than 3,000 transferred cases (as shown in Figure 9.1). The data show that overall, the number of juvenile cases waived to criminal court has been declining since 2006.

From 2005–2022, the largest number of cases waived to adult court involved crimes against persons (Hockenberry & Puzzanchera, 2024). This is expected, as crimes against persons include homicide, rape, robbery, aggravated assault, and so on. Even with this important detail known, it is important to place the number of these cases into further context. Of all the petitioned juvenile delinquency cases for youth sixteen years of age or older, only 2% of cases were waived and only .2% of petitioned delinquency cases were waived for youth ages fifteen or younger. The bottom line is that, once again, only a small fraction of cases are waived in general. Among those cases, delinquent males were more likely to be judicially waived than females, and, in terms of race, Black and Hispanic youth were more likely to be judicially waived to adult court than white youth.

There are several avenues by which a juvenile can be transferred to adult court. These mechanisms are spelled out in a state's legal code. In Table 9.1, note the two main categories of pathways, that is, a juvenile court petition transfer pathway or a criminal court petition pathway. The main difference between the two is where the case originates. If the juvenile case begins in juvenile court, then depending on the case, a petition may be filed to transfer the case from juvenile court to adult court. On the other hand, if the case must begin in adult court given the confines of the state legal code and the alleged offense that was committed by the juvenile, a petition will be filed stating that the youth is to exclusively face charges in the criminal court. Keep in mind that some states may permit two or more of these avenues to transfer a juvenile case to adult court (see Table 9.1). Not shown in the table are those states that allow yet an additional sentencing mechanism called **blended sentencing**. In states like Arkansas, Minnesota, Kansas, and Ohio, judges can impose both a delinquent sentence and an adult sentence.

Table 9.1: Provisions for Imposing Adult Sanctions on Minors, 2019

	Juvenile Court Petition Transfer Pathways			Criminal Court Petition Transfer Pathways		
State	Discretionary	Presumptive	Mandatory	Statutory Exclusion	Once/ Always Adult	Prosecutor Discretion
Number of States	46	12	12	27	35	14
Alabama	✓			✓	✓	
Alaska	✓	✓		✓		
Arizona	✓			✓	✓	✓
Arkansas	✓					✓

California	✓				✓	
Colorado	✓	✓			✓	✓
Connecticut	✓		✓		✓	
Delaware	✓		✓	✓	✓	✓
District of Columbia	✓	✓			✓	✓
Florida	✓				✓	✓
Georgia	✓			✓		✓
Hawaii	✓				✓	
Idaho	✓			✓	✓	
Illinois	✓	✓		✓		
Indiana	✓		✓	✓	✓	
Iowa	✓			✓	✓	
Kansas	✓				✓	
Kentucky	✓		✓			
Louisiana	✓		✓	✓		✓
Maine	✓	✓			✓	
Maryland	✓			✓	✓	
Massachusetts				✓		
Michigan	✓				✓	✓
Minnesota	✓	✓		✓	✓	
Mississippi	✓			✓	✓	
Missouri	✓				✓	
Montana				✓		✓
Nebraska	✓					✓
Nevada	✓	✓		✓	✓	
New Hampshire	✓	✓			✓	
New Jersey			✓			
New Mexico				✓		
New York				✓		
North Carolina	✓		✓		✓	
North Dakota	✓	✓	✓		✓	
Ohio	✓		✓		✓	
Oklahoma	✓			✓	✓	✓
Oregon	✓			✓	✓	
Pennsylvania	✓	✓		✓	✓	
Rhode Island	✓	✓			✓	
South Carolina	✓		✓	✓		

South Dakota	✓			✓	✓	
Tennessee	✓				✓	
Texas	✓				✓	
Utah	✓	✓		✓	✓	
Vermont	✓			✓		
Virginia	✓		✓		✓	✓
Washington	✓			✓	✓	
West Virginia	✓		✓			
Wisconsin	✓			✓	✓	
Wyoming	✓					✓

Note: Table information is as of the end of the 2019 legislative session.

Source: Office of Juvenile Justice and Delinquency Prevention (OJJDP). (2022). Provisions for imposing adult sanctions on minors, 2019. *OJJDP statistical briefing book.* [table modified]. https://ojjdp.ojp.gov/statistical-briefing-book/structure_process/faqs/qa04115

Juvenile Court Petition Transfer Pathways

To date, the most common method of a juvenile case being transferred to adult court is when the case originates in juvenile court (shown in Figure 9.2). Generally speaking, this type of transfer largely involves the decision of a juvenile court judge. Known also as **judicial waiver**, this means formally that the judge has the discretion and legal authorization to waive the juvenile case to adult criminal court. Because the language of each state's legal code varies, the process may also be referred to as "certification," "binding over," or "transfer," for example. One of the most important factors distinguishing judicial waivers from the other types is that juvenile court judges are legally obligated to follow a set of criteria before waiving a juvenile to adult court, as ruled in the U.S. Supreme Court decision *Kent v. United States*. Some of the most pertinent criteria taken into consideration are the seriousness of the offense, the juvenile's prior offense record, and the possibility that they can be rehabilitated. With that said, there are three types of judicial waivers (see Table 9.1). They are discretionary, mandatory, and presumptive. In 2019, forty-six states had provisions for discretionary waiver, twelve states had provisions for presumptive waiver, and twelve states had provisions for mandatory waiver (OJJDP, 2022).

The provisions of a **discretionary waiver** are spelled out in a state's statute describing whether the judge has discretionary power to waive a juvenile's case to adult court or upon request of a motion filed by the prosecutor. Depending on state code, the court may have to consider a specified minimum age, type of offense, prior record of offending, or a combination of these factors (Griffin et al., 2011). In other states, additional legal guidelines are in place where the process for judicial waiver and any consideration for a judicial waiver cannot begin until the prosecuting attorney files the appropriate motion. This demonstrates that the waiver to criminal court is not immediately in effect.

Instead, a hearing is conducted to allow both the prosecutor and the defense counsel to present any evidence that may factor into the judge's waiver decision. Alternatively, some states may allow the probation officer to present their findings of the predisposition report. As shown in Table 9.1, Massachusetts, Montana, New Jersey, New York, and New Mexico are the only states that do not have discretionary waiver provisions.

The second type of judicial waiver is a **presumptive waiver**, where it is the burden of the defense counsel and not the prosecutor to demonstrate clear and convincing evidence to the juvenile court judge that the waiver to the adult court is not justified (Griffin et al., 2011). Most state codes with presumptive waiver cite certain felony offenses as a reason for waiving a juvenile to criminal court. For instance, juveniles who commit the crime of murder are argued as not being amenable to treatment, even though in many ways the juvenile still is a child. Twelve states have presumptive waiver laws, including states like Alaska, Colorado, Illinois, Maine, and Utah (see Table 9.1).

The third type of judicial waiver is a **mandatory waiver**. Here, the state legal code specifies certain conditions that qualify the youth for transfer to criminal court (Griffin et al., 2011). In many states, these conditions may be a certain age of the juvenile, prior offense record, and the seriousness of the offense committed by the juvenile. Ultimately, it is up to the judge to determine if these conditions are satisfied. Thirteen states permit this type of waiver (see Table 9.1), some of which include Connecticut, Delaware, New Jersey, North Carolina, and Ohio.

Criminal Court Petition Transfer Pathways

Another mechanism by which youth can be transferred to adult court is when the juvenile's case must be prosecuted for their crime in criminal court. The mechanisms to do so are also known as a **legislative waiver**. This means that the waiver policy is written into state code; thus, it is virtually automatic as there is no need for the juvenile judge or prosecutor to decide how to handle the case because the juvenile court is excluded. The youth essentially bypasses juvenile court jurisdiction as a result of committing a certain type of offense or because of a certain specified age limit. For example, state code may dictate an automatic waiver for youth ages twelve to sixteen who commit a violent crime such as murder, aggravated robbery, or aggravated sexual assault. In Pennsylvania, for example, a youth regardless of any age can be charged as an adult with the crime of murder. Also, youth ages fifteen and older can be charged as an adult with voluntary manslaughter if a weapon is used in the commission of the crime or in cases where the juvenile has been previously adjudicated for a serious felony offense.

As shown in Table 9.1, thirty-five states also have **"once an adult, always an adult" provisions** (OJJDP, 2022). This means that a juvenile in these states who was tried originally in adult court as a juvenile must also be prosecuted in adult court for any future offense. Another legislative provision is **statutory exclusion**, which exists in twenty-seven states. The most common example of statutory exclusion is where a state legal code stipulates that a juvenile of a certain age, who has committed murder or another serious violent offense, is excluded from juvenile court jurisdiction. One of the more controversial types of legislative waiver is known as a **prosecutorial waiver**, as it places a greater amount of power and discretion in the hands of the prosecutor. This type of waiver is also referred to as direct file (Hess et al., 2013). According to Snyder and colleagues (2000), this type of waiver "is not subject to judicial review and is not required to meet the due process requirements established in *Kent*" (p. 4). As of 2019, fourteen states have prosecutorial waiver provisions (see Table 9.1).

The largest question that has been raised since juvenile waiver laws were put into place is: do they work? More specifically, do youth with "adult" sentences have lower recidivism rates than youth who are processed solely by the juvenile court system? In theory, a youthful offender who is sentenced to adult time for an adult crime should be less likely to reoffend as a result of the long-term punishment and consequences they must face for their actions. However, most studies point to the fact that recidivism actually increased among youth who were given adult sentences (Redding, 2010; Zane et al., 2016). At the same time, a handful of studies have found that juveniles who were tried as adults are no less likely to recidivate than their counterparts who were adjudicated in the juvenile system (Zane et al., 2016). Despite the conflicting results, the consensus among researchers is that the use of juvenile transfer should be limited to older and violent youthful offenders who are a danger to the public because the scientific support for transferring youth to adult court is not overwhelmingly evident (Myers, 2016).

Specialized/Alternative Courts

Another unique feature of the juvenile court is that there are a number of specialty courts. **Specialty courts** are diversionary programs that focus on non-violent offenders and their specific needs by imposing appropriate and non-stigmatizing sanctions and treatment services. Drug courts are the most common type of specialty court, but there are others, including teen courts and mental health courts.

Drug Court

The mid-1980s were punctuated by a shift to imposing tougher sentences for adult drug offenders that resulted in severely constrained court and prison systems. Given the large and growing caseloads of adult offenders, many states could not maintain overcrowded prisons and lacked the funds to build new prisons to house the drug offender population. It became urgent to alleviate these constraints and necessary to provide the offender with an alternative that combined both supervision and treatment. Therein, the dawn of the adult drug court emerged. Even though the rates of substance abuse among juveniles did not climb until later, the juvenile drug court developed as a viable alternative that satisfied lawmakers and correctional administrators. Processing these cases in the traditional juvenile court only meant a delay in service delivery and treatment, whereas drug court could expedite this process. More than 140 juvenile drug courts were created between 1995 and 2001 (Cooper, 2001). As of 2015, the National Institute of Justice estimated that there were roughly 409 juvenile drug courts in the United States.

According to Cooper (2001), juvenile drug courts provide two main types of service. One type of service is intensive supervision of the juvenile delinquent or status offender who has been involved in drugs and/or alcohol. The second type of service is that the juvenile drug court provides countless support services with the primary purpose of addressing the problems that contribute to the juvenile's involvement in the justice system. Service areas include substance abuse treatment, mental health, primary care, family, and education.

Not every juvenile is a candidate for drug court. To qualify in most courts, youth have to be first-time, non-violent offenders with a history of an offense involving substance abuse. In the program, the drug court participant is subjected to weekly drug screens, case hearings, and mandatory attendance in treatment meetings. Nonetheless, some of the goals of the juvenile drug court as stated by Cooper (2001) include:

- Provide immediate intervention, treatment, and structure in the lives of juveniles using drugs through the ongoing, active oversight and monitoring by the drug court judge.
- Improve juveniles' level of functioning in their environment, address problems that may be contributing to their use of drugs, and develop/strengthen their ability to lead crime- and drug-free lives.
- Provide juveniles with skills that will aid them in leading productive substance-free and crime-free lives, including skills relating to their educational development, sense of self-worth, and capacity to develop positive relationships in the community.
- Strengthen the families of drug-involved youth by improving the capacity of families to provide structure and guidance to their children.
- Improve system capacity to promote accountability for both juvenile offenders and the services they are provided. (p. 7)

To date, the research on the effectiveness of juvenile drug courts is inconsistent. Some have even gone so far as to claim that they are not nearly as effective as adult drug courts, while others have found that drug courts are a tremendous benefit in reducing recidivism (Sullivan et al., 2016). According to van Wormer and Lutze (2011), one of the reasons results are mixed is due to the fact that earlier juvenile drug court studies were based on small, unmatched samples that could be characterized as methodologically flawed. Even though Sullivan et al. (2016) found that youth placed on probation had as equally effective outcomes as youth who participated in drug court, they provided sound recommendations and issues to consider. For one, there is great inconsistency among drug court programs regarding how they are administered and the types of clients they serve. Should drug courts focus on habitual drug offenders or occasional drug offenders? So far, the research indicates that more serious offenders benefit more than minor offenders. Also, the length of the program needs to be resolved. Here, too, there is a mixture of program length, which would certainly impact the results. Last, a closer examination of the types of treatment options is needed. One problem that stands out is that some drug courts do not target all of the juvenile's criminogenic needs, but just a few. Treatments were limited in some drug courts to "talk therapy," whereas the use of Multisystemic Therapy and Family Functioning Therapy has been shown to be more successful, which is described further in Chapter 10. Moving forward, the researchers advocate for well-executed juvenile drug courts that are grounded in the risk, need, and responsivity principles.

Teen Court

To date, there are approximately 1,050 teen courts in the United States, serving thousands of youth each year (National Association of Youth Courts , 2020a). More specifically, 45 states have teen court programs (also known as youth courts), and 25 of those states have legislation to support the functioning of the youth court, according to the National Association of Youth Courts (2020b). Since teen or peer courts are a type of diversionary program designed for first-time, non-violent offenders, it is common for youth to have committed crimes like larceny, vandalism, underage drinking, drug possession, or curfew violations, just to name a few. Teen court is also designed to be informal, to hold youth accountable, and to provide an alternative sanction that falls in line with a restorative justice approach. Youth who participate in teen court are commonly around the ages of eleven to seventeen, and in order to participate, the youth has to admit to the charges that have been filed against them. Another notable feature is that this type of diversionary program is voluntary.

Most teen courts employ what is known as an adult judge and peer jury model, where youth are assigned the roles of prosecutor, defense attorney, jury, victims, and so on. (Bouchard & Wong, 2017). Sentencing outcomes are decided by the adult judge or "peer-jury" and are likely to consist of some form of community service, restitution, or an agreement to serve in future teen courts. Depending on the model that is used and the interconnectedness to the community, some courts may even provide participants with referrals to community-based programs. To successfully complete teen court, the youth must comply with the sentencing conditions that were established and refrain from any new offenses during the specified time frame. The maximum benefit the youth receives is having their criminal record expunged.

Many have argued that teen courts are a promising alternative and effectively reduce recidivism. Teen courts are also cost effective, and youth often report high levels of satisfaction, more positive attitudes toward authorities, and increased knowledge about the justice system (Development Services Group, Inc., 2010b). On the other hand, there is still some progress to be made. Bouchard and Wong (2017) conducted a meta-analysis of teen court programs and found that "teen courts are no better at reducing juvenile recidivism than either formal processing or other diversion programs, they are also no worse" (p. 1484). Like others, they too call for more methodologically sound program evaluations. Additionally, steps to create better programs overall are encouraged. One way to improve the effectiveness of teen courts is to embed court programs in evidence-based practice and employ the risk, need, and responsivity principles, which were expressed as a direction for improving drug courts as well.

Mental Health Court

Cocozza and Shufelt (2006) report that as many as 70% of juveniles in the justice system suffer from a mental health issue, many of whom struggle with depression, anxiety, bipolar, and attention deficit hyperactivity disorders. Not only do these youth require a greater level of care and services, but they are also at risk of co-occurring disorders like substance abuse and may be at risk of having suicidal thoughts. With increased awareness about the troubling psychological conditions that plague many youth, mental health courts were considered to be a plausible solution. The first mental health court appeared in 2001 in Santa Clara, California, although others claim the first mental health court for juveniles was created in York County, Pennsylvania, in 1998 (Callahan et al., 2012; Wakefield et al., 2023). Designed after the adult mental health court model, this type of juvenile specialty court diverts youth away from the formal proceedings of the court, while at the same time connecting the youth to appropriate mental health treatment services (Development Services Group, Inc., 2010a). This is not to suggest that mental health courts are "softer" on crime. The court still administers the appropriate sanction, but it is done in tandem with family support services and a comprehensive treatment plan that will afford the youth a greater chance of recovery and a reduced chance of reoffending.

The scope and characteristics of mental health courts across the country vary. Yet, similar to other specialty courts, participation is typically voluntary. Another common condition is that the youth must agree to the charges filed on the petition (a guilty plea) in order to participate in the court (Callahan et al., 2012). In turn, the charges are dropped, so long as the juvenile agrees to the terms of participation in the mental health court and completes the program successfully. Most courts, however, have strict screening processes and will only cater to youth with serious, diagnosable conditions (Cocozza & Shufelt, 2006). Other courts accept youth who self-identify as having a mental health problem. Not all courts have the same admission criteria when it comes to the type of charges filed. Some mental health courts permit youth with violent offenses, while others exclude youth involved in sex offenses, gang-related activities, or drug trafficking crimes. Participation in the program is overseen by a probation officer, and mental health court participants are usually in the program for at least one year. Among nearly a third of the thirty-five courts surveyed by Callahan et al., juveniles ranged from ages thirteen to seventeen, and many were comprised of at least 25%–50% or more male and minority youth.

Today, there are roughly 57 juvenile mental health courts in 15 states across the country (Wakefield et al., 2023). However, research on the effectiveness of mental health courts in general is still at a minimum, and there are many concerns about their use. Since it was the first of its kind, one of the courts that has received the most widespread attention is in Santa Clara County, California. Research evidence has shown the program to be quite successful (Development Services Group, Inc., 2010a). A recent study by Wakefield et al. (2023) found that 48.5% of the 99 mental health court participants completed the program with success. Youth ages 10 to 18 who possessed a positive attitude about the interventions they were receiving were more likely to complete the program with success. Factors associated with a lack of successful program completion were youth who had a history of neglect, removal from their home by CPS, and new charges or a probation violation while they were enrolled in the mental health court. Moreover, youths who had a higher number of previous charges were less likely to complete the program successfully as well. The authors suggest that wrap-around services may complement these efforts and may foreseeably increase the chances of the youth's program success.

On another note, youth with mental health conditions may have increased contact with police officers, and by virtue of their condition, the officer may be more likely to take a youth into custody even for the most minor offense. This widens the net (a term described earlier in Chapter 8) where essentially non-delinquent youth become part of the system, even though they do not pose the same level of threat compared to more serious delinquent offenders. Aside from criminalizing these youth, additional harm comes from the stigmatizing and labeling. One additional concern is whether participation in the mental health court is truly "voluntary." Specifically, youth with mental illnesses may not be fully aware of the decisions they are making about their participation in the court program and may lack the necessary competencies to fully understand the court system processes. A final concern lies with the fact that these courts may be redundant and unnecessary. The juvenile court system is dedicated to treatment and rehabilitation services already, so the need for a separate and specialized mental health court for some seems to be a misuse of resources and duplication of services.

Summary Points

- The juvenile court is a unique and specialized court in that it oversees cases involving delinquent youth, status offenders, and neglected or abused youth of various ages, depending on state legal code.
- Processing a juvenile delinquent or status offender through the entire court process typically involves intake, a detention hearing, and a preliminary hearing, along with an adjudication and disposition hearing. However, youth are often diverted away from the system.
- Key personnel of the juvenile court include the intake officer, probation officer, prosecutor or guardian ad litem, defense counsel, and juvenile court judge.
- The predisposition report is compiled by a probation officer. The report contains a comprehensive background about the juvenile along with a recommendation to the juvenile court judge regarding the most appropriate disposition.

- Clinical and standardized assessments are based on determining a youth's risk level, needs, and responsiveness to individualized treatment services.
- There are three main types of provisions for waiving or transferring a juvenile's case to criminal court. They are judicial, legislative, and prosecutorial waivers.
- An important feature of the juvenile court is that it consists of a variety of specialty courts that are designed to serve targeted groups of offenders with unique needs. Drug courts, teen courts, and mental health courts are just a few of the diversionary mechanisms that exist today.

Key Terms

Adjudication: a stage of the juvenile court where the juvenile is found guilty and adjudicated or charged as a delinquent.

Assessment: more extensive information gathering and detailed interviewing of a youth using a comprehensive psychometric instrument to determine a youth's risk level and to address a youth's needs.

Bail: the conditional and temporary release of an accused person with the conditions that the individual is not a risk to the community and will promise to return to court.

Beyond a Reasonable Doubt: a higher standard of proof with supporting evidence that the juvenile committed said offense.

Blended Sentencing: a type of sentencing mechanism where a judge imposes both a delinquent sentence and an adult sentence.

Defense Counsel: an attorney who may be appointed to the juvenile's case, such as a public defender or a private attorney.

Discretionary Waiver: a type of waiver by which state law describes whether the judge has discretionary power to waive a juvenile's case to adult court or upon the prosecutor's request.

Disposition: a disposition equates to a sentence, but since juveniles are concerned, the disposition refers to treatment and custody options.

Dynamic Factors: characteristics of an individual that can change.

Guardian Ad Litem: a member of the juvenile court who is appointed to investigate and oversee the findings of a case that typically involves a neglected and/or abused youth.

Intake: is a process by which an officer of the court assesses the juvenile's case and decides how to proceed.

Intake Officer: an employee of the juvenile court who gathers information about the youth, which is similar to the booking stage in the adult system.

Judicial Waiver: a mechanism by which a juvenile case is transferred to adult court by a juvenile judge.

Juvenile Court Judge: an administrator of the court who is primarily responsible for overseeing how it is managed.

Juvenile Probation Officer: a member of the juvenile court whose duties involve compiling a predisposition report with a recommendation for the judge on the appropriate disposition and supervising adjudicated youth who have been placed on probation or as deemed necessary by the court.

Legislative Waiver: a type of mechanism where the waiver policy is written into state code; it is virtually automatic as there is no need for the juvenile judge or prosecutor to decide how to handle the case.

Mandatory Waiver: a type of judicial waiver by which state legal code specifies certain conditions that qualify the youth for transfer to criminal court.

Need Principle: a principle of clinical assessment that is comprised of examining criminogenic factors and non-criminogenic factors.

Once an Adult, Always an Adult Provisions: a type of legal statute that sets forth how juveniles tried originally in adult court as a juvenile must also be prosecuted in adult court for any future offense.

Petition: a formal charge filed with the court alleging that the juvenile is an adjudicated delinquent or adjudicated status offender.

Plea Bargain: an agreement made between the prosecutor and the defendant where the defendant enters a guilty plea in order to receive a lighter sentence.

Predisposition Report: an official document that summarizes the juvenile's conduct and current situation with the purpose of providing the juvenile court judge with an appropriate disposition recommendation.

Preponderance of Evidence: a lower standard of proof where the judge will consider the evidence and determine if it is likely that the juvenile committed said offense.

Presumptive Waiver: a type of judicial waiver where it is the burden of the defense counsel and not the prosecutor to demonstrate clear and convincing evidence to the juvenile court judge that the waiver to adult court is not justified.

Preventative Detention: holding a youth temporarily in detention because they are seen as a flight risk, a risk to society, or as in need of protection from their home environment or community.

Prosecutor: a member of the juvenile court who is commonly known for serving the interests of the state.

Prosecutorial Waiver: a type of waiver mechanism that places a greater amount of power and discretion in the hands of the prosecutor when making decisions to waive a juvenile's case to adult court (also known as direct file).

Responsivity: a principle of clinical assessment that suggests how much a youth is amenable to change and is responsive to treatment.

Risk Principle: a principle of clinical assessment that involves predicting the youth's likelihood of reoffending.

Screening: a process of gathering information to reach an immediate conclusion about a youth.

Specialty Courts: diversionary programs that focus on non-violent offenders and their specific needs by imposing appropriate and non-stigmatizing sanctions and treatment services.

Static Factors: characteristics of an individual that are typically fixed and cannot change, such as age, gender, and past delinquent offense history.

Statutory Exclusion: a type of legal statute which stipulates that a juvenile of a certain age who has committed murder or another serious violent offense is excluded from juvenile court jurisdiction.

References

Andrews, D., & Bonta, J. (1994). *The psychology of criminal conduct.* Anderson Publishing.

Andrews, D. A., Bonta, J., & Hoge, R. D. (1990). Classification for effective rehabilitation: Rediscovering psychology. *Criminal Justice and Behavior, 17,* 9–52. https://doi.org/10.1177/0093854890017001004

Baird, C., Healy, T., Bogies, A., Wicke Dankert, E., & Scharenbroch, C. (2013). *A comparison of risk assessment instruments in juvenile justice.* U.S. Department of Justice, Office of Justice Programs, Office of Juvenile Justice and Delinquency Prevention (OJJDP). https://www.ncjrs.gov/pdffiles1/ojjdp/grants/244477.pdf

Bouchard, J., & Wong, J. S. (2017). A jury of their peers: A meta-analysis of the effects of teen court on criminal recidivism. *Journal of Youth Adolescence, 46,* 1472–1487. https://doi.org/10.1007/s10964-017-0667-7

Callahan, L., Cocozza, J., Steadman, H. J., & Tillman, S. (2012). A national survey of U.S. juvenile mental health courts. *Psychiatric Services, 63*(2), 130–134. https://doi.org/10.1176/appi.ps.201100113

Cocozza, J. J., & Shufelt, J. L. (2006). *Juvenile mental health courts: An emerging strategy.* National Center for Mental Health and Juvenile Justice.

Cooper, C. S. (2001). *Juvenile drug court programs.* Office of Juvenile Justice and Delinquency Prevention. https://www.ncjrs.gov/pdffiles1/ojjdp/184744.pdf

Development Services Group, Inc. (2010a). *Mental health courts. Literature review.* Office of Juvenile Justice and Delinquency Prevention. https://www.govinfo.gov/content/pkg/GOVPUB-J32-PURL-gpo121980/pdf/GOVPUB-J32-PURL-gpo121980.pdf

DiIulio, J. J. (1995, November 27). The coming of the super-predators. *The Weekly Standard.* https://fbaum.unc.edu/teaching/articles/DiIulioTheWeeklyStandard1995.pdf

Griffin, P., Addie, S., Adams, B., & Firestine, K. (2011). Trying juveniles as adults: An analysis of state transfer laws and reporting. *Juvenile offenders and victims: National report series.* U.S. Department of Justice, Office of Justice Programs, Office of Juvenile Justice and Delinquency Prevention. https://www.ncjrs.gov/pdffiles1/ojjdp/232434.pdf

Hayes, L. M. (2009). *Juvenile suicide in confinement: A national survey.* National Center on Institutions and Alternatives. National Center on Institutions and Alternatives. Office of Juvenile Justice and Delinquency Prevention. https://www.ojp.gov/pdffiles1/ojjdp/213691.pdf

Hess, K. M., Orthmann, C. H., & Wright, J. P. (2013). *Juvenile justice.* Wadsworth/Cengage.

Ho, A., Lesneskie, E., & Hsu, K. H. (2018). What we don't know may hurt us: An examination of systematic bias in offender risk assessments. *Deviant Behavior, 39*(12), 1566–1577. http://dx.doi.org/10.1080/01639625.2017.1410620

Hockenberry, S., & Puzzanchera, C. (2024). *Juvenile court statistics 2022.* National Center for Juvenile Justice. Office of Juvenile Justice and Delinquency Prevention. https://ojjdp.ojp.gov/publications/juvenile-court-statistics-2022.pdf

Hyland, N. (2018, January). *Delinquency cases in juvenile court, 2014* (NCJ 251107). U.S. Department of Justice, Office of Justice Programs, Office of Juvenile Justice and Delinquency Prevention. https://ojjdp.ojp.gov/sites/g/files/xyckuh176/files/pubs/251107.pdf

Kent v. United States, 383 U.S. 541 (1966).

Lindner, C. (2008). Probation intake: Gatekeeper to the family court. *Federal Probation, 72*(1), 48–53. https://www.uscourts.gov/sites/default/files/72_1_7_0.pdf

McKeiver v. Pennsylvania, 403 U.S. 528 (1971).

Myers, D. L. (2016). Juvenile transfer to adult court: Ongoing search for scientific evidence. *Criminology & Public Policy, 15*(3), 927–938. https://doi.org/10.1111/1745-9133.12232

National Association of Youth Courts. (2020a). *The significance of youth courts: The mission of the National Association of Youth Courts.* https://youthcourt.net/?page_id=121

National Association of Youth Courts. (2020b). *Youth court legislation.* https://youthcourt.net/?page_id=322

National Juvenile Defender Center. (2012). *National juvenile defense standards.* Models for Change. https://njdc.info/wp-content/uploads/2013/09/NationalJuvenileDefenseStandards2013.pdf

Office of Juvenile Justice and Delinquency Prevention (OJJDP). (2021a). Extended age of juvenile court jurisdiction, 2019. *OJJDP Statistical Briefing Book.* U.S. Department of Justice, Office of Justice Programs. https://ojjdp.ojp.gov/statistical-briefing-book/structure_process/faqs/qa04106

Office of Juvenile Justice and Delinquency Prevention (OJJDP). (2021b). Upper and lower age of juvenile court delinquency and status offense jurisdiction: Jurisdictional boundaries 2019. *OJJDP Statistical Briefing Book.* U.S. Department of Justice, Office of Justice Programs. https://ojjdp.ojp.gov/statistical-briefing-book/structure_process/faqs/qa04102

Office of Juvenile Justice and Delinquency Prevention (OJJDP). (2022). Provisions for imposing adult sanctions on minors, 2019. *OJJDP statistical briefing book.* [table modified]. https://ojjdp.ojp.gov/statistical-briefing-book/structure_process/faqs/qa04115

Platt, A. M. (2009). *The child savers: The invention of delinquency.* Rutgers University Press.

Redding, R. R. (2010). Juvenile transfer laws: An effective deterrent to delinquency? *Juvenile Justice Bulletin* (NCJ 220595). U.S. Department of Justice, Office of Justice Programs, Office of Juvenile Justice and Delinquency Prevention. https://www.ncjrs.gov/pdffiles1/ojjdp/220595.pdf

Schall v. Martin, 467 U.S. 253 (1984).

Seymour, M. (2013). Responding to non-compliance with the requirements of community disposals. In M. Seymour (Ed.), *Youth justice in context: Community, compliance and young people* (pp. 9–22). Routledge.

Snyder, H. N., Sickmund, M., & Poe-Yamagata, E. (2000). *Juvenile transfers to criminal court in the 1990's: Lessons learned from four studies.* National Center for Juvenile Justice. https://www.ncjrs.gov/pdffiles1/ojjdp/181301.pdf

Sullivan, C. J., Blair, L., Latessa, E., & Sullivan, C. C. (2016). Juvenile drug courts and recidivism: Results from a multisite outcome study. *Justice Quarterly, 33*(2), 291–318. https://doi.org/10.1080/07418825.2014.908937

Van Voorhis, P., Braswell, M., & Lester, D. (1997). *Correctional counseling and rehabilitation.* Anderson.

van Wormer, J., & Lutze, F. (2011). Exploring the evidence: The value of juvenile drug courts. *Juvenile and Family Justice Today.* https://www.courtswv.gov/sites/default/pubfilesmnt/2023-06/Exploring-the-Evidence.pdf

Vincent, G. M. (2012). *Screening and assessment in juvenile justice systems: Identifying mental health needs and risk of reoffending.* Technical Assistance Partnership for Child and Family Mental Health.

Vincent, G. M., Guy, L. S., & Grisso, T. (2012). *Risk assessment in juvenile justice: A guidebook for implementation*. Models for Change. http://modelsforchange.net/publications/346

Wakefield, S. M., McPherson, P., & Brennan, S. L. (2023). Factors associated with successful completion of juvenile mental health court. *The Journal of the American Academy of Psychiatry and the Law*, *51*(1), 72–81. doi: 10.29158/JAAPL.220035-21

Whitebread, C., & Heilman, J. (1988). An overview of the law of juvenile delinquency. *Behavioral Sciences & the Law*, *6*(3), 285–305. https://doi.org/10.1002/bsl.2370060303

Zane, S. N., Welsh, B. C., & Mears, D. P. (2016). Juvenile transfer and the specific deterrence hypothesis: Systematic review and meta-analysis. *Criminology & Public Policy*, *15*, 901–925. https://doi.org/10.1111/1745-9133.12222

Chapter 10

Juvenile Corrections

Chapter Learning Objectives

Students will be able to:

- Describe the differences between state and local juvenile corrections
- Identify the mission and goals of juvenile corrections
- Explain the significance of the Juvenile Justice Delinquency Prevention Act and its core provisions
- Distinguish residential from non-residential juvenile facilities
- Describe the different types of alternative community sanctions, including probation and intensive supervision probation
- Summarize the different types of juvenile programs
- Outline the main components of the Missouri Model
- Explain the process of juvenile aftercare and effective models for aftercare success

---

Introduction

When it comes to corrections, it is best to think of it as an umbrella term that accompanies an array of services and programs. Juvenile **corrections** involves providing services that occur before adjudication or providing services post-adjudication when the youth is found to be responsible for a crime. In some cases, correctional services can even be provided to youth who are on the verge or periphery of delinquency and are just starting to exhibit troubling behaviors. In other words, preventative or intervention-based services may be provided to youth who have not committed a crime per se but are at risk of doing so. The root of the word "corrections" obviously implies that some form of transformation is to take place, and while most think of prisons and jails as the sole form of corrections, it encompasses a variety of community-based services and aftercare as well. The common thread is that all of these correctional services employ the same common goal and purpose, which is to aid in some type of positive and prosocial transformation of the juvenile while maintaining public safety. It is hoped that programmatic interventions and treatment efforts will correct wayward behaviors and produce law-abiding citizens, who will not be swayed back into a life of crime and delinquency.

The Mission of Juvenile Corrections

The success of juvenile corrections rests on a set of overarching principles, which can be found in each state's juvenile correctional authority's mission statement. Even though a juvenile corrections mission statement may be written differently, there are several common principles. One of the main tenets of juvenile corrections is to maintain public safety for the community. This falls in line with the correctional philosophy of **incapacitation**, which involves removing the juvenile from society and confining them in a secure facility so that future crimes cannot be committed. Following incapacitation, the correctional philosophy of **deterrence** is also evident in juvenile correctional practice as the goal is to prevent future crimes from occurring by providing youth with the opportunity to consider and weigh the consequences of their behavior while under restrictive custody or a supervised community-based program. A third tenet is **rehabilitation**. This includes providing treatment programs for the youth to address factors that may have contributed to their delinquency or misbehavior and in an effort to modify the youth's future behavior. The fourth most common tenet found among juvenile corrections mission statements is a commitment to aftercare and **reintegration**. Providing transitional services to assist the youth back into the community equates to greater success in completing the rehabilitation process. There is one additional correctional philosophy that is worth mentioning, and despite the fact that it appears in juvenile correctional practice and in certain contexts, this philosophy goes against the grain of the overarching value system in which the juvenile court was established. The correctional philosophy of **retribution**, also commonly known as just deserts, revenge, or punishment for the sake of punishment, became the quintessential goal during the "get tough" movement in the mid-1980s and early 1990s, when legislators sought to move delinquency cases to adult courts in order to bestow adult sentences.

As mentioned, the goals of juvenile corrections are found in the mission statements from state to state. For example, the mission of Wisconsin's Division of Juvenile Corrections (DJC) (n.d.) aims not only to provide safety for victims and the community but to reduce recidivism. Wisconsin's Division of Juvenile Corrections states: "The mission of DJC is to promote a juvenile justice system that balances protection of the community, youth accountability, and competency building for responsible and productive community living." Similarly, the mission statement of Florida's Department of Juvenile Justice emphasizes public safety but also rehabilitation service provisions. It reads "to enhance public safety through high-quality, effective services for youth and families delivered by world-class professionals dedicated to building a stronger, safer Florida" (Florida Department of Juvenile Justice, n.d.).

The Juvenile Justice Delinquency Prevention Act

The mission and administration of juvenile corrections are also guided by legislative action. As discussed in Chapter 7, one of the most historic and important pieces of legislation was when Congress enacted the Juvenile Justice and Delinquency Prevention (JJDP) Act in 1974. The provisions of this landmark legislation established the creation of the federal agency, the Office of Juvenile Justice and Delinquency Prevention (OJJDP), which is devoted to training, model programming, and technical assistance, as well as research and evaluation. The provisions also set forth the development of a national advisory council. Moreover, the act included federal funding opportunities for state and local delinquency prevention and intervention programs. The most prominent and impactful provision included the mandatory removal of status offenders from secure detention and correctional facilities and the mandatory separation of juveniles from any institution in which they would be in regular contact with convicted adult offenders.

The JJDP Act was subsequently reauthorized in 1977, 1992, 2002, and 2018. In 1992, the amendments to the JJDP Act that are still followed today include the provision that juveniles who are placed in an adult facility cannot be within sight or sound of an adult offender. Preventative measures must be taken to protect youth from threats, intimidation, coercion, or any type of physical or psychological harm from an adult offender. This means that the juvenile cannot be housed next to an adult cell or be physically present in a dining hall, recreational space, or common space where adult offenders are present. Another provision still in place today pertains to reducing the number of youths of color who come into contact with the juvenile justice system, which was also described in Chapter 8.

In 2018, the Juvenile Justice Reauthorization Act (JJRA) was put into place, amending the previous JJDP Act. Federal legislation was expanded to include removing youth from adult jails when a youth has been charged as an adult. In other words, a fifteen-year-old who has been charged and waived to adult court cannot be held in an adult jail facility pending their court appearance. There are exceptions, but courts must weigh several factors, hold hearings every 30 days to review the case, and remove the youth from the adult jail if 180 days have passed.

To recap, the core provisions of the JJDP Act that stand today are:

- Deinstitutionalizing status offenders
- Removing adjudicated delinquents, status offenders, and non-offending juveniles from adult jails and detention facilities
- Ensuring that youth are removed from sight and sound of adult offenders
- Reducing racial and ethnic disparities

The Two Systems of Juvenile Corrections: State and Local

Aside from the characteristics of juvenile corrections that were just described, there is yet another layer to placing corrections into context. That is, the juvenile correctional system in the United States is characterized at best as either a centralized or decentralized system. Again, here it varies by state. Generally speaking, the administrative powers of juvenile corrections, such as probation and placement in pre-adjudicated detention, are typically orchestrated in a **decentralized system** where administrative authority and responsibility rest with the local government. More long-term confinement in a juvenile correctional facility and aftercare often rests with a state-run administrative authority that is considered to be a **centralized system**. In Florida, for example, this state administrative agency is called the Department of Juvenile Justice, and similarly, in states like Texas, the governing body overseeing juvenile corrections is called the Texas Juvenile Justice Department. It is best to also remember that there is always some variation from state to state and county to county, and a description of these nuances is nearly impossible to cover. For example, probation may be part of the centralized system or the decentralized system. Some states also rely on the social services system or the Department of Health and Human Resources to oversee services for status offenders or foster care youth. No matter how correctional services are administered, the principal goals of corrections are virtually the same.

Community-Based Alternatives: The Local System

Recall from Chapter 9 that after the juvenile has been adjudicated, a disposition hearing takes place to determine which sanction is best to foster rehabilitation for the juvenile, to repair any wrongdoing to the community, and to ensure the safety of the community. Aside from paying restitution, community service, or being returned to the custody of the juvenile's parents, the judge ultimately has to decide the best dispositional alternative. In more serious matters, the judge may place the youth in a group home or residential facility. The most common dispositions involve some type of community-based sanction. Such an alternative can be considered yet another umbrella term that is used in the juvenile justice system. **Community-based alternatives** refer to less restrictive sanctions than incarceration, where the juvenile is immersed in a program or non-secure facility within the community. As stated earlier, these types of sanctions are decentralized, as both local public and private organizations provide the necessary placements and programming for adjudicated or at-risk youth. Among all of the community-based alternatives, the most common disposition is probation. Some of the other most common types of community alternatives include, but are not limited to, day report treatment centers, foster care and group homes, home confinement/electronic monitoring, restitution, and community service.

Day Report Treatment Centers

Day report treatment centers, also referred to as day treatment centers, are non-residential facilities used as a community-based alternative for court-referred, at-risk youth who need additional supervision, counseling, educational, and vocational support services. The origin of these types of centers can be traced to Great Britain, where they were implemented for adult, low-risk drug offenders around the 1970s (Development Services Group, Inc., 2011). At the same time, day report centers can be used as a part of the reintegrative process after a youth has been released from a secure residential facility. Most day report centers operate during the same hours as a public school and provide transportation and meals. Depending on the center, youth may also partake in recreation and community service activities. Some centers may even go so far as to include family support services as well (see Box 10.1).

Youth who attend day treatment receive a highly structured set of services and follow a guided curriculum. Educational and sometimes vocational instruction is matched to the appropriate therapeutic services, given the results of the juvenile's assessment or psychological evaluation. Assessments such as the Juvenile Automated Substance Abuse Evaluation (JASAE), the Youth Level of Service/Case Management Inventory (YLS/CMI), or the Child and Adolescent Functional Assessment Scale (CAFAS) may be administered. As a result, youth may receive tailored services that pertain to life skills, decision-making skills, or peer intervention. Moreover, treatment services may also include substance abuse counseling and/or anger management. Aside from education and therapeutic sessions, youth may partake in group counseling sessions.

The benefits of day report are tremendous as they provide a cost-effective alternative to the taxpayer. Clearly, they also reduce overcrowding in residential facilities and reduce stigma. Youth are easily supervised and receive the necessary educational and counseling support that falls in line with the rehabilitation mission of corrections. However, the success of these programs has not been well documented as research efforts have been mostly devoted to examining adult day report services, and results concerning reducing recidivism with adult offenders have been mixed. Program evaluations about the effectiveness of juvenile day report services at best are scarce. However, in a study of the AMIKids (Associated Marin Institutes) day treatment centers for youth in Florida, Early et al. (2014) found a reduction in felony rearrests among youth who had been released from the program for at least 12 months. Other studies on day treatment for juveniles appear in the psychiatry literature. It is important to note that these programs offer comprehensive clinical treatment services to youth who may or may not have committed status or delinquent offenses, however. These evaluations are directed at examining day treatment programs that cater to youth with diagnosable conditions such as disruptive behavioral disorders, attention deficit hyperactivity disorder, conduct disorder, and so on. For the most part, results are very positive, demonstrating that even short-term intensive services lead to a reduction in problematic behaviors, six to nine months post-program services (Clark & Jerrott, 2012).

Box 10.1: Juvenile Day Reporting Center in North Carolina

The Day Reporting Center in Randolph County, North Carolina, offers a program for court-involved and court-diverted youth not only to address accountability for their actions but to acquire a personal growth mindset. The model the center employs places an emphasis on four core mission-driven areas: positive decision-making skills, developing and enhancing coping skills, stress management, and community service.

One of the main components of the program is devoted to what is known as behavior modification. **Behavior modification** is a type of therapy that involves reducing negative behaviors and increasing appropriate ones. The approach relies on positive reinforcement and the concept of a token economy to promote positive behaviors by rewarding youth when exhibiting prosocial behaviors. The Day Report Center in Randolph County offers a series of evidence-based programs that include aggression replacement training, Botvin's life skills training, Choices and Voices programming, and youth mentoring, just to name a few. Moreover, there are programs to strengthen the family unit. Ultimately, the goal here is to provide at-risk youth with a set of skill sets that will promote positive behavior and increase their capacity to build a successful future.

Source: Randolph County. (n.d.). Day reporting center (JDRC)—Juvenile. https://www.randolphcountync.gov/193/Day-Reporting-Center-JDRC---Juvenile

Foster Care and Group Homes

When it comes to juveniles, the foster care system is used for a myriad of cases. Again, in most states, foster care is part of the social services system and is used most often when a youth's parents or guardians are deemed unfit, and a foster care facility is the more appropriate avenue to serve the best interests of the child. The foster care system is also widely used for status offenders and even for juvenile delinquents. Nonetheless, **foster care** allows a juvenile to reside in the care of a homeowner or family, who may or may not have children of their own. To be a foster family, social service workers screen the intended guardians, ranging from their attitudes about parenting to the physical conditions of the home environment, among other criteria. Foster parents are compensated by the state to cover the expenses of raising the child. Caring for a foster child goes beyond the physical care and emotional support a child needs. Foster parenting may also require additional training to help youth who may have psychological and emotional disorders. In cases like this, the child may need to attend treatment sessions with a licensed therapist. In this type of placement, within a stable family environment, there is a reduced stigma to the youth and a stable family environment that, in theory, allows the youth to thrive.

The concept of foster care appeared during the era of the child-saving movement and is linked specifically to the work of Charles Loring Brace and the New York Children's Aid Society in 1853 (McDonald et al., 1993). Some historians have remarked that the goal at the time was not outright benevolence or concern for children who were the victims of abuse and neglect, but to dispose of vagrant children, many of whom were orphans, and who were seen as a nuisance, riddling the city streets with crime and vice (Platt, 2009). To remedy the situation, the idea was to send these youth to rural communities in the West or South on what became known as "orphan trains." In exchange for labor on a farm, children would be in the custody of a family that would provide adequate food and shelter. The outcome was not always a positive one, as some youths were abused by their foster families. Many historians have argued that this system was similar to slavery or indentured servitude.

For social service agencies, permanent placement in a home with a biological or adopted parent is the key to success as it ultimately will serve the best interests of the child. Unfortunately, this is not always the case. There are many criticisms and consequences of the foster care system. For one, a child is not always placed within one permanent family home or environment. In one study, it was documented that 30% of foster care youth were moved two to nine times while they were placed in the system, and 18% were moved as many as twenty-seven to fifty-six times before their eighteenth birthday (Chambers et al., 2018). Second, the longer a child is in foster care, the more likely the child will become estranged from their biological parents. Third, youth tend to become depressed and anxious as their placement and environment change. Additional challenges are posed to youth who struggle with a diagnosable psychological condition. These are criticisms that social service agencies recognize and continue to improve, but many agencies are limited by the number of foster families that serve them and statewide budget constraints.

Examining over twenty-five studies on the outcomes of youth placed in foster care, the effects can largely be characterized as mixed (McDonald et al., 1993). On one hand, youth placed in foster care fared better than youth who were placed in a group or institutional care setting. Youths also experienced more favorable outcomes when they were placed in the long-term custody of a stable foster family. Also, lower rates of drug and alcohol abuse among foster care youth were reported among the studies that were examined. On the other hand, foster care youth compared to their non-foster care counterparts had lower levels of educational attainment, lower marriage rates, and higher rates of teen pregnancy. Rates of arrest were found to be higher for males who had been formerly placed in foster care versus females in foster care, and again, this was when comparing foster care males and females to those in the general population.

In a more recent but smaller study of dual-status youth, who were both involved in the foster care system and the juvenile justice system, Simmons-Horton (2021) found that foster care served as a common pathway to the juvenile justice system. Among the ten individuals who were interviewed, several of them reported significant trauma before entering either system, such as family abuse, neglect, or exposure to criminal activity. In addition, these youth experienced systemic trauma from multiple placements within the foster care system, abuse from foster families themselves, and neglect, which compounded the trauma that the youth had previously experienced before entering the foster care system. Dual-status youth also stated that they missed out on "normalizing" activities such as participation in sports or clubs that only intensified their feelings of abnormality and feelings of isolation. Despite the small sample size, the take-home messages from the interviewees suggest the need to address lived experiences and that these experiences can be further exacerbated by the foster care system. Trauma-informed care as well as collaboration among practitioners in both the foster care system and the juvenile system is crucial to provide coordinated and comprehensive services.

Group homes or shelters are non-secure residential facilities found within the local community that provide safety and assistance for adjudicated delinquents (Hess et al., 2013). Like foster care homes and even day treatment centers to some degree, group homes can be used for at-risk youth whose best interests are served in a family-like setting or for post-adjudication youth who require aftercare and transitional services back into the community. In some states, these facilities are called therapeutic group homes, and they may be administered by a private or non-profit agency or by the state's social services agency. A typical group home may accommodate as few as four or five youths or as many as twelve to fifteen youths, depending on the size of the facility. Because they are non-secure facilities, one of the most common problems for staff and law enforcement is dealing with youth who commit status offenses such as running away.

Home Confinement/Electronic Monitoring

Commonly referred to as house arrest, **home confinement** involves monitored supervision of a juvenile within the juvenile's home or residence. The youth placed on home confinement may be either an adjudicated delinquent or a pre-adjudicated youth who is awaiting an adjudication hearing. The conditions of home confinement often stipulate the specific time period(s) in which the youth is expected to be at home. That is, the youth may be expected to remain at home all day (lockdown), or for part of the day, where school and work are permissible exceptions, or exclusively during the nighttime hours, much like curfew (Austin et al., 2005). Exceptions are made of course for doctor's appointments, church attendance, and court hearings, but only with permission from the juvenile's probation officer. As an alternative to a more secure placement, home confinement provides substantial cost savings. As a surveillance method, electronic monitoring is typically paired with home confinement.

Electronic monitoring is where a device is placed on the juvenile, such as an ankle or wrist bracelet, or in other cases, a random-dial phone system may be used to place calls to the juvenile's residence. These devices are not only tamper-proof but are accompanied by a Global Positioning System (GPS) or radio frequency system, so that it is easy to determine where the juvenile is at all times (Development Services Group, Inc., 2014). Removal of the device can also be detected. Periods of inactivity or where the device is stationary for a very long period of time may also send an alert to a central monitoring system.

From a systems point of view, there are tremendous benefits to home confinement and electronic monitoring; namely, the juvenile remains within the proper environment, whether that is at school or at home, and within the custody of teachers or guardians who can supervise the youth at all times. In turn, probation officers are also afforded the ability to supervise more youth under these conditions with relative ease. Moreover, these measures remain one of the most cost-effective alternatives to punishment, especially when compared to the cost of incarceration. According to Austin et al. (2005), research studies show that the use of home confinement is successful. Youths are compliant with the conditions of home confinement and are more likely to appear for their adjudication hearings. Other studies conducted in the 1970s and 1980s also found that most youths completed home confinement successfully and that only a smaller percentage of youths either committed new offenses or were sent to a secure facility as a result of violating their home confinement conditions. However, this research is dated. Recent research has examined GPS systems and how they are more effective in monitoring the youth, leading to more favorable outcomes such as successful program completion as opposed to the use of a radio frequency system (Bales et al., 2010).

In contrast, a number of criticisms have surfaced concerning the use of electronic monitoring and home confinement. Arnett (2018) frames a number of problems starting with the fact that surveillance technologies infringe on a juvenile's Fourth Amendment right to privacy, in addition to the juvenile's search and seizure protections. In essence, monitoring devices capture a whole host of data regarding movement for which there is no proper regulation or oversight. Arnett also argues that the terms of home confinement are extremely rigid, vague, lengthy, and set the youth up for failure. In terms of rigidity, the youth and the youth's caregiver(s) must seek permission and approval to leave home for scheduled appointments and emergency situations. This is coupled with rigid rules such as zero tolerance for damaged monitoring device equipment even when the youth was not responsible for the damage to the device themselves. Finally, Arnett states that there is a significant amount of stigma and shame associated with wearing the device in public, which in turn does not align with the goals of juvenile rehabilitation. Yet, in the end, it is important to realize that juvenile probationers do in fact consent to these conditions and may be given the alternative of detention if they prefer.

Probation

The concept of **probation** is based on the notion that wrongdoing can be mended by rehabilitating the juvenile within the community as opposed to a residential institution and is used best with first-time, non-violent offenders. Typically, probation is used as an alternative to more restrictive punishment, where it is emphasized to the juvenile that this is their second or third chance to make behavioral changes and improvements. A probation officer, as described in Chapter 9, takes on the role of supervising and monitoring the youth. It is not uncommon for the youth to have to report to the probationer's office on a scheduled basis or for the probation officer to make unannounced home visits. In theory, probation holds the youth accountable, keeps the community safe, provides the necessary delivery of rehabilitation services, and, like the other community-based approaches, serves as a cost-effective alternative to incarceration.

As discussed earlier, it is important to place into context how correctional services are administrated in each state, whether it be at the state or local level. According to OJJDP (2017), twenty-two states have state-administered juvenile probation services, and twenty states operate juvenile probation services at the local level. At least nine states characterize probation services as "mostly state operated." The majority of these states are in the southeast region of the United States.

To date, and as stated earlier in this chapter, probation is the most common disposition assigned to an adjudicated juvenile delinquent. According to Hockenberry and Puzzanchera (2024), probation was issued to well over half of the adjudicated males and females (67%) as opposed to out-of-home placements or a disposition that involved some other type of sanction, including restitution, community service, or mandated counseling program, in 2022. A breakdown of offense types among those adjudicated youth in 2022 who were placed on probation showed that the majority of cases were for crimes against persons offenses (39%), whereas slightly fewer were for property offenses (29%) or public order offenses (24%). Adjudicated female delinquents (71%) received probation in slightly more instances than adjudicated male delinquents (66%). For both adjudicated male and female delinquents, probation was a likely outcome when the offense involved drugs. In terms of race, probation was assigned to 63% of adjudicated Black youth versus 72% of cases involving adjudicated white youth. Probation was assigned the most to both Black and white adjudicated delinquents in cases that involved a drug offense, followed by offenses that involved persons.

Most county probation offices are equipped with standard form letters that describe the conditions that the juvenile must follow while on probation. A sample of juvenile **probation conditions** can be found in Box 10.2. Such conditions provide the juvenile with a set of rules to follow while maintaining public safety. State law often dictates the mandatory and specific conditions that the juvenile probationer must follow. For example, these conditions stipulate that a juvenile under no circumstances may commit a new delinquent act, that the juvenile is required to report to their juvenile probation officer as directed, and that the juvenile probationer must follow all orders of the court. Moreover, conditions for probation may include a set of specific or special conditions, depending on the individual who is being supervised and the type of crime that was committed. These conditions, however, must fall in line with the best interests of the youth in order to further their rehabilitation. Juveniles who suffer from a substance abuse problem, for instance, may be ordered to attend sobriety counseling as a special condition. It is also possible for parents to have a set of conditions to follow.

Even though standard probation condition letters exist, there are a few considerations that the probation officer must make when using them. For example, probation conditions have to be written using clear and understandable language in order for the juvenile to follow them (Hess et al., 2013). Additionally, probation conditions must be achievable or doable. Most notably, the conditions cannot be written in general or vague terms. Otherwise, the juvenile may unknowingly violate the terms of conditions as they are unable to discern the specific behavior that is forbidden, which could arguably result in a due process rights violation (Fitzgerald, 2011). Vague conditions also place the police or probation officer in a position where they have to speculate as to what type of behavior is prohibitive. Such a case reached the California appellate court, where the vague language read: "That the minor not associate with any *known* probationer, parolee, or gang member" (Fitzgerald, 2011, p. 4). The language was written in the passive voice, where the use of the word "known" was vague, as it did not specify a subject in the sentence. The language of the probation condition was changed by the court in order to make the condition more precise. The revised conditions stated, "You H.C. will not associate with any person known to you to be on probation, on parole or a member of a criminal street gang" (Fitzgerald, 2011, p. 4).

Box 10.2: Sample Juvenile Probation Conditions: Monroe County, Ohio

Obey All Laws

You shall refrain from violation of any law (Federal, State, Local). You shall contact your Probation Officer if arrested or questioned by a Law-Enforcement Officer. (Minor misdemeanor traffic offenses are generally not a basis for the revocation of probation, however you must report them to the Probation Officer.)

Search & Seizure

While on probation I understand I am subject to warrantless searches and consent to the search of my person, residence, out building on my property or under my control, vehicles, as well as all computers, electronics, and cell phones.

Abstain from Drugs

You shall not possess, use, distribute or have under your control any Schedule I, II, III, IV, and V drugs as defined in 3719.41 of the Ohio Revised Code, or instruments for administering them except on prescription of a licensed physician, nor shall you use alcoholic beverages if ordered to abstain by the sentencing judge. It is also your responsibility not to be in the presence of any person using illicit drugs.

Obey Adults

I shall obey the adults in my home and school and police authorities and the Court.

Attend School

I shall attend school regularly and on time.

Curfew/Address/Telephone

I shall keep a 9:00 p.m. curfew and shall be where I live between 9:00 p.m. and 6:00 a.m. I will immediately notify my probation officer of any change in my address and/or telephone number.

Leaving Ohio

I shall not leave the state without the consent of my probation officer.

Contact with Offenders

I shall not contact or be with anyone on probation/community control.

Reporting In (Juvenile)

You shall report to the Probation Officer as ordered. You shall follow his instructions, including any requests for alcohol or drug testing at your own expense. Failure to submit will result in revocation of probation.

Possession of Weapons

I shall not purchase, possess, or have under my control any weapon such as firearms, knives, or dangerous ordinance.

Source: Monroe County, Ohio. (n.d.). *Juvenile rules of probation.* https://www.monroecountyohio.com/government/clerk_of_courts/probate_juvenile_court/standard_rules_of_probation.php

Despite the fact that juvenile probation exists in every state with a set of legislative guidelines, little is known about its effectiveness as a whole. Rather, what has been discussed more extensively are the pros and cons of juvenile probation. The leading positive aspect of juvenile probation is that it is relatively inexpensive. Furthermore, juveniles are held accountable and are easily supervised within the community as a mechanism to reduce stigma. Some of the negative aspects involve the fact that juveniles on probation are often rearrested for new offenses (Steiner et al., 2004). This could be the result of very large caseloads held by overburdened probation officers. Juvenile probation officers who supervise low-risk offenders may be able to effectively supervise as many as fifty to seventy-five juveniles, yet as the risk level increases, the officer should be responsible for fewer probationers. For example, juvenile probation officers with a caseload that requires intensive probation supervision should have only around fifteen to twenty probationers, but this is not always the case.

Intensive Supervision Probation

Some adjudicated delinquents may be spared a trip to a juvenile correctional institution and be placed on **Intensive Supervision Probation (ISP)** instead. ISP is a dispositional alternative for an adjudicated juvenile delinquent who receives a more rigorous level of community supervision by an assigned probation officer, along with increased contacts, drug screenings, and treatment services. ISP is used with adjudicated chronic offenders as well as adjudicated, serious nonviolent juvenile offenders (Krisberg et al., 1994). Thus, ISP lends itself to juveniles who have not succeeded with traditional probation but are on the very cusp of an institutional commitment. While the goal of safety for the community in tandem with rehabilitation for the juvenile delinquent remains at the forefront, intensive supervision probation follows a risk control model. As noted in the literature, the primary focus then is on reducing recidivism. In turn, probation officers have reduced caseloads, since intensive surveillance is required as well as stricter compliance with assigned probation conditions (Tonry, 1990).

Juvenile ISPs were brought about in the 1980s as a way to curb prison overcrowding and as a practical sentencing option since traditional probation practices had seemed to fail (Bouchard & Wong, 2018). The idea to incorporate ISPs made sense given this historical context, when a wider range of correctional alternatives was being explored. Probation on one end was seen as too lenient, while incarceration was seen as too harsh. Intermediate sanctions offered a place in the middle that provided cost savings and with the potential to reduce recidivism. With that said, ISPs offered a viable and attractive solution to several problems and many jurisdictions took hold of the idea.

The use of ISP can be implemented using a variety of intervention strategies. Krisberg et al. (1994) outlined the key components of ISP, which are: case planning and management, program rewards and sanctions, and program services. Case planning and management involves many layers of service delivery from a variety of service providers and professionals, including case managers, probation officers, counselors, teachers, the youth's family, and so on. Like most programs for youth, the use of behavioral modification techniques that utilize positive reinforcement should accompany the youth's programming in an effort to reward and strengthen prosocial behaviors. Furthermore, a mixture of services and programs are offered to the juvenile based on the theoretical model of integrated social control theory. This means that services and programs are needed to strengthen the youth's bonds to conventional activities and persons; to develop personal, social, and technical skills that will allow the youth to function successfully in society; to allow the youth in a guided way to implement and test these skills given meaningful exercises and activities; and to limit the influence of negative and delinquent peer associations. The authors provide a set of core intervention strategies to guide ISP program design and to facilitate its operation. They are:

1. Operate a phase system characterized by an initially high level of external program control to be progressively decreased as the offender displays a greater level of responsibility and internal controls.
2. Deliver or access a range of services guided by a continuously monitored individualized case plan.
3. Develop a constellation of relationships among the youth and law-abiding persons, groups, and institutions that can provide alternative role models, a source of rewards and sanctions external to the program, a network of community support, and a vehicle for disengagement from delinquent peer groups.
4. Teach youth the social and interpersonal skills necessary to maintain positive involvement with family, school, work, prosocial peers, and community institutions.
5. Develop youth competence in life skills, education, and employment.
6. Arrange and advocate for access to opportunities in education and employment that provide meaningful rewards in the short term and long term.
7. Address individualized risk factors that impede functioning or that have weakened the youth's prosocial attachments.
8. Consistently apply graduated rewards and sanctions that recognize youth achievement and provide immediate accountability for violations. (Krisberg et al., 1994, p. 23)

Logically, one would think that an intensive supervisory model would yield reduced recidivism rates, yet research evidence tends to show otherwise. Bouchard and Wong (2018) state that intensive supervision have been known to increase recidivism rather than diminish it. Common sense dictates that any time supervision is heightened for an offender, any wrongdoing will likely be quickly and easily detected. In other words, juveniles assigned to ISP are placed right under the microscope. This suggests that ISPs are more likely to fail in general because stricter supervisory conditions and increased watchfulness afford the probation officer greater chances of detecting whether the conditions for probation have been violated. Youth who violate the conditions for probation, called a **technical violation**, forfeit their right to probation and ultimately may be sent to a secure residential facility. Employing a meta-analysis of twenty-seven studies on juvenile aftercare and intensive supervision programs, Bouchard and Wong (2018) confirmed that aftercare and youth assigned to ISP were more likely to be charged and adjudicated for an offense. Even though a few studies have highlighted some support for ISPs, the existing body of research is very mixed, signaling the need for further discourse about the utility of intensive supervision probation.

Restitution

Yet another common community-based alternative is **restitution**, which is where the offender provides monetary payment of losses to the victim or renders compensation in the form of work or service. At disposition, the juvenile judge will set the amount of restitution, and in some states, the juvenile will be assigned to a probation officer or caseworker in a more formalized restitution program (Schneider & Warner, 1986). The caseworker's primary responsibility is to create a restitution plan with the youth that would include a payment schedule and an identifiable place of employment. If the youth is too young to be employed, they may be assigned community service hours as a way to repay the victim for losses, or the juvenile's parents may have to provide monetary compensation to the victim.

Few studies have examined restitution or court fees and their impact on a juvenile's case. However, in one study, Piquero et al. (2023) examined the impact of monetary sanctions such as fees and restitution on recidivism rates among youth of color compared to white youth. Using a sample of over 12,000 youth who had been assigned to community-based placements in Florida, they found that Black and Hispanic youth received higher fees compared to white youth. For Black youth particularly, when they were assigned restitution, it significantly increased the likelihood of recidivism. Furthermore, when just examining fees assigned to youth alone, recidivism rates were higher than compared to youth who were not assigned fees. While restitution and fees were imposed on a few of the juveniles in this sample overall, it still warrants further exploration as to how monetary sanctions contribute to recidivism and also how monetary sanctions exacerbate racial disparities.

Community Service

For some youth, the best alternative and one that has restorative properties and holds the youth accountable is **community service**. This particular community-based alternative clearly involves compensating and giving back to society by performing a set number of hours or work within the community in some capacity (Thomas & Hunninen, 2008). The type of community service most individuals are familiar with and that is most visible is picking up trash along a major roadway. Volunteer and community service work may also be conducted in a city park or for a county or government agency. Court-appointed community service can be applied as a formal or informal sanction, and it can be coupled with other dispositions as seen fit by the juvenile judge. When it comes to overseeing community service activities, the youth will report to their assigned probation officer. Little is known about how much time is actually devoted to the community by youth assigned to carry out community service. However, some estimates in 2006 in Pennsylvania showed that well over two-thirds of juvenile delinquency cases involved over 500,000 combined hours of service.

An important point of discussion worth mentioning concerning community service is that it can be mandated or voluntary. Some arguments have been raised that for community service to be beneficial, it should be voluntary. In cases involving juveniles, the court typically issues community service as a sanction; thus, service is not voluntary (Thomas & Hunninen, 2008). Even though the service is court-ordered and admittedly coercive, it is still important that the opportunity provides a meaningful experience that rests on the principles of **restorative justice**. The philosophy of restorative justice is hinged on three main components: (1) youth accountability, (2) reparation or restoration to the community, and (3) reparation of harm to the victim. More specifically, Bazemore (2006) elaborates on such a balanced and restorative justice approach, where the offender is accountable to the victim and the community, where the offender develops competency and demonstrable changes in self-concept, and where the community is kept safe from the harms committed by the juvenile. Several states have adopted this approach and have even incorporated it into their administrative goals, much like Wisconsin's mission statement provided earlier in the chapter. Using restorative justice principles, it is also important to link the juvenile to a service project that is related to the juvenile's crime. For instance, if the juvenile painted graffiti on a public structure, it would make sense for the youth to redress the harm by removing the graffiti.

Little research has been conducted on the effectiveness of community service, and among those studies that do exist most of the focus has been on recidivism. Based on a review of several community service initiatives, Bazemore (2006) found that recidivism slightly decreased or did not change much at all among juveniles who participated in community service endeavors. Overall, the research to date trends in a positive direction, but more research is still needed to measure other dimensions, including the perceptions from the offender on the quality of service that is provided and the perception of community stakeholders on the quality of service that is received.

Commitment to the State: Residential Treatment Institutions

In years past, juvenile treatment facilities were known as training schools or reform schools. Even though some states may still refer to them this way, most state-run facilities are called correctional institutions. Juvenile residential **treatment institutions** are secure facilities that are used to house high-risk, pre-adjudicated or adjudicated chronic youthful offenders for a longer period of time. Even though this involves a more extreme form of punishment for youth, the goal and nature of a juvenile residential facility is rehabilitation and treatment. At the same time, the facility serves to house these youth to protect the community as well. These secure institutions include a variety of diagnostic services in order to assist the youth with proper mental health and educational programming during their stay.

To put residential placements into context across the country, among the 134,400 adjudicated cases involving juveniles in 2022, 28% of these cases resulted in place-

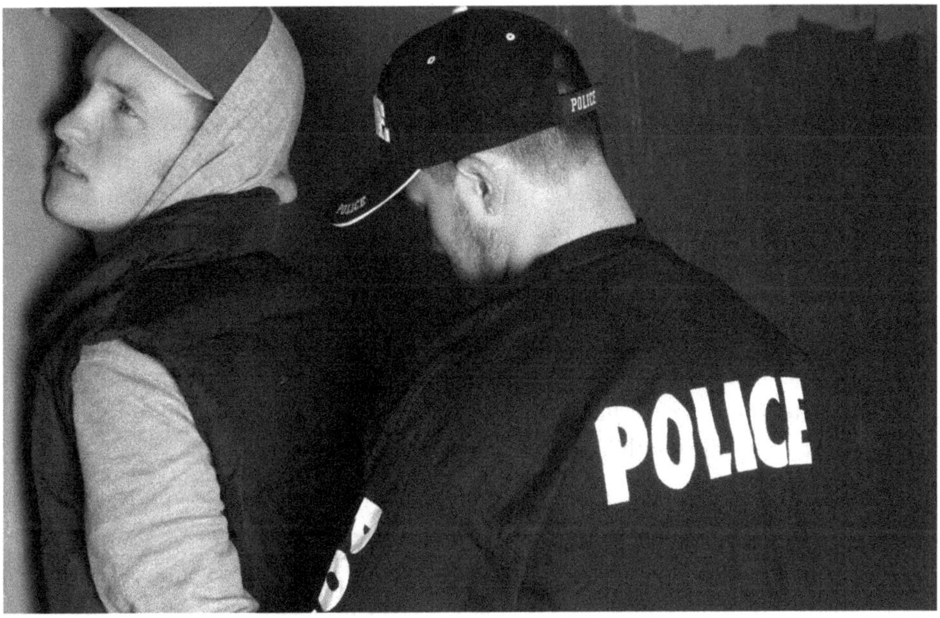

ment in a residential facility (Hockenberry & Puzzanchera, 2024). As of 2022, a census showed that there were 1,277 juvenile residential facilities in the United States (OJJDP, 2024). Of these, 794 were public institutions and 483 were private. Roughly 45,500 juveniles total were in these facilities; the majority of juvenile offenders (78%) resided in public facilities versus private (22%) facilities.

In 2021, states like Texas and California had the largest number of committed juveniles (well over 2,000 juveniles in each state) in a facility that was court ordered as part of their disposition, followed by states like Ohio and Florida, which both had over 1,000 juveniles placed in a residential facility (Puzzanchera et al., 2023a). Similar to the court data that was presented in Chapter 9, residential placement census data showed that placements in juvenile residential facilities are lower than they were in previous years; however, youth of color still comprise a large number of youths held in residential facilities. For example, among juvenile residential facilities in 2021, 37% of youth housed in juvenile residential facilities were Black or white, followed by 20% of youth who were Hispanic, and 3% of youth who were characterized as having more than one race (Puzzanchera et al., 2023b). The remaining 3% percent of youth were categorized as American Indian (2%) or Asian (1%). Thus, youth of color accounted for roughly 64% of the residential population. In terms of gender, females made up roughly 14% of those housed in a residential facility, and younger females (under age 16) were more likely to be placed in a residential facility than their male counterparts. Also, most juveniles were placed in public residential facilities versus privately operated facilities, with Pennsylvania having the most youth held in a private facility in the country.

Detention

As discussed in Chapter 9, it is not uncommon for juveniles to be placed in a juvenile detention facility. Depending on the state, **detention** may simply be used as a temporary holding facility as the youth awaits court proceedings, while other states may utilize the detention center as a part of their disposition. The decision to place a youth in detention as mentioned in Chapter 9 ultimately rests on the judge. Making this decision to place a youth in pre-adjudicated detention is contingent on several factors: (1) the threat the juvenile poses to the safety of the community, (2) the threat the juvenile poses to themselves, and (3) the likelihood that the youth will be present at the adjudication hearing (Hess et al., 2013). Regardless, the youth is constitutionally afforded a detention hearing. Judges must weigh all of these issues and decide whether to continue to keep the youth in detention or release the youth back into society.

Juvenile Correctional Facilities

Remember that correctional institutions are to be used as a last resort in the juvenile system as it is the most restrictive and severe dispositional alternative. Juvenile correctional facilities are essentially prisons and often house more serious, violent, and troubled youthful offenders, who have been adjudicated for a felony or multiple misdemeanor crimes. Much like an adult prison, the day is regimented, and residents are expected to maintain discipline. It varies by state, but some facilities will house juveniles up until age 21, and if the situation dictates, the youth will be transferred to an adult facility. The prison grounds are generally characterized by a secure perimeter with higher levels of internal and external surveillance and monitoring systems. Freedom and movement inside the facility are restricted and limited throughout the day. Similar to an adult facility, juvenile residential facilities have a control center where all doors and cells are operated by staff, who use an extensive surveillance system of cameras. Depending on the state, the juvenile correctional center may be classified by security level, such as maximum security, medium security, or minimum security, whereas other states may label the correctional facility as hardware secure, implying a greater level of security.

Programming

For juveniles, programming is essential to rehabilitation and treatment. If we take away programming, all we are left with is punishment and isolation, which is not only inhumane but ineffective in producing law-abiding young men and women (see Box 10.3). While youth are serving out a disposition in a residential facility or a day report center, there is an excellent window of opportunity to provide them with quality rehabilitative programming. However, looking back at our recent history, this was not always the case. The rhetoric of Martinson's (1974) study, that "nothing works" in rehabilitation, led to the abandonment of prison treatment and rehabilitation programs and ushered in support for "get tough" approaches and harsher, longer sentences. This impacted not only the adult system but the juvenile system as well and coincides with the discussion in Chapter 9 about the fear of the rising number of juvenile "super-predators" in the 1990s. Martinson's sentiments that rehabilitation efforts have failed to reduce recidivism since then have been refuted, and researchers have shown that there are quality, evidence-based programs that do work (Kim et al., 2013). The three main categories of programming that are discussed next include (1) rehabilitation, (2) educational/vocational, and (3) recreational.

Before describing each of these, it is also important to recognize the philosophy that supports why juvenile programming is considered valuable and worthwhile. Youth are viewed as malleable. They are growing and changing, and their ability to reason is adapting as they mature. Also, as youth reach maturity, most will desist from committing future crimes. As mentioned in Chapter 4, desistance or aging-out refers to the process of ceasing to offend, especially as a person gets older, takes on more responsibilities, and has a stake in conformity. After we shake off our adolescence, many of us turn to college, jobs, marriage, military commitments, or starting a family. As we age, these factors make juvenile offending less attractive as our responsibilities increase, and as we invest time and energy into our work and families. Crime is weighed to a point where it is just not worth the risk.

Rehabilitation Programs

Rehabilitation programs are centered on treating the youth along with some type of psychological, behavioral, or social dimension. These programs are therapeutic in nature and can be administered one-on-one or in a group session. The primary focus and most effective way to treat the youth is by altering criminogenic risk factors or traits that are conducive to delinquency such as impulsivity, thrill-seeking, anger, lack of concern for others, substance abuse, and so on. For some youth, their behaviors may be compounded by mental health disorders, in which case, intensive therapy is warranted, and sometimes it is necessary to couple the therapy by administering psychotropic medication to the juvenile. Research has shown that nearly 16% of youth who are not involved in the juvenile justice system have a diagnosable mental health condition compared to studies that show that as many as 65% of juveniles in detention have a diagnosable mental health disorder (Desai et al., 2006). Some of the most common mental health disorders among institutionalized youth are substance abuse disorder, conduct disorder, and post-traumatic stress disorder.

There are numerous treatment programs offered in juvenile correctional facilities across the country. One of the most widely adopted types of treatment approaches is **Cognitive Behavioral Therapy (CBT)**, which is used to treat youth with substance abuse problems, anxiety, depression, and aggression, among other problems (Desai et al., 2006). The underlying principle of CBT is that in order to treat the individual, the individual's thinking has to change or be corrected in some way. Over time and with improper socialization or a lack of socialization, the youth may have developed faulty thinking patterns or learned unhelpful behaviors to address a particular problem. This type of therapy includes, but is not limited to, guiding the youth through a series of exercises that involve problem-solving, confidence building, confronting fears, role-playing, recognizing distorted thinking, and relaxation techniques. The use of CBT among institutionalized and non-institutionalized juvenile justice populations has shown positive results, namely in terms of reducing future episodes of violence, substance abuse, and recidivism.

Box 10.3: Solitary Confinement

One of the major issues that has been called into question in juvenile corrections is the use of solitary confinement, which will also be discussed in greater detail in Chapter 12. It was once believed that isolation provided some type of rehabilitation and allowed a person time for reflection and even repentance. This model, called the silent system, was used in practice in the early 1800s, most notably in the Eastern State Penitentiary for adult offenders in 1829. Eventually, reports came out that prisoners began going insane. Despite what was revealed even back then, the use of solitary confinement, especially when an inmate is a threat to himself or others or has violated a facility policy, continues to be permitted indefinitely in at least ten states, according to the National Conference of State Legislators (e.g., Alabama, Georgia, Kansas, Minnesota, Mississippi, Missouri, Rhode Island, South Dakota, Wisconsin, and Wyoming) (Teigen, 2024). Other states have either banned the use of solitary confinement altogether or limited its use. To date, it is unknown how many youths are placed in solitary confinement and for how long. One estimate from Pennsylvania showed that as many as 10% of juveniles were held in solitary confinement in one facility (Human Rights Watch, 2012).

Solitary confinement can be thought of as a form of long-term isolation and incarceration where an individual is typically housed without any contact with others for at least twenty-two hours a day as a result of violating some type of infraction or for maintaining safety. Remember that youth can be charged as adults and be placed in adult facilities, but not within sight or sound of an adult inmate. This is a form of administrative confinement. The youth may be held in an isolated cell to comply with this federal provision. In disciplinary cases, solitary confinement or restricted housing, as it is also called, can occur for as long as fifteen to ninety days, depending on the number of infractions that were committed (Human Rights Watch, 2012). Arguably, such practices inhibit the growth and development of a juvenile and can lead to hallucinations, suicidal attempts, or even suicide. While in isolation, youth may or may not have a cell with windows, access to proper recreation or exercise, access to educational services, or access to treatment to meet their medical and psychological needs. What compounds this issue is that a number of youths already have a diagnosable mental condition; isolation only exacerbates the youth's symptoms.

From 2011 to 2012, the Human Rights Watch (2012) conducted interviews with youth who were housed in juvenile detention or prison. The majority of the youth were male. In terms of psychological effects, youth reportedly developed imaginary friends in order to cope with the pains of isolation, while others found that the stress of solitary confinement intensified feelings of anger and aggression. Some youth engaged in more serious behaviors such as cutting, which psychologists report is a response to social isolation and a way to force interaction with staff members. Last, at least twelve youths remarked that they contemplated or attempted suicide. One youth spent sixty days in isolation, to the point where he experienced feelings of being trapped, hopelessness, and depression that subsequently led to thoughts of ending his life as not much else mattered to him anymore.

To shift the practice of solitary confinement to being one that is considered a more "humane practice," inmates are often granted at least one hour of recreation time. This can involve moving the inmate to a different part of the facility to walk longer distances in a hallway, placing the youth in a dayroom, or allowing the youth to move around in the appropriate recreation space on the jail or prison grounds (Human Rights Watch, 2012). However, most youths reported that they were denied these opportunities. In Florida, one youth reported that recreation was not provided to him for the first thirty days of isolation. Aside from the psychological harms mentioned earlier, physical harms of solitary confinement included weight loss, and one youth reported the physical transformation of another youth, who started losing his hair. This signals that a lack of exercise and movement, a lack of adequate nutrition, and a lack of physical care all have detrimental effects and take their toll on a youth's growth and development.

Since education is compulsory, youth in solitary confinement cannot be denied an education. However, many youths reported that education was delivered via a packet of materials to the youth for self-study (Human Rights Watch, 2012). Oftentimes, this work was not reviewed or even graded. Around 53% of the youth reported that they were provided with no schooling at all. Several youths also stated that they were not even permitted to have a book or magazine in their cell. What is even more troubling is that many youths struggle with learning disabilities; their needs are simply not met in isolation.

Based on accounts like this, even though a handful of juveniles were interviewed, there is still a need for policy change and reform. Human Rights Watch and the American Civil Liberties Union (2012) call for five areas of policy reform. The first area of reform pertains to the elimination of solitary confinement for any individual under the age of 18. State or federal code needs to be written to prohibit its use. Next, no youth should be detained in an adult prison or jail, as youth are often subjected to the same policies and rules as adults and treated and managed the same way as adult inmates. Another call for reform pertains to isolation and any and all forms of segregation regardless of how many days the youth is kept there. The number of days needs to be limited and highly regulated. Moreover, jails and prisons that utilize this practice should be mandated to provide public reports on the use of solitary confinement. Last, the United States government is called upon to protect youth by ratifying human rights treaties.

Sources: Human Rights Watch. (2012). *Growing up locked down: Youth in solitary confinement in jails and prisons across the United States*. https://www.hrw.org/sites/default/files/reports/us1012ForUpload.pdf; Teigen, A. (2024). States that limit or prohibit juvenile shackling and solitary confinement. NCSL Foundation for State Legislatures. https://www.ncsl.org/civil-and-criminal-justice/states-that-limit-or-prohibit-juvenile-shackling-and-solitary-confinement

Educational Programs

Since education is compulsory, juveniles must attend school, and in correctional settings, school is not optional. Correctional education programs mirror and follow all of the state and national standards for education, using certified instructors, yet there are some distinct differences. For instance, it is not always possible to keep youth separated by grade level or age. Classrooms are often arranged by academic level, requiring the teacher to ensure that the youth is receiving course material at the appropriate level. Some estimates show that youth in the juvenile justice system may be behind as many as two grade levels. Moreover, some youth may have even dropped out of school and need to complete a GED or high school diploma, in which case remedial education and test preparation are essential. The other key difference is that youth may be in mixed classrooms with youth who have a diagnosable learning disorder or deficiency. It is also well known that anywhere from 30% to 35% of incarcerated youth are afflicted with a learning disability (Mallett, 2014). These additional challenges require a well-trained special needs educator to deliver high-quality instruction.

A 2020 census of residential facilities indicated 90% of facilities screened all incoming youth regarding their educational level, and 93% of facilities used previous school records, while 56% used a written assessment or interview from a trained education specialist or counselor to gauge the youth's educational needs (Hockenberry & Sladky, 2024). Youth placed in detention centers and shelters reportedly had greater school attendance versus youth placed in group homes, training schools, or diagnostic centers. Facility reports also showed that a high school level of education was provided in 95% of the facilities, and a middle school level of education was provided in 89% of the facilities. Given the number of youths with learning disabilities, as many as 82% reported a curriculum that provided special education services. With graduation as a common educational goal to prepare juveniles, 74% of facilities offered GED classes.

Recreational Programs

For many youths, recreational programs are a tremendous benefit to reduce stress while adopting prosocial norms and employing communication skills through outlets that involve organized sports or activities. For many taxpayers, recreational facilities inside a juvenile facility are unthinkable. Why would we allow juvenile delinquents to have a full-sized gymnasium when local public schools barely have enough resources or recreational facilities of their own? A slightly different mindset is needed to put this into context. For one, having recreational facilities for juveniles in detention or prison aids in maintaining the safety of staff members. Second, recreation also offers youth a much-needed outlet and an opportunity to release stress or built-up frustration and energy. Third, it also breaks up the monotony for both staff and for juveniles, and at the same time, fosters better staff and juvenile relationships. While it is possible that altercations may occur during "rec-time," the benefits largely outweigh the risks. Recreational programs also fit within the scope of the rehabilitative mission of juvenile corrections.

After the 1974 "nothing works" sentiment swept the justice system and led to more punitive and harsher sentencing, researchers started conducting several meta-analyses demonstrating the positive effects of rehabilitation programs and interventions (Martinson, 1974). Since the 2000s, these efforts can be framed as an evidence-based movement that has been shaped by policymakers and juvenile justice professionals. The three key principles operating now are: (1) limiting the use of detention and incarceration, (2) implementing community-based prevention programs, and (3) creating programs that are based on sound research evidence (Clear et al., 2016). Aside from reducing the number of youths placed in secure institutions and using more community alternatives, the last idea described here is to move away from implementing programs that are unsupported by the research literature, and thereby not worth any financial investment. One of the best methods for examining effective programs is to conduct program evaluations that measure the program's intended outcomes. The outcome could be a behavioral change such as a reduction in the juvenile's violent behavior, a reduction in the juvenile's anger, or a reduction in rearrests. In cases where rearrests are concerned, the researchers would examine recidivism rates.

With evidence-based research in context, it makes sense then that researchers have been invested in examining the outcomes of programs. In a meta-analysis of rehabilitation program-based research, Kim et al. (2013) found the most support among sex offender treatment programs, whereas drug treatment programs and cognitive behavioral programs were not as successful in reducing juvenile recidivism. This body of scientific research does not mean that other types of treatment programs do not work; in fact, rehabilitation programs can reduce recidivism. Besides looking at the outcome of reoffending, researchers like Lipsey (2009) have found support among successful programs when the focus is on a youth's criminogenic needs. Even though recidivism rates are very telling about a program's success, future research must become more tailored by exploring both when programs work best for juveniles and which characteristics of a juvenile that certain programs work best for.

Box 10.4: Wraparound Programs

One well-known type of aftercare program is known as Wraparound. **Wraparound programs** can be characterized as "a philosophy of care" that involves a unique set of community, family-based, and individualized treatment services that allow youth to achieve positive outcomes at present and into adulthood (VanDenBerg et al., 2008). The term "wraparound" is attributed to Dr. Lenore Behar from North Carolina, who implemented this approach as a result of a lawsuit (*Willie M. v. the State of North Carolina*). The case involved a mentally and emotionally troubled juvenile, who had a history of violent and assaultive behaviors and who did not respond to any of the services or institutionalized care provided to him. The goal of the lawsuit was to increase the state's accountability for children like Willie and to mandate that the state develop appropriate and comprehensive services and treatment for the youth and their family. The state of North Carolina complied and began to create alternatives to incarceration that adopted this philosophy.

Wraparound programs are based on ten principles as shown below. Notably, a key feature of the Wraparound program is that it also involves a collaborative and team-based approach to providing the youth with services. Teams are comprised of the youth, the youth's family, and members of the community, along with mental health professionals and educators. These individuals meet regularly and are responsible for creating, implementing, and monitoring plans that meet the youth's and family's unique needs, while maintaining cultural sensitivity. The element that is emphasized here is family. In other words, the child cannot be treated alone successfully without addressing the complex needs of the parents or caregivers. Some of the other key features include understanding that the needs of the family dictate which services are provided instead of simply force-fitting services. Another underlying theme is that treating the family unit as a whole will allow a greater chance for the family and youth to succeed. Moreover, these programs are community-based, and as with many programs, they are outcome driven. To date, research on the wraparound program has been fairly positive, with evidence showing a reduction in problematic behaviors, reductions in residential placements, and increases in educational retention, just to name a few successes.

Ten Principles of the Wraparound Process

1. Family voice and choice. Family and youth/child perspectives are intentionally elicited and prioritized during all phases of the wraparound process. Planning is grounded in family members' perspectives, and the team strives to provide options and choices such that the plan reflects family values and preferences.

2. Team based. The wraparound team consists of individuals agreed upon by the family and committed to them through informal, formal, and community support and service relationships.
3. Natural supports. The team actively seeks out and encourages the full participation of team members drawn from family members' networks of interpersonal and community relationships. The wraparound plan reflects activities and interventions that draw on sources of natural support.
4. Collaboration. Team members work cooperatively and share responsibility for developing, implementing, monitoring, and evaluating a single wraparound plan. The plan reflects a blending of team members' perspectives, mandates, and resources. The plan guides and coordinates each team member's work towards meeting the team's goals.
5. Community-based. The wraparound team implements service and support strategies that take place in the most inclusive, most responsive, most accessible, and least restrictive settings possible and that safely promote child and family integration into home and community life.
6. Culturally competent. The wraparound process demonstrates respect for and builds on the values, preferences, beliefs, culture, and identity of the child/youth and family and their community.
7. Individualized. To achieve the goals laid out in the wraparound plan, the team develops and implements a customized set of strategies, supports, and services.
8. Strengths based. The wraparound process and the wraparound plan identify, build on, and enhance the capabilities, knowledge, skills, and assets of the child and family, their community, and other team members.
9. Persistence. Despite challenges, the team persists in working toward the goals included in the wraparound plan until the team reaches agreement that a formal wraparound process is no longer required.
10. Outcome based. The team ties the goals and strategies of the wraparound plan to observable or measurable indicators of success, monitors progress in terms of these indicators, and revises the plan accordingly. (Bruns et al., 2004, pp. 5–11)

Sources: Bruns, E. J., Walker, J. S., Adams, J., Miles, P., Osher, T. W., Rast, J., VanDenBerg, J. D., & National Wraparound Initiative Advisory Group. (2004). *Ten principles of the wraparound process.* National Wraparound Initiative, Research and Training Center on Family Support and Children's Mental Health, Portland State University. https://nwi.pdx.edu/NWI-book/Chapters/; VanDenBerg, J., Bruns, E. J., & Burchard, J. (2008). History of the wraparound process. In E. J. Bruns & J. S. Walker (Eds.), *The resource guide to wraparound.* National Wraparound Initiative, Research and Training Center for Family Support and Children's Mental Health. https://nwi.pdx.edu/NWI-book/Chapters/

The Missouri Model

The Missouri Division of Youth Services (DYS) touts one of the most successful rehabilitation models for youth in the United States. Commonly referred to as the **Missouri Model**, the model is comprised of a "cottage style" residential program that encapsulates a therapeutic living environment. Initially, the program began with just a small group of troubled youth in the 1970s in response to a draconian model of juvenile reform where physical abuse and extensive use of solitary confinement were taking place at juvenile training schools. The program was later expanded to Missouri's entire juvenile offender population and has been in place for over five decades. The movement to adopt this model not only rested on a statewide juvenile corrections reform movement but also relied on research evidence that called into question the effectiveness of juvenile incarceration.

Housing facilities are one of the most notable features of the Missouri Model. In contrast to concrete cells, a stainless steel sink, and limited furnishings, these facilities incorporate dorm rooms with bunk beds, allowing for as many as ten to twelve youths to sleep in the room (Mendel, 2010). Uniforms are not issued, and instead, youth are permitted to wear their own, albeit appropriate, attire. Personal items are also permitted in their rooms. Since the living environment is dorm-style, it is common to find furnished living rooms with ordinary family-centered fixtures. Some facilities may even go so far as to have a house pet. Living quarters also come equipped with the necessary space to hold team meetings or treatment sessions. On the outside, there is a security fence, but typical hardware security is virtually non-existent on the inside of the facilities. These descriptions certainly signal a departure from the youth facilities that resemble a sterile and cold institution.

Another feature of the Missouri Model is the therapeutic living and treatment environment. Youth spend all of their time in small groups or treatment teams (Mendel, 2010). This provides youth with continuity and allows staff to monitor their behavior more closely. Not unlike adult therapeutic communities and practices used by other residential programs, youth have a set of accountability standards. If a youth acts out or is disruptive, they are expected to explain themselves not only to staff but to the group as a whole. Even though the group setting plays a significant role in daily activities, there are extensive and individualized treatment plans that are overseen by a case management coordinator. Treatment plans are linked to a series of risk and needs assessments, which are completed upon the youth's arrival. One aspect of the risk assessment is to provide the case management coordinator with information to determine the youth's appropriate level of care. This translates to a commitment to build on the youth's academic and pre-vocational skills for the youth to be successful after release.

As mentioned earlier in this chapter, the juvenile's family members are typically brought in for treatment programming themselves (Mendel, 2010). Sometimes there is a need to assist the entire family unit to allow the family to heal. This puts the youth and the family in a better position to achieve success during the aftercare phase of the program. The aftercare phase requires considerable support and supervision of the juvenile, especially as the juvenile transitions from the residential facility to work and school. Reentry programming begins prior to release, where the youth is prepared for the first and most crucial weeks following release from the facility.

The Missouri Model is also known for its high-caliber staff. Here, redefining the traditional role of guards or correctional officers shifted to the role of youth specialist (Mendel, 2010). This meant that coercive job duties such as enforcing rules and punishing wrong behaviors were replaced with the concept of providing safety for youth within a context of care and therapy. To employ the most qualified staff, the Missouri DYS recruits potential employees from colleges and universities. It is expected that candidates have completed at least 60 hours of a college curriculum. Candidates undergo an intensive interviewing process, and those who are successful in becoming youth specialists receive 236 hours of comprehensive training that covers the core beliefs and values about treating youth as shown in Box 10.5.

Box 10.5: Missouri Model: Underlying Beliefs and Values about Youth

- Every young person wants to succeed—and can succeed.
- Public safety is best served not by punishing young people or shaming them for their crimes, but by offering a therapeutic intervention to help them make lasting changes in their attitudes, beliefs, and behaviors.
- These lasting changes cannot be imposed on young people. Youth can't be scared straight, reformed, or deterred from crime by fear of punishment. Rather lasting changes can only result from internal choices made by the young people themselves.
- Like all people, troubled youth tend to resist and fear change. Positive relationships with staff and other youth are critical to overcoming resistance and fostering positive change.
- Every young person requires individual attention. Each DYS youth has chosen to engage in delinquent behaviors based upon their own circumstances, and each will make the decisions to change and grow—or not—for their own personal reasons.
- Some youth lapse into serious and chronic delinquency as a coping mechanism in response to earlier abuse, neglect, or trauma. For other youth, delinquency has less deep-seated roots.
- Regardless of the roots of their behavior problems, delinquent youth typically suffer from a lack of emotional maturity—an absence of insight into their own behavior patterns, an inability to distinguish between feelings and facts, and an underdeveloped capacity to communicate their emotions or express disagreement or anger responsibly.

- All behavior, no matter how destructive, has an underlying emotional purpose. Therefore, rather than punishing or isolating young people when they act out, the best response is to ask probing questions that help the youth understand the roots of the problem and identify more constructive responses.
- Most youth entering custody have very low confidence in their ability to succeed as students—or eventually as workers in the mainstream economy. And most have had limited exposure to mentors and positive role models.
- While the DYS staff and treatment process are important, parents and other family members remain the most crucial people in youths' lives—and the keys to their long-term success. (Mendel, 2010, p. 38)

Source: Mendel, R. A. (2010). *The Missouri model: Reinventing the practice of rehabilitating youthful offenders*. Annie E. Casey Foundation. https://www.aecf.org/resources/the-missouri-model

Since its inception, the Missouri Model has been implemented with great success, one aspect of which is cost savings and the other of which is lower recidivism rates. It may seem alarming, but the state of Missouri spends around $87 million dollars a year on the Division of Youth Services alone (Missouri Division of Social Services, 2017). This equates to around $155 per youth, ten to sixteen years of age. Although the overall price tag appears extraordinary, the bottom line is that this is actually a huge cost savings for taxpayers when it is placed into perspective. The fiscal report also indicated that recidivism rates among youth in the Missouri system are relatively low. To capture this measure, recidivism was defined as youth who either returned to the custody of the Missouri Division of Youth Services or to the adult system in increments of one year post discharge, two years post discharge, and three years post discharge. During the first year, only 10.9% of youth recidivated. Two years after being discharged, 19.7% of youth recidivated, and after three years, the percentage climbed to 27.2%. In comparison to estimates at the national level, recidivism rates after one year of being institutionalized hover around 55% (Snyder & Sickmund, 2006).

Reentry and Aftercare

In 2022, nearly 38,200 youth were in a residential placement facility (also known as out-of-home placement) on any given day (Hockenberry & Puzzanchera, 2024). Many of these youth will eventually be released and require some level of support to transition back into their communities. Contrary to what most would assume, the process of reentry begins months before an individual is released from a secure correctional facility. The misunderstanding is that aftercare begins when the individual is discharged from the facility (Development Services Group, Inc., 2017). More formally, reentry or **aftercare** involves reintegrative services and programs that a youth receives

before release from a secure residential facility and while the youth is being supervised in the community post-institutional release. Depending on the state or local government, some house these services within an actual juvenile probation agency, while others carry out these services via formalized juvenile aftercare programs. Also, the administration may vary based on whether these programs are carried out at the state level or the local level. For instance, in 2017, thirty-eight states were responsible for the administration of juvenile aftercare (OJJDP, 2017). Eight states, Minnesota, Wisconsin, New York, Tennessee, Oklahoma, Georgia, Alabama, and Virginia, were characterized as "mostly state-operated" due to the fact that some of the services are managed by the local government. States like California, Idaho, Kansas, and Pennsylvania were deemed locally operated, again signaling that the local government or local probation department was primarily responsible for the administration of juvenile aftercare services. Regardless of how the services are administered, reintegrative programs ensure that the youth will receive additional support to transition back to society with the hopes of reducing recidivism. Federal monies, known as the Second Chance Act Youth Reentry Program, are also available to the states and local community partners to provide comprehensive services for youth who are returning to their community and to reduce rates of future reoffending. It must be reiterated that the success of reentry and aftercare programs hinges just on that—recidivism. However, no national recidivism data is routinely collected. Some states have compiled these figures on their own, where they define recidivism as the number of youths rearrested within one year after release. Results show, as stated earlier, that as many as 55% of youth released from an institution are rearrested after one year (OJJDP, 2020).

Prior to the youth being released from a secure residential facility, steps must be taken to determine what type of environment or placement is needed for the youth to succeed. For some youth who have reached the age of maturity, this may mean that they return home. For other youth, it may be best to place them in a transitional housing facility or halfway house. In addition, an individualized assessment will be conducted to determine the youth's needs, which will put into motion yet another case plan. Once the youth is placed, they will receive specialized treatment services, along with mentoring, school advocacy, and employment training, as needed. At the same time, they will still be supervised in the community, but to a lesser degree as they complete the various phases of the program and demonstrate successful completion. Some of the most well-known types of reentry programs include **therapeutic communities**, which are residential programs for treating youth with substance abuse disorders (Developmental Services Group Inc., 2017). Other programs follow a family and individual-based treatment service model. These programs are referred to as **Multisystemic Therapy (MST)** programs and are geared toward serving youth who elicit more serious behaviors, such as antisocial behavioral disorders, violent tendencies, severe emotional or disturbance behaviors, or pervasive drug use (see Box 10.4). These programs aim to help the youth within their home environment, to address the origins of the problematic behaviors, and to empower families.

Research on the effectiveness of aftercare has been characterized as mixed. Some studies have found a reduction in recidivism (Weaver & Campbell, 2014), while others find that the aftercare program did not yield any differences in the youth's behavior (Abrams et al., 2014). Yet, the research still provides great insights for future consideration in the development of aftercare programs. In a meta-analysis of twenty-two different studies on juvenile aftercare, James et al. (2013) found that aftercare programs were more beneficial for youth who had a higher risk of reoffending. Specifically, high-risk youth were characterized as those who belonged to ethnic minority groups, coupled with an impoverished background, and gang involvement. Youth characterized as violent also benefited more from aftercare than non-violent youth. The researchers also found aftercare programs were most successful with youth who were in their late adolescence or early adulthood. One would assume that a lengthier aftercare program would produce greater benefits. However, that was not the case. Duration was not as important, but the intensity of the treatment the juvenile received had a larger impact. Moreover, whether the program started while the youth was still in custody or after they were released, did not make a difference. One of the most definitive conclusions and findings to shape and guide successful aftercare programs and reduce recidivism included the use of individualized interventions. This goes back to the concept that was discussed in Chapter 9, that is, the importance of assessing the youth's risks and needs and providing the youth with a customized treatment plan. Last, the researchers found that group therapy was not as beneficial, and programming that catered to a systems approach, such as schools and family, was not as impactful. It was postulated that perhaps youth who return to the community have reached a later stage of adolescence and autonomy where these systems play a reduced role in the young adult's life.

Summary Points

- Corrections is an umbrella term that is used to describe a variety of programs and services. Juvenile corrections can be best characterized as a state-centralized or local-decentralized system. Within the system, the overarching goals of juvenile corrections are based on the principles of public safety, rehabilitation and treatment, and dedication to aftercare and reintegration.
- The Juvenile Justice Delinquency Prevention Act was authorized to put into place a set of standards for states to follow regarding the care and treatment of youth. Aside from the provisions of deinstitutionalizing status offenders and removing adjudicated youth from adult jails and lockups, the other core provisions involve ensuring that youth are removed from sight and sound of adult offenders and assessing and addressing racial and ethnic disparities.
- Community-based sanctions are less restrictive alternatives to incarceration that may include day report treatment centers, group homes, foster homes, house arrest/electronic monitoring, probation, restitution, and community service. Probation is the most commonly used community-based alternative.
- Correctional programs for juveniles are often centered on treating the youth with the notion that they are malleable and at some point will reach the age of maturity. Rehabilitative programs are largely focused on producing cognitive and behavioral changes, and additional programs are offered to bolster a youth's educational and vocational skills. Recreational programs also exist to serve youth and support a healthy lifestyle and well-being.
- Placement in residential facilities is used sparingly for juveniles. Juvenile detention is for temporarily holding a youth as they await court proceedings or as part of the youth's disposition. Secure residential facilities such as juvenile correctional centers hold youth for longer periods of time and typically house youth who have committed more serious crimes or who are repeat serious offenders.
- The process of juvenile reentry begins well before a juvenile is released from a residential facility. A whole host of reintegrative services and support is offered to the youth based on their needs, while the youth maintains accountability. Since the youth's needs are evolving, aftercare programs need to be highly individualized.

- The Missouri Model is one of the most widely successful residential rehabilitation programs for youth where youth thrive in "cottage style" living environments, coupled with supportive and highly trained staff, who work in tandem with the youth's family to provide them the greatest potential for reintegrative success.

Key Terms

Aftercare: reintegrative services and programs that a youth receives prior to release from a secure residential facility and while the youth is being supervised in the community post-institutional release.

Behavior Modification: a type of therapy that involves reducing negative behaviors and increasing appropriate ones using positive reinforcement and the concept of token economy.

Centralized System: a system where administrative authority and responsibility rests with a state or larger governing body.

Cognitive Behavioral Therapy (CBT): a treatment service approach for youth with substance abuse problems, anxiety, depression, and aggression, among other problems, that involves changing the youth's thought process.

Community-Based Alternatives: less restrictive sanctions to incarceration where the juvenile is immersed in a program or non-secure facility within the community.

Community Service: a community-based alternative that involves compensating and giving back to society by performing a set number of hours or work within the community in some capacity.

Corrections: services provided to juveniles prior to adjudication or post-adjudication.

Day Report Treatment Centers: non-residential facilities used as a community-based alternative for court-referred, at-risk youth who need additional supervision, counseling, educational, and vocational support services (also referred to as day treatment centers).

Decentralized System: a system where administrative authority and responsibility rests with the local government.

Detention: a temporary holding facility as the youth awaits court proceedings or a facility where youth are placed as a part of their disposition.

Deterrence: preventing future crimes from occurring by providing youth with the opportunity to consider and weigh the consequences of their behavior while under restrictive custody or a supervised community-based program.

Electronic Monitoring: a surveillance and monitoring device that is placed on the juvenile, such as an ankle or wrist bracelet, or a random-dial phone system that places calls to the juvenile's residence.

Foster Care: residence in the care of a homeowner or family member, who may or may not have children of their own.

Group Homes: non-secure residential facilities found within the local community that provide safety and assistance for adjudicated delinquents (also known as shelters).

Home Confinement: monitored supervision of a juvenile within the juvenile's home or residence.

Incapacitation: removing the juvenile from society and confining them in a secure facility so that future crimes cannot be committed.

Intensive Supervision Probation (ISP): a dispositional alternative for an adjudicated juvenile delinquent who receives a more rigorous level of community supervision by an assigned probation officer along with increased contacts, drug screenings, and treatment services.

Missouri Model: a set of treatment services that are comprised of a "cottage style" residential program that encapsulates a therapeutic living environment.

Multisystemic Therapy (MST): a family and individual-based treatment service model that is geared toward serving youth who elicit more serious behaviors, such as antisocial behavioral disorders, violent tendencies, severe emotional or disturbance behaviors, or pervasive drug use.

Probation: a form of punishment where the juvenile is monitored in the community.

Probation Conditions: conditions that stipulate a set of rules that the juvenile must follow when placed on probation.

Rehabilitation: treatment programs for youth to address factors that may have contributed to their delinquency or misbehavior and in an effort to modify the youth's future behavior.

Reintegration: transitional services to assist the youth back into the community that equates to greater success in completing the rehabilitation process.

Residential Treatment Institutions: secure facilities that are used to house high-risk, pre-adjudicated or adjudicated chronic youthful offenders for a longer period of time.

Restitution: a type of sanction where the offender provides monetary payment of losses to the victim or renders compensation in the form of work or service to the victim.

Restorative Justice: a philosophy hinged on (1) youth accountability, (2) reparation or restoration to the community, and (3) reparation of harm to the victim.

Retribution: punishment for the sake of punishment (also commonly known as just deserts or revenge).

Technical Violation: a violation of the conditions for probation where the juvenile forfeits their right to probation, and ultimately may be sent to a secure residential facility.

Therapeutic Communities: residential programs for treating youth with substance abuse disorders.

Wraparound Programs: "a philosophy of care" that involves a unique set of community, family-based, and individualized treatment services that allow youth to achieve positive outcomes at present and into adulthood.

References

Abrams, L. S., Mizel, M. L., Nguyen, V., & Shlonsky, A. (2014). Juvenile reentry and aftercare interventions: Is mentoring a promising direction? *Journal of Evidence-Based Social Work, 11*, 404–422. https://doi.org/10.1080/10911359.2014.897115

Arnett, C. (2018). Virtual shackles: Electronic surveillance and the adultification of juvenile courts. *The Journal of Criminal Law & Criminology, 108*(3), 399–454. https://scholarlycommons.law.northwestern.edu/jclc/vol108/iss3/1/

Austin, J., Dedel Johnson, K., & Weitzer, R. (2005). *Alternatives to the secure detention and confinement of juvenile offenders.* Office of Juvenile Justice and Delinquency Prevention. https://www.ncjrs.gov/pdffiles1/ojjdp/208804.pdf

Bales, W. D., Mann, K., Blomberg, T. G., Gaes, G., Barrick, K., Dhungana, K., & McManus, B. (2010). *A quantitative and qualitative assessment of electronic monitoring.* Florida State University, College of Criminology and Criminal Justice, Center for Criminology and Public Policy Research. http://criminology.fsu.acsitefactory.com/sites/g/files/upcbnu3076/files/2021-03/A-Quantitative-and-Qualitative-Assessment-of-Electronic-Monitoring.pdf

Bazemore, G. (2006). *Measuring what really matters in juvenile justice.* American Prosecutor's Research Institute. https://www.ojp.gov/pdffiles1/ojjdp/grants/216394.pdf

Bouchard, J., & Wong, J. S. (2018). Examining the effects of intensive supervision and aftercare programs for at-risk youth: A systematic review and meta-analysis. *International Journal of Offender Therapy and Comparative Criminology, 62*(6), 1509–1534. https://doi.org/10.1177/0306624X17690449

Chambers, R. M., Crutchfield, R. M., Willis, T. Y., Cuza, H. A., Otero, A., Goddu Harper, S. G., & Carmichael, H. (2018). "It's just not right to move a kid that many times": A qualitative study of how foster care alumni perceive placement moves. *Children and Youth Services Review, 86*, 76–83. https://doi.org/10.1016/j.childyouth.2018.01.028

Clark, S. E., & Jerrott, S. (2012). Effectiveness of day treatment of disruptive behavior disorders: What is the long-term clinical outcome for children? *Journal of Canadian Academy of Child and Adolescent Psychiatry, 21*(3), 204–212. https://pmc.ncbi.nlm.nih.gov/articles/PMC3413470/

Clear, T. R., Reisig, N. D., & Cole, G. F. (2016). *American corrections.* Cengage.

Desai, R. A., Goulet, J. L., Robbins, J., Chapman, J. F., Migdole, S. J., & Hoge, M. A. (2006). Mental health care in juvenile detention facilities: A review. *Journal of the American Academy of Psychiatry and the Law, 34*(2), 204–214. https://jaapl.org/content/34/2/204

Development Services Group, Inc. (2011). *Day treatment. Literature review.* Office of Juvenile Justice and Delinquency Prevention. https://www.ojjdp.gov/mpg/litreviews/Day_Treatment.pdf

Development Services Group, Inc. (2014). *Home confinement and electronic monitoring. Literature review.* Office of Juvenile Justice and Delinquency Prevention. https://ojjdp.ojp.gov/model-programs-guide/literature-reviews/home_confinement_and_electronic_monitoring.pdf

Development Services Group, Inc. (2017). *Juvenile reentry. Literature review.* Office of Juvenile Justice and Delinquency Prevention. https://www.ojjdp.gov/mpg/litreviews/Aftercare.pdf

Early, K. W., Ryon, S. N., Hand, G. A., & Blankenship, J. L. (2014). Experimental community-based interventions for delinquent youth: An evaluation of recidivism and cost effectiveness. *Contemporary Issues in Juvenile Justice, 8*(1), 29–36. https://digitalcommons.pvamu.edu/cojjp-contemporaryissues/vol8/iss1/4

Fitzgerald, K. (2011, January). *Probation conditions: Adult and juveniles. What types of conditions are unreasonable and unconstitutional?* Revised and updated by R. Braucher, K. Seligman, & J. Price. First District Appellate Project. https://www.fdap.org/wp-content/uploads/2020/11/Seminar2011-ProbationConditions.pdf

Florida Department of Juvenile Justice. (n.d.). *Mission.* https://www.djj.state.fl.us/about-us/mission

Hess, K. M., Orthmann, C. H., & Wright, J. P. (2013). *Juvenile justice.* Wadsworth/Cengage.

Hockenberry, S., & Puzzanchera, C. (2024). *Juvenile court statistics 2022.* National Center for Juvenile Justice. http://www.ncjj.org/Publication/Juvenile-Court-Statistics-2022.aspx

Hockenberry, S., & Sladky, A. (2024). *Juvenile residential facility census 2020: Selected findings.* Juvenile justice statistics national report series bulletin [NCJ 305825]. Office of Juvenile Justice and Delinquency Prevention. https://ojjdp.ojp.gov/publications/juvenile-residential-facility-census-2020-selected-findings.pdf

James, C., Stams, G. J. J. M., Asscher, J. J., De Roo, A. K., & van der Laan, P. H. (2013). Aftercare programs for reducing recidivism among juvenile and young adult offenders: A meta-analytic review. *Clinical Psychology Review, 33*, 263–274. https://doi.org/10.1016/j.cpr.2012.10.013

Kim, B., Merlo, A. V., & Benekos, P. J. (2013). Effective correctional intervention programmes for juveniles: Review and synthesis of meta-analytic evidence. *InternationalJournal of Police Science & Management, 15*(3), 169–189. https://doi.org/10.1350/ijps.2013.15.3.310

Krisberg, B., Neuenfeldt, D., Wiebush, R., & Rodriguez, O. (1994). *Juvenile justice intensive supervision: Planning guide.* National Council on Crime and Delinquency,

Office of Juvenile Justice and Delinquency Prevention. https://www.ojp.gov/ncjrs/virtual-library/abstracts/juvenile-intensive-supervision-planning-guide

Lipsey, M. W. (2009). The primary factors that characterize effective interventions with juvenile offenders: A meta-analytic overview. *Victims and Offenders, 4*, 124–147. https://doi.org/10.1080/15564880802612573

Mallett, C.A. (2014). The "learning disabilities to juvenile detention" pipeline: A case study. *Children & Schools, 36*(3), 147–154. https://doi.org/10.1093/cs/cdu010

Martinson, R. (1974). What works? Questions and answers about prison reform. *The Public Interest, 35*, 22–54.

McDonald, T. P., Allen, R. I., Westerfelt, A., & Pihavin, I. (1993). *Assessing the long-term effects of foster care: A research synthesis.* Child Welfare League of America Press.

Mendel, R. A. (2010). *Missouri model: Reinventing the practice of rehabilitating youthful offenders, summary report.* Annie E. Casey Foundation. https://www.ojp.gov/ncjrs/virtual-library/abstracts/missouri-model-reinventing-practice-rehabilitating-youthful

Missouri Department of Social Services. (2017). *Division of youth services, annual report, fiscal year 2017.* https://dss.mo.gov/re/pdf/dys/youth-services-annual-report-fy17.pdf

Office of Juvenile Justice and Delinquency Prevention (OJJDP). (2017). *Statistical briefing book. Organization and administration of delinquency services. Administration of community supervision (probation), 2017.* https://www.ojjdp.gov/ojstatbb/structure_process/qa04203.asp?qaDate=20177

Office of Juvenile Justice and Delinquency Prevention (OJJDP). (2020). Research central: Measuring what works in juvenile reentry. *OJJDP News @ a Glance.* https://ojjdp.ojp.gov/newsletter/ojjdp-news-glance-novemberdecember-2020/research-central-measuring-what-works-juvenile-reentry

Office of Juvenile Justice and Delinquency Prevention (OJJDP). (2024). Youth in residential placement by facility operation. *Statistical briefing book.* https://ojjdp.ojp.gov/statistical-briefing-book/corrections/faqs/qa08502

Piquero, A. R., Baglivio, M. T., & Wolff, K. T. (2023). A statewide analysis of the impact of restitution and fees on juvenile recidivism in Florida across race and ethnicity. *Youth Violence and Juvenile Justice, 21*(4), 279–308. https://doi.org/10.1177/15412040231180816

Platt, A. M. (2009). *The child savers: The invention of delinquency.* Rutgers University Press.

Puzzanchera, C., Sladky, T.J., & Kang, W. (2023a). *Easy access to the census of juveniles in residential placement.* https://www.ojjdp.gov/ojstatbb/ezacjrp/

Puzzanchera, C., Sladky, T. J., & Kang, W. (2023b). *Offense profile of committed youth by sex and race/ethnicity for United States, 2021.* Easy access to the census of juveniles in residential placement (EZACJRP). https://www.ojjdp.gov/ojstatbb/ezacjrp/

Schneider, A. L., & Warner, J. S. (1986). The role of restitution in juvenile justice systems. *Yale Law & Policy Review*, *5*(2), 382–401. https://openyls.law.yale.edu/handle/20.500.13051/17351?show=full

Simmons-Horton, S. Y. (2021). "A bad combination": Lived experiences of youth in volved in the foster care and juvenile justice system. *Child and Adolescent Social Work Journal*, 38, 583–597. https://doi.org/10.1007/s10560-020-00693-1

Snyder, H. N., & Sickmund, M. (2006, March). *Juvenile offenders and victims: 2006 national report*. Office of Juvenile Justice and Delinquency Prevention. https://www.ojjdp.gov/ojstatbb/nr2006/downloads/NR2006.pdf

Steiner, B., Purkiss, M., Kifer, M., Roberts, E., & Hemmens, C. (2004). Legally prescribed functions of adult and juvenile probation officers: Worlds apart? *Journal of Offender Rehabilitation*, *39*(4), 47–67. https://doi.org/10.1300/J076v39n04_04

Thomas, D., & Hunninen, M. (2008). *Making things right: Meaningful community service for juvenile offenders*. Technical Assistance to the Juvenile Court: Special Project Bulletin. National Center for Juvenile Justice. http://www.ncjj.org/Publication/Making-Things-Right-Meaningful-Community-Service-for-Juvenile-Offenders.aspx

Tonry, M. (1990). Stated and latent functions of ISP. *Crime & Delinquency*, *36*, 174–191. https://doi.org/10.1177/0011128790036001012

Weaver, R. D., & Campbell, D. (2014). Fresh start: A meta-analysis of aftercare programs for juvenile offenders. *Research on Social Work Practice*, *25*(2), 201–212. https://doi.org/10.1177/1049731514521302

Wisconsin Division of Juvenile Corrections. (n.d.). *About the division of juvenile corrections*. https://doc.wi.gov/Pages/AboutDOC/JuvenileCorrections/DivisionOfJuvenileCorrections.aspx

Chapter 11

Juvenile Justice Reform: A Human Rights Perspective

Chapter Learning Objectives

Students will be able to:

- Describe the historical events and decisions that led to a more "just" and reformed juvenile justice system
- Explain how juvenile justice can be examined in a social justice and human rights context
- List some of the current questionable and unfair practices embedded in the juvenile justice system with respect to policing youth, the legal system and the courts, and institutional confinement
- Define the peacemaking approach and explain how it can be used to address social justice and human rights reform for juveniles
- List the key principles of advocacy
- Summarize efforts from lead advocacy groups that have led to reform and change in the juvenile justice system

---

Introduction

Ideally, the juvenile justice system was created and continues to be developed as a solution to the problem of delinquency. Chapter 1 pointed out that the nature of the problem of delinquency must be understood if we are to solve it. It asked, "What is delinquency?" However, we must also know exactly what the solution is to be able to carry it out. A vague or incomplete understanding of what we need to do to prevent and reduce delinquency will inhibit success. Thus, we also need to ask, "What is justice?" As we will see, juvenile justice is more than simply a matter of developing systematic responses to delinquent behavior. As with defining delinquency, we are imperfect and in disagreement in our efforts to define justice as it relates to juvenile crime. In fact, defining delinquency and juvenile justice are inseparable issues. Deciding the nature of delinquency has direct implications for what to do about it, for example determining which behaviors do or do not count as delinquency and thus which ones to sanction (or not), as well as the harm that lies in certain delinquent acts and the appropriate responses to them.

Juvenile Justice as Social Justice

In 1989, the United Nations, comprised of 190 member countries, passed the *Convention on the Rights of the Child* (Attiah, 2014). This landmark piece of international legislation is recognized globally as the single most comprehensive framework when it comes to protecting youth rights. Originally conceived in 1959, the treaty is comprised of over fifty articles. Countries that have signed the treaty agree with utmost certainty to act in the best interests of the child. This includes a demonstration that the laws of that country uphold and provide basic rights to children such as the rights to health care, education, and privacy. Included is the expectation that children are to be protected from exploitation and child labor. Among these provisions, Articles 37 and 40 specifically (as shown in Box 11.1 and Box 11.2) address the rights of a child who is being served by the justice system (Sarri & Shook, 2015). Countries that follow these specific articles are to ensure that youth are afforded appropriate legal counsel and due process rights. Countries also agree not to impose the death penalty for cases involving youth and not to house youth in adult facilities, among other provisions.

Box 11.1: Article 37: Rights of the Child

Article 37

States Parties shall ensure that:

(a) No child shall be subjected to torture or other cruel, inhuman or degrading treatment or punishment. Neither capital punishment nor life imprisonment without possibility of release shall be imposed for offences committed by persons below eighteen years of age;

(b) No child shall be deprived of his or her liberty unlawfully or arbitrarily. The arrest, detention or imprisonment of a child shall be in conformity with the law and shall be used only as a measure of last resort and for the shortest appropriate period of time;

(c) Every child deprived of liberty shall be treated with humanity and respect for the inherent dignity of the human person, and in a manner which takes into account the needs of persons of his or her age. In particular, every child deprived of liberty shall be separated from adults unless it is considered in the child's best interest not to do so and shall have the right to maintain contact with his or her family through correspondence and visits, save in exceptional circumstances;

(d) Every child deprived of his or her liberty shall have the right to prompt access to legal and other appropriate assistance, as well as the right to challenge the legality of the deprivation of his or her liberty before a court or other competent, independent and impartial authority, and to a prompt decision on any such action. (United Nations, 1989, p. 10)

Source: United Nations. (1989). *Convention on the Rights of the Child.* United Nations Human Rights, Office of the Commissioner. https://www.ohchr.org/en/instruments-mechanisms/instruments/convention-rights-child

Among the United Nations affiliates, only three countries did not sign the treaty at that time, which included Somalia, Sudan, and the United States (Attiah, 2014). However, in 2015, both Somalia and Sudan ratified the convention, leaving the United States as the sole country left to ratify it. A discussion about the reasons why the United States failed to ratify the convention is beyond the scope of this chapter, but the primary reason was that the United States did not want to ratify these rights, as it would infringe on the rights of each autonomous state in the nation (Sarri & Shook, 2015). Despite this serious misgiving, it is still of great importance to address the rights of children whether they live in the United States or abroad.

Several egregious cases where juvenile rights were called into question were already mentioned in earlier chapters. Take, for example, false confessions that are bound to occur during police interrogations of youth as described in Chapter 8, or the violations of youth rights that take place in solitary confinement, as mentioned in Chapter 10. As discussed previously, youth in solitary confinement are often deprived of an education, adequate exercise, and suitable mental health treatment. Chapter 8 described the concept of racial and ethnic disparities and the use of extralegal factors in police decision making, which ultimately place youth of color in the hands of the juvenile system more so than their white counterparts. Also in that same chapter, the topic of the school-to-prison pipeline was presented as a consequence of zero-tolerance policies. On its face, zero-tolerance policies were meant to serve and protect youth from the harms of school violence and shootings, but such policies have now led to an additional pathway to filter youth of color and mentally impaired youth into the justice system for trivial infractions.

Based on just a few of the examples previously illustrated, it is evident that reform is still necessary. This means that we must continue to critically examine the human rights issues that still plague our juvenile justice system. There is no denying that such an examination is uncomfortable and unpleasant; however, the first step in making the juvenile justice system more just is to identify the ways in which the system is unjust. Some of the topics that are presented in this chapter are more overt and blatant, while others are barely visible and would have nearly fallen off the radar, had it not been for child advocacy organizations and legal rights associations that have drawn our attention to them.

To better understand the complexity of these issues, each topic will be framed from a human rights and social justice perspective and in a theoretical context when appropriate. According to Capeheart and Milovanic (2007), **social justice** entails not only the aspect of raising awareness but a critical analysis of what is fair and what is just for both society and the individual, while recognizing that society is in a never-ending process of growth and change. For the purpose of analysis in this chapter, the authors also explain how social justice extends beyond criminal justice.

> Criminal justice has been too narrow a focus and pursuit for serious comprehensive endeavors. As we move toward the study and pursuit of social justice, we must first consider what social justice entails. Criminal justice accepts, for the most part, a politically established definition of crime (law, police) and focuses on process (courts) and retribution (corrections). It has traditionally focused on these with little attention to history, political economy, culture, critique, or cross-cultural understanding of the purposes of these institutions. Social justice must consider what is just not only in reaction to "crime" but also in relation to evolving (nonstatic) society. (Capeheart & Milovanic, 2007, pp. 3–4)

Moving forward with this conversation requires an understanding of the concept of human rights. This perspective not only has been echoed by the United Nations' *Convention on the Rights of the Child* but among other national organizations such as the International Federation of Social Workers (IFSW). **Human rights** are fundamental entitlements that are granted to each person regardless of national origin, race, culture, sex, or creed (Mooradian, 2010). The concept of human rights implies a reciprocal relationship where everyone has the responsibility to recognize these rights in a process of "human social transformation" (Ife, 2005). Ultimately, recognizing the rights we possess and the rights of others will lead us to achieve "full humanity" (Mooradian, 2010).

Box 11.2: Article 40: Rights of the Child

Article 40

1. States Parties recognize the right of every child alleged as, accused of, or recognized as having infringed the penal law to be treated in a manner consistent with the promotion of the child's sense of dignity and worth, which reinforces the child's respect for the human rights and fundamental freedoms of others and which takes into account the child's age and the desirability of promoting the child's reintegration and the child's assuming a constructive role in society.

2. To this end, and having regard to the relevant provisions of international instruments, States Parties shall, in particular, ensure that:

   (a) No child shall be alleged as, be accused of, or recognized as having infringed the penal law by reason of acts or omissions that were not prohibited by national or international law at the time they were committed;

(b) Every child alleged as or accused of having infringed the penal law has at least the following guarantees:

(i) To be presumed innocent until proven guilty according to law;

(ii) To be informed promptly and directly of the charges against him or her, and, if appropriate, through his or her parents or legal guardians, and to have legal or other appropriate assistance in the preparation and presentation of his or her defence;

(iii) To have the matter determined without delay by a competent, independent and impartial authority or judicial body in a fair hearing according to law, in the presence of legal or other appropriate assistance and, unless it is considered not to be in the best interest of the child, in particular, taking into account his or her age or situation, his or her parents or legal guardians;

(iv) Not to be compelled to give testimony or to confess guilt; to examine or have examined adverse witnesses and to obtain the participation and examination of witnesses on his or her behalf under conditions of equality;

(v) If considered to have infringed the penal law, to have this decision and any measures imposed in consequence thereof reviewed by a higher competent, independent and impartial authority or judicial body according to law;

(vi) To have the free assistance of an interpreter if the child cannot understand or speak the language used;

(vii) To have his or her privacy fully respected at all stages of the proceedings.

3. States Parties shall seek to promote the establishment of laws, procedures, authorities and institutions specifically applicable to children alleged as, accused of, or recognized as having infringed the penal law, and, in particular:

(a) The establishment of a minimum age below which children shall be presumed not to have the capacity to infringe the penal law;

(b) Whenever appropriate and desirable, measures for dealing with such children without resorting to judicial proceedings, providing that human rights and legal safeguards are fully respected.

4. A variety of dispositions, such as care, guidance and supervision orders; counselling; probation; foster care; education and vocational training programmes and other alternatives to institutional care shall be available to ensure that children are dealt with in a manner appropriate to their well-being and proportionate both to their circumstances and the offence. (United Nations, 1989, p. 11–12)

Source: United Nations. (1989). *Convention on the Rights of the Child.* United Nations Human Rights, Office of the Commissioner. https://www.ohchr.org/en/instruments-mechanisms/instruments/convention-rights-child

Social Justice for Youth: Policing Youth

We know that early policing in the United States evolved from the British system. As our country and our system of law enforcement grew, the concept of night watchmen on foot patrol shifted to the use of motorized patrols, and the use of whistles and bells shifted to the use of radio communications. In the system's infancy, police officers were not trained or equipped to manage wayward youth any differently than adult offenders. As law enforcement agencies evolved into more autonomous organizations, they were fraught with accusations of being incompetent, corrupt, and highly politicized (Vito, 2019). Regardless, the notion of the police officer as a crime-fighter took hold, and treating youth no differently than adults continued. Despite efforts to become more professionalized and specialized, many departments lost sight of the rehabilitative and community-based approaches that best served the needs of youth.

As we learned earlier, this does not suggest that all police departments and officers have blatantly disregarded youth. In Chapter 9, the International Association of Chiefs of Police (IACP) among other national police organizations have acknowledged the need to be a part of juvenile reform efforts. In the past few decades, we have also seen police officers immersed in community-based programs such as Drug Abuse Resistance Education (D.A.R.E.) and Gang Resistance Education and Training (G.R.E.A.T). Additional reforms were put into place to ensure that the rights of youth are fully administered and communicated. To be exact, police officers must consider the youthfulness of the suspect in the *Miranda* custody determination (*J.D.B. v. North Carolina*, 2011).

However, despite our best efforts and attempts to make progress to create a fair and equitable justice system for youth, numerous human rights concerns about police and youth still exist. As stated in earlier chapters, one of the most glaring and unresolved problems in our juvenile justice system is racial and ethnic disparities (R/ED). Recall from Chapter 8 that to understand that racial/ethnic minorities face a higher chance of contact with the justice system and confinement, one must understand the concept of disproportionality or over-representativeness. When people who belong to a group or category are over-represented, their proportion of a specific situation or area is larger than their proportion of a general situation or area. For example, "children of African American descent represent 16% of the total youth population in the United States, 28% of all youth arrested, 35% of youth transferred to adult courts, and 58% of youth sentenced to confinement in adult prisons" (IACHR, 2018, p. 71). Disproportionality is also evident for Hispanic and American Indian youth.

Additional human rights and social justice concerns are before us that have not become as obvious until recently. To protect our youth, most schools are now fitted with a School Resource Officer (SRO), who is a sworn officer of the law dedicated to protecting youth and the local community and to establishing prosocial attitudes about the police. Even though SROs are in place to keep our youth and communities safe, combining these efforts with zero-tolerance policies have only exacerbated the problem of penalizing youth of color.

> African American adolescents as well as those of Hispanic ethnicity are respectively 3.5 and 1.5 times more likely than Caucasian youth to be expelled from schools. Studies show that 70% of all school referrals or arrests nationally involve children of African American or Hispanic background, even though these students make up only 40% of the total population of school enrollment. (IACHR, 2018, p. 71)

Figures like these make it clear that these newer mechanisms are in place to funnel more youth while enrolled in the school system into the justice system. Child advocates call this the school-to-prison pipeline (discussed in Chapter 8) and have sounded the alarm that this may be evidence of new Jim Crow-esque policies that have extended their reach to trap youth of color into the system (Alexander, 2012). Even though the topic of disproportionate minority contact was described and defined in earlier chapters, the following discussion includes examining the issue from other angles and cultivating some of the research findings that inevitably warrant our immediate attention and need for social justice and human rights reform. Moreover, the discussion continues with the ways in which we need to narrow the net. Again, this net has been stretched to capture more and more youth into the system for minor infractions and youthful indiscretions.

Racial and Ethnic Disparities (R/ED)

There has been a lot of discussion about what racial and ethnic disparities are up to this point. The questions that follow are, why are there racial and ethnic disparities in juvenile justice? Is it the result of racial and ethnic discrimination? Or is it because youth of color commit a disproportionately higher amount of delinquency, and therefore get into more trouble with the law? Perhaps since African American, Hispanic, and American Indian youth face more of the stressors associated with crime (e.g., those associated with poverty, unemployment, residential instability, family dysfunction), they as groups commit more crime. However, the evidence does not suggest that minorities generally commit more crimes than whites (Peterson et al., 2007). Albeit some evidence shows that minorities are more likely to commit certain types of crimes (Barkan, 2019), but this difference cannot account for all of the large differences in police-minority contact or confinement. If minorities were indeed at higher risk of committing a violent crime, then it would make sense that they would enter the justice system at higher rates. However, we would expect the justice system to handle white and minority juvenile offenders the same once they are in the system. For example, we would expect that youth of color would not receive tougher sanctions than whites for the same offense. Walker and colleagues (2018) provide compelling evidence that youth of color are more likely to be petitioned, detained before an adjudication hearing, and sentenced to a secure residential facility compared to their white counterparts. These comparisons show that both racial groups are equal in all other aspects (e.g., type of crime committed, prior arrest history, socio-economic status) except in terms of race. With this evidence, it seems that some kind of discrimination is contributing to these disparities.

According to Walker et al. (2018), there are several reasons why youth of color have greater contact with police officers. The examination begins with teasing apart some of the factors related to age, social class, and attitudes. For one, as part of their social lifestyles, juveniles, in general, tend to be out in public and on the streets more than adults, thus being more visible to police officers. This happens to be more likely for some impoverished youth of color, who also have limited personal space or socializing space in confined public housing establishments. In turn, disadvantaged youth of color have a wider range of recreational spaces that include outdoor spaces in their community. For middle-class and upper-class white youth, there are more resources available to socialize, including paid membership to indoor recreational centers, organized sports clubs, or larger fenced-in backyards and private dwellings. Moreover, police are known to patrol public spaces and have a greater presence in surveying disadvantaged communities as opposed to suburban or upper-class neighborhoods (Sarri & Shook, 2015). As discussed in Chapter 9, one of the double-edged swords when it comes to police-youth interactions lies with attitudes. On one hand, youth of color are known to possess less favorable attitudes about the police, especially as more contact with the police occurs (Nordberg et al., 2016). On the other hand, the police do not take kindly to youth who display a disrespectful attitude and may take a youth into custody for what some call "contempt of cop" (Bostic et al., 2014). The mash-up or clash of these two issues may be one of the factors leading to increased arrests of youth of color.

At the individual level, it is possible that discrimination may be committed by well-meaning persons who openly reject bigotry but still have racial and ethnic biases of which they are not consciously aware or which they do not realize are wrong (Merton, 1970). **Racial discrimination** involves treating an individual differently, such as denying rights or opportunities based on a person's race or ethnicity (Barkan, 2019). A person does not have to be "a racist," for example, to commit an act of racial discrimination. We are all raised in a society that is full of stereotypes about certain kinds of people, and only a perfect person could completely avoid thinking in terms of these stereotypes. For example, perhaps because of exposure to media images, one may be more fearful or worried about a juvenile's behavior simply because the juvenile is a Black, Hispanic, or a Muslim male, and react to him on that basis. This kind of stereotype becomes a major problem when a practitioner, or a judge, perhaps without realizing it, uses this kind of information to decide what to do with a juvenile. Penn (2006) echoes a similar sentiment:

> It is not discrimination institutionalized through law or system-wide practice; rather it is entrenched in the minds of police officers, judges, court personnel, child-care workers, and juries. It is discrimination that allows decision makers to believe that Black youths deserve harsher penalties because of the very characteristics they can never change—being Black. (p. 60)

Perhaps the easiest scenario to comprehend is that of the person with overt prejudicial (e.g., racist) beliefs who uses their power to treat minority youth harsher than majority youth. **Racial prejudice** refers to negative attitudes or perceptions about another social category of individuals based on their race or ethnicity (Barkan, 2019). However, juvenile justice workers are mostly highly educated and trained people who are staunchly expected to avoid bias and have the ability to circumvent much of the stereotypical thinking that occurs in the general population. Unfortunately, just like the general population, the population of juvenile justice workers is imperfect, so it likely does have some such people in it. As anyone who has spent much time with juvenile justice workers knows, these people are very rare. These "few bad apples," coupled with the use of overt racial profiling strategies in disadvantaged communities, can account for some but not all racial and ethnic disparities.

The next part of this examination leads to the next question: How does the juvenile justice system discriminate? This set of assumptions moves away from using *only* individual-level explanations of discrimination. In other words, this type of discrimination does not necessarily require individuals to have biased beliefs or subconscious assumptions. Instead, there is indirect or institutional discrimination. **Institutional discrimination** involves "racial and ethnic disparities in outcomes that are the result of the application of racially neutral factors" (Walker et al., 2018, p. 28). One possible form of institutional discrimination includes the risk assessment problem, as racial and ethnic minorities experience some major risk factors at higher rates than whites. For example, racial/ethnic minorities are more likely to live in socially disorganized neighborhoods (e.g., "inner cities") and face family disruption. If decisions to formally handle juveniles are made on the basis of these factors, not just their behavior, then more minorities will come into the system—via their higher exposure to risk factors.

Since these decisions are not made directly on the basis of race or ethnicity, but on a scientifically legitimated process, decisionmakers are "off the hook" so to speak; it is circumstances such as exposure to gangs and poor parenting that are at fault, not their biases, for minority youth's system involvement (Smith, 2011). However, the result may still be unequal treatment by the juvenile justice system.

As we continue to research the origins and sources of discrimination inherent in either working professionals or the juvenile justice system processes and policies therein, it is important to revisit one of the tenets spelled out by the *Convention on the Rights of the Child*, which calls for equal treatment of *all* youth. Any evidence of racial prejudice and discrimination that exists in our juvenile justice system is appalling. Yet, the Inter-American Commission on Human Rights (IACHR) (2018) has noted several states (e.g., Wisconsin, Minnesota, Nebraska, Iowa, and Pennsylvania) where racial disparities were excessive upon entry to the juvenile justice system. To address the problem, some states before 2018 collaborated with an initiative supported by the MacArthur Foundation known as Models for Change. This initiative provided states with support to build and create the necessary mechanisms to collect and analyze data on youth and race and to develop strategies to reduce racial decision making. This was a step in the right direction and coincides with the Rights of the Child Treaty (United Nations, 1989), although it still does not appear to be a widespread concern among all states. If states do not take it seriously or dictate reform, then the responsibility to curb racial and ethnic disparities falls on individual police departments, and after all, this is often the point where the juvenile has the first contact with a member of the system. Attempts to curb arrests of minority youth were also addressed in the *Final Report of the President's Task Force on 21st Century Policing* (2015), including the adoption of procedural justice and community-based policing approaches. At the same time, we cannot ignore the larger social problems that plague inner-city and disadvantaged communities. Here, greater discourse and partnership are needed between professionals and members of the community, where avenues for prevention and early intervention are created instead of imposing stricter social control and punitive measures such as arrest and confinement (Mooradian, 2010).

Narrowing the Net

While we will continue to monitor how youth of color are disproportionately arrested and incarcerated in the system, we must also turn to ways to reduce the harmful impacts of juvenile justice system intervention by limiting its reach. Remember that the majority of youth are processed in the system as juvenile delinquents or status offenders and that very few are serious or chronic offenders. "Status offense" is a very broad term. There are very different types of status offenses and offenders. Each may require a different kind of response. Status offenders' motives and intentions vary; some may resemble those of delinquent offenders while others do not. McNamara (2008) proposed dividing status offenders into three groups. The first is first-time status offenders. Their behavior may be a temporary, minor problem, and the experience of formal juvenile court involvement may only harm them, potentially increasing their problem behavior (Levin & Cohen, 2014). The second is chronic status offenders. These offenders are more problematic and may require more services, but it is still unwarranted to institutionalize them. Repeating a status offense may be due to a persistent external problem rather than criminal intent. For example, it may be expected that a child in a troubled home would run away more than once. Involvement with the juvenile correctional system will not solve their problems. The third is status and delinquent offenders. This category recognizes that youth with delinquency problems will also often engage in status offending. Responses to these offenders must, of course, include remedies for delinquent behavior.

One of the most important principles in juvenile justice is that young people should not have their lives ruined by what may be youthful indiscretions. As discussed earlier in this book, since juveniles are not fully mature, they are more likely to engage in harmful behavior out of temporary ignorance, poor judgment, or emotional impulses. This is why much of their offense details and system involvement are not matters of public record—so that they are not "labeled for life." Members of society find it difficult to embrace someone after they have seriously harmed another. It is understandable that victims and people close to them, especially, may desire that their offenders receive very harsh, long-term (maybe permanent) consequences. However, severe punitive punishment and labeling itself also have great social costs, especially considering that most offenders will remain in or return to our communities. This also contradicts our popular cultural value of forgiveness.

Perhaps it is time to be true to the principle of least intrusive (minimum) intervention (Smith, 2011), which also adheres to the Rights of the Child Treaty (United Nations, 1989). At each phase of justice system contact, decision-making should favor little or no involvement. Police officers might handle more cases informally. When cases must be referred to juvenile court, the court might divert them more often. When the courts must handle cases formally, community-based sanctions could be used more often, especially less punitive ones. When confinement is necessary, less restrictive environments could be used more, and the timely movement of residents out of placement could be emphasized more as a goal. Of course, law and policy would have to enable, if not require, authorities to have these leanings. Moreover, both punitive and rehabilitative policies and practices can widen the net of juvenile justice—they give us reasons to get more youth involved in the system and get them entrenched more deeply (Potter & Kakar, 2002).

Some states are now requiring juvenile sex offenders (JSO) to publicly register as sex offenders, a measure formerly reserved only for adult sex offenders (McNamara & Bucher, 2012). As mentioned in Chapter 5, JSOs tend to be much less violent and predatory and more amenable to treatment, compared to adult sex offenders. Thus, there may be no safety benefit to requiring JSOs to publicly register. Further, such labeling greatly interferes with treatment efforts, which are less likely to be effective when one is stigmatized by community members and denied educational, employment, and other opportunities to engage in productive, prosocial behavior. Sex offender registries have very wide nets (contain a wide range of minor to major offenders). Thus, minor JSOs who stand a high chance of desisting may be grouped in with adult rapists. Even more serious juvenile offenders who should be monitored into adulthood, who for instance should not be employed in childcare, could alternatively be kept off public registries and instead be identified in databases accessible only by necessary criminal justice and youth service authorities. Publicly registering JSOs may be yet another misguided "get tough" policy that results not only in a lack of practical benefits but perhaps public losses such as costs of maintaining registries and re-offending.

Not typically categorized as a status offense, consensual juvenile sexting may be considered one because it is not illegal for adults. "Consensual" here would mean that all parties are willing participants and are at about the same age and cognitive-emotional functioning level, and there is an absence of assaultive or exploitative behavior. Labeling these acts as sex offenses is questionable. For example, prosecuting a juvenile who sends a nude photo of oneself to a romantic partner as if they were the same as a child pornographer is unreasonable. Also, it seems unfair to expect juveniles to overcome the digital nature of modern society and the barrage of sexual imagery in entertainment and advertising to refrain from sexually expressing themselves through modern communication technology. Much juvenile sexting could even be an expression of normal sexual development that is just magnified by modern technology. Sexting can certainly be done without guilty intent. Some research suggests that most juveniles do not view sexting as seriously wrong and are unaware that sexting is illegal (Lamphere, 2014; Le et al., 2014).

Of course, consensual sexting could have very harmful consequences, so this is not to say that we should do nothing about it. Subjects may later regret the activity, especially when images of them somehow circulate to unintended audiences, and one's social and professional reputation suffers. Production and distribution of images may start out consensual but later become non-consensual, as when images are accidentally shared, stolen, or used by former friends and lovers as revenge. Also, sexting may not be as consensual as it seems. While flirting and fun are popular motives, some research also shows that peer pressure and coercion play a role, more so for girls (Lamphere, 2014). Some sexting could also be a form of risky behavior, related to activities such as unprotected sex, promiscuity, and substance abuse (Le et al., 2014). Thus, it may be in the public's interest to discourage sexting altogether.

To illustrate some of the problems inherent in the system even further, the status offense of truancy can be examined more closely. Truancy is formally defined as "habitual unexcused absences from school, exceeding the maximum set by state law" (Mallett, 2016, p. 339). As a category of youthful offending, truants are not a danger to society or themselves. In addition, even though most truants are less likely to step inside the walls of a secure facility, there are exceptions. The current mechanism in place is known as a valid court order (VCO). We hailed the Juvenile Justice and Delinquency Prevention Act of 1979 and the reauthorizations that followed as a starting point for decriminalizing status offenses, but by virtue of a congressional amendment in 1980, that effort was essentially railroaded when the valid court order rule was put into place. The exception allows "judges to confine status offenders in secure detention facilities for limited periods of time and to adjudicate a status offender as a delinquent if the status offender was found to violate a VCO" (Levin & Cohen, 2014, p. 4). In practice, a violation of a VCO is considered a technical violation where the juvenile did not comply with the probation conditions or the conditions that were set forth in an improvement period. It makes sense that if a juvenile violates the conditions, some type of punishment is necessary and must take place; the status offender was given a chance and did not follow the rules. However, is incarceration in a secure residential facility warranted in these cases? To some, only those youth who have exhibited a history of violent behavior or who have violated the VCO with a violent offense necessitate confinement. However, too many status offenders, like truants, may find themselves behind bars, because judges and/or the courts have found ways to bypass the system by either bootstrapping (e.g., raising the youth's status to a delinquent offense, especially for the repeated violation of the same offense) or claiming that the youth suffers from a mental illness (McNamara, 2008).

Given cases like these, many juvenile advocacy groups and non-profit agencies call for reforming the VCO exception. Sending kids to court for minor infractions is impractical and expensive. Also, system contact is stigmatizing and potentially marginalizing. Thus, the system may do more harm than good to environmentally disadvantaged youth with non-criminal behavior problems (Smith, 2011). To do this, states need support and technical assistance. Many non-profit agencies that advocate for youth have the resources to help. Confinement especially could be "taken off the table" for even repeated status offenses, given the lack of evidence showing that residential placement for status offenders helps them and reduces delinquency (McNamara, 2008). This change would eliminate the harm that confinement does to the youth as well as its financial costs. Of course, this recommendation would only apply to juveniles who only commit status offenses. A humane and just approach would incorporate community-based alternatives instead. Another effort to curb the number of truants who reach the juvenile court is for the school system and School Resource Officers to reexamine their zero-tolerance policies. For many youths, the school system is the point of first contact by which truancy is recognized. It does not help that the school's role in disciplinary practice has also become more punitive for minor juvenile indiscretions.

Social Justice for Youth: The Legal System and the Courts

As stated in Chapter 9, the juvenile justice system as a whole is quite remarkable. The first attempt at reforming the system began when Progressives paved the way to create a separate court in 1899 that was dedicated to protecting juveniles, serving their best interests, and providing them with appropriate treatment and rehabilitation services (Grisso, 2017). The design of the original juvenile court was not to follow the same principles of the adult court—seeking guilt or innocence or holding trials for that matter but instead was conceived with several diversionary mechanisms in place, where youth are sometimes given third and fourth chances before a sentence is handed to them (Platt, 2009).

As discussed in Chapter 7, in the 1960s and 1970s, the second wave of reform was punctuated by several United States Supreme Court decisions ensuring that youth were granted certain constitutional due process protections that were originally thought to apply to adults only (Grisso, 2017; Sarri & Shook, 2015). In brief, the Court recognized that youth have the right to be informed in a timely manner of the charges they face on a petition, the right to effective counsel, the right against self-incrimination, and the right to cross-examine witnesses (*In re Gault*, 1967). It was also upheld that youth must be afforded due process when transfer decisions are made to try a youth in criminal court (*Kent v. United States*, 1966). Moreover, the standard of proof was held as beyond a reasonable doubt for youth charged with delinquent offenses (*In re Winship*, 1970), and that youth have similar protections as adults in terms of the double jeopardy clause (*Breed v. Jones*, 1975). Unlike adults, however, youth do not have the same constitutional right to a jury trial (*McKeiver v. Pennsylvania*, 1971).

The twentieth century also ushered in additional and notable policies as outlined in the 1979 Juvenile Justice and Delinquency Prevention Act as well as significant decisions made by the Supreme Court that are indicative of a more "just" system. Falling in line with the Rights of the Child Treaty (United Nations, 1989), the death penalty for juveniles was abolished in 2005 (*Roper v. Simmons*), and five years later, in 2010, life without the possibility of parole for juveniles convicted of non-homicide crimes was abolished (*Graham v. Florida*). This movement was sparked by medical research, as discussed in Chapter 8, which clearly demonstrated that youth are still growing and developing physically, physiologically, and neurologically. Technologies have allowed us to conduct MRIs and brain scans, demonstrating a profound difference in the prefrontal cortex of a youth's brain versus an adult's brain (Blakemore, 2012). Behaviorally this research tells us that youth are more likely to engage in risky and thrill-seeking behaviors and are less likely to consider the consequences of their behavior. If we put our faith in medical research and science, then the bottom line is that a juvenile is not equivalent to a grown adult.

What we have left to address is the result of the reactionary legislation that was hinged on a spike in violent juvenile crime in the late 1980s and the way in which the

political pendulum swung from a treatment-oriented approach to one of punishment and retribution (Merlo & Benekos, 2003; Myers, 2005). The scare of a new generation of teenage super-predators did nothing but further the rhetoric that youth could not be rehabilitated by the juvenile system. The discourse that ensued led to a third wave of reform (Grisso, 2017). While Progressives attempted to remove juveniles from the adult system in the late nineteenth century, we created an avenue to return some of them back to criminal court to serve adult sentences in the late twentieth century. From this standpoint, juvenile waiver to criminal court certainly remains one of the chief concerns we have moving ahead.

Juvenile and Adult Court Jurisdiction

During the Middle Ages, it was believed that children by the age of seven could reason as adults (Sheldon & Vasiliev, 2018). There was no inclination that a period of adolescence existed somewhere in between. Infants simply evolved into miniature adults. Even though Roman law stated that children under the age of seven were immune from criminal responsibility, there were assumptions that young boys around the age of fourteen and young girls around the age of twelve were capable of knowing right from wrong (Menihan, 2014). These presumptions made their way eventually into English common law. It was deemed likewise that children under the age of seven could not be charged with a felony crime; youth over the age of fourteen were deemed adults in the eyes of the law. Menihan points out that there was also this gray area for youth between the ages of seven and fourteen. If it was found that the youth was capable of knowing right from wrong, then the youth was treated as an adult for their crime, and in some cases, even the death penalty was applied. During the time of our country's formation, we borrowed heavily from English common law to establish our laws and governance, adopting similar assumptions about youth culpability.

Jumping forward into the late 1980s and throughout much of the 1990s, states began expanding ways to legally transfer youth to adult court. Today, forty-four states specify that age seventeen is the maximum age for juvenile court jurisdiction. This means that the juvenile's case will fall under the purview of the juvenile court up until the youth's eighteenth birthday (National Conference of State Legislators, 2024). Despite these limits, state codes may stipulate transfer pathways to adult criminal court regardless of age based on the seriousness of the offense or other factors. Nonetheless, most youth who are judicially transferred to criminal court in the United States are sixteen years of age or older (Hockenberry & Puzzanchera, 2024). There are additional characteristics to make note of. Transferred youth are most commonly nonwhite males, and research in the early 1990s showed that the majority of transferred youth were facing charges for violent or personal crimes as opposed to property crimes, which is a trend still evident today. In brief, what we know is that offense seriousness and a youth's prior criminal record play a critical role in transfer decisions. Besides these two main factors, youth are also transferred to criminal court when they have lower levels of educational attainment and suffer from mental health issues. Research indicates that while probation is a very common outcome for youth who have been waived to adult court, this is true for most property offenders. However, sentences are shown to be longer for youth who commit violent offenses, and they are exceptionally longer than if these dispositions were imposed by the juvenile court.

Another way to put this issue to the test is to examine the deterrent effect of juvenile transfer. It seems logical that a punitive approach to managing violent youth could be supported by deterrence theory. If we punish the youth with transfer to adult court and charge the youth with an adult sentence, in theory, the youth will be deterred from future offenses (e.g., specific deterrence), and youth overall in the general population will be persuaded not to commit crimes either (e.g., general deterrence). These concepts fall in line with Becarria's philosophy, that in order for deterrence to be effective, punishment must be "swift, certain, and severe." Lawmakers during the "get tough" movement of the late 1980s and 1990s certainly adopted this line of thinking, especially the notion that punishments must be "severe" to produce some type of deterrent effect. On the contrary, the original school of deterrence thought does not maintain that the more severe the punishment the better. For example, these Classical School philosophers did not support the death penalty. Rather, they maintained that the punishment has to be just enough to make crime undesirable (certain and proportionate to the crime committed). Excessive punishment ("overkill") has no crime reduction value (it may even increase it). "Get tough" laws and policies (e.g., "three strikes" laws, mandatory sentences, juvenile waivers) might be based on the notion that more punishment will reduce crime. Those who favor a simple, consistent, "just desserts" model of justice may consider that draconian sentences and mass incarceration are not only costly and violate human rights principles, but they are inconsistent with deterrence theory.

Some argue that the use of general deterrence to support such policies suggests that we are willing to sacrifice the freedom and liberty of some youth to prevent other youth from committing crimes (Shireman & Reamer, 1986). In and of itself, however, deterrence should not be used as the basis for making policy decisions regarding youth. Stated more pointedly, "under what circumstances is democratic society justified in using the welfare of an individual as a means, rather than as an end, and thus imposing upon him as a means of influencing others?" (Shireman & Reamer, 1986, p. 64). Myers (2005) also explains that among the extant literature, there is a very small or moderate general deterrent effect when it comes to juvenile waiver laws. To account for some of the inconsistencies in previous research studies regarding juvenile transfer, Zane and colleagues (2016) conducted a meta-analysis and found that there was no specific deterrent effect regarding juvenile transfer. In fact, transfer policies may be responsible for increasing recidivism rates among these youthful offenders. If we were to support such policies, we would have to argue for retribution and punishment as the premier justification for upholding juvenile transfer laws—not deterrence.

On another note, it is easy to see that there remains great contradiction and hypocrisy when it comes to our legal age limits in general. In the United States, there are certain ages punctuated by rites of passage, signaling that a person has reached some benchmark of maturity and responsibility. In most states, a sixteen-year-old can drive a car, an eighteen-year-old can vote and join the army, and a twenty-one-year-old can celebrate these accomplishments legally by consuming alcohol. Even the employment of youth is federally restricted by age. In contrast, Chapter 9 presented the process of transferring a juvenile to adult court, and as stated earlier, most states do not specify any age limit for transfer but instead base the transfer on other factors such as the seriousness of the crime, which leaves the door open for judges and prosecutors to transfer certain cases at will. Moreover, depending on state code, some juveniles may be younger than the "age of majority" and still be transferred to criminal court. For example, there have been and are cases where ten-year-olds have been transferred to adult court. Yet, let us bear in mind the hypocrisy of this practice, knowing that in the United States a youth at age ten cannot drive, vote, join the army, or legally drink, but, in turn, a ten-year-old can be held criminally responsible for their actions and handed an adult sentence.

According to Seymour (2013), considering serious offending to be "grown-up" behavior is implausible. If anything, acting with extreme disregard toward others goes completely against our behavioral expectations of a mature, responsible adult. It seems that serious or chronic adolescent and young adult offenders would tend to be less cognitively, emotionally, and socially mature than their non-offending counterparts. Youth offenders are known to have poorer abilities to understand the consequences of their actions, interpret events and circumstances, respond to stimuli in socially acceptable ways, control their impulses, empathize with others, and make good life choices. Indeed, some studies associate psychosocial immaturity with antisocial decision-making, including among juveniles. Thus, serious violent offending may be seen as a sign of not being "an adult." As illustrated in Chapter 9, the push for juveniles to be treated more like adults may be producing more harm than good. While there may not be a problem in reserving adult treatment for the most chronic violent adolescent offenders, there is the potential that less severe juvenile offenders may be caught up in the widening net of treatment as adults.

Regardless, these harsh and punitive measures clearly go against the grain of the Rights of the Child Treaty (United Nations, 1989). The United Nations Committee on the Rights of the Child calls on each state within the United States to adopt legislation specifying the age of criminal responsibility to be between fourteen and sixteen years of age. On the other hand, the Inter-American Commission recommends that states adopt the age of eighteen as the limit for when children are held in the juvenile justice system. To this end, it is uncertain whether each state will adopt these recommended age limits. When it comes to serious youthful offending, the political game and a hyper-sensitive presentation of youthful behavior by the media appear to trump the rights of the child even though research clearly shows that youth who are tried in adult court and who serve adult time are no more rehabilitated or deterred from future crimes than youth who are disposed in the juvenile system (IACHR, 2018). Sarri and Shook (2015) place this into greater context by stating:

> even if we determine that human rights standards should allow for transfer in the limited situations where children are not appropriate for juvenile court treatment, the current situation in the U.S. is well beyond this state. It is a situation where children are treated as adults without clear standards or rationale, clearly in violation of human rights provisions that seek to treat children differently and in the least restrictive way possible. (p. 17)

Social Justice for Youth: Corrections

Correctional reform for youth took hold in the early 1800s in cities like New York, Philadelphia, and Boston (Hess et al., 2013). As stated in Chapter 7, the very first and most well-known reformatory was the House of Refuge, which was opened in New York in 1825. Some of these reform movements were led by upper-class Protestants and other Progressives who were disturbed by the number of wayward and orphaned youth who were plaguing the streets and spiraling deeper into vice. Even more so, child advocates believed it was best to place troubled and orphaned youth in a house of refuge or workhouse where they could learn a respectable trade and adopt a pious lifestyle. Reform schools brought forth the notion that youth also needed to learn the Bible but in an environment that instilled harsh discipline. Even though these were the leading correctional reforms in the 1800s and early 1900s, and meant well, these approaches did little to curb juvenile delinquency or to rehabilitate juveniles, for that matter.

Over time, reform schools transformed into training schools and industrial homes with an emphasis on education and treatment-oriented practice (Sheldon & Vasiliev, 2018). Some of the facilities were developed under a family-style or cottage-style model, holding up to twenty to forty youths. Administrative authority fell into the hands of state and local government instead of philanthropic organizations. Youth were also placed in separate facilities based on gender. However, these facilities were not without problems either. Despite the fact that standards and legal codes were imposed to make youth facilities safe and to increase educational standards, these reform schools and industrial homes were still very punitive in nature, relied heavily on the contract labor system, and did little for youth of color, who were often kept in adult facilities as they were deemed to be unamenable to treatment.

In the twenty-first century, we are still having to address the harms of institutionalizing youth as we did almost two centuries ago. On one hand, however, we have made some strides with creating separate juvenile correctional facilities and juvenile detention facilities and adopting more widespread community corrections alternatives, such as probation. As we stand today, we are still combatting issues related to solitary confinement of youth, a lack of proper education, a lack of specialized medical attention for youth with special needs or diagnosed psychological conditions, and a disproportionate number of youth of color who are sentenced to a residential facility (as described in Chapter 10). None of these problems has been completely extinguished in youth residential facilities and many of these problems are beyond the scope of the chapter. What follows is a critical examination of the damaging effects of labeling and assessing at-risk youth in the context of rehabilitation, along with a discussion about institutional maltreatment of youth and professional misconduct.

Labeling, Exclusion, and Discrimination

Pursuing social justice is more than just rejecting harsh and punitive beliefs, attitudes, policies, and practices. Injustice can also be found in the pursuit of rehabilitation. Treatment is often based on the identification of delinquency risk factors that exist in a juvenile's life. Such risk assessment instruments were described in Chapter 10. While this practice assists probation officers and correctional staff in determining how to help youth, it also possesses several flaws and failings, namely excluding sociostructural factors from the assessment that impact a youth's life and contribute to the risk of delinquency (Smith, 2011).

Goddard and Myers (2016) argue that the system has become too dependent upon the use of risk assessments, which have been hailed as the best examples of evidence-based practice in the twenty-first century. It is true that psychometric risk assessments are grounded in theory, validated, and have been shown to reduce subjective decisions by youth practitioners, yet the issue at stake is that these assessments take into consideration many individual factors/life domains to determine a youth's level of risk that are riddled with racial bias and inequality. For example, some domains include family relations, companions, education/employment, history of perpetration, and history of incarceration. At first glance, it does not seem plausible to suggest that these domains are fraught with bias, although what is inadvertently factored into the equation is how some of these domains of a youth's life are directly impacted or influenced by socioeconomic factors such as poverty, homelessness, and parental incarceration—factors that are beyond a youth's control. Assessing risk level (e.g., high-risk, medium-risk, low-risk) in turn is then ultimately elevated for impoverished youth and youth of color as opposed to white, suburban, or upper-class youth, who may not face the same social constraints or social inequalities. There is a hidden bias where youth of color will also have higher risk scores as they live in areas that are more subject to police presence and increased police contacts. This translates to a juvenile who is not in essence "a bad kid" but who may be classified as "at-risk" because one faces such circumstances.

The other part of fourth-generation risk assessments is to match youth to proper programs, interventions, and treatment services. Youth in the higher-risk categories are generally seen to be in more need of intervention services. While those such as counseling and residential placement may have the best of intentions behind them, they are often, in reality, stigmatizing and punitive. Youth who are being "helped" by juvenile services understand that they are "in trouble." It is therefore possible that youth from bad neighborhoods and homes receive more intrusive sanctions than those who are not so unlucky, even if their actual behavior is about the same. Moreover, Goddard and Myers (2016) also point out that there is an over-emphasis on programming that serves only to address individual factors (treating the "sick" individual) instead of community-level factors (treating the "sick" society). Repair and programming for the community with respect to poverty, homelessness, gang activity, drug addiction, and violence (the "roots of crime," which all contribute to a marginalized youth's risk score) are simply ignored.

Another related problem lies with the issue that the at-risk label may be a way of telling youth "you don't belong here." Youth understand that being classified as at-risk means that authorities believe that they might be likely to keep offending, which is counter-productive if some decide to "accept the label." Recalling labeling theory, definitions of persons give us cues as to how to interpret their behavior. Once youth are labeled deviant—delinquent, antisocial, behavior disordered—their behavior is more likely to be viewed by others (in the community and juvenile justice system) as bad and indicative of their malady. However, much of the behavior of "at-risk youth" could be harmless or the same as that committed by youth who are not labeled deviant—for instance middle-class youth in "good" neighborhoods and homes. Risk assessment creates a double standard between socio-economically disadvantaged and advantaged juvenile offenders (Goddard & Myers, 2016). With problems such as this, the juvenile correctional system, which is meant to be rehabilitative and supportive, marginalizes youth (Smith, 2011).

The discussion earlier in this chapter centered on law enforcement and their interactions with youth, yet it is important to recognize that racial and ethnic disparities can be perpetuated by experiences that occur after youth of color have become deeply involved with the system, in residential placement, for instance. Here, marginalization and discrimination can, again, occur at multiple social levels. At the interpersonal level, some youth workers may have tendencies to treat nonwhite youth more coercively and punitively than white youth, which makes juvenile justice appear illegitimate to youth (Durán, 2012). At the institutional level, white youth and youth of color often have different criminogenic backgrounds, and programs may not be designed specifically enough to improve minorities' ties to family and community, such as through mentoring (Penn, 2012). The result is that the quality of treatment becomes lower for nonwhite youth, who then become more likely to resist treatment, re-offend, and remain in the system.

There are other more overt ways in which Black and Hispanic youth may be treated unfairly in the correctional system. For example, what may exacerbate a staff member's frustration with youth is when a youth acts up or misbehaves. Given what we know about adolescence, it makes perfect sense that youth are going to misbehave and display general discord and sassiness. As a result, a series of miscommunications can creep into staff and youth lives. From the youth's point of view, simple adolescence is one way to explain misbehaving. Another way is by using control balance theory (Tittle, 2004). It is possible that social control (from staff) can be too high, assuming the deficit is substantial and truly exists beyond the individual's perception (i.e., one really is being deprived of autonomy). In certain contexts of juvenile corrections, a certain amount of social control is of course necessary (to keep individuals from causing harm to others or even themselves). To be happy and productive, however, individuals, including children, must possess a great deal of freedom and autonomy. Conceivably, we could produce inappropriate behavior in children by giving them too little control over their every decision making. For instance, this might especially be a problem for institutionalized youth, who get little say over their daily routines. When they misbehave violently, for example, we may assume that the behavior is due to the personal and social factors that led to their placement. While this might be true, it might also be true that the misbehavior is at least partly due to a control deficit caused by institutionalization itself. If a resident becomes discontent with continually being told what to eat, when to wake up and when to go to sleep, and when to go outside and swears at staff, the resident does not necessarily have "anger management issues." It could be that no one, troubled child or not, is naturally accustomed to such control.

Institutional Maltreatment and Professional Misconduct

Both overt and subtle forms of maltreatment exist within our juvenile correctional system. Some youth experience victimization at the hands of a staff member. In a study of state, private, and local juvenile correctional facilities in the entire country, Beck and Rantala (2016) found that there were 1,478 allegations of sexual victimization. Almost a third of these allegations were of staff sexually abusing or harassing the juvenile offender. The rates of sexual abuse are even more staggering when youth are held in adult prisons (IACHR, 2018). That is, youth are "five times more likely to suffer sexual abuse or rape in an adult facility as compared to those held in juvenile facilities, are more likely to be abused by correctional staff and to witness or be the target of violence committed by other prisoners, and have a 50% higher chance of being attacked with a weapon" (IACHR, 2018, p. 11). Rates of abuse also increase the likelihood of suicide and self-injurious behaviors. Additionally, the IACHR observed that in adult facilities, children are subjected to inappropriate use of force by correctional staff, which creates a general climate of fear and dehumanization and are routinely held in solitary confinement, depriving them of physical exercise, education, human contact, and access to mental health services.

Another part of the problem may lie with the fact that employees are reluctant to report misconduct by other employees because of stressful conditions, a defensive staff subculture, and fear of retaliation. It is important to consider that employees work under threats of being harmed by some youth, through physical violence or false complaints, for example. In these types of situations, correctional workers rely on one another to "survive" the work environment—to control youth, look out for each other, and maintain their employment. Indeed, they must work together, very cooperatively, to do their jobs. Under stressful conditions, employees develop "us vs. them" attitudes, for example, staff vs. youth or even staff vs. administration. Also under these conditions, employees may believe that some misconduct is necessary to keep young people in line and to protect themselves.

Since employees must rely on each other for protection from attacks, it is plausible that one may witness misconduct by another employee but be reluctant to report it because one needs that person to "have your back." In the future, the other employee may be less willing to assist during a physical altercation with a youth, and other employees may also act coercively toward the reporting employee because they were disloyal to the group. Additionally, one may feel guilty about "telling" on someone whom one empathizes and identifies with—someone who faces the same work challenges. The offending employee may even be a friend. In practice, reporting another employee for misconduct can indeed be met with hostility, even from supervisors. In one practical setting, Durán (2012) observed that some youth workers subscribed to a "code of silence," whereby they withheld vital information perceived as threatening

to their cohesive group (the staff), demonstrated loyalty to the group (which included "punishment" for those who did not), and felt that they must do whatever is needed to protect the group.

In sum, there are significant and numerous social justice and human rights concerns when it comes to assessing and treating youth and managing youth in juvenile and adult residential facilities. As stated by the Juvenile Justice Reform Act and the IACHR (2018), the primary solution is one of decarceration, and it is a solution that is supported by research evidence (Bonnie et al., 2013) and as described by the Annie E. Casey's Juvenile Detention Alternatives Initiative (JDAI) in Chapter 9. The use of community-based programs has been shown to reduce recidivism as opposed to institutional confinement. In addition, programs are needed to combat and target racial inequality, poverty, and homelessness to strengthen and improve our communities. When it comes to risk assessments, it is time to reexamine how they may be used as instruments of oppression (Goddard & Myers, 2016). Unfair treatment of marginalized youth exacerbates the youth's behavior and is likely to fuel problematic behaviors, thereby increasing rates of reoffending. When and if youth are placed in a residential facility, mechanisms are needed to increase reporting among employees; a subculture that applies group pressure to accept and even use misconduct must be replaced with one that applies group pressure to refrain from misconduct and report it when it does occur. To ensure fair and humane practice with juveniles, the IACHR (2018) recommends that when youth violate criminal law, they should only be punished in proportion to the crime they committed, and confinement needs to be used only as a last resort when all other diversionary or community-based options have been exhausted.

Peacemaking Justice

Our juvenile justice system is, at best, helpful but imperfect, and, at worst, ineffective and unjust. Instead of just repairs, maybe it needs an overhaul. Piecemeal changes will have little or limited impact if the system contains major fundamental flaws. Improving rehabilitation procedures alone will produce limited results. The problem with making internal repairs to the system is that they often focus on what is wrong with offenders, and what can be done better to change them (whether through treatment or punishment), not what is wrong with the system or society itself. When juveniles re-offend, we may simply assume it is because of what is wrong with them, failing to consider that our system is at least partially to blame.

Restorative justice practices as discussed in Chapter 10, for example, are a possible solution. However, programs that embrace this philosophy will do little good if they are housed in a system that is punitive and based on draconian practices that do little to rehabilitate a growing child. In practice, restorative justice programs may focus only on offender responsibility and making amends, values that do not stray far from punitive ideology, while ignoring other important principles such as human rights, collaboration, and healing (Smith, 2011). Thus, broader societal changes are also needed. One way, albeit unconventional, is to make these changes by adopting a peacemaking approach.

Peacemaking criminology is most commonly known as a critical theoretical perspective, situated in a variety of spiritual and religious orientations, namely Buddhism, Hinduism, and Christianity (Klenowski, 2009; Quinney, 1991). Unlike criminological and sociological theories that are based on a set of concrete concepts or propositions, peacemaking is embedded in a belief system that is made up of a set of interrelated principles or core values. Understanding these principles requires a person to think outside the box and to release pre-conceived notions about how best to resolve the crime problem, such as those in existence that involve imposing harsh laws and rules, carrying out these laws within a complex web known as the justice system, and driving and informing these processes by misguided politics. For the sake of ease, the peacemaking orientation will be explained using three main overarching principles.

First, those who follow a peacemaking approach are committed to a society of non-violence and compassion (Fuller, 2003; Quinney, 1991). The history of the United States and even modern-day events have been fraught with "war-making" rather than "peace-making" (Pepinsky, 1999). As a society, we have been known to create initiatives that stimulate agitation and deepen feelings of anger, despair, and hostility. There are many wars to fight—the war on poverty, the war on drugs, the war on terror, and so on. However, we are no closer to ending these wars than when we started them. Moreover, wars incite violence and do not lend themselves to any peaceful resolution that is just or humane. As violence brings on suffering, more suffering brings resentment, furthering the potential for more violence. This never-ending cycle of violence is what disciples of peacemaking seek to correct and prevent.

Second, peacemaking involves an acute awareness of harm and human suffering. For instance, we must face the harsh reality that anywhere from 81% to 93% of detained female juveniles in some states have been prior victims of physical or sexual abuse themselves (Saar et al., 2015). In terms of sexual abuse, research also shows that delinquent girls experience such abuse at a very young age and endure the abuse for a longer duration of time compared to boys. The implication is that the trauma from abuse leads to involvement in future crime and delinquency. We have to ask ourselves when was justice served for these young people when they were victims and before they turned to deviant or delinquent lifestyles? The answer is that they probably never saw justice or even got the chance to begin the healing process or for justice to serve them. This means that we bring into the fold youth who have a history of past victimization that has been unaddressed, but now we are expected to impose undue social control and harsh punitive measures upon them. For peacemaking, a deeper inspection of such criminal justice practices reveals that this only breeds more suffering, deepens the likelihood of oppression, and perpetuates reoffending. In the end, the peacemaking practice calls for a mindful approach to such suffering that is dedicated to strengthening a shared value system of connectedness that is dedicated to caring and nurturing the individual who is suffering and who has been broken, but whom no one has attempted to repair.

Third, following this tradition requires letting go of ego-driven approaches and impulses and turning to methods and solutions that are driven by social justice (Klenowski, 2009; Quinney, 1991). Peacemakers are devoted to promoting peace, consciousness-raising, and spiritual and human transformation. Peacemaking activists call for policies that uphold and respect human rights. Policies that maintain a human rights position are constructed and implemented in such a way that they eliminate harm, eliminate suffering, and eliminate injustice. As a result, the adoption of a peacemaking approach falls in line with meeting the provisions set forth by the *Convention on the Rights of the Child*. It would also greatly improve the juvenile justice system in the United States by addressing numerous human rights concerns outlined by the IACHR (2018) and other advocacy groups.

The current system is undeniably imperfect and there is still much work to be done. This is primarily due to the fact that the system is not completely enclosed; it is embedded in its wider society. To some extent, what is wrong with the system is what is wrong with society. We cannot ignore the early stages of problematic juvenile behavior, but perhaps the community should take charge of interventions instead of just relying on the justice system to solve these problems. Smith (2011) argues that juvenile justice should be kept local, meaning that most interventions should be truly grounded in the community—not just delivered in the community but owned and led by groups and organizations that are not part of the formal justice system. The actors here could include the schools, prosocial peer groups, private non-profit restorative justice groups, and other civic groups. For example, these groups could work with families, neighbors, and youth when disorderly conduct (e.g., loud noise, harassment, vandalism) is noticed to be a problem in the community. Of course, "interventions" here do not include intervening in dangerous situations, which must be left up to formal authorities.

As we have seen, there are a myriad of issues on the table, including but not limited to racial and ethnic disparities, net widening, transfer of youth to adult court and prison, labeling and exclusion, discrimination, institutional maltreatment, and professional misconduct. A number of these issues have been attributed to politicizing delinquency, racial inequality, and the harms of poverty, among others. It behooves us to examine each of these issues further using a different lens. Using a criminological lens has been the tradition, although this has not advanced our juvenile justice system in ways that have eliminated the injustice that many youths continue to endure (Capeheart & Milovanic, 2007). It is time to step outside from this myopic approach and consider other orientations to examine juvenile injustice. This opens the door for considering peacemaking criminology as the mechanism by which we further our understanding of these injustices and use the principles embedded within it to end the suffering and inhumane practices that have fallen on our youth. We also need to adopt a model that will empower youth, not encourage them to be passive recipients of help or view themselves negatively. Many lead advocacy groups in our country have taken on ending the suffering of youth and unfair and inhumane practices. Until we can agree on a model to examine the problems inherent in the juvenile justice system, we rely heavily on the work of these advocates.

Advocacy

With a peacemaking approach in mind, it is helpful to examine how advocacy groups for youth are addressing many of the issues outlined by the Rights of the Child Treaty and the IACHR (2018) firsthand. What can be seen next is how peacemaking and social justice concerns can be put into practice. A humane and just system is what many reformers wanted for children over a century ago. Reformers are still at work today, and while we do not refer to them as "child savers" per se, it is worth noting that they are saving children and youth from the egregious harms and inequality in our justice system that still prevail.

There are numerous child advocacy groups in the United States. Beyond the organizations mentioned in this chapter, firmly established organizations like the Social Work-Child Welfare League, the American Bar Association, the American Psychological Association, the American Pediatric Association, and the American Civil Liberties Union have argued tirelessly for youth rights. **Advocacy** can take on many forms, and given what has been addressed in this chapter, it entails identifying problems, protecting human rights, and serving as a voice or representative for children and young people who are powerless and in need. The efforts described below showcase how advocacy can be administrative-based (where states and non-profit agencies seek to identify problems and solve them), legal-based (allowing for the constitutional rights of juveniles to be fought for and upheld), or community-based (where efforts are furnished from the ground level or local level, involving teachers, families, and religious groups) (Ezell, 2001). A final take-home message is that the efforts carried out by these organizations also demonstrate how we can get involved to improve and reform our juvenile justice system.

Annie E. Casey Foundation

The Annie E. Casey Foundation (2024) is one of the largest philanthropic organizations devoted to advocating for child welfare in the United States. The foundation was created by James E. Casey in 1948 in honor of his mother, who devoted her life to children in the foster care system. Today, the foundation is comprised of several key strategy areas, some of which encompass child welfare, community change, equity and inclusion, evidence-based practice, and leadership development. In the strategy area of juvenile justice, the foundation is devoted to diversion and prevention, reducing youth incarceration, and seeking alternatives to detention—also known as the Juvenile Detention Alternatives Initiative (JDAI) (as discussed in Chapter 9). JDAI includes assisting counties throughout the United States with training and technical assistance, including best practices for reform and assessment.

The Children's Defense Fund

The Children's Defense Fund (CDF) (n.d.) is a national, non-profit organization that was created shortly after the Civil Rights Movement, in 1973, by activist and attorney Marian Wright Edelman. Today, the organization boasts a headquarters located in Washington, DC, along with legislators and advocates stationed at several satellite offices around the country. The defense fund advocates for the rights and well-being of children, and included in their vision is to ensure that marginalized children and youth flourish and that leaders in the community ensure that their well-being is a priority. The organization specializes in providing each child with a healthy start, a head start, a fair start, a safe start, and a moral start in life. Also, the CDF focuses on several key areas, including child health and healing, early childhood development, civic and work life education, family stability and economic mobility, and just and caring communities. They are also committed to a podcast series titled, "Young People Lead." Currently, one of their main ongoing initiatives includes the CDF Freedom Schools program, which promotes literacy, cultural enrichment, and various efforts to address child poverty, gun violence, and the school-to-prison pipeline.

Coalition for Juvenile Justice

The Coalition for Juvenile Justice (n.d.) was established in 1984 and is a national entity comprised of state advisory groups. The coalition principally assists each state advisory group to ensure that youth are diverted from the formal trappings of the system and are handled with the utmost care when managed by the justice system. Essentially, the coalition seeks to assist states in making sure that they are compliant with the core protections as stated in the Juvenile Justice Reform Act. Using evidence-based research as a way to inform policy decisions, the coalition relies on ten core principles to improve the justice system for youth. They are: ensure school engagement; promote the role of prevention; engage youth, family, and community; divert youth from the justice system; reduce institutionalization; eliminate racial and ethnic disparities; ensure access to quality counsel; create a range of effective community-based programs; recognize and serve youth with specialized needs; provide small rehabilitative facilities; improve aftercare and reentry, and keep youth out of adult courts, jails, and prisons. In the end, the organization's overall vision is to reduce the future risk of delinquency and for those delinquent youth who are in the system, to ensure that the process provides safe and healthy alternatives for youth and their families.

Juvenile Law Center

The Juvenile Law Center (2024) was founded in 1975 by four Temple Law School graduates in Philadelphia. The organization is a national, non-profit law firm with a primary focus on advocating for the legal rights of juveniles in the welfare and justice systems. Originally, the group sought to tackle legal rights issues on a smaller scale, but then it turned to address the larger systemic problems throughout the justice system that impact youth around the country by calling for action by the U.S. Supreme Court. To date, the Juvenile Law Center has been instrumental in cases like *Roper v. Simmons* (2005), *Graham v. Florida* (2010), *J.D.B. v. North Carolina* (2011), *Miller v. Alabama* (2012), and *Montgomery v. Louisiana* (2016). Nearly two decades ago, the center played a pivotal role in breaking the *Kids for Cash* scandal, which involved Judge Michael Conahan and Judge Mark Ciavarella in Luzerne County, Pennsylvania. From 2003 to 2008, Judge Ciavarella ordered over 2,000 juveniles to a secure confinement facility, while the judges received $2.2 million dollars in private kickbacks (Getlen, 2014). Fifty percent of the youth who met with the judge did not have any legal representation and were incarcerated for minor offenses. Today, the center remains one of the most recognizable child advocacy leaders in legal reform and for advancing the human rights of youth. They represent youth who have experienced some form of injustice in the juvenile system, youth held in adult prisons, and foster care youth.

National Youth Justice Network

Created in 2005, the National Juvenile Justice Network, now known as the National Youth Justice Network (2025), is a national reform organization dedicated to transforming the juvenile justice system to ensure fairness and equity for all youth. Their mission is to advocate for fair and humane laws, policies, and practices, focusing on the well-being of youths and their families. They serve a diverse group of youth, including those who are disproportionately affected by the justice system, such as youth of color, LGBTQ+ youth, and those from low-income backgrounds. The justice network prides itself on policy and advocacy strategies, transformative leadership by way of their Youth

Justice Leadership Institute, and narrative organizing, which encompasses a shared vision of change and building that change in state and local communities. The organization is dedicated to several key values, which include anti-racism, intersectionality, shifting power, dignity for all youth, community, transformation, and integrity. Today, there are approximately sixty-three member associations across the country.

The Gault Center

The Gault Center (2024), formerly known as the National Juvenile Defender Center, is a nonprofit organization committed to promoting justice for all children by ensuring excellence in youth defense. In 1997, the center began as a project linked to the American Bar Association as a response to address many of the inadequate legal services provided to youth. In 2005, the center separated from the ABA, and in 2022 it took on the name The Gault Center. Their mission is to advocate for a robust youth defense system that provides skilled, well-resourced, and well-trained lawyers to represent juveniles. Similar to many of the efforts discussed in this chapter, the center believes that every child in the legal system deserves the full protection of their constitutional, statutory, and human rights. In turn, they believe in a client-centered, individualized, and developmentally appropriate legal representation, free of bias. In addition, The Gault Center serves to dismantle systemic barriers that impede high-quality representation and barriers that contribute to the disproportionate representation of vulnerable and unserved youth in the juvenile justice system. In brief, they also offer policy development, litigation support, training, and assessment of the juvenile court systems to ensure that young people are fairly and justly represented in the court.

Ending Thoughts

In 2018, the IACHR commented on the current state of affairs for children in the United States, calling for the country to adhere to the international standards and principles of serving the best interests of the child. In essence, the United States was called upon to confirm that the juvenile justice system ensures that rehabilitation remains a priority for youth who are placed in detention while balancing the needs of societal protection; creating a uniform justice system across all levels of jurisdiction across the nation; upholding the constitutional rights of a youth; remaining dedicated to monitoring the current system; evaluating the current system; and making sure that the rights of youth remain at the forefront during these reviews. Moreover, the commission identified the need to develop public policies to protect public safety that do not rely heavily on law enforcement agencies and the criminal justice system. Specifically, the IACHR outlined eleven specific recommendations to the U.S. government. When it comes to juveniles in the justice system, a few of these recommendations are nothing new and echo similar provisions that were stated in the 2018 reauthorization of the Juvenile Justice and Delinquency Prevention Act (now the Juvenile Justice Reform Act), which include:

- implementing legislation guaranteeing access to all persons 18 or younger to the juvenile justice system
- ending the practice of detaining children with adults
- ensuring specialized procedures to protect the due process needs of children
- providing monitoring and protections in the interim for those children kept in adult facilities. (p. 382)

Advocates are still at work to see to it that youth are treated with dignity and respect and afforded universal and constitutional rights that they are entitled to. Policy developments are in place to divert youth out of the system, to uphold youth rights, and to recognize the developmental differences between juveniles and adults, but even though we have made some progress, there is still much more to do. Grisso (2017) frames this reform movement as "fourth wave reform." Unlike the third reform movement of the 1980s and 1990s that sought to punish youth, this reform effort is one that "offers a developmentally appropriate way to assure public safety and the positive growth of adolescents, whose offending most often is a consequence of their immaturity" (p. 2).

In summary and upon review of the existing literature, it is clear that the juvenile justice system is still the most appropriate venue for managing status offenders and delinquents, even though some have called for totally abolishing the juvenile court altogether (Feld, 1999). Reform efforts demand that we abandon the philosophy of retribution in the juvenile justice system and use incarceration as the last resort. The use of community-based interventions needs to be more widespread as they are the most practical, cost-effective, and least stigmatizing ways to assist at-risk youth. The quality of care for youth in residential facilities needs to be improved, including limited to no use of solitary confinement. Youth of color or other marginalized groups, such as those who suffer from mental illness, must be treated fairly (Barkan, 2019). Agencies at all levels of jurisdiction need to end racial discrimination and maltreatment of youth. We must also provide early intervention and family support services and incorporate the community into these processes as well. Last, it is imperative that a culture of advocacy is continued and promoted (Dalrymple, 2004), and in turn that we seek solutions that consider the social, political, and developmental factors that impact youth and crime, and in the context of human rights, awareness of suffering, and social justice. On the horizon still lies a fair and just juvenile system that is certainly within our reach.

Summary Points

- The *Convention on the Rights of the Child* was passed by 190 United Nations members in 1989, providing a comprehensive and international framework for countries to comply with regarding basic rights for children, such as the rights to health care, education, and privacy. Even though the United States signed the treaty, it is the only country that has not ratified the treaty to date.

- It is faulty to assume that justice will prevail using a criminal justice approach alone. Instead, a social justice approach is needed, which entails an examination of what is fair and what is just for both society and the individual as society continues to evolve.
- A human rights approach is also necessary when examining the "justness" of our juvenile justice system. Human rights are a set of basic entitlements or privileges fundamental to the human condition, which should not be denied based on one's national origin, race, culture, sex, or creed.
- Social justice and human rights concerns must remain at the forefront of police organizations. For example, police departments and local jurisdictions need to address reform efforts when it comes to racial and ethnic disparities. Situations and practices that invite racial discrimination, institutional discrimination, and racial prejudice must also remain at the top of the list when it comes to reform. In addition, departments and local jurisdictions, including schools, are urged to examine the ways in which status offenders, youth with mental illness, and nonwhite youth are caught in the wider net for minor infractions and by the use of zero-tolerance policies.
- Over the years, the U.S. Supreme Court has made it clear that juveniles are afforded many of the same constitutional rights as adults. However, our court system and processing are not without their failings. Even though most youth are diverted away from the system or placed on probation, many juveniles are still waived to criminal court and given adult sentences. Although these youth must be sanctioned for their violent crimes, the research shows that the use of adult sanctions for juveniles is ineffective as a deterrent. Moreover, the use of such harsh penalties violates a youth's human rights.
- Even though juvenile corrections has undergone widespread change and reform, the system is still plagued with many problems. Youth are still placed in solitary confinement, and a disproportionate number of minority youth are placed in residential facilities. Risk assessment tools, which appear to be value-neutral, have built-in racial and economic biases that need to be accounted for. In regard to treatment and corrections, youth of color are subject to further discrimination and maltreatment, and ultimately, they are not provided the same quality of care as their white counterparts. In addition, some correctional staff members have been prone to abuse youth physically, emotionally, and sexually.
- A peacemaking approach is a good fit when addressing reform in the juvenile justice system. This perspective is committed to non-violence, awareness of harm and human suffering, and the adoption of policies that are driven by social justice and human rights.
- Numerous youth advocacy organizations in the United States are dedicated to working with state legislators to improve the legal code and practices, to change federal policies, to raise awareness, and to seek justice for youth who have been denied a fair process in the justice system.

Key Terms

Advocacy: identifying problems, protecting human rights, and serving as a voice or representative for an individual who is powerless and in need.

Human Rights: fundamental entitlements that are granted to each person regardless of national origin, race, culture, sex, or creed.

Institutional Discrimination: "racial and ethnic disparities in outcomes that are the result of the application of racially neutral factors" (Walker et al., 2018, p. 28).

Racial Discrimination: treating an individual differently, such as denying rights or opportunities, based on a person's race or ethnicity.

Racial Prejudice: negative attitudes or perceptions about another social category of individuals based on their race or ethnicity.

Social Justice: a concept about raising awareness about what is fair and what is just for both society and the individual, while recognizing that society is in a never-ending process of growth and change.

References

Alexander, M. (2012). *The new Jim Crow: Mass incarceration in the age of colorblindness*. The New Press.

Annie E. Casey Foundation. (2024). *Our big ideas are building a brighter future for America's children, youth, and families*. https://www.aecf.org/

Attiah, K. (2014, November 21). Why won't the U.S. ratify the U.N.'s child rights treaty? *The Washington Post*. https://www.washingtonpost.com/blogs/post-partisan/wp/2014/11/21/why-wont-the-u-s-ratify-the-u-n-s-child-rights-treaty/?noredirect=on&utm_term=.792784c60a27

Barkan, S. E. (2019). *Race, crime, and justice: The continuing American dilemma*. Oxford University Press.

Beck, A. J., & Rantala, R. (2016). *Sexual victimization reported by juvenile correctional authorities, 2007–12*. U.S. Department of Justice, Office of Justice Programs, Bureau of Justice Statistics. https://bjs.ojp.gov/content/pub/pdf/svrjca0712.pdf

Blakemore, S. J. (2012). Imaging brain development: The adolescent brain. *Neuroimage, 61*(2), 397–406. https://doi.org/10.1016/j.neuroimage.2011.11.080

Bonnie, R. J., Johnson, R. L., Chemers, B. M., & Schuck, J. (2013). *Reforming juvenile justice: A developmental approach*. National Academy of Sciences, National Academy Press.

Bostic, J. Q., Thurau, L., Potter, M., & Drury, S. S. (2014). Policing the teen brain. *Journal of the American Academy of Child & Adolescent Psychiatry, 53*(2), 127–129. https://doi.org/10.1016/j.jaac.2013.09.021

Breed v. Jones, 421 U.S. 519 (1975).

Capeheart, L., & Milovanovic, D. (2007). *Social justice: Theories, issues, and movements.* Rutgers University Press.

Children's Defense Fund. (n.d.). Origins and evolution of the CDF freedom schools® program and movement. https://www.childrensdefense.org/our-work/cdf-freedom-schools/cdf-freedom-schools-history/

Coalition for Juvenile Justice. (n.d.). *About us.* http://www.juvjustice.org/

Dalrymple, J. (2004). Constructions of child and youth advocacy: Emerging issues in advocacy practice. *Children and Society, 19,* 3–15. http://dx.doi.org/10.1002/chi.828

Durán, R. J. (2012). An attempt to change disproportionate minority contact by working with youth in corrections. In L. M. Johnson (Ed.), *Experiencing corrections: From practitioner to professor* (pp. 149–164). Sage.

Ezell, M. (2001). *Advocacy in the human services.* Cengage.

Feld, B. (1999). *Bad kids: Race and the transformation of the juvenile court.* Oxford University Press.

Fuller, J. (2003). Peacemaking criminology. In M. D. Schwartz & S. E. Hatty (Eds.), *Controversies in critical criminology* (pp. 85–95). Anderson.

The Gault Center. (2024). *History.* https://www.defendyouthrights.org/about/history/

Getlen, L. (2014, February 23). Corrupt "kids for cash" judge ruined more than 2,000 lives. *New York Post.* https://nypost.com/2014/02/23/film-details-teens-struggles-in-state-detention-in-payoff-scandal/

Goddard, T., & Myers, R. R. (2016). Against evidence-based oppression: Marginalized youth and the politics of risk-based assessment and intervention. *Theoretical Criminology, 21*(2), 151–167. http://dx.doi.org/10.1177/1362480616645172

Graham v. Florida, 560 U.S. 48 (2010).

Grisso, T. (2017). *Policy brief: Assuring the future of developmental reform in juvenile justice: Recommendation of the fourth wave forecasting project.* Models for Change, MacArthur Foundation. http://www.modelsforchange.net/publications/856

Hess, K. M., Orthmann, C. H., & Wright, J. P. (2013). *Juvenile justice.* Wadsworth /Cengage.

Hockenberry, S., & Puzzanchera, C. (2024). *Juvenile court statistics 2022.* National Center for Juvenile Justice. Office of Juvenile Justice and Delinquency Prevention. https://ojjdp.ojp.gov/publications/juvenile-court-statistics-2022.pdf

Ife, J. (2005). Human rights and critical social work. In S. Hick, J. Fook, & R. Pozzuto (Eds.), *Social work: A critical turn* (pp. 55–66). Thompson.

Inter-American Commission on Human Rights (IACHR). (2018). *Children and adolescents in the United States' adult criminal justice system.* International Justice Resource Center. https://www.oas.org/en/iachr/reports/pdfs/children-usa.pdf

In re Gault, 387 U.S. 1 (1967).

In re Winship, 397 U.S. 358 (1970).

J.D.B. v. North Carolina, 564 U.S. 261 (2011).

Juvenile Law Center. (2024). Juvenile Law Center. https://jlc.org/

Kent v. United States, 383 U.S. 541 (1966).

Klenowski, P. M. (2009). Peacemaking criminology: Etiology of crime or philosophy of life? *Contemporary Justice Review, 12*, 207–222. https://doi.org/10.1080/10282580902879344

Lamphere, R. (2014). Prevalence and research methodology. In T. C. Hiestand & W. J. Weins (Eds.), *Sexting and youth: A multidisciplinary examination of research, theory, and law* (pp. 33–60). Carolina Academic Press.

Le, V. D., Temple, J. R., Peskin, M., Markham, C., & Tortolero, S. (2014). Sexual behavior and communication. In T. C. Hiestand & W. J. Weins (Eds.), *Sexting and youth: A multidisciplinary examination of research, theory, and law* (pp. 63–76). Carolina Academic Press.

Levin, M., & Cohen, D. (2014, March). *Kids doing time for what's not a crime: The over-incarceration of status offenders*. Texas Public Policy Foundation. http://modelsforchange.net/publications/521

Mallett, C. (2016). Truancy: It's not about skipping school. *Child and Adolescent Social Work Journal, 33*, 337–347. https://doi.org/10.1007/s10560-015-0433-1

McKeiver v. Pennsylvania, 403 U.S. 528 (1971).

McNamara, R. H. (2008). *The lost population: Status offenders in America*. Carolina Academic Press.

McNamara, R. H., & Bucher, C. C. (2012). *Problem children: Special populations in delinquency*. Carolina Academic Press.

Menihan, C. J. (2014). Criminal mind or inculpable adolescence? A glimpse at the history, failures, and required changes of the American juvenile corrections system. *Pace Law Review, 35*(2), 761–784. https://doi.org/10.58948/2331-3528.1894

Merlo, A. V., & Benekos, P. J. (2003). Defining juvenile justice in the 21st century. *Youth Violence and Juvenile Justice, 1*(3), 276–288. https://doi.org/10.1177/1541204003001003003

Merton, R. K. (1970). Discrimination and the American creed. In P. I. Rose (Ed.), *The study of society* (pp. 449–457). Random House.

Miller v. Alabama, 567 U.S. 460 (2012).

Montgomery v. Louisiana, 577 U.S. (2016).

Mooradian, J. K. (2010). Breaking the lock: Addressing "disproportionate minority confinement" in the United States using a human rights approach. *Journal of Social Work, 12*(1), 37–50. https://doi.org/10.1177/1468017310380087

Myers, D. L. (2005). *Boys among men: Trying and sentencing juveniles as adults*. Praeger.

National Conference of State Legislators. (2024). Juvenile age of jurisdiction and transfer to adult court laws. https://www.ncsl.org/civil-and-criminal-justice/juvenile-age-of-jurisdiction-and-transfer-to-adult-court-laws#:~:text=Five%20states%2D-Georgia%2C%20Louisiana%2C,offense%20is%20serious%20or%20not

National Youth Justice Network. (2025). *About us*. http://www.njjn.org/about-us/

Nordberg, A., Crawford, M. R., Praetorius, R. T., & Hatcher, S. S. (2016). Exploring minority youths' police encounters: A qualitative interpretive meta-synthesis. *Child Adolescent Social Work Journal, 33*, 137–149. https://doi.org/10.1007/s10560-015-0415-3

Penn, E. B. (2006). Black youth: Disproportionality and delinquency. In E. B. Penn, H. T. Green, & S. L. Gabbidon (Eds.), *Race and juvenile justice* (pp. 47–64). Carolina Academic Press.

Penn, E. B. (2012). Working with minority youth in residential treatment. In L. M. Johnson (Ed.). *Experiencing corrections: From practitioner to professor* (pp. 199–212). Sage.

Pepinsky, H. (1999). Peacemaking primer. In B. A. Arrigo (Ed.), *Social justice/Criminal justice: The maturation of critical theory in law, crime, and deviance* (pp. 51–70). Wadsworth.

Peterson, D., Esbensen, F. A., & Taylor, T. J. (2007). Youth violence in context: The roles of sex, race, and community in offending. *Youth Violence and Juvenile Justice, 5*(4), 385–410. https://doi.org/10.1177/1541204006297369

Platt, A. M. (2009). *The child savers: The invention of delinquency*. Rutgers University Press.

Potter, H. R., & Kakar, S. (2002). The diversion decision-making process from the juvenile court practitioners' perspective: Results of a survey. *Journal of Contemporary Criminal Justice, 18*(1), 20–36. http://dx.doi.org/10.1177/1043986202018001003

President's Task Force on 21st Century Policing. (2015, May). *Final report of the President's Task Force on 21st Century Policing*. U.S. Department of Justice, Office of Community Oriented Policing Services. https://www.ojp.gov/ncjrs/virtual-library/abstracts/final-report-presidents-task-force-21st-century-policing

Quinney, R. (1991). The way of peace: On crime, suffering, and service. In H. E. Pepinsky & R. Quinney (Eds.), *Criminology as peacemaking* (pp. 3–13). Indiana University Press Bloomington.

Roper v. Simmons, 543 U.S. 551 (2005).

Saar, M. S., Epstein, R., Rosenthal, L., & Vafa, Y. (2015). *The sexual abuse to prison pipeline: The girls' story*. Center on Poverty and Inequality, Georgetown Law. https://rights4girls.org/wp-content/uploads/r4g/2015/02/2015_COP_sexual-abuse_layout_web-1.pdf

Sarri, R. C., & Shook, J. J. (2015). *Human rights and juvenile justice in the United States.* https://www.researchgate.net/publication/265870037_human_rights_and_juvenile_justice_in_the_united_states

Seymour, M. (2013). *Youth justice in context: Community, compliance, and young people.* Routledge.

Sheldon, R. C., & Vasiliev, P. V. (2018). *Controlling the dangerous classes: A history of criminal justice in America.* Waveland Press.

Shireman, C. H., & Reamer, F. G. (1986). *Rehabilitating juvenile justice.* Columbia University Press.

Smith, R. (2011). *Doing justice to young people: Youth crime and social justice.* Willan Publishing.

Tittle, C. R. (2004). Refining control balance theory. *Theoretical Criminology, 8*(4), 395–428. https://doi.org/10.1177/1362480604046657

United Nations. (1989). *Convention on the Rights of the Child.* United Nations Human Rights, Office of the Commissioner. https://www.ohchr.org/en/instruments-mechanisms/instruments/convention-rights-child

Vito, G. F. (2019). A vision of contemporary policing: Present practices and future developments. In M. Maguire, D. Okada, & A. Sardina (Eds.), *Critical issues in crime and justice thought, policy, and practice* (pp. 249–268). Sage.

Walker, S., Spohn, C., & DeLone, M. (2018). *The color of justice: Race, ethnicity, and crime in America* (6th ed.). Cengage.

Zane, S. N., Welsh, B. C., & Mears, D. P. (2016). Juvenile transfer and specific deterrence hypothesis: Systematic review and meta-analysis. *Criminology and Public Policy, 15*(3), 901–925. https://doi.org/10.1111/1745-9133.12222

Chapter 12

Current Issues in Juvenile Justice

Chapter Learning Objectives

Students will be able to:

- Clarify the "age of criminal responsibility"
- Judge the conditions of juvenile confinement
- Recall major court cases concerning juvenile life without parole sentences
- Deconstruct one's biases concerning controversial juvenile justice issues
- Reflect on one's progress in understanding current juvenile justice issues

---

Introduction

This chapter presents an overview of some of the most prominent current issues facing the juvenile justice system. Within this chapter are discussions about the age of criminal responsibility, conditions of confinement in juvenile correctional facilities, the use of solitary confinement on juveniles, and juvenile life without parole. Within each area, discussions include background information and an overview of current trends. All of the issues extend beyond national concern. The age of criminal responsibility is a very pertinent current international topic of discussion. Conditions of confinement, in part, have to answer the question of what we should provide for children we place in locked, secure correctional facilities. The use of solitary confinement on juveniles is being addressed on a state-by-state basis after being banned at the federal level. The last of these issues has been recently addressed at the Supreme Court level. While examining Juvenile Life without Parole (JLWOP) there are recent Supreme Court cases discussed. Intertwined in all of these issues are three underlining themes:

- the current sentiment of moving away from punishment in the juvenile justice system,
- recent discoveries about the adolescent brain,
- creating an effective, efficient juvenile justice system based on an understanding of and response to adolescent development.

Box 12.1: Is Delinquency "Normal" Adolescent Behavior? A Discussion

We do not want to minimize the seriousness of delinquent acts or delinquency as a social problem. However, we should not exaggerate or "horribilize" them either. Thinking in these two extremes are not likely to lead to just and effective responses to delinquency. Delinquency is a normal part of society, especially the forms that are not seriously violent. As Chapter 2 indicated, this is true statistically. Many delinquent acts occur on a daily basis (high incidence) and many juveniles at any point in time have committed at least one act (high prevalence). Many if not most adults probably committed some kind of act against the law before turning 18, even if a minor one. Include status offenses and nearly all of us have committed a juvenile offense. However, the majority of us do not move on to get into serious trouble with the law.

Adolescence is typically a period during which youth tend to seek more control over their lives, desire more exciting experiences, question authority, and be defiant. Adolescents "experiment" with adult roles and may desire to make "adult decisions" and engage in "adult activities." Some empathy for adolescents is due; they are old enough to *do* the things that adults do but not old enough to be *allowed to* do them. Delinquency is often among the behaviors adolescents engage in to assert themselves and explore new experiences. This "rebellious" stage is a rather necessary transition period from childhood to adulthood. Delinquency is not necessary, but it is necessary for adolescents to begin developing autonomy and independence, which may sometimes bring them into conflict with authorities. We want adolescents to behave well, but we do not want them to be conforming robots either. (Otherwise, what will they be like when they become adults?) By no means is all of this an excuse for delinquent behavior. Much damage can be done by a delinquent act committed while a youth "is going through a phase," even if unintentional. However, a great deal of delinquency is not, by nature, malicious behavior. Much of it could be part of youths' attempts to navigate through the difficult transition into young adulthood. Of course, it is probably safe to say that serious or persistent juvenile offending is not "normal adolescent behavior."

The Age of Criminal Responsibility

As the first juvenile court was created and states began to develop juvenile courts statutes, one area that had to be addressed was the jurisdiction of the juvenile court concerning age. This carries with it two questions: first, at what age does someone become a child with diminished criminal responsibility and at what age does someone become an adult and hold full criminal responsibility?

Besides these being difficult to answer questions, there are unique aspects of the U.S. juvenile justice system that provide additional challenges to this task. Unlike many other countries where there is a singular juvenile justice system, the United States handles juvenile justice at the state level. Thus, there are 56 separate juvenile justice systems in the United States, counting states and American territories. Each state and territory is responsible for setting the age jurisdictional minimum and maximum for their own state (Zang, 2017). The discussion of this issue will begin with an examination and overview of the question of a minimum juvenile age. In other words, should an age be set in juvenile court which excludes children under a certain age because they are simply too young to hold any sort of legal responsibility for their actions?

Minimum Juvenile Age

> One of the most contentious issues in juvenile justice policy is determining the minimum age of criminal responsibility (MACR). There is a large variation around the world on what the appropriate age is, and even within nations differences exist depending upon the nature of the crime and the jurisdiction. (Lash, 2012, para 1)

In the United States, before the first juvenile court was created, young offenders were handled under the **Infancy Defense**, taken from English Common Law. English Common Law held that people under the age of 8 could not be held liable for their actions. Anyone aged 8 or older who committed a crime would have their court appearance in the existing court which heard criminal cases and serve their sentence in existing insti-

Table 12.1: Minimum Juvenile Ages in the U.S.

Minimum Juvenile Age	States/Jurisdiction 29
None Set	Alabama, Alaska, Delaware, Florida, Georgia, Hawaii, Idaho, Illinois, Indiana, Iowa, Kentucky, Maine, Maryland, Michigan, Missouri, Montana, New Hampshire, New Jersey, New Mexico, Ohio, Oklahoma, Oregon, Rhode Island, South Carolina, Tennessee, Virginia, West Virginia, Wyoming
Lower Age Set	18
Age 6	North Carolina
Age 7	Connecticut, New York
Age 8	Washington
Age 10	American Samoa, Arkansas, Arizona, Colorado, Kansas, Louisiana, Minnesota, Mississippi, Nevada, North Dakota, Pennsylvania, South Dakota, Texas, Vermont, Wisconsin
Age 11	Nebraska
Age 12	California, Massachusetts, Utah

Source: National Governor's Association. (2021). *Age boundaries in juvenile justice systems*. https://www.nga.org/publications/age-boundaries-in-juvenile-justice-systems/

tutions designed to hold offenders. There were no other legal avenues or institutions designed to deal with young people who broke the law.

Once the first juvenile court was created in Chicago in 1899, the question of juvenile court jurisdiction had to be addressed. As other juvenile courts were created in different states, the same task had to be completed. While each state and territory set their age jurisdiction at their court's beginnings, it was usually not a permanent "forever" policy. Factors come into play that may affect jurisdictional age policy. For example, public opinion, juvenile crime rates, especially regarding violent crime, and many other variables can come into play in the decision to reexamine and change a minimum age of juvenile court jurisdiction. A good example of this is the changes many states made to juvenile court jurisdiction during the 1990s when an increase in juvenile crime led many states to make changes in jurisdictional policy of the juvenile courts (JJGPS, n.d.).

A current overview of minimum age of criminal responsibility shows that twenty-six states have no specific age set for a juvenile to be referred to the juvenile court. The lowest minimum age of criminal responsibility in the United States, is found in North Carolina. Under North Carolina law, a juvenile as young as 6 years old can be arrested and sent to juvenile courts. Two states have their minimum age of juvenile court jurisdiction set at seven, and one state has the minimum juvenile age at eight. Fourteen states set the lowest age limit for juvenile court jurisdiction at 10, one state has set the age at 11 and three states have a minimum age of 12 years old. States may have additional requirements in play with their jurisdictional age laws. Washington

State has a minimum age of criminal responsibility of 8; however, children between 8 and 12 cannot be charged in juvenile court unless it is first proven that this specific child has "sufficient capacity to understand the act" they will be charged with (National Governor's Association, 2021).

In those states where there is no lower or minimum age of juvenile court jurisdiction set, the Juvenile Court personnel may rely on case law or common law to determine how they proceed with a specific case (Development Services Group, 2024).

Maximum Juvenile Age

Setting the maximum age for juvenile jurisdiction may be an even more controversial matter. In fact, "one of the most difficult areas of criminal justice policy lies in providing appropriate legal mechanisms to reflect the transition from the age of childhood through to maturity and full responsibility under the criminal law" (Urbas, 2000). The maximum juvenile age refers to that age where a youth who breaks the law is considered an adult and faces full criminal responsibility. For example, at the federal level, "the Federal Juvenile Delinquency Act (18 USC § 5031–5042) defines juvenile delinquency as "the violation of a law of the United States committed by a person prior to his 18th birthday which would have been a crime if committed by an adult" (Zang, 2017, p. 1). Thus, the federal age of jurisdiction is through the 17th year of age. In addition, the majority of states also set the age of criminal responsibility at 18, meaning that you are a juvenile through your 17th year. Not all states follow that in their statutes, however, and some states even lowered the age of criminal responsibility during the "get tough" era of the 1990s (Zang, 2017).

Raise the Age

The focus of the Raise the Age movement was to get states to raise juvenile maximum court age at 17 years old (and the age of criminal responsibility at 18 years of age) in those states where it was legally lower than 17. It soon became a widespread movement throughout the United States. The main rationales behind the Raise the Age movement were that juvenile crime rates were decreasing, the Supreme Court had recently overturned capital punishment for crimes committed while a juvenile, and the evolving research of adolescent brain development (Collins and Cooper, 2021). Moreover, "states have raised the age for many reasons, one of which research is showing is that justice-involved teenagers are more likely to move past delinquency and successfully transition to adulthood if they are served by a juvenile justice system, not an adult criminal justice system" (Raise the Age, n.d., p. 5).

Initially, when the movement began, there were fourteen states that had their juvenile court maximum jurisdiction set below the age of 17. Today, there remain only three states that have not changed the maximum age of juvenile court to 17: these are Georgia, Texas, and Wisconsin. All of those states have had legislation introduced that would raise the age (Kelly, 2018, para 6). Georgia has had a bill pass the House, but not the Senate (Bynum, 2023). Both Texas and Wisconsin have a strong Raise the Age presence in their states.

It has not always been a smooth process for all states. Changing the law can sometimes have unintended or unimagined consequences. For example, Missouri had a unique approach to its raise the age jurisdiction. The legislation stated, "The expanded service of the juvenile court system shall not be effective until sufficient funds are appropriated" (Collins & Cooper, 2023, para 3). The bill was passed in 2018 to be enacted in 2021, once the funding question was resolved. Because of the inherent confusion, as well as "a lack of clear direction in the legislation related to funding allocation, several jurisdictions within Missouri are operating under different practices when handling 17-year-olds, with some processing them in their juvenile systems and others still handling them in the adult system or possibly, not at all" (Collins & Cooper, 2023, para 3).

It appears as if we may have a uniform age of criminal responsibility across the United States soon. Even more interesting, some states have set the age of criminal responsibility even higher than 18. "On May 30, 2022, Vermont became the first state in the union to set its juvenile justice age threshold above 18" (Kelly, n.d., para 5.).

Box 12.2: Summary of Act No. 201 in Vermont (2018)

Raising the Jurisdiction of Juvenile Court to Age 19

Act No. 201 Page 1 of 1 2018

VT LEG #334186 v.2

This act summary is provided for the convenience of the public and members of the General Assembly. It is intended to provide a general summary of the act and may not be exhaustive. It has been prepared by the staff of the Office of Legislative Council without input from members of the General Assembly. It is not intended to aid in the interpretation of legislation or to serve as a source of legislative intent.

Act No. 201 (S.234).

Judiciary; human services; juvenile delinquency; youthful offender

An act relating to adjudicating all teenagers in the Family Division, except those charged with a serious violent felony.

This act:

- Creates a new section of law, providing for automatic expungement of criminal history records of qualifying crimes for people who were 18–21 years old at the time they committed the offense, as long as certain criteria are met.

- Requires courts to keep a special index of expunged cases and limits inspection of an expunged record to the person who is the subject of the expunged record.
- Charges the Department for Children and Families (DCF) as the designated agency for supervising preparation and administration of the State plan for the Juvenile Justice and Delinquency Prevention Act.
- Requires the State's Attorney to consider the results of the risk and needs screening in determining whether to file a charge in a juvenile delinquency or youthful offender proceeding, with the presumption that low-to-moderate risk offenders will be referred to diversion.
- Provides that a person placed at Woodside Juvenile Rehabilitation Center can continue to receive treatment past his or her 18th birthday if he or she meets certain criteria.
- Requires DCF and others to report to the General Assembly on the plan for expanding juvenile delinquency and youthful offender status to encompass 18- and 19-year-olds, and requires the Joint Legislative Justice Oversight and Child Protection Oversight Committees to issue findings as to whether key milestones have been met and whether appropriate funding exists for the expansion.
- Expands jurisdiction of the Family Division to 18- and 19-year-olds over the next four years.
- Appropriates funding to DCF for the purpose of the expansion of services to 18- and 19-year-olds. Multiple effective dates, beginning on May 30, 2018. (Legislature, 2018)

Conditions of Confinement

> Deprivation of the liberty of a juvenile should be a disposition of last resort and for the minimum necessary period and should be limited to exceptional cases. The length of the sanction should be determined by the judicial authority, without precluding the possibility of his or her early release (OHCHR, 1990, para 2).

The United States has experienced a long history of juvenile incarceration. In the chapter on juvenile justice history, there is a lengthy discussion of ongoing concerns about conditions of confinement for juveniles. There have been numerous periods of reform, many of which have mandated positive change. This section of the chapter will examine current issues relating to juvenile conditions of confinement.

According to the report *Highlights from the Juvenile Residential Facility Census, 2: Selected Findings*, there were over 30,000 juveniles held in residential correctional placement in the United States in 2022, a 10% increase from 2020. Seventy-seven percent of the offenders were housed in publicly operated facilities. While the majority of surveyed institutions (68%) were small, with 20 or fewer residents, just over 5 out of 10 children institutionalized were being housed in medium-sized facilities, which held between 21–100 youth. Most youth were held in facilities that did not report crowding issues. Most programs offered educational opportunities, and most juveniles attended school. Most juveniles were screened for substance abuse and mental health issues, and most youth were assessed for suicide risk soon after admittance. Publicly and state-run facilities were more likely to have locked sleeping rooms and "one or more confinement features" and were more likely to use them than private facilities (Hockenberry & Sladky, 2024, p. 4). In 2022, ten youth died in custody, with five of those deaths being classified as death by suicide (Hockenberry & Sladky, 2024).

Considering that we do not have a stellar record of conditions of confinement for juveniles in the United States, there obviously have been some changes, both in policy and in procedure. There have been numerous cases brought before the courts resulting in case law as well as some federal statutes that guide us in answering the question "what do we owe youth placed in correctional confinement?" Examining federal statutes and prior case law help us to:

> specify the minimum environmental conditions that juvenile institutions must meet. Under these laws detained youth have a right to protection from violent inmates, abusive staff, unsanitary living quarters, excessive isolation, and unreasonable restraints. They must also receive adequate medical and mental health care, education (including special education for youth with disabilities), access to legal counsel, and access to family communication, recreation, exercise, and other programs. (Puritz & Scali, 1998)

In addition to defining what conditions must be met in juvenile confinement, there have been some additional protections afforded to juveniles through the aforementioned federal statutes.

CIPRA

CIPRA stands for the Civil Rights of Institutionalized Persons Act. Congress enacted it in 1980. "CIPRA gives the Civil Rights Division of the U.S. Department of Justice (DOJ) the power to bring actions against State or local governments for violating the civil rights of persons institutionalized in publicly operated facilities" (Office of Juvenile Justice, n.d., para 1). CIPRA applies to juvenile institutions. CIPRA cannot take cases representing individual concerns, but takes cases that are bigger, those cases that represent systematic issues within correctional institutions (Office of Juvenile Justice, n.d.).

According to the Department of Justice, CIPRA's work with juvenile institutions has made some positive changes:

> Our juvenile work addresses a wide variety of issues, including medical care, mental health care, protection from physical and sexual abuse, equal treatment for youth regardless of race or ethnicity, and fair court procedures. For exam-

> ple, in Terrebonne Parish, Louisiana, we obtained a comprehensive agreement that addresses suicide prevention, how youth are disciplined, keeping youth safe from physical and sexual abuse and staff accountability.... The Section's work helps to ensure that children who were living in dire, often life-threatening, conditions receive adequate medical and mental health care, protection from staff-on-youth or youth-on-youth violence and exploitation, effective programs that encourage juveniles to manage their behavior, adequate educational services, and other protections. We are also working with jurisdictions to explore alternatives to juvenile incarceration. (USDOJ, 2017, para 7–9)

PREA

PREA stands for the Prison Rape Elimination Act. PREA was enacted in 2003 and mandates that correctional institutions must follow certain policies and procedures that are designed with the sole purpose of eliminating sexual abuse in confinement.

> Sexual abuse of people in confinement violates their basic human rights, impedes the likelihood of their successful reentry into the community, and violates the Government's obligation to provide safe and humane conditions of confinement. The government's obligation is even stronger when it comes to ensuring the safety of young people in its custody, youth who by virtue of their age are even more vulnerable to abuse and less likely to be able to protect themselves. (NPREC, n.d., p. 1)

PREA extends its protections to juveniles. The effectiveness of PREA, in both juvenile and adult institutions, remains to be seen.

The Future

Where are we today in regards to conditions of confinement? Unfortunately, both investigative and scholarly work still suggests that we have a ways to go, both in the conditions we say juveniles in confinement should have, as well as in our expectations regarding what juvenile confinement provides for juveniles in the long term. What do we want tomorrow from juveniles we confine today?

There are recent works that suggest that juvenile confinement is really offering us little in the way of public safety, changed juvenile behavior, or fiscal responsibility. A 2011 report entitled *No Place for Kids: The Case for Reducing Juvenile Incarceration*, issued by the Annie E. Casey Foundation, concluded that:

> heavy reliance on correctional confinement exposes incarcerated youth to widespread maltreatment; results in alarming levels of recidivism; incarcerates children who do not pose significant threats to public safety; ignores the emergence of treatment models that produce better outcomes; wastes money with costs that often exceed $100,000 per young person per year; and fails to pro-

> vide adequate mental health, educational, substance abuse and other services. In short, the report found that these institutions are dangerous, ineffective, unnecessary, obsolete, wasteful and inadequate. (Mendel, 2011, para 1)

Five years later, a 2016 report, *The Future of Youth Justice: A Community-Based Alternative to the Youth Prison Model*, from the National Institute of Justice concluded:

> Whether the benefits and costs of youth prisons are weighed on a scale of public dollars, community safety, or young people's futures, they are damaging the very people they are supposed to help and have been for generations. It is difficult to find an area of U.S. policy where the benefits and costs are more out of balance, where the evidence of failure is clearer, or where we know with more clarity what we should be doing differently. (McCarthy et al., 2016, p. 2)

What is the future regarding juvenile confinement and the conditions of confinement? There are suggestions and successes in the juvenile justice arena. Suggestions include looking towards creating and maintaining policy that works based on empirical evidence and good, solid research. One suggestion is that the juvenile justice system continue to rely on current adolescent developmental reform to move juvenile justice in a direction that encapsulates the new developmental adolescent brain research into policies. In addition, we need to understand that weaknesses in policy reform do not mean that the policies coming out of development reform are initially flawed—but may carry unintended consequences (Models for Change, 2017). Some believe that we have some current programs that are empirically tested, successful, and need to be modeled (Ziedenburg, 2006). Juvenile justice is in an exciting time, and we have seen an influx of new policy based on open discussions about the system's shortcomings and current motivation to make things better for the future. We are definitely in a new wave of juvenile justice (Models for Change, 2017).

Juvenile Solitary Confinement

While solitary confinement is a condition of confinement, it is such a major issue in juvenile justice right now that it is presented in this chapter as its own discussion. Solitary confinement can mean a lot of things. According to Teigen and Brown it is "room confinement, isolation, seclusion and segregation" (2016, p. 1). The physical and social isolation can last for 22 to 23 hours a day. This includes limited contact with peers as well as staff and may include canceling or restricting visits from family. In addition, reading materials and radio and television access may be restricted or non-existent. "It is a form of extended sensory and social isolation" (Clark, 2017, p. 350). There are many reasons given as to why solitary confinement is used with juveniles, including assessment, discipline, lack of staff, to keep order, and for personal protection (Clark, 2017).

The *Convention on the Rights of the Child* states that proportionate and appropriate measures shall be used when dealing with juvenile offenders. Many feel that this addresses the use of solitary confinement. The question becomes—what is proportionate and appropriate with juveniles in the use of solitary confinement? An early U.S. Supreme Court case, while holding solitary confinement constitutional, noted the potential harm it could cause (Lessner, 2017).

> In 1890, James Medley, a man awaiting the death penalty for murdering his wife, took his case to court after being held in solitary confinement for forty-five days before his execution. Medley argued that the period of solitary confinement was inhumane, constituting cruel and unusual punishment. Writing for the majority, Supreme Court Justice Samuel Miller recognized the harmful effects of the practice, explaining: "A considerable number of the prisoners fell, after even a short confinement, into a semi-fatuous condition, from which it was next to impossible to arouse them, and others became violently insane; others, still, committed suicide; while those who stood the ordeal better were not generally reformed, and in most cases did not recover sufficient mental activity to be any subsequent service to the community." (Lessner, 2017, para 3)

Solitary confinement is a current issue in juvenile justice because of the fact that the practice grew in both the criminal and juvenile justice arenas in the 1980s as institutional population numbers grew (Clark, 2017). There have been attempts at creating guidelines for the use of solitary confinement with juveniles and at creating reform through establishing best practices.

> In an attempt at reform in 1980, the U.S. Office of Juvenile Justice and Delinquency Prevention created guidelines ("OJJDP Guidelines") that stated juvenile solitary confinement should be limited to twenty-four hours. The same year, the American Bar Association Juvenile Justice Standards Relating to Corrections Administration ("1980 Standards") were promulgated, which stated that juvenile solitary should be limited to ten consecutive days. However, neither the OJJDP Guidelines nor the 1980 Standards were adopted in their entirety in any jurisdiction, and the states that did adopt the 1980 Standards limited their effectiveness by not assigning enough resources to implement them. (Lee, 2016, p. 855)

While in the 1980s there was an attempt to curb the practice of using solitary confinement in juvenile facilities, "the last several years have seen a growing chorus of concern about the deleterious psychological impact of solitary confinement" especially when it comes to juveniles (Clark, 2017, p. 350) Research suggesting that the adolescent brain matures at a much slower rate than previously thought has added more immediacy to determining what solitary confinement can do to an adolescent's mental health. Currently, the practice of using solitary confinement with juveniles and for extended periods of time thrives. "Placing incarcerated teenagers in solitary confinement for prolonged periods is a practice that, although controversial, remains widespread throughout much of the United States" (Clark, 2017, p. 350).

Psychological Concerns

There are concerns that the psychological effects associated with solitary confinement are many and may be exasperated because of age. The American Academy of Child and Adolescent Psychiatry has conducted research that suggests that anxiety, psychological harm, depression, developmental harm, and psychosis may be some of the damaging side effects of putting juveniles in solitary confinement (Terigen & Brown, 2016). In addition, results from the first national survey on suicides in juvenile correctional facilities were published in 2009. This research suggests that:

> About half (50.6 percent) the victims were on room confinement status at the time of death (and 62.0 percent of victims had a history of room confinement). The circumstances that led to room confinement at the time of death included failure to follow program rules/inappropriate behavior (47.3 percent), threat/actual physical abuse of staff or peers (42.1 percent), and other (10.6 percent). (Hayes 2009, p. viii)

The psychological effects of juvenile solitary confinement appear to be well documented. A national task force appointed by the attorney general in 2012 found that "nowhere is the impact on vulnerable children more obvious than when it involves solitary confinement" (cited in Reed, 2017, para 4).

Recent Developments

There have been some substantial changes made at both the federal and state level regarding the use of solitary confinement with juveniles. At the federal level, in late 2015, a bipartisan bill called the Sentencing Reform and Corrections Act was introduced. Part of that bill was the elimination of juvenile solitary confinement in the federal system. In early 2016, President Obama announced that the United States would no longer use solitary confinement with juvenile offenders in federal correctional institutions (Teigen & Brown, 2016). At the state level, by mid-2018, 16 states had banned or limited the use of solitary confinement for juveniles (Teigen, 2018).

Where will these recent developments lead? Will the U.S. Supreme Court accept a case that deals with the use of solitary confinement and juveniles and set some guidelines for its use or maybe even rule on its constitutionality? If so, what would the Supreme Court consider in their decision? The Supreme Court has used the concept of the immature adolescent brain in past decisions (Clark, 2017). Would the adolescent brain development research play as big a role in a solitary confinement case as it did in the U.S. Supreme Court case to end the death penalty for those who are juveniles at the time of crime (see ***Roper v. Simmons***)? States themselves are taking action and creating policy that eliminates or limits the use of solitary confinement within their juvenile correctional facilities, and this might be a trend that continues to grow. Interesting developments are sure to unfold.

Juvenile Life without Parole

The United States is the only member of the United Nations, in fact the only country in that world, that practices juvenile life without parole (JLWOP). It is important to remember for this discussion that Juvenile Life without Parole is referring to the age of the person *at the time of offense*. Even though sentenced through criminal courts, the person was, under law, a juvenile at the age of the crime because they were not yet 18 years old. The juvenile court has no death penalty in its sentencing options.

Once the juvenile death penalty was held unconstitutional in *Roper v. Simmons* in 2005, the harshest sentence left for juvenile offenders was JLWOP. As the sentence began to be used more frequently, its effectiveness and its fairness were examined. To date, there are twenty-seven states, as well as the District of Columbia, which no longer sentence juveniles to life without parole. A recent survey by the Sentencing Project found that nine additional states currently had no one serving JLWOP sentences. The survey also found that there were "1,465 people serving JLWOP sentences at the start of 2020. This number reflects a 38% drop in the population of people serving JLWOP since our 2016 count and a 44% drop since the peak count of JLWOP figures in 2012. This count continues to decline as more states eliminate JLWOP" (Rovner, 2023, para 2).

Recently the Supreme Court of the United States has heard cases dealing with JLWOP and has handed down some parameters about its use in the juvenile court sentencing decisions.

Graham v. Florida *(2010)*

Terrence Graham was convicted of an attempted armed robbery when he was 16 years old. He was tried as an adult and given three years of probation; the first year had to be served in the local jail. He was arrested within six months of his release for an armed home robbery and sentenced to JLWOP. Graham's attorney filed an appeal claiming that the sentence amounted to cruel and unusual punishment, as Graham had not committed a homicide. The issue that the Supreme Court had to decide here was whether Graham's rights were violated based on the Eight Amendment prohibiting cruel and unusual punishment. The court held:

> The Constitution prohibits the imposition of a life without parole sentence on a juvenile offender who did not commit homicide. A State need not guarantee the offender eventual release, but if it imposes a sentence of life it must provide him or her with some realistic opportunity to obtain release before the end of that term. (*Graham v. Florida*, 2010, 982 So. 2d 43)

Miller v. Alabama *and* Jackson v. Hobbs *(2012)*

Evan Miller, 14, and a friend went to a neighbor's trailer where they drank and smoked marijuana. The neighbor lost consciousness, and the teens decided to rob him. The neighbor awoke and physically caught Miller. His friend struck at the neighbor with a baseball bat and once released Miller severely beat him. Then, the teens set the trailer on fire. The neighbor died. Miller was convicted of murder and sentenced to mandatory JLWOP (*Miller v. Alabama*, 2012).

Kuntrell Jackson was 14 years old when he and some friends attempted to rob a video store. One of the other boys had a sawed-off shotgun, and he shot and killed the store clerk. The teens then left the scene and were later apprehended. Jackson was charged with felony capital murder and aggravated robbery and was convicted of both crimes. He was sentenced to mandatory JLWOP. The cases were appealed to the U.S. Supreme Court and the Court issued one holding for both cases (*Miller v. Alabama*, 2012).

> The court in 2012 abolished mandatory life sentences without the possibility of parole in *Miller v. Alabama*. The court in *Miller* ruled that while sentences of life without parole were still permissible, they could only be imposed after judicial consideration of the individual circumstances and the court must consider the offender's maturity level. (Teigen, 2017, para 3)

The Supreme Court had now narrowed the crimes justifying JLWOP to homicide and had ruled that the process of JLWOP could not be given mandatorily; the court had to assess the juvenile's individual characteristics, most specifically their maturity level.

Montgomery v. Louisiana *(2016)*

At 17 years old in 1963, Henry Montgomery killed a deputy sheriff in Louisiana. He was convicted and sentenced to a mandatory JLWOP sentence (*Montgomery v. Louisiana*, 2016.). In 2012, the U.S. Supreme Court decided in the ***Miller*** case that mandatory JLWOP is unconstitutional. Montgomery wanted his mandatory JLWOP sentence set aside as well. His request was denied, and he appealed. The question to the Supreme Court was whether *Miller* had to be applied retroactively.

> On January 25, 2016, the U.S. Supreme Court ruled in *Montgomery v. Louisiana* that its 2012 *Miller* decision which struck down mandatory life imprisonment terms without parole for juveniles must be applied retroactively. States are not required to re-litigate sentences in each case where juveniles received a mandatory sentence of life without parole, but a state must permit juvenile homicide offenders to be considered for parole. (Teigan, 2017)

Box 12.3: Henry Montgomery Today

On April 12, 2019, Henry Montgomery, now 72 years old and serving juvenile life without parole for a crime he committed in 1963 at age 17, was denied parole. Montgomery has served 55 years at the Louisiana State Penitentiary in Angola.

As stated above, it was his case that the Supreme Court took for review and which held that the *Miller* case must be applied retroactively.

> In 2016, after noting the ways that he had become a model prisoner, the Court ruled 6–3 that Mr. Montgomery and people like him were entitled to an individualized review that recognized the hallmark attributes of youth and juvenile offenders' unique capacity to change. "Prisoners like [Mr.] Montgomery must be given the opportunity to show their crime did not reflect irreparable corruption," according to the decision that bears his name. (The Sentencing Project, 2019, para 3)

Thus, Henry Montgomery would have the right to possible parole, as he had been sentenced under a mandatory life without parole sentence.

All but one parole board member of the three-member board voted to release Montgomery on parole, but under Louisiana law a parole board decision must be granted through a unanimous vote.

Montgomery's attorney states, "He's been through all of the programs he could take, ... he started a boxing club that gave young inmates a positive outlet ... was involved in a Methodist church ministry and organized a literacy program for fellow inmates that included helping them write letters home when they could not read or write themselves" (Berman, 2019, para 7).

In 2021, at the age of 75 years old, Henry Montgomery was released from prison.

While the Supreme Court held that the ruling was retroactive, states did not have to retry those juveniles already on JLWOP, but they did have to provide some type of opportunity for possible parole for those juveniles. States had to decide how they would address the cases of those children who were sentenced to JLWOP prior to *Miller* as well as decide what future JLWOP statutes would look like. When *Miller* was decided, 28 states were in direct conflict with the Supreme Court's holding. By 2016, half of those states changed their laws to comply with *Miller*. The laws created in those states, giving juveniles life with the possibility of parole, vary greatly on when a juvenile becomes eligible for parole. Three states (Iowa, South Dakota, and Vermont) do not specify an amount of time until eligibility for parole. States giving the shortest time to eligibility for parole are California and West Virginia at 15 years. There are seven states (Arkansas, Connecticut, Delaware, Michigan, North Carolina, Utah, Washington, and Wyoming) in which parole becomes a possibility in 20–30 years. Three states (Louisiana, Massachusetts, and Pennsylvania) set parole eligibility at 35 years. Nebraska and Texas set the longest time for parole eligibility at 40 years (Teigan, 2017). Will the Supreme Court take that final step of finding that JLWOP is, in and of itself, in violation of the U.S. Constitution under the Eighth Amendment?

Box 12.4: A Brief Discussion about Sexting

Recently, *sexting* has become a problem among youth. In 2017, JAMA Pediatrics published an article stating that one in four teens have received a text message that could be considered a "sext"—a text message that contains something with a sexual content to it (Haelle, 2017).

Containing elements of exhibitionism, voyeurism, and pornography, sexting (a merger of the words sex and texting) "generally refers to using a mobile phone or device to share personal sexually explicit content," usually digital photos (Weins, 2014, p. 3). The term may include both sending and receiving, and images may also be uploaded to the internet such as on social network sites. Commonly, one sends an image of oneself flirtatiously to a romantic or potential romantic partner, or humorously to a friend, but recipients may not be interested in receiving the images. Also, an image may not have been taken of the sender or a willing participant. Producer, sender, and distributor may be different persons, and sexting can be done with hostile intent toward subjects or recipients (e.g., to humiliate or intimidate them). When sexts contain images of persons under 18, it can be treated as criminal child pornography. This charge may be applied even when "the offender" is a juvenile, which is controversial since much consensual juvenile sexting lacks the criminal nature apparent in child pornography produced and consumed by adults (Weins, 2014).

Jones v. Mississippi *(2021)*

Fifteen-year-old Brett Jones murdered his grandfather. Once convicted, he was sentenced to a mandatory sentence of life without parole. His case was appealed to the lower court who upheld the initial conviction.

The Mississippi Supreme Court took the case to decide whether the Eighth Amendment requires that a juvenile must be found as "permanently incorrigible" before sentencing to a mandatory (without any possibility of parole) sentence. In the above mentioned *Miller* case, the U.S. Supreme Court found that JLWOP violated the Eighth Amendment against cruel and unusual punishment. In *Montgomery v. Louisiana*, the Supreme Court held that "*Miller* barred life without the possibility of parole' for all but the rarest of juvenile offenders, those whose crimes reflect permanent incorrigibility" (Oyez, n.d.).

The Mississippi Supreme Court basically held there was no requirement, based on previous court cases, that a judge had to find a juvenile permanently incorrigible before sentencing that juvenile to life without the possibility of parole. To some, "the decision in *Jones* may suggest that the Court is reconsidering its dramatic departure from the traditional deference it had shown in noncapital cases" when it comes to juveniles and JLWOP (*Harvard Law Review*, 2021, para 17).

Conclusion

This chapter presented an overview of some of the most prominent current issues facing the juvenile justice system. Discussions were presented about the age of criminal responsibility, conditions of confinement in juvenile correctional facilities, the use of solitary confinement on juveniles, and juvenile life without parole. Each of these areas represents a very real issue in national and international juvenile justice. We are in a place of change in juvenile justice where the sentiment is moving away from punishment and towards rehabilitation. We have a deeper understanding of the science of the adolescent brain and its development. We are learning to treat trauma and understand that without treating the underlying causes of behavior, behavior is unlikely to change. All of our understanding impacts our policies and practices in the juvenile justice arena. This chapter has presented the abovementioned issues in the context of where we have come from and where we are now. There are still changes on the horizon. The foreseeable future of juvenile justice looks very promising as we continue to develop new ideas, incorporate empirical data, emulate best practices, create effective and efficient policy, and move forward.

Summary Points

MACR

- Currently, many of the juvenile practices and policies that are urgent issues are not new issues in the juvenile justice system. The first juvenile court in Chicago in 1899 had to determine its jurisdiction, and that included the ages of the juveniles whom the court would serve.
- As every state in the country developed juvenile courts, legislators had to determine the age of jurisdiction for their state juvenile courts.
- As we "got tough" "if you're old enough to do the crime, you're old enough to do the time" seemed to sum up the public sentiment toward juvenile offenders. One of the issues that states addressed concerned juvenile jurisdictional age. While some states lowered the age of criminal responsibility through legislative action during this time, most states changed the age of transfer to the criminal courts—lowering the age at which juveniles could be held fully responsible as an adult for their crimes.
- Coming into the current era of juvenile justice, declining crime rates, adolescent brain research, and a developmental model have helped to reshape the discussions regarding the age of criminal responsibility.
- Most states have moved to eighteen as the age to face full criminal responsibility, and the remaining four states are considering change. We will see future developments on this current issue in juvenile justice.

Conditions of Confinement

- Institutionalization represented the initial practice of dealing with troubled juveniles in the United States. Since the New York House of Refuge in the early 1800s there have been reformers expressing concern about the conditions of confinement. Since then, conditions of confinement of juvenile offenders have been in the forefront as a major issue in juvenile justice.
- In the 1970s congressional hearings and class-action lawsuits brought attention to the reality of what was going on in some juvenile institutions. Federal intervention and case law have provided direction and relief. CIPRA and PREA were designed to provide governmental intervention into violations of the rights of incarcerated juveniles.
- Unfortunately, we know that harmful, detrimental, and sometimes even abusive conditions of confinement exist in some juvenile correctional institutions. Suggestions for reform range from creating, embracing, and evaluating new forms of community supervision; to providing alternatives for those youth who do not need to be in secure custody; to recreating new institutions modeled on the most effective existing programs; to eliminating the use of juvenile institutions altogether because we cannot "get them right."

Solitary Confinement

- The use of solitary confinement for juveniles is an issue that seemed to escalate during the "get tough" era of juvenile justice.
- Research on the effects of solitary confinement on adults, when coupled with a deeper understanding of adolescent brain development, indicates that solitary confinement of juveniles can be incredibly detrimental to their well-being.
- Since the 1980s, recommendations for the best practices in using solitary confinement with juveniles have existed. The federal system and some states have eliminated the use of solitary confinement, while other states have limited its use.

Juvenile Life without Parole

- Juvenile Life Without Parole is another issue that is in the spotlight of juvenile justice. JLWOP increased once the Supreme Court ended the death penalty for juveniles. The Supreme Court has decided cases that have really shaped how Juvenile Life Without Parole in the U.S. can be given as a sentence. JLWOP cannot be given for any crime other than homicide, it cannot be a mandatory sentence, and those who were sentenced mandatorily before the Supreme Court case are to be given a chance for parole.
- This represents the major issue that is keeping the United States out of compliance with the United Nations' *Convention on the Rights of the Child* (CRC).
- The future may see the U.S. Supreme Court accepting more cases dealing with JLWOP.
- The juvenile justice system in the United States has gone through a lot of transition in its historically short existence. It has changed focus in terms of its philosophical beliefs and polices. It has considered public opinion, juvenile crime rates, and legislative responses throughout its history. We are in a time when juvenile crime rates and institutional populations have been decreasing. We have come out of the era of fearing and getting tough on juvenile offenders and can collectively begin to assess the juvenile justice system on its effectiveness and efficiency. We can question some of its practices and develop new and more responsive programming, policy, and procedure.

Key Terms

Conditions of Confinement: Conditions that juveniles face while being held in custody.

CIPRA: the Civil Rights of Institutionalized Persons Act enacted by Congress in 1980.

***Graham v. Florida* (2010):** SCOTUS held that life without parole sentences for those who committed a crime other than homicide while a juvenile were unconstitutional.

***Jones v. Mississippi* (2021):** The Mississippi Supreme Court held there was no requirement, based on previous court cases, that a judge had to find a juvenile permanently incorrigible before sentencing that juvenile to life without the possibility of parole.

Juvenile Life without Parole (JLWOP): sentencing someone who commits a crime while a juvenile to a life without parole sentence.

Maximum Age of Criminal Responsibility (MACR): the oldest age at which a person is considered a juvenile for criminal responsibility under state law.

***Miller v. Alabama* and *Jackson v. Hobbs* (2012):** SCOTUS held that mandatory life without parole sentences for juveniles who committed homicide were unconstitutional.

***Montgomery v. Louisiana* (2016):** the SCOTUS held that the *Miller* case (2012) was to be applied retroactively.

PREA: Prison Rape Elimination Act.

Raise the Age: the raise the age movement is pushing for all states to set the maximum juvenile age as 17 and not any lower.

***Roper v. Simmons* (2005):** SCOTUS held that capital punishment for those under age 18 at the time of crime is unconstitutional.

Solitary Confinement: the physical and social separation of someone in correctional custody.

References

Berman, D. A. (2019, April 12). Henry Montgomery (of *Montgomery v. Louisiana*) denied parole yet again at age 72. Sentencing Law and Policy. https://sentencing.typepad.com/sentencing_law_and_policy/2019/04/henry-montgomery-of-montgomery-v-louisiana-denied-parole-yet-again-at-age-72.html

Byrum, R. (2023, March 6). Georgia House votes to prosecute 17 year olds as juveniles. Associated Press.

Clark, A. B. (2017). Juvenile solitary confinement as a form of child abuse. *Journal of the American Academy of Psychiatry Law*, *45*(3), 350–357.

Collins, A. M., & Cooper, M. K. (2023). Raise the age: Perceptions of Missouri juvenile justice actors. *Missouri Policy Journal, 1*(12). https://doi.org/10.62608/2330-930X.1054

Development Services Group, Inc. (2024). *Age boundaries of the juvenile justice system. Literature review: A project of the Model Programs Guide.* U.S. Department of Justice, Office of Justice Programs, Office of Juvenile Justice and Delinquency Prevention. https://ojjdp.ojp.gov/model-programs-guide/literature-reviews/age-boundaries-of-the-juvenile-justice-system

Graham v. Florida, 560 U.S. 48 (2010).

Haelle, T. (2018, February 27). That teen sexting study: What else you need to know before freaking out. *Forbes*. https://www.forbes.com/sites/tarahaelle/2018/02/27/that-teen-sexting-study-what-else-you-need-to-know-before-freaking-out/#eb557f86569e

Harvard Law Review. (2021). *Jones v. Mississippi*. Comment on: 141 S. Ct. 1307. *Harvard Law Review, 135*(1), 381.

Hayes, L. (2009). *Juvenile suicide in confinement: A national survey*. Office of Juvenile Justice and Delinquency Prevention.

Hockenberry, S., & Sladky, A. (2024) *Juvenile residential facility census 2020: Selected findings*. National Report Series Bulletin. NCJ 305825. Office of Juvenile Justice and Delinquency Prevention.

Human Rights Watch. (2012, January 2). *US: Harsh conditions for young lifers*. https://www.hrw.org/news/2012/01/02/us-harsh-conditions-young-lifers

Jackson v. Hobbs, 132 S. Ct. 1733 (2012).

Jones v. Mississippi, 593 S. Ct 98 (2021).

The Justice Policy Institute. (2016). *Raising the age: Shifting to a safer and more effective juvenile justice system*. http://www.justicepolicy.org/uploads/justicepolicy/documents/raisetheagesummary_final_3_6_16.pdf

Juvenile Justice Geography, Policy, Practice & Statistics (JJGPS). (n.d.). *Jurisdictional boundaries*. http://www.jjgps.org/jurisdictional-boundaries

Kelly, J. (2018, June 25). In another big year for "Raise the Age" laws, one state now considers all teens as juveniles. *The Imprint*. https://chronicleofsocialchange.org/youth-services-insider/juvenile-justice-raise-the-age-vermont-missouri-state-legislation

Lash, J. (2012). *Trends around the world in lowering the minimum age of criminal responsibility*. Youth Policy Labs. http://www.youthpolicy.org/blog/justice/trends-in-lowering-the-age-of-criminal-responsibility/

Lee, J. (2016). Lonely too long: Redefining and reforming juvenile solitary confinement. *Fordham Law Review, 85*(2), 845–876.

Legislature of the State of Vermont. (2018). Act No. 201. https://legislature.vermont.gov/Documents/2018/Docs/ACTS/ACT201/ACT201%20Act%20Summary.pdf

Lessner, J. (2017). A cruel and unusual burden: The case for the unconstitutionality of solitary confinement. *Columbia Undergraduate Law Review*. http://blogs.cuit.columbia.edu/culr/2017/11/19/a-cruel-and-unusual-burden-the-case-for-the-unconstitutionality-of-solitary-confinement/

McCarthy, P., Schiraldi, V., & Shark, M. (2016). *The future of youth justice: A community-based alternative to the youth prison model*. Harvard Kennedy School. The National Institute of Justice. https://www.ncjrs.gov/pdffiles1/nij/250142.pdf

Mendel, R. A. (2011, October 4). *No place for kids: The case for reducing juvenile incarceration*. Annie E. Casey Foundation.

Mendel, R. A. (2015, June 24). *Maltreatment of youth in U.S. juvenile corrections facilities: An update on juvenile correctional facility violence*. Annie E. Casey Foundation.

Miller v. Alabama. (n.d.). Oyez. https://www.oyez.org/cases/2011/10-9646

Models for Change. Systems Reform in Juvenile Justice. (2017, March). *Assuring the future of developmental reform in juvenile justice: Recommendations of the Fourth Wave Forecasting Project.* John D. and Catherine T. MacArthur Foundation. http://www.modelsforchange.net/publications/856/Policy_Brief_Assuring_the_Future_of_Developmental_Reform_in_Juvenile_Justice.pdf

Montgomery v. Louisiana, 577 U.S. 190 (2016).

National Governor's Association. (2021). *Age boundaries in juvenile justice systems.* https://www.nga.org/publications/age-boundaries-in-juvenile-justice-systems/

National Prison Rape Elimination Commission (NPREC). (n.d.). *Standards for the prevention, detection, response, and monitoring of sexual abuse in adult prisons and jails.* https://www.ncjrs.gov/pdffiles1/226684.pdf

Office of Juvenile Justice and Delinquent Prevention. (n.d.). Civil Rights of Institutionalized Persons Act in juvenile correctional facilities. https://www.ojjdp.gov/pubs/walls/sect-01.html

Puritz, P., & Scali, M. (1998). *Beyond the walls: Improving conditions of confinement for youth in custody.* American Bar Association. Juvenile Justice Center. Office of Juvenile Justice and Delinquent Prevention.

Reed, D. (2017, November 17). Why solitary confinement is not the right answer for juvenile offenders. CorrectionsOne.com. https://www.correctionsone.com/juvenile-offenders/articles/459872187-Why-solitary-confinement-is-not-the-right-answer-for-juvenile-offenders/

Riley, P. (2023, April 28). Against changing tide, 11 states still haven't limited solitary confinement of juveniles. *Youth Today.* https://youthtoday.org/2023/04/against-changing-tide-11-states-havent-limited-solitary-confinement-of-juveniles/

Roper v. Simmons, 543 U.S. 551 (2005).

Rovner, J. (2023, April 7). *Juvenile life without parole: An overview.* The Sentencing Project. https://www.sentencingproject.org/publications/juvenile-life-without-parole/

The Sentencing Project. (2019, April 15). *Louisiana denies parole to 72-year-old Henry Montgomery.* https://www.sentencingproject.org/news/7186/.

Teigen, A. (2017, April 20). *Miller v. Alabama* and juvenile life without parole laws. National Conference of State Legislators. http://www.ncsl.org/research/civil-and-criminal-justice/miller-v-alabama-and-juvenile-life-without-parole-laws.aspx

Teigen, A. (2020, January 19). *States that limit or prohibit juvenile shackling and solitary confinement.* National Conference of State Legislators. http://www.ncsl.org/research/civil-and-criminal-justice/states-that-limit-or-prohibit-juvenile-shackling-and-solitary-confinement635572628.aspx

Teigen, A., & Brown, A. (2016). *Rethinking solitary confinement for juveniles.* National Conference of State Legislators. http://www.ncsl.org/research/civil-and-criminal-justice/rethinking-solitary-confinement-for-juveniles.aspx

United Nations Office of the High Commissioner for Human Rights (OHCHR). (1990, December 14). *United Nations rules for the protection of juveniles deprived of their liberty*. https://www.ohchr.org/EN/ProfessionalInterest/Pages/JuvenilesDeprivedOf Liberty.aspx

United States Department of Justice (USDOJ). (2017, September 14). Rights of juveniles. https://www.justice.gov/crt/rights-juveniles.

Urbas, G. (2000). *Age of criminal responsibility*. National Criminal Justices Resources Center. https://www.ojp.gov/ncjrs/virtual-library/abstracts/age-criminal-responsibility

Weins, W. J. (2014). Concepts and context. In T. C. Hiestand & W. J. Weins (Eds.), *Sexting and youth: A multidisciplinary examination of research, theory, and law* (pp. 3–32). Carolina Academic Press.

Zang, A. (2017, July). *U.S. age boundaries of delinquency 2016*. Juvenile Justice Geography, Policy, Practice & Statistics. http://www.ncjj.org/pdf/JJGPS%20StateScan /JJGPS_U.S._age_boundaries_of_delinquency_2016.pdf

Ziedenburg, J. (2006, December). *Models for change: Building momentum for juvenile justice reform*. Justice Policy Institute. http://www.justicepolicy.org/uploads /justicepolicy/documents/models_for_change.pdf

Glossary

Adjudication: a stage of the juvenile court where the juvenile is found guilty and adjudicated or charged as a delinquent.

Adolescent-Limited Offenders: the largest category of criminal offenders, who limit their offending to the peak years of adolescence.

Advocacy: identifying problems, protecting human rights, and serving as a voice or representative for an individual who is powerless and in need.

Aftercare: reintegrative services and programs that a youth receives prior to release from a secure residential facility and while the youth is being supervised in the community post-institutional release.

Age-Crime Curve: a graphed pattern that shows that offense or arrest rates rapidly increase in early adolescence, peak in late adolescence/early adulthood, gradually decline during the 20s, and then sharply decline with age.

Age-Graded: a concept that refers to how an individual's experiences (e.g., roles and events) are fairly predictable according to age, based on what commonly occurs in a society.

Aggravated Assault: an unlawful attack wherein the offender uses or presents a weapon or the victim suffers serious bodily injury.

Animal Cruelty: killing or physically abusing or neglecting any animal without just cause.

Antisocial Potential: the varying potential of individuals to engage in antisocial behavior, due to interacting sets of risk and protective factors, which determines whether one offends.

Arson: willful or malicious burning or attempted burning of a house or other building, motor vehicle, aircraft, or personal property of another.

Assessment: more extensive information gathering and detailed interviewing of a youth using a comprehensive psychometric instrument to determine a youth's risk level and to address a youth's needs.

Bail: the conditional and temporary release of an accused person with the conditions that the individual is not a risk to the community and will promise to return to court.

Behavior Modification: a type of therapy that involves reducing negative behaviors and increasing appropriate ones using positive reinforcement and the concept of token economy.

Beyond a Reasonable Doubt: a higher standard of proof with supporting evidence that the juvenile committed said offense.

Biosocial Theories: theories arguing that biological factors—e.g., genes, early health risks, hormones, brain structures, and neurological conditions—interact with the environment ("nature *and* nurture") to produce general types of behavior, including crime.

Blended Sentencing: a type of sentencing mechanism where a judge imposes both a delinquent sentence and an adult sentence.

Bullying: repeated intentional abuse—physical, verbal, or social aggression—committed by an aggressor who has some type of power over the victim.

Burglary/Breaking & Entering: unlawful entry into a structure with the intent to commit a felony or theft.

Capital Disinvestment: a process by which conventional forms of social capital used to sustain valued human activities are reduced or eliminated, such as those initiated by deindustrialization.

Causal Force: the magnitude of a set of factors that varies across individuals—determined by the strength of each factor, the number of factors in the environment, the accumulation of factors weighted by each one's strength or level, and the presence of protective factors.

Centralized System: a system where administrative authority and responsibility rests with a state or larger governing body.

Child Abuse: harmful acts committed against children by older persons including those of a physical (e.g., hitting), emotional (e.g., insults or belittling), and sexual (e.g., inappropriate touch and speech and exposure to pornography) nature.

Child Neglect: the failure of responsible persons to provide for a child's basic physical and psychological needs (e.g., inadequate food, withholding affection, and failure to educate).

Chivalry Hypothesis: the proposition that females are inherently or biologically weaker and in turn are granted more leniency either in arrest or sentencing decisions.

CIPRA: the Civil Rights of Institutionalized Persons Act enacted by Congress in 1980.

Code of the Street: a particular system of street culture beliefs, found primarily in African American inner cities, that emphasizes respect, toughness, bravery, self-protection, and retribution, and advocates violence as a means by which to achieve them.

Cognitive & Social Development Theories: theories that find problems in ways that children learn and acquire reasoning abilities and morals and choose behaviors accordingly, over time.

Cognitive Behavioral Therapy (CBT): a treatment service approach for youth with substance abuse problems, anxiety, depression, and aggression, among other problems, that involves changing the youth's thought process.

Collective Efficacy: mutual trust and solidarity among local residents combined with their willingness to intervene for the common good.

Community-Based Alternatives: less restrictive sanctions to incarceration where the juvenile is immersed in a program or non-secure facility within the community.

Community-Oriented Policing: a problem-solving approach where members of law enforcement serve to protect and secure a safe environment in concert with members of the community.

Community Service: a community-based alternative that involves compensating and giving back to society by performing a set number of hours or work within the community in some capacity.

Computer Security Incidents: attempted or completed crimes involving spyware, adware, hacking, phishing, spoofing, pinging, port scanning, and theft of other information.

Conditions of Confinement: Conditions that juveniles face while being held in custody.

Conflict Model of Legislation: an argument proposing that laws are passed and enforced to represent the interests of the more powerful groups in society.

Conflict Perspective Theories of Crime: theories argue that crime by lower class and other minority individuals is often committed to resist or cope with inequality.

Consensus Model of Legislation: an argument proposing that laws are passed and enforced because the people of a society widely agree upon the laws' value and necessity.

Contextualized Discrimination: occurs in various circumstances or situations where there is some interplay of actions and decisions being made based on a person's race.

Control-Balance Theory: a theory that argues that a person is more likely to offend if one experiences a control imbalance—either a control deficit, which occurs when the control a person can exert is less than that to which they are subjected, or a control surplus, which occurs when the control a person can exert is more than that to which they are subjected.

Control Theories: theories that argue that individuals are more likely to offend if they lack inner inhibitions, self-control abilities, and/or external pressures toward conformity.

Corporal Punishment: the infliction of physical pain, without intent to injure, upon a child with the purpose of correcting the child's behavior.

Correctional Institutions: secure facilities that are used to house high-risk, pre-adjudicated or adjudicated chronic youthful offenders for a longer period of time.

Corrections: services provided to juveniles prior to adjudication or post-adjudication.

Correlation: an empirically verified relationship between two variables, not synonymous with *causation*—a process in which a variable in fact creates a change in another.

Crimes of Accommodation: crimes committed by lower class persons to deal with class disadvantage, such as burglary, robbery, prostitution, and substance abuse.

Crimes of Resistance: crimes committed by socially disadvantaged persons to express dissatisfaction with struggles such as lack of opportunities and interpersonal discrimination.

Criminal Capital: social capital that centers on instrumental crime opportunities.

Criminal Career: The span of an individual's criminal offending, characterized by five key behavioral dimensions: onset, frequency, seriousness, duration, and desistance.

Criminal Embeddedness: a process by which an individual becomes more reliant upon criminal capital and crime opportunities to make a living, and consequently less able to access conventional social capital and opportunities.

Cross-Sectional: a type of research study in which all data are collected at one point in time and thus do not directly show which events or conditions occurred or existed first.

Cumulative Disadvantage: a developmental process by which earlier antisocial behavior is met with sanctions that harm the offender's social bonds, which in turn reduces one's future legitimate opportunities.

Cyber Attacks: offenses targeting computer systems including infecting with viruses, denying service, and electronic vandalism or sabotage.

Cyber Theft: the use of a computer to commit embezzlement or fraud or to steal other things of value such as intellectual property (e.g., piracy and file sharing) and personal or financial data.

Cybercrime: offenses committed with the use of computers and the internet, including cyber attacks, cyber theft, other computer security incidents, "cyberbullying" and "cyberstalking."

Day Report Treatment Centers: non-residential facilities used as a community-based alternative for court-referred, at-risk youth who need additional supervision, counseling, and educational and vocational support services (also referred to as day treatment centers).

Decentralized System: a system where administrative authority and responsibility rests with the local government.

Defense Counsel: an attorney who may be appointed to the juvenile's case, such as a public defender or a private attorney.

Definitions Favorable to Crime: attitudes, beliefs, and perspectives which present offending as somehow good or justified (and perhaps that conforming to the law is bad).

Deindustrialization: a heavy exit of manufacturing industry from an area that results in major job losses and damage to community support.

Delinquency Opportunity Structure: an alternative structure of opportunities made available through exposure to crime and delinquent peers that emerges when conventional opportunities are not available in a community.

Delinquent Act: an act committed by a juvenile, usually a person under the age of 18, that would be considered a criminal act if committed by an adult.

Delinquent Subculture Theories: theories that argue that some youth are distanced from middle-class culture and instead participate in a subculture that espouses beliefs, attitudes, and behaviors—often illegal—that differ from or even oppose those of the dominant culture.

Detention: a temporary holding facility as the youth awaits court proceedings or a facility where youth are placed as a part of their disposition.

Deterrence: preventing future crimes from occurring by providing youth with the opportunity to consider and weigh the consequences of their behavior while under restrictive custody or a supervised community-based program.

Developmental Criminology: an approach based heavily in developmental psychology that describes within-individual changes across the life course for antisocial behavior and explains their development (onset, continuity, and desistence), with a focus on criminal careers.

Deviance: generally, behavior that violates norms.

Deviant Peer Association: having close ties with youth who espouse and encourage antisocial beliefs, values, and behaviors, and who may provide opportunities for delinquency.

Deviant Service Industries: organized economic structures for the sale of illegal goods and services, including those associated with "vice" such as drugs, sex services, and gambling.

Differential Association: a learning theory concept that represents the ratio at which a child spends time with others who advocate crime vs. those who do not.

Differential Reinforcement: the extent to which children recognize, directly or vicariously, that certain behaviors, including crime, are rewarded or not rewarded.

Discretion: the decision-making power afforded to a police officer that may be based on personal opinion but often within a given legal framework.

Discretionary Waiver: a type of waiver by which state law describes whether the judge has discretionary power to waive a juvenile's case to adult court or upon the prosecutor's request.

Disintegrative Shaming: administering retributive sanctions without a reintegration ceremony, which threatens prosocial identity and bonds with prosocial individuals and mainstream institutions and thus increases one's likelihood of re-offending.

Disposition: a disposition equates to a sentence, but since juveniles are concerned, the disposition refers to treatment and custody options.

Diversion: involves the process of referring youth who have committed an offense or exhibit at-risk behaviors to social service and community-based treatment agencies, while still holding the youth accountable for their actions.

Doctrine of Parens Patriae: translates roughly into "father of the child." Used in the history of juvenile justice in the US to give the state the authority to take custody of troubled children.

Driving Under the Influence: operating a motor vehicle while mentally or physically impaired due to alcohol or drug use.

Drug/Narcotic Offenses: illegal production, distribution, or use of certain controlled substances and equipment or devices utilized in preparing or using controlled substances.

Dynamic Factors: characteristics of an individual that can change.

Dynamic Theory: a type of theory that finds explanations for criminal careers in how individuals change throughout life, for example how events or conditions during one stage makes transitions to subsequent stages difficult.

Education: a social institution—a formal system of transmitting the skills, knowledge, and values determined to be needed in a population to make a society function well.

Electronic Monitoring: a surveillance and monitoring device that is placed on the juvenile, such as an ankle or wrist bracelet, or a random-dial phone system that places calls to the juvenile's residence.

Ex parte Crouse: 1839 Pennsylvania Supreme Court case which held that troubled children held no basic constitutional rights and that the authority of the state superseded the rights of parents whose children were troubled. The holdings of the case were widely followed.

Exclusionary Rule: evidence obtained from an unreasonable search is a violation of the Fourth Amendment and cannot be used in court.

Exhibitionism: exposing private body parts (usually genitals) to others in an unwanted way, often to unsuspecting strangers, for sexual arousal.

Extralegal Factors: subjective reasons about a juvenile or their behavior that a police officer may use in arrest decisions that are not found in the legal code.

Factor: a variable that is shown, through statistical analysis or direct observation, to be somehow related to another variable, such as criminal behavior (a.k.a. "correlate").

The Family: the social institution that is initially and primarily responsible for raising children.

Felony: a category representing a range of offenses resulting in serious harm to person or property that are punishable by imprisonment for one year or longer or by death.

Feminist Perspectives on Crime: inquiries into crime causation that seeks better explanations for female offending and gender differences in offending, with a focus on gender inequality.

Formal Social Control: control administered procedurally by official governmental authorities within a social institution designed purposely and primarily for the prevention and punishment of prohibited behavior—the criminal justice system.

Foster Care: residence in the care of a homeowner or family, who may or may not have children of their own.

General Strain Theory: a theory that argues that juveniles engage in delinquency to cope with negative emotions that result from loss of something positive (e.g., a break-up with a romantic partner) or presentation of something negative (e.g., being assaulted or insulted).

***Graham v. Florida* (2010):** SCOTUS held that life without parole sentences for those who committed a crime other than homicide while a juvenile were unconstitutional.

Group Homes: non-secure residential facilities found within the local community that provide safety and assistance for adjudicated delinquents (also known as shelters).

Guardian Ad Litem: a member of the juvenile court who is appointed to investigate and oversee the findings of a case that typically involves a neglected and/or abused youth.

Harsh Corporal Punishment: physical punishment used upon a child either with the intention to injure or without regard to injury (done with excessive force or recklessly).

Hate Crimes: crimes motivated (in whole or in part) by offenders' biases against victims based on race or ethnicity, gender, religion, disability, or sexual orientation.

Home Confinement: monitored supervision of a juvenile within the juvenile's home or residence.

Human Rights: fundamental entitlements that are granted to each person regardless of national origin, race, culture, sex, or creed.

Incapacitation: removing the juvenile from society and confining them in a secure facility so that future crimes cannot be committed.

Incidence: the number of times something occurs in a place or population within a certain time frame (e.g., the number crimes committed in a country for one year).

Infancy Defense: in the young United States, children who broke the law were treated as children were in other countries under English Common Law. If they were younger than seven, they were presumed to not have legal responsibility for their actions, and thus they could not be prosecuted in court.

Informal Social Control: control administered in everyday institutional life, such as home, school, work, place of religious worship, and neighborhood. Informal social control takes place within the context of informal social control institutions (e.g., family, school, and religion).

Institutional-Anomie Theory: a strain theory that argues that a society will experience more crime when its economy dominates over social control institutions (e.g., family and education)—when these other institutions are devalued, altered to accommodate economic requirements, and penetrated by economic norms.

Institutional Discrimination: "racial and ethnic disparities in outcomes that are the result of the application of racially neutral factors" (Walker et al., 2018, p. 28; see Chapter 11).

Intake: a process by which an officer of the court assesses the juvenile's case and decides how to proceed.

Intake Officer: an employee of the juvenile court who gathers information about the youth, which is similar to the booking stage in the adult system.

Integrated Theory: theoretical arguments that are constructed by combining and reconciling aspects of different existing theories, to offer better explanations of behavior.

Intensive Supervision Probation (ISP): a dispositional alternative for an adjudicated juvenile delinquent who receives a more rigorous level of community supervision by an assigned probation officer along with increased contacts, drug screenings, and treatment services.

Interrogation Methods: techniques where a police officer asks questions of a suspect to obtain information that may or may not involve the use of threats or intimidation.

Intimidation: unlawfully threatening a person with words and/or other conduct, excluding displaying a weapon or physically attacking the person.

JJDPA (1974): the Juvenile Justice and Delinquency Prevention Act held a broader mandate aimed at prevention, rehabilitation, and improving the juvenile justice system.

Joyriding: stealing a vehicle for the fun of driving it rather than for material gain.

Judicial Waiver: a mechanism by which a juvenile case is transferred to adult court by a juvenile judge.

Juvenile Court Judge: an administrator of the court who is primarily responsible for overseeing how it is managed.

Juvenile Life Without Parole (JLWOP): sentencing someone who commits a crime while a juvenile to a life without parole sentence.

Juvenile Probation Officer: a member of the juvenile court whose duties involve compiling a predisposition report with a recommendation for the judge on the appropriate disposition and supervising adjudicated youth who have been placed on probation or as deemed necessary by the court.

Labeling Theory: a theory that argues that others' reactions to a person's actual or perceived deviance can itself help bring about future deviant behavior on the part of that person.

Larceny-Theft: unlawful taking of property from the possession of another person (e.g., pocket-picking, purse-snatching, shoplifting, and theft from a building, automobile, or vending machine).

Learning Disabilities: physical or mental conditions (e.g., neurological) that impair the development or acquisition of knowledge and skills, such as being less able to sort and store information due to language or sensory processing problems.

Legal Factors: objective and legally supported reasons about a juvenile's behavior before making an arrest of a juvenile.

Legislative Waiver: a type of mechanism where the waiver policy is written into state code; it is virtually automatic as there is no need for the juvenile judge or prosecutor to decide how to handle the case.

Life Course: "a sequence of age-graded stages and social roles that are socially constructed and recognized as being different from one another" (Benson, 2013, p. 3; see Chapter 4).

Life Course Criminology: a perspective that views criminal behavior as the result of human developmental processes and experiences occurring within social contexts—one that focuses on differences *within*, not just between, individuals in explaining crime.

Life Course Persistent Offenders: the small category of criminal offenders who commit antisocial behavior during early childhood then offend during adolescence and into adulthood.

Life Course Perspective: a multidisciplinary theoretical framework (drawing from fields such as psychology, sociology, and biology) that views human behavior as the result of interactive, multi-level processes and experiences (e.g., biological, psychological, and environmental changes) which occur in sequences or stages across the life span.

Life Stages: socially constructed, culturally relative, and approximately defined periods within the life course.

Longitudinal: type of research study in which data are collected at multiple points in time, often measuring a proposed cause at an earlier time and its proposed effect at a later time.

Low-Level Chronic or Childhood-Limited Offenders: a very small category of offenders who behave antisocially as young children, engage in low-to-moderate delinquency in later adolescence, and then significantly reduce their rate of offending in adulthood.

Low Self-Control: an individual's apparent lack of ability to restrain their behavior in a prosocial manner, characterized by impulsiveness, thrill-seeking, insensitivity, short-sightedness, being nonverbal, and combativeness.

Mala in se: expression used to refer to offenses that are wrong by nature—bad in and of themselves—likely those which cause tangible harm to others (e.g., violent and property crime).

Mala prohibita: expression used to refer to offenses that are wrong simply because the law says they are wrong, not because they are inherently wrong (e.g., public order and status offenses).

Mandatory Waiver: a type of judicial waiver by which the state legal code specifies certain conditions that qualify the youth for transfer to criminal court.

Maximum Age of Criminal Responsibility (MACR): the oldest age at which a person is considered a juvenile for criminal responsibility under state law.

Miller v. Alabama **and *Jackson v. Hobbs* (2012):** SCOTUS held that mandatory life without parole sentences for those who committed homicide while a juvenile were unconstitutional.

Miranda **Warning:** a warning issued by a member of law enforcement that addresses one's right to silence, the consequences of surrendering this right, the privilege and right to receive counsel, the right to obtain indigent defense counsel, and the fact that these rights can be extensive and ongoing as one proceeds up and throughout the processes that may involve interrogation.

Misdemeanor: a category representing a range of less serious offenses punishable by up to one year in jail and/or fines, probation, community service, or restitution.

Missouri Model: a set of treatment services that is comprised of a "cottage-style" residential program that encapsulates a therapeutic living environment.

Monitoring the Future (MTF): an annual survey of self-reported substance use among young people in the U.S. conducted by the University of Michigan's Institute for Social Research with funding from the National Institute on Drug Abuse.

Montgomery v. Louisiana **(2016):** the SCOTUS held that the *Miller* case (2012) was to be applied retroactively.

Motor Vehicle Theft: unlawful taking or attempted taking of a vehicle (e.g., car, truck, van, bus, RV, motorcycle) with the intent to deprive the owner of it.

Multidisciplinary Team Approach: members of the medical profession, law enforcement, child services, victim advocacy, mental health services, and prosecutors who come together in a coordinated and collaborative fashion to respond to the needs of the child or adolescent.

Multisystemic Therapy (MST): a family and individual-based treatment service model that is geared toward serving youth who elicit more serious behaviors, such as antisocial behavioral disorders, violent tendencies, severe emotional or disturbance behaviors, or pervasive drug use.

Murder/Non-Negligent Manslaughter: the willful, unjustifiable killing of another person.

National Crime Victimization Survey (NCVS): an annual survey administered by the Bureau of Justice Statistics (BJS) which asks members of a large representative sample of U.S. households about their experiences with victimization.

National Gang Center (NGC): a project funded by the U.S. Department of Justice that serves as a major source of information on gang activity and intervention in the U.S.

National Survey on Drug Use and Health (NSDUH): an annual survey of self-reported substance use by older adults as well as youth aged twelve or older in the U.S. conducted by the federal government's Substance Abuse and Mental Health Services Administration (SAMHSA).

Need Principle: a principle of clinical assessment that is comprised of examining criminogenic factors and non-criminogenic factors.

Negligent Manslaughter: ("manslaughter") the killing of another person through negligence (carelessness or recklessness).

Net Widening: when attempts made to reduce the number of youths who are formally processed through the juvenile justice system, such early prevention and intervention programs, essentially capture more youth who are subject to formal social control.

Neutralization Techniques: cognitive techniques allegedly used by juvenile offenders to reframe conventional beliefs and values and thus evade moral accountability for offending, including denying responsibility, harm, and victim worth as well as redirecting attention to the hypocrisy of accusers and appealing to higher loyalties.

New York City House of Refuge: The New York House of Refuge opened in New York City on January 1, 1825. It was located in the rural area of Broadway and 23rd Street in Manhattan. The House of Refuge was modeled after adult prisons, but it was unique in that it housed only youth ("A Brief History," n.d.; see Chapter 7).

Norms: culturally relative behavioral expectations or everyday rules of conduct shared by people in a society.

Obstruction of Justice: offenses committed with intent to interfere with the administration of justice (e.g., policing), such as perjury, failure to report crime, and nonviolent resist of arrest.

Office of Juvenile Justice and Delinquency Prevention (OJJDP): an agency within the U.S. Department of Justice that serves as the federal authority on delinquency and juvenile justice, providing important information on research and interventions to professionals and the public.

Once an Adult, Always an Adult Provisions: a type of legal statute that sets forth how juveniles tried originally in adult court as a juvenile must also be prosecuted in adult court for any future offense.

PEACE Model: interrogation techniques used by police officers that are based on a non-accusatory and non-confrontational practice that is widely used in the United Kingdom (Preparation and Planning, Engage and Explain, Account, Closure, and Evaluate).

Personality Trait Theories: theories that implicate pathological qualities in the psychological and behavioral characteristics that set individuals apart.

Petition: a formal charge filed with the court alleging that the juvenile is an adjudicated delinquent or adjudicated status offender.

Petty Offenses: lower level misdemeanor offenses punishable by no more than six months' confinement, $500 fine, or both, such as jaywalking, littering, noise, and minor traffic violations.

Plea Bargain: an agreement made between the prosecutor and the defendant where the defendant enters a guilty plea in order to receive a lighter sentence.

PREA: Prison Rape Elimination Act

Predisposition Report: an official document that summarizes the juvenile's conduct and current situation with the purpose of providing the juvenile court judge with an appropriate disposition recommendation.

Preponderance of Evidence: a lower standard of proof where the judge will consider the evidence and determine if it is likely that the juvenile committed said offense.

Pressured Sex: sex resulting from an aggressor's harassing or manipulative behavior, such as telling lies, making false promises, threatening to break up, threatening to spread rumors, excessive appeals for sex or expressions of unhappiness, and exploiting authority over the victim.

Presumptive Waiver: a type of judicial waiver where it is the burden of the defense counsel and not the prosecutor to demonstrate clear and convincing evidence to the juvenile court judge that the waiver to adult court is not justified.

Prevalence: the number of people or other units (e.g., families) who produce or are affected by incidents (e.g., the number of people victimized by crime in the U.S. last year).

Preventative Detention: holding a youth temporarily in detention because they are seen as a flight risk, a risk to society, or as in need of protection from their home environment or community.

Probable Cause: involves a higher standard of proof where facts support that a crime has been, is being, or will be committed.

Probation: a form of punishment that where the juvenile is monitored in the community.

Probation Conditions: conditions that stipulate a set of rules that the juvenile must follow when placed on probation.

Property Crime: offenses involving the taking of money or property without force or threat of force (e.g., burglary, larceny-theft, motor vehicle theft) and destruction of property (e.g., arson).

Property Crime Index: the Uniform Crime Reporting Program's (UCR) combined measure of burglary, larceny-theft, motor vehicle theft, and arson.

Prosecutor: a member of the juvenile court who is commonly known for serving the interests of the state.

Prosecutorial Waiver: a type of waiver mechanism that places a greater amount of power and discretion in the hands of the prosecutor when making decisions to waive a juvenile's case to adult court (also known as direct file).

Prostitution: engaging in commercial sex acts in exchange for money or other things of value.

Protective Custody: an act where a police or child welfare professional has the authority to remove a child who is reasonably believed to be in imminent danger and to place them in a safe facility.

Protective Factors: variables in a person's life that are (statistically) associated with a *lower* chance that something bad, like criminal behavior, will happen.

Psychopathy Theories: theories of more serious violent and chronic crime that implicate broader criminogenic states of being in which multiple distinct traits comprise "disorders."

Public Order Offenses: acts prohibited by law because they are thought to threaten society's moral well-being (e.g., "vices") more than cause tangible harm to others, such as disorderly conduct, loitering, trespassing, gambling, prostitution, and nonviolent family offenses.

Racial and Ethnic Disparities (R/ED): the examination of data about how youth from different racial and ethnic backgrounds are processed at different stages of the justice system, such as arrest, pre-trial detention, disposition, and transfer to adult court, and for states to develop plans to address any racial and ethnic disparities that are found.

Racial Discrimination: treating an individual differently, such as denying rights or opportunities, based on a person's race or ethnicity.

Racial Prejudice: negative attitudes or perceptions about another social category of individuals based on their race or ethnicity.

Raise the Age: the raise the age movement is pushing for all states to set the maximum juvenile age as 17 and not any lower.

Rape: nonconsensual vaginal or anal penetration of another person with any body part or object, or oral penetration of another person with a sex organ.

Rate: a measure of the quantity of something per a fixed unit of something else—a denominator (e.g., number of arrests per 100,000 citizens) or a percentage of a sample or population (e.g., the percent of juveniles in a study who reported committing offenses).

Rational Choice Theory: a theory that proposes that humans choose actions, including crime, after performing a mental cost-benefit analysis that favors the actions.

Reasonable Suspicion: a standard or presumption made by the officer that under the circumstances there is reason to believe that a person is committing a crime.

Recapitalization: a process, provoked by a loss of capital, in which available resources are collectively reorganized to attain goals.

Rehabilitation: treatment programs for youth to address factors that may have contributed to their delinquency or misbehavior and in an effort to modify the youth's future behavior.

REID Technique: interrogation techniques used by police officers that involves behaviorally provoking questions with the intent of eliciting verbal and nonverbal responses that are subsequently analyzed to determine the truthfulness of the suspect's response.

Reintegration: transitional services to assist the youth back into the community that amounts to greater success in completing the rehabilitation process.

Reintegrative Shaming: administering sanctions that hold offenders accountable and condemn their behavior without segregating them from the community and offer a ceremony or gesture marking one's return to good social standing (e.g., expunging a record or a program graduation).

Religion: as a social institution, is a cultural system of sacred beliefs, values, and rituals that provide adherents with identity and a sense of meaning and purpose in life.

Residential Institutions: secure facilities that are used to house high-risk, pre-adjudicated or adjudicated chronic youthful offenders for a longer period of time.

Responsivity: a principle of clinical assessment that suggests how much a youth is amenable to change and is responsive to treatment.

Restitution: a type of sanction where the offender provides monetary payment of losses to the victim or renders compensation in the form of work or service to the victim.

Restorative Justice: a philosophy hinged on (1) youth accountability, (2) reparation or restoration to the community, and (3) reparation of harm to the victim.

Retribution: punishment for the sake of punishment (also commonly known as just deserts or revenge).

Risk Factors: variables in a person's life that are (statistically) associated with a *higher* chance that something bad, like criminal behavior, will happen.

Risk Principle: a principle of clinical assessment that involves predicting the youth's likelihood of reoffending.

Robbery: the actual or attempted taking of anything of value from a person by force, threat of force, or threat of other immediate harm.

***Roper v. Simmons* (2005):** SCOTUS held that capital punishment for those under age 18 at the time of crime is unconstitutional.

School Resource Officer (SRO): a member of law enforcement in the school system who assumes the responsibilities of a sworn officer with the power to arrest, as well as to serve as a law-related educator and counselor.

School-to-Prison Pipeline: the research-identified pathway from school problems to imprisonment facilitated by school policies and practices, which is experienced more by economically disadvantaged minority youth.

Screening: a process of gathering information to reach an immediate conclusion about a youth.

Search and Seizure: a search of a juvenile and their property by a police officer, but the law reaffirms that the search must be reasonable, that is, the officer must have probable cause, and a warrant is required.

Secondary Deviance: deviant behavior thought to be caused by negatively labeling a person who has committed "primary deviance"—earlier misbehavior not caused by labeling.

Self-Reported Delinquency Surveys: various studies that anonymously and/or confidentially ask juveniles to report their own offending for research purposes.

Self-Selection: a process by which individuals seek out environments and experiences that are consistent with their personality characteristics.

Sexual Assault: Aside from rape or attempted rape, attempted or completed attacks involving unwanted sexual contact between victim and offender, including grabbing or fondling private parts and making verbal threats.

Sexual Harassment: unwelcome sexual conduct that damages the environment (e.g., school) and interferes with the victim's ability to function, such as telling sexual stories or jokes, making sexual gestures or insults, sexual body language, and repeated requests for dates or "hookups."

Simple Assault: an unlawful physical attack without a weapon that does not result in serious bodily injury to the victim.

Social Bonds: individuals' ties or attachments to others that facilitate social control, such as attachment to parents and commitment to school.

Social Capital: resources available to individuals which are embedded in social relations and thus possessed by collective entities such as groups, social networks, communities, and cultures.

Social Control: processes by which the behavior of the people of a society is regulated, which includes mechanisms for ensuring conformity (adherence to norms and values) and responding to deviant behavior.

Social Disorganization Theory: a theory that finds root causes of crime in disadvantages embedded in the structure of neighborhoods, namely poverty, high portions of single-parent homes, high residential mobility, and racial/ethnic background heterogeneity.

Social Enhancement: a process in which a group takes persons inclined to engage in its activities and makes them do more (e.g., an offender committing more serious offenses after joining a gang).

Social Facilitation: a process in which a group instills tendencies to engage in its activities in persons who are not strongly pre-disposed to engage in them (e.g., non-offenders committing delinquency after joining a gang).

Social Institution: a macro-social structure developed within a society to meet social needs—a complex network of interdependent positions that perform social roles that reproduce themselves over time.

Social Justice: a concept about raising awareness about what is fair and what is just for both society and the individual, while recognizing that society is in a never-ending process of growth and change.

Social Learning Theory: a contemporary learning theory that integrates knowledge of interpersonal learning processes with the contextual factors that impact them: differential social organization, differential location in the social structure, theoretically defined structural variables, and differential social location in groups.

Social Process Theories: theories that focus on interpersonal relationships within key socialization environments such as families, peer groups, schools, and religion, and how interaction with others, especially authority figures, shapes our personalities and behavior.

Social Scientific Theory: a proposed explanation of why human behavior, such as crime, occurs.

Social Selection: a process in which persons pre-disposed to engage in activities performed by a type of group gravitate toward that group (e.g., antisocial youth seeking out gang membership).

Social Structural Theories: theories that find causes of behavior in the ways in which society and its parts are organized into patterns of relationships and interactions (e.g., social institutions).

Socially Constructed: a term that refers to how human collective action, rather than "natural forces," create social realities (e.g., morals, law, crime, punishment, and social institutions).

Solitary Confinement: the physical and social separation of someone in correctional custody.

Specialty Courts: diversionary programs that focus on non-violent offenders and their specific needs by imposing appropriate and non-stigmatizing sanctions and treatment services.

Spurious: a type of correlation in which two variables are related because another variable causes them, not because one causes the other.

Stake in Conformity: a person's realization of the relationships and benefits one has to gain by engaging in conventional activities and to lose by engaging in deviance.

Stalking: repeated intrusions such as unwanted monitoring, continuous communication, unwanted physical presence, and intimidating acts which annoy, frighten, or distress victims.

State-Dependent: a concept recognizing that the nature of one's existence at one point in time depends upon its nature at prior points in time.

Static Factors: characteristics of an individual that are typically fixed and cannot change, such as age, gender, and past delinquent offense history.

Static Theory: (a.k.a. propensity theory) a type of theory that identifies a persistent trait or set of traits acquired early in life that causes individuals to offend throughout life.

Status Degradation Ceremony: an often ritualistic event or series of events which shames rule violators, restricts their freedom, and lowers their social standing (e.g., arrest and going to court).

Status Offender: a juvenile who commits an offense that is only an offense because that person is a juvenile and not an adult. Examples include running away from home, truancy, and being beyond parental control.

Status Offenses: noncriminal offenses prohibited for underage persons only, including curfew violations, incorrigibility (being ungovernable), running away, truancy, drinking, and smoking.

Statutory Exclusion: a type of legal statute, which stipulates that a juvenile of a certain age who has committed murder or another serious violent offense is excluded from juvenile court jurisdiction.

Statutory Rape: nonforcible sexual intercourse with a person under the statutory age of consent.

Stigmatization: the process by which a person's identity is degraded because of shaming.

Stolen Property: an offense in which one knowingly receives, buys, possesses, conceals, or transports stolen property.

Strain Theories: theories that argue that juveniles engage in delinquency as an adaptation or reaction to stress or strain they experience from being mistreated or restricted by others.

Subculture of Violence: a subculture found among lower class youth, especially racial minorities, that focuses on violence and presents it as an appropriate or necessary (therefore morally acceptable) response to being attacked, insulted, or otherwise provoked by others.

Super-Predator: scholars warned of juvenile crime rates doubling, of the impending juvenile "super-predator," and of an unsalvageable generation of youth in the early 1990s (Krisberg, 2005; see Chapter 7). Use of the term became widespread.

Systemic Discrimination: widespread discrimination at all stages of the justice system.

Taken into Custody: a process where a juvenile is physically apprehended by a police officer.

Technical Violation: a violation of the conditions for probation where the juvenile forfeits their right to probation and ultimately may be sent to a secure residential facility.

Therapeutic Communities: residential programs for treating youth with substance abuse disorders.

Timing: A life course concept that acknowledges that *when* and in what *order* certain events happen in the life span shapes the impact that these events have upon development.

Trajectories: pathways or developmental lines across the life span which contain transitions across social roles (e.g., education, employment, and criminal behavior).

Transitions: major life events that mark the passage from one social role into another (e.g., high school or college graduation and first marriage).

Turning Points: major changes to individuals' life-course trajectories, often generated by transitions such as adolescence to adulthood (e.g., military service, employment, and marriage).

Uniform Crime Reporting (UCR) Program: the leading source of official crime data provided by the Federal Bureau of Investigation (FBI), which collects data annually on reported crimes, arrests, and cleared (closed) cases from more than 18,000 law enforcement agencies (city, county, state, federal, tribal, and college/university) nationwide.

Vandalism: willful or malicious destruction, damage, defacing, or injuring of property without the consent of the owner or the person responsible for it.

Victimless Crimes: Illegal acts that appear to lack a victim (other than perhaps those committing them), such as many public order, status, and drug offenses.

Violent Crime: offenses involving force or threat of force against a person (e.g., murder, manslaughter, rape, robbery, and assault).

Violent Crime Index: the Uniform Crime Reporting Program's (UCR) combined measure of murder and nonnegligent manslaughter, forcible rape, robbery, and aggravated assault.

Voyeurism: monitoring another person in stealth for sexual arousal (e.g., "peeping Tom" acts).

Weak Social Network: a system of relationships in which the persons who comprise it are unable to pool together and share ample resources such as emotional and financial support and supervision over children.

Weapon Law Violations: offenses involving the manufacture, sale, purchase, transportation, possession, concealment, alteration, or use of firearms, cutting instruments, explosives, incendiary devices, other deadly weapons, or weapon accessories.

Wraparound Programs: "a philosophy of care" that involves a unique set of community, family-based, and individualized treatment services that allow youth to achieve positive outcomes at present and into adulthood.

Youth Risk Behavior Survey (YRBS): a biennial survey conducted by the Centers for Disease Control and Prevention (CDC) to collect data on a variety of self-reported behaviors that affect health, including those which are unlawful, from a nationally representative sample of students in grades 9–12 at public and private schools in the U.S.

Zero-Tolerance Approach: harsher disciplinary codes that are imposed for the most minor offenses or misbehaving.

Index